The Study of Law:
A Critical Thinking Approach

ASPEN PUBLISHERS

The Study of Law
A Critical Thinking Approach
Second Edition

KATHERINE A. CURRIER
Director of Paralegal and Legal Studies Programs
Elms College

THOMAS E. EIMERMANN
Emeritus Professor of Politics and Government
Illinois State University

Wolters Kluwer
Law & Business

AUSTIN   BOSTON   CHICAGO   NEW YORK   THE NETHERLANDS

Aspen Publishers
Attn: Permissions Department
76 Ninth Avenue, 7th Floor
New York, NY 10011-5201

To contact Customer Care, e-mail customer.care@aspenpublishers.com, call 1-800-234-1660, fax 1-800-901-9075, or mail correspondence to:

Aspen Publishers
Attn: Order Department
PO Box 990
Frederick, MD 21705

Printed in the United States of America.

1 2 3 4 5 6 7 8 9 0

ISBN 978-0-7355-6950-8

Library of Congress Cataloging-in-Publication Data

Currier, Katherine A., 1949-
    The study of law: a critical thinking approach/Katherine A. Currier, Thomas E. Eimermann.—2nd ed.
        p. cm.
ISBN 978-0-7355-6950-8
    1. Law—Study and teaching—United States. 2. Legal assistants—United States—Handbooks, manuals, etc. I. Eimermann, Thomas E. II. Title.

    KF386.C88 2009
    340.071'173—dc22

                                                                2009005569

About Wolters Kluwer Law & Business

Wolters Kluwer Law & Business is a leading provider of research information and workflow solutions in key specialty areas. The strengths of the individual brands of Aspen Publishers, CCH, Kluwer Law International and Loislaw are aligned within Wolters Kluwer Law & Business to provide comprehensive, in-depth solutions and expert-authored content for the legal, professional and education markets.

CCH was founded in 1913 and has served more than four generations of business professionals and their clients. The CCH products in the Wolters Kluwer Law & Business group are highly regarded electronic and print resources for legal, securities, antitrust and trade regulation, government contracting, banking, pension, payroll, employment and labor, and healthcare reimbursement and compliance professionals.

Aspen Publishers is a leading information provider for attorneys, business professionals and law students. Written by preeminent authorities, Aspen products offer analytical and practical information in a range of specialty practice areas from securities law and intellectual property to mergers and acquisitions and pension/benefits. Aspen's trusted legal education resources provide professors and students with high-quality, up-to-date and effective resources for successful instruction and study in all areas of the law.

Kluwer Law International supplies the global business community with comprehensive English-language international legal information. Legal practitioners, corporate counsel and business executives around the world rely on the Kluwer Law International journals, loose-leafs, books and electronic products for authoritative information in many areas of international legal practice.

Loislaw is a premier provider of digitized legal content to small law firm practitioners of various specializations. Loislaw provides attorneys with the ability to quickly and efficiently find the necessary legal information they need, when and where they need it, by facilitating access to primary law as well as state-specific law, records, forms and treatises.

Wolters Kluwer Law & Business, a unit of Wolters Kluwer, is headquartered in New York and Riverwoods, Illinois. Wolters Kluwer is a leading multinational publisher and information services company.

About the Authors

Katherine A. Currier, J.D., is director of the Paralegal and Legal Studies programs, housed within the Division of Business and Law, at Elms College. She has developed and taught many law-related courses, including Legal Reasoning, Research, and Writing; Introduction to Legal Studies I and II; Law Office Computer Literacy; Law Office Applications; Interviewing, Counseling, and Negotiating; and Law and Literature. She has publications in the areas of legal ethics as applied to paralegals and law office computing.

Professor Currier is actively involved in the development of undergraduate legal education at both the regional and the national levels, particularly through her work with the American Association for Paralegal Education (AAfPE) and the American Bar Association Approval Commission on Paralegals. Professor Currier has served on the national board of AAfPE, first as its parliamentarian and then later as the elected representative of four-year paralegal programs. She served many years as the AAfPE publications chair, charged with the final responsibility for overseeing the Journal of Paralegal Education and Practice and The Educator. Professor Currier frequently speaks at both the AAfPE Northeast regional meetings and the annual AAfPE conferences on topics as diverse as the of use of computer shareware, paralegals and the unauthorized practice of law, creative teaching techniques, and conducting legal research on the Internet. Professor Currier also chaired the American Bar Association Approval Commission on Paralegals, the body charged with conducting site visits of paralegal programs that are seeking their initial ABA approval or reapproval. Currently, she is a member of the Board of Directors of the International Assembly for Collegiate Business Education (IACBE), an organization dedicated to promoting excellence in business education.

Prior to teaching at Elms College, Professor Currier taught at Suffolk Law School and Western New England College School of Law. She graduated magna cum laude with her B.A. in Political Science from Carelton College in 1971, with her M.A. in Political Philosophy from University of California, Berkeley, in 1973 and with her J.D. from Northeastern University Law School in 1979.

Thomas E. Eimermann is Emeritus Professor of Political Science and a former Director of the Legal Studies Program at Illinois State University. Dr. Eimermann helped establish the paralegal program in 1976 and served as director until 2005. He has taught the Introduction to Paralegal Studies and the Legal Research and Writing courses.

Professor Eimermann was a member of the American Association for Paralegal Education's Board of Directors from 1986 to 1993 and served as president of that organization in 1991-1992. He has also served in the Certification Board and Specialty Task Force of the National Association of Legal

Assistants, as a member of the Illinois State Bar Association Committee on the Delivery of Legal Services, and as a member of the Inquiry Board and the Hearing Board of the Illinois Attorney Registration and Disciplinary Commission. He was also a consultant for the Illinois Department of Corrections, where he designed its Uniform Law Clerk Training Program.

Professor Eimermann's publications include three editions of *Fundamentals of Paralegalism* and journal articles on paralegals, jury behavior, and free speech issues. He earned his B.A. in Political Science at North Central College. He went on to receive an M.A. and a Ph.D. in Political Science from the University of Illinois-Urbana/Champaign campus.

Katherine Currier and Thomas Eimermann also coauthor *Introduction to Law for Paralegals: A Critical Thinking Approach* and *Introduction to Paralegal Studies: A Critical Thinking Approach*.

To our spouses and children
For their understanding and support

Summary of Contents

Contents

List of Illustrations

Preface

NEW TO THIS EDITION

In our ongoing effort to develop a comprehensive introductory law text that is appropriate for use in general education courses and programs in business, criminal justice, paralegal studies, and political science, we have made several significant changes from our previous edition. We have added new topics, reorganized some materials, and incorporated discussions of many recent court decisions.

The most significant of these changes involve placing greater emphasis on the underlying principles of the law and giving less attention to procedural details. Consistent with this shift we have added a new chapter on constitutional law and eliminated the appendices on legal research and legal writing. We also eliminated the Practical Tips as they focused more on what goes on in law offices rather than on the law itself.

We have not changed the use of our "critical thinking approach" throughout the book. Although we no longer have separate chapters on interpreting statutes, interpreting court opinions, and applying the law, we have incorporated the most important principles from these chapters into our new Chapter 1.

The new constitutional law chapter provides an overview of fundamental concepts such as federalism, separation of powers, due process of law, and the equal protection of the laws. In that chapter we also explore the leading approaches used when interpreting some of the vague and often ambiguous language in the federal constitution.

The second edition also adds coverage on affirmative action, capital punishment, hate crimes, homestead exemptions, and sports-related torts. It expands the previous coverage of eminent domain, federal employment discrimination laws, the insanity defense, punitive damages, same-sex marriage and civil unions, and sentencing guidelines.

Coverage of recent Supreme Court cases includes *Grutter v. Bollinger* and *Parents Involved in Community Schools v. Seattle School Dist.* (affirmative action); *Roper v. Simmons* (death penalty); *Kelo v. New London* (eminent domain); and *Blakely v. Washington, United States v. Booker, Scott v. Harris*, and *Hudson v. Michigan* (sentencing guidelines).

Finally, we have updated our NetNotes (references to Internet resources) and incorporated new Discussion Questions, Legal Reasoning Exercises (renamed Critical Thinking Exercises and moved to the end of each chapter for easy reference), and Review Questions.

APPROACH

As the title indicates, in this book we use a critical thinking approach to introduce readers to the study of law. This book is designed for use in introductory law courses for students in any major, but particularly for those in business, criminal justice, paralegal, prelaw, and political science.

Rather than taking an approach that emphasizes the memorization of definitions and rules, *The Study of Law: A Critical Thinking Approach* focuses on the basic foundations of the law and on the legal reasoning process. In addition to presenting an overview of the legal system, this book teaches the basic skills necessary to read and understand statutes and court cases.

We use this critical thinking approach because we believe it is the best way for students to learn the fundamental principles of law. By learning how to read and interpret statutes, cases, regulations, and court documents, students will be better able to learn how the American legal system functions. Therefore this book emphasizes careful reading for detail, analytical thinking, and presentation of arguments. The hypothetical cases, Discussion Questions, and Critical Thinking Exercises incorporated throughout the text all serve to help develop students' critical thinking skills.

ORGANIZATION OF THE BOOK

Part 1, The American Legal System, introduces students to the study of law and the organization of the legal system. It covers such topics as sources of the law, the different ways in which law is classified, and various stages involved in litigation.

Part 2, Substantive Law and Ethical Issues, introduces students to basic concepts and terminology used in the most prominent substantive areas of law. This section leads off with a chapter on constitutional law, because constitutional law stands at the top of the hierarchy of law and establishes the framework within which the legal system operates. We then go on to cover key fundamental concepts in torts, contracts, property and estate law, business law, family law, and criminal law. In each chapter we blend traditional case law with a discussion of cutting-edge developments to give students a solid foundation in traditional concepts and an appreciation of the dynamic nature of law. The final chapter probes the ethical dilemmas attorneys face in the context of our adversary system.

Instructors may wish to alter the sequence in which they cover the chapters, or even skip parts when time is limited. However, it is best if instructors plan on covering Part One before selecting from the substantive law chapters contained in Part Two.

KEY FEATURES

Among the many features that set this book apart are

- the nature of the included cases
- marginal definitions of key terms

■ NetNotes
■ Critical Thinking Exercises
■ Discussion Questions integrated into each chapter
■ Review Questions

Because this book stresses the critical thinking approach, we illustrate our points with hypothetical situations and with real case decisions that students will understand and to which they can relate. The cases cover such topics as AIDS-infected blood transfusions, battered woman's syndrome, same-sex marriage, flag burning, the insanity defense, search and seizure of automobiles, sexual harassment, surrogate motherhood, and spousal immunity. We have also included such "classics" as *McBoyle v. United States, Palsgraf v. Long Island Railroad, Brown v. Board of Education,* and *Mapp v. Ohio.* Our philosophy in editing these and other cases was to retain enough of the court's wording to give students a realistic feel for how judges actually write and to allow students to develop their critical thinking skills. We deleted nonessential information in order to keep each case a reasonable length.

Furthermore, the cases are fully integrated into the text. Many times, these cases are cross-referenced in other cases and used to show how the courts build on precedent and modify it in response to changing societal conditions. Discussion Questions and Critical Thinking Exercises call on students to carefully analyze these cases and apply them to hypothetical situations.

Also of special note are the appendixes. Appendix A includes a complete copy of the United States Constitution and Appendix B contains a convenient listing of websites for legal resources.

An instructor's manual that includes suggested answers for all the Discussion Questions, Review Questions, and Critical Thinking Exercises, as well as teaching tips, is available to help teachers make the most effective use of this book. Also available are PowerPoint slides to assist with classroom lectures and a computerized test bank.

RELATIONSHIP TO THE AUTHORS' OTHER TEXTS

Those familiar with *Introduction to Law for Paralegals: A Critical Thinking Approach* and *Introduction to Paralegal Studies: A Critical Thinking Approach* will recognize many similarities to this text. All three books emphasize the "critical thinking approach" to understanding the law. All three include excerpts from court cases, discussion questions, NetNotes, and references to ethical questions. Topics such as sources of law, classification of the law, structure of the court system, overviews of civil and criminal litigation, overviews of torts, contracts, property law, and criminal law, and analysis of statutes and cases are also covered in all three books.

However, where the other two books are specifically designed for paralegal students, this book is directed at a more general audience. In *The Study of Law* we have dropped appendices on legal research and writing and references to tasks performed by paralegals. To better serve the needs of a more general audience, we have increased our coverage of constitutional law and placed more emphasis on general education goals.

ACKNOWLEDGMENTS

Naturally, we owe a great deal of thanks to the many students, educators, paralegals, and attorneys who contributed ideas for this book. We would also like to recognize Victoria Joseph for her contribution to the criminal law chapter.

We would also like to thank the staff at Aspen Publishers for the excellent support we have received on the books we have done with them. We especially want to thank Betsy Kenny and David Herzig for their roles in helping us develop our books.

Katherine A. Currier
Thomas E. Eimermann
February 2009

Acknowledgments

We are grateful to the following copyright holder for reprint permission:

Supreme Court Historical Society, photograph of the Supreme Court Justices. Collection, The Supreme Court of the United States, courtesy The Supreme Court Historical Society, photographed by Steve Petteway, Supreme Court.

PART 1

The American Legal System

Chapter 1

Introduction to the Study of Law

*The study of the law qualifies a [wo]man to be useful
to self, to neighbors, and to the public.*
Unknown

INTRODUCTION

Why study law? First, law plays an essential role in everyone's life. It provides guidelines on how people should interact with one another. The criminal codes prohibit theft, assault, battery, rape, murder, and many other offenses. The tax codes require that individuals and businesses give part of their income to the government. The environmental laws prohibit the dumping of raw sewage into lakes and rivers. The civil rights laws protect against discrimination and harassment.

In addition to defining what constitutes appropriate behavior, the law provides a mechanism for resolving the conflicts and disagreements that arise among us without resorting to personal violence. When individuals violate a section of the criminal law, the government takes responsibility for bringing them to trial and for administering an appropriate punishment. If one person's negligence injures others, that person can be required to compensate the injured parties for the damages caused by this negligent act. When persons fail to carry out the terms of a contract, the state can either force them to do so or force them to pay damages that resulted from their failure to live up to their agreement.

Legislators, government administrators, and lobbyists focus on developing the statutes and regulations that govern everything from the way we drive our cars to the procedures we have to follow to get a divorce. Many people consult lawyers for advice on what they should do to live within the requirements of the law. For example, a group of entrepreneurs may seek legal advice regarding the best way to organize their new business, or a young married couple may come to an attorney for help with the purchase of their first home. Alternatively, individuals may enlist the aid of an attorney when they have been injured in an automobile accident or have been charged with a crime.

Second, you have no doubt heard the saying "Ignorance of the law is no excuse." Every educated citizen should have a basic understanding of our legal system and our laws.

Third, learning about the law and how the legal system works is a lot of fun. Although most legal disputes never make it to trial, those that do often involve high drama, with captivating rhetoric and surprising testimony. When a select few of those cases reach the appellate level, we see judges crafting new law that can have a tremendous impact on our lives. One only needs to think of the United States Supreme Court case *Roe v. Wade* and the continuing controversy over a woman's right to abortion.

Finally, the study of law is a challenging and rewarding intellectual exercise. Interpretation of the law involves the application of logic and other critical thinking skills. These critical thinking skills can be usefully applied in many different fields of endeavor.

A. OVERVIEW OF LEGAL ANALYSIS

In addition to helping you understand how the American legal system operates and introducing you to the legal principles that form the basis of our law in areas such as criminal law, torts, contracts, property, business organizations, and family law, this text is designed to develop the critical thinking skills you need to understand statutes, court opinions, and administrative regulations. Legal analysis involves:

- Reviewing the underlying situation that is creating the legal problem and analyzing the "relevant" facts;
- Reading and understanding the appropriate legal rules; and
- Applying those legal rules to the relevant facts.

Throughout the text we will be presenting you with short factual scenarios to illustrate how people and businesses turn to the law for help. Take a moment to read the facts of the case of "The Distressed Grandfather" and the case of "The Harassed Student." In addition to studying these cases now, we will refer to them again in later chapters.

Case 1: The Distressed Grandfather

Approximately one year ago, Donald Drake and his six-year-old grandson, Philip, were walking down a residential road on their way home from visiting one of Philip's friends. Philip was walking on the sidewalk approximately thirty feet in front of Mr. Drake. Suddenly, a car sped past Mr. Drake, seemingly went out of control, jumped the curb, and hit Philip. Mr. Drake ran to Philip's side, but it was too late. Philip had been killed instantly. The driver of the car, Mrs. Wilma Small, was unhurt. Based on skid marks and testimony from both Mrs. Small and Mr. Drake, the police investigation following the accident determined that excessive speed was the cause of the accident.

Mr. Drake said that at the time of the accident his only concern was for the welfare of his grandson because he himself was clear of the danger. Naturally, Mr. Drake suffered a great deal of mental pain and shock because of seeing his grandson killed. While being driven home from the accident, he suffered a heart attack that necessitated a lengthy hospital stay.

One year later, he still does not feel completely recovered and often suffers from nightmares reliving the accident and his grandson's death. He wonders if he can sue Mrs. Small to recover for his hospital bills and for his pain and suffering.

Case 2: The Harassed Student

Wanda Smith, a twenty-two-year-old college student, was walking past a construction site on campus when several of the construction workers began to whistle and make cat calls. Wanda did not appreciate being treated as a sex object and greatly resented the way in which these construction workers were behaving.

After talking it over with a few of her friends, Wanda decides to talk to an attorneys to see if she can take legal action. She does not want other women to have to undergo similar treatment and wonders if she can collect damages for mental suffering.

Keep these two situations in mind as we give you a quick overview of the three basic steps in analyzing a legal situation.

B. IDENTIFYING THE RELEVANT FACTS

The first step in legal analysis is to review and identify the relevant facts. The answer to any legal question depends on the specific facts of the individual case. Even a minor change in the facts may alter the outcome of the case.

Just as a medical doctor cannot give a competent medical diagnosis without a thorough examination of the patient, a lawyer cannot render legal advice without a complete understanding of all the relevant facts. Some areas of the law, such as those dealing with negligence or landlords and tenants, are particularly **fact bound**. For example, assume a stranger approaches an attorney at a party with a question such as: "My landlord is trying to evict me. Can he do that?" or "My husband is trying to get custody of my kids. Will he succeed?" It would be impossible for the attorney to answer without gathering a lot more information and personally reviewing key documents.

Fact bound
Legal issues are said to be fact bound when even a minor change in the facts can change the outcome.

C. READING AND UNDERSTANDING THE APPROPRIATE LEGAL RULES

Cause of action
A claim that, based on the law and the facts, is sufficient to support a lawsuit.

After meeting with a potential client, the first thing that an attorney needs to determine is whether the client has a valid cause of action. A **cause of action** can be defined as a claim that, based on the law and the facts, is sufficient to support a lawsuit. For example, in Wanda Smith's case, she was clearly upset and disturbed by what had happened to her. However, that does not mean she has a legal remedy. Her lawyers will have to prove not only that the construction workers harassed and upset her, but also that these actions violated some law. It is important to understand that not every problem is a problem for which the courts will supply a remedy.

Thus, the second stage of legal analysis involves the identification of the specific provisions of the law that are applicable to the situation. Because there are so many laws at the federal, state, and local levels, and because the law covers such a wide variety of topics, it is impossible for anyone to know everything there is to know about the law. The law is far too complex for any individual to be able to commit it all to memory. Furthermore, because the law is constantly changing, one's legal knowledge must be continually updated. Therefore, even lawyers who specialize and strive to keep current by reading legal newspapers, journals, and bar publications on a daily basis may still need to do legal research. Law books and online computer databases are the tools of the trade for the legal professional.

When conducting legal research, attorneys focus on the two main sources of law:

1. court-made law (common law) and
2. enacted law.

Constitution
The fundamental law of a nation or state.

Enacted law can be further subdivided into constitutional, statutory, and administrative law. We will be discussing these sources of law in more depth in Chapter 2.

Statute
A law enacted by a state legislature or by Congress.

1. Understanding Enacted Law: Constitutions, Statutes, and Regulations

While some of the most important laws, such as freedom of speech, can be found in the U.S. and state **constitutions**, most everyday legal problems are governed by statutes, local ordinances, or agency regulations. **Statutes** are enacted by the U.S. Congress or state legislatures; **ordinances** are laws enacted by local governments; and **regulations** are laws promulgated by state and federal administrative agencies. All three lay down general rules that apply to future conduct.

Ordinance
A law enacted by a local government; a subcategory of statutory law.

When a legislative body formulates a statute, it is setting down general rules that will be applied to a variety of future situations. Trying to lay down rules today for situations that will arise in the future is a difficult task, as illustrated by the following classic example.

Assume a town council passed the following ordinance:

Regulation
A law promulgated by an administrative agency.

It shall be unlawful to operate any vehicle on town park paths. Violators will be subject to a $100 fine for the first offense and up to a $500 fine for each additional offense.

The council passed the ordinance in response to citizen complaints about a group of teenagers who had been riding their motorcycles on the paths of the town's parks. Not only are motorcycles noisy, but also the citizens were afraid that one day an accident would occur and a child walking down one of the paths would be injured.

Following the passage of this ordinance the following four events took place in a town park:

1. For a "lark," two teenagers drove a Jeep Cherokee down one of the park paths.
2. The garbage collector backed his truck approximately six feet down one of the park paths to pick up garbage from one of the trash receptacles.
3. A child pushed her doll's baby carriage along a park path.
4. An ambulance drove down one of the park paths to pick up a man who had collapsed in the middle of the park.

Based on a literal reading of the town's new ordinance, all four of these situations are violations of the law. All four involve a "vehicle" being on a park path. However, while the town council undoubtedly wished to ban joyriding Jeep Cherokee drivers as much as it wanted to ban joyriding motorcycle riders, it is highly unlikely that it actually wished to prohibit situations 2, 3, and 4. The problem is that the town council members chose language that was more inclusive than they really intended, and now all four parties are technically guilty of violating the ordinance.

This example illustrates how slippery language can be and how difficult it is to draft a law that encompasses only what you are trying to prohibit. It also illustrates how ambiguities in a statute may not appear until you apply it to individual factual situations. Therefore, though on its face a statute may seem straightforward, always remember that even the most seemingly clear language can be ambiguous when applied to a new factual situation.

Sometimes statutory ambiguities result from sloppy draftsmanship. More often, however, ambiguities arise when the statute is applied to unanticipated circumstances. There are also times when the drafters purposely write the ambiguity into the statute in order to provide a basis for compromise by glossing over conflicts among the legislators. Throughout this text, we will see examples of the courts grappling with such problems of statutory interpretation.

2. Understanding Court Opinions

In this text, you will be reading many court opinions. In court opinions, the judge drafting the opinion will give a summary of the relevant facts—the law that is being applied to those facts and the court's decision as to the outcome of the case. The law being discussed could be based upon enacted law, a constitutional provision, statutory language, or a regulation, or it could be based on something known as the common law. Common law is court-made law created when there is no enacted law covering the situation.

Mandatory authority
Court decisions from a higher court in the same jurisdiction

Persuasive authority
Court decisions from an equal or a lower court from the same jurisdiction or from a higher court in a different jurisdiction.

Stare decisis
The doctrine that normally once a court has decided an issue, other courts in the same jurisdiction will decide the same way.

a. How to Read a Court Opinion

The first thing you need to do, when reading a court opinion, is to take note of the court—for example, whether it is a state or federal court—and the date on which the case was decided. These are critical factors because they relate to the very important differences between **mandatory authority** and **persuasive authority**. Whereas judges are expected to decide cases consistently with those of higher courts in the same system, they can consider but do not have to follow the decisions of other courts at their same level or from another system.

Figure 1-1 shows the hierarchical nature of mandatory authority. A decision handed down by a court is mandatory authority for those courts below it connected by an arrow. For example, a federal district court in the First Circuit is required to follow the decisions of the federal court of appeals for the First Circuit. But the decisions of the Second Circuit court of appeals are only persuasive authority for the First Circuit district courts. Likewise, the decisions of state A's highest appellate court are mandatory authority for state A's intermediate appellate and trial courts, but they are only persuasive authority for state B's courts This process of looking to precedent—prior cases—for guidance is known as following the doctrine of **stare decisis.** Stare decisis literally means the decision stands.

The first section of a court opinion usually starts with a discussion of the facts of the case. These facts can be divided into two groups: substantive facts and procedural facts.

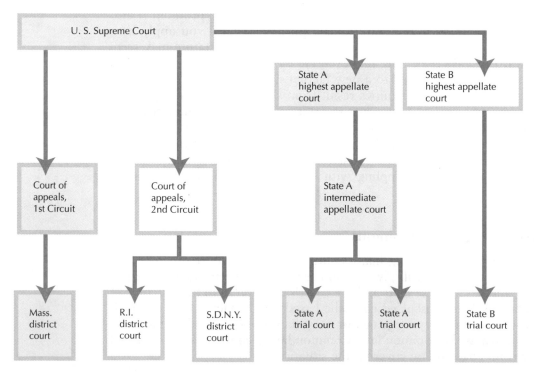

Figure 1-1   Mandatory Authority

The **substantive facts** deal with what happened to the parties before the litigation began—that is, with why one party is suing the other.

When reading a court opinion, look for answers to the following questions:

- Who were the parties in this legal dispute?
- Who did what to whom that created the conflict being litigated?
- Which party initiated the legal action (either civil suit or criminal prosecution)?
- What did the various parties want the court to do?

Procedural facts refer to what happened in the lower courts or administrative agencies as well as the action taken by the appellate court issuing the opinion. For example, in the trial court did the plaintiff win after a jury verdict, or did the plaintiff lose on a motion to dismiss? These procedural facts are sometimes referred to as the **judicial history** of the case.

After reviewing the facts, the court will move on to discuss the **legal issues** raised in the case. It is not unusual for a court opinion to address multiple issues in a single opinion. These legal issues usually relate to how the law should be interpreted or applied to the facts of the case being decided. The discussion of the issue will often include references to cases that the court wishes to rely on as precedent. There may also be references to prior cases that the court rejects as precedent either because they are not relevant to the precise issue being decided or because the court disagrees with the prior court's reasoning.

The opinion will conclude with a section that announces the official decision reached by the majority of the participating judges. In addition to declaring how the law is to be interpreted, it will usually include directions as to what is to happen next. These directions constitute what is called the **disposition of the case**. If the court agreed with the actions of a lower court, it will simply **affirm** the lower court's decision. If the court found that an error was committed, it will **reverse** the actions of the lower court and **remand** the case back for further actions consistent with the way the court interpreted the law.

In cases where there is more than one judge, those not fully agreeing with the majority may choose to file either a **concurring** or **dissenting** opinion. While these concurring and dissenting opinions have no legal affect on the outcome of the case, concurring opinions can affect the way the law is interpreted in the future, and dissenting opinions can provide arguments that may sway other judges in future cases.

The following is a court opinion dealing with facts similar to those Mr. Drake experienced. As you read the case, pay careful attention to the facts, the rule the court applied to those facts, how the court resolved the case, and finally its reasoning for finding as it did. Keep in mind that court decisions can be quite complex, and judges often use a writing style that is different from the sorts of writing to which you have become accustomed. Therefore, always plan on reading the case at least twice. The first time, focus on getting the "big picture." On the second reading you can pay more attention to the details and take notes. We will be discussing one method of note taking, called briefing a case, in the next section, after you have read *Dillon v. Legg*.

Substantive facts
Things that happened to the parties before the litigation began and that are relevant to their claims.

Procedural facts
Actions taken by lower courts or administrative agencies before the case reached the court issuing the opinion you are reading.

Legal issues
Questions about the interpretation and application of the law.

Affirm
When the higher court agrees with what the lower court has done.

Reverse
When the higher court disagrees with what the lower has done.

Remand
When an appellate court sends a case back to the trial court for a new trial or other action.

Concurring opinion
An opinion that agrees with the majority's result but disagrees with its reasoning.

Dissenting opinion
An opinion that disagrees with the majority's decision and reasoning.

b. Sample Case: Dillon v. Legg

Dillon v. Legg
68 Cal. 2d 728, 441 P.2d 912 (1968)

TOBRINER, Justice.

[O]n . . . September 27, 1964, defendant drove his automobile in a southerly direction on Bluegrass Road near its intersection with Clover Lane in the County of Sacramento, and at that time plaintiff's infant daughter, Erin Lee Dillon, lawfully crossed Bluegrass Road. [D]efendant's negligent operation of his vehicle caused it to "collide with the deceased Erin Lee Dillon resulting in injuries to decedent which proximately resulted in her death."

Plaintiff's [complaint] alleged that [the mother] "was in close proximity to the . . . collision and personally witnessed said collision." She further alleged that "because of the negligence of defendants [she] sustained great emotional disturbance and shock and injury to her nervous system" which caused her great physical and mental pain and suffering.

[D]efendant . . . moved for judgment on the pleadings, contending that "No cause of action is stated in that allegation that plaintiff sustained emotional distress, fright or shock induced by . . . witnessing of negligently caused injury to a third person." The court granted a judgment on the pleadings against the mother [and she] appealed from the judgment.

That the courts should allow recovery to a mother who suffers emotional trauma and physical injury from witnessing the infliction of death or injury to her child for which the tortfeasor is liable in negligence would appear to be a compelling proposition. . . .

Nevertheless, past American decisions have barred the mother's recovery. Refusing the mother the right to take her case to the jury, these courts ground their position on an alleged absence of a required "duty" of due care of the tortfeasor to the mother. [They state] the imposition of duty here would work disaster because it would invite fraudulent claims and it would involve the courts in the hopeless task of defining the extent of the tortfeasor's liability. In substance, they say, definition of liability being impossible, denial of liability is the only realistic alternative.

We have concluded that neither of the feared dangers excuses the frustration of the natural justice upon which the mother's claim rests. . . .

1. This court in the past has rejected the argument that we must deny recovery upon a legitimate claim because other fraudulent ones may be urged. . . .

The possibility that some fraud will escape detection does not justify an abdication of the judicial responsibility to award damages for sound claims: if it is 'to be conceded that our procedural system for the ascertainment of truth is inadequate to defeat fraudulent claims . . . , the result is a virtual acknowledgment that the courts are unable to render justice in respect to them.'

Indubitably juries and trial courts, constantly called upon to distinguish the frivolous from the substantial and the fraudulent from the meritorious, reach some erroneous results. But such fallibility, inherent in the judicial process, offers no reason for substituting for the case-by-case resolution of causes an artificial and indefensible barrier. Courts not only compromise their basic responsibility to decide the merits of each case individually but destroy the public's confidence in them by using the broad broom of 'administrative convenience' to sweep away a class of claims a number of which are admittedly meritorious. . . .

2. The alleged inability to fix definitions for recovery on the different facts of future cases does not justify the denial of recovery on the specific facts of the instant case; in any event, proper guidelines can indicate the extent of liability for such future cases.

In order to limit the otherwise potential infinite liability which would follow every negligent act, the law of torts holds defendant amenable only for injuries to others which to defendant at the time were reasonably foreseeable. . . .

Since the chief element in determining whether defendant owes a duty or an obligation to plaintiff is the foreseeability of the risk, that factor will be of prime concern in every case. Because it is inherently intertwined with foreseeability such duty or obligation must necessarily be adjudicated only upon a case-by-case basis. We cannot now predetermine defendant's obligation in every situation by a fixed category; no immutable rule can establish the extent of that obligation for every circumstance of the future. We can, however, define guidelines which will aid in the resolution of such an issue as the instant one.

. . . In determining, in such a case, whether defendant should reasonably foresee the injury to plaintiff, or, in other terminology, whether defendant owes plaintiff a duty of due care, the courts will take into account such factors as the following: (1) Whether plaintiff was located near the scene of the accident as contrasted with one who was a distance away from it. (2) Whether the shock resulted from a direct emotional impact upon plaintiff from the sensory and contemporaneous observance of the accident, as contrasted with learning of the accident from others after its occurrence. (3) Whether plaintiff and the victim were closely related, as contrasted with an absence of any relationship or the presence of only a distant relationship.

The evaluation of these factors will indicate the degree of the defendant's foreseeability: obviously [a] defendant is more likely to foresee that a mother who observes an accident affecting her child will suffer harm than to foretell that a stranger witness will do so. Similarly, the degree of foreseeability of the third person's injury is far greater in the case of his contemporaneous observance of the accident than that in which he subsequently learns of it. The defendant is more likely to foresee that shock to the nearby, witnessing mother will cause physical harm than to anticipate that someone distant from the accident will suffer more than a temporary emotional reaction. All these elements, of course, shade into each other; the fixing of obligation, intimately tied into the facts, depends upon each case.

In light of these factors the court will determine whether the accident and harm was reasonably foreseeable. Such reasonable foreseeability does not turn on whether the particular defendant as an individual would have in actuality foreseen the exact accident and loss; it contemplates that courts, on a case-to-case basis, analyzing all the circumstances, will decide what the ordinary man under such circumstances should reasonably have foreseen. The courts thus mark out the areas of liability, excluding the remote and unexpected.

In the instant case, the presence of all the above factors indicates that plaintiff has alleged a sufficient prima facie case. Surely the negligent driver who causes the death of a young child may reasonably expect that the mother will not be far distant and will upon witnessing the accident suffer emotional trauma. . . .

We are not now called upon to decide whether, in the absence or reduced weight of some of the above factors, we would conclude that the accident and injury were not reasonably foreseeable and that therefore defendant owed no duty of due care to plaintiff. In future cases the courts will draw lines of demarcation upon facts more subtle than the compelling ones alleged in the complaint before us. . . .

To deny recovery would be to chain this state to an outmoded rule of the 19th century which can claim no current credence. No good reason compels our captivity to an indefensible orthodoxy.

The judgment is reversed.

BURKE, J., Dissenting

The majority, obviously recognizing that they are . . . embarking upon a first excursion into the "fantastic realm of infinite liability," undertake to provide so-called "guidelines" for the future. But notwithstanding the limitations which these "guidelines" purport to impose, it is only reasonable to expect pressure upon our trial courts to make their future rulings conform to the spirit of the new elasticity proclaimed by the majority.

. . . Upon analysis, [the majority's guidelines'] seeming certainty evaporates into arbitrariness. . . . What if the plaintiff was honestly mistaken in believing the third person to be in danger or to be seriously injured? . . . How "close" must the relationship be between the plaintiff and the third person? I.e., what if the third person was the plaintiff's beloved niece or nephew, grandparent, fiancé, or lifelong friend, more dear to the plaintiff than her immediate family? Next, how "near" must the plaintiff have been to the scene of the accident, and how "soon" must shock have been felt? Indeed, what is the magic in the plaintiff's being actually present? Is the shock any less real if the mother does not know of the accident until her injured child is brought into her home? On the other hand, is it any less real if the mother is physically present at the scene but is nevertheless unaware of the dan-ger or injury to her child until after the accident has occurred? No answers to these questions are to be found in today's majority opinion. . . .

It appears to me that in the light of today's majority opinion the matter at issue should be commended to the attention of the Legislature of this state. . . . [I]f all alleged California tortfeasors, including motorists, home and other property owners, and governmental entities, are now to be faced with the concept of potentially infinite liability beyond any rational relationship to their culpability, then surely the point has been reached at which the Legislature should reconsider the entire subject and allow all interests affected to be heard.

I would affirm the judgment.

Now that you have read *Dillon v. Legg,* it is time to turn our attention to stylized legal note taking, called case briefing.

c. Briefing Court Opinions

The word *brief* has several meanings in the legal field. When we refer to briefing a case or to case briefs, we are referring to a written summary of a court opinion. This is to be contrasted with an appellate brief, which is a formal written argument to an appellate court, in which a lawyer argues why that court should affirm or reverse a lower court's decision.

(1) Reasons for Briefing Cases

Case Briefing
A method for summarizing court opinions.

Briefing court opinions serves two purposes. First, and most important, it makes you read the case thoroughly. You have to go back and dig out the essentials, organize them, and state them in your own words. This is necessary for an adequate understanding of the court opinion. Second, it is a form of note taking that provides a condensed record of the most important information about the case you briefed. You can use these case briefs to refresh your memory when preparing for class or studying for exams.

(2) Format of a Case Brief

While most case briefs share many common features, there is no single format that is universally accepted within the legal community. Indeed, there are almost as many different briefing styles as there are attorneys writing briefs. What we present here is an approach that we think will help you organize your thoughts and understand the opinion.

The case briefing method described here breaks the case down into the following elements: (a) case citation, (b) facts—both procedural and substantive, (c) rule, (d) issue, (e) holding, (f) reasoning, and (g) criticism. Although you list the items in a specific order, you may find yourself filling them in out of order. That is fine because case briefing is a circuitous process. You will often rewrite one part of your brief as your understanding of that part changes based on your work on other parts. As with any type of writing, thinking and writing are intertwined.

A more detailed explanation of the content and purpose of each section of a case brief is provided below. As you finish reading the specific directions for each part of the brief, try your hand at briefing *Dillon v. Legg*. Then look at how that section was worded in the sample case brief beginning on page 15.

(a) *Case Citation* The case citation goes at the top. The citation should contain enough information to let the reader know (1) the name of the case, (2) the court that decided it, (3) where the reader can locate it, and (4) the year of decision. You may also want to indicate the page number in your textbook.

(b) *Facts* Include a summary of both substantive and procedural facts. The most difficult part of this section is determining how much detail to include. Omit any facts that you think did not form the basis of the court's decision, but be sure to include all facts that the court relied on in reaching its decision, being as precise as possible. For example, if the case involves an eight-year-old girl, and you think her age and sex matter, do not simply say the case involved a child. However, if an accident occurred at 222 Main Street, but the precise location is not important, there is no need to mention the address.

For the procedural facts, be sure to include what happened in the lower court or courts. For example, indicate which party won at the trial court level. Also, report the final disposition of the case—for example, did the court affirm or reverse, and if it reversed, did it also remand? Some legal writers prefer to put the court's disposition in a separate section rather than including it with the other procedural facts. If you include the disposition with the procedural facts, however, then the reader can see the "whole story" right at the beginning of the brief.

(c) *Rule* The **rule** is a general legal principle in existence before the case began that the court uses to reach the decision in this case. These rules can come from a constitution, statute, regulation, or a previous court decision.

(d) *Issue(s)* A court opinion will include one or more issues. An **issue** is the legal question created by the facts and relevant rule that the court must resolve. Traditionally, issue statements start with the word *whether* and include enough of the relevant facts and law for the reader to be able to see why the parties are in court, that is, what the fight is all about. Learning to state the issue precisely is one of the most difficult parts of the case brief, so do not get discouraged if this takes some practice.

(e) *Holding* The **holding** is the court's answer to the issue. The holding is the new version of the rule, a rule that future courts will look to for assistance in deciding similar cases.

If you have given a complete issue statement, technically the holding could be a simple yes or no answer. However, it is always best to give the holding as a complete declarative sentence using the same elements as you did for the issue.

One of the most difficult aspects of developing the holding is determining how narrow or broad it should be. A **narrow holding** contains many of the case's specific facts, thereby limiting its future applicability to a narrow range of cases. A **broad holding** states the facts in very general terms so that the holding will apply to a wider range of cases. See Figure 1-2.

Rule
In a case brief, the general legal principle in existence before the case began.

Issue
In a case brief, the legal question facing the court.

Holding
In a case brief, the court's answer to the issue presented to it; the new legal principle established by the court opinion.

Narrow holding
A statement of the court's decision that contains many of the case's specific facts, thereby limiting its future applicability to a narrow range of cases.

Broad holding
A statement of the court's decision in which the facts are either omitted or given in very general terms so that it will apply to a wider range of cases.

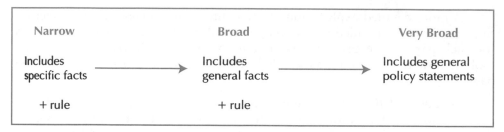

Figure 1-2   Possible Holdings for a Case

To be useful, a holding should be broad enough to help courts resolve similar cases, but not so broad as to stand for no more than a general legal principle. Learning how to state a holding either very narrowly, by including very specific facts, or very broadly, by stating the facts as generalizations only, is a skill you will acquire over time. It is best to start with a narrow holding because you will find it easier to amend a narrow holding to make it broader than you will to amend a broad holding to make it narrower. However, even with a narrow holding, include only those facts that you think truly affected the court's decision.

Also be sure to include any possible limitations to the holding. If the court specifically states that its decision covers only a certain set of circumstances, your brief should make that clear. For example, in a case dealing with a social host's liability for serving alcohol to a minor, a court might relieve the social host of any responsibility but limit its holding to situations where alcohol is not being served for a profit.

Finally, note that the court's procedural answer—reversed, remanded, affirmed, and so on—can never be the holding. The holding is always a statement of the new rule that results from the court's decision.

(f) Reasoning   In this section of the brief you explain, in your own words, *why* the court ruled as it did. The court's reasoning gives you your best clue as to how the court may act in the future in a different but similar situation.

Pinpoint as far as is possible the explicit and implicit reasons that the court gave to justify its holding. But do not quote the court's exact language unless the precise phrasing is critical. It will be easier for the reader to understand your summary if it is primarily in your own words.

In analyzing the reasoning, you need to distinguish between the ratio decidendi and obiter dictum. The **ratio decidendi** is a decision on the legal issues raised in that specific case, whereas **obiter dictum** (sometimes just referred to as dicta) refers to a comment a judge makes that is not necessary to the resolution of the case. For example, it is dictum when a judge talks about what might have been if the facts had been different from the ones presented. Even though courts have power to decide only the precise case with which they are faced, human nature being what it is, judges often cannot resist discussing issues that were not really presented to them. While that part of the opinion will have no effect on the litigants, it could give you a very good clue as to how the court might decide a different case in the future.

(g) Criticism   You should use this section of the brief to evaluate the court's decision. Do you think it was appropriate and well justified? If not, why not? If you agree with the result, do you think the court gave the best or only

Ratio decidendi
The court's reason for its decision.

Dictum
A statement in a judicial opinion not necessary for the decision of the case.

reasons for reaching that result? If the court included a limitation in the holding, what problems do you think that will cause for future litigants?

If there were concurring or dissenting opinions, include a discussion of their reasoning. While only the majority opinion represents the court's view, what individual concurring and dissenting judges have to say can influence later courts. Do not be discouraged if you find the criticism section one of the most difficult parts of the brief to write. It is the court's job to convince you that it has reached the right result for the right reasons. Therefore, your first reaction may be to simply agree with everything it says. Resist that inclination. Remember that the case would not have been appealed unless someone thought there were two sides to the issue. Take a look at Figure 1-3 for some additional helpful hints for briefing a case.

d. Sample Brief for Dillon v. Legg

Dillon v. Legg
68 Cal. 2d 728, 441 P.2d 912 (1968)

Facts: Mother saw her daughter run over and killed by a negligent driver. She sued for the emotional distress she suffered in witnessing the accident. The trial court dismissed her claim; reversed.

Rule: There can be no recovery for emotional distress from simply observing the death of another.

Issue: Whether a mother can recover for the emotional distress she suffered upon seeing the negligently caused death of her daughter despite the current rule that denies recovery for an injury caused by observing the death of another.

Holding: Yes, a mother who witnesses the negligently caused death of her child can recover for emotional distress.

Reasoning: Traditionally, there have been two arguments advanced for precluding such suits: 1) a fear of fraudulent claims and 2) a fear of indefinable claims. The court discounted both fears. As to the fear of fraudulent claims, the court stated that even if some fraud were to occur, that does not justify denying recovery for valid cases. Besides, in every type of case, it is ultimately the responsibility of the courts to distinguish the valid from the fraudulent claim. As to the second concern, a fear of indefinable claims, the court said that was no reason to deny recovery in this specific case, where no one would deny that a mother seeing her child killed would suffer great harm, and that guidelines could be established to set the extent of liability in future cases. The guidelines the court developed provide that the following factors should be taken into account: 1) how close the plaintiff was to the scene of the accident; 2) whether the plaintiff observed the accident or heard about it later; and 3) how closely related the plaintiff was to the victim.

Criticism: The dissenting judge thought the guidelines raised more questions than they answered and that such an important change in the law should come from the legislature, not the courts.

I agree that the guidelines are a bit vague and will be difficult to apply in new situations. For example, will "closely related" be determined by familial status or by an actual investigation into how involved the plaintiff was in the victim's life?

1. Read the Case First, Then Brief
Do not try to brief the case as you read it for the first time. Read it through, underlining if you wish and making notes in the margin, before you start your brief.

2. Develop a Workable Style
Develop a briefing style that works best for you. As mentioned above, there is no right or wrong method. However, if your brief is to serve its intended purpose, you must write it in such a way that you can return to it later and easily find the information for which you are looking.

3. Write Based on the Needs of Your Reader
If you will be using the brief just as a reference for yourself, abbreviate commonly used terms. For example, use π or P. for plaintiff and Δ or D. for defendant. You may also want to write in phrases rather than complete sentences.

4. Cross-reference
Develop a cross-reference system that will allow you to find the court's full discussion of the points you summarized in your brief. For example, you could place numbers in the margin of the case to correspond to the points you discuss in your brief.

5. Paraphrase
Write the brief in your own words. A brief should not be a long series of quotations, so do not copy large parts of the opinion. A brief is your summary of the case, not merely a listing of quotations from it.

6. Use a Dictionary
Make sure you understand every unfamiliar legal term. Initially, you will find the courts using many unfamiliar terms, some of which will be specialized legal terms. Others, however, will simply be "normal English" you do not know. Do not hesitate to turn to a legal dictionary or an English language dictionary for help.

Figure 1-3   Six Hints for Better Brief Writing

3. Applying the Legal Rules to the Facts

Legal reasoning
The application of legal rules to a client's specific factual situation; also known as *legal analysis*.

The final stage of legal analysis involves applying the legal rules to a specific set of facts. This is called **legal reasoning.** If the legal research discussed above sufficiently identifies unambiguous legal rules that clearly apply to the client's situation, an attorney can confidently advise clients as to the legal consequences of anticipated acts or recommend steps that they should take to protect themselves.

Frequently, however, the law will be ambiguous, and there will be no prior cases with the exact same set of facts. Then there will be no clear answer as to how the rules should be applied until the issue is resolved by an appellate court. Those are the cases that are often the most interesting to read as the ambiguity in the law's language or its applicability to a new set of facts forces the court to also consider the policy concerns behind the law.

For example, think about Mr. Drake's situation and the *Dillon v. Legg* court decision. If a court were asked to apply that decision to Mr. Drake's facts, how do you think he would fare? Factually, do you think the court would view a mother and a grandfather as similar? On policy grounds, do you think the court would tend to resolve the issue of recovering for emotional distress the same in those situations involving mothers and those involving grandfathers?

If you discuss this with your classmates, you may find that you differ as to the "right" answer. But in reality, there are no "right" answers, only better or worse arguments. Any decision about what the law should be is a choice between competing values.

Finally, sometimes there are no rules that govern the situation. For example, while there are both federal and state statutes that protect employees from sexual harassment, under current law Ms. Smith does not appear to have a cause of action against the construction workers.

Twenty-five years ago, Ms. Smith would not even have had a cause of action if she had been harassed by her employer. But as societal values change, the law usually changes as well. In recent years our society has become more sensitive to issues of gender equality, and new laws have been developed to provide new protections. Twenty years from now, someone in Ms. Smith's position may have a cause of action that does not exist today. Societal values will change, and the law will continue to evolve in order to respond to those changes.

DISCUSSION QUESTIONS

1. Why do you suppose there are certain types of harm, such as the humiliation Ms. Smith felt when the construction workers whistled at her, that courts will not help individuals resolve?

2. Do you think it is right that employees can go to court and sue their bosses for sexual harassment? Why? If the harasser were a co-worker instead of a boss, how would you view the situation?

SUMMARY

Law is an important topic for study because it directly or indirectly affects almost every aspect of your daily life. Besides defining what constitutes appropriate behavior, the law also provides a mechanism for resolving conflicts and disagreements without resorting to personal violence. It is also good to study the law because it is a challenging intellectual exercise that involves the application of logic and other critical thinking skills that can be useful in many different endeavors.

Legal analysis involves analyzing the "relevant" facts, reading and understanding the appropriate legal rules, and applying those rules to the relevant facts. In order to understand legal rules, you need to learn how to read and interpret constitutions, statutes, and court decisions.

A case brief provides a condensed record of the most important information about the case you read, and the process of briefing a case helps you to understand what was actually decided and how the court justified its decision.

Do not be dismayed if you are sometimes overwhelmed by the complexity and the sheer volume of legal concepts and materials. Learning law is a lot like learning a foreign language. Although many of these terms may be new to you now, they will become increasingly familiar as you progress through the text. In the end you will be amazed at how these diverse pieces end up fitting into a logical and effective system.

CRITICAL THINKING EXERCISES

1. Assume John shipped obscene music CDs from Massachusetts to California. He has been charged with violating a federal criminal statute that prohibits interstate shipment of any obscene "book, pamphlet, picture, motion-picture film, paper, letter, writing, print or other matter of indecent character." Has he violated the statute?

2. John Smith tried to buy cocaine from an undercover officer. Instead of cash, he offered to sell his fully automatic MAC-10 firearm. According to the court, the MAC-10 is "a favorite among criminals. It is small and compact, lightweight, and can be equipped with a silencer. Most important of all, it can be devastating: A fully automatic MAC-10 can fire more than 1,000 rounds per minute." After Mr. Smith was arrested, he was charged with drug-trafficking crimes, including an attempt to possess cocaine with intent to distribute. He was also charged with violating a federal statute that mandates a 30-year sentence if a defendant "during and in relation to any crime of drug trafficking uses a firearm." The defendant argued that within the context of the statute, "uses" means to use the firearm as a weapon, which he did not do. The prosecution argued that in the plain dictionary meaning of the term "uses," the defendant "used" the firearm to try to purchase the cocaine. If you were the judge, how would you resolve the case?

3. List all of the ways in which you think Mr. Drake's case is similar to that of *Dillon v. Legg*. Then list all of the ways in which you think Mr. Drake's case could be likened to that of a bystander. Do you think a court would see Mr. Drake's case as more similar to that of the mother in *Dillon v. Legg* or to that of a bystander? Are there additional facts that you think the court would want to know before reaching its decision?

REVIEW QUESTIONS

1. Why does the study of law involve more than simply memorizing rules?
2. What is legal reasoning?
3. What is the doctrine of stare decisis, and why is it important?
4. Why is it important to know whether a set of facts are analogous to or distinguishable from those in prior court decisions?
5. What is a cause of action? What does it mean to say that a person does not have a valid cause of action?
6. Why does law change? Should it?
7. Why is there no one "right" answer to a legal problem?

Chapter 2

Functions and Sources of Law

We hold these truths to be self-evident....
Declaration of Independence

INTRODUCTION

No modern society can exist without a strong legal system, and when a person has a problem or is trying to avoid a problem, that person frequently turns to lawyers and the legal system for help. In this chapter we explore the role of law in American society and the sources of that law. As we begin that discussion, let us first introduce you to Diane Dobbs, who met with attorney Pat Harper of the law firm of Darrow and Bryan. She related the following story.

Case 3: The Pregnant Waitress

Ms. Diane Dobbs had been employed by the Western Rib Eye Restaurant for the past three years. Throughout that time her work record had been exemplary. Customers often spoke to the manager to tell him how Diane's service and personality contributed to their especially enjoyable dining experience at the restaurant.

Six months ago Diane, who is not married, found out that she was pregnant. When she approached her manager, Ben, to discuss arrangements for a maternity leave, instead of the favorable reception she had expected, Ben reached over, patted her stomach, and said, "Well, I guess we can't have you working for us any longer." Ben then grabbed her by the arm and escorted her out of the restaurant. Diane protested and asked to be allowed to collect her personal belongings from her locker, but the manager just laughed and said she was "history." When Diane began to cry, he softened his demeanor a little and said, "Look, we simply can't have a pregnant lady working here. It just wouldn't be good for business."

Although she has been actively looking, Diane has not yet been able to find suitable employment.

When a client presents a problem to an attorney, the attorney may feel confident that the legal system can provide a remedy, but that will not always be so. As we indicated in Chapter 1, not every problem can be resolved by the legal system. In order to better appreciate why this is so, we need to study the function of law, the history of our American legal system, and the sources of our laws.

A. FUNCTIONS AND THEORIES OF LAW

The development and enforcement of the law are essential governmental functions in all developed societies. Although the laws themselves sometimes differ, they serve the same essential functions in all fifty states and at the federal level.

1. Definition of Law

Laws
Rules of conduct promulgated and enforced by the government.

It is our **laws**—rules of conduct promulgated and enforced by the government—that define the types of conduct that are either prohibited or required. For example, a criminal code usually prohibits the unauthorized taking of property that belongs to someone else. Tax laws require that certain types of individuals or corporations give part of their income to the government. The laws can apply to the behavior of individuals, businesses, and even governments themselves. Thus, municipalities may be prohibited from dumping raw sewage into lakes and rivers and the police prohibited from conducting unreasonable searches and seizures.

To be considered laws, these rules of conduct must be promulgated and enforced by the appropriate governmental bodies. For example, only the U.S. Congress can make federal statutory law, and only a state's highest court can authoritatively interpret the meaning of that state's laws.

These rules of conduct also carry with them certain sanctions that can be imposed on those who fail to follow the rules. When individuals violate a section of the criminal law, they may be fined, sent to prison, or in some cases even suffer loss of life. Persons who are found liable under the civil law may be forced to pay various penalties or damage awards or to perform some action, such as carrying out the terms of a contract. Police who conduct illegal searches and seizures may be denied the right to use in court any evidence they find and may even be forced to pay damages to the injured parties. Even presidents can be cited for contempt of court if they fail to turn over subpoenaed materials.

2. Functions of Law

While there may be a great deal of debate over the wisdom and appropriateness of a particular law (as there is, for example, over a mandatory seat belt law), there is general agreement that laws themselves are necessary. As the Task Force on Law and Law Enforcement reported to the National Commission on the Causes and Prevention of Violence:

> Human welfare demands, at a minimum, sufficient order to insure that such basic needs as food production, shelter and child rearing be satisfied, not in a state of constant chaos and conflict, but on a peaceful, orderly basis with a reasonable level of day-to-day security. . . . When a society becomes highly complex, mobile, and pluralistic; the beneficiary, yet also the victim, of extremely rapid technological change; and when at the same time, and partly as a result of these factors, the influence of traditional stabilizing institutions such as family, church, and community wanes, then that society of necessity becomes increasingly dependent on highly structured, formalistic systems of law and government to maintain social order. . . . For better or worse, we are by necessity increasingly committed to our formal legal institutions as the paramount agency of social control.[1]

It has thus been increasingly left to the legal system to define and enforce the rules of society. Some of these rules, such as restrictions on abortions, pornography, and gambling, are heavily influenced by the religious and moral beliefs of various groups in the society, while others, such as traffic regulations, have no moral content at all. In either case they help to provide the type of order and predictability that are essential elements of our modern society.

3. Theories of Jurisprudence

To help explain what the purpose of law is and how laws work (or should work in a just society), various theories of legal philosophy have been developed. This area of study, known as **jurisprudence,** has had an important impact on the development of our legal system and on the thinking of many judges.

Jurisprudence
The study of law and legal philosophy.

One part of jurisprudence deals with theorizing about the source of laws. For example, since the time of the ancient Greeks, **natural law** theorists have believed that man-made law should be based on timeless and immutable principles that can be discovered through careful thought and humanity's innate sense of right and wrong. The purpose of having governments and laws is to protect the natural rights that are inherent in these principles. Therefore, the laws that governments enact are to be respected when they reflect these natural laws but should be resisted when they do not conform to these natural laws.

Natural law
A legal philosophy whose proponents think there are ideal laws that can be discovered through careful thought and humanity's innate sense of right and wrong.

This natural law philosophy has had a great influence on the development of the American legal system and is reflected in our Declaration of Independence, which includes the following:

> We hold these truths to be self-evident, that all men are created equal, that they are endowed by their Creator with certain unalienable Rights, that among these are Life, Liberty, and the Pursuit of Happiness.

The Reverend Martin Luther King, Jr. used natural law as a justification for civil disobedience in his fight against racial segregation.

---

[1] J. Campbell, J. Sahid, & D. Strang, Law and Order Reconsidered: Report of the Task Force on Law and Law Enforcement to the National Commission on the Causes and Preventions of Violence 3, 5 (1970).

Legal positivism
A legal theory whose proponents believe that the validity of a law is determined by the process through which it was made rather than by the degree to which it reflects natural law principles.

Legal Formalism
A legal theory that views the law as a complete and autonomous system of logically consistent principles within which judges find the correct result by simply making logical deductions.

Legal realism
A legal philosophy whose proponents think that judges decide cases based on factors other than logic and preexisting rules, such as economic and sociological factors.

The alternative to the natural law theory is known as **legal positivism.** Supporters of this approach believe that the validity of a law is determined by the process through which it was made rather than by the degree to which it reflects natural law principles. To a legal positivist a law is valid as long as it was passed by the appropriate lawmaking agency.

A second area of jurisprudence is concerned with the extent to which judges simply apply the law versus create the law. **Formalists** believe that the proper role of the judge is to do the former—that is, simply to apply the law. They view the law as a complete and autonomous system of logically consistent principles. Judges can find the "correct result" by simply making logical deductions. Judges serve as impartial technicians who simply identify the proper, preexisting rule and then apply it to the facts of the case. Social policy and the judge's private views are considered irrelevant.

Legal realists, on the other hand, reject the formalist's assertion that judges' decisions are reached by a strict application of the principles of logic. First, judges must frequently decide between contradictory rules. Second, legal realists point to instances in which the law is vague and ambiguous. Because of the elastic nature of the English language, it is always possible for judges to expand or contract the meaning of any given rule. In these situations, the realists assert that judges can interpret the wording of the statutes and prior cases to justify different outcomes. The number of five-to-four split votes in controversial Supreme Court cases is often cited as proof of this assertion that there are always counterarguments.

But if, as the realists assert, logic alone is insufficient to explain judicial decisions, what then does determine how judges decide cases? Some realists suggest that judges simply seek interpretations that will advance the public values and social goals to which they subscribe. Others argue that realism involves going beyond the confines of the law to determine the social consequences of the alternative outcomes. To assist in this process, judges should look to the expertise that can be provided by the social sciences, specifically psychology, sociology, and economics.

An illustration of the realist approach can be found in the 1954 Supreme Court case of *Brown v. Board of Education.*[2] That case raised the question of whether segregated public schools could provide "separate but equal" education. In 1896 in *Plessy v. Ferguson*[3] the Court had found that segregated railway cars did not violate the Fourteenth Amendment so long as they provided "equal" accommodations. However, rather than relying on the legal precedent established by *Plessy*, the Court in *Brown* looked beyond the law and recognized studies done by social scientists that concluded that segregation in the public schools had a detrimental effect upon black children because it generated feelings of inferiority "that may affect their hearts and minds in a way unlikely ever to be undone."[4] Based upon this data, the Court concluded that "[s]eparate educational facilities are inherently unequal."[5] Today, lawyers routinely present

---

[2]347 U.S. 483 (1954).
[3]163 U.S. 537 (1896).
[4]347 U.S. at 494.
[5]Id. at 495.

policy arguments in support of their client's position in an effort to convince the court that finding for their side is not only "legally" but also "socially" desirable.

While few still argue that judicial decisions are determined solely by the rules of logic, there remains considerable disagreement as to how far judges should be given discretion, especially in the area of constitutional interpretation. Prominent political conservatives such as Supreme Court Justice Antonin Scalia argue for a strict construction that narrowly interprets the text of the Constitution in a manner that is consistent with what most people understood those words to mean at the time that they were written.[6] This view is often referred to as **originalism.** Scalia argues that such an approach will keep judges from substituting their own political views for those of the original drafters.

In contrast to this strict construction approach, others argue that judges should seek to determine the underlying goal or value that the drafters had in mind at the time they wrote the law. Then they should select the modern-day option that best advances that goal or value. This view is sometimes labeled the **evolutionary** or "living law" approach. We discuss both of these approaches in greater detail in "Approaches to Constitutional Interpretation" on pages 129–131 in Chapter 6.

Of course, many legal thinkers embrace more than one theory of how law should be viewed. Consider the following remarks of Justice Benjamin Cardozo:

> My analysis of the judicial process comes then to this, and little more: logic, and history, and custom, and utility and the accepted standards of right conduct, are the forces which singly or in combination shape the progress of the law.[7]

As you read the cases that are contained in this book, stop and analyze them in terms of these different perspectives of the role of law and how law is made. Did they include references to the natural law? How much discretion did the precedents leave to the judge? What values were aligned with each of the possible outcomes?

DISCUSSION QUESTIONS

1. Do you agree with the statement "Laws are necessary"? Many believe we have too many laws today. Do you agree? If you do, which laws should be eliminated? Do we need additional laws in some areas?

2. Can you think of ways, other than those mentioned in the text, that natural law theory has influenced the development of American law?

3. One of the basic principles of the natural law theory is that people should not have to obey an unjust law. Should it be left to the individual or to a judge to determine when a human-made law is unjust? If it is left to the judge, what criteria should the judge use?

4. Which of the theories of jurisprudence discussed in the text do you think best explains how law should work?

Originalism
An approach to constitutional interpretation that narrowly interprets the text of the Constitution in a manner that is consistent with what most people understood those words to mean at the time that they were written.

Evolutionary approach
An approach to constitutional interpretation in which judges seek to determine the underlying purpose that the drafters had in mind at the time they wrote the law and the modern-day option that best advances that purpose.

---

[6]Antonin Scalia, A Matter of Interpretation: Federal Courts and the Law (1997).
[7]Benjamin Cardozo, The Nature of the Judicial Process 112 (1949).

5. There is an old joke about a lawyer who was asked, "What is two plus two?" The lawyer responded, "What do you *want* it to be?" Which legal theory does this best exemplify? Is it necessarily a bad thing that we live in a world where two plus two does not always have to be four?

B. SOURCES OF LAW

Most people can recall something from their high school civics class about the legislature making the law, the executive branch enforcing the law, and the courts interpreting the law. The truth is that the legislative, executive, and judicial branches are all involved in making the law.

1. Constitutional Law

Constitutional law
A body of principles and rules either explicitly stated in, or inferred from, the U.S. Constitution and those of the individual states.

Constitutions are usually written by specially selected delegates to a "constitutional convention." The text that is agreed upon by these delegates then has to be "ratified" (approved) by either a direct vote of the people or by approval by some representative body.[8] The procedures for amending a constitution are included in the text of the document and usually involve either the general electorate or some representative body approving amendments that were formally proposed through legislative action, special conventions, or referendums.[9]

The United States was the first nation to adopt a written constitution, and it is that Constitution that provides the framework within which all our laws are made. The first major function of the federal Constitution is to establish an organizational structure that allocates governmental powers. On the national level, the Constitution divides governmental powers among the legislative, executive, and judicial branches. This is commonly referred to as the **separation of powers.**

Separation of powers
The division of governmental power among the legislative, executive, and judicial branches.

The separate branches of government share power and have the ability to limit the actions of the other branches. In the Federalist Papers, James Madison explained that this system of **checks and balances** is designed to guard against "a gradual concentration of the several powers in the same department." Under the Constitution, Congress has the power to make laws, but the President has the power to veto them. The executive branch is responsible for administering the law, but it cannot spend money to do so unless Congress provides for the appropriate funding in the budget.

Checks and balances
Division among governmental branches so that each branch acts as a check on the power of the other two.

The Constitution also divides governmental power between the national government and the states. This division of power between the national government and the states is referred to as **federalism.** Certain powers are

Federalism
A system of government in which the authority to govern is split between a single, nationwide central government and several regional governments.

---

[8]The U.S. Constitution had to be ratified by conventions of at least nine states. Most state constitutions require ratification by a majority vote of the general electorate.

[9]Article V of the U.S. Constitution requires that amendments be proposed by two-thirds of both Houses or by a special convention called at the request of the legislatures of two-thirds of the states. The proposed amendment must then be ratified by the legislatures of three-fourths of the states or by conventions in three-fourths of the states.

explicitly granted to the federal government, while all others are reserved to the states and the people.

The second major function of the Constitution is to protect individual rights from governmental overreaching. Because our founding fathers perceived a lack of such protection in the Constitution, as soon as it was ratified, the first Congress began work on the first ten amendments, commonly known as the **Bill of Rights**. These ten amendments include protections for freedom of speech and press, freedom of religion, a privilege against self-incrimination, the right to an attorney and a trial by jury, and protections against unreasonable searches and seizures. Along with the Thirteenth, Fourteenth, and Fifteenth Amendments (added during the Civil War), these amendments serve to prevent state or federal government officials from interfering with our civil rights and liberties.

Bill of Rights
The first ten amendments to the U.S. Constitution.

The Constitution and its amendments constitute the "supreme law of the land." To be enforceable, all other laws must not conflict with the principles laid down in the Constitution. When there is a challenge to the constitutionality of a law, it is the courts that determine whether or not the law is valid. The process by which the courts make these types of judgments is referred to as **judicial review**.

Power of judicial review
A court's power to review statutes to decide if they conform to the U.S. or state constitutions.

It could be argued that since the Constitution established three coequal branches, each branch should be free to interpret the Constitution as it sees fit. However, there are times in which there is disagreement among the three branches about the interpretation of the Constitution, and in those situations, someone has to have the final say.

In *Marbury v. Madison*[10] the U.S. Supreme Court claimed this power for itself. The Court held it was inherent in the nature of a court's work to have to resolve conflicting interpretations of the law before it can carry out its assigned task of applying the law. If a Court determines that a statute does not conform to the Constitution, then the statute is invalid and the court cannot enforce it.

> It is emphatically the province and duty of the judicial department to say what the law is. Those who apply the rule to particular cases, must of necessity expound and interpret that rule. If two laws conflict with each other, the courts must decide on the operation of each.
>
> So if a law be in opposition to the constitution; if both the law and the constitution apply to a particular case, so that the court must either decide that case conformably to the law, disregarding the constitution; or conformably to the constitution, disregarding the law; the court must determine which of these conflicting rules governs the case. This is of the very essence of judicial duty.
>
> If then the courts are to regard the constitution; and the constitution is superior to any ordinary act of the legislature; the constitution, and not such ordinary act, must govern the case to which they both apply.[11]

---

[10]5 U.S. (1 Cranch) 137 (1803).

[11]Id. at 177-78.

Over the years, the U.S. Supreme Court has used this power of judicial review to invalidate a number of federal and state laws that it found to be in conflict with the U.S. Constitution. Some of the most controversial of the more recent applications of judicial review include decisions invalidating state laws involving racial segregation, abortion, and school prayer.

DISCUSSION QUESTION

6. Arguably, if Congress passes a statute, it means that the majority of both the House and the Senate believed it was not in conflict with the constitution. Why should the decision of the people's elected representatives be overridden by unelected, appointed judges?

In addition to determining the constitutionality of statutes, the courts are often called upon to determine the meaning of the Constitution itself. The Constitution was written more than 200 years ago and uses broad, sweeping terminology such as "freedom of speech," "establishment of religion," "unreasonable searches and seizures," and "cruel and unusual punishment." It is often difficult to determine the meaning of such ambiguous phrases, especially when applied to a specific situation. Under the power of judicial review, the U.S. Supreme Court has the final say regarding the interpretation of those ambiguous constitutional provisions. Therefore, in order to study constitutional law, one must look beyond the text of the document and also review relevant court decisions. In Chapter 6 you will have the opportunity to learn more about constitutional law and to read some of the most important court decisions that have shaped its interpretation.

Each of the fifty states also has a written constitution that defines the organization and powers of its government. Most also include an equivalent of the federal Bill of Rights. In the past many attorneys tended to ignore their own state's constitutional provisions. Recently, however, there has been an increase in litigation based on state constitutional law. This is partly because many state constitutions provide for more protection of individual rights than does the federal Constitution. The highest court in each state is the final arbiter of what its state constitution means.

In the following case, a school board instituted random drug testing of its student athletes in response to a survey that found significant drug and alcohol problems in the student body: 40 percent of sophomores reported having used illegal drugs. The United States Supreme Court had ruled that a similar drug testing program in another state did not violate the Fourth Amendment of the U.S. Constitution. Therefore, the plaintiffs in this case, parents of student athletes, brought this lawsuit in state court, alleging that the drug testing violated their children's rights under their state constitution.

York v. Wahkiakum School District No. 200
163 Wash. 2d 297, 178 P.3d 995 (2008)

SANDERS, J.

The question before us is whether random and suspicionless drug testing of student athletes violates article I, section 7 of the Washington State Constitution.[1]

... The school district claims random drug testing, without any individualized suspicion, is constitutional. ...

As part of the policy, all student athletes must agree to be randomly drug tested as a condition of playing extracurricular sports. The drug testing is done by urinalysis, with the student in an enclosed bathroom stall and a health department employee outside. The sample is then mailed to Comprehensive Toxicology Services in Tacoma, Washington. ...

We are aware there are strong arguments, policies, and opinions marshaled on both sides of this debate, but we are concerned only with the policy's constitutionality. And while we are loath to disturb the decisions of a local school board, we will not hesitate to intervene when constitutional protections are implicated.

... The United States Supreme Court has held such activity does not violate the Fourth Amendment to the federal constitution. *Vernonia Sch. Dist.*, 515 U.S. 646, 115 S. Ct. 2386, 132 L. Ed. 2d 564. But we have never decided whether a suspicionless, random drug search of student athletes violates article I, section 7 of our state constitution. ...

The Wahkiakum School District modeled its policy after the one used by the Vernonia School District. But simply passing muster under the federal constitution does not ensure the survival of the school district's policy under our state constitution. The Fourth Amendment provides for "[t]he right of the people to be secure in their persons, houses, papers, and effects, against unreasonable searches and seizures." U.S. Const. amend. IV. Therefore, a Fourth Amendment analysis hinges on whether a warrantless search is

reasonable, and it is possible in some circumstances for a search to be reasonable without a warrant. ...

Our state constitution provides, "No person shall be disturbed in his private affairs, or his home invaded, without authority of law." Wash. Const. art. I, § 7. It is well established that in some areas, article I, section 7 provides greater protection than its federal counterpart—the Fourth Amendment. ...

This requires a two-part analysis. First, we must determine whether the state action constitutes a disturbance of one's private affairs. Here that means asking whether requiring a student athlete to provide a urine sample intrudes upon the student's private affairs. Second, if a privacy interest has been disturbed, the second step in our analysis asks whether authority of law justifies the intrusion. The "authority of law" required by article I, section 7 is satisfied by a valid warrant, limited to a few jealously guarded exceptions. Because the Wahkiakum School District had no warrant, if we reach the second prong of the analysis we must decide whether the school district's activity fits within an exception to the warrant requirement.

[T]he school district claims student athletes have a lower expectation of privacy. Certainly, students who choose to play sports are subjected to more regulation. ... And certainly there is generally less privacy in locker rooms than in other parts of a school. But the district does not link regulations and the communal atmosphere of locker rooms with a student's lowered expectation of privacy in terms of being subjected to suspicionless, random drug testing. We do not see how what happens in the locker room or on the field affects a student's privacy in the context of compelling him or her to provide a urine sample. ...

Because we determine that interfering with a student athlete's bodily functions disturbs one's private affairs, we must address the second prong of the article I, section 7 analysis: does the school

---

[1]Article I, section 7 of the Washington Constitution provides:
No person shall be disturbed in his private affairs, or his home invaded, without authority of law.

district have the necessary authority of law to randomly drug test student athletes?

We have long held a warrantless search is per se unreasonable, unless it fits within one of the "jealously and carefully drawn exceptions." ...

Though we have not considered drug testing in public schools, we have a long history of striking down exploratory searches not based on at least reasonable suspicion. *State v. Jorden,* 160 Wash. 2d 121, 127, 156 P.3d 893 (2007) ("[T]his court has consistently expressed displeasure with random and suspicionless searches, reasoning that they amount to nothing more than an impermissible fishing expedition.") ... In *Kuehn,* this court held a search of student luggage required by school officials as a condition of participation in a school-sponsored trip to Canada violated both the Fourth Amendment and article I, section 7. *Kuehn,* 103 Wash. 2d at 595, 694 P.2d 1078. We opined, "[i]n the absence of individualized suspicion of wrongdoing, the search is a general search. '[W]e never authorize general, exploratory searches,'" and such searches are "anathema to the Fourth Amendment and Const. art. 1, § 7 protections." Id. at 599, 694 P.2d 1078 (quoting *State v. Helmka,* 86 Wash. 2d 91, 93, 542 P.2d 115 (1975)).

The few times we have allowed suspicionless searches, we did so either relying entirely on federal law or in the context of criminal investigations or dealing with prisoners. ... In *Olivas,* 122 Wash. 2d at 83, 856 P.2d 1076, we upheld blood tests of convicted felons without individualized suspicion. And recently in *State v. Surge,* 160 Wash. 2d 65, 156 P.3d 208 (2007), we held a DNA sampling of convicted felons did not violate article I, section 7. That case allowed for warrantless testing without individualized suspicion because we asserted such testing did not disturb a reasonable right to privacy. But these cases present far different factual situations from drug testing student athletes. A felon has either already pleaded guilty or been found guilty beyond a reasonable doubt of a serious crime; a student athlete has merely attended school and chosen to play extracurricular sports. Most troubling, however, is that we can conceive of no way to draw a principled line permitting drug testing only student athletes. If we were to allow random drug testing here, what prevents school districts from either later drug testing students participating in any extracurricular activities, as federal courts now allow, or testing the entire student population?

We cannot countenance random searches of public school student athletes with our article I, section 7 jurisprudence. As stated earlier, we require a warrant except for rare occasions, which we jealously and narrowly guard. We decline to adopt a doctrine similar to the federal special needs exception in the context of randomly drug testing student athletes. In sum, no argument has been presented that would bring the random drug testing within any reasonable interpretation of the constitutionally required "authority of law."

Accordingly, we hold the school district's policy 3515 is unconstitutional and violates student athletes' rights secured by article I, section 7.

CASE DISCUSSION QUESTIONS

1. In addressing the issue of whether student athletes have the constitutional right to be free from suspicionless random drug testing, the Washington Supreme Court engaged in a two-part analysis. In the first part of that analysis, the court discussed whether student athletes have a lower expectation of privacy. How did the court resolve that question? Do you agree with its reasoning?

2. In the second part of its analysis, the court discussed whether it should carve out an exception for schools to the normal constitutional requirement of obtaining a warrant prior to a search. It concluded it should not. How did the differing language in the Fourth Amendment of the U.S. Constitution and section 7 of the Washington Constitution help the Court in reaching that conclusion?

3. After this decision, student athletes in Washington could no longer be subjected to random drug testing. However, in the neighboring state of Oregon students have no such protection. Under our federal system, how is that possible? Do you think that is a fair result?

NETNOTE

You can read the full text of the Declaration of Independence, the Constitution, and the Bill of Rights at the National Archives Web site: *www.archives.gov.*

The Declaration of Independence:

> *www.archives.gov/exhibits/charters/declaration.html*

The Constitution:

> *www.archives.gov/exhibits/charters/constitution.html*

The Bill of Rights:

> *www.archives.gov/exhibits/charters/bill_;of_;rights.html*

You can also view the Constitution and the Bill of Rights at Find Law:

> *http://caselaw.lp.findlaw.com/data/constitution/articles.html*

> *http://caselaw.lp.findlaw.com/data/constitution/amendments.html*

(Note: The last two addresses do not start with www.)

---

2. Statutory Law

As explained above, federal and state constitutions delineate the general framework within which the government must operate. Although these documents do list some major substantive and procedural rights, they were not designed to contain the types of detailed laws and regulations we need to operate in today's complex society. Rather, the federal and state constitutions specifically delegate the power to make these laws to the legislative branches of government.

At the federal level, the legislative power rests with the U.S. Congress. At the state level, it is exercised by state legislatures and a variety of local bodies such as city councils and village boards. Congress and state legislatures enact **statutes,** while city councils and village boards enact **ordinances.**

These statutes and ordinances lay down general rules that govern future conduct. They are general in the sense that they apply to broad categories of people rather than to specific individuals. Furthermore, the requirements they impose generally cannot be applied to actions taken *before* the law went into effect.

Statute
A law enacted by a state legislature or by Congress.

The formulation of such future-oriented rules is a difficult task, because legislatures cannot foresee all the possible circumstances that might arise. Statutes therefore often contain general prohibitions that are somewhat ambiguous and open to differing interpretations. Ambiguity in statutes can also result from sloppy draftsmanship or be intentionally inserted to avoid creating conflicts among the legislation's supporters.

An example of the ambiguity contained in statutes can be found in the following excerpt from Title VII of the 1964 Civil Rights Act. It states:

> It shall be an unlawful employment practice for an employer (1) to . . . discriminate against any individual . . . because of such individual's race, color, religion, sex, or national origin.[12]

Recall the situation of Diane Dobbs mentioned at the beginning of the chapter. Was the restaurant manager discriminating against Diane Dobbs because of her sex when he fired her for being pregnant? While the statute clearly states that employers cannot discriminate on the basis of sex, it is not clear what types of actions should be considered sex discrimination. After the enactment of Title VII some people argued that pregnancy discrimination should be considered a form of sex discrimination because only women can become pregnant. Others argued that it should not be considered sex discrimination because the differential treatment is based on the condition of being pregnant rather then on the employee's sex. Although only women can become pregnant, the employer was legitimately differentiating between two different types of women—those who were pregnant and those who were not—rather than discriminating between women and men.

As with ambiguities in constitutional provisions, when disagreements such as this arise over the meaning of a statute, a court must resolve the ambiguity. Thus in *Gilbert v. General Electric*,[13] the U.S. Supreme Court was called upon to determine if discrimination based on pregnancy was a form of sex discrimination under Title VII. The Supreme Court ruled in *Gilbert* that Title VII allowed employers to discriminate based on pregnancy.

The Supreme Court's interpretation would have left Diane without a remedy under the statute. However, luckily for her, if the legislative branch disagrees with the interpretation a court gives to one of its statutes, Congress can always introduce new legislation that amends the original statute to make clear that a different result or interpretation was intended. If this new legislation passes, the court's interpretation is superseded by the new statute. In this instance, Congress reacted by amending the statute to include pregnancy discrimination in the definition of sex discrimination.[14] Thus, under the amended statute, it was unlawful for Diane's employer to fire her based upon her pregnancy.

Note, however, the difference between interpreting a statute and making a determination that it is unconstitutional. Whereas the legislative branch can amend one of its statutes to override a judicial interpretation, the courts retain the final authority with respect to deciding whether it is constitutional.

---

[12]42 U.S.C. § 2000e-2(a) (2008).

[13]429 U.S. 125 (1976).

[14]Bennett Amendment, 42 U.S.C. § 2000e(k) (2008).

3. Administrative Law

Administrative agencies create administrative law. **Administrative law** is similar to statutory law in that it lays down rules designed to regulate future conduct. However, these rules are usually drawn more narrowly and directed to a more specialized group. Often the legislative branch intentionally leaves it to the executive branch and to independent regulatory agencies to "fill in the details" of the law within a general structure set down by the legislature. Through the process of filling in these details the executive branch is actually making the law.

Administrative law
Rules and regulations created by administrative agencies.

Assume a taxpayer wins $50 in the lottery. Must he pay taxes on it? The Internal Revenue Code, a federal statute, provides that he must pay tax on income but only includes general categories of income. The Internal Revenue Service (IRS), a federal agency, has developed **regulations** that define in much more detail what the word *income* means. Without the IRS, Congress would be forced to make constant revisions in the federal tax laws and would be hard-pressed to see that they were enforced.

Regulation
A law promulgated by an administrative agency.

Other examples of federal agencies include the Occupational Safety and Health Administration (OSHA), which oversees the federal statute requiring safe working conditions, and the Environmental Protection Agency (EPA), which oversees the federal statute governing the environment.

Just as the courts are drawn into the lawmaking process when they must interpret constitutions and statutes, so too are they called on to be the final arbiters of the meaning of administrative regulations. If someone disagrees with the administrative interpretation of a statute, the dissatisfied party can go to court to challenge the agency's interpretation. The court must support the agency's interpretation unless the court determines that the regulation is outside the authorization Congress gave to the administrative agency or that the regulation is unconstitutional. To determine whether the agency has stepped out of the bounds created for it by Congress, the court will examine the **enabling act,** the statute that created the agency. The court will also seek to determine the underlying legislative intent of the statute that the agency is attempting to interpret through its regulations.

Enabling act
A statute establishing and setting out the powers of an administrative agency.

Returning once again to the case of our pregnant waitress, attorney Pat Harper may also wish to consider suing Diane Dobbs's employer for sexual harassment. A sexual harassment case would be based on the same federal statute, Title VII, that we discussed above. The statute makes no specific reference to sexual harassment. However, the Equal Employment Opportunity Commission (EEOC), acting under authority given to it in the statute, has declared that acts of sexual harassment are a form of sex discrimination. One of its administrative regulations states:

> Unwelcome sexual advances, requests for sexual favors, and other verbal or physical conduct of a sexual nature constitute sexual harassment when (1) submission to such conduct is made either explicitly or implicitly a term or condition of an individual's employment, (2) submission to or rejection of such conduct by an individual is used as the basis for employment decisions affecting such individual, or (3) such conduct has the purpose or effect of unreasonably interfering with an individual's work performance or creating an intimidating, hostile, or offensive working environment.[15]

---

[15]29 C.F.R. § 1604.11 (2008).

Note how much more specific the wording of the regulation is in comparison to the wording of the statute.

Recall that Diane Dobbs alleged that the manager patted her on the stomach as he was firing her for being pregnant. Do you think that is sufficient to support a claim of sexual harassment? Is there any language in the regulation that could support such a claim?

In addition to their power to promulgate regulations, and as part of their enforcement powers, most agencies have investigatory and adjudicative powers. For example, if Diane Dobbs wants to pursue her claim of sexual harassment, Title VII mandates that she first take her complaint to the EEOC or a comparable state agency. The agency will investigate her case and, if it deems it appropriate, will hold a hearing to determine the truth of her claims. If she or her employer is not satisfied with the results obtained at the agency, then either of them can take the case to court. Ultimately, the court would be the final arbiter of whether Diane Dobbs's situation fits within the agency definition of sexual harassment.

Fourth branch of government
Administrative agencies.

Because administrative agencies combine legislative, executive, and judicial functions, they are sometimes referred to as the **fourth branch of government.**

The following case illustrates the interaction between the courts and administrative agencies when the interpretation of a federal statute is called into question. As you know, Congress has enacted a federal statute, the Internal Revenue Code, to set out the requirements that individuals and businesses must follow regarding the payment of federal taxes. The Code also provides certain exemptions for charitable organizations that operate for educational purposes. In 1970 the Internal Revenue Service (IRS), an administrative agency, interpreted that provision to mean that an organization could not be given tax exempt status if it engaged in racially discriminatory policies. Based on fundamentalist religious beliefs, Bob Jones University followed a policy that denied admission to applicants who advocated interracial marriage or dating. Based on this racially discriminatory admissions policy, the IRS denied Bob Jones University tax exempt status. The University sued in federal court seeking a refund of federal unemployment tax payments. The following excerpt is from the decision of the U.S. Supreme Court in which the Court determined that nonprofit private schools such as Bob Jones University that follow racially discriminatory admission practices, even if based on religious beliefs, do not qualify as tax exempt organizations under the Internal Revenue Code.

Bob Jones University v. United States
461 U.S. 574 (1983)

Chief Justice BURGER delivered the opinion of the Court.

. . . Charitable exemptions are justified on the basis that the exempt entity confers a public benefit—a benefit which the society or the community may not itself choose or be able to provide, or which supplements and advances the work of public institutions already supported by tax revenues. . . . [However, the] institution's purpose must not be so at odds with the common community conscience as to undermine any public benefit that might otherwise be conferred.

[A] declaration that a given institution is not "charitable" should be made only where there can be no doubt that the activity involved is contrary to a fundamental public policy. But there can no longer be any doubt that racial discrimination in education violates deeply and widely accepted views of elementary justice. . . . Over the past quarter of a century, every pronouncement of this Court and myriad Acts of Congress and Executive Orders attest a firm national policy to prohibit racial segregation and discrimination in public education.

An unbroken line of cases following *Brown v. Board of Education* establishes beyond doubt this Court's view that racial discrimination in education violates a most fundamental national public policy, as well as rights of individuals. . . .

Petitioners contend that, regardless of whether the IRS properly concluded that racially discriminatory private schools violate public policy, only Congress can alter the scope of [a federal statute]. Petitioners accordingly argue that the IRS overstepped its lawful bounds in issuing its 1970 and 1971 rulings.

Yet ever since the inception of the Tax Code, Congress has seen fit to vest in those administering the tax laws very broad authority to interpret those laws. In an area as complex as the tax system, the agency Congress vests with administrative responsibility must be able to exercise its authority to meet changing conditions and new problems. Indeed as early as 1918, Congress expressly authorized the Commissioner "to make all needful rules and regulations for the enforcement" of the tax laws. The same provision, so essential to efficient and fair administration of the tax laws, has appeared in Tax Codes ever since; and this Court has long recognized the primary authority of the IRS and its predecessors in construing the Internal Revenue Code.

Congress, the source of IRS authority, can modify IRS rulings it considers improper; and courts exercise review over IRS actions. In the first instance, however, the responsibility for construing the Code falls to the IRS. Since Congress cannot be expected to anticipate every conceivable problem that can arise or to carry out day-to-day oversight, it relies on the administrators and on the courts to implement the legislative will. Administrators, like judges, are under oath to do so. . . .

The actions of Congress since 1970 leave no doubt that the IRS reached the correct conclusion in exercising its authority. It is, of course, not unknown for independent agencies or the Executive Branch to misconstrue the intent of a statute; Congress can and often does correct such misconceptions, if the courts have not done so. Yet for a dozen years Congress has been made aware—acutely aware—of the IRS rulings of 1970 and 1971. As we noted earlier, few issues have been the subject of more vigorous and widespread debate and discussion in and out of Congress than those related to racial segregation in education. Sincere adherents advocating contrary views have ventilated the subject for well over three decades. Failure of Congress to modify the IRS rulings of 1970 and 1971, of which Congress was, by its own studies and by public discourse, constantly reminded, and Congress' awareness of the denial of tax-exempt status for racially discriminatory schools when enacting other and related legislation make out an unusually strong case of legislative acquiescence in and ratification by implication of the 1970 and 1971 rulings. . . .

Petitioners contend that, even if the Commissioner's policy is valid as to nonreligious private schools, that policy cannot constitutionally be applied to schools that engage in racial discrimination on the basis of sincerely held religious beliefs. As to such schools, it is argued that the IRS construction of § 170 and § 501(c)(3) violates their free exercise rights under the Religion Clauses of the First Amendment. . . .

The governmental interest at stake here is compelling. . . . [T]he Government has a fundamental, overriding interest in eradicating racial discrimination in education—discrimination that prevailed, with official approval, for the first 165 years of this Nation's constitutional history. That governmental interest substantially outweighs whatever burden denial of tax benefits places on petitioners' exercise of their religious beliefs.

CASE DISCUSSION QUESTIONS

1. What type of law (constitutional, statutory, or administrative) is being challenged in this case?
2. How is statutory law relevant to this case?
3. Why do you think the Court gives so much deference to the IRS's determination as to the meaning of the Internal Revenue Code?
4. Why is constitutional law relevant to this case?

4. Judicial Interpretation and the Common Law

As we have noted above, courts play a vital role in interpreting constitutions and the laws created by the legislatures and agencies. The courts also apply and interpret the **common law** when there is no statute, administrative regulation, or constitutional provision governing the case they are adjudicating.

Common law
Law created by the courts.

The common law consists of various legal principles that have evolved through the years from the analysis of specific court decisions. Ultimately, these principles can be traced back to early medieval England, though they have been modified through the years by various state courts. When a legal dispute involves a subject that is not adequately covered by the other types of law, the judge applies the principles of the common law. In other words, in the absence of pronouncements from the constitution or a legislative or administrative body, the judge looks to the earlier decisions of other judges in similar circumstances.

Indeed, courts existed in England long before there was a democratically elected legislature to enact legislation. The roots of the court's power to create law go back to the eleventh century and the Norman Conquest. Although reading about medieval history may seem irrelevant to your study of the modern American legal system, the principles followed by our American legal system originated in England in 1066. Until 1066 Anglo-Saxon kings ruled England. There was no central legislature or centralized court system. Disputes were decided locally based on local custom. In 1066 the king, Edward the Confessor, died without children. This left the succession to the throne to either his brother-in-law, Harold, a powerful English baron, or his French cousin, William, Duke of Normandy. Harold was elected king. Immediately William assembled an army of soldiers, knights, and horses.[16]

In the fall of 1066 William landed on the south coast of England with his soldiers and knights, mounted on horseback. The mounted Norman knights overwhelmed the English foot soldiers, defeating the English army. On Christmas Day, 1066, William, the Duke of Normandy, had himself crowned king of England.

England became a country where everyone who spoke English owned no land and was impoverished. The king and the upper classes spoke French and used French in the courts. As a result, one enduring reminder of the Norman Conquest was the infusion of French words, such as **acquit** and **voir dire,** into our legal vocabulary. In addition, Norman kings used Latin in their written

---

[16] This is a good illustration of what occurs when there is no established governmental structure for settling disagreements. The disputants resort to violence.

documents, so many Latin words, such as **certiorari** and **actus reus,** were incorporated into our legal language.

The Norman Conquest left a much greater legacy, however, than the French and Latin words in our legal vocabulary. It created an entirely new method for resolving disputes. Before the Conquest most disputes were decided locally, and the "law" would vary from town to town. As part of unifying England, the English kings wanted to create a common law throughout the land.

How was this uniformity created? Remember that there was no central legislature. The solution was for the king to appoint judges and establish a court system so that disputes could be settled in a uniform manner. Initially, the "courts" were simply individual judges appointed by the king to "ride a circuit" around the countryside, settling disputes in the name of the king. Over time the judges realized that rather than deciding each case as though it were the first of its kind, it would be more efficient to share the results of their prior decisions with each other so that similar cases could be decided similarly. The resulting court-made law became known as the common law.

Unless a good reason dictated otherwise, it became the policy to follow the rules laid down in prior decisions. This was how the doctrine of **stare decisis** developed. Once courts had determined the law in an area, other courts followed that rule unless a court thought there was a good reason to change it.

By about 1200 the main structure of the common law system was in place. A body of centrally appointed judges applied a common law throughout the country, and a tradition of following precedent had been established. The commencement of a series of Year Books, each collecting cases from the most important courts for that year, further solidified this development. In 1535 this system was replaced by reporters, collections of court opinions as "reported" by various authors. Finally, in 1865 this process culminated in the United States with the practice of publishing official law reports.

Meanwhile, the common law had come to America and had formed the basis for our legal system. There are areas of the law that are still totally governed by the common law, such as most matters dealing with torts. However, over the years more and more areas of the common law have been enacted into statutes; that process is known as the **codification of the common law.** When the common law has been changed through legislation, the statute is said to be in **derogation of the common law.**

Before abandoning our history lesson, we need to briefly mention one more development in the English court system that has had a great impact on our system, and that was the development of equity courts. The courts we have discussed up to now had the power to settle disputes by requiring one party to compensate the other with money damages. But there are times when money is not what the litigants want. Rather they would like the court to order the other party to do something, such as living up to contractual obligations, or to cease doing something, such as having loud parties in the wee hours of the morning. In response to this need, the English created the **equity** courts.

Judges in the equity courts used their powers to "do justice." For example, equity powers allow judges to take preventive action when the law would otherwise limit their decisions to monetary awards after the damage has been done. Equity powers include a judge's ability to issue an **injunction** or to order

Stare decisis
The doctrine stating that normally once a court has decided one way on a particular issue, it and other courts in the same jurisdiction will decide the same way on that issue in future cases given similar facts, unless they can be convinced of the need for change.

Codification of the common law
The process of legislative enactment of areas of the law previously governed solely by the common law.

Derogation of the common law
Used to describe legislation that changes the common law.

Equity
Fairness; a court's power to do justice. Equity powers allow judges to take action when otherwise the law would limit their decisions to monetary awards. Equity powers include a judge's ability to issue an injunction and to order specific performance.

Injunction
A court order requiring a party to perform a specific act or to cease doing a specific act.

Specific performance
A requirement that a party fulfill his or her contractual obligations.

specific performance. An injunction is a court order requiring someone to act or to refrain from acting. Specific performance requires that a party fulfill his or her contractual obligations. In the 1800s most states merged their law and equity courts. Therefore, today judges have the power to give either monetary awards or equitable relief or both, as they deem appropriate.

DISCUSSION QUESTIONS

7. For each of the following, which source of law—a constitution, a statute, an administrative regulation, or a court opinion—would be best able to handle the problem and why?

    a. A requirement that all motorcycle riders wear helmets.

    b. A rule making a bar owner liable for any injuries caused by a patron to whom the bar sold drinks.

    c. A rule that all semi-trailers traveling on interstate highways use concave mud flaps.

    d. A requirement that employers not discriminate on the basis of religion or sexual orientation.

    e. A requirement that no more than a certain percentage of a known pollutant be released by factory smokestacks.

    f. A question as to whether a person not wearing a seat belt should be able to recover for injuries that person sustained in an automobile accident that was not his fault.

    g. A law prohibiting government from interfering with an individual's right to freedom of speech.

SUMMARY

Laws are rules of conduct that are enforced by the government. They play an important role in managing conflict and ensuring the rule of law in modern democratic societies. In this chapter we have looked at four sources of law: constitutions, statutes, administrative regulations, and the common law.

Our country was the first to adopt a written constitution, and it is our federal constitution that provides the framework within which all our laws are made. Similarly, states' constitutions provide the legal basis for their governments to act.

Even though traditionally we say that the legislature makes the law, the executive branch enforces the law, and the courts interpret the law, the truth is that the legislative, executive, and judicial branches, as well as administrative agencies, are all involved in making the law. Legislatures create law by enacting statutes, agencies create law by promulgating regulations, and appellate courts create law through their written opinions known as court decisions. In addition, the executive branch occasionally creates law through executive orders.

The example with which we began this chapter provides a good illustration of how statutory, regulatory, and court-made law work together. Congress enacted a statute that prohibited "sex discrimination." Because this phrase is so broad, the EEOC, an administrative agency, has issued regulations that more clearly define some types of sex discrimination, such as sexual harassment. Finally, even the most detailed regulation cannot cover every individual case. Therefore, the courts are constantly called on to interpret the meaning of both statutes and regulations.

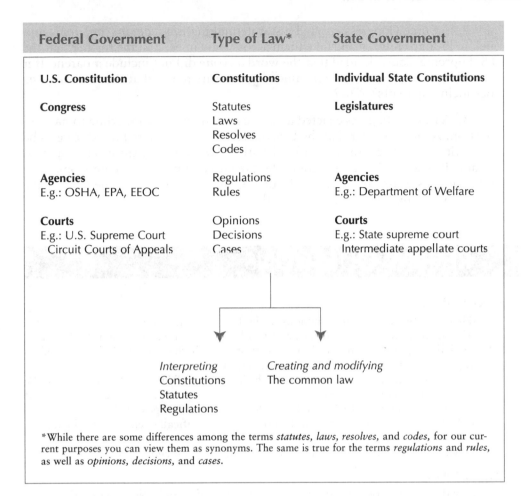

Federal Government	Type of Law*	State Government
U.S. Constitution	**Constitutions**	**Individual State Constitutions**
Congress	Statutes Laws Resolves Codes	**Legislatures**
Agencies E.g.: OSHA, EPA, EEOC	Regulations Rules	**Agencies** E.g.: Department of Welfare

Courts
E.g.: U.S. Supreme Court
   Circuit Courts of Appeals
	Opinions
	Decisions
	Cases
		Courts
		E.g.: State supreme court
		   Intermediate appellate courts

Interpreting
Constitutions
Statutes
Regulations

Creating and modifying
The common law

*While there are some differences among the terms *statutes, laws, resolves,* and *codes,* for our current purposes you can view them as synonyms. The same is true for the terms *regulations* and *rules,* as well as *opinions, decisions,* and *cases.*

Figure 2-1   Sources of Law

Where no constitution, statute, or administrative regulation applies, the courts rely on the common law to resolve the problem. But it is through the power of judicial review and in their role as interpreters of constitutional, statutory, and administrative provisions that courts have the greatest power: By interpreting the law, the courts end up creating the law. Figure 2-1 summarizes the major sources of law.

CRITICAL THINKING EXERCISES

1. Would you expect to hear a follower of natural law, legal positivism, or legal realism making the following statements?
   a. The killing of another human is wrong.
   b. The penalty for first degree murder is life imprisonment or death.
   c. Studies have shown that a disproportionate number of minority men are sentenced to the death penalty.

2. Assume Congress enacted a statute making it a federal crime for "anyone" to kidnap children and take them across state lines. Assume further that the U.S. Supreme Court decided that the word *anyone* did not include a parent. If it wanted to do so, could Congress amend the statute to say that the word *anyone* does include parents? Why?

3. Assume Congress enacted a statute making it a federal crime to have an abortion. Assume further that the U.S. Supreme Court declared the statute to be unconstitutional because it interfered with a woman's constitutional right to privacy. If it wanted to do so, could the executive branch prosecute women for violating the statute? In other words, does Congress or the Supreme Court have the final word on what is constitutional? Why?

‖‖ REVIEW QUESTIONS

Pages 19 through 29

1. What are the two primary functions of the U.S. Constitution?
2. What is the power of judicial review, and why is it so important to our legal system?
3. Read the excerpts from the U.S. Constitution and the Bill of Rights located in Appendix A. Then answer the following questions:
   a. Which article deals specifically with the legislature? With the executive? With the judiciary? (This may seem like trivia necessary only for *Jeopardy* contestants, but lawyers often refer to Article I, Article II, or Article III powers.)
   b. Which amendment states that the powers not specifically delegated to the federal government are reserved to the states?
   c. Make a list of the rights protected by the first ten amendments.

Pages 29 through 30

4. Why do constitutions and statutes frequently include ambiguous language?
5. How do courts become involved in the legislative process?
6. Who has the final say as to what a statute means, the legislature or the courts?
7. Who has the final say as to the constitutionality of a statute, the legislature or the courts?

Pages 31 through 34

8. How are statutes and administrative regulations similar? How do they differ?
9. Why are administrative agencies referred to as the fourth branch of government?

Pages 34 through 37

10. What impact did the Norman Conquest have on the American legal system?
11. What is the common law?
12. Why were equity courts created, and what special powers were they given?

Chapter 3

Classification of the Law

Logically, everything ought to come first.
Jean Jacques Rousseau

INTRODUCTION

In the previous chapter, we explained how law is made not only by legislatures, but also by administrative agencies and courts. Based on its source, we classified law in terms of constitutional, statutory, administrative, or common law. You can also classify law based on whether it involves

1. state, federal, or local law (every state as well as the federal government has its own laws);
2. civil and/or criminal law (**civil law** deals with harm against an individual—for example, a broken contract—whereas **criminal law** deals with harm against society as a whole—as when violence leads to someone's death); and
3. substantive and/or procedural law (**substantive law** defines our legal rights and duties—for example, the duty to obey speed limits and the right of freedom of speech—whereas **procedural law** is comprised of the rules that govern how the legal system operates).

Knowledge of these classification schemes is a necessary part of understanding how our legal system is organized. Often these classifications will be clear-cut, but at times, the categorizations are not so obvious.

Recall the case of Diane Dobbs, the pregnant waitress introduced at the beginning of the last chapter. In analyzing Diane's story, an attorney would think in terms of the three categories we just listed. While it is not necessary to

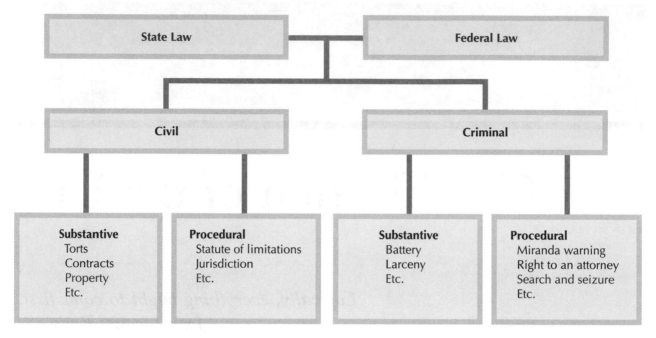

Figure 3-1   How Lawyers Classify the Law

proceed in any particular order in applying the three categories listed above to Diane's situation, all three must be evaluated. First, do Diane's problems relate to state or federal law? Are both state and federal laws involved? Second, does her situation involve any criminal laws, or does only civil law apply? Third, in addition to examining the substantive law issues, what procedural issues might be involved? As we proceed through the chapter, we will discuss each of these classifications.

Note that these are not mutually exclusive categories. A particular situation may involve both federal and state laws, both civil and criminal issues, and procedural as well as substantive questions. Figure 3-1 illustrates how these different categories relate to each other. At this point do not be concerned about understanding all of the terms listed in the figure. As the chapter proceeds, we will discuss each term in more detail.

A. FEDERAL VERSUS STATE LAW

Federalism
A system of government in which the authority to govern is split between a single, nationwide central government and several regional governments that control specific geographical areas.

Each of the fifty states, along with the federal government, has its own legal system. Each determines how its court system will be organized and what laws it will enforce. Although the laws of one state are often similar to the laws of another, each state ultimately decides for itself what those laws will be. This is because, as we mentioned in the last chapter, the United States operates under a system of government known as **federalism.** In our federal system the power to make various types of laws is divided between the federal government in Washington, D.C., and the fifty state governments. A legal problem may involve state law or federal law or both state and federal law.

1. Federal Law

You will be in an area covered by federal law if the problem deals with any of the following:

1. a U.S. constitutional issue (such as freedom of speech or the rights of a criminal defendant),
2. a federal statute (such as the Internal Revenue Code), or
3. regulations of a federal agency (such as the IRS).

When a legal problem involves one of these three areas, this is known as raising a federal issue or a federal question. As we will see later in the chapter on civil litigation, categorizing a legal problem in this way is very important as generally federal courts can only hear cases that either involve parties from different states or that raise a federal question.

When you hear people complaining about what they believe to be the excessive reach of the federal government, they are frequently referring to the second area of federal law, federal statutes. However, despite its growth in recent years, it is not true that eventually all areas of the law will be governed by federal law. The Constitution imposes important limits on the scope of Congress's law-making power. Congress can enact legislation only if the Constitution has given Congress the power to legislate in that particular area. These delegated powers can be found in Article I, Section 8. In addition, several constitutional amendments, such as Section 5 of the Fourteenth Amendment, have provisions enabling Congress to pass legislation necessary to enforce that amendment.

For example, Congress could and does enact legislation regarding taxation because Article I, Section 8 provides that "[t]he Congress shall have Power To lay and collect Taxes, Duties, Imposts and Excises." On the other hand, Congress could not enact a national divorce law, as there is nothing in the Constitution to give Congress that power. Furthermore, under the Tenth Amendment any power not specifically given to Congress by the Constitution is reserved to the people or to the states.

It is important to note, however, that after enumerating powers such as those to lay and collect taxes, establish post offices and post roads, raise armies, and declare war, Section 8 states that Congress has the power "to make all Laws which shall be necessary and proper for carrying into Execution" the specifically enumerated powers. The U.S. Supreme Court broadly interpreted this last clause in the 1819 case of *McCulloch v. Maryland*.[1] Even though the Constitution did not explicitly delegate to Congress the power to create banks, the Court ruled that Congress could create and operate a national bank as part of the exercise of its expressly delegated powers to collect taxes and to borrow money. This is known as the "**doctrine of implied powers.**"

In addition, Congress has sweeping powers under Article I, Section 8. That section provides: "Congress shall have power to regulate commerce . . . among the several states." This has come to be known as the "interstate commerce clause." Originally, the courts interpreted "interstate commerce" to mean exactly that: the movement of goods across state lines. However, in *Gibbons v.*

Doctrine of implied powers
Powers not stated in Constitution but that are necessary for Congress to carry out other, expressly granted powers.

---

[1] 17 U.S. 316 (1819).

Ogden[2] the Supreme Court interpreted this clause as giving the federal government the authority not only to regulate products that actually travel in interstate commerce, but also to regulate anything that has an "effect upon" interstate commerce.

In the 1930s Congress used this expansive reading of the interstate commerce clause as the basis for much of its "New Deal" economic legislation, including the Unfair Labor Standards Act (controlling the hours and wages of employees who manufactured goods destined for interstate commerce) and the National Labor Relations Act (creating the National Labor Relations Board and authorizing it to enjoin unfair labor practices).

Then, from the 1960s through the 1990s, this expansive reading of the commerce clause allowed Congress to address a wide range of social problems through federal statutes, such as the 1964 Civil Rights Act. We will discuss further the limits of Congress's commerce clause power in Chapter 6, Constitutional Law. For now, consider the recent 2005 decision in which the U.S. Supreme Court addressed the question of whether the commerce clause gave the federal government the power to prohibit the cultivation and use of marijuana. The marijuana was grown and used within a single state for medical purposes, pursuant to a physician's orders and was authorized by state law.

Gonzales v. Raich
545 U.S. 1 (2005)

SCALIA, J., delivered the opinion of the Court.

In 1996, California voters passed Proposition 215, now codified as the Compassionate Use Act of 1996 (CSA). The proposition was designed to ensure that "seriously ill" residents of the State have access to marijuana for medical purposes. . . . The Act creates an exemption from criminal prosecution for physicians, as well as for patients and primary caregivers who possess or cultivate marijuana for medicinal purposes with the recommendation or approval of a physician. . . .

Respondents Angel Raich and Diane Monson are California residents who suffer from a variety of serious medical conditions and have sought to avail themselves of medical marijuana pursuant to the terms of the Compassionate Use Act. They are being treated by licensed, board-certified family practitioners, who have concluded, after prescribing a host of conventional medicines to treat respondents' conditions and to alleviate their associated symptoms, that marijuana is the only drug available that provides effective treatment. Both women have been using marijuana as a medication for several years pursuant to their doctors' recommendation, and both rely heavily on cannabis to function on a daily basis. Indeed, Raich's physician believes that forgoing cannabis treatments would certainly cause Raich excruciating pain and could very well prove fatal.

Respondent Monson cultivates her own marijuana, and ingests the drug in a variety of ways including smoking and using a vaporizer. . . .

On August 15, 2002, county deputy sheriffs and agents from the federal Drug Enforcement Administration (DEA) came to Monson's home. After a thorough investigation, the county officials concluded that her use of marijuana was entirely lawful as a matter of California law. Nevertheless, after a 3-hour standoff, the federal

---

[2] 22. U.S. 1 (1824).

agents seized and destroyed all six of her cannabis plants.

Respondents thereafter brought this action against the Attorney General of the United States and the head of the DEA seeking injunctive and declaratory relief prohibiting the enforcement of the federal Controlled Substances Act (CSA), 84 Stat. 1242, 21 U.S.C. § 801 *et seq.*, to the extent it prevents them from possessing, obtaining, or manufacturing cannabis for their personal medical use. . . .

The case is made difficult by respondents' strong arguments that they will suffer irreparable harm because, despite a congressional finding to the contrary, marijuana does have valid therapeutic purposes. The question before us, however, is not whether it is wise to enforce the statute in these circumstances; rather, it is whether Congress' power to regulate interstate markets for medicinal substances encompasses the portions of those markets that are supplied with drugs produced and consumed locally. Well-settled law controls our answer. The CSA is a valid exercise of federal power, even as applied to the troubling facts of this case. . . .

[Respondents] argue that the CSA's categorical prohibition of the manufacture and possession of marijuana as applied to the intrastate manufacture and possession of marijuana for medical purposes pursuant to California law exceeds Congress' authority under the Commerce Clause. . . .

The Commerce Clause emerged as the Framers' response to the central problem giving rise to the Constitution itself: the absence of any federal commerce power under the Articles of Confederation. For the first century of our history, the primary use of the Clause was to preclude the kind of discriminatory state legislation that had once been permissible. Then, in response to rapid industrial development and an increasingly interdependent national economy, Congress "ushered in a new era of federal regulation under the commerce power," beginning with the enactment of the Interstate Commerce Act in 1887 and the Sherman Antitrust Act in 1890. . . .

[There are] three general categories of regulation in which Congress is authorized to engage under its commerce power. First, Congress can regulate the channels of interstate commerce. Second, Congress has authority to regulate and protect the instrumentalities of interstate commerce, and persons or things in interstate commerce. Third, Congress has the power to regulate activities that substantially affect interstate commerce. Only the third category is implicated in the case at hand.

Our case law firmly establishes Congress' power to regulate purely local activities that are part of an economic "class of activities" that have a substantial effect on interstate commerce. See, *e.g., Wickard v. Filburn,* 317 U.S. 111 (1942). As we stated in *Wickard,* "even if appellee's activity be local and though it may not be regarded as commerce, it may still, whatever its nature, be reached by Congress if it exerts a substantial economic effect on interstate commerce." *Id.,* at 125.

. . . In *Wickard,* we upheld the application of regulations promulgated under the Agricultural Adjustment Act of 1938, which were designed to control the volume of wheat moving in interstate and foreign commerce in order to avoid surpluses and consequent abnormally low prices. The regulations established an allotment of 11.1 acres for Filburn's 1941 wheat crop, but he sowed 23 acres, intending to use the excess by consuming it on his own farm. Filburn argued that even though we had sustained Congress' power to regulate the production of goods for commerce, that power did not authorize "federal regulation [of] production not intended in any part for commerce but wholly for consumption on the farm." *Wickard,* 317 U.S., at 118, 63 S. Ct. 82. Justice Jackson's opinion for a unanimous Court rejected this submission. He wrote:

> . . . That appellee's own contribution to the demand for wheat may be trivial by itself is not enough to remove him from the scope of federal regulation where, as here, his contribution, taken together with that of many others similarly situated, is far from trivial.

Id., at 127-128, 63 S. Ct. 82.

Wickard thus establishes that Congress can regulate purely intrastate activity that is not itself "commercial," in that it is not produced for sale, if it concludes that failure to regulate that class of activity would undercut the regulation of the interstate market in that commodity.

The similarities between this case and *Wickard* are striking. Like the farmer in *Wickard,* respondents are cultivating, for home consumption, a fungible commodity for which there is an established, albeit illegal, interstate market. Just as the Agricultural Adjustment Act was designed "to control the volume [of wheat] moving in interstate and foreign commerce in order to avoid surpluses . . ." and consequently control the market price, a primary purpose of the CSA is to control the supply and demand of controlled substances in both lawful and unlawful drug markets. In *Wickard,* we had no difficulty concluding that Congress had a rational basis for believing that, when viewed in the aggregate, leaving home-consumed wheat outside the regulatory scheme would have a substantial influence on price and market conditions. Here too, Congress had a rational basis for concluding that leaving home-consumed marijuana outside federal control would similarly affect price and market conditions.

. . . In both cases, the regulation is squarely within Congress' commerce power because production of the commodity meant for home consumption, be it wheat or marijuana, has a substantial effect on supply and demand in the national market for that commodity.

[The Court concluded that the application of the federal statute criminalizing the manufacture, distribution, or possession of marijuana to intrastate growers and users of marijuana for medical purposes did not violate the Commerce Clause.]

CASE DISCUSSION QUESTIONS

1. The Court reasoned that the marijuana used for local, medicinal purposes could find its way into the interstate market and therefore have an economic effect on interstate commerce. Do you agree? Do you think that possibility is enough to validate Congress's power to regulate in this case?

2. After noting that "foregoing cannabis treatments would certainly cause Raich excruciating pain and could very well prove fatal," the Court emphasized it was ruling only on the constitutionally of Congress's actions, not on the wisdom of those actions. Does this seem like a valid approach to you?

3. Although judges are supposed to be immune from political pressure and are to decide cases solely based on the law and facts before them, some have argued that the nationwide emphasis on the "war on drugs" influenced the outcome of this case. What do you think?

2. State Law

Whereas the federal government must trace all of its powers back to a specific constitutional authorization, the states are allowed to make any laws they deem appropriate for the health, welfare, safety, and morals of their citizens as long as those laws are not prohibited by the U.S. Constitution.[3] Typical examples of areas covered by state law are criminal behavior, contracts, torts, property, marriage, and family matters. While much of the law from one state to the next is quite similar, the states are free to create their own unique laws. Whereas one state may choose to legalize gambling, another may not; whereas one state may choose to allow no-fault divorces, another may not.

---

[3] The Tenth Amendment to the U.S. Constitution declares that "powers not delegated to the United States by the Constitution, nor prohibited by it to the States, are reserved to the States respectively, or to the people."

Some see this diversity as one of the great strengths of our political system. They argue that it encourages experimentation and innovation by allowing the residents of Georgia, for example, to establish rules of conduct that differ from those established by the residents of Nevada. Critics, on the other hand, point to the problems it creates for interstate business and travel—for example, forcing large corporations and other out-of-state parties to hire local attorneys and making it difficult for an attorney to move a practice from one state to another. They also point out that states are sometimes reluctant to impose needed regulations (in areas such as environmental protection and worker safety) for fear that the affected businesses will move to another state with fewer restrictions.

As we become an ever more interdependent nation, however, state laws are tending to become more and more uniform, especially in the area of commercial law. Businesses with dealings in more than one state do not like having to worry about a multiplicity of state laws. Therefore, most states have voluntarily moved to adopt uniform laws in areas such as commercial sales.

3. Preemption

Frequently, both the federal and state governments pass laws covering the same general area of law. For example, federal, state, and local governments have all passed laws prohibiting discrimination in the rental or sale of residential property. In situations such as this, the doctrine of preemption comes into play.

The doctrine of preemption allows the federal government to prevent state and local governments from passing laws that conflict with federal laws and sometimes even to prohibit states from passing any laws on a particular subject. For example, it would create chaos if every state could individually regulate railroad safety. Instead, under the Federal Railroad Safety Act,[4] the federal government created uniform standards related to railroad safety, such as maximum train speed and train length.

A recent example of the federal government's power of preemption occurred in the *Gonzales v. Raich* case discussed above. In addition to validating Congress's use of its commerce-clause power to regulate the intrastate noncommercial use of marijuana, the Court held that the California laws providing for the medicinal use of marijuana could not be used to protect California residents from federal prosecution. The Constitution's Supremacy Clause "unambiguously provides that if there is any conflict between federal and state law, federal law prevails."[5]

While the preemption doctrine prohibits state or local regulations that conflict with federal constitutional or legislative law, generally state and local governments can pass additional regulations or protections for their citizens as long as they do not conflict with federal laws. You already saw one example of this in the last chapter in the case involving the right of students to be free from random drug testing. The Washington Supreme Court found that the Washington constitution provided more protections for their citizens than did the U.S. Constitution. As another example, consider that federal statutes prohibit employers from discriminating on the basis of race or sex if that employer

Preemption
The power of the federal government to prevent the states from passing conflicting laws, and sometimes even to prohibit states from passing any laws on a particular subject.

---

[4] 49 U.S.C.A. § 20106 (2008).
[5] 545 U.S. at 29.

employs fifteen or more employees. These laws do not prevent state or local governments from enacting laws against discrimination on the basis of sexual orientation or from prohibiting race or sex discrimination by employers who have less than fifteen employees. For example, a Massachusetts statute states that an employer of six or more employees may not discriminate on the basis of race, color, religious creed, national origin, sex, sexual orientation, genetic information, or ancestry. This is perfectly valid as it does not conflict with the federal statute.

In summary, a legal problem could be governed by federal law, or state law, or both. Keep these three possibilities in mind.

■ First, there are some areas in which only the states can legislate—areas reserved to the states—such as divorce.
■ Second, there are some areas in which both the states and Congress can legislate—such as criminal behavior that crosses state lines.
■ Third, there are a few areas in which only Congress can legislate—areas of total preemption—such as certain safety issues involving trains traveling across state lines.

DISCUSSION QUESTIONS

1. Following several well-publicized instances in which travelers were kept for hours on airplanes on airport runways without food, water, or adequate bathroom facilities, legislatures in several states considered enacting airline passenger bill of rights laws requiring airlines to provide food, water, clean toilets, and fresh air to passengers stuck in a non-airborne plane for more than an hour. The airline industry threatened to file suit to block the legislation on the grounds that the federal government has preempted regulation of the airline industry. What types of arguments would you make on behalf of the states? What do you think the role of the state should be in this type of situation?

2. Can you think of any areas of the law that are not now regulated on a federal level but should be? What are those areas, and why do you think the federal government should take on a more active role?

3. Can you think of any areas of the law that should be left solely to state and local governments? If so, what are they, and why do you think the federal government should not be involved?

4. In what areas of the law do you think there should be uniformity across all of the states? In what areas should there be diversity? Why?

B. CRIMINAL VERSUS CIVIL LAW

Another major classification within the law is the division between criminal law and civil law. Both provide mechanisms for addressing violations of the law, but they differ regarding the procedures that must be used and the types of sanctions or remedies that are available. In this section we will first compare criminal and civil law. Next, we will take a quick look at the major substantive areas of criminal and civil law.

	Civil	Criminal
Type of harm	Private injury	Harm to society
Names of the parties	Plaintiff/defendant	State*/defendant
"Prosecutor" of the claim	Usually an individual; sometimes the government	Government
Standard of proof	Proponderance of the evidence	Beyond a reasonable doubt
Judgment	Liable/not liable	Guilty/not guilty
Sanctions/remedies	Damages/injunction	Imprisonment/fines/death
Source of law	Common law/statutes	Statutes

*The State may also be referred to as the Commonwealth or the People. Although the state is the named party, it is actually a government employee, the prosecutor (also known as the district attorney, state's attorney, or attorney general), who brings the lawsuit as the state's representative.

Figure 3-2   A Comparison of Civil and Criminal Law

1. A Comparison of Criminal and Civil Law

Some of the major differences between criminal and civil law are listed in Figure 3-2.

a. Type of Harm

Civil law is invoked when one individual harms another. When an individual violates a part of the **criminal law,** society considers itself the offended party and takes an active role in the sanctioning process. Thus, if Peter Jones burglarizes Sam Smith's home, the criminal law views that act as an offense against society itself rather than simply as a matter between Smith and Jones.

But what determines when an act such as burglarizing someone's home is a wrong against society as a whole? It is up to the legislative branch of government to decide when the consequences of certain acts are viewed as grave enough to classify the act as a crime against the state. Thus, when the legislature perceives that a particular act, such as drunk driving, has that broader impact, it can criminalize.

b. Names of the Parties and the "Prosecutor" of the Claim

The person who brings the civil suit (also known as a civil action or a civil lawsuit) is known as the **plaintiff,** and the person sued is called the **defendant**. For example, recall the situation involving the pregnant waitress presented at the beginning of Chapter 2. If Diane Dobbs were to sue the restaurant, she would be the plaintiff. Both the corporation that owns the Western Rib Eye

Civil law
Law that deals with harm to an individual.

Criminal law
Law that deals with harm to society as a whole.

Plaintiff
A person who initiates a lawsuit.

Defendant
In a lawsuit, the person who is sued; in a criminal case, the person who is being charged with a crime.

Restaurant and the restaurant manager would probably be named as defendants. Although civil suits are usually between individuals, a governmental unit (federal, state, or local) can become a plaintiff in a civil suit. In a criminal case, the case is listed as *People v. Jones* or *State v. Jones*. Governmental attorneys prosecute the accused party (the defendant), and the victim is merely a witness.

c. Standard of Proof

Beyond a reasonable doubt

The standard of proof used in criminal trials. The evidence presented must be so conclusive and complete that there are no reasonable doubts regarding the guilt of the accused.

Preponderance of the evidence

The standard of proof most commonly used in civil trials. The evidence presented must prove that it is more likely than not the defendant committed the wrongful act.

Clear and convincing

The standard of proof used in some civil trials. The evidence presented must be greater than a preponderance of the evidence but less than beyond a reasonable doubt.

Because of the serious consequences of violating criminal laws, the standard of proof is different from that used in civil cases. On the criminal side, the prosecution is required to prove its case **beyond a reasonable doubt**. Judges usually explain the beyond a reasonable doubt standard to jurors as the degree of doubt that causes a reasonable person to refrain from acting. The proof must be so conclusive and complete that all reasonable doubts regarding the facts are removed from the jurors' minds.

In most civil actions the plaintiff need only meet the **preponderance of the evidence** standard. A preponderance of the evidence is usually understood to mean that the facts asserted are more likely to be true than not true. One study showed that judges equate "beyond a reasonable doubt" with a median probability of approximately 8.8 out of 10. Jurors averaged approximately 8.6 out of 10. The judges interpreted preponderance of the evidence as a median probability of 5.4 out of 10. For jurors the median was 7.1 out of 10.[6] These results indicate that although judges and jurors may disagree as to the precise meaning of the standards, they agree that the criminal law requires a greater degree of proof before its sanctions can be applied.

There are a few occasions in which a higher, **clear and convincing evidence** standard, is used in civil actions. Examples include situations in which someone is being denied an important government benefit or is facing involuntary commitment to a mental institution. The court in the case of *In re D.T.*, beginning on page 49, was faced with deciding which standard should be applied when the state wishes to terminate a parent's rights.

The termination process involves two stages. At the first stage the state must prove the parent is "unfit" by clear and convincing evidence. If the state is able to do so, then the state must prove that it is in the best interests of the child for parental rights to be terminated. At this second stage, rather than using either the clear and convincing or preponderance of the evidence standard, the trial court simply relied on its "sound discretion." After finding that "sound discretion" is not a recognized standard of proof, the Illinois Supreme Court addressed the issue of which recognized standard, clear and convincing evidence or preponderance of the evidence, should have been used during this second stage.

DISCUSSION QUESTION

5. What do you think of the differences between judges' and jurors' definitions of "beyond a reasonable doubt" and a "preponderance of the evidence"? Do you think this causes any problems for our legal system?

[6]Simon & Mahan, Quantifying Burdens of Proofs, 5 Law & Soc'y Rev. 39 (1971).

In re D.T., A Minor (The People of the State of Illinois et al., Appellants, v. Brenda T., Appellee). Supreme Court of Illinois 212 Ill. 2d 347; 818 N.E.2d 1214 (2004)

Justice FITZGERALD delivered the opinion of the court

Background

On February 1, 1998, respondent, Brenda T., took her four-year-old son, D.T., to the emergency room of Ravenswood Hospital. D.T. was in severe pain from an injury to his scrotum inflicted by respondent's boyfriend at least 48 hours earlier. The injury was caused by repetitive blunt blows to the scrotum. D.T. was transferred to Children's Memorial Hospital, where he underwent surgery to determine whether castration would be necessary. In addition to this injury, multiple bruises to D.T.'s face, arm, back, buttock and thigh were apparent. A linear bruise on his cheek had the characteristic appearance of a mark left by an open-hand slap. D.T. tolerated the surgery well, and although castration was unnecessary, the injury left D.T. with an increased risk of infertility later in life.

D.T. was discharged from the hospital on February 4, 1998, and taken into protective custody. The trial court later placed guardianship of D.T. in the Department of Children and Family Services (DCFS) and appointed the Cook County public guardian as D.T.'s attorney and guardian ad litem (GAL). . . .

On July 19, 1999, the State filed a petition seeking termination of respondent's parental rights and appointment of a guardian with the right to consent to adoption. . . . [O]n April 6, 2001, after hearing testimony from respondent, the foster mother, the DCFS investigator, case workers, counselors, and other service providers, the trial court determined that the State had demonstrated, by clear and convincing evidence, that respondent was unfit in that she failed to protect D.T. from an environment injurious to his welfare. Hearing on the best-interests portion of the State's petition commenced the following month, and on June 8, 2001, the trial court found,

within its "sound discretion," that it was in D.T.'s best interest to terminate respondent's parental rights. . . .

The appellate court affirmed the finding of unfitness [but] held that a preponderance of the evidence standard, which the State had failed to satisfy, applies at a best-interests hearing. . . .

Analysis

Proceedings to terminate parental rights are governed principally by the Juvenile Court Act of 1987 (705 ILCS 405/1-1 et seq. (West 2000)) and the Adoption Act (750 ILCS 50/1 et seq. (West 2000)). Generally, under the Juvenile Court Act, where a child is adjudicated abused, neglected or dependent, and the State seeks to free the child for adoption, unless the parent consents, the State must first establish that the parent is "unfit" under one or more of the grounds set forth in the Adoption Act. If the trial court finds the parent to be unfit, the court then determines whether it is in the best interests of the minor that parental rights be terminated. . . .

We turn to the issue of whether the preponderance standard, adopted by the appellate court, or the clear and convincing standard, urged by respondent, is applicable. . . .

In any given proceeding, the minimum standard of proof the due process clause permits reflects the weight of the private and public interests affected, as well as a societal judgment about how the risk of error should be allocated between the parties. . . . "The more stringent the burden of proof a party must bear, the more that party bears the risk of an erroneous decision." . . . For example, in a criminal case the private interests of the defendant are of such magnitude that society imposes the risk of error almost entirely on itself by requiring the State to prove the defendant's guilt "beyond a reasonable doubt." . . . This high standard of proof reduces the risk of finding an innocent person guilty, but increases the risk of acquitting a guilty person. . . .

In contrast, civil cases generally require the lesser "preponderance" standard of proof. This standard allocates the risk of error roughly equally between the litigants, reflecting the view that the interests at stake are of relatively equal societal importance. In some civil cases, however, the interests at stake are deemed to be more substantial, requiring a higher standard than a preponderance. In these cases, a clear and convincing standard is imposed. The clear and convincing standard requires proof greater than a preponderance, but not quite approaching the criminal standard of beyond a reasonable doubt. A party burdened with a clear and convincing standard shoulders a greater share of the risk of an erroneous determination.

In determining whether, as argued by respondent, a clear and convincing standard is the minimum burden of proof at a best-interests hearing that the due process clause will allow, we apply the test developed in *Mathews v. Eldridge,* 424 U.S. 319 (1976). . . . Under *Mathews,* the dictates of due process require consideration of three factors: "first, the private interest that will be affected by the official action; second, the risk of an erroneous deprivation of such interest through the procedures used, and the probable value, if any, of additional or substitute procedural safeguards; and finally, the Government's interest, including the function involved and the fiscal and administrative burdens that the additional or substitute procedural requirement would entail." . . .

Two private interests are at stake in a proceeding to terminate parental rights: the parent's fundamental liberty interest in the care, custody and management of his or her child and the child's interest in a . . . "loving, stable and safe home environment" . . . At the unfitness stage, the interests of the parent and the child coincide to the extent that they both "share a vital interest in preventing erroneous termination of their natural relationship." The alignment of these interests at the unfitness hearing favors the use of error-reducing procedures, i.e., use of a more stringent burden of proof than a preponderance. The same, however, is not true at a best-interests hearing. Once the State proves parental unfitness, the interests of the parent and the child diverge. Thus, at a best-interests hearing, the parent and the child may become adversaries, as the child's interest in a loving, stable and safe home environment become more aligned with the State's interest in terminating parental rights and freeing the child for adoption. Although the parent still possesses an interest in maintaining the parent-child relationship, the force of that interest is lessened by the court's finding that the parent is unfit to raise his or her child.

The second *Mathews* factor requires us to consider the risk of an erroneous deprivation of the parent's and child's interests resulting from the use of a preponderance standard and the likelihood that a higher evidentiary standard— clear and convincing—would reduce the risk of error. At the unfitness hearing, the focus is on the parent's conduct relative to the ground or grounds of unfitness alleged by the State. The trial court is not permitted to consider the child's interests. A clear and convincing standard underscores the importance of the parent's interest and the fact that such interest will not be extinguished lightly. A clear and convincing standard reduces the risk that a fit parent will be found unfit.

Following a finding of unfitness, however, the focus shifts to the child. The issue is no longer whether parental rights *can* be terminated; the issue is whether, in light of the child's needs, parental rights *should* be terminated. Accordingly, at a best-interests hearing, the parent's interest in maintaining the parent-child relationship must yield to the child's interest in a stable, loving home life. The stricter clear and convincing burden of proof would place a greater share of the risk of an erroneous determination on the State, operating to the benefit of the parent, but to the detriment of the child. This is so because an erroneous finding that termination of parental rights is not in the child's best interests results in preservation of the parent-child relationship, to the obvious favor of the unfit parent. Such an erroneous finding, however, would also deprive the child of the opportunity for permanency, one of the stated goals of the Juvenile Court Act, and subject the child to the frequently uncertain and fluctuating world of foster care. Thus, application of a clear and convincing burden of proof at the best-interests hearing does not adequately safeguard the interest of the child in a "normal family home" Imposition of a preponderance standard, however, would distribute the risk of error relatively equally, reflecting the roughly equal interest the parents, the State, and the child have in the outcome of the proceeding.

Turning to the final *Mathews* factor, two governmental interests are at stake in a parental rights termination proceeding: the state's "parens patriae interest in preserving and promoting the welfare of the child and a fiscal and administrative interest in reducing the cost and burden of such proceedings." . . . Use of a clear and convincing standard of proof at the best-interests hearing would likely not impose an increased fiscal burden on the state, since the higher evidentiary burden is already required at the unfitness hearing. Further, unlike other procedural safeguards, such as the right to counsel in criminal proceedings, no additional state resources would be called into play simply by virtue of a stricter evidentiary standard.

Use of a clear and convincing standard at the best-interests hearing would, however, frustrate the state's *parens patriae* interest in protecting the welfare of its children. Although the state's *parens patriae* interest generally favors preservation of

the minor's family ties, it may also encompass an interest in severing family ties. . . . As this court has recognized, "once a court has found by clear and convincing evidence that a parent is unfit, the state's interest in protecting the child is sufficiently compelling to allow the termination of parental rights." . . . The increased burden on the State resulting from imposition of a clear and convincing standard of proof will hinder this substantial public interest.

Based on the foregoing analysis of the *Mathews* factors, we conclude, as did the appellate court, that due process does not require imposition of a clear and convincing standard of proof at a best-interests hearing, and that the preponderance standard of proof adequately ensures the level of certainty about the court's factual conclusions necessary to satisfy due process. In the present case, the trial court declined to recognize a particular burden of proof and instead indicated that its best-interests ruling was based on its "sound discretion." The trial court erred.

[W]e remand this matter to the trial court for a new best-interests hearing to be conducted under the constitutionally proper standard—a preponderance of the evidence.

Case Discussion Questions

1. What is the difference between each of the following standards of proof?
   a. beyond a reasonable doubt
   b. preponderance of the evidence
   c. clear and convincing evidence
2. What factors are to be considered in determining which standard should be applied, and why in this particular case did the court choose preponderance of the evidence?
3. Do you agree that preponderance of the evidence is the appropriate standard when determining whether to terminate the parental rights of an "unfit" parent? Why?

d. Judgment

The result of the court's actions in a civil suit is a finding of liability or no liability. Do not use the term *guilty* when referring to a civil defendant. In a criminal case we say that the defendant was found guilty or not guilty.

e. Sanctions/Remedies

Damages
Monetary compensation, including compensatory, punitive, and nominal damages.

The typical remedy in a civil case is either **damages,** where the defendant pays the plaintiff for the harm he or she has done, or an **injunction,** where the court orders the defendant to take some specific action or to cease acting in a specific way. For example, in Diane's situation she might ask to be paid for the time she has been out of work (damages) and request a court order requiring the restaurant to rehire her (an injunction).

While the focus of civil law is on redressing the losses of the plaintiff, in the criminal law the sanctions are designed to punish the offender and deter future offenders. If a court of law determines that a provision of the criminal law has been violated, it may impose two broad types of sanctions—loss of liberty and financial penalty. The loss of liberty can range from receiving unsupervised probation to spending a few days in the county jail to serving several years in a state penitentiary to receiving the death penalty. The fines assessed as part of the criminal process become the property of the state rather than the victim. Only occasionally will a negotiated settlement with a criminal defendant contain some provisions for restitution for the victim. Usually, if the victim wishes to receive money from the criminal defendant to compensate her for the harm done to her, she must hire a lawyer and initiate a civil suit.

f. Sources of Law

A final difference relates to the sources of criminal and civil law. Criminal law is almost entirely statutory, while civil law is rooted in the common law (court-made law). Gradually, however, this distinction is being eroded as more and more areas of the civil law are becoming controlled by statutory law.

As noted above, single event can become the basis for actions in both the criminal and the civil courts. For example, the victim of a battery could sue the attacker for civil damages at the same time the state is prosecuting the attacker on a criminal charge. The driver of an automobile involved in a traffic accident may receive a traffic ticket from the police and at the same time be sued by someone else involved in the accident. In certain types of antitrust cases the government can choose between seeking criminal charges and seeking civil damages. As noted earlier regarding Diane's case, she might bring a civil action to recover money and obtain a court order. In addition, she might want to press criminal charges for the restaurant's refusal to let her collect her personal belongings. Charging a person with a criminal violation and suing that person civilly do not constitute **double jeopardy.** Double jeopardy is defined as being prosecuted twice for the same criminal offense.

Double jeopardy
A constitutional protection against being tried twice for the same crime.

In summary, common ways of differentiating criminal from civil law include the following: In a civil case the harm is to an individual, while in a criminal case the action is said to harm society itself; in a civil case the parties are labeled the plaintiff and the defendant, whereas in a criminal case they are the state and the defendant; the government prosecutes criminal cases, while individual plaintiffs initiate civil cases; in a criminal case the government must prove its case beyond a reasonable doubt, whereas in a civil case the plaintiff must prove his or her case by a preponderance of the evidence; a finding of guilt in a criminal case results in a fine or imprisonment, while a finding of liability in a civil case results in a monetary award or an injunction; and the source of law for civil cases is both court-made law and statutes, whereas almost all criminal law is based in statutes. (Refer again to Figure 3-2 on page 47.)

Finally, even though we sometimes talk about civil versus criminal law, keep in mind that the same facts may give rise to both civil and criminal lawsuits. If a potential defendant in a civil case has been convicted at a criminal trial that will make it easier for the plaintiff to win a civil case. However, even if the defendant was acquitted at the criminal trial, because of the different standards of proof and evidentiary requirements the plaintiff may still win in a civil case.

2. Criminal Law

Murder, robbery, and arson are examples of criminal behavior. However, it is much easier to list types of criminal behavior than it is to define the difference between criminal and civil law. As mentioned earlier, usually it is said that a criminal act harms not just the victim but also society as a whole. That definition does not get us very far. What is a wrong against society as a whole? One way of viewing this is to say that the act hurts not only the individual victim, but also society as a whole because the act's consequences are so grave as to cause concern to the rest of the population. When the legislature perceives that a particular act such as arson has that broader impact, it enacts a statute outlining the elements of the crime and its punishment.

In this section we will discuss the major types of criminal behavior, what is necessary to prove to a court that a crime has been committed, and what defenses might be raised to try to show the court that the defendant was justified in acting as he or she did.

a. Types of Crimes

Serious crimes, such as murder, rape, armed robbery, and aggravated assault, are classified as **felonies**, and they generally involve a punishment that can include a year or more in a state prison. **Misdemeanors** include such lesser charges as disorderly conduct and criminal damage to property. When incarceration is called for in these cases, it usually is for less than one year and is served in a county jail. Today the criminal law in most jurisdictions is entirely statutory in nature, and the legislature determines whether a given act is to be considered a felony or a misdemeanor.

The criminal codes of most states typically divide crimes into the following categories:

1. crimes against persons (homicide, kidnapping, sex offenses, assault, and battery),
2. crimes against property (theft, robbery, burglary, arson, and trespass),
3. crimes against the public health or decency (drug offenses, bribery, gambling, prostitution, and disorderly conduct), and
4. crimes against the government itself (treason and official misconduct).

The focus of federal criminal law is on interstate activities and unlawful interference with a federal agency or its workers.

Felony
A serious crime, usually carrying a prison sentence of one or more years.

Misdemeanor
A minor crime not amounting to a felony, usually punishable by a fine or a jail sentence of less than a year.

b. Establishing a Prima Facie Case

In order for a person to be convicted in a criminal trial, the prosecution must establish that the defendant committed an act defined as being illegal in the criminal code. This involves proving that the accused both had the requisite bad intent (called **mens rea**) and committed the requisite bad behavior (called **actus reus**). Different acts—killing someone, burning down a building, robbing a store—can give rise to different crimes. It is also true that the same act accompanied by different types of intent can give rise to different crimes. For example, the act of killing could be categorized as murder or manslaughter depending on the defendant's state of mind when he or she committed the act.

At the trial the prosecution must first present a **prima facie case**, one that establishes the elements of the crime, the requisite bad intent and bad behavior. A prima facie case contains enough evidence to support a finding of guilty if the defense presents no contrary evidence. If the prosecution fails to present a prima facie case, the judge must issue a not guilty verdict without the defense even presenting its case.

c. Defenses

If the prosecution does present a prima facie case, the defense then has the opportunity to present evidence that either contradicts that presented by the prosecutor or establishes a legally recognized justification. This evidence could involve witnesses who contradict the testimony of prosecution witnesses or evidence that establishes an alibi, self-defense, or insanity.

There are essentially two types of criminal **defenses**. The first type justifies the act. The second type negates the requisite mens rea. An example of the first type of defense, which justifies the act, is self-defense. The defendant admits killing the victim but argues that he or she had no choice. Examples of the second type of defense, which negates the requisite intent, are insanity, infancy, and intoxication. Each of these defenses has as its premise the fact that the defendant was incapable of forming the requisite intent to commit the crime.

After the defense has presented its evidence, the prosecution has a chance to respond with rebuttal witnesses to attack these defenses and reestablish the credibility of its own witnesses.

3. Civil Law

Civil law involves private actions brought by individuals to address perceived wrongs. In this section we will discuss what is necessary to prove a civil prima facie case, the defenses to a civil suit, the damages that a plaintiff can recover, and the main areas of civil law.

a. Establishing a Prima Facie Case

Just as the prosecution has the burden of establishing a prima facie case in a criminal case, so, too, the plaintiff shares a similar burden in a civil case. The plaintiff has the burden of proving the various elements listed in his or her

---

Mens rea
Bad intent.

Actus reus
Bad act.

Prima facie case
What the prosecution or plaintiff must be able to prove in order for the case to go to the jury— that is, the elements of the prosecution's case or the plaintiff's cause of action.

Defense
A fact or legal argument that would relieve the defendant of liability in a civil case or guilt in a criminal case.

complaint that show the plaintiff has a valid **cause of action**. A cause of action is a claim that, based on the law and the facts, is sufficient to demand judicial action. The plaintiff must prove these elements by a preponderance of the evidence, which means it is more likely than not that the defendant committed the wrong.

For example, assume a car and a truck collided at an intersection. The driver of the car is injured and wants to sue the truck driver, alleging the truck driver ran a red light. The car driver will be the plaintiff, and his cause of action will be based on the law of **negligence** (acting unreasonably under the circumstances) and the facts of what happened at the intersection. To succeed in a lawsuit, the plaintiff will have to present evidence that it is more likely than not that the truck driver was negligent. If the plaintiff/driver is able to do so, then he has satisfied his prima facie case. Every area of civil law has its own required elements that constitute the plaintiff's prima facie case. Later in this chapter as you read about torts, contracts, and property law, note the requirements of each for the plaintiff to prove a prima facie case.

Cause of action
A claim that based on the law and the facts is sufficient to support a lawsuit. If the plaintiff does not state a valid cause of action in the complaint, the court will dismiss it.

Negligence
The failure to act reasonably under the circumstances.

b. Defenses

The defendant/truck driver can respond first by trying to negate the plaintiff's case. Perhaps he has a witness who will testify that the light was green for the truck driver and red for the plaintiff. In addition to attempting to negate the plaintiff's case, the defendant can raise defenses of his own, known as **affirmative defenses**. In effect, the defendant is saying this: Even if you are right and I did something wrong, I have a good excuse or a reason why my liability should be reduced.

For example, in the accident mentioned above, the truck driver might ask the car driver's passenger to testify that the car driver was not being as attentive to his driving as he should have been. This behavior could have contributed to the accident, thereby decreasing the defendant's share of the liability.

It is very important to keep these two approaches separate: First, the defendant tries to negate the plaintiff's case. Second, the defendant raises defenses that could limit his liability even if the plaintiff's version of the law and facts is true.

Depending on the area of law, different defenses will be available. For example, it might be a valid defense to a contract claim that the defendant was only fifteen years old when he signed the contract. However, being fifteen years old may not be a defense to an intentional tort, such as battery.

In some cases, statutes or constitutions protect certain classes of people or institutions from being sued by granting them either full or partial immunity. One of the oldest and most important forms of immunity is **sovereign immunity**. Historically, the doctrine of sovereign immunity prohibited injured parties from suing the government, unless the government gave its consent. This protection can be traced back to the concept of the divine right of kings and the idea that "the king can do no wrong." In Chapter 7 we discuss how the doctrine of sovereign immunity has been modified over the years. Later in this book we also discuss the related concepts of spousal and parental immunity.

Affirmative defense
A defense whereby the defendant offers new evidence to avoid judgment.

Sovereign immunity
The prohibition against suing the government without the government's consent.

c. Damages

Compensatory damages
Money awarded to a plaintiff in payment for his or her actual losses.

Punitive damages
Money awarded to a plaintiff in cases of intentional torts in order to punish the defendant and serve as a warning to others.

Nominal damages
A token sum awarded when liability has been found but monetary damages cannot be shown.

Contract
An agreement supported by consideration.

Consideration
Something of value exchanged to form the basis of a contract.

Property law
Law dealing with ownership.

Real property
Land and objects permanently attached to land.

Personal property
All property that is not real property.

If a court determines that the plaintiff should recover, the issue of damages (monetary compensation) arises. There are three types of damages: compensatory, punitive, and nominal. **Compensatory damages** are intended to compensate the plaintiff for the harm done to her or him. In a tort action involving harm to a person, that might mean the cost of medical bills, lost time from work, and pain and suffering. **Punitive damages** are designed to punish the defendant and typically are awarded only for intentional torts when the court deems that the **tort-feasor** (the person who committed the tort) deserves an additional punishment beyond just compensating the plaintiff for the harm done to him or her. Finally, **nominal damages** are awarded when the law has been violated but the plaintiff cannot prove any monetary harm. As mentioned earlier, in addition to or instead of damages, the court might issue an injunction, an order to the defendant telling the defendant to do a specific act or to cease doing a specific act.

d. Areas of Civil Law

Civil law covers a very broad range of subjects, including adoption, admiralty collections, corporate, divorce, employment, environmental, intellectual property, personal injury, probate, and real estate law. However, we believe it is helpful to think of civil law as falling into three main categories: making deals, owning property, and protecting people and property from harm. The most basic principles of each are covered in the standard law school courses of contracts, property, and torts, respectively. The various specialty fields listed above all involve applications of the principles taught in these three courses.

(1) Contracts

The formal definition of a **contract** is an agreement supported by consideration. Therefore, contract law deals with two-sided agreements or bargains. I agree to sell you my diamond ring, and you agree to give me $500 in return. We have struck a bargain, entered into a contract. If something should go wrong—if I refuse to hand over the ring or you refuse to give me the money—we would find our actions governed by contract law. For a contract to be valid, there must be an offer, an acceptance of the offer, and **consideration**—that is, something of value must be exchanged. It is the consideration that differentiates a contract from a gift. Common defenses to a contract action include breach by the other side and incapacity to contract, as when one party is underage.

(2) Property

Property law deals with ownership. If two neighbors have a dispute over the correct placement of the boundary separating their land, property law will resolve it. Property law is divided into two main categories: (1) **real property,** land and objects permanently attached to land, and (2) **personal property,** all other property.

The first issue raised in a property law case may be how to classify the property. For example, is a room air conditioner real or personal property? If it is simply sitting in a window opening and can be easily removed without damage to the window, it is personal property. But what if the window has been taken out and the air conditioner screwed into the window frame? Is it now "permanently attached"? How you classify property is important because different rules may apply to real versus personal property.

Another common dispute that arises under property law relates to gift law. Above we noted that the difference between a contract and a gift is that a contract is two-sided (each party gives something to the other), while a gift is one-sided. The necessary elements for a valid gift include an offer, an acceptance of the offer, and delivery. Usually, the first two elements are not at issue, but the last element, delivery, can become a problem, especially when the gift is delivered symbolically, as by handing over the keys to a car. The question is, Has the car been delivered? The deciding factor is usually whether the owner has relinquished all control over the object. In the case of a car, that probably involves more than simply handing over a set of keys. This type of delivery is known as **constructive delivery.** (*Note:* A constructive delivery is one example of a **legal fiction.** Courts create a legal fiction when they need to make an assumption that is not based in fact in order to resolve a dispute. For example, courts frequently speak of corporations as though they were persons.) No actual delivery of the car is made, but the owner takes the necessary actions to allow the new owner to gain control over the gift.

(3) Torts

Issues of **tort law** arise when one person harms another person or that person's property. A tort is defined as a private wrong (other than a breach of contract) in which a person is harmed because of another's failure to carry out a legal duty. Through the common law, the courts have defined legal duties as occasionally including the affirmative obligation to take action to protect others. More commonly, courts require that everyone refrain from taking actions that inflict harm on others. Torts are traditionally categorized as intentional, negligent, or the result of strict liability.

As the name indicates, an **intentional tort** occurs when someone intentionally harms a person or that person's property. If one of your classmates deliberately hits you, your classmate has committed the intentional tort known as battery. **Battery** is the intentional, harmful or offensive physical contact by one person with another person. Libel, slander, invasion of privacy, and false imprisonment are other examples of intentional torts.

The most common category of tort law is that of **negligence.** Negligence is the failure to act as a reasonably prudent and careful person is expected to act under the circumstances. This used to be known as the reasonable man standard but has more recently become known as the reasonable person standard.

Constructive
Not factually true, but accepted by the courts as being legally true.

Legal fiction
An assumption that something that is not real is real—for example, saying that a corporation is a person for purposes of its being able to sue and be sued.

Tort law
Law that deals with harm to a person or a person's property.

Intentional tort
A tort committed by one who intends to do the act that creates the harm.

Case 4: Mr. Whipple

Mr. Whipple owns a grocery store. A customer breaks a bottle of apple juice and promptly reports it to Mr. Whipple. Nonetheless, Mr. Whipple fails to have the broken jar and spilled juice cleaned up. Twenty minutes later another customer slips on the wet floor, breaking her leg.

Mr. Whipple would probably be found liable for negligence. Clearly he did not intend for the customer to slip and break her leg. Therefore, there was no intentional tort. But a jury might find that a reasonable store owner would have ordered the spill cleaned up within twenty minutes after learning of it.

In order for a plaintiff to prove negligence, he or she must show that

1. the defendant owed the plaintiff a duty of care,
2. the defendant breached that duty,
3. and the breach caused
4. the plaintiff harm.

These four basic prerequisites (elements) in a negligence case are known as duty, breach, causation, and harm. In the case just mentioned, Mr. Whipple had a duty to act as a reasonable store owner would under the circumstances. The circumstances were a broken jar of apple juice about which Mr. Whipple was informed and a twenty-minute time period in which he did nothing. If the jurors believe Mr. Whipple breached his duty to act as a reasonable store owner, then they will find liability if they also think that breach caused the customer harm.

Ethics Alert

You are walking along the beach and see a young child drowning. No one else is in sight. Should the law require you to try to save the child? Should it matter if you are an off-duty lifeguard?

As the store owner, Mr. Whipple would, of course, try to defend himself through rebutting the plaintiff's evidence. Perhaps it had only been two and not twenty minutes since he learned of the spill. In addition, he might try to raise an affirmative defense. As mentioned previously, an affirmative defense is a defense whereby the defendant offers new evidence to avoid or limit the judgment. The two main affirmative defenses to negligence are **contributory negligence** and **assumption of the risk.** Contributory negligence means that the plaintiff was also negligent and through that negligence contributed to his or her own injury. In Mr. Whipple's case, perhaps the customer was in a hurry and was not looking where she was going. Assumption of the risk means that the plaintiff voluntarily and knowingly subjected himself or herself to a known danger. Perhaps the customer saw the spilled juice but chose to walk through it anyway. In many states assumption of the risk is no longer a separate defense to negligence, as it has been subsumed under the more general category of contributory negligence.

Historically, any showing of contributory negligence or assumption of the risk meant that the plaintiff could recover nothing from the defendant even if the defendant's actions were much more culpable than those of the plaintiff. Legislatures and courts in many states have tried to rectify that situation by replacing contributory negligence with a new defense known as

Contributory negligence Negligence by the plaintiff that contributed to his or her injury. Normally, any finding of contributory negligence acts as a complete bar to a plaintiff's recovery.

Assumption of the risk Voluntarily and knowingly subjecting oneself to danger.

comparative negligence. Under comparative negligence, instead of the plaintiff's own negligence relieving the defendant of liability, the jury compares the negligence of the plaintiff to that of the defendant and apportions the responsibility. The plaintiff's recovery is reduced by his or her degree of negligence.

The third category of tort law is called **strict liability.** In some cases persons or corporations can be held liable for injuries that resulted from their actions, even when their actions were reasonable under the circumstances and they did not intend to harm anyone. The doctrine of strict liability holds that persons who engage in activities that are inherently dangerous are responsible for injury that results, even though they carried out the activities in the safest and most prudent way possible. For example, someone who uses explosives or who keeps wild animals is liable for all resulting injuries, even if that person used the utmost care. In recent years many courts have held manufacturers and sellers to be strictly liable when a defective product the defendant manufactured or sold caused harm to the user or consumer, even when the user or consumer could not show that the manufacturer's negligence caused the defect.

Comparative negligence
A method for measuring the relative negligence of the plaintiff and the defendant, with a commensurate sharing of the compensation for the injuries.

Strict liability
Liability without a showing of fault.

DISCUSSION QUESTIONS

6. For each question, decide whether the facts raise an issue of tort, contract, or property law or more than one area of law.

    a. You buy a new car. Two days later as you are driving, the brakes fail, and you go off the road, hitting a telephone pole. Luckily you are unhurt, but the car is badly damaged.

    b. You rent an apartment. One night as you are leaving the building through the central stairway, the railing gives way, and you fall down, breaking your leg.

7. For each of the following situations decide if you think liability should be found based on an intentional tort, negligence, or strict liability or whether no liability should be found.

    a. Sally was angry with Martha. One night after leaving class, she deliberately drove her car into the side of Martha's car.

    b. One night after leaving class, Sally was in a hurry. When she arrived at the stop sign at the student parking lot entrance to Main Street, she did a "rolling stop." Martha was driving by on Main Street. Sally's auto hit the side of Martha's car.

    c. One night after leaving class, Sally got into her brand new Dodge van. When she arrived at the stop sign at the student parking lot entrance to Main Street, she pressed on the brakes, but nothing happened. Martha was driving by on Main Street. Sally's auto hit the side of Martha's car.

    d. One night after leaving class, Sally got into her car. When she arrived at the stop sign at the student parking entrance to Main Street, she suddenly got a tremendous cramp in her side and momentarily lost control of her car. Martha was driving by on Main Street. Sally's auto hit the side of Martha's car.

C. SUBSTANTIVE VERSUS PROCEDURAL LAW

Substantive law
Law that creates rights and duties.

In addition to being categorized on the basis of its source, we also classify law as being either substantive or procedural. **Substantive law** refers to the part of the law that defines our rights and duties. It defines what actions will violate the criminal law and what our obligations are to each other. For example, substantive law includes the statutes that govern the legal speed limits, the circumstances under which someone can be convicted of robbery, and when a contract is enforceable. **Procedural law,** on the other hand, deals with how the legal system operates. It defines the steps that someone must go through to file a lawsuit and the procedures the police must follow in conducting a search or interrogating a suspect.

Procedural law
Law that regulates how the legal system operates.

Every case is founded in substantive law, and attorneys must determine what their client's obligations and liabilities are. However, they must be equally aware of the procedural aspects of the case. Even if the substantive law is on the client's side, the case may be lost if a claim is not filed within the time prescribed in the **statute of limitations.** The legal system imposes a limitation on how long a plaintiff has before he or she can no longer bring suit. Those limitations vary given the type of case involved. A plaintiff could also lose if the complaint, the initial document that starts a lawsuit, fails to include all the required information.

Statute of limitations
The law that sets the length of time from when something happens to when a lawsuit must be filed before the right to bring it is lost.

We have all heard of the criminal who was set free due to a "technicality." The rules of criminal procedure have their roots in the Constitution and are intended to protect the innocent from the overreaching of possibly overzealous law enforcement officials. These rules govern everything from the way in which the arresting police officer must inform a suspect of his or her rights to how evidence is introduced at trial.

Civil law is also controlled by very specific rules of procedure. Those rules of civil procedure will be the focus of Chapter 5. Criminal procedure will be discussed in Chapter 12. You will be studying the various areas of substantive law throughout this book and throughout your career.

DISCUSSION QUESTION

8. Review the hypothetical case that began Chapter 2. How would you categorize Diane's legal problems?

SUMMARY

We have seen how law can be categorized as either state or federal, civil or criminal, and substantive or procedural. The first category, state or federal, arises because the United States operates under a system of federalism. Under our federal system, governmental authority is split between the national government and the fifty state governments. Some areas of the law, such as divorce, are reserved exclusively to the states; some are reserved to the federal government; and some are shared by the states and the federal government. Federal law will be involved only if the federal Constitution, a federal statute, or a federal regulation is involved.

Civil law involves harm to an individual, while criminal law deals with harms to society as a whole. In both criminal and civil cases, the party with the burden of proof must first establish a prima facie case. Once that is established, the other side is given the opportunity to negate the prima facie case or to raise affirmative defenses. While the law has become increasingly specialized, the main areas of civil law are contracts, property, and torts. Tort law can be further subdivided into those involving intentional acts, those based on negligent behavior, and those that result from an imposition of strict liability. Finally, substantive law defines our rights and duties. Procedural law deals with how the legal system operates.

CRITICAL THINKING EXERCISES

1. Diana Levine, a professional musician, went to the hospital for treatment of a headache. By the time she left the hospital, her headache was gone, but so was one of her arms. The hospital staff had injected her with the drug Phenergan to alleviate her nausea caused by the migraine headache. The drug entered an artery, her arm became gangrenous, and several weeks later, her hand and lower arm were amputated. The drug's manufacturer knew that directly injecting the drug (as opposed to administering it through an IV drip) carried a risk of injury. The drug's label warned of the dangers associated with direct injection but did not prohibit that method of giving the drug. The label as written was approved by the federal Food and Drug Administration (FDA) in 1974. The FDA is the federal agency created by Congress responsible for approving all drug labeling. A Vermont jury determined that the drug's manufacturer did not adequately warn against that method of administration in its drug labeling and awarded Ms. Levine $5 million in compensatory damages, and the Vermont Supreme Court affirmed. The drug manufacturer appealed the case to the U.S. Supreme Court arguing that the FDA's authority over drug labeling preempts any state laws regarding product liability. What policy arguments would you advance for arguing that Ms. Levine's state products liability case is not preempted? What policy arguments would you advance for arguing that her case should be preempted by federal law?

2. For each question determine whether you think the law involved is federal, state, or both.
   a. A person is liable for slander if that person intentionally says that someone is a thief when she knows it is not true.
   b. To be valid, a contract for the sale of real estate must be in writing.
   c. Trucks traveling on interstate highways must be equipped with concave mud flaps.
   d. No employer with ten or more employees may discriminate on the basis of race, color, religion, sex, or national origin.
   e. A manufacturer of inherently dangerous products will be liable for any defective product that causes injury.

3. Take a moment to read the following Massachusetts statute regarding larceny: "Whoever steals . . . and with intent to steal . . . the property of another . . . shall be guilty of larceny. . . ."[5]

---

[5]Mass. Gen. Laws ch. 266, § 30 (2008).

a. Assume Alan got into a car, knowing that it was not his, "hot wired" it, and then drove off in it. Is he guilty of violating the statute? Why?

b. Assume Bill approached a car that he intended to steal but was scared away by a passerby. Is he guilty of violating the statute? Why?

c. Assume Charles got into a car, thinking he was getting into his friend's car, and "hot wired" it but only meant to borrow it. Is he guilty of violating the statute? Why?

||| REVIEW QUESTIONS

Pages 39 through 40

1. What are the three major ways in which attorneys categorize the law?
2. What is the difference between substantive and procedural law?
3. In terms of the type of harm caused, what is the difference between civil and criminal law?

Pages 40 through 46

4. What is federalism?
5. True or false: Every state must have the same laws regarding gambling. Why?
6. What does it mean to say that the federal government is a government of limited powers?
7. Do you think Congress could (not should) enact a national divorce statute? Why?
8. Why are some areas of the law preempted by the federal government?

Pages 46 through 53

9. Name at least four ways in which civil law differs from criminal law.
10. When is the burden of proof "beyond a reasonable doubt" and when is it a "preponderance of the evidence"? What is the difference between them?
11. In a civil case, if a jury is evenly split, leaning equally toward the plaintiff's and the defendant's views of the facts, who will win, the plaintiff or the defendant? Why?

Pages 53 through 56

12. What two basic elements must be established for the government to prove the prima facie case in a criminal case?
13. Why can the same act constitute several different crimes?
14. What are the two basic defenses to a criminal action?
15. In a criminal case, does the government or the defendant present its case first? Why?
16. What is the general definition of a civil cause of action?
17. In a civil case, does the plaintiff or the defendant present its case first? Why?
18. What are the three types of damages available in a civil case?
19. In addition to damages, what might a plaintiff seek in a civil case?

Pages 56 through 61

20. What must be present for a contract to be valid?
21. What is the basic difference between a contract and a gift?
22. What are the three main areas of tort law?
23. Give the general definition of negligence, and list the elements necessary to prove a prima facie case.
24. What are the main defenses to negligence?

Chapter 4

Structure of the Court System

*Trial courts search for truth and appellate courts
search for error.*
Unknown

INTRODUCTION

The law provides rules about how people should behave in different types of situations and provides remedies for when those rules are broken. However, these rules are not self-enforcing. In order to enforce these rules, people often have to go to court to have a judge or jury settle disputes for them. A court is a unit of the judicial branch of government that has authority to decide legal disputes. **Jurisdiction** refers to the ability of a specific court to hear a particular type of case.

One major way of classifying courts is in terms of whether they are trial or **appellate courts**. They can also be classified in terms of whether they are federal or state courts. In this chapter we will examine the structure of the various court systems, the concept of jurisdiction, and the roles played by those who work in the court system.

A. TRIAL VERSUS APPELLATE COURTS

Most court cases begin in a **trial court**.[1] Trial courts are said to be courts of **original jurisdiction** because trial courts are where actions are initiated and

---

[1]The primary exception to this pattern occurs when a dispute is adjudicated in an administrative agency and then appealed to the courts. In very rare circumstances a case can be filed directly with the U.S. Supreme Court under its original jurisdiction.

Jurisdiction
The power of a court to hear a case.

Appellate courts
Courts that determine whether lower courts have made errors of law.

Trial courts
Courts that determine the facts and apply the law to the facts.

Original jurisdiction
The authority of a court to hear a case when it is initiated (as opposed to appellate jurisdiction).

heard for the first time. In addition to conducting trials, much of a trial court's time is spent in far less dramatic proceedings, such as receiving plea agreements and ratifying out-of-court settlements. When a trial is held, attorneys present witness testimony and other evidence. After considering the evidence and the attorneys' arguments, trial courts have two functions. First, they must determine whose version of the facts is most credible. Second, they must apply the law to those facts to reach a decision. Therefore, trial courts must determine both questions of fact and questions of law.

Questions of fact
Questions relating to what happened: who, what, when, where, and how.

Questions of fact relate to the determination of what took place: who, what, when, where, and how? **Questions of law** relate to how the judge interprets and applies the law and include such issues as how a statute is to be interpreted and whether a specific piece of evidence is admissible. In a jury trial questions of fact are determined by the jury, while questions of law are determined by the judge. If it is a **bench trial** rather than a **jury trial,** the judge will decide the factual questions as well as the legal ones.

Questions of law
Questions relating to the interpretation or application of the law.

In most cases that go to trial, the meaning of the law is clear, but the facts themselves are very much in dispute. For example, under the criminal codes of most states it is a violation of the law for a person to forcibly take someone else's property without the owner's permission. When someone is tried for robbery, the trial usually focuses on such factual questions as the identification of the alleged robber and the ownership of the property taken.

Bench trial
A trial conducted without a jury.

Although the primary focus of most trials is on factual issues, at times legal issues are involved as well. For example, a trial judge may have to decide if certain testimony or evidence is admissible. That is a question of law. If the judge decides that the testimony or evidence is not admissible, then the trial proceeds without it. Also, if the judge rules that a search was illegal or that disputed pictures are too prejudicial, then the objects discovered in that search or the pictures in dispute are not admitted as evidence. Based on the evidence that has been allowed, the jury then resolves the questions of fact.

Jury trial
When a jury decides the facts and determines liability or guilt.

Consider the following example: In most states it is a crime for someone other than a physician, pharmacist, or other authorized medical person to sell or distribute narcotic drugs. When someone is on trial for selling narcotics, the prosecution must present evidence that shows the accused did in fact sell a substance that fits the legal definition of a prohibited narcotic drug. These are issues of fact. The evidence usually consists of an undercover police agent testifying that the accused did sell the agent a substance that laboratory reports identify as a narcotic.

Entrapment
A defense requiring proof that the defendant would not have committed the crime but for police trickery.

It is possible, however, that the defendant might admit to selling the drug but then claim **entrapment.** The entrapment doctrine prohibits law enforcement officers from instigating criminal acts to lure otherwise innocent persons into committing a crime. One question of fact relating to the entrapment defense is whether the defendant ever committed such a criminal act or thought of committing such an act before. However, in addition to the factual questions and depending on the circumstances of a given case, a legal issue of what constitutes entrapment could arise. For example, assume government agents supplied the defendant with a drug and then later arrested him for selling the very same drug to another government agent. Here no one would be disputing what happened—the facts. But an appellate court could be asked to decide whether such actions legally qualify as entrapment. In *Hampton v. United States*[2] the U.S. Supreme Court held that as long as the defendant is predisposed to commit the crime, it is not entrapment when government agents supply the defendant with a drug and then later arrest him for selling the very same drug to another government agent.

In sum, legal issues can arise in three ways:

- First, legal issues can arise regarding the meaning of the underlying cause of action, as in the example given above regarding whether entrapment had occurred. You saw another example of this in Chapter 2 in the case of *Bob Jones University* when the court had to determine whether a school that followed racially discriminatory admission practices qualified for a charitable exemption under the Internal Revenue Code.
- Second, during a trial numerous legal issues may be raised involving the conduct of the trial itself. To give but a few examples, such issues might include whether a particular piece of evidence should be excluded because it is the product of an illegal search and seizure, whether the plaintiff's attorney should be allowed to pursue a certain line of questioning, whether the judge should present a particular set of instructions to the jury, and whether prejudicial publicity has tainted the defendant's trial.
- Finally, legal issues can involve challenges to the constitutionality of the law that is being applied. For example, a doctor charged with performing an illegal abortion could argue that the law he is charged with violating is itself unconstitutional.

Appellate courts review the actions taken by trial courts (and in some cases the actions of administrative agencies). Therefore, the person who loses in a trial court may be able to appeal the decision to an appellate court. The party filing the appeal is called the **appellant** or the **petitioner**. The party who won in the trial court is called the **appellee** or the **respondent**. Most states and the federal government provide for one appeal as a matter of right. Additional appeals are usually at the discretion of the higher court.

Appellant or petitioner
The party in a case who has initiated an appeal.

Unlike trial courts, appellate courts do not hear testimony. They rely on the written record of what occurred in the trial court to determine whether the trial court made an error regarding the law. They do so because when conducting a review, appellate courts limit themselves to "legal" as opposed to "factual" issues that are specifically raised by the party who is bringing the appeal. Therefore, you can appeal a lower court decision only when you raise a valid legal issue. Appellate courts will not reconsider the facts; they will consider only whether the trial court made an error of law. Case 5: Alibi to a Murder on page 66 illustrates this point.

Appellee or respondent
The party in a case against whom an appeal has been filed.

---

[2]425 U.S. 484 (1976).

Case 5: Alibi to a Murder

Frederick Jones could not believe it when he was arrested for murder because he thought he had an ironclad alibi.

At his trial an elderly gentleman testified that he saw Mr. Jones near the scene of the murder shortly after it took place. At one point in the trial, over the objection of the defendant's attorney, the prosecutor showed the jury bloody and gruesome pictures of the deceased victim.

Mr. Jones testified that not only did he not commit the murder, but also he was attending an out-of-town wedding at the time the murder was supposed to have taken place. Ten witnesses then took the stand in succession and testified that they had been at the wedding and seen the defendant there.

At the end of the trial the jury convicted Mr. Jones.

Do you think there is any basis for launching an appeal in Mr. Jones's case? It is a question of fact whether on the night of the murder Mr. Jones was present at the scene of the murder (as testified to by one elderly witness) or out of town attending a wedding (as testified to by ten other witnesses). Therefore, his whereabouts on the night of the murder cannot form the basis for an appeal.

On the other hand, it is a question of law as to whether the judge should allow the jury to see pictures of the victim's bloody corpse. It can be argued that the viewing of those pictures was so inflammatory as to prejudice the jury. Therefore, the showing of the pictures could form the basis of an appeal. Keep in mind that this does not mean that Mr. Jones would win at the appellate level. It simply means that he would be given the opportunity to argue his case to the appellate court.

There is one exception to the rule that appellate courts review only questions of law. Occasionally they will review a case because they believe that what the jury did was something that no reasonable jury could do. Because appellate courts review only legal issues, normally they do not engage in this type of second-guessing regarding the trial court's findings. For example, in Mr. Jones's situation mentioned above, even though ten eyewitnesses testified that Mr. Jones was out of town on the night of the murder, Mr. Jones's attorney cannot appeal on the grounds that the jury was mistaken about his whereabouts on the night of the murder. Appellate courts will accept a jury's determination as to which witnesses were most credible. Only in rare instances will appellate courts reexamine the evidence.

If the appellate court determines that a legal error occurred but that it was minor and did not affect the result, the court labels it a **harmless error** and allows the decision to stand. If the court finds that a significant legal error was made in the way the trial was conducted, it will usually cancel the original outcome by **reversing** the trial court's decision. It may also direct that the case be retried by **remanding** the case to the trial court for further consideration.

In criminal cases a reversal of a conviction does not necessarily mean that the defendant will go free, as the government then has the option of retrying the case. However, if the appellate court rules that a key piece of evidence is

Harmless error
A trial court error that is not sufficient to warrant reversing the decision.

Reverse
A decision is reversed when an appellate court disagrees with the decision of a lower court.

Remand
When an appellate court sends a case back to the trial court for a new trial or other action.

inadmissible, the government may choose not to retry the defendant because it may feel that its case is too weak without the excluded evidence.

If the government chooses to proceed with a new trial, this does not violate the constitutional provision regarding **double jeopardy**. Double jeopardy occurs when a person is tried more than once for the same criminal offense. The Fifth and Fourteenth Amendments to the Constitution prohibit various forms of double jeopardy. However, when a defendant voluntarily appeals a conviction, he or she waives the right not to be retried for the same crime.

Appellate court judges reach their decisions by majority vote. Someone from the majority writes the **majority opinion** explaining the court's decision and how that decision was reached. In cases where the decision is not unanimous, judges may also write concurring or dissenting opinions to explain the nature of their disagreements. In a **concurring opinion** the judge agrees with the result reached by the majority but not with its reasoning. In a **dissenting opinion** the judge disagrees with the result and with the reasoning.

Majority opinion
An opinion in which a majority of the court joins.

Concurring opinion
An opinion that agrees with the majority's result but disagrees with its reasoning.

In summary, there are several major differences between trial and appellate courts. At the trial-court level the parties are called the plaintiff and the defendant in a civil case and the state and the defendant in a criminal case. At the appellate-court level the party who lost in the trial court is called either the appellant or the petitioner, while the party who won is called either the **appellee** or the **respondent**. In the trial court either a single judge or a jury decides the facts, and the judge determines the law. In the appellate court, a panel of three or more judges decides questions of law based on the attorneys' briefs (written arguments) and oral arguments. There are no witnesses who give testimony in the appellate courts and no juries. The judges merely review the trial transcript and the written briefs from the lawyers. Sometimes oral arguments from the opposing attorneys are heard, during which the judges have an opportunity to pose questions. Lower-level appellate judges usually work in rotating panels of three, while in the upper-level appellate courts all the judges jointly decide each case.

Dissenting opinion
An opinion that disagrees with the majority's decision and its reasoning.

Most of these differences are directly related to the most important distinction between trial and appellate courts: Trial courts determine the facts and apply the law to those facts; appellate courts deal only with questions of law. Three basic types of legal questions can arise at the appellate level. First are those that relate to the meaning of the underlying legal cause of action or defense, such as what qualifies as entrapment. Second, one of the parties can argue that the law being applied is unconstitutional, as when the doctor challenged an abortion law. Finally, legal issues can arise that have nothing to do with the underlying legal claim but rather relate to how the trial was conducted. Figure 4-1 summarizes the differences between trial and appellate courts.

DISCUSSION QUESTIONS

1. Do you think it is a good or a bad idea that only questions of law can be appealed?

2. Can you think of a situation when an appellate judge might reverse and remand a case? When a judge might reverse but not remand a case?

	Trial Court	Appellate Court
Parties' names	Plaintiff/defendant State/defendant	Appellant/appellee or petitioner/respondent
Decision maker	Judge and sometimes a jury	Majority vote of three or more judges
Attorney arguments	Yes	Yes
Witness testimony	Yes	No
Evidence introduced	Yes	No
Questions of fact decided	Yes	No
Questions of law decided	Yes	Yes

Figure 4-1   Comparison of Trial and Appellate Courts

B. FEDERAL AND STATE COURT SYSTEMS

Trial and appellate courts exist in both the federal and the state court systems. At first glance the federal and state judicial systems of this country present a confusing mixture of titles and functions. In large part this is because there are actually fifty-one different court systems (the federal system plus one for each state). To complicate matters, the same types of courts often have different names. For example, the basic trial court is called the court of common pleas in Pennsylvania, the district court in Minnesota, the circuit court in Illinois, the superior court in California, and the supreme court in New York. Although New York uses the "supreme court" designation for its trial courts, most states reserve that title for their highest appellate court. Out of this confusion we will try to create some order by discussing the basic structure of both the federal court system and a typical state court system. Although both systems can seem quite complex, the federal system has just three levels, as do most state systems: the trial courts, the intermediate appellate courts, and one appellate court of last resort.

1. The Federal System

A simplified organizational chart of the federal court system is shown in Figure 4-2. As you can see, it follows the basic pattern described above: trial courts, intermediate appellate courts, and one highest appellate court. The federal court system also includes a variety of other less well-known judicial bodies, such as the U.S. Court of International Trade, which are not listed here. The arrows indicate the avenues for appeals.

U.S. Supreme Court
The highest federal appellate court, consisting of nine appointed members.

The **U.S. Supreme Court** sits at the top of the federal judicial branch, where it hears appeals from both federal and state courts. However, as we will discuss more fully later in this chapter, not all state cases can be appealed to the U.S.

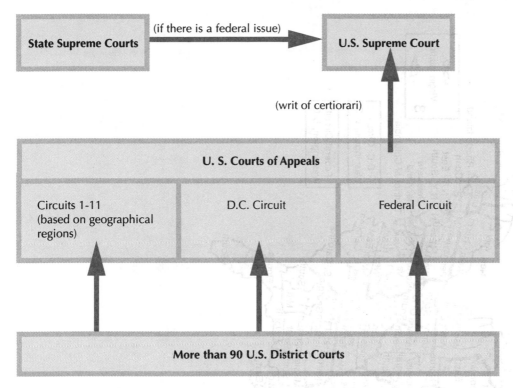

Figure 4-2 The Federal Court System

Supreme Court. Cases are appealed from state supreme courts only when federal issues are involved.

Immediately below the Supreme Court are the **U.S. courts of appeals.** Both the Supreme Court and the courts of appeals are appellate courts. The Supreme Court is the highest appellate court, while the courts of appeals are intermediate-level appellate courts. The country is divided geographically into twelve circuits, which include eleven numbered circuits and the District of Columbia as a separate circuit. The thirteenth circuit is called the Federal Circuit, where appeals in specialized cases from the entire country are heard. There is a court of appeals for each of the thirteen circuits. Most of the work, however, is done in the federal trial courts, the ninety-three **U.S. district courts** spread among the fifty states. There is at least one district court for each state. Most district court cases are appealed to the U.S. court of appeals in the circuit in which the district court is located. To gain an appreciation for how the circuits are organized, look at the map in Figure 4-3, page 70.

The basic outline for this three-tiered judicial structure is set forth in the federal Constitution. Article III, Section 1, provides that "[t]he judicial Power of the United States, shall be vested in one supreme Court, and in such inferior Courts as the Congress may from time to time ordain and establish." Those **"inferior Courts"** are the district courts and courts of appeals. Congress established the first inferior courts through the Judiciary Act of 1789. That act provided for thirteen districts and three circuits. Over the years, through further

U.S. courts of appeals
The intermediate appellate courts in the federal system.

U.S. district courts
The general jurisdiction trial courts in the federal system.

Inferior courts
In the federal system, all courts other than the U.S. Supreme Court.

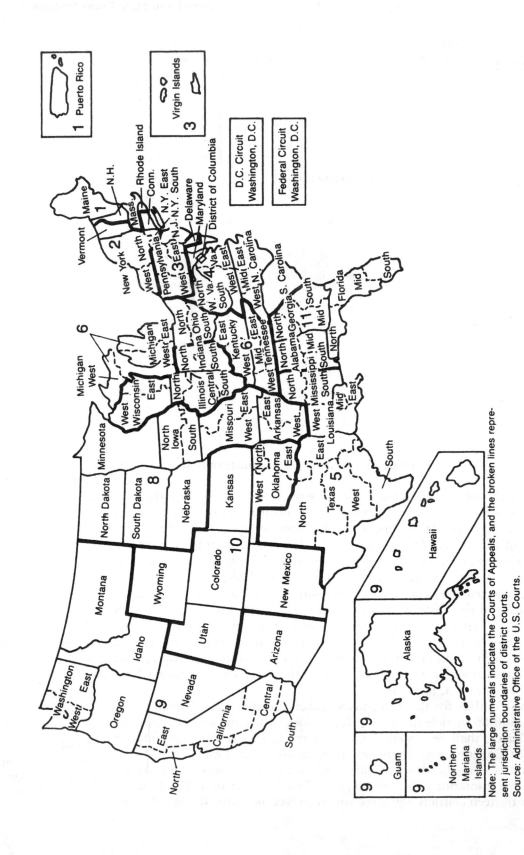

Figure 4-3 District and Circuit Court Boundaries

Note: The large numerals indicate the Courts of Appeals, and the broken lines represent jurisdiction boundaries of district courts.

Source: Administrative Office of the U.S. Courts.

legislative action, the number of both district and federal circuits has grown to its present-day level.

a. The Primary Federal Courts

In the federal system, cases normally begin in one of the district courts, which serve as the federal trial courts. These district courts are courts of **general jurisdiction.** That means they are authorized to adjudicate all types of civil and criminal cases. Courts of **limited jurisdiction** hear only a narrow range of cases on a specific subject (such as probate, domestic relations, or traffic).

The number of judges assigned to each district varies from one to twenty-seven depending on the caseload of the district. Usually, cases are heard by a single judge or a judge and a jury. The district court judges are assisted by **magistrate judges** and **bankruptcy judges.**

The magistrate judges supervise court calendars, hear procedural motions, issue **subpoenas,** hear minor criminal offense cases, and conduct civil pretrial hearings. In some district courts the magistrate judges, with the consent of the parties involved, conduct trials and enter judgments in civil cases. Bankruptcy judges handle most bankruptcy cases entirely on their own. In a limited number of cases they conduct the trial but then must submit their proposed findings of fact to the district judge, who enters the final order or judgment.

The losing party takes an appeal from a district court decision to the appropriate court of appeals. For example, cases from California district courts are appealed to the Court of Appeals for the Ninth Circuit. Each of the twelve regular circuits has from four to twenty-three judges. In courts of appeals, a panel, normally composed of three judges, hears appeals and reaches its decision through a majority vote. Occasionally all the judges sit together and decide a case **en banc.** This happens most frequently when the losing party in a case already decided by a panel of the court requests a rehearing before the full membership of the court.

Sitting at the top of the federal judicial system is the U.S. Supreme Court. The Court is composed of nine justices, who hear all appeals as a group. It is interesting to note that the Judiciary Act of 1789, mentioned above, provided for a Supreme Court with one chief justice and five associate justices. As with the number of courts, the number of Supreme Court justices has also grown over the years as the volume of the Court's work has increased. The Supreme Court justices also reach their decisions by majority vote.

A case seldom goes any further than a court of appeals, as the U.S. Supreme Court rarely is required to hear a case on appeal. Most cases that do reach the U.S. Supreme Court do so because the litigants have requested a **writ of certiorari.** In this writ the losing party asks the Supreme Court to review the case. The decision of whether to grant a writ of certiorari is discretionary. The Supreme Court usually hears no more than 200 of the approximately 4,000 requests it receives each year. For the request to be granted, four of the nine justices must agree to hear the case. If the request is denied, this does not mean that the Court agrees with the lower court's decision. It simply means that the Court does not want to hear the case. When discussing the Court's response to a writ of certiorari, you will often hear lawyers refer to the granting or denial of cert.

General jurisdiction
A court's power to hear any type of case arising within its geographical area.

Limited jurisdiction
A court's power to hear only specialized cases.

Subpoena
A court order requiring a person to appear to testify at a trial or deposition.

En banc
When an appellate court that normally sits in panels sits as a whole.

Writ of certiorari
A means of gaining appellate review; in the U.S. Supreme Court the writ is discretionary and will be issued to another court to review a federal question if four of the nine justices vote to hear the case.

NETNOTE

The official Web site of the federal judiciary is *www.uscourts.gov/*. It contains links to the U.S. Supreme Court, the U.S. courts of appeals, the U.S. district courts, and the U.S. bankruptcy courts. Emory University's Web site at *www.law. emory.edu/index.php?id=2997/* has a map of the federal circuits that allows you to link to a wide variety of information on each of the circuits. The U.S. Supreme Court's site at *www.supremecourtus.gov/* contains helpful information on the Court's procedures, its caseload, and biographies and pictures of the justices.

DISCUSSION QUESTIONS

3. Why do you think the framers of the Constitution chose to give federal judges lifetime tenure and to protect them from salary reduction? Do you think that was a wise decision?

4. Do you think it is appropriate that the Supreme Court hears no more than 200 of the approximately 4,000 requests it receives each year? What criteria should the Court use in deciding which cases it will hear?

b. Other Federal Courts

Figure 4-4, page 73, shows where the "core" courts, shown in Figure 4-2, fit into a more complete organizational chart of the federal court system. In addition to the primary courts discussed above, Congress has created more specialized courts, known as **legislative courts,** under Article I of the federal Constitution. These legislative courts include the U.S. Court of Military Appeals, the U.S. Tax Court, the U.S. Claims Court, and the U.S. Court of International Trade.

The U.S. Court of Military Appeals is the final appellate tribunal for court-martial convictions. The U.S. Tax Court (formerly the Board of Tax Appeals) considers challenges to Internal Revenue Service rulings. The U.S. Claims Court (formerly the Court of Claims) decides the validity of specific types of claims against the U.S. government, and the U.S. Court of International Trade (formerly the U.S. Customs Court) reviews decisions and appraisals of imported merchandise made in collecting customs duties.

2. State Court Systems

Due to the controversial nature of many of its decisions, the U.S. Supreme Court gets the lion's share of the media coverage given to the courts on the evening news. While many important cases and significant constitutional issues are decided in the federal courts, it is in state courts that over 98 percent of all legal business occurs.[3]

---

[3]Cooke & Goodman, The State of the Nation's State Courts, Nat'l. L.J., Mar. 19, 1984, at 23.

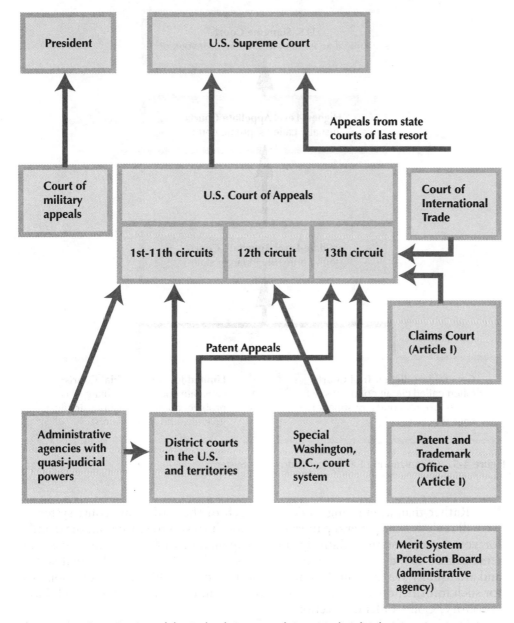

Figure 4-4 Organization of the Federal Courts and Quasi-Judicial Administrative Agencies

Many states have court systems that are very similar to the federal system. Cases begin in a trial court and then proceed through one or two levels of appellate courts. Figure 4-5, on page 74, shows the organization of a typical state court system. Note how closely it parallels Figure 4-2, showing the core of the federal court system. The path for appeals in most state court systems is from the trial court to an intermediate appellate court (if one exists) and then to the state's highest appellate court (usually called the supreme court).

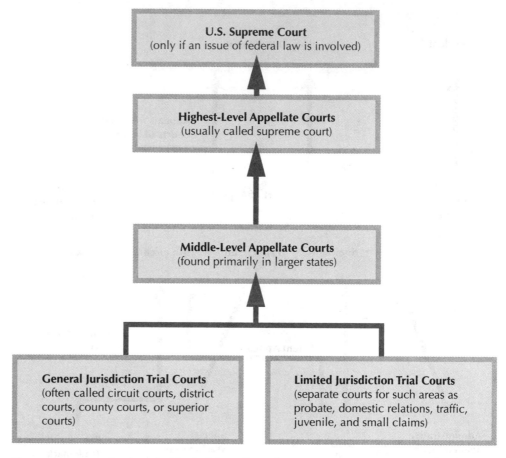

Figure 4-5 Organization of a Typical State Court System

Rather than attempting to describe each of these fifty-one court systems, we will review some general patterns and leave it to you to search out the details for your specific state. Relatively simple explanations of most state court systems can be found in books and pamphlets published by the individual states and are usually available in the reference section of local libraries. Other sources for such information are The American Bench and the Martindale-Hubbell Law Directory, Court Calendar section.

Starting at the bottom of Figure 4-5, you will find the trial courts. In some states, below the trial courts shown in Figure 4-5 is a system of inferior courts with names such as justice of the peace, city, and magistrate courts. Those courts are not **courts of record**. No permanent record is kept of the testimony, lawyers' remarks, or judges' rulings. The absence of a record eliminates the possibility of an appeal and requires the losing party to initiate a completely new trial in a higher-level trial court if that party wishes to have the matter reconsidered.

Many states have one basic trial court, similar to federal district courts, that can hear any type of case (i.e., it has **general jurisdiction**). This court typically carries a name such as circuit court, district court, county court, or superior court. On the other hand, other states have a confusing variety of specialized courts with **limited jurisdiction**. These courts hear a narrow range of cases on a specific subject (such as probate, domestic relations, or traffic) and sometimes even overlap regarding the types of cases they can hear. For example, in Massachusetts both the probate court and the superior court can hear divorce cases.

States maintain either one or two levels of appellate courts. The larger states have generally gone to a two-tiered system like that in operation at the federal level. The intermediate-level appellate courts usually sit in panels, while the court of last resort sits **en banc.** On some matters appeals to the highest court are discretionary, while on others they are a matter of right. A few states have established separate courts to handle criminal versus civil appeals at the intermediate or highest level. Finally, as noted earlier in this chapter, even the name of the highest-level appellate court varies from state to state. While most states identify their highest court as the state supreme court, in New York and Maryland it is called the court of appeals.

In most cases a state's top appellate court is the end of the road because cases can be appealed to the U.S. Supreme Court only if they raise a federal issue. For example, in criminal cases state courts must accord the due process rights guaranteed by the U.S. Constitution. This can involve resolving issues regarding the right to counsel, the admissibility of evidence resulting from an allegedly illegal search, jury selection procedures, and so on. If the defendant thinks these constitutional rights have been violated, she or he may be able to appeal the case to the federal courts on the basis that a federal issue is involved. Whenever a federal law or a provision of the U.S. Constitution is involved, the federal courts have the right to make the final determination as to what that law or constitutional provision means. But remember that a criminal defendant has no right to appeal his or her conviction in a state court to a federal court unless such federal issues are raised. Under the principles of federalism the state courts are the final arbiters as to the meaning of state statutes and state constitutional provisions.

3. Exclusive and Concurrent Jurisdiction

If a specific court is the only one authorized to hear a particular type of case, it has **exclusive jurisdiction.** If more than one court is authorized to hear the same type of case, they each have **concurrent jurisdiction.** Where concurrent jurisdiction exists, a case can be heard by more than one court, and the parties can select the one they wish to use.

As we mentioned in Chapter 3, the federal government is a government of limited powers. Just as Congress can legislate only if the Constitution has given it the power to do so, federal courts can hear cases only if the Constitution has given them the power to do so. Article III, Section 2, of the Constitution spells out the jurisdiction of the federal courts in terms of (1) the nature of the subject matter of the case and (2) the parties involved. Figure 4-6 on page 76 lists the requirements for federal court jurisdiction. Two of the grounds for federal court jurisdiction require particular emphasis, as they account for the bulk of federal cases. The federal courts have jurisdiction when the case involves

1. federal law. This is known as **federal question jurisdiction** and includes cases involving a federal statute, a federal regulation, or the U.S. Constitution.

Exclusive jurisdiction
When only one court has the power to hear a case.

Concurrent jurisdiction
When more than one court has jurisdiction to hear a case.

Federal question jurisdiction
The power of the federal courts to hear matters of federal law.

Based on the subject matter (federal question):
Any case involving the interpretation or application of
1. the U.S. Constitution,
2. a federal law or regulation,
3. a treaty, or
4. admiralty and maritime laws.

Based on the parties involved:
Any case or controversy in law and equity in which
1. the case affects ambassadors or other public ministers and counsels,
2. the United States is a party to the suit,
3. the controversy is between two or more states,
4. the controversy is between a state and citizens of another state,*
5. the parties are citizens of different states (known as diversity jurisdiction),
6. the controversy is between citizens of the same state claiming lands under grants of different states, or
7. the controversy is between (a) a state or the citizens thereof and (b) foreign states, citizens, or subjects.*

Based on the amount of money involved:
In addition to the constitutional requirements stated above, Congress has the power to add a minimum dollar value to suits between citizens of different states. The current federal statute states that the amount in controversy in diversity actions must exceed $75,000 to qualify for original federal jurisdiction.

*The Eleventh Amendment modified this to exclude situations where the suit was commenced or prosecuted against a state by an individual.

Figure 4-6   Jurisdiction of Federal Courts

Diversity jurisdiction
The power of the federal courts to hear matters of state law if the opposing parties are from different states and the amount in controversy exceeds $75,000.

2. opposing litigants from different states where the amount in controversy exceeds $75,000. This is known as **diversity jurisdiction.**

If a lawsuit does not fall within one of the categories listed in Figure 4-6, the parties have no choice but to bring the matter in a state court.

That federal courts have jurisdiction over cases involving federal law seems obvious. But why should federal courts have jurisdiction over matters relating to state law simply because the litigants are from differing states and the amount in controversy exceeds $75,000? Traditionally it has been argued that diversity jurisdiction is necessary to protect out-of-state litigants from the biases they would suffer in state court. Today, however, many disagree as to whether there is a continuing need for diversity jurisdiction.

While it might seem as though it should be relatively easy to decide whether there are valid grounds for finding federal jurisdiction based on the case involving either a federal question or citizens of differing states, this is not always so. In fact, before the parties can resolve the underlying legal issues, they often have to litigate whether a state or federal court is the proper forum. Questions of diversity jurisdiction can be particularly troubling. For the litigants to be able to proceed in federal court there must be complete diversity of citizenship. This means that no plaintiff and defendant can be from the same state.

If they are, then they must proceed in state court. In 2006, the United States Supreme Court was confronted with this issue when it had to resolve whether a national bank was a "citizen" of every state in which it maintained a branch office.

Wachovia Bank v. Schmidt
546 U.S. 303 (2006)

GINSBURG, J., delivered the opinion of the Court.

This case concerns the citizenship, for purposes of federal-court diversity jurisdiction, of national banks, *i.e.*, corporate entities chartered not by any State, but by the Comptroller of the Currency of the U.S. Treasury. Congress empowered federal district courts to adjudicate civil actions between "citizens of different States" where the amount in controversy exceeds $75,000. 28 U.S.C. § 1332(a)(1). . . . For diversity jurisdiction purposes . . . Congress has . . . provided that national banks "shall . . . be deemed citizens of the States in which they are respectively located." § 1348.

The question presented turns on the meaning, in § 1348's context, of the word "located." Does it signal . . . that the bank's citizenship is determined by the place designated in the bank's articles of association as the location of its main office? Or does it mean, in addition . . . that a national bank is a citizen of every State in which it maintains a branch? . . .

I

Petitioner Wachovia Bank, National Association (Wachovia), is a national banking association with its designated main office in Charlotte, North Carolina. Wachovia operates branch offices in many States, including South Carolina.

The litigation before us commenced when plaintiff-respondent Daniel G. Schmidt III and others, citizens of South Carolina, sued Wachovia in a South Carolina state court for fraudulently inducing them to participate in an illegitimate tax shelter. Shortly thereafter, Wachovia filed a petition in the United States District Court for the District of South Carolina, seeking to compel arbitration of the dispute. As the sole basis for federal-court jurisdiction, Wachovia alleged the parties' diverse citizenship. . . .

The Court of Appeals' [determination was that] Wachovia is "located" in, and is therefore a "citizen" of, every State in which it maintains a branch office. Thus Wachovia's branch operations in South Carolina . . . rendered the bank a citizen of South Carolina. Given the South Carolina citizenship of the opposing parties, the majority concluded that the matter could not be adjudicated in federal court. . . .

III

The Fourth Circuit panel majority advanced three principal reasons for deciding that Wachovia is "located" in, and therefore a "citizen" of, every State in which it maintains a branch office. First, consulting dictionaries, the Court of Appeals observed that "[i]n ordinary parlance" the term "located" refers to "physical presence in a place." Banks have a physical presence, the Fourth Circuit stated, wherever they operate branches. Next, the court noted, "Section 1348 uses two distinct terms to refer to the presence of a banking association: 'established' and 'located.'" "To give independent meaning" to each word, the court said, "it is most reasonable to understand the place where a national bank is 'established' to refer to a bank's charter location, and to understand the place where it is 'located' to refer to the place or places where it has a physical presence." Finally, the Court of Appeals stressed that in *Citizens & Southern Nat. Bank v. Bougas*, 434 U.S. 35, 98 S.Ct. 88, 54 L.Ed.2d 218 (1977), this Court interpreted the term "located" in the former venue statute for national banks as encompassing any county in which a bank maintains a branch office. Reasoning that "the jurisdiction and venue statutes pertain to the same subject matter, namely the amenability of national banking associations to suit in federal court," the panel majority concluded that, "under the *in pari materia* canon[,] the two statutes should be interpreted" consistently.

IV

None of the Court of Appeals' rationales persuade us to read § 1348 to attribute to a national bank, for diversity jurisdiction purposes, the citizenship of each State in which the bank has established branch operations. First, the term "located," as it appears in the National Bank Act, has no fixed, plain meaning. . . .

Second, Congress may well have comprehended the words "located" and "established," as used in § 1348, not as contrasting, but as synonymous or alternative terms. . . .

Finally, *Bougas* does not control the meaning of § 1348. . . . True, under the *in pari materia* canon of statutory construction, statutes addressing the same subject matter generally should be read "as if they were one law." But venue and subject-matter jurisdiction are not concepts of the same order. Venue is largely a matter of litigational convenience; accordingly, it is waived if not timely raised. Subject-matter jurisdiction, on the other hand, concerns a court's competence to adjudicate a particular category of cases; a matter far weightier than venue, subject-matter jurisdiction must be considered by the court on its own motion, even if no party raises an objection. . . .

V

To summarize, "located" . . . is a chameleon word; its meaning depends on the context in and purpose for which it is used.

. . . Concerning access to the federal-court system, § 1348 deems national banks "citizens of the States in which they are respectively located." There is no reason to suppose Congress used those words to effect a radical departure from the norm. An individual who resides in more than one State is regarded, for purposes of federal subject-matter (diversity) jurisdiction, as a citizen of but one State. . . . Similarly, a corporation's citizenship derives, for diversity jurisdiction purposes, from its State of incorporation and principal place of business. § 1332(c)(1). It is not deemed a citizen of every State in which it conducts business or is otherwise amenable to personal jurisdiction. Reading § 1348 in this context, one would sensibly "locate" a national bank for the very same purpose, *i.e.,* qualification for diversity jurisdiction, in the State designated in its articles of association as its main office. . . .

For the reasons stated, the judgment of the United States Court of Appeals for the Fourth Circuit is reversed, and the case is remanded for further proceedings consistent with this opinion.

CASE DISCUSSION QUESTIONS

1. What three main arguments did the Court of Appeals use to reach its conclusion that national banks are "located," for diversity jurisdiction purposes, in every state where they have branch offices?

2. Why did those arguments fail to persuade the U.S. Supreme Court?

3. How do you reconcile the theory that diversity jurisdiction is for the protection of out-of-state "citizens" with the U.S. Supreme Court's holding that national banks with in-state branch offices should receive the benefit of federal court jurisdiction?

Unlike the federal courts, state courts generally have the power to hear any type of case. The only time state courts are prohibited from hearing cases involving federal law is when Congress has expressly included that limitation in a federal statute.

In situations where both the state and the federal courts have concurrent jurisdiction, the plaintiff makes the initial decision as to which court to use.

However, when the plaintiff selects a state court and the federal courts also have jurisdiction, the defendant may be able to **remove** the case to federal court.

It is very important to understand that deciding whether to go to state or federal court is not the same as deciding whether the court will apply state or federal law to the case. See Figure 4-7. For example, in a negligence case a federal court might have jurisdiction based on the diversity of citizenship of the parties. However, the federal court must follow state negligence law in deciding the case. If the case involves an area of unsettled state law, the federal court must base its decision on its best guess as to what the state's highest court would do if faced with the same situation. Because the federal court is only guessing at what the state court would do, the federal court's decision is binding on the current litigants but is not binding on the state courts. Therefore, no matter how the federal court decides the case, it will still be open to the state courts to change the law in that area the next time a litigant brings a case on the same issue to the state courts. Likewise, when a state court hears a case involving a federal matter, it must follow the guidance of the federal courts.

Removal
The transfer of a case from state court to federal court.

DISCUSSION QUESTION

5. As the federal courts face an increasingly heavy workload, many have argued that it is time to either raise the required amount in controversy or eliminate diversity jurisdiction entirely. The requirement that the amount in controversy exceed $75,000 is to help ensure that federal courts are not inundated with cases of minimal importance. In 1789 Congress set the figure at $500, but over the years it has increased the amount to the present-day figure of $75,000. Would you be in favor of such changes?

C. COURT PERSONNEL

It takes many different participants to make the judicial system work effectively. Court personnel include not only the judges and attorneys appearing before them but also court clerks, court reporters, and bailiffs. Some states also use **justices of the peace, court commissioners,** and **magistrates** in their court systems. Individuals

Does State or Federal Law Apply?	Do the State or Federal Courts have Jurisdiction?
Federal Law—restricted to (1) issues arising from the U.S. Constitution, (2) statutes Congress has enacted pursuant to its limited powers under the U.S. Constitution, such as the interstate commerce clause, or (3) agency regulation.	**Federal Courts—only if** (1) the case involves federal law (federal question jurisdiction) or (2) the case involves state law but the parties are from different states and the amount in controversy is over $75,000 (diversity jurisdiction).
State Law—unless preempted by federal law, generally **anything** states deem to be in the best interests of their citizens.	**State Courts**—generally **any type of case** unless Congress has provided for exclusive federal jurisdiction.

Figure 4-7   Two Separate Questions: State or Federal Law *and* State or Federal Court?

holding these titles are lower-level court personnel who perform limited judicial duties but are not considered full-fledged judges. In some states they do not have to be lawyers to perform these duties.

1. Judges

It is the responsibility of the trial court judge to decide whether to dismiss a case before it reaches trial, to determine the extent of pretrial discovery, and to set the amount of time the lawyers will have to prepare their cases. Once the trial is under way, the judge acts as the presiding officer, rules on objections, and determines when recesses will occur. If a jury is involved, the judge supervises its selection, removes jury members from the courtroom at key times to protect them from improper influences, and instructs them on the meaning of the law they are to apply. When a jury is not involved, the judge also acts as the fact finder and decides whether the defendant is guilty (in criminal cases) or liable (in civil cases). In criminal cases the judge is also responsible for sentencing the convicted defendant. If the litigants want to contest a trial judge's findings, they must present their arguments to appellate judges.

Appellate court judges review lower court decisions and decide whether they should be affirmed or reversed. As discussed at the beginning of this chapter, they focus on questions of law rather than second guessing the trial court's findings of fact.

In the federal system, the president, with the approval of the U.S. Senate,[4] appoints district court, court of appeals, and Supreme Court judges. The U.S. Constitution, Article III, Section 1, provides that "[t]he Judges, both of the supreme and inferior Courts, shall hold their Offices during good Behaviour, and shall, at stated Times, receive for their Services, a Compensation, which shall not be diminished during their Continuance in Office." This means that "constitutional" judges are guaranteed lifetime tenure unless they resign or are impeached and that they are protected from any salary reductions.

Unlike these "constitutional" judges, other federal judges do not hold lifetime appointments. For example, the court of appeals in each circuit appoints bankruptcy judges for fourteen-year terms. District courts appoint magistrate judges for eight-year terms.

Dating back to the 1968 Nixon/Humphrey presidential campaign, there has been increased attention paid to the legal philosophy of judicial appointees— especially those being considered for the U.S. Supreme Court. (See discussion of Theories of Jurisprudence in Chapter 2.) The potential nominee's views on controversial issues, such as abortion rights, same-sex marriage, and affirmative action have become critical.

In 2005 Associate Justice Sandra Day O'Connor announced her retirement from the court to spend time with a husband battling Alzheimer's, and Chief Justice William Rehnquist died of thyroid cancer. This gave President George W. Bush the opportunity to significantly change the ideological balance on the Supreme Court. Based on the decisions handed down since his appointments of

---

[4]Federal judicial appointments, particularly at the district court level, have frequently been used as a form of political patronage to reward attorneys who have been loyal supporters of the party. The "senatorial courtesy" tradition gives senators from the president's party a veto power over district court appointments from their state.

John Roberts and Samuel Alito, Bush clearly moved the Supreme Court in a more conservative direction. So far new Chief Justice Roberts's voting pattern has been similar to that of Rehnquist, but Alito has voted much more conservatively than had Justice O'Connor—especially on cases involving affirmative action and abortion. Figure 4-8 shows a picture of the U.S. Supreme Court taken in the spring of 2006. The caption includes biographical information about the justices.

States vary widely with respect to how they select their judges. Only a few states follow the federal model of executive appointments. Most states have voters choose their judges in either partisan or nonpartisan elections or use a variant of the "Missouri Plan" in which the governor selects from candidates recommended by a nonpartisan commission.

2. Jurors

For most civil and criminal trials, the parties have the option of having their case heard solely by the judge or by a judge and a jury. This is in stark contrast to most European courts where the jury trial is reserved almost exclusively for criminal cases. We will discuss the role of jurors and how they are selected in Chapters 4 and 12.

3. Attorneys

In our "adversarial" legal system, attorneys are responsible for effectively presenting all of the relevant facts and arguments that favor their clients. But, in addition to being advocates for their clients, attorneys are considered officers of the court. As such, they are responsible for maintaining proper decorum in the courtroom and acting within the ethical restraints imposed on them by the courts and their profession.

Figure 4-8 The U.S. Supreme Court, 2006. **Standing, from left to right**: *Stephen Breyer*— appointed by President Clinton (D) in 1994; a former law clerk for Justice Goldberg, a law professor, and a federal appellate court judge. *Clarence Thomas*—appointed by President George H. Bush (R) in 1991; the second African American to reach the Supreme Court and a federal appellate court judge when appointed; his confirmation hearings included the examination of charges that he had sexually harassed a female employee while he was Chairman of the U.S. Equal Employment Opportunity Commission. *Ruth Bader Ginsburg*—appointed by President Clinton (D) in 1993; the second woman to reach the Supreme Court; had been the General Counsel for the ACLU, a law professor, and a federal appellate judge. *Samuel Alito*— the most recent member to join the court, appointed by President George W. Bush (R) in 2006; was Deputy Assistant U.S. Attorney General and a federal appellate court judge. **Sitting, from left to right**: *Anthony Kennedy*—appointed by President Reagan (R) in 1988; a law professor and federal appellate judge. *John Paul Stevens*—appointed by President Ford (R) in 1975; served as a law clerk for Justice Rutledge, was an antitrust lawyer, and served as a federal appellate court judge. *John Roberts,* Chief Justice—appointed by President George W. Bush (R) in 2005; a former law clerk to Justice Rehnquist, worked for the Justice Department during the Reagan administration, and was a federal appellate court judge. *Antonin Scalia*—appointed by President Reagan (R) in 1986; a law school professor and a federal appellate court judge. *David H. Souter*—appointed by George H. Bush (R) in 1990; a New Hampshire Supreme Court justice and a federal appellate court judge.

4. Support Personnel

Court clerks are responsible for keeping the court files in proper condition and ensuring that the various motions filed by lawyers and the actions taken by judges are properly recorded. A head clerk of the courts is usually responsible for running the central records section of the courthouse; his or her assistants are assigned to sit in on the actual courtroom proceedings.

The **court reporter** prepares verbatim transcripts of courtroom proceedings. Most reporters use a stenotype machine rather than shorthand. Because it is expensive, they prepare a written transcript only if the case is being appealed.

Bailiffs are responsible for maintaining order in the courtrooms. They are also responsible for watching over the juries when they are in recess or when they have been sequestered. When a jury is sequestered, the members sleep at a hotel and are kept isolated from the public and their families to prevent them from being exposed to prejudicial publicity, threats, bribes, or any other improper influences.

Finally, sheriffs and marshals also serve as officers of the court. They serve summonses and other court documents, collect money as required by court judgments, and otherwise help in carrying out the court's orders.

SUMMARY

In this chapter we have seen that although the American legal system may seem to involve a confusing mix of names and functions, all courts can be classified in two ways:

1. They are either trial or appellate courts. Some trial courts have only limited jurisdiction; for example, they only hear cases in which less than a certain amount of money is in dispute.
2. They are part of either the federal or a state system.

The federal court system and most state court systems are based on a three-tier model. At the bottom are the trial courts, which decide both factual and legal issues. Generally, above the trial courts is an intermediate appellate court. At the top of every system is the highest appellate court. Appellate courts decide questions of law only. In the federal system the trial courts are called district courts, the intermediate appellate courts are called courts of appeals, and the highest court is the U.S. Supreme Court.

The power of a particular court to hear certain types of cases is known as its jurisdiction. The federal Constitution limits all federal courts' jurisdiction by allowing them to hear only the types of cases listed under Article III, Section 2. The two most common grounds for federal court jurisdiction are federal question and diversity of citizenship.

CRITICAL THINKING EXERCISES

1. As discussed above, it is not always easy to know whether something is a question of fact or a question of law. In fact, there have been cases when the issue on appeal was whether something was a question of fact or a question of law.

That question is itself a question of law. To see how that can happen, assume there was a negligence trial in which a grocer was sued when a customer slipped and fell. The customer testified that she slipped on a banana peel in the produce section. The grocery store owner testified that when he came to the assistance of the customer, there was no peel on the floor. One of the store employees also testified that he had mopped the floor in that area just five minutes before the accident and that there were no banana peels on the floor. Nonetheless, the jury found the store liable. Can the store appeal on the grounds that it was telling the truth and the customer was lying? Why? Can the store appeal on the grounds that the jury should not have found that it acted negligently because even if there was a banana peel, such hazards are to be expected in the produce section and the store had done all it could to make the area safe? Is that issue—that is, whether the store acted as a reasonable store should—a question of fact or a question of law?

2. For each of these situations determine whether you think the matter should be heard in state or federal *court*. Also decide whether you think a court would apply state or federal *law*.

    a. A wife wants to divorce her husband.

    b. Martha, a Massachusetts resident, wants to sue Susan, a Massachusetts resident, for $80,000 based on breach of contract.

    c. Sam, a Massachusetts resident, wants to sue Jill, a Vermont resident, for $80,000 based on breach of contract.

    d. A teacher in a public school wants to challenge a state law requiring all teachers to start each day of class with a minute of silent prayer.

||| REVIEW QUESTIONS

Pages 63 through 68

1. What are the two basic functions of trial courts?
2. What is the difference between questions of law and questions of fact? Why is it important to know the difference?
3. Give an example of a question of fact that might arise during a murder trial. Give an example of a question of law that might arise in that same trial.
4. What is the difference between a bench and a jury trial?
5. What will an appellate court usually do if it finds that the trial court made a harmless error?
6. What is the difference between reversing and remanding a case?
7. How do majority, dissenting, and concurring opinions differ from each other?
8. List the major differences between trial and appellate courts.

Pages 68 through 72

9. In the federal court system what are the names given to
    a. the highest appellate court?
    b. the intermediate appellate courts?
    c. the trial courts?
10. Look at the map in Figure 5-3. How many district courts are there in your state? In which circuit is your state located?

11. If you hear that "cert." has been denied in a case, what does that mean?
12. In the federal system, what are the "inferior Courts"?

Pages 72 through 84

13. Describe a typical state court system. How is your state court system similar to or different from the "typical" state system?
14. True or false: In every state the highest appellate court is called the supreme court.
15. Jurisdiction refers to the power a court has to hear a case. Define each of the following types of jurisdiction:
    a. general jurisdiction
    b. limited jurisdiction
    c. original jurisdiction
    d. appellate jurisdiction
    e. exclusive jurisdiction
    f. concurrent jurisdiction
16. What are the two major grounds for gaining federal court jurisdiction?

Chapter 5

Civil Litigation and Its Alternatives

Discourage litigation. Persuade your neighbors to compromise whenever you can. As a peacemaker the lawyer has superior opportunity of being a good man. There will still be business enough.
Abraham Lincoln

INTRODUCTION

Litigation is the process of using the courts to settle disputes. In this chapter we provide an overview of the litigation process, including the procedural steps involved in initiating, trying, and appealing civil cases. Because litigation can be a very expensive, stressful, and lengthy process, various alternatives to litigation have developed. Therefore, in addition to the litigation process, we will also look at these alternative approaches to litigation, such as arbitration and mediation, known collectively as **alternative dispute resolution (ADR).**

We will use the cases of Donald Drake, which we introduced in Chapter 1, and Diane Dobbs, which we introduced in Chapter 2, to illustrate litigation and its alternatives. You will recall that Mr. Drake witnessed the death of his grandson, Philip, when Philip was struck by the car Wilma Small was driving. Diane Dobbs was the waitress who was fired when she announced to her boss that she was pregnant. Here are the cases again for your review.

Alternative dispute resolution (ADR) Techniques for resolving conflicts that are alternatives to full-scale litigation. The two most common are arbitration and mediation.

Case 1: The Distressed Grandfather

Approximately one year ago Mr. Drake and his six-year-old grandson, Philip, were walking down a residential road on their way home from visiting one of Philip's friends. Philip was walking on the sidewalk approximately thirty feet in front of Mr. Drake. Suddenly, a car sped past Mr. Drake, seemingly went out of control, jumped the curb, and hit Philip. Mr. Drake ran to Philip's side, but it was too late. Philip had been killed instantly. The driver of the car, Mrs. Wilma Small, was unhurt.

At the time of the accident Mr. Drake's only concern was for the welfare of his grandson because he himself was clear of the danger. Naturally, Mr. Drake suffered a great deal of emotional pain and shock because of seeing his grandson killed. While being driven home from the accident, he suffered a heart attack that necessitated a lengthy hospital stay.

One year later, he still does not feel completely recovered and often suffers from nightmares reliving the accident and his grandson's death. Mr. Drake would like to sue Mrs. Small to recover for his hospital bills and for his pain and suffering.

Case 3: The Pregnant Waitress

Ms. Diane Dobbs had been employed by the Western Rib Eye Restaurant for the past three years. Throughout that time her work record had been exemplary. Customers often spoke to the manager to tell him how Diane's service and personality contributed to their especially enjoyable dining experience at the restaurant.

Six months ago Diane, who is not married, found out that she was pregnant. When she approached her manager, Ben, to discuss arrangements for a maternity leave, instead of the favorable reception she had expected, Ben reached over, patted her stomach, and said, "Well, I guess we can't have you working for us any longer." Ben then grabbed her by the arm and escorted her out of the restaurant. Diane protested and asked to be allowed to collect her personal belongings from her locker, but the manager just laughed and said she was "history." When Diane began to cry, he softened his demeanor a little and said, "Look, we simply can't have a pregnant lady working here. It just wouldn't be good for business."

Although she has been actively looking, Diane has not yet been able to find suitable employment.

Because this is a textbook, we have no choice but to present topics in a linear fashion. Therefore, in this chapter, we will first discuss the various alternatives to litigation and then proceed to the litigation process. However, you should keep in mind that real life does not proceed in such a straightforward manner. Although informal negotiations may begin the moment a dispute arises, there is no set order in which the parties are required to proceed. They may decide to file a complaint immediately, initiating the litigation process, but then suspend their litigation efforts while trying to resolve the dispute through arbitration or mediation. Should those efforts fail, the parties may then pick up where they left off in the litigation process. At other times, however, the parties may turn first to an alternative dispute resolution process and only then proceed with initiating a lawsuit if that process fails. Therefore, as you read this chapter, keep in mind that the various forms of alternative dispute resolution, including informal negotiations, mediation, and arbitration, can arise at any time from before formal litigation has begun to well after a lawsuit has been filed and the litigation process is under way.

A. ALTERNATIVE DISPUTE RESOLUTION

In general terms, litigation involves lawsuits, whereas ADR is any other method for resolving a dispute. ADR can take many forms, ranging from very informal negotiations, which usually begin as soon as a dispute arises and may not end until the final appeal has been filed, to the more formal approaches of mediation and arbitration. Those more formal approaches require the involvement of a neutral third party, as either a mediator or arbiter. The main difference between mediation and arbitration is that in mediation, the third party acts as a facilitator who tries to help the parties reach their own resolution. In arbitration, the third party is a decision maker who acts much like a judge would at a trial. While mediation and arbitration are the most commonly used forms of formal ADR, the term sometimes includes other activities such as mini-trials and summary jury trials, which are designed to encourage out-of-court settlements.

Alternative dispute resolutions can be used before or after litigation has begun. Recognizing that ADR can be effective after litigation has commenced, Congress enacted legislation in 1998 requiring that each U.S. district court establish and implement a plan to decrease costs and delays in the federal court system. Specifically, the legislation mandated that all district courts establish programs to offer alternative dispute resolution to litigants. In addition, nearly all of the U.S. courts of appeals have established mediation programs to assist parties in resolving their appeals. Similarly, many state and local court systems have also incorporated ADR, especially in the area of family law, where the parties are often required to participate in formal mediation regarding issues of child custody and visitation.

NETNOTE

If you are interested in learning more about various forms of ADR, there are several Web sites you can visit, including the American Arbitration Association at *www.adr.org,* the Mediation Information and Resource Center at *www.mediate.com,* and the ABA Section on Dispute Resolution at *www.abanet.org/dispute.* A Particularly interesting site is that of the Victim Offender Mediation Association (VOMA) at *www.voma.org.* VOMA supports mediation between victims and offenders, so that victims are given an opportunity to have their questions answered and their emotional and other needs met, and offenders are held accountable and given an opportunity to make restitution to their victims and the community.

While such required mediation may at first appear to be a contradiction in terms, many states are now imposing "mandatory mediation" in selected types of disputes. It is mandatory in the sense that both parties are required to engage in a formal mediation process before a court can hear the case. However, if the mediation is not successful, the parties can still end the mediation process and continue with the court proceedings.

The business community has long been a strong supporter of ADR because it is viewed as a faster and less expensive means of settling disputes that arise in the course of doing business. It is common practice for businesses to include arbitration clauses in their contracts. Under these clauses the parties are legally bound to refer disputes over the interpretation of a contract to arbitration rather than take them to court. In addition to saving time and money, ADR often allows a company to settle a dispute without attracting the public attention that may accompany a lawsuit.

1. Arbitration

Arbitration
An ADR mechanism whereby the parties submit their disagreement to a third party, whose decision is binding.

When a dispute is sent to **arbitration**, the matter is delegated to a neutral third-party arbitrator. Both parties agree in advance to accept the arbitrator's decision. In many cases the arbitrator's decision is binding, and the dissatisfied party may not challenge it in court unless the award was obtained by fraud.

An arbitrator functions much like a judge in a court of law, but the arbitrator follows a much simpler set of procedures that do not require as much time or expense. The arbitrator is usually selected from a panel of individuals who have special training in the area. These individuals are often affiliated with the American Arbitration Association or one of the other organizations set up specifically to provide arbitration services. In addition to being speedier and less expensive than traditional litigation, the results of arbitration can frequently be kept confidential.

In the field of labor law, arbitration is often used as a way of avoiding strikes. Sports fans are familiar with the role arbitration has played in determining the salaries of baseball players. Also, public employees are often required to use arbitration when state law prohibits them from striking.

Arbitration also plays an important role in Internet commerce. In 1999, the Internet Corporation for Assigned Names and Numbers (the entity that has sole responsibility for assigning domain names ending in .com, .net, .org, and more than fifty country codes) began requiring that everyone who registers for an Internet address must agree to arbitration under the terms of their Uniform Domain Name Dispute Resolution Policy (UDRP).

In 2006, there were approximately 4,000 arbitration demands relating to allegedly abusive domain names.[1] Many of these disputes are the result of cybersquatting, which occurs when someone registers the name of a trademark, famous person, or business with the intent of reselling the name to that organization or person or profiting directly from the public's confusion as to the real identity of the site. For example, Disney Enterprises recently filed a complaint against DisneyComics.com. The arbitration panel that considered the case found that the domain name was confusingly similar to the Disney trademark

---

[1] "Domain Name Arbitrations," *The National Law Journal*, p. 17, July 23, 2007.

and was being used in bad faith to take advantage of the famous mark. Therefore, they granted the request to transfer DisneyComics.com to Disney.[2] As reported by the main service providers for domain-name dispute resolution, arbitration of these cases is much faster (usually accomplished within two months) and much cheaper (usually costing no more than $4,000) than litigation.[3]

Case 3: The Pregnant Waitress (continued)

Many employees are members of unions and hence subject to a collective bargaining agreement negotiated between labor and management. If Diane Dobbs had been a member of a union and had filed a grievance, her union representative would first have tried to negotiate a resolution with management. If that was not successful, most likely the collective bargaining agreement would have included a mandatory arbitration clause that would require Ms. Dobbs to submit her grievance to arbitration.

---

2. Mediation

Although both arbitration and **mediation** involve the disputants meeting with a neutral third party, they differ greatly with respect to the role this third party plays. Whereas an arbitrator imposes a solution, a mediator attempts to guide the disputants toward a compromise that is voluntarily accepted by both sides.

Mediation
An ADR mechanism whereby a neutral third party assists the parties in reaching a mutually agreeable, voluntary compromise.

The basic premise of mediation is that the best solution is the solution that the parties themselves devise. After all, they (not the mediator) best understand their positions, and they (not the mediator) will have to live with the solution they reach.

The mediator's role is therefore like that of a Sherpa guide. The guide's role is not to tell the explorers which mountain to climb or even whether to climb a mountain at all. The guide simply helps the climbers find the best way to reach whatever summit they have chosen to climb. In mediation, the mediator helps the disputants identify the issues that divide them and explore possible solutions for bridging the divide.[4]

Generally, some types of cases are better suited for mediation than others. Mediation is particularly appropriate in those situations where the parties will be required to deal with each other in the future, such as after a divorce when children are involved, or when the parties simply wish to have amiable future relations, such as in the case of a dispute between neighbors. It is hoped that the mediation process will not only resolve the current situation but will also improve the participants' interpersonal and conflict management skills as they continue to deal with each other in the future.

---

[2]National Arbitration Forum Issues Three Decisions on Internet Domain Name Disputes (May 23, 2007), http://www.arb-forum.com/newsroom.aspx?itemID=1250.

[3]World Intellectual Property Organization, Frequently Asked Questions: Internet Domain Names, http://wio.iint.org/amc/en/center/faq/domains.html.

[4]*See* Mori Irvine, Serving Two Masters: The Obligation under the Rules of Professional Conduct to Report Attorney Misconduct in a Confidential Mediation, 26 Rutgers L.J. 155, 158 n. 13 (1994).

In tort cases, mediation works best in situations where liability is clear-cut and the dispute is primarily over the amount of the damages. In this type of situation, both sides can usually see the advantage in settling for an "average" damage award rather than spending a significant amount of money on trial preparation and then gambling on the outcome.

There are, of course, some situations that do not lend themselves to mediation. For example, Rosa Parks, a black woman, was arrested in 1955 for refusing to give up her seat on a city bus to a white person. Civil rights leaders used her situation to bring public attention to racial discrimination in the South and organized the famous Montgomery bus boycott. This type of political mobilization could not have happened through mediation.[5]

Mediation may also not be appropriate in situations involving domestic violence. Not only may the contact between the abuser and the victim during mediation result in further violence following the mediation session, but the victim may perceive the mediation session itself as another form of abuse. Furthermore, because mediation works best when the parties are of fairly equal bargaining power, it is not as effective in situations of abuse, where the victim often perceives him- or herself as powerless against the abuser.

3. Summary Jury Trials

Summary jury trial
A nonbinding process in which attorneys for both sides present synopses of their cases to a jury, which renders an advisory opinion on the basis of these presentations.

Summary jury trials are nonbinding mock trials in which attorneys for both sides present synopses of their cases to a jury, which then renders an advisory opinion on the basis of these presentations. Time is saved because the attorneys give summaries of what key witnesses are expected to say rather than going through complete direct and cross-examinations. It is hoped that the parties will agree to a settlement that approximates the results reached by the mock jury.

4. Evaluation of ADR Techniques

Proponents of ADR argue that its use saves time and avoids at least some of the expenses associated with going to court. It is also generally thought that the parties will feel better about a solution they worked out through mediation than they will about a decision imposed on them by the courts. This is especially true in child custody cases, where the parents should feel as though they "own" the decision, as they will often need to continue to have regular contact with each other and to consult with each other about the welfare of their children.

Not everyone agrees with this assessment. For example, a study conducted by the Rand Institute for Civil Justice found that ADR was not extensively used when it was voluntary and that when it was used, it did not result in great savings of time or expenses. Furthermore, its use was not found to affect the participants' views of fairness or attorney satisfaction.[6]

Nevertheless, other studies indicate that ADR participants are extremely satisfied with both the process and the result, at least when the ADR method used is mediation, not arbitration. For example, a recent survey conducted by the National Law Journal and the American Arbitration Association found that

---

[5]Drew Peterson, Getting Together: Conflict—Appropriate and Inappropriate Cases for Mediation, 23 Alaska Bar Rag 9 (1999).

[6]Van Duch, Case Management Reform Ineffective, Nat'l. L.J., Feb. 3, 1997, at A3.

of those who responded to the survey, a majority of litigators and in-house counsel preferred nonbinding mediation over binding arbitration. Not only did mediation save money and time, but the respondents felt it provided a more satisfactory process, as it was most likely to preserve the relationship between the disputing parties. The attorneys' complaints about arbitration included distrust of the arbiters themselves, the costs (which can approach those of litigation), and the inability to appeal an arbiter's decision.

DISCUSSION QUESTIONS

1. If two disputants want to settle their differences other than by going to court, what options do they have?

2. If you were involved in a dispute, which alternative dispute resolution method would you prefer?

3. Do you think either mediation or arbitration would be appropriate in Mr. Drake's case? Why or why not?

When alternative dispute resolution methods fail, the parties may decide to proceed to litigation. That process of litigation is the subject of the next section.

Case 1: The Distressed Grandfather (continued)

Mr. Drake's attorney, attorney Harper prefers to use a form of ADR whenever possible as it may save her clients time, stress, and expense. Also, if there is a chance for an ongoing relationship between the parties, mediation, because it is less adversarial than litigation or arbitration, may help to preserve that relationship. Mrs. Small's attorney, however, has refused to engage in informal negotiations or in more formal ADR methods, such as mediation or arbitration. He informed attorney Harper that it is his position that, as Mr. Drake was not Philip's parent, there is no legal basis for making Mrs. Small responsible for Mr. Drake's injuries. Attorney Harper informed Mr. Drake that they have no choice, if they want to proceed, except to turn to the court system and litigation.

B. LITIGATION

The procedures that govern the litigation process are spelled out in formal rules that are published under names such as the Federal Rules of Civil Procedure, the Massachusetts Rules of Civil Procedure, the Illinois Criminal Law and Criminal Procedure, and the Federal Rules of Evidence. Although the specific stages in the process and the specific court documents that must be completed differ in federal and state court systems, they also have much in common. Because most state rules are based on the federal rules, the focus of this book is on the federal rules. However, even though most states base their rules on those developed for the federal system, the procedures followed in state and federal courts do vary somewhat. In both federal and state courts, there are three basic stages of litigation: pretrial, trial, and appeal. Take a few moments to study Fig 5-1, on page 94, which provides an overview of the litigation process. Refer to it as you proceed with the remainder of this chapter to help you keep track of the various stages.

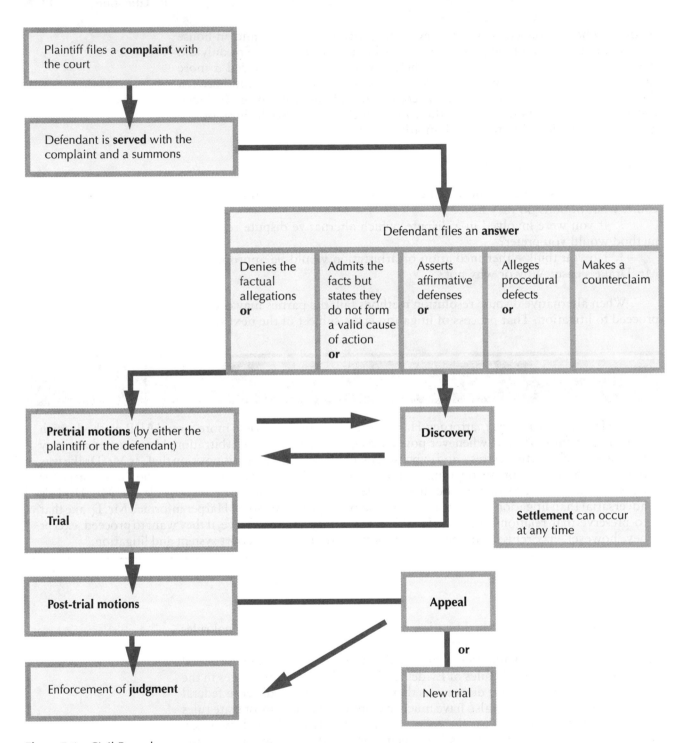

Figure 5-1 Civil Procedure

1. The Pretrial Stage

A lawsuit officially begins when the plaintiff files the appropriate legal documents with the clerk of the court. However, before this can occur, the attorney must handle some preliminary matters, including determining the following:

- whether a legal basis for the suit exists,
- who should be sued,
- in which court the case should be brought,
- whether the statute of limitations has expired, and
- whether any administrative agency must be consulted before filing suit.

Once those issues have been resolved and a determination to sue has been made, the lawsuit enters the pleadings stage. The **pleadings** are the documents each side files with the court and serves on the other side to commence the lawsuit. In order to narrow the issues, either party may file **pretrial motions**. Finally, the parties will engage in **discovery**, an attempt by both sides to gather as much information as possible. The end result of this process may be a negotiated settlement, a court determination to dismiss the suit, or a decision to proceed to the trial stage.

Pleadings
The papers that begin a lawsuit—generally, the complaint and the answer.

Pretrial motion
A motion brought before the beginning of a trial either to eliminate the necessity for a trial or to limit the information that can be heard at the trial.

Discovery
The modern pretrial procedure by which one party gains information from the adverse party.

a. Preliminary Matters

The decisions as to these preliminary matters are not always easy to make and may involve extensive factual and legal research in order to determine the best course of action.

(1) Legal grounds for the suit

As you will recall from Chapter 1, not every problem is a legal problem for which the courts can provide a remedy. Therefore, before an attorney can initiate a lawsuit, the attorney must be convinced that the client has a valid cause of action—that is, based on the law and the facts, that the client's claim is sufficient to support a lawsuit. This determination involves answering two questions affirmatively. First, does the attorney believe that there are sufficient credible facts to support the plaintiff's position? Second, does the attorney believe that there is a valid legal theory to support the claim?

NETNOTE

On the Internet you can find all sorts of useful information about the courts—everything from their fax numbers to the location of a specific courthouse. To find the address of any state court, a good place to start is at the home page for the National Center for State Courts, *www.ncsconline.org/D_KIS/info_court_web_sites.html*. The center maintains a complete listing for all fifty states. For information on federal courts, you can visit either the federal judiciary home page at *www.uscourts.gov* or the Federal Judicial Center home page at *www.fjc.gov*. Finally, the U.S. Supreme Court has its own Web site at *www.supremecourtus.gov*.

In determining whether their client's position is supported by credible facts, attorneys must review relevant documents and interview witnesses. This requirement that the attorney make a reasonable inquiry into the factual and legal bases for the claim is dictated in the federal system by Rule 11 of the Federal Rules of Civil Procedure. If a court determines that the attorney has not conducted a reasonable inquiry or has filed suit for an improper purpose, then it may impose monetary sanctions on the attorney and on the parties.

(2) Parties to the suit

Standing
The principle that courts cannot decide abstract issues or render advisory opinions; rather they are limited to deciding cases that involve litigants who are personally affected by the court's decision.

Under the legal principle called **standing**, only parties with a real stake in the outcome are allowed to participate in a lawsuit. Generally, courts are not supposed to decide abstract issues or render advisory opinions. (The one exception occurs in some states where courts are authorized to respond to requests for advice from other governmental bodies.) By requiring courts to decide concrete rather than abstract cases, they will have the benefit of parties who have a vested interest in the outcome and who will therefore vigorously argue their positions.

> Why limit lawsuits to people who have been hurt? One reason is that they're likely to marshal the strongest arguments. It brings to mind the old line about the role of the chicken and the pig in furnishing your breakfast: The chicken is involved, but the pig is *committed*. Let chickens file lawsuits against bacon-and-egg combos, and they may lack the motivation to do a good job.[7]

Because of this requirement of standing, persons and organizations cannot file lawsuits simply because they do not approve of a certain governmental policy or some corporation's building project. For example, only persons who have been sentenced to death can challenge the death penalty. If the court determines that the parties do not have standing, it simply dismisses the case without making a determination on the merits.

A classic example of how the requirement of standing affects who can sue occurred in conjunction with the litigation that led up to the famous case of *Brown v. Board of Education*.[8] Although the National Association for the Advancement of Colored People (NAACP) was opposed to the Kansas policy of segregating its public school system, it had no standing on its own to challenge the constitutionality of that policy. Before it could proceed, the organization had to recruit an African American child who was actually turned away when she attempted to enter an all-white school located in her neighborhood.[9] Eventually, the NAACP was able to find thirteen parents and their children who were willing to serve as plaintiffs in the case.

---

[7]Steve Chapman, No Decision Sometimes Best Decision, The Republican, June 22, 2004, at A9.
[8]347 U.S. 483 (1954).
[9]Paul E. Wilson, A Retrospective of *Brown v. Board of Education*: The Genesis of *Brown v. Board of Education*, 6 Kan. J.L. & Pub. Pol'y 7 (1996).

After having determined that the plaintiff has the required standing to sue, the attorney must decide who should be named as defendants. Naturally the attorney will choose to sue the person who caused his or her client harm. However, the most logical person to sue may not be worth suing because he or she may not have money to pay the damages that a court might award. This is referred to as being **judgment proof**. If there is more than one possible defendant, the plaintiff will want to make sure to include the one with the deepest pockets (most assets).

For example, under a theory known as **respondeat superior** an employer can sometimes be held responsible for the acts of its employees. Because employers usually have more money than employees, persons injured by an employee will frequently also sue the employer. Similarly, in an automobile accident case the plaintiff may sue the manufacturer of the auto or the governmental unit responsible for maintaining the roadway.

Finally, in special circumstances when a number of people have been injured, such as in an airplane crash, the plaintiff may also wish to consider the possibility of a **class action suit**. The named plaintiff brings the suit on behalf of a large class of additional plaintiffs who are in a similar situation with respect to having been wronged by the defendant.

(3) Selection of the court

The last preliminary issue requires the attorney to decide which court should hear the case. From your readings in Chapter 3 you know that lawsuits begin in a trial court and not an appellate court, but which trial court? That will depend on which trial courts have **jurisdiction** over the type of case that the attorney will be filing. Recall that jurisdiction relates to the power of a particular court to hear a case brought before it. In some cases the attorney may have the option of selecting among several different courts and must evaluate the advantages and disadvantages of using one versus the other.

In determining whether jurisdiction exists, you must consider both **subject matter jurisdiction** and **personal jurisdiction**. If a court does not have both subject matter jurisdiction and personal jurisdiction, it cannot hear the case.

(a) Subject matter jurisdiction   As the term implies, subject matter jurisdiction is determined by the subject matter of the case—that is, the type of law that is involved. Take a moment to review the material in Chapter 4 on the jurisdiction of the federal and state courts. Do you think Mr. Drake's case could be filed in federal court? Federal courts and state courts are empowered to hear different types of cases. Generally, as we discussed in Chapter 4, federal courts can hear only cases relating to federal law (such as federal constitutional or statutory issues) or cases in which the plaintiff and defendant are from different states and the amount in dispute exceeds $75,000.

Cases involving diversity of citizenship and more than $75,000 can usually be started in either federal or state court. In deciding which court to choose, an attorney will consider matters such as filing requirements, deadline dates, the current backlog of cases, discovery procedures, the rules of evidence, and the personalities of the judges. The convenience of the physical location of the court may also be a factor.

Judgment proof
When the defendant does not have sufficient money or other assets to pay the judgment.

Class action suit
A lawsuit brought by a person as a representative for a group of people who have been similarly injured.

Jurisdiction
The power of a court to hear a case.

Subject matter jurisdiction
The power of a court to hear a particular type of case.

Personal jurisdiction
The power of a court to force a person to appear before it.

Case 1: The Distressed Grandfather (continued)

Mr. Drake's case does not involve federal law, as negligence is strictly a matter of state law. However, Mr. Drake is a resident of Massachusetts, and Mrs. Small, the defendant, is a resident of New Hampshire. Because they are residents of different states, attorney Harper will be able to file the complaint for Mr. Drake's case in federal court if the amount in dispute exceeds $75,000. Recall from Chapter 4, however, that even if she brings the case in federal court, because the accident happened in Massachusetts, the federal court will apply Massachusetts state law. Attorney Harper could also commence Mr. Drake's lawsuit in state court. For his case, the federal and state courts have concurrent jurisdiction. Attorney Harper is free to search for the best available forum.

Minimum contacts
A constitutional fairness requirement that a defendant have at least a certain minimum level of contact with a state before the state courts can have jurisdiction over the defendant.

(b) Personal jurisdiction   Personal jurisdiction relates to the court's power to force a person to appear before it—hence the name personal jurisdiction. Generally, for a state court to have personal jurisdiction over a defendant, the defendant must either be a resident of that state, be served with process within the state, consent to the lawsuit, or have some **minimum contacts** with the state. For example, a state court would have jurisdiction over a nonresident defendant who caused an automobile accident within that state's borders. States exercise this jurisdiction over nonresidents through "long arm statutes." Typically, such statutes allow the states to exercise jurisdiction if the subject matter of the lawsuit is a tort the defendant committed within the state, a contract the defendant entered into within the state, or a harm the defendant caused as a result of business conducted within the state. Each of these activities would satisfy the minimum contacts requirement so long as exercising jurisdiction does not offend "traditional notions of fair play and substantial justice."

The widespread use of the Internet to conduct business has raised interesting new issues regarding personal jurisdiction. In the following case a North Carolina resident sued a Georgia resident in South Carolina for allegedly libelous statements the defendant had posted on the Internet in Georgia, but which the North Carolina resident had read in North Carolina.

Dailey v. Popma
662 S.E.2d 12 (N.C. App. 2008)

GEER, Judge.

Plaintiff Jack Dailey appeals from an order dismissing his claims against defendant Donald Popma on the ground that defendant has insufficient contacts with the State of North Carolina for personal jurisdiction to exist in this State. Plaintiff, a resident of North Carolina, claims that defendant, a resident of Georgia, posted defamatory statements about plaintiff on the internet. According to plaintiff, because the effect of the defamation occurred in North Carolina, sufficient minimum contacts exist.

The internet presents unique considerations when it comes to issues of personal jurisdiction. . . .

Facts

On 1 September 2006, plaintiff filed a complaint that asserted claims for libel . . . arising out of internet postings. According to the complaint:

> During July and August, 2006, defendant posted numerous false and defamatory statements about plaintiff on the internet, these statements including that the plaintiff, (a) committed embezzlement; (b) committed theft; (c) is a cheat and a liar; (d) is going to be wearing an orange jumpsuit; (e) is a crook; (f) committed felonies; (g) is an asshole; (h) acted clandestinely and illegally; (i) is dishonest; (j) is a devious con man; (k) is a scumbag; (l) is the equivalent of a molester of boys; (m) will be convicted on multiple counts; (n) is extremely underhanded; (o) is a lying fraud. . . .

With respect to the July and August 2006 internet postings that were the subject of the complaint, defendant stated that all internet postings made by him during that period were done while in Georgia. . . .

Substantively, in deciding whether a North Carolina court has personal jurisdiction over a nonresident defendant, we must apply a two-step analysis: "First, the transaction must fall within the language of the State's 'long-arm' statute. Second, the exercise of jurisdiction must not violate the due process clause of the fourteenth amendment to the United States Constitution." Since neither plaintiff nor defendant disputes the applicability of the long-arm statute, the sole issue before this Court is whether the trial court properly concluded that asserting jurisdiction over defendant would violate due process.

To satisfy the due process prong of the personal jurisdiction analysis, there must be sufficient "minimum contacts" between the nonresident defendant and our state "such that the maintenance of the suit does not offend traditional notions of fair play and substantial justice." *Int'l Shoe Co. v. Washington*, 326 U.S. 310 (1945). Our Supreme Court has noted that "[t]he concept of 'minimum contacts' furthers two goals. First, it safeguards the defendant from being required to defend an action in a distant or inconvenient forum. Second, it prevents a state

from escaping the restraints imposed upon it by its status as a coequal sovereign in a federal system." *Miller v. Kite*, 313 N.C. 474, 477, 329 S.E.2d 663, 665 (1985).

. . . What constitutes "minimum contacts" depends on the quality and nature of the defendant's contacts on a case-by-case basis, but, regardless of the circumstances, there must be "'some act by which the defendant purposefully avails itself of the privilege of conducting activities within the forum State.'" The defendant's contact with the forum state must be "'such that he should reasonably anticipate being haled into court there.'"

. . . The question presented in this appeal becomes, therefore: Did defendant, through his internet postings, manifest an intent to target and focus on North Carolina readers?

. . . Defendant's affidavit indicates that he participated in a number of internet bulletin board discussions related to shooting "camps" conducted by plaintiff in at least North Carolina and Alabama, which camps were attended "by enthusiasts from a number of locations across the southeastern United States. . . ." Defendant further stated that he understood that some of the participants in the bulletin board discussions were not located in North Carolina. These assertions are evidence of a lack of focus on North Carolina residents. . . .

Plaintiff's primary argument is that the effect the postings had on him in North Carolina is sufficient to establish personal jurisdiction over defendant. [H]owever . . . for internet activity the effect on a plaintiff is not enough. A holding otherwise would confer jurisdiction in each state in which a plaintiff was affected by internet postings. The defense of lack of personal jurisdiction would, in effect, be eliminated from all cases involving defamation on the internet because:

> [T]he Internet is omnipresent-when a person places information on the Internet, he can communicate with persons in virtually every jurisdiction. If we were to conclude as a general principle that a person's act of placing information on the Internet subjects that person to personal jurisdiction in each State in which the information is accessed, then the defense of personal jurisdiction, in the sense that a State has geographically limited judicial power,

would no longer exist. The person placing information on the Internet would be subject to personal **jurisdiction** in every State.

ALS Scan, Inc. v. Digital Serv. Consultants, Inc., 293 F.3d 707, 712 (4th Cir. 2002). . . .

In sum, whether internet postings confer jurisdiction in a particular forum hinges on the manifested intent and focus of the defendant.

Because plaintiff has failed to establish that defendant posted the material in the bulletin board discussions with the intent to direct his content to a North Carolina audience, personal jurisdiction does not exist over defendant in North Carolina courts. Accordingly, we affirm the trial court's dismissal of plaintiff's complaint for lack of personal jurisdiction.

CASE DISCUSSION QUESTIONS

1. How did the court resolve the case? Did the North Carolina courts have jurisdiction over the Georgia resident based on his Internet postings?
2. What was the rationale the court gave for its decision.
3. What do you think the plaintiff would have had to prove to establish North Carolina jurisdiction over the defendant?
4. Do you agree with the court's holding? Why?

Case 1: The Distressed Grandfather (continued)

Because Mr. Drake's accident happened in Massachusetts, the accident supplies the minimum contacts that Massachusetts courts need to hear the lawsuit. Mr. Drake may sue Mrs. Small in Massachusetts.

To better understand this concept of personal jurisdiction, just for a moment assume the situation had been different, as illustrated in Fig 5-2. Assume that Mr. Drake, a Massachusetts resident, had been vacationing in Maine when the accident happened, and assume that Mrs. Small, a New Hampshire resident, was also vacationing in Maine. Then the issue of personal jurisdiction would be much more complicated. As he lives in Massachusetts, Mr. Drake would like to commence his lawsuit there. Under these revised facts, however, Mrs. Small has had no contact with Massachusetts, and as at least minimum contacts are required, Mr. Drake would not be allowed to sue her in Massachusetts. He could sue her in New Hampshire because, as a resident of that state, the New Hampshire courts would have jurisdiction over Mrs. Small. He could also sue her in Maine, as the accident in that state provides the minimum contacts necessary to satisfy personal jurisdiction.

Statutes of limitations
The law that sets the length of time from when something happens to when a lawsuit must be filed before the right to bring it is lost.

(4) Statutes of limitations

Statutes of limitations set the amount of time that a person has before he or she is forever barred from bringing a lawsuit. Such statutes vary depending on the type of situation involved. Some statutes of limitations set very short deadlines. A person complaining of discrimination at work has only 180 days in which to bring a complaint. Other statutes of limitations, such as that for murder, are essentially without limit. Typically, persons have two years from

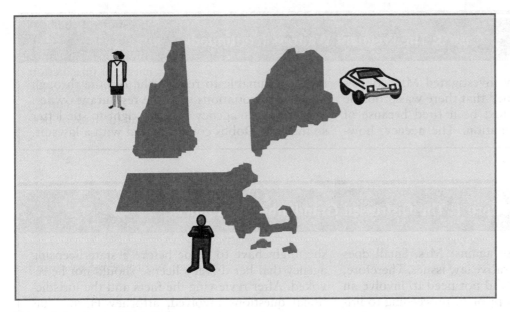

Figure 5-2   Personal Jurisdiction

the date of a negligent act to file a lawsuit. Mr. Drake is fortunate in that he sought legal advice well within the time frame allowed by the statute of limitations.

(5) Exhaustion of administrative remedies

If Mr. Drake's claim had involved a matter coming under the jurisdiction of an administrative agency, he might have had to consult that agency before being allowed to sue in a court of law. Such a requirement is known as the **exhaustion of administrative remedies**. The purpose behind this rule is to give the administrative agency a chance to resolve the problem before the parties resort to a lawsuit.

Exhaustion of administrative remedies
The requirement that relief be sought from an administrative agency before proceeding to court.

Case 3: The Pregnant Waitress (continued)

In employment discrimination cases, there is a requirement that an employee who has experienced discrimination at work first complain to the state or federal agency that handles such claims before being allowed to proceed with a lawsuit. Therefore, Ms. Dobbs's attorney would first instruct Diane to file a complaint with the local agency handling employment discrimination claims.

Once a person has filed a complaint with an administrative agency, that agency usually tries to resolve the issue by getting the parties to reach a mutually agreeable resolution. If those efforts are not successful, the process may proceed to a formal hearing. Such a hearing is similar to a trial but is less formal. An administrative law judge, rather than a trial court judge, oversees the proceeding. Usually there is no requirement that the rules of evidence be strictly

---

Case 3: The Pregnant Waitress (continued)

The state agency investigated Ms. Dobbs's situation and determined that there was probable cause to believe she had been fired because of unlawful sex discrimination. The agency, however, was unable to resolve the dispute through informal negotiations with the restaurant owner. Therefore, the agency issued a right-to-sue letter so that Ms. Dobbs could proceed with a lawsuit.

Case 1: The Distressed Grandfather (continued)

Mr. Drake's case against Mrs. Small does not raise any administrative law issues. Therefore, Mr. Drake's attorney did not need to involve an administrative agency prior to proceeding to litigation. However, separate from Mr. Drake's claims against her, Mrs. Small may find herself before an administrative agency if the police determine the accident was her fault. For example, she might have to argue before a state licensing agency that her driver's license should not be revoked. After reviewing the facts and the jurisdictional questions involved, attorney Harper has determined that the best court in which to proceed with Mr. Drake's case is federal district court. Her first step in initiating the lawsuit will be to draft a complaint.

Complaint
The pleading that begins a lawsuit.

Answer
Defendant's reply to the complaint. It may contain statements of denial, admission, or lack of knowledge and affirmative defenses.

Counterclaim
A claim by the defendant against the plaintiff.

Cross-claim
A claim by one defendant against another defendant or by one plaintiff against another plaintiff.

Third-party claim
A claim by a defendant against someone in addition to the persons the plaintiff has already sued.

followed. Some administrative agencies also allow for nonattorney representatives. Often, the hearing officer's decision resolves the dispute. However, if one of the parties is dissatisfied with the decision, depending on the agency, that party may have the option either to appeal the decision to a higher body within the agency itself, to appeal the decision to a court, or to start the whole process anew with a lawsuit.

b. Pleadings

The pleadings are the documents that each side files with the court and serves on the other side in order to commence the lawsuit. Their purpose is to narrow and focus the issues involved. The initial document the plaintiff files is logically called a **complaint** because the plaintiff is the person starting the lawsuit and hence complaining of some behavior. A complaint states the allegations that form the basis of the plaintiff's case. The document the defendant files in response to the complaint is called an **answer** because it contains the defendant's answers to the charges laid out in the complaint. There are various other pleadings, including a **counterclaim** (a countersuit by the defendant against the plaintiff), a **cross-claim** (a suit by one defendant against another defendant), and a **third-party claim** (a suit by a defendant against someone not originally part of the lawsuit), but in most litigation the pleadings are simply the complaint and the answer.

(1) The complaint

The body of the complaint consists of the allegations of facts that constitute the cause of action. The federal rules allow for **notice pleading**—that is, the complaint must simply identify the transaction from which the plaintiff's claim arises. In many states, however, the facts being pleaded must be "ultimate" facts as opposed to conclusions of law.

Notice pleading
A method adopted by the federal rules in which the plaintiff simply informs the defendant of the claim and the general basis for it.

Case 1: The Distressed Grandfather (continued)

In Mr. Drake's case the complaint includes a statement indicating why he believes the federal district court has jurisdiction, a statement showing why Mr. Drake has a valid claim against Mrs. Small, and finally what relief he would like the court to grant him. See Exhibit 5-1 on page 104.

---

(2) The summons

The plaintiff must arrange to have the defendant notified that the suit has been filed. The plaintiff's attorney does this by preparing a **summons** and then having that summons and a copy of the complaint served on (given to) the defendant. Proper service usually requires that the local sheriff (or a U.S. marshal in federal cases) personally deliver the notice in the form of a summons to the defendant. There are occasions where proper notice can be satisfied by mailing the summons to the defendant's last known address, publishing copies of it in newspapers of general circulation, or delivering it to an authorized agent.

Courts require such **service** for reasons of basic fairness. Before a court will hear a lawsuit, it must be convinced that the defendant has received proper **notice** that the suit has been filed against him or her.

Summons
A notice informing the defendant of the lawsuit and requiring the defendant to respond or risk losing the suit.

Service
The delivery of a pleading or other paper in a lawsuit to the opposing party.

Case 1: The Distressed Grandfather (continued)

You can see the summons prepared for the Drake case in Exhibit 5-2 on page 105. This would be served along with a copy of the complaint in order to notify defendant Small of the nature of the claim.

---

(3) The answer

Upon receiving the summons, the defendant has a designated time within which to file a formal answer to the complaint. For example, the summons in the Drake case indicates that after Mrs. Small receives the complaint and summons, she has twenty days in which to answer the complaint. In an answer, a defendant can choose a combination of responses from among the following alternatives:

Notice
Being informed of some act done or about to be done.

- ∎ deny the facts that the plaintiff says took place,
- ∎ admit the facts but assert that those facts do not provide the plaintiff with a legal remedy,

UNITED STATES DISTRICT COURT FOR THE DISTRICT OF MASSACHUSETTS

Civil Action, File Number_____

Donald Drake, Plaintiff   }

v.   }   COMPLAINT

Wilma Small, Defendant   }

1. Jurisdiction of this court is founded on diversity of citizenship. Plaintiff is a citizen of Massachusetts, and defendant is a citizen of Connecticut. The matter in controversy exceeds, exclusive of interest and costs, the sum of seventy-five thousand dollars.

2. The plaintiff, Donald Drake, is a natural person residing at 56 Bancroft Way, Springfield, Massachusetts.

3. The defendant, Wilma Small, is a natural person residing at 106 Hemingway Lane, Keene New Hampshire.

4. On September 1, 2008, while the plaintiff was walking on the sidewalk along a public way called Bishop Street in Springfield, Massachusetts, the defendant negligently drove a motor vehicle onto the sidewalk where the plaintiff's grandson, Philip Drake, was walking approximately thirty feet ahead of the plaintiff.

5. As a result of the defendant's negligence, the plaintiff's grandson was struck by the defendant's motor vehicle and instantly killed. The plaintiff viewed the entire accident.

6. As a direct result of viewing the death of his grandson, the plaintiff suffered a heart attack, great physical pain, mental suffering, and expenses for medical attention and hospitalization in the sum of one million dollars.

WHEREFORE the plaintiff demands judgment against the defendant in the sum of one million dollars, interest, and costs.

Plaintiff demands trial by jury.

Dated: _____

_____
Pat Harper
333 Main St.
Springfield, MA 01009
413-787-9999

Exhibit 5-1 Complaint

- claim that additional facts give rise to an **affirmative defense,**
- assert that there are procedural defects in the complaint, and
- bring a claim of one's own against either the plaintiff or another defendant.

These options are not considered mutually exclusive.

A sixth alternative is simply not to respond at all—that is, not to file any documents with the court. However, the failure to take any action is viewed as an admission of the allegations contained in the complaint and creates a situation in which the plaintiff can seek a **default judgment.** In a default judgment the judge awards the judgment against the party who fails to appear in court to contest the matter. While the plaintiff must still convince the judge that the claim is legitimate, the defendant has no right either to challenge the evidence presented or to present contrary evidence. Although it is possible to have a default judgment set aside, it is a very difficult task.

Mrs. Small's answer might look like Exhibit 5-3 on page 106.

Affirmative defense
A defense whereby the defendant offers new evidence to avoid judgment.

Default judgment
A judgment entered against a party who fails to complete a required step, such as answering the complaint.

UNITED STATES DISTRICT COURT FOR THE DISTRICT OF MASSACHUSETTS

Civil Action, File Number_____

Donald Drake, Plaintiff   }
                               }
              v.   }   SUMMONS
                               }
                               }
Wilma Small, Defendant   }

To the above-named Defendant:

    You are hereby summoned and required to serve upon Pat Harper , plaintiff's attorney, whose address is 333 Main St., Springfield, MA 01009 , an answer to the complaint which is herewith served upon you, within 20 days after service of this summons upon you, exclusive of the day of service. If you fail to do so, judgment by default will be taken against you for the relief demanded in the complaint.

                    Witness _____ , Esq.
at _____ , the _____ day of _____ 20____ .

                    _____
                    Clerk of Court

(Seal of Court)

    This summons is issued pursuant to Rule 4 of the Federal Rules of Civil Procedure.

Exhibit 5-2   Summons

UNITED STATES DISTRICT COURT FOR THE DISTRICT OF MASSACHUSETTS

Civil Action, File Number 09-483

Donald Drake, Plaintiff	}	
v.	}	PLAINTIFF'S INTERROGATORIES
Wilma Small, Defendant	}	TO WILMA SMALL

[The interrogatories start with fairly standard boilerplate language. Attorneys use the word **boilerplate** to refer to standard language found in a particular type of legal document. In the case of interrogatories the boilerplate language at the beginning sets out basic information such as to whom the interrogatory answers are to be returned, the deadline for their return, and instructions for answering the interrogatories. This language is then followed by the specific questions.]

1. State your full name, age, full address, and telephone number.

2. At the time of the events referred to in paragraphs 4 and 5 of the complaint, did you have a valid driver's license?

3. Has your driver's license ever been suspended or revoked, and if so, state
    a. When and where it was suspended or revoked;
    b. The grounds upon which the license was suspended or revoked. . . .

15. During the 24 hours preceding the events referred to in paragraphs 4 and 5 of the complaint, had you consumed any medicines, drugs, or alcoholic beverages of any type, and if so, state
    a. The type and amount consumed;
    b. The length of time over which the substance was consumed;
    c. The names, addresses, and telephone numbers of every person who has knowledge as to your consumption of the substance. . . .

Dated: _____

_____
Pat Harper
333 Main St.
Springfield, MA 01009
413-787-9999

Exhibit 5-3 Answer

Case 1: The Distressed Grandfather (continued)

(a) Deny the facts that the plaintiff says took place. Mrs. Small will naturally deny as many of the complaint's allegations as she can. She must be careful, however, to deny only those allegations that she truly intends to dispute. As to the other matters, she must either admit their validity or state that she is without the knowledge to form a belief as to the truth or falsity of the statements.

(b) Admit the facts but assert that those facts do not provide the plaintiff with a legal remedy. As suggested earlier, under Massachusetts law it is unclear whether grandfathers can sue for the emotional distress they experience when seeing a grandchild harmed. Therefore, Mrs. Small may want to take advantage of the second option, arguing that even if the facts as alleged are true, they do not form a basis for a lawsuit.

(c) Claim that additional facts give rise to an affirmative defense. As to the third option, in her answer Mrs. Small will also include any affirmative defense that she thinks may decrease or even eliminate her liability. In this case there does not appear to be any such defense, but let us assume the facts were different. Assume that instead of walking down the sidewalk Mr. Drake was driving his car. Assume further that just as he was approaching an intersection, the light turned from green to yellow. He might have had time to stop, but he chose to proceed through the intersection. Mrs. Small, speeding toward him from his right, ran her red light and struck his car, killing Philip in the passenger seat. Clearly Mrs. Small was negligent, and Mr. Drake would want to sue her. However, Mrs. Small might feel that Mr. Drake was also negligent given these changed facts. Therefore, in her answer Mrs. Small would allege the affirmative defense of contributory negligence.

(d) Assert that there are procedural defects in the complaint. This option is usually raised through a separate motion. A motion is simply a request made to the court, asking for a court ruling on a particular matter. The assertion that the complaint is defective will be discussed below under the heading "Pretrial Motions."

(e) Bring a claim of one's own against either the plaintiff or another defendant. Finally, if Mrs. Small has a claim that she would like to bring against Mr. Drake based on the same factual situation on which he is relying, then she must bring that claim as part of her answer. In this case it does not appear that Mrs. Small has any basis for a counterclaim. However, let us suppose the same altered facts laid out in option (d), where both Mr. Drake and Mrs. Small were driving their own vehicles. If Mrs. Small had been injured, in addition to alleging that she does not owe Mr. Drake any money because of his contributory negligence, she might countersue Mr. Drake to try to recover some money from him to compensate her for her own injuries.

c. Pretrial Motions to End Part or All of the Litigation

Sometimes the parties feel they have grounds for having the lawsuit dismissed without a trial. Therefore, in addition to or instead of filing an answer, the defendant may file a motion asking that the court immediately dismiss the case. A **motion** is a written request directed to the court. There are two basic motions that can end part or all of a lawsuit: Rule 12 motions, known as motions to dismiss, and Rule 56 motions, known as motions for summary judgment.

Motion
A request made to the court.

(1) Rule 12 motions to dismiss

Rule 12 outlines the basic types of pretrial motions, as well as how they are presented to the court. For example, if Mrs. Small's attorney thinks the complaint is defective, the attorney can bring a motion under Rule 12. Potential problems with the complaint include the following:

(1) lack of jurisdiction over the subject matter,
(2) lack of jurisdiction over the person,
(3) improper venue,
(4) insufficiency of process,
(5) insufficiency of service of process,
(6) failure to state a claim upon which relief can be granted,
(7) failure to join a party under Rule 19. . . .

12(b)(6) motion
A request that the court find the plaintiff has failed to state a valid claim and dismiss the complaint.

The most important of the Rule 12 motions is (6), commonly referred to as a **12(b)(6) motion.** If the defendant can convince the court that she has a solid foundation for such a motion—that is, that the plaintiff has stated a claim for which the court cannot give relief—then the court will be forced to dismiss the complaint. This means that there will be no trial. No judge or jury will ever hear about the accident or about Mr. Drake's injuries. In Mr. Drake's case the defendant might very well file such a motion, arguing that, in Massachusetts, trial courts have no right to grant relief to a grandfather who suffers injury upon seeing a grandchild negligently killed.

(2) Rule 56 motions for summary judgment

Rule 56 motion (summary judgment motion)
A request that the court grant judgment in favor of the moving party because there is no genuine issue as to any material fact and the moving party is entitled to judgment as a matter of law. It is similar to a 12(b)(6) motion except that the court also considers matters outside the pleadings.

Another method that attorneys may use to try to end a case before trial is through filing a Rule 56 motion, known as a motion for **summary judgment.** An attorney's objective in filing a summary judgment motion is generally the same as that in filing a 12(b)(6) motion—to end the case without the need for a trial. The main difference between the two motions is that when faced with a 12(b)(6) motion, the court must make a determination based only on the facts as alleged in the complaint, and it must assume those facts are true for purposes of deciding the motion. (If the court denies the motion, all parties treat the facts as once again being in dispute.) In a summary judgment motion, however, the court will consider additional evidence as presented in documents other than the pleadings, such as depositions, answers to interrogatories, admissions on file, and affidavits. Rule 56 provides that if those documents show that

■ there is no genuine issue as to any material fact and
■ the moving party is entitled to a judgment as a matter of law,

then the court will grant the motion and enter judgment for the moving party.

As with the motion to dismiss, if the court grants the summary judgment motion and there are no other unresolved factual issues, then there will be no trial. This is a very important fact to keep in mind.

Case 1: The Distressed Grandfather (continued)

Assume in our case that the complaint did not state that Mr. Drake is Philip's grandfather but rather had simply stated that he is a relative. The defendant's attorney could request that Mr. Drake admit he is the grandfather. With that admission in hand, the defendant, Mrs. Small, could then proceed to file a summary judgment motion on the same grounds as she would have filed a motion to dismiss.

---

(3) Appealing a summary judgment or motion to dismiss

A court's decision to grant a motion to dismiss or for summary judgment is considered a final decision and as such is appealable. If the losing party convinces the appellate court to reverse the trial court's decision, the case will then be returned to the trial court so that the parties can proceed with the litigation. In other words, having an appellate court reverse the decision to grant a motion to dismiss or a summary judgment motion does not mean that the prevailing party will have won on the merits. All the prevailing party will have won is the right to proceed with the litigation.

Case 1: The Distressed Grandfather (continued)

Mrs. Small's attorney filed a summary judgment motion on the grounds that Mrs. Small owed Mr. Drake, a grandfather, no duty of care. The trial court granted this motion. Attorney Harper appealed this decision and convinced the court to reverse the trial court's decision. At that point what has she won for Mr. Drake? Only the right to continue with the lawsuit from where they left off.

Before leaving summary judgment motions, consider these two brief points. First, plaintiffs as well as defendants can bring summary judgment motions. The purpose of the motion is to avoid the necessity of a trial if there are no material facts in dispute. The purpose of a trial is to ferret out the facts. If the facts are already known, there is no need for a trial. Therefore, once the facts are known, either side can ask the court to determine that there is no need for a trial

---

Case 1: The Distressed Grandfather (continued)

Assume in Mr. Drake's situation that during her deposition Mrs. Small broke down and admitted that her speeding caused the accident. Her medical experts informed her, however, that they did not think Mr. Drake's heart attack was caused by seeing his grandson's death but rather by a combination of old age and poor eating habits. The plaintiff might be able to convince the court based on Mrs. Small's deposition testimony to grant summary judgment on the issue of the defendant's negligence. However, a trial would still be necessary in order to determine whether Mr. Drake's heart attack was caused by witnessing the accident and, if so, the amount of damages he suffered.

and to declare him or her the winner. Second, motions to dismiss and summary judgment motions can relate to just part of the case.

d. Discovery

Once the defendant files an answer, each side frequently begins using various **discovery** devices to find out more about the strength of the other side's case. The purpose of discovery is to help each side find out as much information as possible so that each can fairly evaluate the case and prepare for trial or settlement. The parties seek to discover information about the identification of witnesses, the nature of the testimony that such witnesses can be expected to provide, and the contents of relevant contracts, medical reports, and so forth. Such information is acquired through various discovery tools, including interrogatories, depositions, requests for admissions, motions to produce documents, and motions for physical and mental exams. What follows is a discussion of the most important methods.

Interrogatories
Written questions sent by one side to the opposing side, answered under oath.

(1) Interrogatories

Interrogatories are written questions sent by one party in a lawsuit to another party to obtain written answers in return. **Interrogatories** are used to help locate potential witnesses, establish dates, determine a person's medical or financial condition, and inquire about the existence of documentary evidence.

Rule 33 provides that "[a]ny party may serve upon any other party written interrogatories." Note therefore that interrogatories may not be served on nonparties. Also, in the federal system the number of interrogatories is limited to twenty-five. States usually impose a similar limitation.

When a law office receives interrogatories directed to its client, the client usually is instructed to write out the answers as fully as possible. An attorney may then edit these answers and prepare the formal responses, which will be returned to the other party's attorney.

Case 1: The Distressed Grandfather (continued)

A sample of the types of questions that might be drafted in Mr. Drake's case can be found in Exhibit 5-4. In addition to these questions, what other types of information do you think Mr. Drake's attorney should attempt to gather through the use of interrogatories?

A major advantage of interrogatories is that they are relatively inexpensive to prepare. A major disadvantage is that the answers can be closely reviewed by that person's attorney or paralegal before they are returned to the party submitting the questions.

(2) Depositions

Deposition
The pretrial oral questioning of a witness under oath.

If an attorney would like to ask questions of a nonparty, such as the doctor who treated Mr. Drake, or would like to ask questions of either a party or a nonparty in person, that attorney will consider taking a deposition. A **deposition** is sworn testimony that is taken outside the courtroom without a judge being

UNITED STATES DISTRICT COURT FOR THE DISTRICT OF MASSACHUSETTS

Civil Action, File Number 09-483

Donald Drake, Plaintiff   }

v.   }   PLAINTIFF'S INTERROGATORIES

Wilma Small, Defendant   }   TO WILMA SMALL

[The interrogatories start with fairly standard boilerplate language. Attorneys use the word **boilerplate** to refer to standard language found in a particular type of legal document. In the case of interrogatories the boilerplate language at the beginning sets out basic information such as to whom the interrogatory answers are to be returned, the deadline for their return, and instructions for answering the interrogatories. This language is then followed by the specific questions.]

1. State your full name, age, full address, and telephone number.

2. At the time of the events referred to in paragraphs 4 and 5 of the complaint, did you have a valid driver's license?

3. Has your driver's license ever been suspended or revoked, and if so, state
    a. When and where it was suspended or revoked;
    b. The grounds upon which the license was suspended or revoked. . . .

15. During the 24 hours preceding the events referred to in paragraphs 4 and 5 of the complaint, had you consumed any medicines, drugs, or alcoholic beverages of any type, and if so, state
    a. The type and amount consumed;
    b. The length of time over which the substance was consumed;
    c. The names, addresses, and telephone numbers of every person who has knowledge as to your consumption of the substance. . . .

Dated: _____

_____
Pat Harper
333 Main St.
Springfield, MA 01009
413-787-9999

Exhibit 5-4 Interrogatories

present. Although a judge is not present, there is a court reporter who administers the oath and records the testimony. The format of a deposition is similar to that of a trial in that one attorney questions the witness and the opposing attorney has an opportunity to make objections and to cross-examine the witness.

Depositions are used primarily to preserve the testimony of a witness when that witness may not be available for the trial (as in the case of a physician) or when the attorney wants to ensure that the story of the individual being deposed cannot be changed. Because a person can be subpoenaed to be deposed, a statement may be obtained from a witness otherwise unwilling to talk to the attorney or to an investigator.

Deponent
The person who is being asked questions at a deposition.

An attorney is responsible for asking the questions during a deposition. The advantages of a deposition over interrogatories are that the deposing attorney is not limited in the number of questions he or she can ask, the **deponent's** answers are usually more spontaneous, the deposing attorney can view the demeanor of the person answering the questions, and under certain circumstances the answers may be used later in a court trial. The major disadvantages are the time and cost involved. At a minimum a deposition requires the time and presence of both attorneys, a court reporter, and the deponent. Without a special court order federal rules limit the number of depositions to ten.

Case 1: The Distressed Grandfather (continued)

The attorney representing Ms. Smith arranged for a deposition of Dr. Gary Booth, one of the doctors who treated Mr. Drake after his heart attack.

---

(3) Requests for admissions

Request for admissions
A document that lists statements regarding specific items for the other party to admit or deny.

A **request for admissions** is a written document that lists statements regarding specific facts for the other party to admit or deny. Once admitted, a matter cannot be contested. The purpose of the request for admissions is to clarify what is not in dispute and what therefore will not need to be resolved through a trial. Paralegals frequently draft requests for admissions.

(4) Requests for documents and physical examinations

Subpoena duces tecum
A court order that a person who is not a party to litigation appear at a trial or deposition and bring requested documents.

The motion to produce documents is used to obtain documents in the possession of one of the parties. Documents in the possession of third parties can be obtained through a **subpoena duces tecum.** The motion for a physical examination is usually used in personal injury cases or other situations where the health of one of the parties is at issue.

Traditionally, discovery requests resulted in the production of one or more boxes of printed documents. However, as law firms and businesses in general have become more and more computerized, reports, memos, letters, e-mails, and so on frequently originate in electronic form (for example, as Microsoft Word, Microsoft Excel, or Adobe Acrobat PDF files). Although these files take far less room to store and are typically easier to send to interested parties, the trend toward using electronic documents also creates new challenges. The sheer volume of electronic data can be overwhelming. Think how a single e-mail can be duplicated many times over when the receiver sends a reply to the sender or forwards the e-mail to others. Hence, a single e-mail can turn into many "documents." Also, there is the problem of metadata. Metadata is stored in electronic documents and contains identifying information, such as the name of the document's author, when the document was originally created, and when and how it was last modified. This can create problems if there is information contained in that metadata the attorneys would rather the other side not know. For example, assume a proposed settlement letter went through several revisions. If an attorney were to forget to erase the information tracking each of those changes, an astute opponent might be able to learn that originally the client was willing to settle for much less than the current offer contained in the letter.

DISCUSSION QUESTIONS

4. If expense and time were not obstacles, do you think most attorneys would prefer to use interrogatories or depositions? Why?

5. If you were doing the discovery plan for Mr. Drake, what methods of discovery would you prefer? Why? Would your answer change if you were representing Mrs. Small? Why or why not?

e. Settlement

Most cases settle rather than going to trial. Settlement is a possibility at any time, even before the commencement of a lawsuit, but human nature being what it is, it often seems to happen on the very eve of trial.

2. The Trial

If the case is not settled, then it proceeds to trial. Although the majority of lawsuits filed never reach the trial stage, the results of those that are tried influence the results of future settlements. For example, some companies compile and publish reports of recently decided personal injury cases in different areas of the country. When parties learn of the amount of damages being awarded in similar cases, they may see the necessity for settling their case out of court.

a. The Right to a Jury Trial

The use of juries in our legal system is a product of our English common-law heritage. The system originated as a means of limiting the powers of the English monarchy and safeguarding citizens against corrupt or biased judges and prosecutors. Today the use of the jury system is most strongly entrenched in criminal cases, but it continues to play an important role in civil cases as well.

The Seventh Amendment to the U.S. Constitution states that the right to a trial by jury shall be preserved in suits at common law where the value in the controversy exceeds $20. Although the word *preserved* might suggest that the constitutional right to a jury trial is limited to those actions tried by a jury in 1791, the right to a jury trial now extends to most types of federal civil cases. Because there is no federal right to a jury in civil cases tried in state courts, each state has defined for itself the extent to which juries are to be available in state courts. In most states you will not find juries in divorce and probate cases. But you will find juries provided for, either by statute or by constitution, in contractual and tort matters exceeding a specific dollar limit.

The basic function of the jury is to resolve the factual, as opposed to the legal, questions raised in the case. Generally, this comes down to deciding how much credibility to give to the often conflicting testimony of various witnesses. When damage awards are called for, the jury must decide how to measure pain and suffering in terms of dollars and cents. In cases where a jury is not used, the judge takes over the jury's function in addition to her or his normal duties of presiding over the trial and resolving the legal questions raised.

Finally, a word about the number of people on a jury: Under the common law a jury consisted of twelve people. However, the courts have ruled that there is nothing that is constitutionally significant about that number, and six-person juries have been used in civil cases at both the federal and the state levels. Furthermore, it is not unusual to select one or two extra jurors as alternates, especially where the trial is expected to last for more than a few days. These alternates sit in the jury box with their fellow jurors throughout the trial and are used as substitutes if regular jurors are unable to continue. An alternate does not participate in the deliberations, however, unless he or she has replaced one of the original jurors.

b. Jury Selection

Voir dire
An examination of a prospective juror to see if he or she is fit to serve as a juror on a specific case.

The first formal step in a jury trial is the selection of individual jurors from a pool of jurors. The modern trend is to require almost everyone to serve as a juror. This process of selecting individual jurors is known as **voir dire** and marks the start of the trial. The voir dire itself consists of questioning potential jurors to determine whether they are fit to serve on the jury for that specific case. For example, a potential juror would be disqualified if he or she had a personal relationship with a party in the case or with one of the attorneys involved. Potential jurors may also be disqualified if they have been exposed to a great deal of prejudicial pretrial publicity or if they have been involved in similar lawsuits themselves.

Challenge for cause
A method for excusing a prospective juror based on the juror's inability to serve in an unbiased manner.

Attorneys use two types of challenges when seeking to prevent specific individuals from serving on the jury in their case. The first line of attack is usually a **challenge for cause.** To exercise this challenge, the attorney must convince the judge that something about the juror's background or answers demonstrates that the person has some type of bias. If the judge agrees, the person will not be seated. There is no limit on the number of such challenges that can be raised or granted. In some well-publicized and highly controversial cases, attorneys have gone through hundreds of jurors before arriving at the final twelve.

Peremptory challenge
A method for excusing a prospective juror; no reason need be given.

Attorneys can also exercise **peremptory challenges.** These allow an attorney to have a potential juror removed without giving a reason for the dismissal. However, peremptory challenges are limited in number. In deciding whether to use one of these valuable peremptory challenges on a questionable juror, attorneys must weigh the risk of having to accept a worse juror later because they will have exhausted their limited supply of challenges.

DISCUSSION QUESTIONS

6. Many people argue that life and lawsuits have become too complex for the average juror. For example, how can anyone but an economist understand the intricacies of an antitrust lawsuit or anyone but a computer expert comprehend the concept of reverse engineering? Do you think there are certain types of lawsuits where the jury should be composed only of experts in that field? Should jury trials be eliminated entirely in some areas of the law?

7. When litigants have sufficient money, they often hire jury experts, people who specialize in studying the characteristics of various groups. The theory is that certain types of people will be likely to favor one side over the other; for example, in a medical malpractice case, a person may lean toward the doctor, while others will favor the patient. Can you think of any groups that you could characterize in this way? Do you think this is a valid approach to choosing a jury? Even if valid, should it be used?

c. Opening Statements

Once the jury is selected, the attorneys make opening statements in which they outline the evidence they hope to present. In these presentations the plaintiff's and defendant's attorneys state their theories of the case and describe, from their respective points of view, what allegedly took place and to what they expect the witnesses to testify. The jury is thus presented with a framework for viewing the upcoming testimony.

Because the plaintiff has the burden of proving his or her case, the plaintiff's attorney presents the first opening argument. In most cases the defendant's attorney makes an opening statement immediately following that of the plaintiff's attorney. At other times the defense waits until the plaintiff's attorney has finished presenting the plaintiff's witnesses and exhibits and the defense is about to present its case.

d. Presentation of Evidence

After the opening statements the plaintiff's attorney presents evidence in the form of witness testimony and exhibits. The exhibits consist of such things as medical records, accident reports, and photographs of the accident scene. Specific rules of evidence dictate what types of evidence can be admitted and the manner in which witnesses can be questioned.

In considering evidence it is essential to be aware of the differences between facts and opinions. When a witness testifies that he saw the defendant's automobile strike the plaintiff's car broadside, he is testifying about a fact he observed. But when that same witness says the defendant was driving too fast for the icy condition of the road, he is stating an opinion. Generally, only expert witnesses, such as doctors and police officers, can testify as to their opinions, based on their expert knowledge.

In conducting the **direct examination** of a witness, an attorney usually cannot ask leading questions. A **leading question** is one that suggests the answer. For example, "Wouldn't you say the defendant appeared to be very angry at that point in time?" is a leading question.

Once the plaintiff's attorney has completed questioning a witness, the defendant's attorney may **cross-examine** that same witness. The cross-examination clarifies any potentially misleading statements or half-truths and attacks the credibility of the witness. Therefore, the defense attorney attempts to bring out possible biases or the inability of the witness to have seen clearly what she or he claims to have seen. On cross-examination a lawyer may ask leading questions.

The defendant's cross-examination is then followed by redirect examination, where the plaintiff's attorney has the opportunity to ask additional questions of the witness. The plaintiff's attorney uses redirect questions to rehabilitate the witness after the defense's attack on the witness's credibility. These questions cannot be used to raise new subjects or to explore topics that were not covered as

Direct examination
The questioning of your own witness.

Leading question
A question that suggests the answer; generally, leading questions may not be asked during direct examination of a witness.

Cross-examination
The questioning of an opposing witness.

part of the cross-examination. The redirect is then followed by an opportunity for recross-examination by the defendant's attorney, but that must, in turn, be limited to topics raised during the redirect. At that point the witness is finally excused, and the plaintiff's attorney then proceeds to call the next witness.

Throughout the process of questioning witnesses and presenting evidence, the attorneys must keep in mind that appellate courts usually require them to raise appropriate objections at the proper times during the trial. An attorney cannot complain later to an appellate court about something that he or she did not complain about at the proper time to the trial judge.

This requirement for "laying a proper foundation" places additional pressures on the trial attorney. A careless or incompetent attorney can simultaneously destroy the client's chances to win at the trial level and to successfully appeal an adverse decision. Attorneys will make objections for the record even when they do not expect the trial judge to accept them. This is sometimes called protecting the record or making a record for appeal.

Directed verdict

A verdict ordered by a trial judge if the plaintiff fails to present a prima facie case or if the defendant fails to present a necessary defense.

After the plaintiff's attorney has finished calling witnesses and presenting evidence, the defense has its opportunity. Before this occurs, it is not unusual for the defense attorney to move for a **directed verdict**. This motion requests that the judge end the trial at that point and find in favor of the defendant on the basis that the plaintiff's side failed to meet its obligation of presenting a prima facie case supporting its position. The judge will enter a directed verdict if the judge concludes that the plaintiff's evidence is so weak that even considered in its most favorable light (without considering any rebuttal evidence from the defendant) it is not sufficient as a matter of law to merit a verdict in the plaintiff's favor.

Case 1: The Distressed Grandfather (continued)

To present the prima facie case of negligence, attorney Harper must enter evidence of each element of negligence: duty, breach, cause, and harm. If she inadvertently omits one of the elements, then there is no way for the court to find a basis for the negligence claim, and a directed verdict in the defendant's favor would be appropriate.

If the court grants the motion, the trial is over. However, it is very unusual for a judge to accept a motion for a directed verdict at this point in the trial. Typically, the judge denies the motion, and the defense attorney goes on to present his or her witnesses. The same process of direct, cross, redirect, and recross is used. The defense strategy involves presenting evidence that contradicts evidence presented by the plaintiff and possibly attempting to raise a legally accepted defense for that particular type of case.

Once the defendant's case is complete, the plaintiff can ask for a directed verdict on the basis that even if the defendant's evidence is taken in its most favorable light, it would be insufficient to rebut the plaintiff's case. If the judge also denies this motion, as is usually the case, then the plaintiff can present witnesses who will attempt to rebut testimony and evidence presented by the defense. After that, either side can again renew its motion for a directed verdict. If these motions are again denied, both sides then give their closing arguments.

DISCUSSION QUESTIONS

8. Do you agree with the rule that only experts should be allowed to state their opinions? Why should it matter if a witness who saw Mrs. Small stumble just before she entered her car testifies that "Mrs. Small was drunker than a skunk"?

9. One of the all-time famous leading questions is "So, when did you stop beating your wife?" What is the problem with asking your witness this type of question during direct examination?

NETNOTE

You can read about and see video clips of current trials on www.cnn.com/crime.

e. Closing Arguments

Perhaps the most dramatic part of any trial is the closing arguments. Here the attorneys review and interpret the evidence in its most favorable light and develop emotional appeals. Closing arguments are their final chance to persuade the jury. Although both the plaintiff and the defendant receive equal time, in some states the plaintiff has the advantage of splitting the time and speaking both first and last. The plaintiff is given this advantage because the plaintiff also has the burden of proof to overcome.

f. Jury Instructions

Before sending the jury members out to deliberate, it is the judge's responsibility to properly instruct them about the nature of their duties and the requirements of the law. The jury's duty is to determine the facts and then apply the requirements of the law to those facts. However, the jury is composed of a group of lay persons who do not know what the law requires. Therefore, it is the duty of the judge to explain the law in terms the jury can understand.

g. Jury Deliberations, Verdict, and Judgment

Once they have been properly instructed, the jurors retire to a special room where they deliberate in private until they reach their **verdict,** or they report they cannot reach a consensus and the judge declares a **mistrial.** In most cases the jurors must come to a unanimous agreement regarding the verdict, although some states have provisions for less-than-unanimous verdicts in certain types of cases.

Usually, evidence is presented at the trial regarding the question of liability and the amount of damages. If the jurors find that the defendant is liable, they next consider the amount of damages. In some cases, however, a bifurcated trial is held. During the first phase of the trial the jury hears testimony regarding liability and then deliberates on that issue alone. If the jury finds the defendant

Verdict
The opinion of a jury on a question of fact.

Mistrial
A trial ended by the judge because of a major problem, such as a prejudicial statement by one of the attorneys.

liable, the trial enters a second stage, in which the jury hears evidence about the nature of the damages. The jury then deliberates regarding the amount of damages to award.

Once a verdict is reached, the court enters its official **judgment** regarding the rights and obligations of the parties involved in the case, and the clerk enters it into the record. It is this entering of the judgment that gives the parties the right to enforce the court's decision. Then, for example, if the defendant fails to pay damages that were part of the judgment, the plaintiff can request a **writ of execution.** The writ instructs the sheriff to seize the defendant's property, sell it at public auction, and then use the proceeds to pay the plaintiff. Usually, if the losing party does not appeal within a specified time period, the judgment automatically becomes effective. If the losing party does appeal, the court stays the judgment until the appellate court reaches its decision.

h. Post-Trial Motions

After the verdict has been announced, the losing party has a certain time period within which to file post-trial motions. The most common motions are a motion for judgment notwithstanding the verdict and a motion for a new trial. Both motions are frequently made but seldom granted.

The motion for a **judgment notwithstanding the verdict,** also known as a **judgment N.O.V.** (judgment non obstante veredicto), is a request to the judge to reverse the jury's decision on the basis that the evidence was legally insufficient to support its verdict. If the judge grants the motion, the case is over, and the moving party has won.

An attorney usually bases the **motion for a new trial** on the assertion that some procedural error has tainted the outcome. The losing party might argue, for example, that some piece of evidence was admitted that should not have been admitted or that someone made improper contacts with a juror on the case. If the court grants the motion, the case has to be retried.

3. The Appeal

"I'll take my case all the way to the Supreme Court" is a battle cry that has been echoed by many concerned litigants. No one likes to lose, and there are few attorneys who have not dreamed of arguing a case before the U.S. Supreme Court.

On the other hand, appeals consume time and money. The client's initial desire for appeal often pales because of costs. In addition, the option to appeal may be either very limited or even nonexistent. If the attorney did not make the correct objections during the trial or if the client's case did not involve any questions of law, then there will be no basis for an appeal.

a. The Timing and Filing of the Appeal

A case cannot be appealed until a final judgment has been entered. This can occur at any time during the trial if the court grants a final judgment. For example, the court can grant a motion to dismiss, a summary judgment motion, a motion for a directed verdict, or one of the post-trial motions. Most commonly a final judgment comes after a jury verdict. The party wishing to have the case reviewed must file a notice of appeal within a specified time period after the final judgment is entered.

Judgment
The decision of the court regarding the claims of each side. It may be based on a jury's verdict.

Writ of execution
A court order authorizing a sheriff to take property in order to enforce a judgment.

Judgment notwithstanding the verdict (judgment N.O.V.)
A judgment that reverses the verdict of the jury when the verdict had no reasonable factual support or was contrary to law.

Motion for a new trial
A request that the court order a rehearing of a lawsuit because irregularities, such as errors of the court or jury misconduct, make it probable that an impartial trial did not occur.

The side bringing the appeal, the appellant, files an **appellate brief**. The brief explains the facts of the case, lists the relevant statutes and court cases, and then presents legal arguments for overturning the lower court's decisions. Then the other side, the appellee, files its brief. Finally, the appellant has the opportunity to file a reply brief in response to the appellee's argument and to any new authorities cited in the appellee's brief.

b. The Scope of the Review

When an appellate court considers a case, it does not conduct a new trial. It simply reviews the official record of the proceedings at the trial court. Moreover, it limits its review to specific appealable issues, for which the party appealing the case must have laid a proper foundation at the trial level.

As you know, in general appellate courts consider only legal issues. Recall that legal issues involve the interpretation and application of the law; factual issues involve the determination of whether a given event took place as alleged.

Sometimes, however, appellate courts are asked to review a trial court's findings of fact. When they do so, it is on a very limited basis. Generally, appellate courts will resolve conflicts in the testimony and questions of the credibility of the witnesses in favor of the trial judge's position. They cannot disregard a trial court's findings of fact unless they determine that the findings were **clearly erroneous**. This means not simply that the appellate court would have found otherwise but that the appellate court is convinced that the trial court made a mistake, as, for example, when the trial court did not base its findings on sufficient evidence.

However, when an appellate court reviews legal issues, it gives no deference to the trial court's findings but rather makes its own independent review. A legal issue might involve reviewing a trial judge's interpretation of a statute or legal document, such as a will or a lease. Similarly, questions about the nature of the jury instructions and the trial court's decision on the admissibility of evidence present legal issues.

Sometimes the resolution of a legal issue requires the court to review the facts. This creates a situation that is hard to categorize as either factual or legal. For example, when a party appeals based on the trial judge's decision to deny a motion for a directed verdict, the appellant is arguing that the evidence was so one-sided that it could support only one conclusion. Because it is a ruling on a motion, it is a legal question; but to reach a decision, the appellate court must make a judgment about the strength of the evidence itself. In these mixed fact/law situations, an appellate court often does an independent review—especially if the court believes the legal aspects predominate. An appellate court uses the clearly erroneous standard when factual aspects predominate, such as in questions involving negligence.

If the appellate court decides that the trial judge made a legal error, it must determine whether that error was prejudicial or merely harmless. Errors are defined as prejudicial when they probably affected the results. **Harmless errors** are errors so minor and peripheral that they had no significant effect on the outcome. Only prejudicial errors are considered to be **reversible errors**.

Examples of harmless errors include (1) a mistake in the pleadings if the facts can be determined at trial; (2) errors in jury instructions unless there is reason to believe that they actually misled the jury; and (3) the failure to strictly

Appellate brief
An attorney's written argument presented to an appeals court, setting forth a statement of the law as it should be applied to the client's facts.

Clearly erroneous
Standard used by appellate courts when reviewing a trial court's findings of fact.

Harmless error
A trial court error that is not sufficient to warrant reversing the decision.

Reversible error
An error made by the trial judge sufficiently serious to warrant reversing the trial court's decision.

follow the rules of evidence in a bench trial, as it is assumed a judge is unlikely to be affected by incompetent evidence.

Finally, sometimes an appeal is based upon a challenge to a trial judge's decision as to court procedure or how the case should be managed. Examples include permission to amend a complaint, denial of a request for a continuance, imposition of sanctions for filing an improper pleading, and the awarding of prejudgment interest. Because these types of decisions are generally left to the discretion of the trial judge, appellate courts review them using an abuse of discretion standard. They will reverse a trial court only if the appellant can prove the judge committed a clear error of judgment, lacked the authority to act, or acted with prejudice or malice.

c. Oral Arguments

Depending on the rules of the particular appellate court, the court may hear oral arguments on appeal. During oral argument the attorneys present their clients' positions. The court gives the attorneys a limited time to speak (often no more than twenty minutes), and the judges frequently interrupt the attorneys with questions. The purpose of the questioning is to probe weak points in the argument and to explore the implications of the attorney's line of reasoning.

d. The Decision and Its Publication

Affirm
When a higher court agrees with what a lower court has done.

Reverse
When an appellate court disagrees with the decision of a lower court.

Remand
When an appellate court sends a case back to the trial court for a new trial or other action.

With or without the benefit of oral argument, the judges study the matter until they reach a decision by majority vote. Usually, the case is assigned to one of the judges in the majority to prepare the official opinion of the court. As part of this process the judge's law clerks verify the authorities cited in the briefs, sometimes finding additional cases that apply. The clerks typically prepare a rough draft of the opinion for the majority judges to edit and polish. The other judges on the court have the right to prepare either concurring or dissenting opinions if they want the record to reflect their differences. You will recall that in a concurring opinion the judge agrees with the outcome but disagrees with the reasoning in the court's opinion. In a dissenting opinion the writer disagrees with both the outcome and the reasoning. The court's decision is then published in the appropriate **reporters**, law books that contain all of an appellate court's opinions.

Usually, the appellate decision is either to **affirm** the lower court's action or to **reverse** and **remand** (return) the case to the lower court for reconsideration. Sometimes, based on the nature of the case, a new trial is not needed to supplement the factual record. Then the judges may simply enter a final judgment based on the existing record.

e. Further Appeals

Depending on the court structure and the nature of the case, the party that loses at the appellate level (regardless of which party lost at the trial-court level) may have the option of appealing to yet a higher-level appellate court. The general rule, however, is that there is only one right of appeal. A second appeal to a higher court is usually discretionary rather than a matter of right: The judges on the higher appellate court choose to hear only the cases that they believe have the greatest judicial significance. For example, to have a case heard by the U.S. Supreme Court, the losing party must first petition the Court and request that it grant a writ of certiorari. In support of this request the applicant will file a written brief. The purpose of the brief is not to argue the merits of the case but to convince the Court to agree to hear the case. Common reasons are the importance of the case for others beyond the immediate litigants and the need to resolve conflicts among the circuits. For example, for many years the federal courts of appeals were reaching different results in sexual harassment cases. Some courts of appeals thought such situations were covered by Title VII, while others disagreed. In a federal system, leaving such a conflict unresolved is obviously undesirable, as the outcome of a case will vary based on where it is brought. Eventually the Supreme Court agreed to hear a case involving sexual harassment and resolved the issue by deciding that such situations are covered by Title VII.[10]

If the Court grants the petition for a writ of certiorari, the litigants will then file briefs arguing the merits of the case. However, the Court denies most petitions for certiorari.

Most state courts follow a similar procedure. For example, in Massachusetts there is one right of appeal to the intermediate appellate court. If a party wishes to be heard by the state's highest court, the Massachusetts Supreme Judicial Court, that person must file an application for **leave to obtain further appellate review**.

If the higher appellate court accepts the appeal, then the parties file new briefs, and the process described above begins all over again.

SUMMARY

When people have a dispute they cannot settle themselves, they typically turn to the courts to have a judge or jury settle it for them. This process of using the courts is referred to as litigation. Because it is such a complex, time-consuming, and expensive way of settling disputes, people are increasingly turning to various forms of alternative dispute resolution (ADR).

The most common types of ADR are arbitration, mediation, and summary jury trials. Increasing numbers of courts are requiring litigants to try different types of mediation before they allow a case to come to trial. Many business contracts include provisions for mandatory arbitration.

In some circumstances it may be necessary to exhaust administrative remedies prior to filing a lawsuit. Adjudicatory hearings in administrative agencies follow the general outline of a civil trial, but they are less formal and do not involve as many due process protections. A hearing officer presides over the hearing, acting much like a judge would. Although it is relatively easy to get evidence admitted into the record, the hearing officer has a great deal of discretion over the weight given to that evidence. Once all avenues of appeal within an agency have been exhausted, a party can often seek review within the judicial system.

The three main stages of litigation are pretrial, trial, and post-trial. In the pretrial stage the parties use pleadings, discovery, and pretrial conferences to identify the facts and the legal issues involved in the dispute. The majority of cases are settled "out of court" during this stage.

---

[10]Meritor Savings Bank v. Vinson, 477 U.S. 57 (1986).

At the trial stage the parties present their evidence to either a judge or a jury. The rules of evidence dictate the form in which the evidence must be presented and what types of questions witnesses can be required to answer. Following the trial verdict, the losing party may challenge the trial court's decision in an appellate court.

CRITICAL THINKING EXERCISES

1. Assume Mary was injured in an automobile accident while vacationing in California. Joe was driving the car that hit her. Mary is a resident of Michigan. Joe is a resident of Florida. In which state(s) may Mary bring suit? Why?

2. Four Seasons Campground rents campground spaces in New Jersey, the state in which it is also incorporated. John Haas, a resident of Pennsylvania, learned about the campsite on its Web site, www.fourseasonscamping.com, and decided he wanted to lease campground space for the next summer. Because the website did not allow for such seasonal purchases to be made online, Mr. Haas drove to New Jersey, where he signed a contract. Later that year while at his leased campsite, a branch fell from a tree, striking him on his head and causing him to fall into a brick fireplace and then to the ground. When he sued the campground in Pennsylvania for the injuries he suffered, the defendant Campground filed a motion to have the case dismissed for lack of personal jurisdiction. How do you think the court ruled and why?

3. Some have likened the current discovery process to a guessing game whereby one side tries to guess what information the other side has and attempts to ferret it out through the clever use of interrogatories and depositions. Do you think the system would work better if all parties were automatically required to hand over all relevant information at the beginning of the lawsuit? Do you think that would be a workable system? A fair system? Recently the federal rules were amended to require automatic disclosure in certain circumstances. The change is contained in Rule 26(a)(1). It is too early to tell if the attempt to increase voluntary cooperation among attorneys will be successful.

REVIEW QUESTIONS

Pages 87 through 93
1. What are the most common forms of ADR, and how do they differ from each other?
2. What types of disputes are best suited to resolution through ADR? Which are least appropriate?
3. What do the proponents of ADR see as the advantages of ADR over traditional litigation?

Pages 93 through 102
4. What are the three basic stages of civil litigation?
5. What rules govern civil litigation in federal courts?
6. What issues have to be considered in deciding who should be sued?
7. How does a class action lawsuit differ from one brought by and on behalf of one individual?

8. If someone says that a particular court does not have jurisdiction over a lawsuit, what is meant by that?
9. What is the difference between subject matter jurisdiction and personal jurisdiction?
10. What is the purpose of requiring litigants to first exhaust their administrative remedies?
11. How does an administrative hearing differ from a civil trial?

Pages 102 through 107

12. What is the purpose of each of the following pleadings:
    a. the complaint
    b. the answer
    c. a counterclaim
    d. a cross-claim
    e. a third-party claim
13. Under the federal rules what three items must be included in a complaint?
14. What is a caption?
15. What is the purpose of a summons?
16. What is the danger to the defendant in failing to answer a complaint?
17. What are the five basic ways that a defendant can respond to a complaint, and what is the purpose of each?

Pages 107 through 109

18. What are the grounds for a 12(b)(6) motion, and what is its purpose?
19. What is the difference between a 12(b)(6) motion and a summary judgment motion?

Pages 110 through 113

20. What is the main goal of discovery?
21. What are interrogatories and depositions, and how do they differ?
22. Besides interrogatories and depositions, what are the main discovery tools available to the parties?

Pages 113 through 118

23. What is the function of the jury?
24. What is a voir dire, and what is its purpose?
25. What are the differences between challenges for cause and peremptory challenges, and what is the function of each?
26. What do attorneys hope to accomplish in their opening statements?
27. Who presents evidence first, the plaintiff or the defendant, and why?
28. When can either side move for a directed verdict? What is the purpose of that motion?
29. What is the difference between a verdict and a judgment?
30. What is the difference between the motion for a judgment notwithstanding the verdict (a judgment N.O.V.) and a motion for a new trial? Give an example of when each could be used.

Pages 118 through 121

31. Describe the limitations on a litigant's right to appeal.
32. What is the difference between a harmless error and a reversible error?

PART 2

Substantive Law and Ethical Issues

Chapter 6

Constitutional Law

The great generalities of the constitution have a content and a significance that vary from age to age.
Benjamin Cardozo

INTRODUCTION

Constitutional law involves some of the most fundamental concepts in our legal system and many of the most controversial issues of our day. These issues range from the powers of the President to carry on wars to the way that police conduct searches and interrogate suspects. It also includes issues such as the use of affirmative action, the right to an abortion, and prayer in schools.

While the U.S. Constitution receives far more attention than do our state constitutions, the latter also play an important role in our legal system. Although our focus in this chapter will be on the federal constitution, you will find that what you learn here about the federal constitution will also help you understand and interpret state constitutions.

Our current U.S. Constitution did not go into effect until 1789–fifteen years after the first formal meeting of the first Continental Congress and thirteen years after the signing of the Declaration of Independence. That Continental Congress was composed of representatives from what were then the British colonies. It functioned as a de facto government while we declared our independence from England and fought the Revolutionary War. It raised an army and a navy, appointed George Washington to lead its armed forces, and sent representatives to seek alliances with foreign countries.

The Continental Congress also developed a document, known as the Articles of Confederation, which established a government structure that was in effect from 1781 until our current constitution superseded it in 1789. The

Constitutional law
A body of principles and rules either explicitly stated in, or inferred from, the U.S. Constitution and those of the individual states.

Articles created a confederation made up of "states" (rather than colonies) and formally named this country the United States of America. Under the terms of these Articles, the member states retained all sovereign powers, and the national government could only do what the states' delegates voted to authorize. All governmental functions were concentrated in a single legislative chamber where each state had one vote. It is especially important to note that the national government had no authority to levy taxes, and therefore had to rely on voluntary contributions from its member states.

These and other inherent weaknesses led to calls for changes in the governing structure and eventually to the Constitutional Convention held in Philadelphia in 1787. The delegates to this convention went on to draft the document that, with its twenty-seven amendments, still governs us today.

Two major factors set constitutional law apart from the other areas of law we cover in this book. The first is its relative importance in relationship to the other types of law. As we discussed in Chapter 2, common law can be overridden by the passage of a statute. Administrative regulations are only valid where they have been specifically authorized by statute and are ruled invalid if they exceed the terms of that statutory authorization. Statutes, in turn, are only valid if they were enacted by legislative bodies with constitutional authority to enact them and if they do not conflict with provisions of the Constitution. Thus, if any statute, regulation, or interpretation of the common law is deemed to be in conflict with any aspect of the Constitution, then that statute, regulation, or aspect of the common law is treated as invalid and unenforceable. It is therefore said that constitutional law sits at the top of the hierarchy of law.

Based on the principle of judicial review (also discussed in Chapter 2), it is within the inherent powers of the judiciary for judges to make determinations as to whether a specific statute, regulation, or common law decision conflicts with the constitution. Because any lower court decisions involving applications of the U.S. Constitution are ultimately reviewable by the U.S. Supreme Court, it is the justices of our highest judicial body who determine the meaning of our constitutional law.

The second major distinguishing factor of constitutional law is the degree to which many of its key provisions use language that is quite vague and ambiguous. Although the U.S. Constitution is quite specific about things like the number of senators and representatives, and their minimum ages, there are many other clauses that use extremely broad language, which is open to a variety of different interpretations. A few examples include the following:

- Article I, Section 8: "Congress shall have power to . . . *regulate commerce* with foreign Nations, and among the several States, and with the Indian Tribes.
- Article II, Section 4: "The President, Vice President and all civil Officers of the United States, shall be removed from Office on Impeachment for, and Conviction of, Treason, Bribery, or *other high Crimes and Misdemeanors.*"
- Amendment IV: "The right of the people to be secure in their persons, houses, papers, and effects, against *unreasonable* searches and seizures, shall not be violated . . . ."
- Amendment V: "No person shall . . . be deprived of life, liberty, or property, without *due process of law;* nor shall private property be taken for *public use,* without just compensation."

DISCUSSION QUESTION

1. Some argue that the ambiguities found in many of the constitutional provisions are actually a source of strength as they allow for flexibility in interpretation; others argue that they weaken the Constitution because they leave us without a fixed content. What do you think? Do you think the often vague and ambiguous constitutional provisions are a source of strength or weakness?

In the first section of this chapter, we explore how judges go about interpreting this type of vague and ambiguous language. This is followed by an overview of the most important concepts of constitutional law including federalism, separation of powers, due process of law, and the equal protection of the laws. Our focus is on helping you develop an understanding of the basic principles the Supreme Court has identified and the major "tests" or standards that the courts typically apply.

A. APPROACHES TO CONSTITUTIONAL INTERPRETATION

There is no universally agreed upon approach to constitutional interpretation. Indeed, most judges utilize a combination of four different approaches.

Literal interpretation
An approach in which judges use common dictionary definitions for terms used in the document they are interpreting.

1. A Literal Reading of the Text

The interpretation of constitutions, like the interpretation of statutes and regulations, begins with an examination of the text of the document. Most scholars and legal practitioners believe that, *in most situations,* judges should stick to a **literal interpretation** and apply commonly accepted dictionary definitions for interpreting the words used in the document.

Consider the use of this method for interpreting the Second Amendment to the U.S. Constitution. It reads:

> A well regulated Militia, being necessary to the security of a free State, the right of the people to keep and bear Arms, shall not be infringed.

When the U.S. Supreme Court was called upon to interpret this amendment in *District of Columbia v. Heller,*[1] both the majority and the dissent supported their interpretation with dictionary definitions of what it meant to "keep and bear arms." A resident of the District of Columbia had challenged the constitutionality of a local gun control law that prohibited possession of handguns (unless specifically authorized by the police chief) and required residents to keep lawfully owned firearms unloaded and either disassembled or with a trigger lock on. Writing for the majority, Justice Scalia concluded that "keep" means to possess and "bear" means to carry. He defined "arms" as both offensive and defensive weapons[2] and then concluded that individuals have a right to possess

---

[1] 128 S. Ct. 2783 (2008).
[2] Id. at 2793.

and use firearms for purposes of self-defense[3] and other "lawful purposes,"[4] in addition to service in the militia.

> The prefatory clause does not suggest that preserving the militia was the only reason Americans valued the ancient right; most undoubtedly thought it even more important for self-defense and hunting.[5]

In his dissenting opinion, Justice Stevens cited the Oxford English Dictionary's definition that "bear arms" means "to serve as a soldier, do military service, fight."[6] Based in part on this definition he concluded that the Second Amendment only protects the possession and use of weapons in the context of formal regulated militias.

Note that while Justices Scalia and Stevens both relied on dictionary definitions, they came to opposite conclusions about what the Second Amendment means.

DISCUSSION QUESTION

2. If two justices of the United States Supreme Court can both use the "literal reading" approach and yet still reach opposite results, do you think there is any value in judges using this approach as a starting place for their analysis?

Contextual analysis
An approach whereby judges examine other parts of the same document or similar documents to see how the same words or phrases were used in these related contexts.

2. Contextual Analysis

Sometimes, the same word can mean different things in different contexts. Consider the difference between a hit in a baseball game, a hit on Broadway, and a hit in Blackjack. Therefore, when interpreting words in the Constitution, judges often consider the context in which those words appear.

Once again consider the wording of the Second Amendment. It consists of two clauses joined into a single sentence. The first clause, "[a] well regulated Militia, being necessary to the security of a free state," is a preamble or introduction, while the second identifies the specific right, the right of the people to "keep and bear Arms." What does the preamble clause tell you about what it means to "keep and bear Arms"?

In the *Heller* decision, Justice Stevens concluded that

> [t]he preamble to the Second Amendment makes three important points. It identifies the preservation of the militia as the Amendment's purpose; it explains that the militia is necessary to the security of a free State; and it recognizes that the militia must be "well regulated."[7]

In light of these references to the role of the militia, Justice Stevens argued that the restriction contained in the second clause should be limited to prohibitions that interfere with the militia.

---

[3]Id at 2816.
[4]Id. at 2813.
[5]Id. at 2801.
[6]Id. at 2828 (Stevens, JJ., dissenting).
[7]Id. at 2824 (Stevens, JJ., dissenting).

In contrast, Justice Scalia's opinion declared that the operative restrictions on keeping and bearing arms are not limited by the introductory clause. In support of his position, he cited the following quote in a 1982 text on statutory construction:

> The settled principle of law is that the preamble cannot control the enacting part of the statute in cases where the enacting part is expressed in clear, unambiguous terms.[8]

Because the "operative clause" of the amendment refers to the "right of the *people*," rather than to a right of people *in the Militia,* Justice Scalia interprets the "operative clause" of the amendment as creating a general right that is not limited to participation in the militia.

Contextual analysis can also involve examination of other sections of the constitution or related legislation. For example, Justice Scalia argued that the right to keep and bear arms is an "individual right," rather than one reserved for members of the militia. Scalia pointed out that "Nowhere else in the Constitution does a 'right' attributed to 'the people' refer to anything other than an individual right."[9]

Another example of contextual analysis can be found in the interpretation of the Fourth Amendment. The Fourth Amendment provides:

> The right of the people to be secure in their persons, houses, papers, and effects, against unreasonable searches and seizures, shall not be violated, and no Warrants shall issue, but upon probable cause, supported by Oath or affirmation, and particularly describing the place to be searched, and the person or things to be seized.

The first clause establishes, but does not define, a right against *unreasonable* searches and seizures. The second clause declares that search warrants should only be issued in situations where probable cause has been found and that these warrants must specifically describe the places to be searched and the items or persons to be seized. The obvious implication is that a search pursuant to a properly issued warrant based on probable cause is not an unreasonable search.

Sometimes judges even look to statutes to help resolve the meaning of a provision in the Constitution. Suppose, for example, prior to our last presidential election, someone had brought a suit challenging John McCain's eligibility to be President of the United States on the grounds that he was not a "natural born citizen," because he had been born on a military base in the Panama Canal Zone. An examination of Article II, Section 1 reveals the following relevant text:

> Article II, Section 1: "No person except a natural born Citizen, or a Citizen of the United States, at the time of the Adoption of this Constitution, shall be eligible to the Office of President."

"Natural born citizen" is not a commonly used or universally understood term in the English language and is not defined in Article II, Section 1. A search of other parts of the Constitution reveals that the first section of the Fourteenth

---

[8]Id. at 2790, n.3.
[9]Id. at 2790.

Amendment includes a definition of citizenship[10] but does not specify what it means to be a "natural born citizen." The Constitution does, however, contain a provision, Article I, Section 8, that gives Congress the power to establish a "uniform Rule of Naturalization." An examination of the statutes that Congress has passed in the exercise of this power reveals that Section 1403 of Title 8 of the U.S. Code states:

> Any person born in the Canal Zone on or after February 26, 1904, . . . whose father or mother or both at the time of the birth of such person was or is a citizen of the United States, is declared to be a citizen of the United States.

Therefore, while a reading of the Constitution alone might have led one to think that John McCain could not qualify to run for President, a search of the statutes that Congress has passed interpreting that language shows that indeed McCain, even though born in the Canal Zone, does qualify as a "natural born citizen."

3. Historical Analysis

In situations where contextual analysis does not resolve the textual ambiguities, judges will often utilize an historical analysis designed to identify either what the common understanding of words and phrases was at the time the constitutional provision was ratified or what the people who drafted the language were trying to accomplish. The first approach is popularly known as "originalism" or "semantic originalism." The second approach is often referred to as the "intent of the framers" approach. We will illustrate the difference between these two approaches by examining cases interpreting the Eighth Amendment.

> Excessive bail shall not be required, nor excessive fines imposed, nor cruel and unusual punishments inflicted.

The first part of this amendment prohibits *excessive* bail and *excessive* fines. We will return to these clauses later. At this point we focus our attention on the clause that prohibits the infliction of *cruel and unusual* punishments.

a. Originalism

The originalism approach holds that the Constitution should be interpreted to reflect what the average person thought it meant at the time the provision in question was adopted.[11] In applying this approach to cases involving the issue of capital punishment, one must seek to determine if the average person in 1791 considered the death penalty to be "cruel and unusual" punishment. Such an analysis strongly suggests that they did not because the death penalty was commonly used both before and for many years after the Eighth Amendment was adopted. Also, the Fifth Amendment (adopted at the same time as the Eighth) authorizes deprivation of life as long as there is due process.

---

[10] All persons born or naturalized in the United States, and subject to the jurisdiction thereof, are citizens of the United States and of the State wherein they reside.

[11] Justice Antonin Scalia is among the most prominent advocates for this approach.

While this approach works well when considering whether the Eighth Amendment prohibits all forms of the death penalty, it is far more difficult to apply it to determining the nature of the crimes to which the death penalty can be applied or the specific method used to bring about the condemned person's death.

Examples of originalism can also be found in the *Heller* case. The Court's majority employed an originalist approach when it asserted that the common understanding of keeping and bearing arms was that ordinary citizens had a right to possess and carry firearms so they could be ready at all times to defend their homes and the country. On the other hand, the Court's dissent disputed this assertion by citing a study that found that, of 115 references to the "bear arms" found in books disseminated in the period between the Declaration of Independence and the adoption of the Second Amendment, 110 of them clearly used it in a military context.[12]

b. Intent of the Framers

Another problem with the approach just discussed is that even if one limits the timeframe to when the Constitution was adopted, a term or phrase may mean different things to different people. A phrase may have one meaning for the educated middle class and yet another meaning among lower-class working people or to specific ethnic groups.

A second type of historical analysis focuses on the intentions of the elites rather than on the common understanding of the average person. When using this approach, judges seek to determine what the people who drafted and voted for the provision wanted to achieve through its adoption and then interpret the language in a way that is consistent with that objective.

As you can imagine, it is extremely difficult to determine what the framers actually intended. Judges may review the minutes of the Constitutional Convention, may examine the legislative history of the amendments, and may look at public statements made to convince others to vote for the provision in question, but different participants may have had different intentions.

A good example of this approach is found in the Supreme Court's cases involving the establishment of religion clause of the First Amendment. The exact wording used in the amendment is "Congress shall make no law respecting an establishment of religion."[13] Because the Constitution does not define what constitutes "an establishment of religion," and because there is no clear understanding as to what it meant to the ordinary person at that time, Supreme Court opinions in this area often discuss the presumed intentions of the men who drafted the First Amendment.

In these types of cases judges frequently quote from the writings of the men who drafted the sections that are being interpreted. For example, in *Reynolds v. United States,* the justices referred to Thomas Jefferson's letter to the Danbury Baptist Association as "an authoritative declaration of the scope and effect" of the First Amendment.[14] In that letter Jefferson penned his famous lines that the establishment clause built "a wall of separation between church and State." In

---

[12]Heller, 128 S. Ct. at 2790, n.9 (Stevens, JJ., dissenting).

[13]Due to the passage of the Fourteenth Amendment, this First Amendment protection has also been applied to the states. *See* discussion on pages 152-156.

[14]98 U.S. 145, 164 (1879).

Everson v. Board of Ed. of Ewing, Justice Black wrote, "In the words of Jefferson, the clause against establishment of religion by law was intended to erect 'a wall of separation between church and State.'"[15]

In *Lee v. Weisman* Justice Souter carefully examined the various House and Senate drafts of what was to become the First Amendment and concluded that "[t]he sequence of the Senate's treatment of this House proposal, and the House's response to the Senate, confirm that the Framers meant the Establishment Clause's prohibition to encompass nonpreferential aid to religion."[16] He also noted that "Jefferson necessarily condemned what, in modern terms, we call official endorsement of religion. He accordingly construed the Establishment Clause to forbid not simply state coercion, but also state endorsement, of religious belief and observance."[17] He noted that President Jefferson steadfastly refused to issue Thanksgiving proclamations of any kind because he thought they violated the religion clauses and cited a letter from Thomas Jefferson to Rev. S. Miller written in 1808.[18]

James Madison, who later became our second President, was also influential in drafting the First Amendment. In *Lee v. Weisman,* Souter quoted Madison as having concluded that "[r]eligious proclamations by the Executive recommending thanksgivings & fasts" violated the First Amendment because "the members of a Govt . . . can in no sense, be regarded as possessing an advisory trust from their Constituents in their religious capacities."[19]

A problem with this approach is that while the primary drafters, Jefferson and Madison, may have intended to create a clear separation between church and state, other legislators who voted to adopt the First Amendment may have only intended to prohibit the practice of having the government favor one religious group over other religious groups. Opponents of the strict separation of church and state point out that the early Presidents included religious messages in their inaugural and Thanksgiving Day addresses. In his dissent in *Lee v. Weisman,* Justice Scalia declared:

> From our Nation's origin, prayer has been a prominent part of governmental ceremonies and proclamations. The Declaration of Independence, the document marking our birth as a separate people, "appealed to the Supreme Judge of the world for the rectitude of our intentions" and avowed "a firm reliance on the protection of divine Providence." In his first inaugural address, after swearing his oath of office on a Bible, George Washington deliberately made a prayer a part of his first official act as President.[20]

In response, Justice Souter countered:

> To be sure, the leaders of the young Republic engaged in some of the practices that separationists like Jefferson and Madison criticized. The First Congress did hire institutional chaplains, and Presidents Washington and Adams unapologetically marked days of "public thanksgiving and prayer." Yet in the face of the separationist dissent,

---

[15]330 U.S. 1, 16 (1947).

[16]505 U.S. 577, 613 (1992).

[17]Id at 623.

[18]Id.

[19]Id. at 624-25 (quoting James Madison, "Detached Memoranda" at 558).

[20]Id. at 633 (Scalia, JJ., dissenting).

those practices prove, at best, that the Framers simply did not share a common understanding of the establishment clause, and, at worst, that they, like other politicians, could raise constitutional ideals one day and turn their backs on them the next.[21]

4. Living/Evolving Constitution

So far, we have looked at three different approaches courts use to help resolve ambiguous words and phrases found in constitutions. When literal and contextual approaches do not resolve the ambiguity, judges turn to the historical record in an effort to find either the "original understanding" of the words or the intent of those who drafted them. All of these approaches are based on the assumption that the constitution has a fixed meaning that does not change from one decade to another.

Advocates of what is variously called the "living constitution," the "evolving constitution," or the "subjective intent" approach believe the constitution was intentionally designed to be able to change with the times. They assert that terms like "unreasonable searches and seizures," "due process of law," and "equal protection of the laws" were designed to identify fundamental values rather than specific rules, and that it is the proper task of contemporary judges to apply these fundamental values to changing circumstances.[22]

Take, for example, the Fourth Amendment prohibition against *unreasonable* searches and seizures. In 1791, when the amendment was ratified, its drafters and the common man of the times were thinking of situations in which police or soldiers would physically enter a house and look through a person's possessions and private papers. Of course they had no way of knowing that, 200 years later, there would be miniature cameras and microphones that could be secretly hidden in a person's house and thermo-imaging devices that could practically look though walls. In light of these new developments, how should the Fourth Amendment's prohibition against unreasonable searches be interpreted?

In 1929, in the context of deciding if a federal prosecutor could use evidence obtained from electronic eavesdropping on private telephone conversations, Justice Brandeis wrote:

> When the Fourth and Fifth Amendments were adopted, "the form that evil had theretofore taken," had been necessarily simple. Force and violence were then the only means known to man by which a Government could directly effect self-incrimination. It could compel the individual to testify—a compulsion effected, if need be, by torture. It could secure possession of his papers and other articles incident to his private life—a seizure effected, if need be, by breaking and entry. Protection against such invasion of "the sanctities of a man's home and the privacies of life" was provided in the Fourth and Fifth Amendments by specific language . . . .

> Moreover, "in the application of a constitution, our contemplation cannot be only of what has been but of what may be." The progress of science in furnishing the Government with means of espionage is not likely to stop with wire-tapping. Ways may some day be developed by which the Government, without removing papers from

---

[21]Id. at 626.

[22]Advocates of this approach include prominent legal scholars such as Ronald Dworkin and Lawrence Tribe, and Supreme Court Justices such as William Brennan, Thurgood Marshall, and Stephen Breyer.

secret drawers, can reproduce them in court, and by which it will be enabled to expose to a jury the most intimate occurrences of the home.[23]

Justice Brandeis's position was rejected by a majority of the Court, which ruled that the Fourth Amendment only applied to physical trespass. However, seventy-three years later, when deciding if it was a violation of the Fourth Amendment for government agents to use a thermal-imaging device (a method not in general public use) aimed at a private home from a public street for the purpose of detecting evidence of a crime, Justice Scalia wrote:

> It would be foolish to contend that the degree of privacy secured to citizens by the Fourth Amendment has been entirely unaffected by the advance of technology. For example, as the cases discussed above make clear, the technology enabling human flight has exposed to public view (and hence, we have said, to official observation) uncovered portions of the house and its curtilage that once were private . . . . The question we confront today is what limits there are upon this power of technology to shrink the realm of guaranteed privacy.[24]

The Court concluded that the government use of thermo-imaging technology had violated the Fourth Amendment.

Another striking application of the living/evolving constitution approach can be found in cases interpreting the equal protection clause of the Fourteenth Amendment. This clause reads, "Nor shall any State . . . deny to any person within its jurisdiction the equal protection of the laws."

A literal reading does not provide an understanding of what the "equal protection of the laws" means. The dictionary defines "equal" as having the same capability, quantity, or effect as another, as in equal strength or equal weight, but what does it mean to assert that a state cannot deny equal protection of its laws. Does it mean that governments must always treat everyone the same way? If so, it would appear to void any law that makes a distinction in how different classes of people are treated. But governments set different rules for different types of people all the time. Consider how little children, teenagers, and adults are treated differently for such things as curfews, consumption of alcohol and tobacco, driving automobiles, and voting.

DISCUSSION QUESTION

3. Read the Fourteenth Amendment again. Under its provisions, do you think men can be drafted into military service without equal numbers of women also being drafted? If so, how do you justify that distinction? Also, do you think the government could force people of different races to eat in different restaurants as long as the food selection, prices, and service were equal? Why or why not?

Use of a contextual analysis reveals that the equal protection clause was part of a set of three amendments that all sprang from the Civil War conflict.

---

[23]Olmstead v. United States, 277 U.S. 438, 473 (1929).
[24]Kyllo v. United States, 533 U.S. 27 (2002).

The Thirteenth Amendment abolished slavery and involuntary servitude. The Fourteenth Amendment

- made the former slaves citizens of the United States and states wherein they resided;
- prohibited states from abridging the privileges or immunities of citizens of the United States;
- prohibited states from depriving any person of life, liberty, or property without due process of law; and
- prohibited states from denying any person within its jurisdiction of the equal protection of the laws.

The Fifteenth Amendment prohibited denial of the right to vote on the basis of race, color, or previous condition of servitude.

But while contextual analysis thus suggests that the equal protection clause was designed to protect newly freed slaves, there is nothing in the wording of the amendment that would limit its application to situations in which distinctions are based on having been a slave. The right to equal protection of the law can be seen as protecting all persons within the jurisdiction of the states.

Furthermore, even in the context of race-based distinctions, it is not clear what the equal protection clause actually requires. In 1896, the U.S. Supreme Court in *Plessy v. Ferguson*[25] developed the "separate but equal" concept to explain its ruling that as long as everyone could ride in a railway car that was "equal" to others on the same train, it did not violate the equal protection clause for a state to require "colored people" to be segregated from "whites" riding in railway cars traveling within the state. On the other hand, in 1954, a very different Supreme Court rejected the application of the separate but equal doctrine to the field of public education and ruled that the equal protection clause prohibited states from segregating public schools on the basis of the race of the students attending them.

As you read the following excerpts from Chief Justice Earl Warren's landmark opinion in *Brown v. Board of Education,* pay special attention to his discussion of various approaches to interpreting the meaning of the equal protection clause.

Brown v. Board of Education of Topeka
SUPREME COURT OF THE UNITED STATES
347 U.S. 483 (1954)

Mr. Chief Justice WARREN delivered the opinion of the Court.

These cases come to us from the States of Kansas, South Carolina, Virginia, and Delaware. They are premised on different facts and different local conditions, but a common legal question justifies their consideration together in this consolidated opinion.

[25]163 U.S. 537. *See* discussion from Chapter 2 on page 22.

In each of the cases, minors of the Negro race, through their legal representatives, seek the aid of the courts in obtaining admission to the public schools of their community on a nonsegregated basis.... The plaintiffs contend that segregated public schools are not "equal" and cannot be made "equal," and that hence they are deprived of the equal protection of the laws....

[A review of the historical records surrounding the adoption of the Fourteenth Amendment] convince us that, although these sources cast some light, it is not enough to resolve the problem with which we are faced. At best, they are inconclusive. The most avid proponents of the post-War Amendments undoubtedly intended them to remove all legal distinctions among "all persons born or naturalized in the United States." Their opponents, just as certainly, were antagonistic to both the letter and the spirit of the Amendments and wished them to have the most limited effect. What others in Congress and the state legislatures had in mind cannot be determined with any degree of certainty.

An additional reason for the inconclusive nature of the Amendment's history, with respect to segregated schools, is the status of public education at that time. In the South, the movement toward free common schools, supported by general taxation, had not yet taken hold. Education of white children was largely in the hands of private groups. Education of Negroes was almost nonexistent, and practically all of the race were illiterate. In fact, any education of Negroes was forbidden by law in some states.... It is true that public school education at the time of the Amendment had advanced further in the North, but the effect of the Amendment on Northern States was generally ignored in the congressional debates.... As a consequence, it is not surprising that there should be so little in the history of the Fourteenth Amendment relating to its intended effect on public education.

In the first cases in this Court construing the Fourteenth Amendment, decided shortly after its adoption, the Court interpreted it as proscribing all state-imposed discriminations against the Negro race. The doctrine of "separate but equal" did not make its appearance in this Court until 1896 in the case of *Plessy v. Ferguson*, involving not education but transportation....

In the instant cases, ... there are findings ... that the Negro and white schools involved have been equalized, or are being equalized, with respect to buildings, curricula, qualifications and salaries of teachers, and other "tangible" factors. Our decision, therefore, cannot turn on merely a comparison of these tangible factors in the Negro and white schools involved in each of the cases. We must look instead to the effect of segregation itself on public education.

In approaching this problem, we cannot turn the clock back to 1868 when the Amendment was adopted, or even to 1896 when *Plessy v. Ferguson* was written. We must consider public education in the light of its full development and its present place in American life throughout the Nation. Only in this way can it be determined if segregation in public schools deprives these plaintiffs of the equal protection of the laws.

Today, education is perhaps the most important function of state and local governments. Compulsory school attendance laws and the great expenditures for education both demonstrate our recognition of the importance of education to our democratic society. It is required in the performance of our most basic public responsibilities, even service in the armed forces. It is the very foundation of good citizenship. Today it is a principal instrument in awakening the child to cultural values, in preparing him for later professional training, and in helping him to adjust normally to his environment. In these days, it is doubtful that any child may reasonably be expected to succeed in life if he is denied the opportunity of an education. Such an opportunity, where the state has undertaken to provide it, is a right which must be made available to all on equal terms.

We come then to the question presented: Does segregation of children in public schools solely on the basis of race, even though the physical facilities and other "tangible" factors may be equal, deprive the children of the minority group of equal educational opportunities? We believe that it does.

... To separate [school children] from others of similar age and qualifications solely because of their race generates a feeling of inferiority as to their status in the community that may affect their hearts and minds in a way unlikely ever to be undone. The effect of this separation on their educational opportunities was well stated by a finding in the Kansas case by a court which nevertheless felt compelled to rule against the Negro plaintiffs:

> "Segregation of white and colored children in public schools has a detrimental effect upon the colored children. The impact is greater when it has the sanction of the law; for the policy of separating the races is usually interpreted as denoting the inferiority of the negro group. A sense of inferiority affects the motivation of a child to learn. Segregation with the sanction of law, therefore, has a tendency to the educational and mental development of negro children and to deprive them of some of the benefits they would receive in a racial[ly] integrated school system."

Whatever may have been the extent of psychological knowledge at the time of *Plessy v. Ferguson,* this finding is amply supported by modern authority. Any language in *Plessy v. Ferguson* contrary to this finding is rejected.

We conclude that in the field of public education the doctrine of "separate but equal" has no place. Separate educational facilities are inherently unequal. Therefore, we hold that the plaintiffs and others similarly situated for whom the actions have been brought are, by reason of the segregation complained of, deprived of the equal protection of the laws guaranteed by the Fourteenth Amendment . . . . It is so ordered.

CASE DISCUSSION QUESTIONS

1. Why does Chief Justice Warren believe the case cannot be resolved by looking at the historical records that surrounded the adoption of the Fourteenth Amendment? On what body of authority does he rely instead?

2. Do you agree with the approach followed by Justice Warren or do you think one of the other approaches we have discussed would have been more appropriate for interpreting the meaning of the equal protection clause?

B. DIVISION OF POWERS

Having covered the major methods used for interpreting ambiguous constitutional words and phrases, we now move on to a discussion of the most important substantive constitutional principles and some of the cases that have applied these principles.

As discussed in Chapter 2, one of the major functions of the Constitution is to allocate governmental powers—between the states and the federal government and within the federal government. The allocation of power between the states and the federal government raises the issue of federalism, while that of the allocation of power within the federal government raises issues of separation of powers and checks and balances.

1. Federalism

As noted earlier, one of the most significant features of the U.S. Constitution was the creation of a federalist system of government in which governmental powers are divided between a national/central government and the state/regional governments. The Constitution specifically delegates key powers, such

Federalism
A system of government in which the authority to govern is split between a single, nationwide central government and several regional governments that control specific geographical areas.

as the power to levy taxes, declare war, raise armies, and regulate interstate and foreign commerce, to the national government, and in the Tenth Amendment reserves all others "to the states and to the people."

In the early years of our nation, there was a debate over whether the Constitution should be viewed as a creation of the states or of the people themselves. The Preamble[26] declares that it is being established by the people, but the ratification of the document was based on the actions of the states. This debate became an important part of the conflicts between Northern and Southern states leading up to the Civil War.[27] When the federal government passed laws that Southern states opposed, the leaders of some of these states developed the doctrines of nullification and secession. Those who believed in nullification thought that states could refuse to accept or enforce federal laws they viewed as incompatible with the existence of the Union. They furthermore contended that a belief in the right of secession meant that individual states could withdraw from the Union. Both of these concepts were based on the theory that the Constitution was a pact among the states, rather than a creation of the people. These issues were eventually settled by force of arms, when President Lincoln refused to accept the Southern states' attempts to secede. After the Civil War was over, the U.S. Supreme Court ruled in *Texas v. White* that once a state has joined the Union, the relationship is "perpetual and indissoluble."[28]

a. Roles of the Federal and State Governments

The Constitution lists the following as the primary responsibilities of the federal government:

- guaranteeing a republican form of government,
- protecting the people from Indians, foreign invasion and internal insurrections (including declaring war and raising and regulating armies, navies, and the militia),
- regulating commerce with foreign nations and among the several states and Indian Tribes,
- establishing uniform rules of naturalization and bankruptcies,
- coining money and regulating its value,
- fixing standards of weights and measures,
- establishing post offices and post roads, and
- promoting the progress of science and useful arts by granting patents and copyrights.

Rather than listing either the states' responsibilities or their powers, the Constitution simply lists things that states are prohibited from doing. The list of prohibitions on state activities includes the following:

- entering into treaties or alliances,
- coining money and emitting bills of credit,

---

[26]"We the People of the United States, . . . do ordain and establish this Constitution for the United States of America."

[27]Alternatively referred to as the "War between the States."

[28]74 U.S. 700 (1869).

- passing bills of attainder, passing ex post facto laws, impairing the obligation of contracts, or granting titles of nobility, and
- imposing duties on imports or exports, keeping troops, or engaging in war without the consent of Congress.

Finally, the Tenth Amendment states:

> The powers not delegated to the United States by the Constitution, nor prohibited by it to the States, are reserved to the States respectively, or to the people.

Based on what is commonly called the "state police power," states have a residual power to protect the health, welfare, safety, and morals of their citizens. Because it is hard to think of an action that would not be considered relevant to the health, welfare, safety, or morals of the people, this means that states can legislate in any area not explicitly prohibited by the Constitution.

b. Implied Powers

When analyzing the powers of the federal government, it is important to note that at the end of the list of the powers delegated to the federal government in Article I, Section 8, the Constitution states that Congress has the power "to make all Laws which shall be necessary and proper for carrying into Execution the foregoing Powers, and all other Powers vested by this Constitution in the Government of the United States, or in any Department or Officer thereof." As you will recall from our discussion in Chapter 3 on page 41, this so-called necessary and proper clause is the basis for what is known as the "**doctrine of implied powers.**"

Starting with *McCulloch v. Maryland*,[29] when the U.S. Supreme Court held that Congress could create and operate national banks even though the Constitution did not explicitly delegate this power to Congress, the Court has broadly interpreted the necessary and proper clause. This gives Congress the power to take actions not specifically listed in the constitution but which are reasonably related to carrying out specifically delegated powers.

However, even this broad granting of federal power has limits. In *McCulloch,* the Court also noted:

> Should congress, in the execution of its powers, adopt measures which are prohibited by the constitution; or should congress, under the pretext of executing its powers, pass laws for the accomplishment of objects not intrusted to the government; it would become the painful duty of this tribunal, should a case requiring such a decision come before it, to say, that such an act was not the law of the land.[30]

An example of such a case occurred in 1972 when the Court had to determine the constitutionality of a federal statute governing low-level radioactive waste. In that statute Congress had attempted to compel states to develop regulations regarding the disposal of radioactive waste generated within their

Doctrine of implied powers
Powers that are not stated in the Constitution but which are necessary for Congress to carry out other, expressly granted powers.

---

[29]17 U.S. 316 (1819).
[30]Id. at 423.

borders. The Court held that while Congress itself could regulate in the area of radioactive waste disposal, the constitution does not give Congress the power to compel states to regulate in any particular way.[31]

c. The Commerce Power

In addition to the necessary and proper clause, the commerce clause has been the basis for a broad range of federal laws. The commerce clause provides, "Congress shall have power to regulate commerce with foreign nations and among the several states and Indian Tribes." As you will recall from Chapter 3, pages 41–42, the Supreme Court has interpreted this clause as giving the federal government the authority not only to regulate products that actually travel in interstate commerce but also to regulate anything that has an "effect upon" interstate commerce.

Congress used this expansive interpretation of its commerce power in the 1930s when it passed extensive New Deal legislation in order to address the economic crisis brought on by the stock market crash of 1929 and the ensuing Great Depression. For example, Congress created new federal entities, such as the National Labor Relations Board, and promoted economic recovery through legislation, such as the Unfair Labor Standards Act. Then in the 1960s, Congress relied upon the commerce clause as its constitutional justification for the passage of the 1964 Civil Rights Act provisions making it unlawful to discriminate in a place of public accommodation on the basis of race, color, religion, sex, or national origin. The Supreme Court endorsed this approach in *Heart of Atlanta Motel, Inc. v. United States,* where it held that the law was within the scope of the commerce clause because the existence of racially discriminatory practices made it more difficult for racial minorities to travel from one state to another and that this in turn had a negative impact on the free flow of interstate commerce.[32] In a related case, the Court found that even a small, local, family-owned restaurant catering to local customers had enough of an impact on interstate commerce to justify Congress's actions in prohibiting discrimination.[33]

From the 1960s through the 1990s, this expansive reading of the commerce clause continued. This allowed Congress to address a wide range of social problems through federal statutes. It was not until the 1995 case of *United States v. Lopez*[34] that the U.S. Supreme Court began striking down federal statutes on the basis that they had exceeded congressional power under the interstate commerce clause.

In *Lopez,* the Court reversed a conviction under a federal statute that made it a federal crime to possess a firearm in a school zone. The Court found that the interstate commerce clause did not give the federal government authority to regulate the possession of guns on public school grounds because Congress had failed to show a sufficient connection between the unlawful possession of guns near schools and an economic impact on interstate commerce. Five years later, in *United States v. Morrison,*[35] the Supreme Court struck down a federal statute,

---

[31]New York v. U.S. 505 U.S. 144 (1992).

[32]379 U.S. 241 (1964).

[33]Katzenback v. McClung, 379 U.S. 294 (1964).

[34]514 U.S. 549 (1995).

[35]529 U.S. 598 (2000).

the Violence Against Women Act of 1994, aimed at protecting women from acts of criminal violence, holding that Congress had exceeded its powers under the commerce clause. The Court held that Congress had overstepped its powers because gender-motivated crimes were not the kind of *economic* activity that Congress has the power to regulate.[36]

Many commentators thought the *Lopez* and *Morrison* decisions signaled the Court's return to a more conservative judicial philosophy that stressed the limitations of federal powers and the preservation of states' rights. But then in 2005, as you saw from your reading of *Gonzales v. Raich,*[37] in Chapter 3, on pages 42–44, the Court held that the commerce clause gave the federal government the power to prohibit the cultivation and use of marijuana, even when the marijuana was grown and used within a single state for medical purposes, pursuant to a physician's orders and authorized by state law. The Court reasoned that the marijuana used for local, medicinal purposes could find its way into the interstate market and therefore had an economic effect on interstate commerce.[38]

d. Preemption

As we discussed in Chapter 3 on pages 45–46, the **preemption** doctrine allows the federal government to prevent the states from passing laws that conflict with federal laws, and in some cases even prohibits states from passing any laws on a particular subject. However, in areas generally preempted by federal law, if there are areas left unregulated, the states may still enact "gap filler" legislation. In addition, if a state law would not conflict with federal law, nor unreasonably burden interstate commerce, it may coexist with federal laws. For example, as we have seen, Title VII, a federal statute, prohibits employers from discriminating on the basis of race, sex, color, religion, or national origin. While no state may allow such discrimination, states may create more stringent standards, such as stating that in addition to the above-listed categories no employer may discriminate on the basis of sexual orientation.

Preemption
The power of the federal government to prevent the states from passing conflicting laws, and sometimes even to prohibit states from passing any laws on a particular subject.

e. Relations among the States

In addition to defining the relationship between the national government and the state governments, the Constitution also contains provisions relating to the relationship among the states. Article IV, Section 1 states, "Full Faith and Credit shall be given in each State to the public Acts, Records, and judicial Proceedings of every other State." For example, if someone has won a judgment in a court in one state, it should be enforceable against a person who has moved to a different state.

In recent years, several states have authorized marriages, "civil unions," or "domestic partnerships" between two people of the same sex.[39] These actions

---

[36]Id. at 618.

[37]545 U.S. 1 (2005).

[38]Noting the "troubling facts" of the case, in which Raich's physician had testified that "forgoing cannabis treatments would certainly cause Raich excruciating pain and could very well prove fatal, the Court emphasized it was ruling only on the constitutionality of Congress's actions, not on the wisdom of those actions. Id. at 9.

[39]As of the time this section was written, the Supreme Courts of Hawaii, Massachusetts, California, and Connecticut had all ruled that their state constitutions allowed same-sex couples to marry. However,

have set the stage for a future legal battle regarding the recognition of these legal relationships by other states. Can states that have laws limiting marriage to a union of a man and a woman be forced to recognize a same-sex couple married in Massachusetts or Connecticut? If a same-sex couple formed a "civil union" that guaranteed them the same rights and benefits as married couples, would other states to which they might move also have to provide them with the same rights and benefits as married couples?

Although a literal reading of the Full Faith and Credit clause would seem to require states to accept marriages that were considered valid in the state in which they were performed, the courts have also developed a judicial doctrine that recognizes an exception to this general rule when the action in question is contrary to the public policy of the state that is being asked to accept the action of another state. Examples would include the acceptance of common law marriages and the degree of kinship involved in marriages with cousins. On this basis, a state that specifically rejected same-sex marriages might be able to refuse to accept one that occurred in another state.[40]

The second section of Article IV provides additional interpretive challenges. It provides, "The citizens of each state shall be entitled to all privileges and immunities of citizens in the several states." The first problem presented by this section is that the Constitution does not define the terms "privileges" and "immunities." Over the years, the courts have held that these privileges and immunities include a right to pass through or reside in other states for purposes of a trade or profession.[41] However, states can charge nonresidents more for some state privileges, such as college tuition or sporting licenses.[42]

DISCUSSION QUESTION

4. Some writers have suggested that Article IV, Section 2 could be used to protect the rights of same-sex couples that were married or that formed civil unions in other states. What do you think? If a person is married in Massachusetts should Mississippi be required to recognize that marriage? If not, what does this say about ours being a *United* States?

Separation of powers
The division of governmental power among the legislative, executive, and judicial branches.

2. Separation of Powers

In addition to allocating governmental powers between the federal and the state governments, the Constitution divides the federal government into three separate branches: legislative, executive, and judicial. The Constitution specifies the eligibility criteria for serving in various positions in these branches[43] and lists the powers that are allocated to each branch.

---

constitutional amendments to limit marriage to situations involving one man and one woman were later passed in Hawaii and California. California, Connecticut, New Hampshire, New Jersey, Oregon, and Vermont have all passed civil union/domestic partnership laws that grant same-sex couples legal rights that are similar to those of married couples. *See* Chapter 11, pages 398–405.

[40]*See* cases such as DeSanto v. Barnsley, 476 A.2d 952 (Pa. Super. 1984); Brogan v. Brogen, 261 N.W.2d 606 (Minn. 1977); and In re Estate of Bivians, 652 P.2d 744 (N.M. 1982).

[41]Corfield v. Coryell, 6 Fed. Cases 3230 (1823).

[42]Vlandis v. Kline, 412 U.S. 441 (1973).

[43]*See* discussion of criteria to serve as President on page 131–132.

Although the Constitution contains separate lists of powers for each of the three branches of government, some of these powers are overlapping. In effect the Constitution creates a system of separate branches exercising shared powers. It is this sharing of powers that creates our system of **checks and balances.** In the Federalist Papers, James Madison explained that this system of checks and balances was designed to guard against "a gradual concentration of the several powers in the same department." Thus, while Congress is given the power to make laws, the President is given the power to veto them. While the executive branch is responsible for administering the law, only Congress can provide for the appropriate funding in the budget.

DISCUSSION QUESTION

5. It is sometimes said that separation of powers is a misnomer. Why do you think that is?

a. Legislative Branch

The legislative branch consists of the House of Representatives and the Senate. Collectively, they are known as the Congress. In addition to vesting all legislative powers in the Congress, the Constitution also assigned it the following tasks:

- authorizing governmental expenditures,
- proposing amendments to the constitution,
- counting the ballots of the Electoral College and breaking ties if they occur;
- impeaching Presidents, Vice Presidents, and "all civil officers of the United States," and
- approving presidential appointments for judges, heads of federal agencies, and other high-level federal officials.

Although they are not specifically listed in the Constitution, it has long been recognized that, based on English tradition, the legislature also has the power to investigate matters relevant to the operation of the government and to imprison people for contempt for such things as disrupting the legislative chamber, attempting to bribe members of Congress, and refusing to testify before Congress after having been properly served.

b. Executive Branch

Article II begins with the declaration that "The executive power shall be vested in a President of the United States of America." The general executive powers include the power to appoint (with the advice and consent of the Senate) "ambassadors, other public ministers and consuls, judges of the Supreme Court, and all other officers of the United States, whose appointments are not herein otherwise provided for, and which shall be established by law; but the Congress may by law vest the appointment of such inferior officers, as they think proper, in the President alone, in the courts of law, or in the heads of departments."

Related to this general executive power are the doctrines of **executive privilege** and **presidential immunity.** The former is the right to be able to keep

Executive privilege
A legal doctrine that exempts some members of the executive branch from having to disclose information in situations where nondisclosure is deemed necessary to the discharge of executive responsibilities.

Presidential immunity
A legal doctrine that exempts the President of the United States from being criminally prosecuted or from being civilly sued for actions taken as President.

certain types of information confidential and to be able to protect some levels of subordinates from being required to testify before Congress. A claim of presidential immunity involves an assertion that the President cannot be criminally prosecuted or have a civil action brought against him or her for actions taken as President. Both doctrines are justified on the basis that they are necessary for the President to effectively carry out the duties of the office.

Both executive privilege and presidential immunity were raised during the Watergate scandal when President Richard Nixon was named an "unindicted coconspirator," and a Special Prosecutor subpoenaed recorded tapes of presidential conversations. In *U.S. v. Nixon,* the Supreme Court rejected Nixon's claim of executive privilege because his claim was not based on protection of military or diplomatic secrets.[44] The question of whether he could be criminally prosecuted for his attempts to cover up the White House scandal became moot when his successor, Gerald Ford, granted Nixon a pardon for any actions he had taken while President.

The question of a President's immunity from civil suit was addressed by the Supreme Court in 1982 in *Nixon v. Fitzgerald.*[45] In a 5-4 decision the Court ruled that Richard Nixon had absolute (as opposed to qualified) immunity from a civil action brought by a former federal employee who alleged that he had been fired for his "whistle blowing" testimony. The majority argued that absolute immunity was necessary to ensure that the President was not timid or hesitant to carry out his constitutional duties for fear of civil liability.

In 1997, the Supreme Court was called upon to decide if then-President Bill Clinton was immune from a sexual harassment civil suit by Paula Jones for acts that allegedly took place before he became President.[46] The Court ruled that President Clinton was not immune from Ms. Jones's suit because he had not established that the burdens of responding to the litigation would impair the effective performance of his presidential duties.[47]

As part of our checks and balances system, the Constitution gives the President a "qualified veto" power over legislation passed by Congress. It is classified as qualified (as opposed to absolute) because a presidential veto can be overridden by a two-thirds vote of both the House and the Senate. Whereas the governors of some states have a "line item veto" that allows them to strike down parts of a bill while still allowing other parts to become law, the President must either accept or veto the entire bill.[48]

In the past few years, the practice of Presidents stating constitutional objections in "**signing statements**" has become a controversial political and constitutional issue. While the practice of Presidents issuing a statement that comments on a law they are signing goes back to the early nineteenth century, these signing statements typically focused either on defining vague terms or on mobilizing political constituencies. However, starting in the 1980s, President Ronald Reagan and his successors began using these signing statements not only

Signing statement
A written pronouncement issued by the President at the time a bill is signed into law.

---

[44]418 U.S. 683 (1974).

[45]457 U.S. 731.

[46]Ms. Jones alleged that her state job duties had been changed and that she had suffered hostile treatment after she rejected sexual advances from Bill Clinton when he was governor of Arkansas.

[47]Clinton v. Jones, 520 U.S. 681 (1997). Before the case went to trial, Bill Clinton, without admitting any liability, agreed to settle the lawsuit for $850,000.

[48]Some governors even have an amendatory veto that allows them to make changes in parts of the bill.

to express constitutional objections to parts of the law but also to declare that parts of the law did not need to be enforced as they were written.[49]

This practice appears to be a strategy for creating a de facto line item veto, even though the Constitution does not allow for one. In 2006, a task force of the American Bar Association asserted that it was "contrary to the rule of law and our constitutional system of separation of powers" to use signing statements to modify the meaning of duly enacted laws.[50] The practice certainly contradicts the provision in Article II, Section 3, which requires the President to "take care that the laws be faithfully executed." In *Hamdan v. Rumsfeld*,[51] the opinion of the Court appears to not give any weight to a signing statement attached to the Detainee Treatment Act of 2005. However, as of the writing of this text, the courts have not yet ruled directly on the constitutionality of this practice.

Another key area of conflict between the executive and legislative branches involves military involvement in nondeclared wars. Article II, Section 2 reads, "The President shall be Commander and Chief of the army and navy of the United States, and of the militia of the several states, when called into the actual service of the United States," while Congress is given the power to "declare war, grant Letters of Marque and Reprisal, and make Rules concerning Captures on Land and Water" in Article I, Section 8 (11). Several scholars have concluded that the original understanding of this clause was to give Congress the power to "commence" war, whether formally declared or not.[52]

In practice, Presidents have frequently committed U.S. military forces to armed conflict without Congress having declared a war. The only armed conflicts for which Congress officially declared a war were the War of 1812 and the Spanish-American War of 1898. In the Mexican War of 1846 and World Wars I and II, Congress officially recognized that a state of war already existed. For the wars in Korea, Vietnam, and Iraq, Congress passed various resolutions of support rather than issuing a formal declaration of war.

Through the years there have been many attempts to get the U.S. Supreme Court to limit the President's war powers and to require a formal declaration of war, but due to the justiciability issues discussed in the next section, the courts have consistently avoided ruling on this issue.[53]

c. Judicial Branch

Article III states that "The judicial power of the United States shall be vested in one supreme court, and in such inferior courts as the Congress may from time to time, ordain and establish." The judicial power referred to in the Constitution includes the power to decide cases and controversies, the power to issue writs, the contempt power, and the power to make rules that govern

---

[49]According to a 2007 study by the Congressional Research Service, 34 percent of Reagan's signing statements contained objections to one or more provisions of the statute. Comparable figures for his successors were 47 percent for George H. W. Bush, 18 percent for William J. Clinton, and 78 percent for George W. Bush.

[50]American Bar Association press release, "Blue-Ribbon Task Force Finds President Bush's Signing Statements Undermine Separation of Powers," July 24, 2006.

[51]548 U.S. 557 (2006).

[52]*See* Charles A. Lofgren, "War-Making under the Constitution: The Original Understanding," 81 Yale L.J. 672 (1972).

[53]*See, e.g.,* Dellums v. Bush, 752 F. Supp. 1141 (D.D.C. 1990).

judicial proceedings. The various courts that Congress has established and how they relate to other courts in the state and federal systems was discussed in Chapter 4.

Since the courts have neither the power of the purse (which rests with the legislature), nor that of the sword (which rests in the executive branch), Alexander Hamilton wrote in *Federalist* No. 78 that the judiciary was the weakest of the three departments of power. However, as a result of our common law tradition and the doctrine of judicial review,[54] the courts in this country have far more power and influence than do those in most other countries.

John Marshall, one of our greatest jurists, was able to lay the foundation for this strong judiciary without provoking destructive confrontations. In *Marbury v. Madison* (discussed in Chapter 2 on pages 25–26), he successfully established the doctrine of judicial review without giving his political opponents the opportunity to defy the Supreme Court's ruling.[55]

Judicial self-restraint
A self-imposed restraint that judges exercise to avoid having to decide controversial issues and political confrontations.

One of the reasons for the wide acceptance of the doctrine of judicial review is that, throughout our nation's history, judges have exercised what is called **judicial self-restraint**. Judges have avoided direct confrontations with other branches of government on politically volatile issues by narrowly limiting standing to sue, strictly enforcing the case or controversy rule, refusing to deal with "political questions," and delaying a decision until the political climate has cooled down.

Justiciable controversy
A court case involving parties with opposing interests that will be personally affected by the court's decision.

The requirement of **justiciability** is based on the wording of Article III, Section 2 where it states that "The judicial power shall extend to all Cases . . ." and "to controversies . . . ." This is interpreted as requiring the controversy to be definite and concrete rather than abstract or theoretical. Therefore, the federal courts refuse to give advisory opinions and require there to be a true controversy between parties that are in an adversarial relationship.[56]

Standing to sue doctrine
The requirement that a potential litigant have a sufficient stake in the outcome of the case before being accepted as a party in the case.

In addition to being in an adversarial relationship, **standing** requires that the litigants have a personal stake in the outcome of the case. Thus, even though you might be passionately against capital punishment, you would not have standing to challenge it in court unless you had been convicted of a capital offense and already been given a death sentence.[57]

An interesting case illustrating the importance of standing involved an attempt to challenge a public school district's practice of beginning each school day with a recitation of the Pledge of Allegiance on the basis that the inclusion of the phrase "under God" violated the establishment of religion clause of the First Amendment.[58] The plaintiff in the case, Michael Newdow, filed suit on behalf of his daughter, who was an elementary school student in the district. (Because minors are not allowed to file suits on their own, their legal guardians are allowed to do so on their behalf.) In this case Newdow shared physical custody

---

[54]*See* discussion of judicial review in Chapter 2 on page 25.

[55]It is widely thought that Madison would have ignored the writ of mandamus if it had been issued. However, by ruling that the Supreme Court lacked authority to issue the writ, Marshall left Madison and Jefferson without any effective way to dispute the Court's ruling.

[56]The plaintiff and the defendant cannot be seeking the same result or making the same arguments.

[57]While people who are not personally affected do not have standing to sue, they may, in some situations, be able to participate in the litigation by providing financial support to litigants that do have standing or by filing amicus briefs.

[58]*See* pages 132–135 and 165–170 for a discussion of this clause.

of his daughter with her mother, but the mother had exclusive legal custody. By ruling that shared physical custody was insufficient to authorize filing a suit on behalf of a minor, the Supreme Court dismissed the case for lack of standing and therefore avoided ruling on the controversial establishment of religion question.

DISCUSSION QUESTION

6. The standing doctrine requires that the plaintiff be personally affected by the action he or she is challenging. Do you think a taxpayer should be deemed to have standing to challenge government expenditures such as for building roads and bridges, for special education programs, or for sex education programs? Why or why not?

The **political question doctrine** is another example of judicial self-restraint. Cases are typically considered political questions when there is a lack of objective criteria by which to decide the case or when the nature of the decision is one that belongs to one of the other branches of government. This doctrine is typically invoked in cases involving foreign policy and war powers.

The following excerpt from *Corrie v. Caterpillar* is an example of a case in which the defendant sought to have a suit dismissed on the grounds that the political question doctrine prevented this type of case from being heard in federal court. The plaintiffs filed the suit after their family members were killed or injured when the Israeli Defense Forces (IDF) demolished homes in the Palestinian Territories. They named Caterpillar, Inc., as a defendant because the IDF had used bulldozers manufactured by this U.S.-based company.

Political question doctrine

The practice of not deciding cases in situations where their resolution is committed to another branch of government or because those issues are not capable of judicial resolution.

Corrie v. Caterpillar, Inc.
United States Court of Appeals for the Ninth Circuit
503 F.3d 974 (2007)

I. Facts and Background

... Following the Six Day War in 1967, Israel occupied and took control of the West Bank and Gaza Strip. Caterpillar is the world's leading manufacturer of heavy construction and mining equipment. Among its customers is the IDF [Israeli Defense Forces], which since 1967 has utilized Caterpillar bulldozers to demolish homes in the Palestinian Territories. According to plaintiffs' complaint, Caterpillar sold the bulldozers to the IDF despite its actual and constructive notice that the IDF would use them to further its home destruction policy in the Palestinian Territories; a policy plaintiffs contend violates international law. Seventeen members of plaintiffs' families—sixteen Palestinians and one American—were killed or injured in the course of the demolitions ....

III. Political Question Doctrine

... Plaintiffs' complaint does not reference the government's role in facilitating the sales at issue, but undisputed evidence in the record suggests that the United States pays for every bulldozer the IDF purchases from Caterpillar. Before considering that evidence at the pleadings stage, we must decide whether the presence of a political question deprives a court of subject matter jurisdiction. To the extent the answer to that question is "unclear," we now hold that it does.

The political question doctrine first found expression in Chief Justice Marshall's observation that "[q]uestions, in their nature political, or which are, by the constitution and laws, submitted to the executive, can never be made in this court." *Marbury v. Madison*, (1803). The Supreme Court has since explained that "[t]he nonjusticiability of a political question is primarily a function of the separation of powers." *Baker v. Carr*, (1962). *Baker* outlined six independent tests for determining whether courts should defer to the political branches on an issue:

> Prominent on the surface of any case held to involve a political question is found [1] a textually demonstrable constitutional commitment of the issue to a coordinate political department; or [2] a lack of judicially discoverable and manageable standards for resolving it; or [3] the impossibility of deciding without an initial policy determination of a kind clearly for nonjudicial discretion; or [4] the impossibility of a court's undertaking independent resolution without expressing lack of the respect due coordinate branches of government; or [5] an unusual need for unquestioning adherence to a political decision already made; or [6] the potentiality of embarrassment from multifarious pronouncements by various departments on one question.

The Supreme Court has indicated that disputes involving political questions lie outside of the Article III jurisdiction of federal courts. *See Schlesinger v. Reservists Comm. to Stop the War*, (1974) . . . .

"The conduct of the foreign relations of our government is committed by the Constitution to the executive and legislative [branches] . . . and the propriety of what may be done in the exercise of this political power is not subject to judicial inquiry or decision." *Oetjen v. Cent. Leather Co.*, (1918). However, it is "error to suppose that every case or controversy which touches foreign relations lies beyond judicial cognizance." *Baker*, 369 U.S. at 211. We will not find a political question "merely because [a] decision may have significant political overtones." *Japan Whaling Ass'n v. Am. Cetacean Soc'y*, (1986) . . . .

The decisive factor here is that Caterpillar's sales to Israel were paid for by the United States . . . . Allowing this action to proceed would necessarily require the judicial branch of our government to question the political branches' decision to grant extensive military aid to Israel. It is difficult to see how we could impose liability on Caterpillar without at least implicitly deciding the propriety of the United States' decision to pay for the bulldozers which allegedly killed the plaintiffs' family members.

Several of the six *Baker* tests are implicated by the United States government's role in financing the Caterpillar bulldozer purchases by the IDF. We begin with the first: Whether there is "a textually demonstrable constitutional commitment of the issue to a coordinate political department." . . . It is well established that the conduct of foreign relations is committed by the Constitution to the political departments of the Federal Government; [and] that the propriety of the exercise of that power is not open to judicial review . . . .

Whether to grant military or other aid to a foreign nation is a political decision inherently entangled with the conduct of foreign relations . . . .

. . . Plaintiffs' action also runs head-on into the fourth, fifth, and sixth *Baker* tests because whether to support Israel with military aid is not only a decision committed to the political branches, but a decision those branches have already made . . . . A court could not find in favor of the plaintiffs without implicitly questioning, and even condemning, United States foreign policy toward Israel.

. . . It is not the role of the courts to indirectly indict Israel for violating international law with military equipment the United States government provided and continues to provide. "Any such policy condemning the [Israeli government] must first emanate from the political branches." *Vatican Bank*, 410 F.3d at 561. Plaintiffs may purport to look no further than Caterpillar itself, but resolving their suit will necessarily require us to look beyond the lone defendant in this case and toward the foreign policy interests and judgments of the United States government itself.

We therefore hold that the district court did not err in dismissing the suit under the political question doctrine. Because we affirm on this ground, we do not reach the other issues raised on appeal.

CASE DISCUSSION QUESTIONS

1. The Court refers to six independent tests for determining whether courts should defer to another political branch on a specific issue. Which of the six tests did the court think were particularly implicated in this case?

2. Do you agree that the presence of a political question should deprive this court of subject matter jurisdiction?

3. Because the Court found that it lacked subject matter jurisdiction, the plaintiffs were left without a remedy. Does that seem right to you?

Another method the courts sometimes use to avoid controversial cases is delay. The Supreme Court has often put off hearing controversial cases until after the political pressures have died down. For example, the Supreme Court delayed consideration of the WWII Japanese Internment until after the war was over in 1946. It also put off a full review of the constitutionality of the anti-communist Smith Act until 1957, well after the red scare and Senator Joseph McCarthy's influence had diminished.

d. Structural Amendments

Since the Constitution went into effect in 1789, twenty-seven amendments have been added to it.[59] A listing of those involving governmental organization and powers is provided below.

- Eleventh Amendment [ratified in 1795] prohibits the federal courts from hearing civil suits in which a citizen of one state or a foreign country sued a different state.
- Twelfth Amendment [ratified in 1804] requires electors in the Electoral College to vote for a President and for a Vice President rather than for two choices for President.[60]
- Sixteenth Amendment [ratified in 1913] authorizes the federal government to levy an income tax on individuals and corporations.
- Seventeenth Amendment [ratified in 1913] requires the direct election of Senators.[61]
- Twentieth Amendment [ratified in 1933], commonly referred to as the Lame Duck Amendment, shortens the period of time between when elections are held and when Congress and the President formally take office.
- Twenty-second Amendment [ratified in 1951] imposes a two-term limit on the office of President.[62]

---

[59]Proposed amendments that failed to be ratified include the Equal Rights Amendment and the D.C. Voting Amendment. The Eighteenth Amendment (prohibition) was later repealed by the Twenty-first Amendment.

[60]This change was made to eliminate the situation where the runner-up in the Presidential vote became the Vice President.

[61]Prior to the amendment, Senators were chosen by state legislatures.

[62]If a person becomes President by virtue of having filled a mid-term vacancy (as when Vice President Johnson took over after the assassination of President Kennedy), then that person can only be elected President once if he or she has already served two years or more.

- Twenty-fifth Amendment [ratified in 1967] clarifies the line of succession if the President dies in office, provides a procedure for dealing with situations in which the President becomes disabled, and provides for appointment of a new Vice President when that office becomes vacant between election cycles.
- Twenty-seventh Amendment [ratified in 1992] prohibits Senators and Representatives from receiving a salary increase they voted on until after the next election cycle for the House of Representatives.

Amendments involving civil rights and civil liberties will be discussed in the next section of this chapter.

C. CIVIL RIGHTS AND CIVIL LIBERTIES

A second major function of the Constitution is to protect individual rights from governmental overreaching. When the lack of specific protections for individual rights became an issue in the debates over ratification, the federalists quickly responded to these concerns by promising to amend the Constitution to add these types of protections.

Bill of Rights
The first ten amendments to the U.S. Constitution.

When the new government was formed in 1789, Thomas Jefferson and James Madison led the way in formulating the ten amendments that became commonly known as the **Bill of Rights**. These ten amendments include freedom of speech and press, freedom of religion, the privilege against self-incrimination, the right to an attorney and a trial by jury, and protections against unreasonable searches and seizures.

Following the Civil War, additional constitutional rights were added through the adoption of the Thirteenth, Fourteenth, and Fifteenth Amendments. Whereas the Thirteenth Amendment abolished slavery and the Fifteenth Amendment states that the right to vote cannot be based on race, the Fourteenth Amendment guarantees "privileges and immunities of citizens," "due process," and "equal protection" of the law without any reference to slavery or race. These "Civil War amendments" were briefly covered in our discussion of the living/evolving constitution approach on pages 135–137. In this section we will also be discussing the Fourteenth Amendment in relation to how it has affected the application of the Bill of Rights to the states, on pages 153–155, and with regard to its equal protection clause on pages 173–183.

1. Basic Concepts

Before beginning our coverage of the specific rights protected by the Constitution, we need to clarify some of the terminology used and discuss some of the basic concepts involved in this area of constitutional interpretation.

a. Rights and Liberties

Legal right
A legally enforceable claim to use something or to be treated in a particular way.

When we speak of something being a right, we usually think of something that is considered a privilege or a prerogative. In the legal context we define it as a legally enforceable claim to use something or to be treated in a particular way.

Human rights are rights that all humans are thought to have regardless of where they live. They are loosely defined by the United Nations and other international bodies, but are not very effectively enforced. Civil rights are rights that are associated with being a citizen or an inhabitant of a country and are enforced by the government of that country.

You will frequently see the terms **civil rights** and **civil liberties** used interchangeably, though scholars will sometimes distinguish between them on the basis that civil rights involve getting something from the government (for example, the opportunity to be represented by an attorney or the opportunity to have a trial by jury) while civil liberties involve the government not interfering with aspects of people's personal lives (for example, freedom of expression, freedom of religion, and the right to privacy).

b. Constitutional versus Statutory Rights

Civil rights and liberties can be based on clauses found either in the Constitution or in statutes. We tend to focus on rights that are contained in the Bill of Rights and other parts of the Constitution because they are generally considered to be the most important and the most secure. However, it is important to note that statutes can also create legally enforceable rights and liberties that provide additional protections. See, for example, the coverage of employment law in Chapter 10.

It is particularly important to note that, unlike statutory protections, constitutional rights apply to governmental actions only. This **"state action" requirement**, means that persons seeking to enforce the constitutional right to free speech or to be free from unreasonable searches and seizures must first establish that the right in question was violated by actions of government officials. Thus, the First Amendment does not apply if your neighbor or a private employer attempts to prevent you from speaking freely. While the equal protection clause may prevent a governmental agency from treating you unfairly, it has no impact on how a private employer or a local coffee shop might treat you.

On the other hand, legislative bodies can create legally enforceable rights that do apply to private individuals and nongovernmental entities. Civil rights laws have been passed that prohibit public places such as stores, restaurants, and movie theatres from discriminating on the basis of specific categories, such as race, color, religion, sex, or national origin.

c. Application of the Bill of Rights to the States

Prior to discussing the specific clauses contained in the Bill of Rights, we need to see how these amendments apply to the actions of state governments. While it is quite clear that the drafters of the Bill of Rights intended that the amendments protect individuals from actions of the new federal government, it is less clear as to the extent to which they were also intended to limit actions of the state governments.

The First Amendment begins with the words "Congress shall make no law respecting an establishment of religion . . . ." A literal interpretation would lead one to conclude that this is a restriction only on laws passed by Congress (the legislative branch of the new federal government). However, the Fourth Amendment simply states "The right of the people to be secure in their persons, houses, papers, and effects, . . . shall not be violated . . . " without any reference

Human rights
Legal rights that all human beings are thought to have regardless of where they live.

Civil rights
Legal rights that (1) are associated with being a citizen or an inhabitant of a country and are enforced by the government of that country, and (2) involve having the government do something for its citizens.

Civil liberties
Legal guarantees that the government will not interfere with aspects of people's personal lives.

State action requirement
A court-imposed requirement that most constitutional protections apply only if a governmental entity is involved.

as to which governmental units it applies. Similarly, the Sixth Amendment states "In all criminal prosecutions, the accused shall enjoy the right to . . . ." This wording would also seem to apply to all criminal prosecutions brought by either federal or state authorities.

The Supreme Court first addressed the issue of the application of the Bill of Rights to the states in 1833 in *Barron v. Baltimore*.[63] An action by the city of Baltimore to redirect the course of several streams caused large deposits of sand and dirt to accumulate in the area of a harbor wharf owed by Barron. Because these deposits made his wharf inaccessible to the ships that had been using it, he sought compensation from the city for his losses. When the city refused to provide compensation, he brought suit alleging the city had violated the Fifth Amendment to the U.S. Constitution by depriving him of his property rights without due process of law. Writing for a unanimous Supreme Court, Chief Justice John Marshal ruled that the Fifth Amendment did not apply to the states for the following reasons:

- Where limitations are placed on state powers in other sections of the Constitution, it explicitly mentions states in the text of the document. The Fifth Amendment does not contain this type of explicit reference to the states.
- The people who proposed and supported the Bill of Rights were concerned about limiting the powers of the federal government rather than those of the states. If they had been concerned about protecting individuals from state governments, they would have simply amended their state constitutions instead of seeking a federal amendment.

While *Barron v. Baltimore* remains settled law, the passage of the Fourteenth Amendment due process clause had the effect of applying various rights found in the Bill of Rights to the states. Although the Fourteenth Amendment was clearly intended to establish and protect legal rights for former slaves, the amendment did not limit these newly created rights to any one race or to those who had been slaves.[64]

In *Hurtado v. California*,[65] the Supreme Court was called upon to determine whether the due process clause of the Fourteenth Amendment contains a right to have a grand jury in a state criminal prosecution. Hurtado's attorney argued that "due process" should mean the same thing it does when it is was used in the Fifth Amendment, and therefore that the Fourteenth Amendment should also be interpreted as guaranteeing a right to a grand jury.

Unfortunately for Hurtado, the majority of the justices rejected this argument and instead ruled that the due process clause of the Fourteenth Amendment did not have the same meaning as the due process clause of the Fifth Amendment. The opinion of the court declared that the general concept of "due process" has a distinct meaning that does not necessarily include all the provisions listed in the Bill of Rights.

---

[63]32 U.S. 243.

[64]*See* discussion on page 137.

[65]110 U.S. 516 (1884).

Having ruled that the Fourteenth Amendment's due process requirements were not the same as those imposed by the Fifth Amendment's due process clause, the Supreme Court was left with the task of specifying how they differed. Rather than setting out a comprehensive listing, the justices chose to consider potential applications on a case-by-case process frequently referred to as "selective incorporation."

Throughout the years, various justices have used a variety of different standards for determining whether a particular practice was, or was not, required by the Fourteenth Amendment. The most famous and widely used standard was announced in 1937 in *Palko v. Connecticut*.[66] In *Palko* Justice Benjamin Cardozo announced that the standard for what does or does not violate the due process clause of the Fourteenth Amendment is whether the challenged practice violates "fundamental principles of liberty and justice which lie at the base of all our civil and political institutions."[67] Other tests used by various judges have included "case by case fairness," whether the right was "fundamental to ordered liberty," and whether it reflected the "fundamental principles of liberty and justice which lie at the base of all our civil and political institutions."

In applying these various standards, the Supreme Court has found that most of the rights contained in the Bill of Rights are in fact also applicable to the states through the due process clause of the Fourteenth Amendment. Exhibit 6.1 presents a partial listing of the rights found in the Bill of Rights that have also been applied to the states through the Fourteenth Amendment.

The only major provisions that have not been applied to the states are the provisions or partial provisions of the

- Second Amendment (right to bear arms)
- Third Amendment (right not to have to quarter soldiers in your home)
- Fifth Amendment (right to indictment by a grand jury)
- Seventh Amendment (right to a jury trial in civil cases)
- Eighth Amendment (right against excessive bail and excessive fines)

2. The Right to Vote

At the core of any democracy is the right to vote. When the constitution was drafted, it left the question of who could vote up to the states, and most of them limited the right to vote to white men who owned property. However, the Fifteenth, Nineteenth, Twenty-third, Twenty-fourth, and Twenty-sixth Amendments were eventually added to expand and protect citizens' rights to vote.

- The Fifteenth Amendment (ratified in 1870) states that the right to vote cannot be denied or abridged on account of race, color, or previous condition of servitude.
- The Nineteenth Amendment (ratified in 1920) states that the right to vote cannot be denied or abridged on account of sex.

---

[66]302 U.S. 319 (1937).

[67]Although the Court in Benton v. Maryland, 395 U.S. 784 (1969) reversed *Palko*'s finding that the Fifth Amendment double jeopardy provisions were not incorporated into the Fourteenth Amendment due process clause, it did not specifically reject the *Palko* standard. Rather it ruled that bans on double jeopardy represented a "fundamental ideal in our constitutional heritage."

Provision	Case
Freedom of speech	*Gitlow v. New York* (1925)
Freedom of the press	*Near v. Minnesota* (1931)
Right to counsel in capital cases	*Powell v. Alabama* (1932)
Freedom to petition and assembly	*DeJonge v. Oregon* (1937)
Free exercise of religion	*Cantwell v. Connecticut* (1940)
Establishment of religion	*Everson v. Bd. of Ed.* (1947)
Right to public trial	*In re Oliver* (1948)
Protection against unreasonable search and seizure	*Wolf v. Colorado* (1949)
Freedom of association	*NAACP v. Alabama* (1958)
Right against cruel and unusual punishment	*Robinson v. California* (1962)
Right to counsel in all felony cases	*Gideon v. Wainwright* (1963)
Privilege against self-incrimination	*Malloy v. Hogan* (1964)
Right to confront and cross-examine	*Pointer v. Texas* (1965)
Right to privacy	*Griswold v. Connecticut* (1965)
Right to an impartial jury	*Parker v. Gladden* (1966)
Right to a speedy trial	*Klopfer v. North Carolina* (1967)
Right to a jury trial for serious offenses	*Duncan v. Louisiana* (1968)
Right against double jeopardy	*Benton v. Maryland* (1968)

Exhibit 6.1   Bill of Rights Provisions Applied to the States

- The Twenty-third Amendment (ratified in 1961) allows residents of the District of Columbia to vote for presidential electors.
- The Twenty-fourth Amendment (ratified in 1964) prohibits the use of poll taxes (which prevents a form of economic discrimination).
- The Twenty-sixth Amendment (ratified in 1971) states that the right to vote cannot be denied or abridged on account of age unless the person is younger than 18.

3. Freedom of Expression

Freedom of expression
A term used to include a group of First Amendment provisions designed to protect people's ability to inform and influence others.

Freedom of expression is a term used to incorporate a group of First Amendment rights designed to protect people's ability to inform and influence others. These rights include freedom of speech, freedom of the press, freedom of association, the right to peacefully assemble, and the right to petition the government for redress of grievances. These rights are generally considered to be essential for the operation of a successful democracy. They foster a more stable society because people are more willing to accept decisions, even those with which they disagree, when they believe they have had a chance to influence the decision-making process.

These rights come with limitations on their use. In deciding First Amendment cases, the courts must balance the values of free expression against the government's interests in maintaining order and preserving the existence of the nation. In the oft quoted words of Justice Oliver Wendell Homes,

> [T]he character of every act depends upon the circumstances in which it is done. The most stringent protection of free speech would not protect a man in falsely shouting fire in a theatre and causing a panic.[68]

From the passage of the Alien and Sedition Acts in 1798 to the Patriot Act in 2001, our nation's history is replete with legislation that has limited free expression in situations where it is deemed to pose a threat to our national security. To again quote Justice Holmes,

> When the nation is at war many things that might be said in time of peace are such a hindrance to its effort that their utterance will not be endured so long as men fight and that no Court could regard them as protected by any constitutional right.[69]

Time and place restrictions
Governmental restrictions that limit when and where free expression activities can take place.

With varying degrees of success, governments at all levels have also sought to justify limitations on free expression based on their desire to preserve the peace and to protect citizens from having their sensibilities offended. Examples include restrictions on mass gatherings and protest marches. In cases dealing with whether to award damages for libel, courts have struggled for years trying to develop standards that will allow communities to ban obscene and offensive words and images without interfering with legitimate political and artistic expression. The courts have also grappled with whether reporters have a constitutional right to protect the identity of their sources and the extent to which special rules can be applied to broadcast media and the Internet.

Content neutrality
A court-imposed requirement that government regulations of free expression not be based on the viewpoint being expressed.

One of the most important principles of First Amendment jurisprudence is the distinction between what are referred to as **"time and place restrictions"** and content regulation. Although government cannot prohibit many types of speech, it can require demonstrators to get permits, it can limit the use of sound amplification equipment, and it can prevent protesters from blocking access to buildings. Such regulations must, however, be **content neutral**. That is to say, they must not discriminate on the basis of the points of view being presented. A government cannot give a permit to hold a Republican or Democratic Party rally and then refuse to grant the same permit to the Green or Libertarian Party. It cannot block anti-war protests while allowing demonstrations to support the troops.

Symbolic speech
The use of physical actions, rather than words, to express a point of view.

Another key concept of First Amendment law involves what is called **"symbolic speech."** This occurs when nonverbal actions are taken for the purpose of expressing a point of view. Some of the most controversial examples have included flag burning and the destruction of draft cards. Take a few moments to examine the Supreme Court's handling of the Texas flag desecration

---

[68]Schenck v. United States, 249 U.S. 47 (1919).

[69]Id.

statute in *Texas v. Johnson*. Note how the Court evaluates the various arguments Texas put forth to justify this application of its flag desecration law.

Texas v. Johnson
491 U.S. 397 (1989)

Justice BRENNAN delivered the opinion of the Court.

After publicly burning an American flag as a means of political protest, Gregory Lee Johnson was convicted of desecrating a flag in violation of Texas law. This case presents the question whether his conviction is consistent with the First Amendment. We hold that it is not.

I

While the Republican National Convention was taking place in Dallas in 1984, respondent Johnson participated in a political demonstration dubbed the "Republican War Chest Tour." . . . [T]he purpose of this event was to protest the policies of the Reagan administration and of certain Dallas-based corporations . . . .

The demonstration ended in front of Dallas City Hall, where Johnson unfurled the American flag, doused it with kerosene, and set it on fire. While the flag burned, the protestors chanted: "America, the red, white, and blue, we spit on you." . . . Of the approximately 100 demonstrators, Johnson alone was charged with a crime. The only criminal offense with which he was charged was the desecration of a venerated object in violation of Tex. Penal Code Ann. § 42.09(a)(3) (1989). After a trial, he was convicted, sentenced to one year in prison, and fined $2,000. The Court of Appeals for the Fifth District of Texas at Dallas affirmed Johnson's conviction, 706 S.W.2d 120 (1986), but the Texas Court of Criminal Appeals reversed, 755 S.W.2d 92 (1988), holding that the State could not, consistent with the First Amendment, punish Johnson for burning the flag in these circumstances . . . .

We granted certiorari, 488 U.S. 907 (1988), and now affirm.

II

. . . The First Amendment literally forbids the abridgment only of "speech," but we have long recognized that its protection does not end at the spoken or written word. While we have rejected "the view that an apparently limitless variety of conduct can be labeled "speech" whenever the person engaging in the conduct intends thereby to express an idea," *United States v. O'Brien*, supra, at 376, we have acknowledged that conduct may be "sufficiently imbued with elements of communication to fall within the scope of the First and Fourteenth Amendments," [*Spence v. Washington*, 418 U.S. 405, 409 (1974) (reversing the conviction of a college student who displayed the flag with a peace symbol affixed to it by removable black tape)] . . . .

The State of Texas conceded for purposes of its oral argument in this case that Johnson's conduct was expressive conduct, . . . and this concession seems to us as prudent . . . . Johnson burned an American flag as part—indeed, as the culmination—of a political demonstration that coincided with the convening of the Republican Party and its re-nomination of Ronald Reagan for President. The expressive, overtly political nature of this conduct was both intentional and overwhelmingly apparent . . . .

III

. . . The State offers two separate interests to justify this conviction: preventing breaches of the peace and preserving the flag as a symbol of nationhood and national unity. We hold that the first interest is not implicated on this record and that the second is related to the suppression of expression.

A

Texas claims that its interest in preventing breaches of the peace justifies Johnson's conviction for flag desecration. However, no disturbance of the peace actually occurred or threatened to occur because of Johnson's burning of the flag . . . .

The State's position, therefore, amounts to a claim that an audience that takes serious offense at particular expression is necessarily likely to disturb the peace and that the expression may be prohibited on this basis. Our precedents do not countenance such a presumption. On the contrary, they recognize that a principal "function of free speech under our system of government is to invite dispute. It may indeed best serve its high purpose when it induces a condition of unrest, creates dissatisfaction with conditions as they are, or even stirs people to anger." . . .

Nor does Johnson's expressive conduct fall within that small class of "fighting words" that are "likely to provoke the average person to retaliation, and thereby cause a breach of the peace." *Chaplinsky v. New Hampshire*, 315 U.S. 568, 574 (1942). No reasonable onlooker would have regarded Johnson's generalized expression of dissatisfaction with the policies of the Federal Government as a direct personal insult or an invitation to exchange fisticuffs . . . .

We thus conclude that the State's interest in maintaining order is not implicated on these facts. The State need not worry that our holding will disable it from preserving the peace . . . .

B

[T]he State's claim is that it has an interest in preserving the flag as a symbol of nationhood and national unity, a symbol with a determinate range of meanings. According to Texas, if one physically treats the flag in a way that would tend to cast doubt on either the idea that nationhood and national unity are the flag's referents or that national unity actually exists, the message conveyed thereby is a harmful one and therefore may be prohibited . . . .

If there is a bedrock principle underlying the First Amendment, it is that the government may not prohibit the expression of an idea simply because society finds the idea itself offensive or disagreeable . . . .

To conclude that the government may permit designated symbols to be used to communicate only a limited set of messages would be to enter territory having no discernible or defensible boundaries. Could the government, on this theory, prohibit the burning of state flags? Of copies of the Presidential seal? Of the Constitution? In

evaluating these choices under the First Amendment, how would we decide which symbols were sufficiently special to warrant this unique status? To do so, we would be forced to consult our own political preferences, and impose them on the citizenry, in the very way that the First Amendment forbids us to do . . . .

The way to preserve the flag's special role is not to punish those who feel differently about these matters. It is to persuade them that they are wrong . . . . And, precisely because it is our flag that is involved, one's response to the flag burner may exploit the uniquely persuasive power of the flag itself. We can imagine no more appropriate response to burning a flag than waving one's own, no better way to counter a flag burner's message than by saluting the flag that burns, no surer means of preserving the dignity even of the flag that burned than by—as one witness here did—according its remains a respectful burial. We do not consecrate the flag by punishing its desecration, for in doing so we dilute the freedom that this cherished emblem represents.

V

Johnson was convicted for engaging in expressive conduct. The State's interest in preventing breaches of the peace does not support his conviction because Johnson's conduct did not threaten to disturb the peace. Nor does the State's interest in preserving the flag as a symbol of nationhood and national unity justify his criminal conviction for engaging in political expression. The judgment of the Texas Court of Criminal Appeals is therefore affirmed.

Justice KENNEDY, concurring.

. . . The hard fact is that sometimes we must make decisions we do not like. We make them because they are right, right in the sense that the law and the Constitution, as we see them, compel the result. And so great is our commitment to the process that, except in the rare case, we do not pause to express distaste for the result, perhaps for fear of undermining a valued principle that dictates the decision. This is one of those rare cases . . . .

Though symbols often are what we ourselves make of them, the flag is constant in expressing beliefs Americans share, beliefs in law and peace and that freedom which sustains the human spirit. The case here today forces recognition of the costs to which those beliefs commit us. It is poignant but fundamental that the flag protects those who hold it in contempt.

For all the record shows, this respondent was not a philosopher and perhaps did not even possess the ability to comprehend how repellent his statements must be to the Republic itself. But whether or not he could appreciate the enormity of the offense he gave, the fact remains that his acts were speech, in both the technical and the fundamental meaning of the Constitution. So I agree with the Court that he must go free.

Chief Justice REHNQUIST, with whom Justice WHITE and Justice O'CONNOR join, dissenting.

. . . For more than 200 years, the American flag has occupied a unique position as the symbol of our Nation, a uniqueness that justifies a governmental prohibition against flag burning in the way respondent Johnson did here . . . .

. . . In *Chaplinsky v. New Hampshire*, 315 U.S. 568 (1942), a unanimous Court said: "Allowing the broadest scope to the language and purpose of the Fourteenth Amendment, it is well understood that the right of free speech is not absolute at all times and under all circumstances. There are certain well-defined and narrowly limited classes of speech, the prevention and punishment of which have never been thought to raise any Constitutional problem. These include the lewd and obscene, the profane, the libelous, and the insulting or "fighting" words—those which by their very utterance inflict injury or tend to incite an immediate breach of the peace. It has been well observed that such utterances are no essential part of any exposition of ideas, and are of such slight social value as a step to truth that any benefit that may be derived from them is clearly outweighed by the social interest in order and morality." The Court upheld Chaplinsky's conviction under a state statute that made it unlawful to "address any offensive, derisive or annoying word to any person who is lawfully in any street or other public place." . . .

Here it may equally well be said that the public burning of the American flag by Johnson was no essential part of any exposition of ideas, and at the same time it had a tendency to incite a breach of the peace. Johnson was free to make any verbal denunciation of the flag that he wished; indeed, he was free to burn the flag in private. He could publicly burn other symbols of the Government or effigies of political leaders. He did lead a march through the streets of Dallas, and conducted a rally in front of the Dallas City Hall. He engaged in a "die-in" to protest nuclear weapons. He shouted out various slogans during the march, including: "Reagan, Mondale which will it be? Either one means World War III"; "Ronald Reagan, killer of the hour, Perfect example of U.S. power"; and "red, white and blue, we spit on you, you stand for plunder, you will go under." . . .

The result of the Texas statute is obviously to deny one in Johnson's frame of mind one of many means of "symbolic speech." Far from being a case of "one picture being worth a thousand words," flag burning is the equivalent of an inarticulate grunt or roar that, it seems fair to say, is most likely to be indulged in not to express any particular idea, but to antagonize others . . . . It was Johnson's use of this particular symbol, and not the idea that he sought to convey by it or by his many other expressions, for which he was punished . . . .

I would uphold the Texas statute as applied in this case.

CASE DISCUSSION QUESTIONS

1. What justifications did the state of Texas give for limiting free expression rights with regard to criminalizing flag burning?

2. What reasons did Justice Brennan give for rejecting each of the state's justifications?

3. Under what circumstances, if any, should the government be able to prohibit the expression of an idea simply because society finds the idea offensive or disagreeable?

4. If the special significance of the flag justifies special protections, what other types of symbols—for example, a Bible, sacred writings of other religions, or a copy of the Constitution—should receive similar protection?

5. In a dissenting opinion that was not included here, Justice Stevens argued that the government should be able to protect the flag in the same way it can prohibit people from writing graffiti on the Washington Monument or the Lincoln Memorial. How would you respond to that argument?

4. The Relationship between Government and Religion

One of the most controversial and most misunderstood topics in constitutional law is the relationship between church and state. It is controversial because there is strong disagreement as to what the founding fathers intended, as well as what in a religiously diverse country they thought the relationship should be between church and state. Confusion in this area is also caused because many people react on a very emotional level to cases involving religion and yet know little about the rationale for the Court's decisions. For example, many people believe that our country was founded as a Christian nation. But despite this popular misconception, there is no mention of such a commitment in the Preamble to the Constitution:

> We the People of the United States, in Order to form a more perfect Union, establish Justice, insure domestic Tranquility, provide for the common defense, promote the general Welfare, and secure the Blessings of Liberty to ourselves and our Posterity, do ordain and establish this Constitution for the United States of America.

Nor is such a belief in Christian fundamentals found anywhere else in the Constitution. In fact, rather than making one's acceptance of Christianity a prerequisite for holding public office, Article VI actually contains a prohibition against using any type of religious test for office.

The only direct discussion of the nature of the relationship between religion and government is found at the beginning of the First Amendment where it states, "Congress shall make no law respecting an establishment of religion or prohibiting the free exercise thereof . . . ." Note that this language consists of two distinct clauses, involving two very different focuses. The declaration that Congress shall make no law respecting an establishment of religion is commonly referred to as the **establishment clause**. It deals with the extent to which the government can recognize and support religious groups. The second clause, commonly referred to as the **free exercise clause**, prohibits the government from interfering with people's religious activities.

a. The Free Exercise Clause

We begin with a discussion of the **free exercise clause** because it is easier to understand and somewhat less controversial. Most Americans accept the idea that people should be allowed to practice the religion of their own choosing and in the manner of their own choosing. For example, most would agree that Christians under the age of 21 should be allowed to drink wine as part of their communion rituals. But should Native Americans be able to use hallucinogenic drugs in their religious ceremonies? Should Mormons be allowed to practice

Free exercise of religion clause
A clause in the First Amendment that prohibits government from taking actions to prevent people from adopting any type of religious beliefs or following religious practices that do not violate general, religiously neutral laws.

polygamy? Should Christian Scientists be allowed to withhold needed medical treatment from their children on the basis of their religious beliefs, or Satanic cult members be able to incorporate human sacrifice into their religious rituals?

To analyze whether such activities are protected under the free exercise clause, the courts look to two key issues. First, the courts must determine what should be considered a religious activity. Second, the courts must decide what, if any, limitations should be placed on the exercise of that activity.

In determining what constitutes a religious activity, the courts have generally been quite inclusive. In *Davis v. Beason,*[70] the court wrote:

> The term "religion" has references to one's views of his relations to his Creator, and to the obligations they impose of reverence for his being and character, and of obedience to his will . . . ."

In *United States v. Seeger,*[71] the Court ruled that it was religiously based conscientious objection when the person's objections were based on beliefs that held the same place as traditionally defined religious beliefs.

However, even though an activity may be religiously motivated, it is not necessarily immune from governmental regulation. While the government cannot dictate what people must believe, it can place some limitations on how they act. Therefore, sincerely held religious beliefs do not immunize adherents from criminal laws, such as murder, assault, or theft. Under the prevailing interpretations of the free exercise clause, the courts are required to balance the person's religious rights against the government's interest in preserving the general welfare of society and the protection of third parties who might be injured in the process. Thus, the government cannot force a Christian Scientist to accept medical treatment, but it may be able to keep parents from preventing their minor children from receiving it.

A good example of this type of balancing act is found in *Wisconsin v. Yoder,* in which Amish and Mennonite parents were convicted of violating the state's compulsory public school attendance law because they refused to send their children to school beyond the eighth grade. The parents argued that it was a violation of their free exercise of religion for the state to require them to send their children to public schools after the eighth grade because it exposed the children to ideas that threatened their unique, religiously based life style. On appeal, the state supreme court agreed with the parents that applying the compulsory school attendance law to them violated their rights under the free exercise clause of the First Amendment, made applicable to the states by the Fourteenth Amendment. After granting a writ of certiorari, the U.S. Supreme Court delivered the following opinion:

---

[70]133 U.S. 333 (1890).
[71]380 U.S. 163 (1965).

Wisconsin v. Yoder
406 U.S. 205 (1972)

Mr. Chief Justice BURGER delivered the opinion of the Court.

. . . In support of their position, respondents presented as expert witnesses scholars on religion and education whose testimony is uncontradicted. They expressed their opinions on the relationship of the Amish belief concerning school attendance to the more general tenets of their religion, and described the impact that compulsory high school attendance could have on the continued survival of Amish communities as they exist in the United States today. The history of the Amish sect was given in some detail, beginning with the Swiss Anabaptists of the 16th century who rejected institutionalized churches and sought to return to the early, simple, Christian life de-emphasizing material success, rejecting the competitive spirit, and seeking to insulate themselves from the modern world. As a result of their common heritage, Old Order Amish communities today are characterized by a fundamental belief that salvation requires life in a church community separate and apart from the world and worldly influence. This concept of life aloof from the world and its values is central to their faith.

A related feature of Old Order Amish communities is their devotion to a life in harmony with nature and the soil, as exemplified by the simple life of the early Christian era that continued in America during much of our early national life. Amish beliefs require members of the community to make their living by farming or closely related activities . . . .

Formal high school education beyond the eighth grade is contrary to Amish beliefs, not only because it places Amish children in an environment hostile to Amish beliefs with increasing emphasis on competition in class work and sports and with pressure to conform to the styles, manners, and ways of the peer group, but also because it takes them away from their community, physically and emotionally, during the crucial and formative adolescent period of life . . . .

The Amish do not object to elementary education through the first eight grades as a general proposition because they agree that their children must have basic skills in the "three R's" in order to read the Bible, to be good farmers and citizens, and to be able to deal with non-Amish people when necessary in the course of daily affairs. They view such a basic education as acceptable because it does not significantly expose their children to worldly values or interfere with their development in the Amish community during the crucial adolescent period . . . .

There is no doubt as to the power of a State, having a high responsibility for education of its citizens, to impose reasonable regulations for the control and duration of basic education. See, e.g., *Pierce v. Society of Sisters,* 268 U.S. 510, 534 (1925). Providing public schools ranks at the very apex of the function of a State. Yet even this paramount responsibility was, in *Pierce,* made to yield to the right of parents to provide an equivalent education in a privately operated system . . . .

It follows that in order for Wisconsin to compel school attendance beyond the eighth grade against a claim that such attendance interferes with the practice of a legitimate religious belief, it must appear either that the State does not deny the free exercise of religious belief by its requirement, or that there is a state interest of sufficient magnitude to override the interest claiming protection under the Free Exercise Clause . . . .

[T]he unchallenged testimony of acknowledged experts in education and religious history, almost 300 years of consistent practice, and strong evidence of a sustained faith pervading and regulating respondents' entire mode of life support the claim that enforcement of the State's requirement of compulsory formal education after the eighth grade would gravely endanger if not destroy the free exercise of respondents' religious beliefs.

We turn, then, to the State's broader contention that its interest in its system of compulsory education is so compelling that even the established religious practices of the Amish must give way . . . .

The State advances two primary arguments in support of its system of compulsory education. It notes, as Thomas Jefferson pointed out early in our history, that some degree of education is necessary to prepare citizens to participate effectively and intelligently in our open political system if we are to preserve freedom and independence. Further, education prepares individuals to be self-reliant and self-sufficient participants in society. We accept these propositions.

However, the evidence adduced by the Amish in this case is persuasively to the effect that an additional one or two years of formal high school for Amish children in place of their long-established program of informal vocational education would do little to serve those interests. Respondents' experts testified at trial, without challenge, that the value of all education must be assessed in terms of its capacity to prepare the child for life. It is one thing to say that compulsory education for a year or two beyond the eighth grade may be necessary when its goal is the preparation of the child for life in modern society as the majority live, but it is quite another if the goal of education be viewed as the preparation of the child for life in the separated agrarian community that is the keystone of the Amish faith.

The State attacks respondents' position as one fostering "ignorance" from which the child must be protected by the State. No one can question the State's duty to protect children from ignorance but this argument does not square with the facts disclosed in the record. Whatever their idiosyncrasies as seen by the majority, this record strongly shows that the Amish community has been a highly successful social unit within our society, even if apart from the conventional "mainstream." . . .

Affirmed.

CASE DISCUSSION QUESTIONS

1. On what basis did the Court conclude that Wisconsin's compulsory school attendance laws could not be applied to the Amish parents?

2. The Court's opinion went to great lengths to document the history of the Amish and how their beliefs were endangered by the state's mandatory attendance law. How do you think a judge would respond to a situation in which parents who live in an urban area and are not part of a long-established religious group choose not to send their children to school beyond the eighth grade on the basis that they did not want them exposed to students with values that differed from their own?

3. In light of our increasingly technologically advanced society, should states alter their compulsory school attendance laws from age 16 to age 18? What are the pros and cons of such a change?

4. Note the opinion's reference to *Pierce v. Society of Sisters*. In that case, the Supreme Court struck down an Oregon compulsory attendance law that did not allow students to attend private schools as an alternative to public schools. Under what circumstances do you think states should allow parents to "home school" their children? What kinds of checks should the government institute to ensure the quality and content of the children's education?

5. In a dissenting opinion in *Yoder,* Justice Douglas argued that it was in the Amish children's best interest to receive a high school education so they would know what their alternatives were and be prepared if they sought a different type of lifestyle. He therefore argued that the state's compulsory attendance law should be applied to the Amish children, even though the parents

wanted to shelter them from outside interests. What do you think of Justice Douglas's position? To what extent should parents be able to shelter their children from ideas or religious beliefs to which they do not want them exposed?

As we have seen in the *Yoder* case, the free exercise of religion cases require judges to balance the general public interest against the right of individuals to follow their religious beliefs. But how are judges supposed to determine what the appropriate balance should be? In 1963, the U.S. Supreme Court ruled that the government had to establish that any restrictions on the free exercise of religion were necessary to achieve a *compelling state interest* and that the means had to be *narrowly tailored* to achieve that interest.[72] This is the test the Court applied in *Yoder*. In 1990, however, the Supreme Court announced a new standard that made it easier for the government to justify restrictions on the free exercise of religion. In *Employment Division v. Smith*,[73] the Court upheld the application of a comprehensive ban on all uses of various types of controlled substances to situations where hallucinogenic drugs were used in Native American religious ceremonies. In doing so, it stated that as long as the law in question was neutral on its face and of general applicability, it was not a violation of the free exercise clause, even if it had the incidental effect of burdening a particular religious practice.

DISCUSSION QUESTION

7. If the Court were asked today to apply the test developed in *Employment Division v. Smith* to the facts of *Yoder*, do you think it would change the result? Which test do you think best balances the needs of society and of individuals to practice their religion as they wish?

Even though the *Smith* test makes it more difficult to win a free exercise challenge, plaintiffs can still prevail when the prohibition is not truly neutral. In *Church of Lukumi Balbalu v. Hialeah*,[74] the Court struck down an ordinance passed by Hialeah, Florida, that prohibited the killing of animals as part of a religious ceremony. The legislative history indicated that it had been passed to try to prevent a religious group that practiced animal sacrifice from building a church in their community. The Court ruled that it was clearly directed at a specific religious group and that it could not be justified as a secular public health regulation because it did not apply to slaughterhouses and other situations where animals were killed.

b. The Establishment Clause

As we have seen, the free exercise clause serves to protect a person's right to practice religion without undue governmental interference. The **establishment clause** focuses on the extent to which the state can recognize and support religious groups.

Establishment of religion clause
A clause in the First Amendment that restricts the types of actions government can take to recognize and support religious groups and religious principles.

---

[72]Sherbert v. Verner, 374 U.S. 398 (1963).

[73]464 U.S. 872

[74]508 U.S. 520 (1993).

Both liberals and conservatives agree that, at a minimum, the establishment clause prohibits the establishment of an official national religion. However, they disagree as to whether it should be interpreted as requiring a "strict separation of church and state" or merely a requirement that the state treat all religions evenhandedly. The difficulties of determining the intentions of the drafters and supporters of this clause were discussed earlier in this chapter on pages 133–135.

Supporters of the accommodation approach believe the country would be a better place in which to live if more people followed religious teachings, and that publicly supported religious activities, such as prayer in schools, would help hold families together and reduce crime. In recent years they have gained considerable political influence, and President George W. Bush's administration backed many "faith-based initiatives."

On the other hand, supporters of the strict separation of church and state position fear that government support of religion inevitably ends up fostering and legitimizing the religious beliefs of the majority at the expense of religious minorities. They argue that government support of religious activities inevitably leads to greater religious conflict in society because it invites religious groups to compete against each other for governmental rewards.

One of the things that makes this a particularly challenging area of constitutional law is that the Supreme Court has had difficulty agreeing on the specific standards that should be used in judging the constitutionality of challenged activities. Going back to 1947 when the Supreme Court approved a school bussing program that included students going to religiously affiliated schools,[75] the Supreme Court has focused on the idea that government activities affecting religion must have a valid government purpose that is not related to fostering religion. In 1971, the Supreme Court formally announced a three-part test, commonly known as the *Lemon* test[76], that incorporated this secular purpose component, along with consideration of the impact the program had on religion[77] and the extent to which it involved "excessive government entanglements."[78]

Over the years, the Court has not consistently applied the Lemon test, and at times it has completely ignored it.[79] It has also developed several variations of the test. These variations continue to stress secular purpose, primary effect, and avoidance of government entanglements, but they also place emphasis on concepts such as perceived endorsement of religion,[80] coercion,[81] and social conflict.[82]

---

[75]Everson v. Bd of Education, 330 U.S. 1 (1947).

[76]Lemon v. Kurtzman, 468 U.S. 602 (1971). The case involved a challenge to a Pennsylvania law providing various types of financial aid for religiously affiliated schools.

[77]The primary effect of the program had to be neutral. It could neither advance nor retard religion. However, an indirect, secondary effect on religion was permissible.

[78]Part of the program in question failed this part of the test because it would require government inspectors to be in the classroom, and that would create excessive government entanglements.

[79]*See, e.g.,* Marsh v. Chambers, 463 U.S. 783 (1983). The Court never directly explained why it did not apply the *Lemon* test. However, whereas *Lemon* dealt with activities in public schools, this case involved prayers by a chaplin in a state legislature.

[80]Advocated by O'Connor in Lynch v. Donnely, 465 U.S. 668 (1984).

[81]Advocated by Kennedy in Allegheney v. ACLU, 492 U.S. 573 (1989).

[82]Advocated by Breyer in Zelman v. Simmons-Harris, 536 U.S. 639 (2002).

The following excerpts from *Van Orden v. Perry* provide an example of how the current Supreme Court uses these tests. This case involved a challenge to the constitutionality of the display, on the Texas State Capitol grounds, of a large stone monument inscribed with the Ten Commandments. In another case decided on the same day, the Supreme Court struck down a Ten Commandments display in a Kentucky courthouse.[83] Four of the justices (Stevens, O'Connor, Souter, and Ginsburg) found both displays unconstitutional, while another four justices (Rehnquist, Scalia, Kennedy, and Thomas) came to the opposite conclusion. Justice Breyer, the crucial fifth vote, struck down the courthouse display while upholding the display on the capitol grounds.

Van Orden v. Perry
545 U.S. 677 (2005)

Chief Justice REHNQUIST announced the judgment of the Court and delivered an opinion, in which Justice SCALIA, Justice KENNEDY, and Justice THOMAS join.

. . . The 22 acres surrounding the Texas State Capitol contain 17 monuments and 21 historical markers commemorating the "people, ideals, and events that compose Texan identity." . . .

The legislative record surrounding the State's acceptance of the monument from the Eagles—a national social, civic, and patriotic organization—is limited to legislative journal entries. After the monument was accepted, the State selected a site for the monument based on the recommendation of the state organization responsible for maintaining the Capitol grounds. The Eagles paid the cost of erecting the monument, the dedication of which was presided over by two state legislators.

Petitioner Thomas Van Orden is a native Texan and a resident of Austin . . . . Forty years after the monument's erection and six years after Van Orden began to encounter the monument frequently, he sued numerous state officials in their official capacities . . . seeking both a declaration that the monument's placement violates the Establishment Clause and an injunction requiring its removal . . . .

Our cases, Januslike, point in two directions in applying the Establishment Clause. One face looks toward the strong role played by religion and religious traditions throughout our Nation's history . . . . The other face looks toward the principle that governmental intervention in religious matters can itself endanger religious freedom.

. . . In this case we are faced with a display of the Ten Commandments on government property outside the Texas State Capitol. Such acknowledgments of the role played by the Ten Commandments in our Nation's heritage are common throughout America. We need only look within our own Courtroom. Since 1935, Moses has stood, holding two tablets that reveal portions of the Ten Commandments written in Hebrew, among other lawgivers in the south frieze. Representations of the Ten Commandments adorn the metal gates lining the north and south sides of the Courtroom as well as the doors leading into the Courtroom. Moses also sits on the exterior east facade of the building holding the Ten Commandments tablets.

Similar acknowledgments can be seen throughout a visitor's tour of our Nation's Capital . . . .

Of course, the Ten Commandments are religious—they were so viewed at their inception and so remain. The monument, therefore, has religious significance. According to Judeo-Christian belief, the Ten Commandments were given to Moses by God on Mt. Sinai. But Moses

[83]McCreary County, Kentucky v. American Civil Liberties Union of Kentucky, 545 U.S. 844 (2005).

was a lawgiver as well as a religious leader. And the Ten Commandments have an undeniable historical meaning, as the foregoing examples demonstrate. Simply having religious content or promoting a message consistent with a religious doctrine does not run afoul of the Establishment Clause . . . .

There are, of course, limits to the display of religious messages or symbols. For example, we held unconstitutional a Kentucky statute requiring the posting of the Ten Commandments in every public schoolroom. *Stone v. Graham,* (1980). In the classroom context, we found that the Kentucky statute had an improper and plainly religious purpose. [W]e have "been particularly vigilant in monitoring compliance with the Establishment Clause in elementary and secondary schools," *Edwards v. Aguillard,* (1992) . . . .

The placement of the Ten Commandments monument on the Texas State Capitol grounds is a far more passive use of those texts than was the case in *Stone,* where the text confronted elementary school students every day. Indeed, Van Orden, the petitioner here, apparently walked by the monument for a number of years before bringing this lawsuit. The monument is therefore also quite different from the prayers involved in *Schempp and Lee v. Weisman.* Texas has treated her Capitol grounds monuments as representing the several strands in the State's political and legal history. The inclusion of the Ten Commandments monument in this group has a dual significance, partaking of both religion and government. We cannot say that Texas' display of this monument violates the Establishment Clause of the First Amendment.

The judgment of the Court of Appeals is affirmed.

It is so ordered.

Justice BREYER, concurring in the judgment.

. . . Thus, as Justices Goldberg and Harlan pointed out, the Court has found no single mechanical formula that can accurately draw the constitutional line in every case . . . .

In certain contexts, a display of the tablets of the Ten Commandments can convey not simply a religious message but also a secular moral message (about proper standards of social conduct). And in certain contexts, a display of the tablets can also convey a historical message (about a historic relation between those standards and the law)—a fact that helps to explain the display of those tablets in dozens of courthouses throughout the Nation, including the Supreme Court of the United States . . . .

Here the tablets have been used as part of a display that communicates not simply a religious message, but a secular message as well. The circumstances surrounding the display's placement on the capitol grounds and its physical setting suggest that the State itself intended the latter, nonreligious aspects of the tablets' message to predominate. And the monument's 40-year history on the state grounds indicates that that has been its effect.

The group that donated the monument, the Fraternal Order of Eagles, a private civic (and primarily secular) organization, while interested in the religious aspect of the Ten Commandments, sought to highlight the Commandments' role in shaping civic morality as part of that organization's efforts to combat juvenile delinquency . . . .

The physical setting of the monument, moreover, suggests little or nothing of the sacred. The monument sits in a large park containing 17 monuments and 21 historical markers, all designed to illustrate the "ideals" of those who settled in Texas and of those who have lived there since that time. The setting does not readily lend itself to meditation or any other religious activity . . . .

If these factors provide a strong, but not conclusive, indication that the Commandments' text on this monument conveys a predominantly secular message, a further factor is determinative here. As far as I can tell, 40 years passed in which the presence of this monument, legally speaking, went unchallenged (until the single legal objection raised by petitioner). And I am not aware of any evidence suggesting that this was due to a climate of intimidation. Hence, those 40 years suggest more strongly than can any set of formulaic tests that few individuals, whatever their system of beliefs, are likely to have understood the monument as amounting, in any significantly detrimental way, to a government effort to favor a particular religious sect, primarily to promote religion over nonreligion . . . .

This case, moreover, is distinguishable from instances where the Court has found Ten

Commandments displays impermissible. The display is not on the grounds of a public school, where, given the impressionability of the young, government must exercise particular care in separating church and state.

This case also differs from McCreary County, where the short (and stormy) history of the courthouse Commandments' displays demonstrates the substantially religious objectives of those who mounted them, and the effect of this readily apparent objective upon those who view them . . . .

For these reasons, I believe that the Texas display—serving a mixed but primarily nonreligious purpose, not primarily "advanc[ing]" or "inhibit[ing] religion," and not creating an "excessive government entanglement with religion,"—might satisfy this Court's more formal Establishment Clause tests. But, as I have said, in reaching the conclusion that the Texas display falls on the permissible side of the constitutional line, I rely less upon a literal application of any particular test than upon consideration of the basic purposes of the First Amendment's Religion Clauses themselves. This display has stood apparently uncontested for nearly two generations. That experience helps us understand that as a practical matter of degree this display is unlikely to prove divisive. And this matter of degree is, I believe, critical in a borderline case such as this one.

At the same time, to reach a contrary conclusion here, based primarily upon on the religious nature of the tablets' text would, I fear, lead the law to exhibit a hostility toward religion that has no place in our Establishment Clause traditions. Such a holding might well encourage disputes concerning the removal of longstanding depictions of the Ten Commandments from public buildings across the Nation. And it could thereby create the very kind of religiously based divisiveness that the Establishment Clause seeks to avoid . . . .

I concur in the judgment of the Court.
Justice STEVENS, with whom Justice GINSBURG joins, dissenting.

The message transmitted by Texas' chosen display is quite plain: This State endorses the divine code of the "Judeo-Christian" God . . . .

Even if, however, the message of the monument, despite the inscribed text, fairly could be said to represent the belief system of all Judeo-Christians, it would still run afoul of the Establishment Clause by prescribing a compelled code of conduct from one God, namely a Judeo-Christian God, that is rejected by prominent polytheistic sects, such as Hinduism, as well as non theistic religions, such as Buddhism . . . . And, at the very least, the text of the Ten Commandments impermissibly commands a preference for religion over irreligion . . . . Any of those bases, in my judgment, would be sufficient to conclude that the message should not be proclaimed by the State of Texas on a permanent monument at the seat of its government.

. . . The judgment of the Court in this case stands for the proposition that the Constitution permits governmental displays of sacred religious texts. This makes a mockery of the constitutional ideal that government must remain neutral between religion and irreligion. If a State may endorse a particular deity's command to "have no other gods before me," it is difficult to conceive of any textual display that would run afoul of the Establishment Clause . . . .

I respectfully dissent.

CASE DISCUSSION QUESTIONS

1. The monument on the grounds of the Texas State Capitol displayed one version of the Ten Commandments:

- I am the Lord thy God. Thou shalt have no other gods before me.
- Thou shalt not make to thyself any graven images.
- Thou shalt not take the Name of the Lord thy God in vain.
- Remember the Sabbath day, to keep it holy.

- Honor thy father and thy mother, that thy days may be long upon the land which the Lord thy God giveth thee.
- Thou shalt not kill.
- Thou shalt not commit adultery.
- Thou shalt not steal.
- Thou shalt not bear false witness against thy neighbor.
- Thou shalt not covet thy neighbor's house. "Thou shalt not covet thy neighbor's wife, nor his manservant, nor his maidservant, nor his cattle, nor anything that is thy neighbor's."

a. Which of these commandments would you characterize as having a religious message and what is the nature of those messages?
b. What, if any, bias is shown to any particular religion?
c. Which commandments relate to our civil or criminal laws?
d. What overall message do you think this display sends to the average person viewing it? Do you think the main message is one of endorsing a particular religion or is it more historical and tied to the state's secular moral message about appropriate social conduct?
e. The Texas display was donated to the state by the Eagles (a national, civic/fraternal group) for the expressed purpose of combating juvenile delinquency. Do you think it is an effective means of achieving that goal?

2. Why does Justice Rehnquist think this monument does not run afoul of the Establishment Clause?

3. While Justice Breyer agrees with the Court's decision, he presents different reasoning. On what basis would he allow the monument to stand? Do you agree with his assertion that the Texas Capitol display differed enough from those in public schools and the Kentucky courthouse display to justify upholding the former while striking down the later? Why or why not?

Other controversial applications of the establishment clause have involved school prayer and the teaching of evolution. The Supreme Court has consistently ruled against having state/school-sponsored prayers at the beginning of the school day and at school-sponsored events, but it has also held that the free exercise clause gives students the right to pray on their own before school or at lunch. States cannot prohibit the teaching of evolution, nor can they require that "creation science" or "intelligent design" be taught in schools.

Although the establishment clause prohibits various types of direct government aid to religious schools, the courts have allowed various forms of indirect aid and some voucher systems that can be used to pay tuition at religiously affiliated schools.

5. Due Process

The right to due process of law is protected by both the Fifth and Fourteenth Amendments. The Fifth states:

No person shall ... be deprived of life, liberty, or property, without due process of law.

The Fourteenth states:

> ... nor shall any State deprive any person of life, liberty, or property, without due process of law ....

Earlier in this chapter we discussed the way in which the Fourteenth Amendment due process clause has been used to apply most of the Bill of Rights to the states. In this section we discuss the difference between procedural and substantive due process.

a. Procedural Due Process

Procedural due process involves the legal procedures used in processing criminal prosecutions and various civil claims. The purpose of due process protections is to ensure that before the government takes away someone's property or liberty, the person is put on notice and given a chance to present his or her case. Due process can include such things as giving notice, providing for a neutral fact-finder, and requiring that witnesses be available for cross-examination.

Generally, the seriousness of the proposed deprivation of property or life will determine the amount of due process that someone receives. For example, a student facing expulsion from a state university might only have the right to notice and a hearing before a neutral fact-finder, whereas someone charged with murder would have a number of other procedural rights, such as the right to an attorney, the right to a jury trial, and the right to confront witnesses.

The most important of these procedural safeguards are listed in the Fourth (search and seizure), Fifth (grand juries, double jeopardy, and self-incrimination), Sixth (speedy trial, public trial, jury trial with right to confront accusers; compulsory process for obtaining witnesses; and assistance of counsel), Seventh (jury trial in civil suits), and Eighth (right to bail) Amendments. We discuss them in detail in the Criminal Procedure section of Chapter 12.

Procedural due process The requirement that governments follow certain procedures when seeking to deprive people of life, liberty, or property.

b. Substantive Due Process

Whereas procedural due process relates to *how* the government must go about depriving people of their lives, liberty, or property, substantive due process relates to the substance of the law that was violated. Substantive due process prohibits the government from depriving anyone of life, liberty, or property when the law being violated is found to be arbitrary or unreasonable. Whereas laws, such as those against theft, assault, or murder, are not considered to be arbitrary or unreasonable, some laws regulating various business practices, abortions, and homosexuality have at various times been found to violate substantive due process rights.

In 1890, the Supreme Court first struck down a state economic regulation on the basis that it violated substantive due process.[84] Similar decisions striking down various economic regulations continued until the 1930s when the Court signaled the end of the substantive due process application of the liberty of contract.[85]

Substantive due process The requirement that governments not deprive anyone of life, liberty, or property where the law being violated is found to be arbitrary or unreasonable.

---

[84]Chicago, M. & St. P. R. Co. v. Minnesota, 134 U.S. 418.

[85]*See, e.g.,* Nebbia v. New York, 291 U.S. 502 (1934), and West Coast Hotel v. Parish, 300 U.S. 379 (1937).

The recognition of personal privacy as a liberty interest began in 1942 with *Skinner v. Oklahoma* where the Supreme Court struck down a state statute that authorized the sexual sterilization of persons convicted two or more times of felonies involving moral turpitude.[86] It was the Court's 1965 decision in *Griswald v. Connecticut,*[87] however, that brought the concept of a constitutional right to privacy to public attention. In that case, the Court ruled that a Connecticut statute prohibiting the use of any drug, medical article, or instrument for the purpose of preventing conception violated the due process clause of the Fourteenth Amendment when applied to married couples.

Writing for the Court, Justice Douglas deduced the existence of a liberty interest in privacy from a "penumbra" formed by "emanations from" various sections of the Bill of Rights, including the following:

- First Amendment freedom of association,
- Third Amendment prohibition against quartering of soldiers,
- Fourth Amendment search and seizure protection,
- Fifth Amendment self-incrimination, and
- Ninth Amendment rights reserved to the people.

On the other hand, in his concurring opinion, Justice Goldberg concluded that "liberty" is not confined to rights specifically mentioned in the first eight amendments, but as indicated by the Ninth Amendment, includes other rights "rooted in the traditions and conscience of our people." Justices Harlan and White believed the right to marital privacy was implicit in the liberty referred to in the due process clause.

Eight years later, when the Supreme Court decided *Roe v. Wade,*[88] seven of the nine justices ruled that a Texas anti-abortion statute violated the right of privacy involving sex and procreation that had been recognized in *Griswold.*

Once they recognized that a protected liberty was involved, they then had to determine if the governmental interests asserted by the state justified limiting the woman's right to choose. The Court found that the state's asserted interest in protecting the health of pregnant women was not advanced by the anti-abortion law because modern medical techniques had made early abortions safer for the woman than going through normal childbirth.

The state also asserted an interest in the protection of prenatal life. However, an extensive review of the law showed that the unborn had never been recognized in the law as legal persons.

> When those trained in the respective disciplines of medicine, philosophy, and theology are unable to arrive at any consensus [about when life begins], the judiciary, at this point in the development of man's knowledge, is not in a position to speculate as to the answer.[89]

Therefore, the majority of the justices chose not to recognize a governmental interest in protecting potential life prior to the point of "viability."[90] Based on

---

[86] 316 U.S. 535.

[87] 381 U.S. 479.

[88] 410 U.S. 113 (1973).

[89] Id. at 159.

[90] The point at which the fetus is presumably capable of meaningful life outside the mother's womb.

this, they ruled that the state could proscribe abortion after the point of viability *except* where it is necessary to preserve the life or health of the mother.

The *Roe v. Wade* decision soon became a central rallying point for a "pro-life" political movement that proved quite successful at gaining control of many state legislatures and created a powerful voting block in Congress. While they never mustered enough votes in the Senate to pass any of their proposed "human life" constitutional amendments, they were quite successful in passing laws that made it more difficult for women to get abortions. These statutes, in turn, were promptly challenged in court by "pro-choice" groups.[91]

While all this legislating and adjudicating was going on, the "pro-life" groups also worked hard to elect presidential candidates who would presumably appoint Supreme Court justices who would vote to overturn *Roe v. Wade*. When Samuel Alito replaced Sandra Day O'Connor in 2006, many thought the ideological balance had shifted to the point where *Roe* might finally be reversed. The first opportunity for these new justices to overturn *Roe* came in a case challenging the constitutionality of the Partial-Birth Abortion Ban Act of 2003, which proscribed a particular method of ending fetal life in the later stages of pregnancy.[92] While a 5-4 majority of the justices held that the statute was constitutionally valid on its face,[93] they did not overrule what they interpreted to be the basic holding of *Roe v. Wade*.

The right to privacy also served as the constitutional basis for invalidating a Texas law criminalizing homosexual sodomy. In 2003 the Court ruled that state laws prohibiting sexual activities between consenting adults of the same sex violated right to privacy interests protected by the due process clause of the Fourteenth Amendment.[94]

6. Equal Protection

The equal protection clause is found at the end of Section 1 of the Fourteenth Amendment. The key language is

> Nor shall any State . . . deny to any person within its jurisdiction the equal protection of the laws.

While the legislative history indicates that the Fourteenth Amendment was designed to protect the newly freed slaves, nothing in the wording of the clause limits it to situations involving former slaves or distinctions based on race. The Supreme Court has applied the clause to a wide variety of discriminatory criteria including sex, age, ethnicity, religion, and region of the country.

Note further that this clause protects "any person within its [the state's] jurisdiction"—not just citizens of the state. In 1886, the Supreme Court had

---

[91]*See, e.g.,* Planned Parenthood v. Danforth, 428 U.S. 52 (1976); Planned Parenthood v. Casey, 505 U.S. 833 (1992); Akron v. Akron Center for Reproductive Health, 462 U.S. 416 (1983); Webster v. Reproductive Health Services, 492 U.S. 490 (1989); Stenburg v. Carhart, 530 U.S. 914 (2000). Some of the restrictions were upheld as reasonable, while others were struck down on the basis that they placed too great a burden on the woman's right to control her own body.

[92]Gonzales v. Carhart, 550 U.S. 124 (2007).

[93]It left open the possibility of someone later challenging the way it was being applied in a specific situation.

[94]Lawrence v. Texas, 539 U.S. 558.

ruled that it was a violation of the equal protection clause for a state to prohibit a noncitizen from China from starting a laundry business.[95] More recently, the Supreme Court ruled that children of undocumented aliens could not be discriminated against with respect to receiving a public education.[96]

As has been the case with most of the other rights discussed in this chapter, it is important to note that these rights are not absolute. The Supreme Court has never ruled that the government has to treat all people the same at all times and regardless of their particular circumstances. Rather, it has interpreted the Fourteenth Amendment as prohibiting *some, but not all,* forms of differential treatment. In determining if a specific type of differential treatment violates the equal protection clause, judges examine the appropriateness of the criteria being used and the way in which those criteria are being applied.

a. Standards/Test Applied

Over the years, the Supreme Court has developed a set of legal "tests" or "standards" that are to be applied when judging equal protection claims. In reading equal protection cases, it is important to note which of three basic standards is being applied.

(1) Standard scrutiny (or the rational basis test)

Rational Basis Test
Applied to cases of alleged discrimination when there is no suspect classification nor fundamental right involved; the plaintiff must prove the challenged action is not reasonably related to achieving a legitimate government purpose

In cases in which the **rational basis test** is used, the plaintiff has the burden of convincing the Court that the policy or action being challenged is not *reasonably related* to achieving a *legitimate government purpose.* To be a legitimate purpose, the government must be able to relate it to some grant of constitutional power. This is the most commonly used standard in equal protection analysis. It is used when neither of the others apply.

(2) Strict scrutiny (or the compelling interest test)

Strict Scrutiny Test
Applied to cases of alleged discrimination when there is a suspect classification or a fundamental right involved; the government must prove the challenged action was necessary to achieve a compelling government interest and was the least restrictive means available.

The **strict scrutiny** standard lies at the opposite end of the spectrum. Whereas it is relatively easy for the government to prevail under standard scrutiny, it is much more difficult for the government to prevail when strict scrutiny is applied.

In these types of cases the burden of proof rests with the government rather than with the alleged victim of the unequal treatment. To win the case, the government must be able to establish that (1) its action was necessary to achieve a *compelling government interest,* and (2) it is the *least restrictive means available.* Notice that, under this standard, the government's interest must be *compelling* as opposed to simply being *legitimate* when using standard scrutiny analysis. Notice also that whereas standard scrutiny only requires that the policy being challenged be *reasonably* related to the government's interest, strict scrutiny requires the government establish that it could not have achieved its goal through a less restrictive alternative. As we will see, this standard is applied in cases involving race discrimination or fundamental rights.

[95]Yick Wo v. Hopkins, 118 U.S. 356 (1886).
[96]Plyler v. Doe, 457 U.S. 202 (1982).

(3) Intermediate (or heightened scrutiny) standard

The third standard used in equal protection analysis lies somewhere between the other two. It is more demanding than the rational basis standard but not as demanding as strict scrutiny. Under this standard the government's objective has to be *important,* and the challenged policy must be *substantially related.* While these terms are difficult to quantify, *important* is more demanding than *legitimate* but less than *compelling,* and being *substantially* related falls between being *reasonably* related and being the *least restrictive* means available. This standard was first applied to cases of sex discrimination.

(4) Choosing the proper standard

There are many occasions when the outcome of an equal protection case will depend upon which of these three standards a court chooses to apply. Practices that might be acceptable under one test may not be acceptable under one of the other tests.

The rational basis test (standard scrutiny) is the "default" standard in equal protection cases. It is the standard that is used when the facts of the case do not invoke a more specialized and more demanding standard.

The compelling interest test (strict scrutiny standard) is used when the party claiming to be discriminated against is a member of what is called a "suspect class" *or* is being denied a "fundamental right." As to the first basis for using the strict scrutiny test, in determining if someone is a member of a suspect class, the Supreme Court considers

- the extent to which its members are easily identifiable,
- how difficult it is to change one's identity, and
- if there is a long history of discrimination against members of that group.

Note that African Americans have always been considered to be a suspect class for purposes of equal protection analysis, but the courts have vacillated in their categorization of some other groups.

As to the second basis for using the strict scrutiny test, in order to be considered a fundamental right, it must not only be an important right but one that is explicitly stated in the Constitution. Examples of fundamental rights are freedom of speech and freedom of the press.

The intermediate standard was first announced in a sex discrimination case in 1976.[97] Its creation followed an ongoing disagreement between justices as to whether the rational basis or the strict scrutiny standards should be applied in sex discrimination claims. Justices Brennan, Douglas, White, and Marshall had argued that strict scrutiny should be applied because sex, like race, alienage, and national origin, was an inherently suspect classification. Unable to get a decisive fifth vote for this approach, they eventually developed intermediate scrutiny as a compromise solution. Used primarily in sex discrimination cases, it has also been applied in some cases involving discrimination against aliens.

Intermediate scrutiny test
Usually applied to cases of alleged gender discrimination; the government must show the challenged action was substantially related to an important government interest.

---

[97]Craig v. Boren, 429 U.S. 190 (1976).

As you read the following excerpts from *San Antonio Independent School Dist. v. Rodriguez* think about how the Supreme Court decides which test to apply and how this can make such a significant difference in the outcome of the case.

San Antonio Independent School Dist. v. Rodriguez
411 U.S. 1 (1973)

This class action on behalf of certain Texas school children was instituted against state school authorities in the United States District Court for the Western District of Texas. The plaintiffs argued that the state's statutory system for financing public education based on property taxes violated the equal protection clause because it resulted in substantial interdistrict disparities in per-pupil expenditures.

Mr. Justice POWELL delivered the opinion of the Court.

. . . The precedents of this Court provide the proper starting point. The individuals, or groups of individuals, who constituted the class discriminated against in our prior cases shared two distinguishing characteristics: because of their impecunity they were completely unable to pay for some desired benefit, and as a consequence, they sustained an absolute deprivation of a meaningful opportunity to enjoy that benefit.

. . . [I]n support of their charge that the system discriminates against the "poor," appellees have made no effort to demonstrate that it operates to the peculiar disadvantage of any class fairly definable as indigent, or as composed of persons whose incomes are beneath any designated poverty level. Indeed, there is reason to believe that the poorest families are not necessarily clustered in the poorest property districts . . . . [T]here is no basis on the record in this case for assuming that the poorest people—defined by reference to any level of absolute impecunity—are concentrated in the poorest districts.

Second, neither appellees nor the District Court addressed the fact that, . . . lack of personal resources has not occasioned an absolute deprivation of the desired benefit. The argument here is not that the children in districts having relatively low assessable property values are receiving no public education; rather, it is that they are receiving a poorer quality education than that available to children in districts having more assessable wealth. Apart from the unsettled and disputed question whether the quality of education may be determined by the amount of money expended for it, a sufficient answer to appellees' argument is that, at least where wealth is involved, the Equal Protection Clause does not require absolute equality or precisely equal advantages . . . .

For these two reasons—the absence of any evidence that the financing system discriminates against any definable category of "poor" people or that it results in the absolute deprivation of education—the disadvantaged class is not susceptible of identification in traditional terms.

. . . We thus conclude that the Texas system does not operate to the peculiar disadvantage of any suspect class . . . . They also assert that the State's system impermissibly interferes with the exercise of a "fundamental" right and that accordingly the prior decisions of this Court require the application of the strict standard of judicial review . . . . It is this question—whether education is a fundamental right, in the sense that it is among the rights and liberties protected by the Constitution—which has so consumed the attention of courts and commentators in recent years.

. . . Education, of course, is not among the rights afforded explicit protection under our Federal Constitution. Nor do we find any basis for saying it is implicitly so protected. [T]he undisputed importance of education will not alone cause this Court to depart from the usual standard for reviewing a State's social and economic legislation. It is appellees' contention, however, that education is distinguishable from other services and benefits provided by the State because it bears a peculiarly close relationship to other rights and liberties accorded protection under the Constitution. Specifically, they insist that education is itself a fundamental personal right because it is essential to the effective exercise of First Amendment freedoms and to intelligent utilization of the right to vote. In asserting a nexus between speech and education, appellees urge that the right to speak is meaningless unless the speaker is capable of articulating his thoughts intelligently and persuasively. The "marketplace of ideas" is an empty forum for those lacking basic communicative tools. Likewise, they argue that the corollary right to receive information becomes little more than a hollow privilege when the recipient has not been taught to read, assimilate, and utilize available knowledge.

A similar line of reasoning is pursued with respect to the right to vote. Exercise of the franchise, it is contended, cannot be divorced from the educational Foundation of the voter. The electoral process, if reality is to conform to the democratic ideal, depends on an informed electorate: a voter cannot cast his ballot intelligently unless his reading skills and thought processes have been adequately developed . . . .

Even if it were conceded that some identifiable quantum of education is a constitutionally protected prerequisite to the meaningful exercise of either right, we have no indication that the present levels of educational expenditure in Texas provide an education that falls short . . . . Whatever merit appellees' argument might have if a State's financing system occasioned an absolute denial of educational opportunities to any of its children, that argument provides no basis for finding an interference with fundamental rights where only relative differences in spending levels are involved and where—as is true in the present case—no charge fairly could be made that the system fails to provide each child with an opportunity to acquire the basic minimal skills necessary for the enjoyment of the rights of speech and of full participation in the political process.

. . . It should be clear, for the reasons stated above and in accord with the prior decisions of this Court, that this is not a case in which the challenged state action must be subjected to the searching judicial scrutiny reserved for laws that create suspect classifications or impinge upon constitutionally protected rights.

. . . In sum, to the extent that the Texas system of school financing results in unequal expenditures between children who happen to reside in different districts, we cannot say that such disparities are the product of a system that is so irrational as to be invidiously discriminatory. Texas has acknowledged its shortcomings and has persistently endeavored—not without some success—to ameliorate the differences in levels of expenditures without sacrificing the benefits of local participation . . . . In its essential characteristics, the Texas plan for financing public education reflects what many educators for a half century have thought was an enlightened approach to a problem for which there is no perfect solution. We are unwilling to assume for ourselves a level of wisdom superior to that of legislators, scholars, and educational authorities in 50 States, especially where the alternatives proposed are only recently conceived and nowhere yet tested. The constitutional standard under the Equal Protection Clause is whether the challenged state action rationally furthers a legitimate state purpose or interest. We hold that the Texas plan abundantly satisfies this standard.

CASE DISCUSSION QUESTIONS

1. Why is it relevant to decide if "poor people" constitute a special class of people? What conclusion does Justice Powell reach?

2. Justice Powell distinguished between an absolute deprivation and a partial deprivation of a benefit. Why is this important to the outcome of the case?

3. What is a "fundamental right," and why is it important in this case?

4. In what ways did the plaintiffs argue that education is related to the First Amendment? Why did they attempt to make this link? What was the basis upon which the majority rejected the plaintiff's argument on this point?

5. Which standard of review did Justice Powell apply, and why did he use it?

6. Why did the Texas system meet that standard?

7. In *Rodriguez* the Court was forced to choose between the standard and strict scrutiny tests as it had not yet developed the intermediate standard. If the *Rodriguez* case had been argued in 1983 instead of 1973, after the creation of the intermediate standard, do you think the final result would have been different? Why or why not?

b. Race Discrimination

As previously mentioned, the drafters of the Fourteenth Amendment clearly intended for it to protect against racial discrimination. However, in *Plessy v. Ferguson,*[98] the Supreme Court used a "separate but equal" interpretation of the equal protection clause to subvert its original intent. Indeed, it was not until the Court's 1954 decision in *Brown v. Bd. of Education*[99] that the equal protection clause began to be enforced in a way that truly protected African Americans. (See Chapter 2, pages 22–23, for a further discussion of these landmark cases.)

In addition to desegregating public schools, the equal protection clause was used to stop racial discrimination in public services and public employment. The Court in *Shelley v. Kraemer*[100] prevented judicial enforcement of racially restrictive covenants in real estate and in *Loving v. Virginia*[101] struck down state laws prohibiting interracial marriages.

In recent years, the Supreme Court has reached several decisions in which the equal protection clause has been the basis for striking down various "affirmative action" programs. These cases have involved situations in which racial criteria were being used to increase racial diversity in public schools or certain types of jobs. In 1995 in *Adarand Constructors, Inc. v. Pena,*[102] the Supreme Court ruled that all uses of racial criteria, even those designed to help racial minorities, had to be judged by the strict scrutiny standard. In 2003, they approved an affirmative action program used for law school admissions at the University of Michigan while on the same day striking down an affirmative action admissions program used for undergraduate admissions at Michigan.[103] In 2007, the Court held that K-12 public school districts could not use race-based criteria for the purpose of achieving racial diversity in their schools.[104]

c. Sex Discrimination

The first major women's rights case was decided by the Supreme Court in 1873 when they ruled in *Bradwell v. Illinois*[105] that it was not a violation of the

---

[98]163 U.S. 537 (1896).

[99]349 U.S. 294 (1954).

[100]334 U.S. 1 (1948).

[101]388 U.S. 1 (1967).

[102]515 U.S. 2000 (1995).

[103]*See* Grutter v. Bollinger, 539 U.S. 306 (2003); Gratz v. Bollinger, 539 U.S. 244 (2003).

[104]Parents Involved in Community Schools v. Seattle School Dist. No. 1, 127 S. Ct. 2738 (2007).

[105]83 U.S. 130 (1873).

Fourteenth Amendment for a state to limit the practice of law to males. While the Nineteenth Amendment gave women the right to vote in 1920, it was not until 1971 that the Supreme Court used the equal protection clause to strike down a statute discriminating against women.[106]

Since then, the Court has gone on to decide a number of significant sex discrimination cases including ones that established different ages for consuming alcoholic beverages; that limited selected college programs to members of a single sex; that held a male, below a certain age, criminally responsible for having voluntary sex with a female of that same age while not imposing any comparable criminal liability on the female; and that required males to register for the draft without requiring females to do the same. In some cases, the Court has upheld the sex-based discrimination, and in others it has been struck down.[107]

United States v. Virginia provides a good example of the type of reasoning used in sex discrimination cases.

United States v. Virginia
518 U.S. 515 (1996)
June 26, 1996, Decided

Justice GINSBURG delivered the opinion of the Court.

Virginia's public institutions of higher learning include an incomparable military college, Virginia Military Institute (VMI). The United States maintains that the Constitution's equal protection guarantee precludes Virginia from reserving exclusively to men the unique educational opportunities VMI affords. We agree.

Founded in 1839, VMI is today the sole single-sex school among Virginia's 15 public institutions of higher learning. VMI's distinctive mission is to produce "citizen-soldiers," men prepared for leadership in civilian life and in military service. VMI pursues this mission through pervasive training of a kind not available anywhere else in Virginia.

. . . Inherent differences between men and women, we have come to appreciate, remain cause for celebration, but not for denigration of the members of either sex or for artificial constraints on an individual's opportunity. Sex classifications may be used to compensate women "for particular economic disabilities [they have] suffered," *Califano v. Webster,* 430 U.S. 313, 320, 51 L. Ed. 2d 360, 97 S. Ct. 1192 (1977) (*per curiam*), to "promote equal employment opportunity," see *California Fed. Sav. & Loan Assn. v. Guerra,* 479 U.S. 272, 289, 93 L. Ed. 2d 613, 107 S. Ct. 683 (1987), to advance full development of the talent and capacities of our Nation's people. But such classifications may not be used, as they once were, to create or perpetuate the legal, social, and economic inferiority of women.

---

[106]Reed v. Reed, 414 U.S. 71. (1971). The statute in question made a presumption that a man would be a better executor of an estate than a woman.

[107]Discrimination favoring men over women was struck down in United States v. Virginia, 518 U.S. 515 (1996) (male only military academy). Discrimination favoring women over men was struck down in Craig v. Boren, 429 U.S. 190 (1976) (drinking ages), and Mississippi University for Women v. Hogan, 458 U.S. 718 (1982) (female only nursing program), but was upheld in Michael M. v. Superior Court of Sonoma County, 450 U.S. 464 (1981) (statutory rape laws), and Rostker v. Goldberg, 453 U.S. 57 (1981) (male only draft registration requirement).

. . . [W]e conclude that Virginia has shown no "exceedingly persuasive justification" for excluding all women from the citizen-soldier training afforded by VMI . . . .

Single-sex education affords pedagogical benefits to at least some students, Virginia emphasizes, and that reality is uncontested in this litigation. Similarly, it is not disputed that diversity among public educational institutions can serve the public good. But Virginia has not shown that VMI was established, or has been maintained, with a view to diversifying, by its categorical exclusion of women, educational opportunities within the Commonwealth. In cases of this genre, our precedent instructs that "benign" justifications proffered in defense of categorical exclusions will not be accepted automatically; a tenable justification must describe actual state purposes, not rationalizations for actions in fact differently grounded . . . .

Virginia next argues that VMI's adversative method of training provides educational benefits that cannot be made available, unmodified, to women. Alterations to accommodate women would necessarily be "radical," so "drastic," Virginia asserts, as to transform, indeed "destroy," VMI's program. Neither sex would be favored by the transformation, Virginia maintains: Men would be deprived of the unique opportunity currently available to them; women would not gain that opportunity because their participation would "eliminate the very aspects of [the] program that distinguish [VMI] from . . . other institutions of higher education in Virginia."

. . . It may be assumed, for purposes of this decision, that most women would not choose VMI's adversative method. As Fourth Circuit Judge Motz observed, however, in her dissent from the Court of Appeals' denial of rehearing en banc, it is also probable that "many men would not want to be educated in such an environment. (On that point, even our dissenting colleague might agree.) Education, to be sure, is not a "one size fits all" business. The issue, however, is not whether "women—or men—should be forced to attend VMI"; rather, the question is whether the Commonwealth can constitutionally deny to women who have the will and capacity, the training and attendant opportunities that VMI uniquely affords.

The notion that admission of women would downgrade VMI's stature, destroy the adversative system and, with it, even the school, is a judgment hardly proved, a prediction hardly different from other "self-fulfilling prophec[ies]." . . . When women first sought admission to the bar and access to legal education, concerns of the same order were expressed.

. . . Women's successful entry into the federal military academies, and their participation in the Nation's military forces, indicate that Virginia's fears for the future of VMI may not be solidly grounded. The Commonwealth's justification for excluding all women from "citizen-soldier" training for which some are qualified, in any event, cannot rank as "exceedingly persuasive," as we have explained and applied that standard.

. . . There is no reason to believe that the admission of women capable of all the activities required of VMI cadets would destroy the Institute rather than enhance its capacity to serve the "more perfect Union."

CASE DISCUSSION QUESTIONS

1. Justice Ginsburg notes that there are "inherent differences" between men and women. Do you agree, and if so, list some that you think are the most important.

2. Are any of these differences relevant to this case, and if so, what kinds of accommodations would VMI need to make to accommodate those differences?

3. At one point in this litigation, Virginia started a separate, women's only, program at a different location in the state. Do you think a separate program for women is an acceptable solution? Why or why not?

4. Some people believe that girls develop more self-confidence and leadership skills when they attend single-sex schools. Do you agree? Does this belief hold true for elementary, secondary, and college levels? If this is true, does it justify having single-sex schools? Are there situations in which boys would do better in single-sex schools?

d. Discrimination Based on Sexual Orientation

In recent years, a number of cases challenging laws and administrative practices against same-sex marriage have received national media attention. While this issue certainly raises federal equal protection issues, to date, these cases have involved state supreme courts applying state constitutions rather than interpretations of the U.S. Constitution. (See discussion in Chapter 11, pages 398–405. The full faith and credit clause issues raised by these situations were discussed earlier in this chapter on pages 143–144.)

The most significant gay rights–related decision to reach the U.S. Supreme Court has been *Romer v. Evans*.[108] Gay rights supporters sued to block the passage of an amendment to the Colorado constitution. The amendment would have prevented the enactment of any state or local laws prohibiting discrimination on the basis of "homosexual, lesbian or bisexual orientation, conduct, practices or relationships." Plaintiffs argued that the amendment violated the equal protection clause because it was state action that discriminated against them on the basis of their sexual orientation. If the amendment were allowed to be implemented, then they would have to go through the difficult process of getting another state constitutional amendment before they could get the legislature to include them in any statutes or ordinances that would protect them from discrimination. Other groups, however, were free to seek laws that would protect them without first having to pass constitutional amendments.

The case is significant, not only for the result—the Court found for the plaintiffs—but also for the test used and the way it was applied. The Court struck down the amendment even though it only applied the rational basis standard rather than either of the more demanding mid-level or strict scrutiny standards. In finding that the state had failed to show that the amendment was reasonably related to a legitimate government purpose, Justice Kennedy wrote:

> The amendment's sheer breadth is so discontinuous with the reasons offered for its passage that it seems inexplicable by anything but animus toward the class that it affects . . . . The breadth of the Amendment is so far removed from these particular justifications that we find it impossible to credit them.

Furthermore, since the justices never really discussed why they used the rational basis test rather than either mid-level or strict scrutiny, it could be argued that they left the door open for application of a stricter test at a later date.

e. Discrimination Based on Age

Courts apply the least demanding rational basis standard to cases involving age discrimination. Because people's ages are constantly changing, they do not fit the requirements for being treated as a suspect class. That is not to say,

---

[108]517 U.S. 620 (1996).

however, that all forms of age discrimination are necessarily reasonably related to a legitimate government purpose.

Lower courts around the country have upheld challenges to laws establishing minimum ages for drivers' licenses, right to drink alcoholic beverages, and curfew laws. In *Massachusetts Board of Retirement v. Murgia*,[109] the Supreme Court held that it was not a violation of the Fourteenth Amendment equal protection clause for a state to establish a mandatory retirement age of 50 for uniformed state police officers. That is not to say, however, that a mandatory retirement age for members of other professions, such as college professors, would be reasonably related to a legitimate government purpose.

f. Economic Discrimination

As anyone who has paid taxes knows, the federal government uses a graduated income tax that charges a higher rate on those who make more money. On the face of it, this discriminates against the rich. On the other hand, there are more tax deductions available to the rich, and studies consistently show that many people with higher incomes actually pay a lower percentage of that income for taxes. Because the Courts only apply the rational basis standard, the only question relevant to constitutional law is whether a graduated system is reasonably related to the legitimate government objective of raising money to pay for the services it provides.

There are several interesting cases in which plaintiffs have argued that they are being discriminated against because of their lack of wealth. The *San Antonio Independent School Dist. v. Rodriguez* case reprinted on pages 176–177 is an example of this type of litigation. Because the status of being poor is not sufficient to create a suspect class, and because not everyone in the school district was poor, the Court applied the rational basis test. While the Court noted that there were clearly better, more equitable ways of financing schools, the current system was not irrational. Therefore, it did not violate the equal protection clause.

Another case involving alleged discrimination against the poor was *Maher v. Roe*,[110] a test case brought to challenge Connecticut administrative regulations limiting Medicaid benefits for abortions to those that were "medically necessary." The plaintiffs were low-income women (who qualified for a government medical assistance program) who wished to have abortions but could not afford to pay for them on their own. They argued that they were being denied the equal protection of the law because the state policies kept poor women from having abortions that women with more money could have.

As it had done in *San Antonio v. Rodriguez*, the Court ruled that the plaintiffs did not constitute a suspect class. It also rejected the claim that the state's actions violated the women's fundamental right to have an abortion.[111] Because there was no suspect class and no fundamental right, the Court applied

---

[109]427 U.S. 307 (1976).

[110]432 U.S. 464 (1977).

[111]The Court ruled that the state's refusal to pay for abortions did not amount to a denial of the right to have an abortion because, while *Roe v. Wade* prohibits the government from imposing criminal penalties on those who have or perform abortions, the constitutional right to an abortion does not extend to having the government pay for it.

the rational basis test and found that it was not unreasonable for a state to make a value judgment preferring childbirth to abortion or to insist upon a prior showing of medical necessity to ensure that its money was being spent for authorized purposes.

SUMMARY

Constitutional law involves some of the most fundamental concepts in our legal system and many of the most controversial issues of our day. Constitutions define the organization and powers of the government and grant basic civil rights and civil liberties.

Because some sections of our constitutions include very general and somewhat ambiguous terminology, one often has to turn to court decisions in order to gain a better understanding of their meaning. The most common approaches that courts use to interpret constitutions include the literal approach, the contextual approach, the two historical approaches, and the living/evolving constitution approach.

The primary function of the original Constitution was to explain how the new central government was to be organized and its relationship to the state governments. To create a federalist form of government, the document lists specific powers that are delegated by the people to the federal government, lists some that are prohibited to the states, and then reserves all other powers to the states. To implement the concept of separation of powers, the Constitution divides the federal government's powers among the three branches of government: the legislative, executive, and judicial.

Over the years, the constitution has had twenty-six amendments—one of which was later repealed. Some have made structural changes, such as altering the way we choose the Vice President or limiting the number of years that a President can serve. Others have established or expanded civil rights and civil liberties. These rights include the right to vote, freedom of expression, freedom of religion, due process rights, and the equal protection of the law.

CRITICAL THINKING EXERCISES

1. Review the clauses of the U.S. Constitution quoted on page 128, and then for each one
   a. state what you think are the two most logical alternative meanings and
   b. give arguments for how a judge should go about deciding which meaning is the most appropriate interpretation.

2. The Fourth Amendment establishes a protection against "unreasonable searches and seizures," but it does not directly define what is or is not an unreasonable search and seizure. The amendment consists of a number of clauses. Analyze how each clause contributes to a better understanding of what constitutes an unreasonable search and seizure.

The right of the people to be secure in their persons, houses, papers, and effects, against unreasonable searches and seizures, shall not be violated, and no Warrants shall issue, but upon probable cause, supported by Oath or affirmation, and particularly describing the place to be searched, and the person or things to be seized.

a. This first clause refers to a "right of the people." What can be inferred from the text of the amendment as to who the people are who have this right?

b. What can be inferred from the text of the amendment as to whether this amendment includes a right to be secure in one's automobile?

c. The amendment states that this right of the people should not be violated. But by whom? What can be inferred from the text of the amendment as to who the violators might be? For example, does this amendment protect the security of your house from actions of your neighbors?

d. It is important to understand the meaning of all the words contained in this amendment, but it may contain words with which you may not be familiar. If so, consult a good legal dictionary or some other reliable source and then answer the following. What are warrants? What is probable cause?

e. Why do you think the warrant must be "supported by Oath or affirmation" and must particularly describe the place to be searched and the person or things to be seized?

f. What relevance do the clauses about the issuance of warrants have to do with the question of what constitutes an "unreasonable search and seizure"?

3. In his book *The Myth of Judicial Activism,* Kermit Roosevelt III states that when using its powers of judicial review, the Court can make two kinds of mistakes. "It can uphold laws that are in fact unconstitutional, and it can strike down laws that are constitutionally sound."[112] Which type of decision, if wrong, is harder to correct? Which type of decision do you think carries the greatest possibility of harm?

4. Although Article II, Section 2 of the Constitution states that the President shall be "Commander in Chief of the Army and Navy of the United States, and of the Militia of the several States," Article I, Section 8, Clause 11 gives Congress the power to "declare war." When President George W. Bush sent United States military forces into Iraq in March 2003, he did so without first having asked Congress for a formal declaration of war.

a. Who, if anyone, would have standing to challenge the constitutionality of the President's action in federal court? Any citizen of the United States? Anyone who paid federal taxes? A soldier who was being sent into combat in Iraq? A U.S. Senator or a member of the House of Representatives?

b. How do you think a judge would apply the political question doctrine to this type of case? If a judge were to determine that the plaintiffs had standing and that the issue was justiciable, what arguments could be made that it was constitutional for the President to invade Iraq without first getting a declaration of war from Congress? That it was unconstitutional?

5. Several years ago, a suit was filed challenging the constitutionality of displaying a 43-foot Christian cross on city-owned property on top of an 800-foot-

---

[112]Kermit Roosevelt III, The Myth of Judicial Activism (Yale University Press 2006), p. 29.

high hill. The 24-ton cross was donated by a private association committed to advancing religious interests and then maintained with public funds. It was easily visible for miles. There were no other religious symbols that were similarly visible in the area. For fifty years, the cross was the site of numerous religious events, such as weddings, baptisms, and Easter sunrise services. During the first thirty-eight years of its existence, there was no placard or marker indicating a reason for the cross being there. However, after objections to its presence were raised in the 1990s, a marker with a "Veterans" memorial inscription was placed at its foot.

    a. What types of legal arguments would you make if you were an attorney representing the plaintiffs in this case? Representing the defendants?

    b. Following a favorable ruling for the plaintiffs, the city attempted to sell a small parcel of land beneath the cross to a private association seeking to preserve the cross. What would be its reason for doing so, and how do you think a reviewing judge would respond?

6. Assume Congress passed a law forbidding all postal workers from speaking publicly in favor of any political candidate. If a worker was found to be violating this law, that worker would be immediately fired with no right to a hearing. How would you evaluate the validity of this statute under the Fifth Amendment's due process guarantees?

7. A state enacted administrative regulations limiting Medicaid benefits for abortions to those that were "medically necessary." Welfare recipients who wanted to have nontherapeutic abortions brought a suit challenging these regulations as being a violation of the Fourteenth Amendment's equal protection clause.

    a. If you were an attorney for the plaintiffs, which of the various equal protection standards would you want the court to apply? Why? What arguments would you use to support your position?

    b. If you were an attorney for the state, which of the various equal protection standards would you want the court to apply? Why? What arguments would you use to support your position?

    c. How is *Roe v. Wade* relevant to resolving the issues involved in this case? To what extent are the facts of the cases similar? In what ways do they differ?

    d. Do you think the Court would ultimately uphold or strike down the state's regulations? Why?

REVIEW QUESTIONS

Pages 127 through 139

1. What are the two main functions of the U.S. Constitution?
2. Define judicial review. What is it about the nature of our Constitution that makes judicial review so important?
3. What are the four main approaches that judges use when interpreting ambiguous or vague constitutional words and phrases?
4. What difficulties are posed by taking a literalist approach to the Constitution?
5. When a court uses a contextual analysis, on what types of text is it likely to rely?
6. There are two variations of historical analysis. What are they and how do they differ from each other?

7. What is the living/evolving approach to constitutional analysis? What are its advantages and disadvantages as compared to the other three approaches?

Pages 139 through 152

8. What are the advantages and disadvantages of federalism?
9. How has the doctrine of implied powers been used over the years to expand congressional power?
10. The Constitution gives Congress the power to regulate commerce. How have the courts interpreted this power, and why has its application in specific situations caused a great deal of controversy?
11. What is the doctrine of preemption, and what purpose does it serve in our federalist system of government?
12. In what way does the "full faith and credit clause" govern the relationship among the states?
13. The Constitution provides for a separation of powers among the three federal branches of government, thereby creating a system of checks and balances. What does that mean?
14. What is judicial self-restraint? How does it relate to justiciability and standing?
15. When the courts determine that something is a "political question," what does that mean, and what effect will that have on the litigation?
16. What does the Twenty-fifth Amendment do, and why is it important?

Pages 152 through 170

17. Where can you locate the Bill of Rights, and what protections does it contain?
18. What is the difference between civil rights and civil liberties?
19. To what extent is the Bill of Rights applicable to the states?
20. Which amendments impact the right to vote?
21. Describe some of the limitations that the courts have placed on our freedom of expression.
22. When is a "time and place restriction" valid?
23. What is meant by "content neutrality"?
24. Define symbolic speech. Under what circumstances is it protected?
25. The First Amendment contains two clauses dealing with religion. What are they, and how do they differ from each other?
26. How do the courts decide whether a particular activity should be protected under the First Amendment's free exercise clause?
27. What is the *Lemon* test, and how has the Court used it to determine whether a particular state action is in violation of the First Amendment freedom of religion clause?

Pages 170 through 185

28. The Fifth Amendment provides both procedural and substantive due process. How do they differ from each other?
29. What and whom does the equal protection clause protect?
30. What standards are applied in equal protection cases, and what determines which one will be used in a specific case? How does the selection of the standard to be used affect the outcome of the case?
31. When faced with a claim of discrimination based on sexual orientation, how has the Supreme Court's approach differed from the way it has handled cases of discrimination based on sex?
32. Why is discrimination based on age treated differently than discrimination based on sex or race?
33. Has the Supreme Court found that poverty is a suspect classification? Why does this matter?

Chapter 7

Torts

*The risk reasonably to be perceived defines
the duty to be obeyed.*
Justice Benjamin Cardozo

INTRODUCTION

A **tort** can occur when someone injures you, slanders your reputation, or damages your property. A tort is defined as a private wrong (other than a breach of contract) in which a person or property is harmed because of another's failure to carry out a legal duty. In most instances this legal duty is an obligation to refrain from taking actions that harm others. Occasionally, a duty will consist of an affirmative obligation to act in order to protect others.

A tort is considered to be a "private wrong," as opposed to criminal acts, which are seen as "public wrongs." Therefore, while the state prosecutes crimes, the individual harmed must pursue a tort action. The end results of a criminal action and a civil tort suit also differ: a finding of guilt in a criminal action can result in a fine paid to the state or in imprisonment, while a finding of liability in a tort action usually leads to a damage award to the harmed party. However, as we discussed in Chapter 3, because both criminal acts and torts can result in harm to a person or property, sometimes the same set of facts will give rise to both a tort action and a criminal action.

Tort actions must also be distinguished from contract actions. In a tort action the legal duties are established by the courts through the common law and more recently also by statutory modifications of the common law. In contrast, contract actions are based on the legal duties the parties established in their contract. A further difference between a contract action and a tort action lies in the remedy sought. In a contract action the purpose of the lawsuit is to give the injured party the benefit of the bargain. In a tort action the purpose is to compensate the plaintiff for any losses suffered. For example, assume you purchase an automobile with defective brakes. Because of the defect you are unable to stop at a red light and are in a minor accident. The purpose of a breach of contract action would be to "get the benefit of your bargain"—that is, a car without defective brakes. The purpose of a tort action would be to fully compensate you for any harm to yourself or the car, including your medical bills, lost time from work, and pain and suffering. As this example suggests, at times one set of facts can give rise to both a breach of contract action and a tort action. For example, if a manufacturer intentionally lies about a product he is selling and the buyer relies on that lie to her detriment, the buyer might be able to sue for both breach of contract (thereby invalidating the sale) and fraud (thereby recovering for damages caused by the product).

Tort law has ancient roots, and tort rules have been created by the courts on a case-by-case basis. Therefore, looking to precedent for analogous situations plays a large role in any analysis of a tort problem. In addition, the courts frequently look to an authoritative secondary source, the **Restatement of the Law of Torts, Second**. This Restatement was drafted by a group of legal scholars in order to summarize the existing common-law rules in a set of black letter principles. At times, instead of simply "restating" the law, the drafters also included their vision of what tort law should become. This is most notable in the area of products liability. Although the Restatement is a secondary source and is therefore only persuasive authority, you will frequently see courts citing it and even formally adopting some of its provisions.

In spite of its ancient common-law roots, tort law has never been static. Historically, judges have seen the need to adapt the common-law principles to changing conditions. Most recently some of those conditions have included the development of modern modes of transportation and other scientific advances, such as the ability to artificially create and prolong life. In addition, when the need arises, instead of simply adapting the currently existing common-law rules, the courts will even recognize new torts. One example is the new tort of battered woman's syndrome, which we will discuss later in this chapter.

While tort law is still predominantly court-created law, legislatures are playing an increasingly active role. For example, both Congress and state legislatures have enacted "tort reform" statutes, with the purpose of modifying some of the perceived abuses of the tort system. One example is legislation to place limits on the amount of damages that can be awarded in certain types of tort cases. Such tort reform measures have even been included in the national platforms of the major political parties.

Torts have traditionally been classified into three major categories: intentional acts, negligence, and strict liability. See Figure 7-1. In any one of these three areas, the person who commits the tort is known as the **tortfeasor**.

When people intentionally seek to violate a duty toward others, their purposeful conduct is classified as an **intentional tort**. Those who commit intentional torts are subject to punitive in addition to compensatory damages. If John intentionally drives his car into Jill's car, damaging her car and injuring Jill, John has committed an intentional tort. As we will see later in this chapter, John's motive (reason) for hitting Jill's car is irrelevant. All that matters is that he intended to do so.

Restatement of the Law of Torts, Second
An authoritative secondary source, written by a group of legal scholars, summarizing the existing common law, as well as suggesting what the law should be.

Figure 7-1 Degrees of Fault

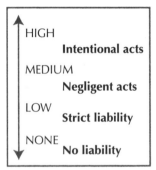

When the harm occurs as a result of a careless act done with no conscious intent to injure anyone, the act is classified as **negligence**. Negligent actors are subject to compensatory but not to punitive damages. If the reason John's car struck Jill's was not because he had intended to do so but because he had carelessly taken his eyes off the road to adjust his radio, John's behavior may be classified as negligent.

There are times when for policy reasons the defendant is held responsible even though the defendant did not act negligently nor intentionally to harm the plaintiff. These are classified as **strict liability** torts. Strict liability is usually limited to situations involving an ultrahazardous activity, such as dynamiting, or the manufacture or sale of a potentially dangerous product. For example, if the reason John ran into Jill's car was because his brakes failed, the car manufacturer may be held strictly liable.

Finally, it is important to realize that the law does not provide for compensation for all injuries. There are true accidents, when either no one is at fault or the fault rests solely with the person injured. In those situations, the injured party cannot recover damages.

A. INTENTIONAL TORTS

An intentional tort occurs whenever someone intends an action that results in harm to a person's body, reputation, emotional well-being, or property. Almost any harm that you can imagine, if caused intentionally, can be classified as an intentional tort. In this section of the chapter we will discuss just a few of the most common intentional torts. First, there are the torts that cause harm to a person's body, reputation, or emotional well-being: assault and battery, false imprisonment, defamation, invasion of privacy, and intentional infliction of emotional distress. Second, there are the torts that cause harm to a person's property: trespass, trespass to personal property, and conversion. Third, we will briefly discuss a variety of other torts, including false arrest, malicious prosecution, abuse of process, fraud, and business torts.

In order to prove that an intentional tort occurred, the plaintiff must prove each of that tort's elements. The defendant then has the opportunity to raise any defenses. The primary defenses available in intentional tort cases are consent, self-defense, defense of third parties, and various types of privilege.

As we will see, one set of facts can give rise to more than one type of intentional tort. In addition, many intentional torts are also crimes. Consider the following fact scenario.

Case 6: The Abused Spouse

Mrs. Day has been living with Mr. David Day for the past five years. While their marriage has never been a happy one, Mrs. Day never thought of divorce until last night. Mr. Day came home very late from an adult co-ed softball game. Mrs. Day said it was obvious that he had been drinking. They soon got into a verbal fight. Among other things, Mr. Day yelled at Mrs. Day that he had told her boss she had been skimming money from the company's petty cash drawer.

Mrs. Day had never done any such thing. He also told her that he had received a call earlier in the day from the local hospital, telling him that Mrs. Day's mother had been admitted following a massive heart attack. (Later Mrs. Day found out that this was not true, but at the time she believed Mr. Day and became very upset.) The fight escalated, and Mr. Day began waving his baseball bat in front of Mrs. Day. Mrs. Day said that she was not frightened, as Mr. Day had never hit her, and she did not believe he would do so then. In fact, she turned her back on him and started to leave the room. He then yelled at her and, before she could turn around, hit her on the back of her arm with the bat, breaking her arm. Mrs. Day then fled to the bathroom, locking the door behind her. Mrs. Day remained in the bathroom for over two hours until she felt it was safe to leave. She found Mr. Day asleep on the living room couch. She fled to a neighbor's, who drove her to the hospital. The next morning Mrs. Day returned home to find Mr. Day as well as her purse gone. There was a message on the answering machine from her boss saying that she was fired.

While Mrs. Day is contemplating divorce proceedings, her more immediate concern is to learn what legal actions she can take to compensate her for her broken arm, emotional distress, missing purse, and lost job.

1. Harm to a Person's Body, Reputation, or Emotional Well-Being

The following torts will be discussed in this section: assault and battery (harm or threatened harm to a person's body), false imprisonment (a wrongful detention), defamation (harm to a person's reputation), and invasion of privacy and the intentional infliction of emotional distress (harm to a person's emotional well-being).

a. Assault and Battery

Assault
An intentional act that creates a reasonable apprehension of an immediate harmful or offensive physical contact.

Battery
An intentional act that creates a harmful or offensive physical contact.

An **assault** occurs when someone reasonably fears that he or she is about to suffer a harmful or offensive physical contact. A **battery** is the intentional harmful or offensive physical contact. While we usually think of assault and battery as one tort, in reality they are two torts. They can be present together, as, for example, when Tom first waves a fist in front of Sam's face and then proceeds to punch Sam in the nose. However, there can also be an assault with no battery whenever there is the threat of a battery but no ensuing physical contact. And there can also be a battery with no assault, as, for example, when the person being attacked does not see the threat of physical contact before it actually occurs.

(1) The elements of assault and battery

To prove an assault, the plaintiff must show that each of the following elements occurred:

1. an intentional act
2. that creates a reasonable apprehension of
3. an immediate harmful or offensive physical contact.

Notice the requirement in element 3 that the apprehension be of an *immediate* physical contact. A threat to go and get a gun is not an assault because there is no threat of an immediate contact.

To prove a battery, the plaintiff must show that each of the following elements occurred:

1. an intentional act
2. that creates a harmful or offensive physical contact.

Notice that for both assault and battery the contact does not have to actually be physically painful. It simply must be harmful or offensive. An unwanted kiss from a stranger could qualify as an offensive contact.

Contact also includes contact with anything attached to the person, such as clothing. In the classic case of *Fisher v. Carrousel Motor Hotel, Inc.,*[1] the court found that a battery had been committed when a hotel employee grabbed a plate from a customer. Also, the defendant need not actually do the touching if the defendant set the action in motion, such as by throwing a rock or ordering a dog to attack.

In discussing battery there are three important concepts to keep in mind. First, the intent involved must be the intent to perform the act, not necessarily to cause the plaintiff harm. Assume a boy, as a practical joke, pulls out a chair just as his friend is about to sit on it. The friend falls to the ground, breaking his arm. Even though the boy did not mean to hurt his friend, he is liable for battery. He intentionally did an act that caused physical injury. This example also illustrates the difference between intent, the desire to do an act, and motive, the reason for the act. The court is concerned with the intent (the boy's desire to pull out the chair) and not with his motive (his wish to play a practical joke).

Second, usually defendants will be liable for any consequences of their actions, even if the consequences were unforeseeable. Often this is phrased as follows: "The defendant must take the plaintiff as the defendant finds her." For example, if the plaintiff has an "eggshell skull" and the defendant merely taps the plaintiff's head lightly, the tap may seriously injure the plaintiff. The defendant is liable, even if such a tap would not have harmed most people.

Third, assume John swung his fist, meaning to hit Bill. However, Bill moved aside and John hit Sara instead. John is liable to Sara for battery under the theory of **transferred intent**.

The following case involves a friendly backyard touch football game that unfortunately ends in injury. While reading the case, decide for yourself whether you think the plaintiff should have been allowed to succeed on her claim of battery.

Transferred intent
A legal fiction that if a person directs a tortious action toward A but instead harms B, the intent to act against A is transferred to B.

---

[1] 424 S.W.2d 627 (Tex. 1967).

Knight v. Jewett
3 Cal. App. 4th 1022, 275 Cal. Rptr. 292 (1990)

TODD, Acting P.J.

Kendra Knight appeals a summary judgment granted in favor of Michael Jewett in her lawsuit against Jewett for . . . assault and battery stemming from a touch football game in which she was injured. . . .

Facts

On January 25, 1987, Knight and several other individuals, including Jewett, gathered at the Vista home of Ed McDaniels to observe the Super Bowl football game. Knight and Jewett were among those who decided to play a game of coed touch football during half-time using a "peewee" football often used by children. Apparently, no explicit rules were written down or discussed before the game, other than the requirement that to stop advancement of the player with the ball it was necessary to touch that player above the waist with two hands. Knight and Jewett were on different teams.

Previously, Knight had played touch football and frequently watched football on television. Knight voluntarily participated in the Super Bowl half-time game. It was her understanding that this game would not involve forceful pushing, hard hitting or hard shoving during the game. She had never observed anyone being injured in a touch football game before this incident.

About five to ten minutes after the game started, Jewett ran into Knight during a play and afterward Knight asked Jewett not to play so rough. Otherwise, she told him, she would stop playing.

On the next play, Knight suffered her injuries, when she was knocked down by Jewett and he stepped on the little finger of her right hand.

Kendra had three surgeries on the finger, but they proved unsuccessful. The finger was amputated during a fourth surgery.

According to Jewett, he had jumped up to intercept a pass and as he came down he knocked Knight over. When he landed, he stepped back and onto Knight's hand.

According to Knight's version, her teammate, Andrea Starr, had caught the ball and was proceeding up the field. Knight was headed in the same direction, when Jewett, in pursuit of Starr, came from behind Knight and knocked her down. Knight put her arms out to break the fall and Jewett ran over her, stepping on her hand. Jewett continued to pursue Starr for another 10 to 15 feet before catching up with her and tagging her. Starr said the tag was rough enough to cause her to lose her balance and fall and twist her ankle. . . .

Discussion . . .

Inasmuch as this case reaches us on appeal from a summary judgment in favor of Jewett, it is only necessary for us to determine whether there is any possibility Knight may be able to establish her case.

A requisite element of assault and battery is intent. Here, however, there is no evidence that Jewett intended to injure Knight or commit a battery on her. Moreover, the record affirmatively shows Knight does not believe Jewett had the intent to step on her hand or injure her.[7] Without the requisite intent, Knight cannot state a cause of action for assault and battery. . . .

Affirmed.

---

[7]The deposition of Kendra Knight was taken on October 19, 1988, and offered in support of the motion for summary judgment. Ms. Knight testified as follows:

"Q. Do you believe that Mr. Jewett was trying to step on your hand? Do you have any reason to believe he had any intention to hurt you?"

"A. No."

CASE DISCUSSION QUESTIONS

1. Did the court think that a battery had occurred? Why?
2. What role do you think Ms. Knight's deposition played in the court's reasoning?
3. Do you think the result would have been different if Ms. Knight had never watched football or played touch football prior to her accident?

(2) The defenses to assault and battery

The first step in winning a tort claim is for the plaintiff to prove each of the elements of that tort. Then, only if the plaintiff is able to do so, the defendant raises any defenses. The defenses that can be raised to an assault or battery claim are consent, self-defense, defense of others, and sometimes defense of property.

Consent to a tortious act can sometimes be implied from the nature of the plaintiff's conduct. When one goes to a barber or hair stylist, there is an implied consent for that person to touch and cut the customer's hair. Some types of consent are implied by law, such as when a doctor administers medical treatment in an emergency. Because the court in *Knight v. Jewett* did not think that Ms. Knight had established a prima facie case for battery, it did not consider whether the defendant had any valid defenses. If the court in *Knight* had thought Mr. Jewett intentionally stepped on Ms. Knight, it next would have discussed the issue of whether she had consented to the battery. How do you think the court would have resolved that issue?

For self-defense and defense of others to be valid, the plaintiff must reasonably believe that a threat exists and then must use only as much force as is necessary to stop the battery. Self-defense, for example, could be used as a valid defense against a battery charge if the plaintiff had threatened the defendant with a knife and the defendant had defended himself with his fists. However, if the plaintiff was unarmed and struck the defendant with his fists, it might not be a valid self-defense for the defendant to stab the plaintiff with a knife.

Perhaps one of the most controversial defenses is that of defense of property. The following case from Iowa illustrates a rejection of its use.

Katko v. Briney
183 N.W.2d 657 (Iowa 1971)

MOORE, C.J.

The primary issue presented here is whether an owner may protect personal property in an unoccupied boarded-up farm house against trespassers and thieves by a spring gun capable of inflicting death or serious injury.

We are not here concerned with a man's right to protect his home and members of his family. Defendants' home was several miles from the scene of the incident to which we refer infra.

Plaintiff's action is for damages resulting from serious injury caused by a shot from a 20-gauge spring shotgun set by defendants in a bedroom of an old farm house which had been uninhabited for several years. Plaintiff and his companion, Marvin McDonough, had broken and entered the house to find and steal old bottles and dated fruit jars which they considered antiques.

At defendants' request plaintiff's action was tried to a jury consisting of residents of the community where defendants' property was located. The jury returned a verdict for plaintiff and against defendants for $20,000 actual and $10,000 punitive damages.

After careful consideration of defendants' motions for judgment notwithstanding the verdict and for new trial, the experienced and capable trial judge overruled them and entered judgment on the verdict. Thus we have this appeal by defendants. . . .

II. Most of the facts are not disputed. In 1957 defendant Bertha L. Briney inherited her parents' farm land in Mahaska and Monroe Counties. Included was an 80-acre tract in southwest Mahaska County where her grandparents and parents had lived. No one occupied the house thereafter. . . .

For about 10 years, 1957 to 1967, there occurred a series of trespassing and housebreaking events with loss of some household items, the breaking of windows and "messing up of the property in general." The latest occurred June 8, 1967, prior to the event on July 16, 1967 herein involved.

Defendants through the years boarded up the windows and doors in an attempt to stop the intrusions. They had posted "no trespass" signs on the land several years before 1967. The nearest one was 35 feet from the house. On June 11, 1967 defendants set "a shotgun trap" in the north bedroom. After Mr. Briney cleaned and oiled his 20-gauge shotgun, the power of which he was well aware, defendants took it to the old house where they secured it to an iron bed with the barrel pointed at the bedroom door. It was rigged with wire from the doorknob to the gun's trigger so it would fire when the door was opened. Briney first pointed the gun so an intruder would be hit in the stomach but at Mrs. Briney's suggestion it was lowered to hit the legs. He admitted he did so "because I was mad and tired of being tormented" but "he did not intend to injure anyone." He gave no explanation of why he used a loaded shell and set it to hit a person already in the house. Tin was nailed over the bedroom window. The spring gun could not be seen from the outside. No warning of its presence was posted.

Plaintiff lived with his wife and worked regularly as a gasoline station attendant in Eddyville, seven miles from the old house. He had observed it for several years while hunting in the area and considered it as being abandoned. He knew it had long been uninhabited. In 1967 the area around the house was covered with high weeds. Prior to July 16, 1967 plaintiff and McDonough had been to the premises and found several old bottles and fruit jars which they took and added to their collection of antiques. On the latter date about 9:30 P.M. they made a second trip to the Briney property. They entered the old house by removing a board from a porch window which was without glass. While McDonough was looking around the kitchen area plaintiff went to another part of the house. As he started to open the north bedroom door the shotgun went off striking him in the right leg above the ankle bone. Much of his leg, including part of the tibia, was blown away. Only by McDonough's assistance was plaintiff able to get out of the house and after crawling some distance was put in his vehicle and rushed to a doctor and then to a hospital. He remained in the hospital 40 days. . . .

III. Plaintiff testified he knew he had no right to break and enter the house with intent to steal bottles and fruit jars therefrom. He further testified he had entered a plea of guilty to larceny in the nighttime of property of less than $20 value from a private building. . . .

Prosser on Torts, Third Edition, pages 116–118, states:

> . . . the law has always placed a higher value upon human safety than upon mere rights in property, it is the accepted rule that there is no privilege to use any force calculated to cause death or serious bodily injury to repel the threat to land or chattels, unless there is also such a threat to the defendant's personal safety as to justify self-defense. . . . spring guns and other man-killing devices are not justifiable against a mere trespasser, or even a petty thief. They are privileged only against those upon whom the landowner, if he were present in person would be free to inflict injury of the same kind.

Restatement of Torts, section 85, page 180, states: . . . A possessor of land cannot do indirectly and by a mechanical device that which, were he present, he could not do immediately and in person. . . . Study and careful consideration of defendants' contentions on appeal reveal no reversible error.

Affirmed.

All Justices concur except LARSON, J., who dissents.

CASE DISCUSSION QUESTIONS

1. Why did the court uphold the jury's verdict in favor of the plaintiff trespasser?

2. The dissent stated: "When such a windfall comes to a criminal as a result of his indulgence in serious criminal conduct, the result is intolerable and indeed shocks the conscience. If we find the law upholds such a result, the criminal would be permitted by operation of law to profit from his own crime." What do you think?

3. Because the defendants did not raise the issue, this court did not deal directly with whether punitive damages were appropriate. What facts would support such a finding; what facts would argue against such a finding? Do you think punitive damages were appropriate in this case? Why?

4. Should a landowner who sets a trap such as in this case also be found criminally liable if an intruder is seriously injured? Why?

5. Do you think the result in this case would have been different if the house had been occupied? Why?

6. At trial Mr. Briney testified that "[p]rior to this time . . . he had locked the doors, posted seven no trespassing signs on the premises, and complained to the sheriffs of two counties on numerous occasions. . . . [A]ll these efforts were futile and the vandalism continued." What else could the defendants have done to protect their property?

b. False Imprisonment

False imprisonment occurs whenever one person, through force or the threat of force, unlawfully detains another person against his or her will. Issues of false imprisonment most frequently arise in situations in which store employees seek to detain suspected shoplifters or employers wish to detain and interview employees they suspect of unlawful activities.

False imprisonment
Occurs whenever one person, through force or the threat of force, unlawfully detains another person against his or her will.

(1) The elements of false imprisonment

In order to prove false imprisonment, the plaintiff must show the following:

1. an intentional act
2. that caused confinement or restraint
3. through force or the threat of force.

The plaintiff must actually be confined with no means of escape. For example, leaving someone alone in an unlocked office does not constitute false imprisonment.

(2) Defenses to false imprisonment

The most common defense to false imprisonment is that the defendant was justified in restraining the plaintiff. For example, many states have enacted statutes to protect merchants who want to question a suspected shoplifter. Usually, these statutes provide that a shopkeeper may detain a suspected shoplifter only if the shopkeeper can show probable cause to justify the delay and that even then the shopkeeper may detain the suspected shoplifter only for a reasonable time and in a reasonable manner. As you can imagine, because of the way these three statutory requirements are worded, each has given rise to a great deal of litigation.

In the following case, notice how each individual fact becomes very important in determining, first, whether the shopkeeper had falsely imprisoned the plaintiff and, second, whether the shopkeeper could prove a valid defense.

Coblyn v. Kennedy's, Inc.
359 Mass. 319, 268 N.E.2d 860 (1971)

SPIEGEL, JJ.

This is an action of tort for false imprisonment. At the close of the evidence the defendants filed a motion for directed verdicts which was denied. The jury returned verdicts for the plaintiff in the sum of $12,500. The case is here on the defendants' exceptions to the denial of their motion and to the refusal of the trial judge to give certain requested instructions to the jury.

We state the pertinent evidence most favorable to the plaintiff. On March 5, 1965, the plaintiff went to Kennedy's, Inc. (Kennedy's), a store in Boston. He was seventy years of age and about five feet four inches in height. He was wearing a woolen shirt, which was "open at the neck," a topcoat and a hat. "[A]round his neck" he wore an ascot which he had "purchased . . . previously at Filenes." He proceeded to the second floor of Kennedy's to purchase a sport coat. He removed his hat, topcoat and ascot, putting the ascot in his pocket. After purchasing a sport coat and leaving it for alterations, he put on his hat and coat and walked downstairs. Just prior to exiting through the outside door of the store, he stopped, took the ascot out of his pocket, put it around his neck, and knotted it. The knot was visible "above the lapels of his shirt." The only stop that the plaintiff made on the first floor was immediately in front of the exit in order to put on his ascot.

Just as the plaintiff stepped out of the door, the defendant Goss, an employee, "loomed up" in front of him with his hand up and said: "Stop. Where did you get that scarf?" The plaintiff responded, "[W]hy?" Goss firmly grasped the plaintiff's arm and said: "[Y]ou better go back and see the manager." Another employee was standing next to him. Eight or ten other people were standing around and were staring at the plaintiff. The plaintiff then said, "Yes, I'll go back in the store" and proceeded to do so. As he and Goss went upstairs to the second floor, the plaintiff paused twice because of chest and back pains. After reaching the second floor, the salesman from whom he had purchased the coat recognized him and asked what the trouble was.

The plaintiff then asked: "[W]hy 'these two gentlemen stop me?'" The salesman confirmed that the plaintiff had purchased a sport coat and that the ascot belonged to him.

The salesman became alarmed by the plaintiff's appearance and the store nurse was called. She brought the plaintiff into the nurse's room and gave him a soda mint tablet. As a direct result of the emotional upset caused by the incident, the plaintiff was hospitalized and treated for a "myocardial infarct."

Initially, the defendants contend that as a matter of law the plaintiff was not falsely imprisoned. They argue that no unlawful restraint was imposed by either force or threat upon the plaintiff's freedom of movement. However, "[t]he law is well settled that '[a]ny general restraint is sufficient to constitute an imprisonment . . . ' and '[a]ny demonstration of physical power which, to all appearances, can be avoided only by submission, operates as effectually to constitute an imprisonment, if submitted to, as if any amount of force had been exercised.' If a man is restrained of his personal liberty by fear of a personal difficulty, that amounts to a false imprisonment' within the legal meaning of such term." *Jacques v. Childs Dining Hall Co.*, 244 Mass. 438, 438–439.

We think it is clear that there was sufficient evidence of unlawful restraint to submit this question to the jury. Just as the plaintiff had stepped out of the door of the store, the defendant Goss stopped him, firmly grasped his arm and told him that he had "better go back and see the manager." There was another employee at his side. The plaintiff was an elderly man and there were other people standing around staring at him. Considering the plaintiff's age and his heart condition, it is hardly to be expected that with one employee in front of him firmly grasping his arm and another at his side the plaintiff could do other than comply with Goss's "request" that he go back and see the manager. . . .

In addition, as this court observed in the *Jacques* case, supra, at p. 441, the "honesty and veracity [of the plaintiff] had been openly . . . challenged. If she had gone out before . . . [exonerating herself], her departure well might have been interpreted by the lookers on as an admission of guilt." . . .

The defendants next contend that the detention of the plaintiff was sanctioned by G.L. c. 231, § 94B, inserted by St. 1958, c. 337. This statute provides as follows: "In an action for false arrest or false imprisonment brought by any person by reason of having been detained for questioning on or in the immediate vicinity of the premises of a merchant, if such person was detained in a reasonable manner and for not more than a reasonable length of time by a person authorized to make arrests or by the merchant or his agent or servant authorized for such purpose and if there were reasonable grounds to believe that the person so detained was committing or attempting to commit larceny of goods for sale on such premises, it shall be a defense to such action. . . ."

The defendants argue in accordance with the conditions imposed in the statute that the plaintiff was detained in a reasonable manner for a reasonable length of time and that Goss had reasonable grounds for believing that the plaintiff was attempting to commit larceny of goods held for sale.

It is conceded that the detention was for a reasonable length of time. We need not decide whether the detention was effected in a reasonable manner for we are of opinion that there were no reasonable grounds for believing that the plaintiff was committing larceny and, therefore, he should not have been detained at all. However, we observe that Goss's failure to identify himself as an employee of Kennedy's and to disclose the reasons for his inquiry and actions, coupled with the physical restraint in a public place imposed upon the plaintiff, an elderly man, who had exhibited no aggressive intention to depart, could be said to constitute an unreasonable method by which to effect detention.

The pivotal question before us as in most cases of this character is whether the evidence shows that there were reasonable grounds for the detention. . . .

The defendants assert that the judge improperly instructed the jury in stating that "grounds are reasonable when there is a basis which would appear to the reasonably prudent, cautious, intelligent person." In their brief, they argue that the "prudent and cautious man rule" is an objective standard and requires a more rigorous and restrictive standard of conduct than is contemplated by G.L. c. 231, § 94B. The defendants' requests for instructions, in effect, state that the proper test is a subjective one, viz., whether the defendant Goss had an honest and strong suspicion that the plaintiff was committing or attempting to commit larceny.

We do not agree. . . . [T]he words "reasonable grounds" and "probable cause" have traditionally been accorded the same meaning. In the case of *Terry v. Ohio,* 392 U.S. 1, involving the question whether a police officer must have probable cause within the Fourth Amendment to "stop-and-frisk" a suspected individual, the Supreme Court of the United States held that the "probable cause" requirement of the Fourth Amendment applies to a "stop-and-frisk" and that a "stop-and-frisk" must "be judged against an objective standard: would the facts available to the officer at the moment . . . 'warrant a man of reasonable caution in the belief' that the action taken was appropriate? . . . Anything less would invite intrusions upon constitutionally guaranteed rights based on nothing more substantial than inarticulate hunches, a result this Court has consistently refused to sanction." Pp. 21–22.

If we adopt the subjective test as suggested by the defendants, the individual's right to liberty and freedom of movement would become subject to the "honest . . . suspicion" of a shopkeeper based on his own "inarticulate hunches" without regard to any discernible facts. In effect, the result would be to afford the merchant even greater authority than that given to a police officer. . . .

Applying the standard of reasonable grounds as measured by the reasonably prudent man test to the evidence in the instant case, we are of opinion that the evidence warranted the conclusion that Goss was not reasonably justified in believing that the plaintiff was engaged in shoplifting. There was no error in denying the motion for directed verdicts and in the refusal to give the requested instructions.

Exceptions overruled.

CASE DISCUSSION QUESTIONS

1. Why did the court think that there was sufficient evidence of unlawful restraint? Do you agree?

2. Did the court think that the detention had taken place in a reasonable manner? Why?

3. Did the court think that finding reasonable grounds to detain someone should be based on an objective or a subjective standard? Why? Do you agree?

DISCUSSION QUESTION

1. Many argue that shoplifting is a major cause of increased costs. Do you think shopkeepers should be given more or less leeway in deciding when to detain suspected shoplifters?

c. Defamation

Defamation
The publication of false statements that harm a person's reputation.

Slander
Spoken defamation.

Libel
Written defamation.

Defamation can consist of either oral or written remarks that harm a person's reputation. Oral defamation is known as **slander** (remember "s" for spoken), and written defamation is known as **libel** (remember "l" for literary). To be considered defamatory, the material must tend to injure a person's reputation, to hold a person up to ridicule, or to excite adverse, derogatory, or unpleasant feelings or opinions about that person. Furthermore, the statement must present the defamatory information as being factual rather than merely the opinion of the speaker. For example, a movie review or editorial is generally viewed as a statement of opinion rather than fact.

(1) The elements of defamation

Whether it is oral or written, defamation consists of the following elements:

1. publication
2. of false statements
3. that cause harm to reputation.

The first element, publication, means that someone other than the plaintiff and the defendant must read or hear the defamatory comments. The offending material cannot harm someone's reputation if it is never seen or heard by a third party.

Second, and perhaps most important, the defamatory material must be false. No matter how damaging the information, a tort of defamation has not been committed if the statement was true. Note, however, that the plaintiff may still be able to recover damages by suing under the theory of invasion of privacy or intentional infliction of emotional distress.

As to the third element, the plaintiff must show that the publication of this false information damaged his or her reputation. This is usually established by showing that the plaintiff lost a job, a contract, or something else of value as a result of people having read or heard the defamatory material. However, historically some remarks are considered to be so bad that they are automatically viewed as damaging and thus constitute **defamation per se**. Examples of such remarks include the following:

Defamation per se
Remarks considered to be so harmful that they are automatically viewed as defamatory.

1. that someone has a loathsome communicable disease,
2. that someone committed business improprieties,
3. that someone has been imprisoned for a serious crime, and
4. that an unmarried woman is unchaste.

When dealing with comments that are defamatory per se, the plaintiff does not need to prove the statements caused him or her harm, as it is presumed they did so.

(2) Defamation of public figures

In order to protect the First Amendment rights of a free press to act as a watchdog and critic of government, the courts have made it more difficult for certain classes of people, public officials and "public figures," to win defamation suits. This rule was first enunciated by the U.S. Supreme Court in *New York Times Co. v. Sullivan,*[2] when the Court stated: "The constitutional guarantees require, we think, a federal rule that prohibits a public official from recovering damages for a defamatory falsehood relating to his official conduct unless he proves that the statement was made with 'actual malice'—that is, with knowledge that it was false or with reckless disregard of whether it was false or not."[3] This rule was extended to "public figures" in a 1974 Supreme Court case.[4]

What this means in practical terms is that when the plaintiff is a public official or public figure, the plaintiff must prove a fourth element, actual malice, in addition to the three elements that everyone else has also to prove—that is, (1) publication (2) of false statements (3) that cause harm to reputation. While it is clear that this fourth requirement comes into play only if the plaintiff is a public official or a public figure, it is less clear whether the defendant must also be a member of the media.

First, to qualify as a public figure, a person must either have achieved widespread fame or notoriety or be someone who became well known through involvement in a public controversy. Second, as noted above, to prove actual **malice**, the plaintiff must show that the defendant either knew the material was false but went ahead and published it anyway or acted with a "reckless disregard"

Malice
Making a defamatory remark either knowing the material was false or acting with a "reckless disregard" for whether or not it was true.

---

[2] 376 U.S. 254 (1964).
[3] Id. at 279-280.
[4] Gertz v. Robert Welch, Inc., 418 U.S. 323 (1974).

for whether or not it was true. This can involve an examination of the editors as to what they knew and when they knew it in reaching their decision to publish the material. The courts take into consideration such factors as the nature of the news being reported, the historical trustworthiness of the source of the information, and the time constraints publishers are under to meet a deadline.

A prominent California case involving television personality Carol Burnett illustrates how these principles have been applied. In *Burnett v. National Enquirer, Inc.*,[5] Burnett sued the National Enquirer for publishing a four-sentence item that read:

> In a Washington restaurant, a boisterous Carol Burnett had a loud argument with another diner, Henry Kissinger. Then she traipsed around the place offering everyone a bite of her dessert. But Carol really raised eyebrows when she accidentally knocked a glass of wine over one diner and started giggling instead of apologizing. The guy wasn't amused and "accidentally" spilled a glass of water over Carol's dress.[6]

As a preliminary matter the court determined that the National Enquirer should be viewed as a magazine rather than a newspaper. In defamation cases, courts show more leniency toward newspapers because their short deadlines prevent them from having enough time to fully investigate their stories. The Enquirer's normal lead time, however, was one to three weeks, during which time staff could verify the accuracy of its stories.

Next the court determined that the story was patently false and that the Enquirer knew that to be so: "There was no 'row' with Mr. Kissinger, nor any argument between the two, and what conversation they had was not loud or boisterous. Respondent never 'traipsed around the place offering everyone a bite of her dessert,' nor was she otherwise boisterous, nor did she spill wine on anyone."[7] Further, the court held that the statement was libelous on its face: "a message which reasonably carried the implication respondent's actions were the result of some objectionable state of inebriation."[8]

The jury awarded Ms. Burnett $300,000 in compensatory damages and $1.3 million in punitive damages. The trial court reduced this to $50,000 compensatory damages and $750,000 punitive damages. On appeal the court sustained the compensatory award but remanded the case for a retrial on the issue of punitive damages, stating that the amount of the punitive damages was disproportionate when compared to the compensatory award. The dissent disagreed, stating:

> The fact is that this is a publication read nationally by 16 million people. The potential for harm through a repetition of a libel by such an institution is tremendous. There are others to be protected from the harm. If the risk to an intentional wrongdoer that he will be adequately punished is slight, the defendant may well chance it again. It can in effect "write it off" as an expense or cost of doing business. Thus punitive damages

---

[5] 144 Cal. App. 3d 991 (1983).
[6] Id. at 997.
[7] Id. at 999.
[8] Id. at 1013.

need to be more than "an expense" item or "cost of doing business" which the defendant can calculate and absorb. . . . [9]

(3) Defenses to defamation

Because one of the elements of defamation is that the statement is false, truth is an absolute defense. There are also some circumstances when even the publication of a false statement can be privileged. For example, judges, attorneys, jurors, and other court personnel are protected against being held liable for comments that are made as part of their official duties, even if the statements turn out to be false. In 1979, in *Hutchinson v. Proxmire*,[10] the U.S. Supreme Court held that Wisconsin's Senator William Proxmire could not be sued for derogatory comments he made on the Senate floor when giving out one of his "Golden Fleece Awards." However, he could be sued for making those same remarks at a press conference and in a press release.

DISCUSSION QUESTION

2. In the case against the National Enquirer, Carol Burnett testified that the statements were particularly offensive to her because of her nationally known work against alcoholism.
    a. Do you think that should affect the amount of the damage award?
    b. During the trial, Johnny Carson on his program The Tonight Show denounced the National Enquirer. How do you think the trial judge should have handled that situation?
    c. Do you agree with the dissent that a large punitive award was justified in this case? Why?

d. Invasion of Privacy

The tort of **invasion of privacy** covers a variety of different situations. They include

1. disclosure,
2. intrusion,
3. appropriation, and
4. false light.

Disclosure and intrusion best fit our common conception of what would be an invasion of privacy. **Disclosure** is the publicizing of embarrassing private affairs, and **intrusion** is the unjustified intrusion in another's private activities. Examples of intrusion include a neighbor eavesdropping and a photographer hounding a movie star by following that person everywhere he or she goes. **Appropriation** is defined as the unauthorized exploitive use of one's personality, name, or picture for the defendant's benefit. For example, Johnny Carson sued a Michigan corporation for renting and selling "Here's Johnny" portable toilets.

Invasion of privacy
An intentional tort that covers a variety of situations, including disclosure, intrusion, appropriation, and false light.

Disclosure
The intentional publication of embarrassing private affairs.

Intrusion
The intentional unjustified encroachment into another person's private activities.

Appropriation
An intentional unauthorized exploitive use of another person's personality, name, or picture for the defendant's benefit.

---

[9]Id. at 1020 (dissenting opinion).
[10]443 U.S. 111 (1979).

The corporation acknowledged that "Here's Johnny" was the introductory slogan for The Tonight Show and in fact coupled the phrase with a second one, "The World's Foremost Commodian." The court determined that the defendant unfairly appropriated Carson's identity and used it for the sale of its products.[11] Finally, **false light** involves the use of a picture or some other means to infer a connection between the person and an idea or a statement for which the individual is not responsible.

False light
The intentional false portrayal of someone in a way that would be offensive to a reasonable person.

In cases involving invasion of privacy, truth is not considered to be a valid defense. For example, it is not considered acceptable to publicize that someone is having an affair with his or her neighbor, even if it is true. However, "newsworthiness" is a valid defense. If the material is of legitimate public interest—for example, the mayor having an affair with a member of city council—then its publication is considered to be privileged unless it was done with malice. That is why it is so difficult for movie stars to prove this tort against tabloids and gossip columnists. Finally, as with other intentional torts, consent is a defense.

e. Intentional Infliction of Emotional Distress

Traditionally, plaintiffs could recover for their emotional distress that was caused by another tort, such as battery or false imprisonment. More recently the courts have created a new tort that allows plaintiffs to recover for emotional distress even absent another type of injury. This tort of intentional infliction of emotional distress is sometimes referred to as the tort of outrage. In order to ensure that such claims are valid, most courts have placed severe restrictions on what the plaintiff must prove, such as requiring that the intentional act that causes the emotional distress be extreme and outrageous and the emotional distress suffered be severe.

Therefore, to prove the intentional infliction of emotional distress, a plaintiff must show

1. an intentional act
2. that is extreme and outrageous
3. and causes
4. severe emotional distress.

As to the fourth requirement some courts add that the emotional distress must be so severe that it results in physical injury.

In the following case a restaurant manager was concerned about stealing occurring in the restaurant. He lined up the waitresses and told them that until he found out who the culprit was, he would fire them in alphabetical order. Plaintiff Debra Agis had the misfortune of having a name at the top of the alphabet. As you read this case, ask yourself whether you think the manager's actions were such that they would give rise to a claim of intentional infliction of emotional distress. This case also raises issues of **loss of consortium**. The loss of consortium is the loss by one spouse of the other spouse's companionship, services, or affection.

Loss of consortium
The loss by one spouse of the other spouse's companionship, services, or affection.

---

[11]Carson v. Here's Johnny Portable Toilets, Inc., 698 F.2d 831 (6th Cir. 1983).

Agis v. Howard Johnson Company
371 Mass. 140, 355 N.E.2d 315 (1976)

QUIRICO, JJ.

This case raises the issue, expressly reserved in *George v. Jordan Marsh Co.*, 359 Mass. 244, 255 (1971), whether a cause of action exists in this Commonwealth for the intentional or reckless infliction of severe emotional distress without resulting bodily injury. Counts 1 and 2 of this action were brought by the plaintiff Debra Agis against the Howard Johnson Company and Roger Dionne, manager of the restaurant in which she was employed, to recover damages for mental anguish and emotional distress allegedly caused by her summary dismissal from such employment. Counts 3 and 4 were brought by her husband, James Agis, against both defendants for loss of the services, love, affection and companionship of his wife. This case is before us on the plaintiffs' appeal from the dismissal of their complaint.

Briefly, the allegations in the plaintiffs' complaint, which we accept as true for purposes of ruling on this motion, are the following. Debra Agis was employed by the Howard Johnson Company as a waitress in a restaurant known as the Ground Round. On or about May 23, 1975, the defendant Dionne notified all waitresses that a meeting would be held at 3 P.M. that day. At the meeting, he informed the waitresses that "there was some stealing going on," but that the identity of the person or persons responsible was not known, and that, until the person or persons responsible were discovered, he would begin firing all the present waitresses in alphabetical order, starting with the letter "A." Dionne then fired Debra Agis.

The complaint alleges that, as a result of this incident, Mrs. Agis became greatly upset, began to cry, sustained emotional distress, mental anguish, and loss of wages and earnings. It further alleges that the actions of the defendants were reckless, extreme, outrageous and intended to cause emotional distress and anguish. In addition, the complaint states that the defendants knew or should have known that their actions would cause such distress.

The defendants moved to dismiss the complaint pursuant to Mass. R. Civ. P. 12(b)(6) on the ground that, even if true, the plaintiffs' allegations fail to state a claim on which relief can be granted because damages for emotional distress are not compensable absent resulting physical injury. The judge allowed the motion, and the plaintiffs appealed. . . .

The most often cited argument for refusing to extend the cause of action for intentional or reckless infliction of emotional distress to cases where there has been no physical injury is the difficulty of proof and the danger of fraudulent or frivolous claims. There has been a concern that "mental anguish, standing alone, is too subtle and speculative to be measured by any known legal standard," that "mental anguish and its consequences are so intangible and peculiar and vary so much with the individual that they cannot reasonably be anticipated," that a wide door might "be opened not only to fictitious claims but to litigation over trivialities and mere bad manners as well," and that there can be no objective measurement of the extent or the existence of emotional distress. There is a fear that "[i]t is easy to assert a claim of mental anguish and very hard to disprove it."

While we are not unconcerned with these problems, we believe that "the problems presented are not . . . insuperable" and that "administrative difficulties do not justify the denial of relief for serious invasions of mental and emotional tranquility. . . ." "That some claims may be spurious should not compel those who administer justice to shut their eyes to serious wrongs and let them go without being brought to account. It is the function of courts and juries to determine whether claims are valid or false. This responsibility should not be shunned merely because the task may be difficult to perform." . . .

In light of what we have said, we hold that one who, by extreme and outrageous conduct and without privilege, causes severe emotional distress to another is subject to liability for such emotional distress even though no bodily harm may result. However, in order for a plaintiff to prevail in a case for liability under this tort, four elements must be established. It must be shown (1) that the actor intended to inflict emotional distress or that he knew or should have known that emotional distress was the likely result of his conduct, (2) that the conduct was "extreme and outrageous," was "beyond all possible bounds of decency" and was "utterly intolerable in a civilized community," (3) that the actions of the defendant were the cause of the plaintiff's distress, and (4) that the emotional distress sustained by the plaintiff was "severe" and of a nature "that no reasonable man could be expected to endure it." These requirements are "aimed at limiting frivolous suits and avoiding litigation in situations where only bad manners and mere hurt feelings are involved," and we believe they are a "realistic safeguard against false claims. . . ."

Testing the plaintiff Debra Agis's complaint by the rules stated above, we hold that she makes out a cause of action and that her complaint is therefore legally sufficient. . . . While the judge was not in error in dismissing the complaint under the then state of the law, we believe that, in light of what we have said, the judgment must be reversed and the plaintiff Debra Agis must be given an opportunity to prove the allegations which she has made.

2. Counts 3 and 4 of the complaint are brought by James Agis seeking relief for loss of consortium as a result of the mental distress and anguish suffered by his wife Debra. There is no question that an action for loss of consortium by either spouse may be maintained in this Commonwealth where such loss is shown to arise from personal injury to one spouse caused by the negligence of a third person. The question before us is whether an action for loss of consortium may be maintained where the acts complained of are intentional, and where the injuries to the spouse are emotional rather than physical.

[T]he fact that there is no physical injury should not bar the plaintiff's claim. . . . [T]he underlying purpose of such action is to compensate for the loss of the companionship, affection and sexual enjoyment of one's spouse, and it is clear that these can be lost as a result of psychological or emotional injury as well as from actual physical harm.

Accordingly, we hold that, where a person has a cause of action for intentional or reckless infliction of severe emotional distress, his or her spouse also has a cause of action for loss of consortium arising out of that distress. . . .

CASE DISCUSSION QUESTIONS

1. The court stated that "for purposes of ruling on the motion dismissing plaintiff's complaint" it was accepting as true the allegations in the plaintiff's complaint. Why?

2. What is the most common reason given for refusing to allow a claim for intentional infliction of emotional distress when there is no physical injury? What was the court's response?

3. What four elements does the court require for a successful claim for intentional infliction of emotional distress?

4. Procedurally, what had to happen next in this case for the plaintiff to recover?

Discussion Questions

3. What constitutes "extreme and outrageous" conduct is obviously a troubling issue, as is how debilitating the emotional distress must be to be seen as "severe." Consider the facts of *Harris v. Jones,* 380 A.2d 611 (1977). The plaintiff sued his employer (General Motors) and one of his supervisors, H. Robert Jones. Jones knew that the plaintiff suffered from a speech impediment that caused him to stutter. Jones also knew that the plaintiff was very sensitive about his disability. "Jones approached Harris over 30 times at work and verbally and physically mimicked his stuttering disability. . . . As a result of Jones' conduct Harris was 'shaken up' and felt 'like going into a hole and hide.'" However, the court concluded that Harris's humiliation was not so intense as to meet the requirement of being severe. Do you agree?

4. The March 1984 issue of Hustler magazine ran a parody of an advertisement for Campari Liqueur that featured various celebrities describing the first time they tasted Campari. Hustler's version presented a supposed interview with the Reverend Jerry Falwell, a nationally prominent Protestant minister, conservative political figure, and head of the now defunct "Moral Majority." The "advertisement" claimed that Falwell's first experience with Campari was part of an incestuous sexual encounter with his mother in an outhouse. Shortly after the issue hit the newsstands, Falwell sued the magazine for libel, invasion of privacy, and intentional infliction of emotional distress. If you were the judge, how would you rule on each of these issues?

2. Harm to a Person's Property

Property can be classified as either real property (land and anything permanently attached to land) or personal property. When someone invades your rights to real property, that is the tort of trespass. An invasion of your rights to personal property can be classified as either trespass to personal property or conversion.

a. Trespass to Land

A trespass occurs whenever

1. someone enters or causes something to enter or remain
2. on the land of another
3. without permission.

Examples of trespass include entering land that is posted with "No Trespassing" signs, standing alongside someone else's property and throwing rocks onto the property, and tying your boat to someone else's dock during a storm. The last situation raises the most common defense to trespass—that is, that the trespass was warranted to save the defendant's property or life.

b. Trespass to Personal Property and Conversion

Trespass to personal property occurs when someone harms or interferes with the owner's exclusive possession of the property but has no intention of keeping the property. For example, if your neighbor intentionally lets your dog loose, hoping it will never return, your neighbor has committed the tort of trespass to personal property. **Conversion** is considered the "big brother" of trespass in that it involves the more serious taking of someone else's property with the intent of permanently depriving the owner. It is the civil side of theft.

c. Defenses to Torts against Property

As mentioned above, private necessity, such as the need to tie up a boat to someone else's dock during a storm, may serve as a defense to trespass. Also, generally there is the right to invade another's land as a public necessity (such as to put out a fire or to catch a fleeing felon). Another defense to trespass to personal property and conversion is rightfully retaining someone's property. For example, a car mechanic may rightfully retain an auto on which he has worked until he is paid for his labor. This is known as an **artisan's lien.**

3. Other Intentional Torts

False arrest, malicious prosecution, and abuse of process are all intentional torts that are designed to provide some protection against misuse of the legal system. **False arrest** occurs when a person is arrested (by either a law officer or a citizen) without probable cause and when not covered by special privilege. **Malicious prosecution** and **abuse of process** both involve malicious and improper use of the courts or other forms of legal proceedings. Note that the plaintiff must prove that the behavior was malicious (that is, that the person proceeded even though the charges were known to be invalid) and not just a mistake.

Finally, there are intentional torts related to business dealings. **Fraud,** or intentional misrepresentation, involves (1) the intent to induce reliance on the misrepresentation, (2) knowledge that the misrepresentation is false or a reckless disregard for the truth, (3) justifiable reliance, and (4) harm. Fraud can form the basis for either a tort or a contract claim. We will discuss it more fully in the next chapter on contracts. The tort of **interference with a contractual relationship** prohibits one from inducing a party to breach a contract or interfering with the performance of a contract. Intentionally breaching a contract can prove to be very expensive, as is illustrated by the case of *Pennzoil v. Texaco*. Pennzoil had contracted with the Getty Oil Company to purchase Getty Oil at $122.05 per share. Before they could do so, however, Texaco offered Getty a high price per share, which Getty accepted. Pennzoil took Texaco to court and won a $10.53 billion judgment on its claim of tortuous interference. Although that amount was later reduced to a $3 billion dollar settlement, the case still stands as a powerful warning against intentionally derailing contractual arrangements.[12]

Interference with a contractual relationship An intentional tort that occurs if someone induces a party to breach a contract or interferes with the performance of a contract.

Figure 7-2 on page 207 summarizes the elements and defenses of the most common intentional torts.

B. NEGLIGENCE

The most common tort actions involve **negligence.** Negligence is a failure to act as a reasonably prudent and careful person is expected to act in similar circumstances. It is a careless inflicting of an injury as opposed to an intentional one. Negligence actions can arise from such diverse circumstances as a slip on a

---

[12]Stephen Labaton, *Texaco Reported to Reach Accord on Pennzoil Suit*, N.Y. Times, Dec. 19, 1987.

Prima Facie Case	Defenses
Assault 1. an intentional act 2. that creates a reasonable apprehension of 3. an immediate harmful or offensive physical contact	1. consent 2. self-defense 3. defense of others 4. sometimes defense of property
Battery 1. an intentional act 2. that creates a harmful or offensive physical contact	
False imprisonment 1. an intentional act 2. that caused confinement or restraint 3. through force or the threat of force	1. consent 2. justification (e.g., shopkeeper's statute)
Defamation 1. publication 2. of false statements 3. that cause harm to reputation	1. truth 2. privilege
Invasion of privacy covers a variety of different situations, including 1. disclosure 2. intrusion 3. appropriation 4. false light	1. consent 2. newsworthiness
Intentional infliction of emotional distress 1. an intentional act 2. that is extreme and outrageous 3. and causes 4. severe emotional distress	1. consent
Trespass to land 1. someone enters or causes something to enter or remain 2. on the land of another 3. without permission	1. consent 2. private necessity 3. public necessity
Trespass to personal property 1. interference with the owner's exclusive possession 2. of personal property	1. rightful retention (e.g., under a mechanic's lien) 2. necessity
Conversion 1. taking 2. personal property 3. of another 4. with the intent of permanently depriving the owner	

Figure 7-2 Summary of Intentional Torts

wet spot on a supermarket floor to alleged medical malpractice. The four basic elements in a negligence case are duty, breach of duty, causation, and harm.

1. The Elements of Negligence

To be found negligent, a person must have acted unreasonably under the circumstances. More specifically, the courts look to the following four elements to establish negligence:

1. The defendant must owe a duty to the plaintiff to act reasonably, and
2. the defendant must have breached that duty
3. thereby causing
4. the plaintiff harm.

a. Duty

The law imposes a duty to act with "due care." This due care standard is defined in terms of how a "reasonably prudent person" would act in the same situation. If the person has some specialized type of training, such as a medical degree, then that individual is expected to act not just as a reasonable person would act but also as a reasonable person with medical training would act. Furthermore, the greater the inherent danger is in a particular situation, the more cautious the individual is expected to be. The duty is owed by all persons within the society to a degree that is consistent with their ages and physical and mental conditions. Jurisdictions differ, however, as to whom it is owed. Most states take the position that this duty to act with due care is owed to anyone who suffers injuries as a proximate or direct result of the person's actions. Other states say the duty applies only to those persons for whom there was a foreseeable risk.

What legal duty you owe to others also varies depending on your relationship to that other person. The closer and more direct the relationship, the greater the likelihood that a court will find a duty. For example, a doctor clearly has a duty to use due care in treating her patients. However, does the doctor also owe a duty to the patient's family? For instance, if the doctor failed to diagnose a contagious disease and the patient transmitted that disease to his wife, should the wife be able to sue the doctor?

Another example of how the relationship between the parties can determine the degree of duty owed is seen in the varying levels of duty a landowner owes to different types of people on his or her land. Many states, using a standard based solely on the status of the person injured, hold that a higher duty is owed to someone lawfully invited and present than to a trespasser. Further, they may view the duty owed to an adult trespasser as less than that owed to a child trespasser. Other states simply say that landowners owe a duty of care to everyone on their land. However, the level of duty varies with the circumstances, including whether the person harmed was a trespasser. While the result may be the same, the approaches are fundamentally different. A court in the latter type of jurisdiction would not base its analysis solely on the status of the person injured but would take into account everything that contributed to the injury.

One of the circumstances that might influence a finding of negligence is whether the defendant was acting under an emergency situation. For example, in a very colorful opinion, *Cordas v. Peerless Transportation Co.*,[13] New York's highest court was faced with the following situation: A thief was running down a Manhattan street being chased by his victim and a group of concerned citizens. The thief, armed with a pistol, jumped into a parked taxicab and ordered the driver to drive. The driver proceeded about fifteen feet and then quickly threw his car out of first speed in which he was proceeding, pulled on the emergency, jammed on his brakes, and, although he [thought] the motor was still running, swung open the door to his left and jumped out of his car. He confesses that the only act that smacked of intelligence was that by which he jammed the brakes in order to throw off balance the hold-up man who was half-standing and half-sitting with his pistol menacingly poised.[14] Mrs. Cordas and her two children were standing on an adjacent sidewalk and were injured by the driverless taxi. They sued the taxicab company, claiming that the driver acted negligently in jumping to safety and leaving the moving vehicle uncontrolled.

The court stated that "the test of actionable negligence is what reasonably prudent men would have done under the same circumstances."[15] The court then held that when faced with an emergency a person is not required to exercise the same mature judgment that is expected under circumstances where there is an opportunity for deliberation. In this case the driver "—the ordinary man in this case—acted in a split second in a most harrowing experience. . . . The court is loathe to see the plaintiffs go without recovery even though their damages were slight, but cannot hold the defendant liable upon the facts adduced at the trial."[16] Therefore, plaintiffs were not entitled to recover from the cab driver.[17]

Finally, the courts sometimes couch their discussion of duty in terms of **misfeasance** versus **nonfeasance**. Generally, you only owe a duty to refrain from harming someone. If you do actually harm someone, that is misfeasance. Further, there is no duty to prevent harm to those with whom you have no direct contact. Therefore, generally nonfeasance, the absence of action, cannot lead to liability. However, in order to find liability, a court might label an activity as misfeasance even though on the surface it appeared as though the defendant had not directly caused the injury. This was the case in *Weirum v. RKO General Inc.*[18] In order to increase its listening audience, a rock station held a contest wherein a traveling disk jockey gave out clues to his location. The first to arrive on the scene would receive a prize. Two teenagers, in an attempt to beat each other to the prize, drove in excess of eighty miles an hour and forced the plaintiff's car off of the road. The court stated:

Misfeasance
Acting is an improper or a wrongful way.

Nonfeasance
Failing to act.

> The primary question for our determination is whether defendant owed a duty to decedent arising out of its broadcast of the giveaway contest. The determination of duty is primarily a question of law. It is the court's "expression of the sum total of those considerations of policy which lead the law to say that the particular plaintiff is entitled to protection" (Prosser, Law of Torts (4th ed. 1971) pp. 325-326). Any number of considerations may justify the imposition of duty in particular circumstances, including

---

[13]27 N.Y.S.2d 198 (1941).

[14]Id. at 199-200.

[15]Id. at 200.

[16]Id. at 202.

[17]Id.

[18]539 P.2d 36 (Cal. 1975).

the guidance of history, our continually refined concepts of morals and justice, the convenience of the rule, and social judgment as to where the loss should fall. While the question whether one owes a duty to another must be decided on a case-by-case basis, every case is governed by the rule of general application that all persons are required to use ordinary care to prevent others from being injured as the result of their conduct. However, foreseeability of the risk is a primary consideration in establishing the element of duty.[19]

The court found that the risk to the plaintiff was foreseeable. While acknowledging that normally, absent a special relationship, no one owes a duty to control the conduct of third parties, the court stated that the rule does not apply in a case such as this one where the radio station's conduct is what created the undue risk of harm.

Misfeasance exists when the defendant is responsible for making the plaintiff's position worse, i.e., defendant has created a risk. Conversely, nonfeasance is found when the defendant has failed to aid plaintiff through beneficial intervention. As section 315 [of the Restatement of the Law of Torts, Second] illustrates, liability for nonfeasance is largely limited to those circumstances in which some special relationship can be established. If, on the other hand, the act complained of is one of misfeasance, the question of duty is governed by the standards of ordinary care discussed above. Here, there can be little doubt that we review an act of misfeasance to which section 315 is inapplicable. Liability is not predicated upon defendant's failure to intervene for the benefit of decedent but rather upon its creation of an unreasonable risk of harm to him.[20]

DISCUSSION QUESTION

5. In the *Weirum* case the defendants argued that finding them liable would lead to situations in which "entrepreneurs will henceforth be burdened with an avalanche of obligations: an athletic department will owe a duty to an ardent sports fan injured while hastening to purchase one of a limited number of tickets; a department store will be liable for injuries incurred in response to a 'while-they-last' sale."[21] How do you think the court responded?

As the *Weirum* court noted, issues of duty usually revolve around whether the plaintiff was someone whom the defendant could foresee would be harmed by his actions. Courts frequently say that duty is a question of law to be determined by the judge, while foreseeability is a question of fact to be determined by the jury.

It is always to the defendant's benefit to end a lawsuit as early as possible to save litigation expenses and to put the matter to rest. On the other hand, it is often to the benefit of the plaintiff to go to trial, especially when the facts may arouse the jury's sympathy. Therefore, in a negligence action the defendant will try to argue whenever possible that the defendant owed no duty to the plaintiff.

---

[19]Id. at 39.

[20]Id. at 41.

[21]Id.

As duty is a question of law, the judge can resolve the matter on a motion to dismiss. If the judge determines that there was no duty, then the plaintiff loses, and the case is dismissed. However, the plaintiff will try to characterize the issue as a question of foreseeability, thereby necessitating a trial. Then the jury, after hearing all of the evidence and seeing the extent of the plaintiff's injuries, can resolve the issue of foreseeability as a question of fact.

At times, even though the person injured was a "foreseeable plaintiff," for policy reasons the courts will state that no duty is owed to the plaintiff. For example, in New York, until the courts were confronted with the following case, an infant harmed while a fetus had no right to sue for his or her negligently caused injuries. While reading the case, pay particular attention to the reasons the court gives for its decision to expand the range of those to whom a duty is owed to include a viable fetus.

Woods v. Lancet
303 N.Y. 349, 102 N.E.2d 691 (1951)

DESMOND, J.

The complaint served on behalf of this infant plaintiff alleges that, while the infant was in his mother's womb during the ninth month of her pregnancy, he sustained, through the negligence of defendant, such serious injuries that he came into this world permanently maimed and disabled. Defendant moved to dismiss the complaint as not stating a cause of action, thus taking the position that its allegations, though true, gave the infant no right to recover damages in the courts of New York. The Special Term granted the motion and dismissed the suit, citing *Drobner v. Peters* (232 N.Y. 220). In the Appellate Division one Justice voted for reversal with an opinion in which he described the obvious injustice of the rule, noted a decisional trend (in other States and Canada) toward giving relief in such cases, and suggested that since *Drobner v. Peters* (supra) was decided thirty years ago by a divided vote, our court might well re-examine it.

The four Appellate Division Justices who voted to affirm the dismissal below, wrote no opinion except that one of them stated that, were the question an open one and were he not bound by *Drobner v. Peters* (supra), he would hold that "when a pregnant woman is injured through negligence and the child subsequently born suffers deformity or other injury as a result, recovery therefore may be allowed to the child, provided the causal relation between the negligence and the

damage to the child be established by competent medical evidence." (278 App. Div. 913.) It will hardly be disputed that justice (not emotionalism or sentimentality) dictates the enforcement of such a cause of action. The trend in decisions of other courts, and the writings of learned commentators, in the period since *Drobner v. Peters* was handed down in 1921, is strongly toward making such a recovery possible. The precise question for us on this appeal is: shall we follow *Drobner v. Peters,* or shall we bring the common law of this State, on this question, into accord with justice? I think, as New York State's court of last resort, we should make the law conform to right.

Drobner v. Peters (supra), like the present case, dealt with the sufficiency of a complaint alleging prenatal injuries, tortiously inflicted on a nine-month foetus, viable at the time and actually born later. There is, therefore, no material distinction between that case and the one we are passing on now. However, *Drobner v. Peters* must be examined against a background of history and of the legal thought of its time and of the thirty years that have passed since it was handed down. . . . The movement toward a more just treatment of such claims seems to have commenced with the able dissent in the *Allaire* case, which urged that a child viable but in utero, if injured by tort, should, when born, be allowed to sue. . . .

In *Drobner v. Peters* (supra), this court, finding no precedent for maintaining the suit, adopted the general theory of *Dietrich v. North-ampton* (supra), taking into account, besides the lack of authority to support the suit, the practical difficulties of proof in such cases, and the theoretical lack of separate human existence of an infant in utero. It is not unfair to say that the basic reason for *Drobner v. Peters* was absence of precedent. However, since 1921, numerous and impressive affirmative precedents have been developed. . . . Of law review articles on the precise question there is an ample supply. They justify the statement in Prosser on Torts, at page 190, that: "All writers who have discussed the problem have joined in condemning the existing rule, in maintaining that the unborn child in the path of an automobile is as much a person in the street as the mother, and urging that recovery should be allowed upon proper proof."

What, then, stands in the way of a reversal here? Surely, as an original proposition, we would, today, be hard put to it to find a sound reason for the old rule. Following *Drobner v. Peters* (supra) would call for an affirmance but the chief basis for that holding (lack of precedent) no longer exists. And it is not a very strong reason, anyhow, in a case like this. Of course, rules of law on which men rely in their business dealings should not be changed in the middle of the game, but what has that to do with bringing to justice a tortfeasor who surely has no moral or other right to rely on a decision of the New York Court of Appeals? Negligence law is common law, and the common law has been molded and changed and brought up-to-date in many another case. Our court said, long ago, that it had not only the right, but the duty to re-examine a question where justice demands it. That opinion notes that Chancellor Kent, more than a century ago, had stated that upwards of a thousand cases could then be pointed out in the English and American reports "which had been overruled, doubted or limited in their application," and that the great Chancellor had declared that decisions which seem contrary to reason "ought to be examined without fear, and revised without reluctance, rather than to have the character of our law impaired, and the beauty and harmony of the system destroyed by the perpetuity of error." And Justice Sutherland, writing for the Supreme Court in *Funk v. United States* (290 U.S. 371, 382), said that while legislative bodies have the power to change old rules of law, nevertheless, when they fail to act, it is the duty of the court to bring the law into accordance with present day standards of wisdom and justice rather than "with some outworn and antiquated rule of the past." No reason appears why there should not be the same approach when traditional common-law rules of negligence result in injustice.

The sum of the argument against plaintiff here is that there is no New York decision in which such a claim has been enforced. Winfield's answer to that (see U. of Toronto L.J. article, supra, p. 29) will serve: "if that were a valid objection, the common law would now be what it was in the Plantagenet period." And we can borrow from our British friends another mot: "When these ghosts of the past stand in the path of justice clanking their mediaeval chains the proper course for the judge is to pass through them undeterred" (Lord Atkin in *United Australia, Ltd., v. Barclay's Bank, Ltd.*, [1941] A.C. 1, 29). We act in the finest common-law tradition when we adapt and alter decisional law to produce common-sense justice.

The same answer goes to the argument that the change we here propose should come from the Legislature, not the courts. Legislative action there could, of course, be, but we abdicate our own function, in a field peculiarly nonstatutory, when we refuse to reconsider an old and unsatisfactory court-made rule. . . .

Two other reasons for dismissal (besides lack of precedent) are given in *Drobner v. Peters* (supra). The first of those, discussed in many of the other writings on the subject herein cited, has to do with the supposed difficulty of proving or disproving that certain injuries befell the unborn child, or that they produced the defects discovered at birth, or later. Such difficulties there are, of course, and, indeed, it seems to be commonly accepted that only a blow of tremendous force will ordinarily injure a foetus, so carefully does nature insulate it. But such difficulty of proof or finding is not special to this particular kind of lawsuit (and it is beside the point, anyhow, in determining sufficiency of a pleading). Every day in all our trial courts (and before administrative tribunals, particularly the Workmen's Compensation Board), such issues are disposed of, and it is an inadmissible concept that uncertainty of proof can ever destroy a legal right. The questions of causation, reasonable certainty, etc., which will arise in these cases are no different, in kind, from the ones which have arisen in thousands of other negligence cases decided in this State, in the past.

The other objection to recovery here is the purely theoretical one that a foetus in utero has no existence of its own separate from that of its mother, that is, that it is not "a being in esse." We need not deal here with so large a subject. It is to be remembered that we are passing on the sufficiency of a complaint which alleges that this injury occurred during the ninth month of the mother's pregnancy, in other words, to a viable foetus, later born. Therefore, we confine our holding in this case to prepartum injuries to such viable children. Of course such a child, still in the womb is, in one sense, a part of its mother, but no one seems to claim that the mother, in her own name and for herself, could get damages for the injuries to her infant. To hold, as matter of law, that no viable foetus has any separate existence which the law will recognize is for the law to deny a simple and easily demonstrable fact. This child, when injured, was in fact, alive and capable of being delivered and of remaining alive, separate from its mother. We agree with the dissenting Justice below that "To deny the infant relief in this case is not only a harsh result, but its effect is to do reverence to an outmoded, timeworn fiction not founded on fact and within common knowledge untrue and unjustified."

The judgments should be reversed, and the motion denied, with costs in all courts.

LEWIS, J. (dissenting). I agree with the view of a majority of the court that prenatal injury to a child should not go unrequited by the one at fault.

If, however, an unborn child is to be endowed with the right to enforce such requital by an action at law, I think that right should not be created by a judicial decision on the facts in a single case. Better, I believe, that the right should be the product of legislative action taken after hearings at which the Legislature can be advised, by the aid of medical science and research, not only as to the stage of gestation at which a foetus is considered viable, but also as to appropriate means—by time limitation for suit and otherwise—for avoiding abuses which might result from the difficulty of tracing causation from prenatal injury to post-natal deformity. . . .

Accordingly, I dissent and vote for affirmance.

CASE DISCUSSION QUESTIONS

1. Reading this case we learned almost nothing about the facts that gave rise to this lawsuit. What procedural reason explains why we do not know very many of the facts?

2. Why did the court decide to overrule *Drobner v. Peters?*

3. What limitations did the court put on its holding? What difficulties can you foresee this creating for future litigants?

4. Do you agree with the court that this issue was a matter for judicial as opposed to legislative change? Why?

5. In 2004, the Massachusetts Supreme Judicial Court was faced with the following fact scenario. A daughter wished to sue her mother for negligence that stemmed from a car accident while the child was a fetus. The mother allegedly drove her car through an intersection, causing a collision with another vehicle. The daughter was born prematurely four days later. Her premature birth caused her a number of respiratory problems that plagued her with severe breathing difficulties. Assuming the court were to follow the reasoning of the *Woods v. Lancet* decision, how do you think the Massachusetts court decided? Why?

b. Breach

In order to determine if someone has breached the duty of due care, the court considers all the circumstances. In evaluating those circumstances, the actions of the defendant are measured by an objective standard. That is, the jury is asked to consider what a reasonable person would have done.

In order to prove how a reasonable professional would have acted, the plaintiff will be required to call an expert witness to testify as to the professional standard of care and how in the expert's opinion the defendant breached that standard. For example, in a case involving alleged medical malpractice by a pediatric oncologist, the plaintiff would call as an expert witness a doctor specializing in that field.

Sometimes the defendant's actions violate a statute. If that statute's purpose is to protect the public, the plaintiff belongs to the group of persons the statute was meant to protect, and violation of the statute was a direct cause of the plaintiff's injury, then some states will hold that violation of the statute is negligence per se. In other states violation of such a statute is only evidence of negligence and can be rebutted. For example, assume there is a state statute prohibiting the sale of firearms to minors. A store owner sells a gun to a minor, and the minor, while playing a game of "chicken," discharges the gun, injuring another minor. If the injured minor sued the store owner, he would argue that the purpose of the statute was public protection, that he belonged to that group the statute was designed to protect, and finally that the seller's violation of the statute directly caused his injury. In those states that hold that violation of such a statute is negligence per se, the store owner would be found liable based on his violation of the statute. In those states where the presumption of negligence can be rebutted, the store owner would try to introduce evidence showing that his act of selling the gun and its accidental discharge were too removed from each other to make it fair to hold him responsible.

Res ipsa loquitur
"The thing speaks for itself"; the doctrine that suggests negligence can be presumed if an event happens that would not ordinarily happen unless someone was negligent.

Another concept that can sometimes be used by the plaintiff to show negligence is the doctrine of **res ipsa loquitur**—the thing speaks for itself. Res ipsa loquitur applies in those situations where the event ordinarily would not have happened unless someone was negligent, the cause of the injury was under the defendant's exclusive control, and the injury was not due to the plaintiff's actions. For example, elevators usually do not drop, panes of glass usually do not fall out of windows, and planes do not crash absent someone's negligence. In those types of situations the court will assume that the defendant was negligent without the plaintiff having to prove the precise nature of that negligence.

Because in each case involving breach the court must evaluate the behavior given all the circumstances, the specific facts become very important. In reading the following case pay attention to the particular facts that you think influenced the court's determination that there was no breach of duty. Even though the plaintiff in this case was thirteen, notice how the court uses the archaic term "infant" when referring to him.

Sauer v. Hebrew Institute of Long Island, Inc.
17 A.D.2d 245, 233 N.Y.S.2d 1008 (1962)

BERGAN, J.

The infant plaintiff, a camper at defendant's Summer camp, was injured while playing a game supervised by defendant's personnel. The infant was 13 years old and the game was a "water fight" between groups of campers of similar age, played on a grass-covered area in which opposing groups of boys doused each other with water from cups or water pistols.

In running away from an opponent, the infant plaintiff slipped on the grass and struck his head on a concrete walk at the side of the grass area. After a trial before the court without a jury, an award of $15,000 has been made to infant plaintiff and nominal damages to his father.

In our view of the record, this result is not warranted. The defendant, as the operator of a camp for boys, could not reasonably be made responsible in damages for the consequences of every possible hazard of play activity. It was required, rather, to guard against dangers which ought to have been foreseen in the exercise of reasonable care.

It has not been demonstrated that the water fight game was more hazardous than any ordinary camp activity involving running. It was inevitable in the game that the grass would become wet; and, indeed, in any such game among 13-year-old boys, that there would be tumbles and falls whether it was wet or dry.

To impose liability in this situation is to interdict the game itself, which in turn would so sterilize camping activity for boys as to render it sedentary. It would take a keen sense of the prescient to envisage that in running in the game the infant plaintiff would slip at the very point in the area where there was a concrete walk. Nor is it, indeed, clearly demonstrated that, in view of the infant's plaintiff's bare feet, the wetness of the grass played any effective part in his falling.

The Trial Judge felt that the game itself "[had] every aspect of innocent play"; that the supervision was adequate and there was no "defect in the grounds on which the contest took place." (33 Misc. 2d 785, 786.) He felt, however, that the game should have been played on sand and not on grass. This retrospective view of how the camp should have managed the game, upon which there can be reasonable difference of opinion, is insufficient to impose a liability on defendant, either as an evaluation of the facts of the case, or as a matter of law.

The judgment for plaintiffs should be reversed on the law and the facts and judgment entered for defendant, without costs. . . .

CASE DISCUSSION QUESTIONS

1. Why did the court find that the camp was not liable for the boy's injury? Do you agree with that decision? Why?

2. What facts do you think were most important in helping the court reach its decision?

DISCUSSION QUESTIONS

6. Most states have statutes prohibiting the sale of alcohol to a minor. If a store sold alcohol to a minor and the minor while intoxicated drove an automobile that collided with and killed a cyclist, would the liquor store owner be held liable as to the deceased cyclist?

7. On an icy, snow-covered road the plaintiff lost control of her car, skidded across the center line, and collided with a road grader, driven by the defendant. The defendant did not have the statutorily required class B driver's license. The

plaintiff, who was severely injured in the accident, sued the defendant under the theory of negligence per se. How do you think the court ruled and why?

c. Cause

In a tort action the defendant's actions must be the cause of the plaintiff's injuries. Under one commonly used test, referred to as the **"but for" standard**, it is necessary to establish that if the defendant had not acted in that manner, the plaintiff would not have been injured. This is also known as the **actual cause** or **cause in fact.** Sometimes there is more than one "cause" of an injury. When there are concurrent causes, the court asks if any one of them was a substantial factor in causing the injury. Under the "substantial factor" test, liability is imposed if the defendant's action is shown to be a substantial factor in causing the plaintiff's injuries.

Actual cause
Also known as cause in fact, this is measured by the "but for" standard: But for the defendant's actions, the plaintiff would not have been injured.

Sometimes it is impossible for the plaintiff to know who of several defendants was responsible for the injury. Such was the situation in the classic case of *Sumers v. Tice.*[22] The two defendants and the plaintiff had gone hunting. Both defendants shot at the same time, and the plaintiff was injured. The plaintiff was unable to show whose gun had caused the injury. The court held that the burden was on the defendants to show who was liable, and absent such a showing, both were liable. A more modern variant of this theory was adopted by the California Supreme Court in *Sindell v. Abbott Laboratories.*[23] In that case the plaintiff had developed cancer, allegedly because her mother took the product diethylstilbestrol (DES) while pregnant. The plaintiff's major roadblock in proving her case was that approximately 200 manufacturers had produced DES, and she had no way of knowing which specific company had produced the DES her mother had taken. Under a **market share theory**, the court held that each of the manufacturers would be held responsible based on its market share at the time the mother took DES.

Market share theory
A legal theory that allows plaintiffs to recover proportionately from a group of manufacturers when the identity of the specific manufacturer responsible for the harm is unknown.

The second prong of the requirement that the defendant's actions "cause" the injury is known as **proximate cause**. For a defendant's actions to be considered the proximate cause, a natural and continuous causal sequence must be shown between action and harm that is unbroken by any efficient intervening cause. In deciding cases in which determining the proximate cause is a key issue, the courts frequently wrestle with unforeseeable consequences and intervening forces. For example, the courts are sometimes faced with chain-reaction situations in which a person's actions lead to an event that in turn leads to several other events that eventually impact other people. Is everyone along the chain to be held responsible under the theory that but for their actions, no injury would have happened, or is it more just to say that only those actors most immediately involved in the injury should be held responsible?

Proximate cause
Once actual cause is found, as a policy matter, the court must also find that the act and the resulting harm were so foreseeably related as to justify a finding of liability.

As you will see, this notion of proximate cause is not really about cause at all but rather represents a policy decision that at some point a defendant will not be held responsible for every consequence of every action. Just as a pebble thrown into a pond sends out ripples of ever-decreasing strength, every action sends out repercussions of ever-decreasing importance. At some point we say that the consequences are too remote from the original action to hold the actor responsible.

---

[22] 199 P.2d 1 (Cal. 1948).
[23] 607 P.2d 924 (Cal. 1980).

Assume Ms. Farmer takes a lantern with her to her barn in order to milk her cow and thoughtlessly places the lantern next to the cow, who kicks it over. The barn catches on fire. The fire spreads to the neighbor's field, which also catches on fire. No major harm is done except that the ensuing group of gawkers, as well as the multiple fire-fighting and police vehicles, blocks traffic for over an hour. As a result, Mr. Smith, who is on his way to an important appointment, misses the appointment and consequently is fired. Should the neighbor be able to sue Ms. Farmer for the damage to his field? Most certainly. Should Mr. Smith be able to sue Ms. Farmer for his lost job? Most likely no. Why? In both cases Ms. Farmer was the "but for" cause of the injury. But most courts would probably say that the foreseeability of the harm to Mr. Smith was too remote to hold Ms. Farmer accountable. They might phrase this either as a lack of duty to Mr. Smith (an unforeseeable plaintiff) or as a lack of proximate cause (an unforeseeable injury). In either case the issue boils down to one of policy; that is, is this the type of injury for which we want to hold Ms. Farmer accountable?

As you read negligence cases, you will notice that the courts often confuse the issues of duty of care and proximate cause. This is because both are based on the concept of foreseeability. In order for a duty to be present, harm to that person must be foreseeable. However, even if the defendant's actions caused the harm, if that particular harm was not foreseeable, the concept of proximate cause says that, for policy reasons, we will no longer hold the defendant liable.

(1) Palsgraf v. Long Island Railroad Company

The following classic case is probably the most famous tort decision ever written. However, as you will see from reading the case, even the most gifted legal jurists have difficulty differentiating between duty and proximate cause, as both are based on the concept of foreseeability. As you read the case, ask yourself, Was the railroad not liable because it owed no duty to Mrs. Palsgraf or because its employee's actions were not the proximate cause of her harm?

Palsgraf v. Long Island Railroad Company
248 N.Y. 339, 162 N.E. 99 (1928)

CARDOZO, Ch. J.

Plaintiff was standing on a platform of defendant's railroad after buying a ticket to go to Rockaway Beach. A train stopped at the station, bound for another place. Two men ran forward to catch it. One of the men reached the platform of the car without mishap, though the train was already moving. The other man, carrying a package, jumped aboard the car, but seemed unsteady as if about to fall. A guard on the car, who had held the door open, reached forward to help him in, and another guard on the platform pushed him from behind. In this act, the package was dislodged, and fell upon the rails. It was a package of small size, about fifteen inches long, and was covered by a newspaper. In fact it contained fireworks, but there was nothing in its appearance to give notice of its contents. The fireworks when they fell exploded. The shock of the explosion threw down some scales at the other end of the platform, many feet away. The scales struck the plaintiff, causing injuries for which she sues.

The conduct of the defendant's guard, if a wrong in its relation to the holder of the package, was not a wrong in its relation to the plaintiff, standing far away. Relatively to her it was not negligence at all. Nothing in the situation gave notice that the falling package had in it the potency of peril to persons thus removed. Negligence is not actionable unless it involves the invasion of a legally protected interest, the violation of a right. "Proof of negligence in the air, so to speak, will not do" (Pollock, Torts [11th ed.], p. 455). . . . If no hazard was apparent to the eye of ordinary vigilance, an act innocent and harmless, at least to outward seeming, with reference to her, did not take to itself the quality of a tort because it happened to be a wrong, though apparently not one involving the risk of bodily insecurity, with reference to some one else. "In every instance, before negligence can be predicated of a given act, back of the act must be sought and found a duty to the individual complaining, the observance of which would have averted or avoided the injury" (McSherry, C.J., in *W. Va. Central R. Co. v. State*, 96 Md. 652, 666). The plaintiff sues in her own right for a wrong personal to her, and not as the vicarious beneficiary of a breach of duty to another.

A different conclusion will involve us, and swiftly too, in a maze of contradictions. . . . One who jostles one's neighbor in a crowd does not invade the rights of others standing at the outer fringe when the unintended contact casts a bomb upon the ground. The wrongdoer as to them is the man who carries the bomb, not the one who explodes it without suspicion of the danger. Life will have to be made over, and human nature transformed, before prevision so extravagant can be accepted as the norm of conduct, the customary standard to which behavior must conform.

The argument for the plaintiff is built upon the shifting meanings of such words as "wrong" and "wrongful," and shares their instability. What the plaintiff must show is "a wrong" to herself, i.e., a violation of her own right, and not merely a wrong to some one else, nor conduct "wrongful" because unsocial, but not "a wrong" to any one. . . . The risk reasonably to be perceived defines the duty to be obeyed. . . . Here, by concession, there was nothing in the situation to suggest to the most cautious mind that the parcel wrapped in newspaper would spread wreckage through the station. . . .

The judgment of the Appellate Division and that of the Trial Term should be reversed, and the complaint dismissed, with costs in all courts.

ANDREWS, J. (dissenting). . . .

What is a cause in a legal sense, still more what is a proximate cause, depend in each case upon many considerations, as does the existence of negligence itself. Any philosophical doctrine of causation does not help us. A boy throws a stone into a pond. The ripples spread. The water level rises. The history of that pond is altered to all eternity. It will be altered by other causes also. Yet it will be forever the resultant of all causes combined. Each one will have an influence. How great only omniscience can say. You may speak of a chain, or if you please, a net. An analogy is of little aid. Each cause brings about future events. Without each the future would not be the same. Each is proximate in the sense it is essential. But that is not what we mean by the word. Nor on the other hand do we mean sole cause. There is no such thing. . . .

As we have said, we cannot trace the effect of an act to the end, if end there is. Again, however, we may trace it part of the way. A murder at Serajevo may be the necessary antecedent to an assassination in London twenty years hence. An overturned lantern may burn all Chicago. We may follow the fire from the shed to the last building. We rightly say the fire started by the lantern caused its destruction. A cause, but not the proximate cause. What we do mean by the word "proximate" is, that because of convenience, of public policy, of a rough sense of justice, the law arbitrarily declines to trace a series of events beyond a certain point. This is not logic. It is practical politics. Take our rule as to fires. Sparks from my burning haystack set on fire my house and my neighbor's. I may recover from a negligent railroad. He may not. Yet the wrongful act as directly harmed the one as the other. We may regret that the line was drawn just where it was, but drawn somewhere it had to be. We said the act of the railroad was not the proximate cause of our neighbor's fire. Cause it surely was. The words we used were simply indicative of our notions of public policy. . . .

The act upon which defendant's liability rests is knocking an apparently harmless package onto the platform. The act was negligent. For its proximate consequences the defendant is liable. If its contents were broken, to the owner; if it fell upon and crushed a passenger's foot, then to him. If it exploded and injured one in the immediate vicinity, to him also. . . . Mrs. Palsgraf was standing some distance away. How far cannot be told from the record—apparently twenty-five or thirty feet. Perhaps less. Except for the explosion, she would not have been injured. . . .

Under these circumstances I cannot say as a matter of law that the plaintiff's injuries were not the proximate result of the negligence. That is all we have before us. The court refused to so charge. No request was made to submit the matter to the jury as a question of fact, even would that have been proper upon the record before us.

The judgment appealed from should be affirmed, with costs.

CASE DISCUSSION QUESTIONS

1. Why did the majority hold that there was no negligence as to Mrs. Palsgraf? Do you agree?

2. The dissent stated: "What we do mean by the word 'proximate' is, that because of convenience, of public policy, of a rough sense of justice, the law arbitrarily declines to trace a series of events beyond a certain point. This is not logic. It is practical politics." Compare that to the quote at the beginning of this chapter.

3. Part of the dissent that we omitted included the following illustration: "A chauffeur negligently collides with another car which is filled with dynamite, although he could not know it. An explosion follows. A, walking on the sidewalk nearby, is killed. B, sitting in a window of a building opposite, is cut by flying glass. C, likewise sitting in a window a block away, is similarly injured. And a further illustration. A nursemaid, ten blocks away, startled by the noise, involuntarily drops a baby from her arms to the walk." Who out of A, B, C, and the baby should recover from the chauffeur? Why?

(2) Intervening cause

Sometimes after the defendant has acted negligently, another factor intervenes that contributes to the plaintiff's injury. If the intervening cause is great enough, the court may find that the defendant's negligence is no longer the proximate cause. In those situations the intervening cause is deemed to be a **superseding cause,** and the defendant's negligence no longer makes him or her liable. If, however, the intervening cause was foreseeable, the court may still find the defendant liable. Perhaps surprisingly, the classic case of a foreseeable intervening cause is malpractice. For example, assume a man is injured through a motorcyclist's negligent driving. If the injured man is taken to the hospital and his injuries are made worse through a doctor's malpractice, the motorcyclist will be responsible for all the injuries, not just those caused by the initial accident. Also, tavern owners are liable for injuries caused by their intoxicated patrons. An interesting variant of that will be discussed in the next section of this chapter when we look at two different approaches to the issue of social host liability. The following case graphically illustrates the problem of deciding where liability should end.

Anglin v. State Department of Transportation
472 So. 2d 784, 10 Fla. Law W. 1622 (Dist. Ct. App. 1985)

ZEHMER, JJ.

In these consolidated personal injury cases, plaintiffs below appeal a final summary judgment, contending the trial court erred in ruling as a matter of law that appellees were insulated from liability by unforeseeable independent intervening causes. We reverse.

On the night of September 3, 1979, Cleopatra Anglin, her husband, and her brother were traveling through drizzling rain in a 1965 Chevrolet pickup truck. Upon crossing a Seaboard Coastline Railroad track on Alternate U.S. 27 in rural Polk County, they unexpectedly hit an accumulation of water that covered both lanes of travel and was approximately six inches deep. The truck motor was doused with water, sputtered for some distance after hitting the pool of water, and then died. The Anglins attempted to start the motor by pushing the truck down the road and then "popping" the clutch once the truck reached a moderate speed. Approximately fifteen minutes after their truck hit the water, during which time they attempted in vain to push-start the truck several times, a car driven by Edward DuBose passed the Anglin truck heading in the opposite direction. A short distance after passing the truck, which was still on the road and, according to some witnesses, still being pushed, Mr. DuBose turned his car around and headed back toward the truck to render assistance. Unfortunately, Mr. DuBose failed to timely see the truck, hit his brakes, slid into the rear of the truck, and pinned Mrs. Anglin between the two vehicles, causing injury resulting in amputation of both legs. The distance between the pool of water and the accident scene was estimated by some witnesses as approximately 200 yards, by others up to three-tenths of a mile.

On February 16, 1981, Mrs. Anglin and her husband filed a complaint against the state Department of Transportation and Seaboard Coastline Railroad Company, alleging negligence in the design and maintenance of the road and railroad tracks by allowing the accumulation of water on the roadway immediately adjacent to the railroad tracks. Defendants filed a motion for summary judgment and, in addition to numerous depositions already taken, plaintiffs filed affidavits in opposition to the motion. A final summary judgment in favor of the defendants was entered on June 9, 1983, upon the trial judge's ruling as a matter of law that the actions of the plaintiffs in attempting to push-start their disabled pickup truck and the actions of Mr. DuBose in negligently losing control of his car and colliding with the plaintiffs' truck were independent, efficient intervening causes of the accident that were unforeseeable by the defendants, thereby breaking the chain of causation between the purported negligence of the defendants and the injury.

As a general rule, a tortfeasor is liable for all damages proximately caused by his negligence. The term "proximate cause" (or "legal cause," in the language of the standard jury instructions) consists of two essential elements: (1) causation in fact, and (2) foreseeability. See generally, 38 Fla. Jur. 2d, Negligence, §§ 29–48. Causation in fact is often characterized in terms of a "but for" test, i.e., but for the defendant's negligence, the resulting damage would not have occurred. In the present case, there is no question as to causation in fact because "but for" the defendants' alleged negligence in causing the pooling of water on the highway, there would have been no accidental stopping of plaintiff's truck and resulting injury.

The second element of proximate cause, foreseeability, is, unlike causation in fact, a concept established through considerations of public policy and fairness whereby a defendant whose conduct factually "caused" damages may nevertheless be relieved of liability for those damages. Thus, proximate cause may be found lacking where the type of damage or injury that occurred is not within the scope of danger or risk created by the defendant's negligence and, thus, not a reasonably foreseeable result thereof. . . . It is not necessary, however, that the defendants "be able to foresee the exact nature and extent of the injuries or the precise manner in which the injuries occur"; all that is necessary to liability is that "the tortfeasor be able to foresee that some injury will likely result in some manner as a consequence of his negligent acts." . . . In the instant case, it cannot be said as a matter of law that an injury to plaintiff was not within the scope of danger or risk arising out of the alleged negligence. In the field of human experience, one should expect that negligently permitting a pool of water on an open highway would likely pose a substantial hazard to motorists because a vehicle crashing unexpectedly into the water is likely to experience a stalled motor or other difficulty causing the vehicle to stop on the highway, thereby subjecting its occupants to the risk of injury from collision by other cars.

Proximate cause may be found lacking, however, where an unforeseeable force or action occurring independently of the original negligence causes the injury or damage. This force or action is commonly referred to as an "Independent, efficient intervening cause." For the original negligent actor to be relieved of liability under this doctrine, however, the intervening cause must be "efficient," i.e., truly independent of and not "set in motion" by the original negligence. The trial court's ruling that the conduct of the plaintiffs in pushing their truck down the road was an independent, efficient intervening cause of the accident was error because the existence of the pool of water set into motion the plaintiffs' subsequent actions in attempting to restart the motor that was stalled by driving through the water. These actions, having been "set in motion" by defendants' negligence, did not constitute an independent, efficient intervening cause. Whether the plaintiffs' conduct was negligent and caused the injury should be submitted to the jury under appropriate instructions on comparative negligence.

The trial court correctly characterized Mr. DuBose's negligent operation of his car as an independent intervening cause. The negligent pooling of water did not cause Mr. DuBose to negligently operate his vehicle into collision with the plaintiffs.[2] The trial court erred, however, in ruling as a matter of law that such intervening cause warranted entry of summary judgment for defen-

dants. If an intervening cause is reasonably foreseeable, the negligent defendants may be held liable. Whether an intervening cause is foreseeable is ordinarily for the trier of fact to decide. Only if reasonable persons could not differ as to the total absence of evidence to support any inference that the intervening cause was foreseeable may the court determine the issue as a matter of law. In the circumstances of this case (the night was dark, it was raining, and the collision occurred in a rural area where traffic customarily moves rapidly), had DuBose come on the scene and collided with plaintiffs' stalled truck immediately after plaintiffs hit the pooled water, the question of foreseeability of that occurrence would most assuredly present a jury issue. The fact that plaintiffs attempted to push-start their stalled truck for approximately fifteen minutes and that Mr. DuBose collided with it while attempting to stop and provide assistance does not change this jury issue to a question of law. The plaintiffs' exposure to danger was created by defendants' negligence, and the fact that a collision might occur while plaintiffs were extricating themselves from such danger up to fifteen minutes later presents a jury issue on foreseeability. That is so because the defendants need not have notice of the particular manner in which an injury would occur; it is enough that the possibility of some accidental injury was foreseeable to the ordinarily prudent person.

Reversed and Remanded.

BOOTH, J., Dissenting

We should affirm the summary judgment entered below based on lack of proximate cause. The chain of events here between alleged negligent act and injury is too attenuated and is broken, in fact, by the independent, intervening actions of others.

For the purpose of this appeal, we assume that defendants were negligent in maintaining a depression on a rural roadway, a depression which, in the aftermath of Hurricane David, was filled with six inches of water. It would be foreseeable that a driver who unexpectedly traversed such a depression in the road could lose control of

---

[2]The result would be otherwise if, for example, Mr. DuBose had driven through the pool of water and failed to stop because his brakes became wet and ineffective.

his vehicle, causing an accidental injury to himself or others. Stalling and the immediate consequences thereof are also not unforeseeable. Other results of the puddle could be termed as "foreseeable" in a philosophical, but not a legal, sense. For example, the disabled vehicle could have been struck by lightning, or the occupants could have been robbed or become ill but unable to seek medical care. In each instance, it could be said that, but for the stalling of their car caused by the defendant these subsequent events would not have occurred. Although there would be cause and effect relationship, such consequences would generally not be within the scope of the risk created by the negligent party who caused the vehicle to become immobile. The law does not impose liability because of the concept of "proximate cause," as stated in Prosser and Keeton:

> In a philosophical sense, the consequences of an act go forward to eternity, and the causes of an event go back to the dawn of human events, and beyond. But any attempt to impose responsibility upon such a basis would result in infinite liability for all

wrongful acts, and would "set society on edge and fill the courts with endless litigation." As a practical matter, legal responsibility must be limited to those causes which are so closely connected with the result and of such significance that the law is justified in imposing liability. Some boundary must be set to liability for the consequences of any act, upon the basis of some social idea of justice or policy.

Therefore, I would agree with the majority that there could be a jury question as to causation in fact. But, as to proximate cause, in this case at least, the principle is one of law. . . .

The issue, then, is the scope of the legal duty to protect the plaintiff against intervening causes which are possible but not probable. . . . Plaintiff's injury occurred more than a quarter of an hour after, and three-tenths of a mile down the road from, the puddle. The accident occurred after, and as the result of, negligence of others, each acting independently of defendants.

The law does not impose unlimited liability for all consequences that may result from a puddle of water on the road. . . .

CASE DISCUSSION QUESTIONS

1. Do you agree with the majority or the dissent? Why?

2. Two years later, in 1987, this decision was reversed by the Supreme Court of Florida in *Department of Transp. v. Anglin*, 502 So. 2d 896, 900 (Fla. 1987) (as they so quaintly put it in Florida, "[W]e quash the decision below and remand for proceedings consistent with this opinion"). On what basis do you think the court reached its decision?

(3) Duty of care to third parties

As we have seen, sometimes the court will hold a person responsible for the actions of someone else. For example, traditionally a bar owner can be held responsible if an intoxicated patron negligently injures a third party. Liability is based on what are known as **dramshop laws**. In a sense the bar owner is held responsible for the patron's negligence.

A related and emerging area of the law is the degree of responsibility a social host has for the actions of an intoxicated guest. In some states the courts have refused to find liability, stating that such a change in the law is better left to the legislature. For example, in *Charles v. Seigfried*,[24] Alan Seigfried held a party at which he provided drinks for everyone, including sixteen-year-old Lynn Sue. Alan knew of Lynn Sue's "advanced state of drunkenness," knew that she had

---

[24]651 N.E.2d 154 (Ill. 1995).

driven her own car to the party, and allowed her to leave the party while still extremely intoxicated. While driving, Lynn Sue died in a fatal collision. In refusing to find the host liable for Lynn Sue's death, the court noted that "the drinking of the intoxicant, not the furnishing it, is the proximate cause of the intoxication and the resulting injury. As a matter of public policy, the furnishing of alcoholic beverages is considered as too remote to serve as the proximate cause of the injury."[25] The court also based its decision on the belief that such a change in the law should come from the legislature.[26]

Other courts have disagreed. For example, the Massachusetts Supreme Judicial Court thought it was appropriate for the court, and not the legislature, to tackle the problem of social host liability. In *McGuiggan v. New England Telephone & Telegraph Co.*[27] the court concluded that "in certain circumstances liability properly could be imposed on such a social host."[28] Those circumstances arise when the social host knew or should have known the guest was drunk, knowingly gave the guest an alcoholic drink anyway, and knew or should have known that the guest would operate a motor vehicle.[29] The court noted that every case

in which social host liability was acknowledged as a possibility or as a fact has been decided in the past decade. This trend toward imposing liability is no doubt a response to the greater concern of society in recent years regarding the problems of drunken driving. It is understandable that the law of torts, which in many aspects measures one's duty by what is reasonable conduct in the circumstances, should begin to respond to society's increasing concern.[30]

NETNOTE

The Internet contains many sources for medical information. For example, you can find current medical news at *www.medscape.com*. The Cancer Web at *http://cancerweb.ncl.ac.uk/omd/* contains an online medical dictionary.

d. Harm

As we have seen, the purpose of negligence law is to compensate the plaintiff for any harm suffered. Until recently, however, that harm could include emotional distress only if the plaintiff also suffered physical harm and only if the plaintiff was in the "zone of danger" created by the defendant's actions.

---

[25]Id. at 157.

[26]Id. at 160.

[27]496 N.E.2d 141 (Mass. 1986).

[28]Id. at 141.

[29]Id. at 146.

[30]Id.

Therefore, a parent standing at her kitchen window, seeing her child negligently harmed by a speeding motorist, could not recover for her emotional distress. Then, as you read in Chapter 1 in a landmark decision, *Dillon v. Legg*,[31] the California Supreme Court held that a mother could recover for her emotional distress caused by seeing her daughter negligently injured. This was the result even though the mother was not "in the zone of danger," as she never feared for her own safety. Since *Dillon* many state courts have followed the lead of the California courts by adopting the tort of negligent infliction of emotional distress. Others have expanded on the *Dillon* holding, both as to how contemporaneous the injury and the plaintiff's emotional distress must be and as to who beyond parents and children is covered. For example, in *Leong v. Takasaki*[32] a ten-year-old boy was allowed to recover for nervous shock and psychic injuries after he witnessed his step-grandmother's death, when she was struck by the defendant's vehicle. In 1979 the New Hampshire Supreme Court held that the trial court erred in dismissing a case where the father did not hear the accident that harmed his daughter but was near enough to immediately become aware of the accident and go to her aid.[33]

DISCUSSION QUESTION

8. A woman sees her live-in boyfriend run over by a car and killed. Should she be allowed to sue for emotional distress? Why?

2. Defenses to Negligence

In representing the defendant in a negligence case the attorney usually attempts to rebut the plaintiff's evidence on as many of the above four elements as possible. In other words, the defense tries to show that no duty was owed to the plaintiff, that no breach occurred, and that the defendant's action was not the cause of the plaintiff's injuries. Another approach to defending such cases involves raising an affirmative defense, in which it is admitted that negligence was established, but it is argued that the defendant should not be held liable because of actions taken by the plaintiff. Traditionally, the two major affirmative defenses were contributory negligence and assumption of the risk. Today most states have adopted a form of comparative negligence.

a. Contributory Negligence

Contributory negligence Negligence by the plaintiff that contributed to his or her injury. Normally, it is a complete bar to the plaintiff's recovery.

The doctrine of contributory negligence asserts that the plaintiff contributed to his or her own injuries or otherwise failed to protect himself or herself from risks that were foreseeable. In other words, it was the plaintiff's breach of a duty to protect himself or herself that was the proximate cause of the injuries. The defendant therefore is relieved of any liability connected with the defendant's negligence, no matter how great the defendant's negligence and how slight the plaintiff's contributory negligence.

---

[31]441 P.2d 912 (Cal. 1968).

[32]520 P.2d 758 (Haw. 1974).

[33]Corso v. Merrill, 406 A.2d 300 (N.H. 1979).

One way that a plaintiff can sometimes avoid the defense of contributory negligence is to argue that the defendant had the **last clear chance** to avoid the accident. Applied mainly in automobile accident cases this doctrine states that the negligence of the plaintiff does not preclude a recovery for the negligence of the defendant where it appears that the defendant, by exercising reasonable care and prudence, might still have been able to avoid the accident or at least reduce some of the plaintiff's injuries. For example, assume the plaintiff driver is hit by the defendant driver's car. The defendant was speeding at the time and therefore was negligent. However, the plaintiff was contributorily negligent in that she ran a stop sign. In a state that follows contributory negligence, the plaintiff will be barred from recovery. However, if she can show that the defendant had the last clear chance to avoid the accident, perhaps by veering off the road or shifting lanes, then she may be able to shift responsibility back to the defendant.

One area that has given the courts a great deal of difficulty is whether a plaintiff's failure to wear a seat belt should be considered a defense in a negligence action. Some courts have held that the failure to wear a seat belt, especially when there is a statutory duty to do so, shows a lack of ordinary care and hence is contributory negligence. Others have pointed out that as the failure to wear a seat belt did not cause the accident, such a failure cannot be seen as contributory negligence. However, if the failure to wear a seat belt caused an increase in the injuries, then that could be factored into the question of damages, analogously to the contract concept of mitigation of damages. Finally, a third approach is to ignore the presence or absence of a seat belt. These courts agree with the second approach—that failure to wear a seat belt is not contributory negligence, as it had no part in causing the accident—but disagree that it should be a factor in reducing the damage award. These courts argue that the failure to wear a seat belt is not analogous to the duty to mitigate damages. The duty to mitigate arises only after and not before an injury occurs.

b. Assumption of the Risk

Another affirmative defense involves the concept of **assumption of the risk**. According to this doctrine a plaintiff may not recover for an injury received as a result of voluntarily subjecting himself or herself to a known danger. Successful use of this defense requires proof that the plaintiff knew about the dangerous nature of the situation before voluntarily exposing himself or herself to that danger. It is argued, for example, that when people choose to attend a baseball game, they assume the risk of being hit by a foul ball. Take another example: if you know that a parking lot is covered with ice and yet you proceed to walk across it, the court will probably say that you assumed the risk of any injury from falling on the ice.

Notice that assumption of the risk involves a subjective standard. The plaintiff must voluntarily and knowingly assume the danger; that is, he or she must actually understand the risk. This can be contrasted with contributory negligence, which is measured not by what the plaintiff was thinking but by what a reasonable person would have done.

Under the traditional view, assumption of the risk, like contributory negligence, was a complete bar to recovery. Today many states have eliminated assumption of the risk as a separate defense, having subsumed it under the defense of comparative negligence. This eliminates many of the proof problems

Last clear chance
The doctrine that states that despite the plaintiff's contributory negligence, the defendant should still be liable if the defendant was the last one in a position to avoid the accident.

Assumption of the risk
Voluntarily and knowingly subjecting oneself to danger.

(i.e., having to prove what the plaintiff was actually thinking) and the problems of categorizing specific behavior as either negligence or assumption of the risk. For example, if you get into a car being driven by someone you know is intoxicated, is that an unreasonable act on your part (contributory negligence) or assumption of the risk (knowingly subjecting yourself to a dangerous situation)? In those states that have subsumed assumption of the risk under comparative negligence, the plaintiff's recovery can be reduced either if it can be shown that a reasonable person would have acted differently or if the plaintiff actually knew and voluntarily assumed the risk.

Exculpatory clause
A provision that purports to waive liability.

An example of an express assumption of the risk is the signing of a waiver of liability. Such waivers are frequently called **exculpatory clauses** because their purpose is to relieve tortfeasors of liability. In certain circumstances the courts have upheld such waivers, particularly when the parties are of fairly equal bargaining power and the event involves inherent danger, such as skydiving or mountain climbing. Increasingly, however, courts are refusing to enforce such waivers. Sometimes the refusal is based on the public policy argument that the parties were of very unequal bargaining power. Other times the courts have invalidated such waivers by requiring specific language or by finding an ambiguity and construing the language against the drafter. In addition, the courts usually disallow exculpatory clauses in cases of gross negligence.

An example of the recent trend disfavoring releases is the Virginia Supreme Court case of *Heitt v. Lake Barcroft Community Assn.*[34] The plaintiff was injured while participating in an athletic event sponsored by a homeowners' association. During the swimming portion of the event he dove into the water, struck his head, and sustained severe injuries, leaving him a quadriplegic. Prior to entering the event, he had signed an entry form that provided in part:

> "In consideration of this entry being accepted to participate in the Lake Barcroft Teflon Man Triathlon I hereby . . . waive, release and forever discharge any and all rights and claims for damages . . . for any and all injuries suffered by me in said event."[35]

The Virginia Supreme Court held that "an agreement entered into prior to injury, releasing a tortfeasor from liability for negligence resulting in personal injury, is void because it violates public policy."[36] The court distinguished prior decisions upholding waivers as having been limited to situations involving only property damage.

c. Comparative Negligence

Comparative negligence
A method for measuring the relative negligence of the plaintiff and the defendant, with a commensurate sharing of the compensation for the injuries.

Both contributory negligence and assumption of the risk prevent a plaintiff from being compensated for very serious injuries, even when the injuries resulted from rather minor breaches when compared to the extreme negligence of the defendant. In response to the perceived unfairness of this situation, all but a handful of states, through statutes and court decisions, have moved to adopt **comparative negligence**. Under comparative negligence, negligence is measured

---

[34] 418 S.E.2d 894 (Va. 1992).
[35] Id. at 895.
[36] Id.

in terms of percentages, and damages are distributed proportionately. There are three alternative theories of comparative negligence:

1. A plaintiff can recover when the plaintiff's negligence is slight but may not recover when the plaintiff's negligence is gross.
2. Under a "pure" comparative negligence statute a plaintiff can recover actual damages less a percentage, calculated as the amount of negligence attributable to the plaintiff.
3. Under modified comparative negligence a plaintiff's recovery is reduced by the percentage of the plaintiff's own negligence if the defendant's negligence is greater than that of the plaintiff. However, the plaintiff is barred from recovering anything if the plaintiff's negligence is greater than the defendant's.

d. Immunities

For policy reasons certain defendants, even though negligent, are immune from suit. Traditionally, immunity meant a complete bar to recovery. Recently, however, the courts have been reexamining many immunities and in some instances limiting their effect or even eliminating them entirely. For example, some states have removed the bar of spousal immunity, and others have eliminated parental immunity, thereby allowing spouses to sue each other and children to sue their parents. The doctrine of charitable immunity has also been abolished or limited in most states.

The doctrine of **sovereign immunity** prohibits suits against the government without the government's consent. It can be traced back to the concept of the divine right of kings and the idea that the king could do no wrong. In modern times federal and state governments have passed legislation that modifies this concept. For example, at the federal level Congress has enacted the Federal Tort Claims Act (FTCA).[37] Under that statute someone can sue the government for harm caused by a government employee's negligence but not for an intentional tort or for something that resulted from a discretionary function. These limitations are a cause for much litigation, as it is often difficult to determine whether a particular action is the result of negligence or an intentional act and whether the action falls within a "discretionary function." Similarly, on the state and local level, governmental acts are often protected from suit if the public employee's action involved basic policy choices.

In circumstances where one is prohibited from suing the government for the employee's actions, he or she may sometimes be able to sue the government official directly. Limitations apply here as well. For example, judicial and legislative officials have an absolute privilege against being held liable for any actions performed as part of their official duties. The reasoning behind this absolute bar is that such officials must be able to perform their daily work without constant fear of being sued. Other administrative personnel receive only a qualified immunity. In order to recover damages under the terms of this qualified immunity, the plaintiff must prove that the defendant acted in bad faith.

---

[37] 28 U.S.C.S. § 1346(B) (2008).

In the following case the police stopped an intoxicated driver. An eyewitness stated that the driver "Fuller was swaying, unsteady on his feet, holding his hands up to his head, moving back and forth and holding onto the top of the door to steady himself." The police officer talked to Fuller for about one minute, did not conduct a field sobriety test, and did not detain him. Ten minutes later, driving at approximately seventy-five miles per hour, Fuller's car collided head-on with a car being driven by Mark Irwin. The collision killed Fuller, Mark Irwin, and a passenger in Irwin's car and seriously injured Debbie Irwin and her son. When Mrs. Irwin brought suit against the town, the court had to determine whether the town should be held liable for the police officer's actions. Massachusetts has a tort claims act that is similar to the federal statute in that it prohibits lawsuits based on a "discretionary function."

Irwin v. Town of Ware
392 Mass. 745, 467 N.E.2d 1292 (1984)

Judges HENNESSEY, C.J., WILKINS, LIACOS, ABRAMS, NOLAN, LYNCH, & O'CONNOR, JJ. NOLAN, J., dissenting, with whom LYNCH and O'CONNOR, JJ., join.

HENNESSEY, C.J.

The plaintiffs commenced this action against the defendant town of Ware (town). They charge that police officers of the town negligently failed to take into protective custody a motor vehicle operator who was under the influence of intoxicating liquor and who subsequently caused an accident resulting in harm to the plaintiffs. The jury returned special verdicts for the plaintiffs in the amount of $873,697. . . .

2. Applicability of G.L. c. 258, § 2.

Whether the town is liable to the plaintiffs for the negligence of its police officers depends initially upon the scope of G.L. c. 258, the so-called Massachusetts Tort Claims Act (Act). As to scope, the Act provides in relevant part that "[p]ublic employers shall be liable for injury or loss of property or personal injury or death caused by the negligent or wrongful act or omission of any public employee while acting within the scope of his office or employment, in the same manner and to the same extent as a private individual under like circumstances." G.L. c. 258, § 2, as appearing in St. 1978, c. 512, § 15. The Act exempts from such liability, how-ever, "any claim based upon the exercise or performance or the failure to exercise or perform a discretionary function or duty on the part of a public employer or public employee, acting within the scope of his office or employment, whether or not the discretion involved is abused." G.L. c. 258, § 10(b). As a threshold matter, therefore, we must determine whether the challenged actions of the police officers were outside the Act as "discretionary functions" within the meaning of G.L. c. 258, § 10(b).

The town contends that the statutes setting forth an officer's authority with respect to intoxicated motor vehicle operators "indicate that the arrest of Fuller, assuming, arguendo, that he was intoxicated, was discretionary and not mandatory." Whether an act is itself discretionary, of course, does not turn on whether that act was negligently or nonnegligently performed. Therefore, we need not consider how the act was performed in this case to determine whether it is discretionary. Rather, we must address only a more general question: Is the decision of a police officer to remove from the roadways a driver who he knows or has reason to know is intoxicated a discretionary act within the meaning of G.L. c. 258, § 10(b). We conclude it is not.

. . . In *Whitney v. Worcester*, 373 Mass. 208, 219 (1977), we noted that immunity for discretionary functions did not extend to all acts requiring judgment because "the performance of all functions involves the exercise of discretion and judgment to some degree." We described discretionary acts as those "characterized by the high degree of discretion and judgment involved in weighing alternatives and making choices with respect to public policy and planning." In contrast, we explained that not counted among such acts are those which involve "the carrying out of previously established policies or plans." Id. at 218.

No reasonable basis exists for arguing that a police officer is making a policy or planning judgment in deciding whether to remove from the roadways a driver who he knows is intoxicated. Rather, the policy and planning decision to remove such drivers has already been made by the Legislature. ["Any officer authorized to make arrests . . . may arrest without warrant any person . . . who the officer has probable cause to believe has operated or is operating a motor vehicle while under the influence of intoxicating liquor," G.L. c. 90, § 21.] This is not to say every harm resulting from the conscious failure of a police officer to remove an intoxicated driver from the roadway will give rise to liability for the public employer. There may be situations in which an officer's failure to remove an intoxicated driver from the roadway will not lead to such liability. Where liability does not result, however, it will be because some element of the tort alleged will not have been established. It will not be because the act of the officer is discretionary within the meaning of G.L. c. 258, § 10(b). . . .

7. Conclusion.

In sum, we conclude that, under G.L. c. 258, a town or city may be held liable in damages for the negligent failure of its police officers to remove from the highway a motor vehicle operator who is under the influence of intoxicating liquor and who subsequently causes injuries or death to other travelers. . . . [The case was remanded for a new trial because of erroneously admitted evidence regarding Fuller's blood alcohol content.]

CASE DISCUSSION QUESTIONS

1. Why didn't the court think the police officer's actions fell under the "discretionary functions" exception?

2. This case established that the defense of sovereign immunity was not available in these circumstances. However, to recover, the plaintiff still had to establish that the police officer was negligent. What elements of the negligence claim do you think might give the plaintiff problems?

3. Many charitable and sovereign immunity statutes cap the allowable recovery. In the *Irwin* case the statute provided that the public employer would not be liable "for any amount in excess of one hundred thousand dollars." There were four plaintiffs in this case. How do you think the parties argued this language should be interpreted?

3. Reckless Behavior

In between the two main categories of torts that we have discussed thus far, intentional torts and negligence, is an area of liability variously described as gross negligence, or willful or wanton behavior, or **recklessness**. The courts disagree as to whether these are forms of "super negligence" or are more akin to intentional behavior. They also disagree as to whether they represent different mental states or are simply different ways of describing the same thing.[38]

Recklessness
Disregarding a substantial and unjustifiable risk that harm will result.

---

[38]Sawyer v. Food Lion, Inc., 549 S.E.2d 867, 870 (N.C. 2001) ("gross negligence requires a finding that the conduct is willful, wanton, or done with reckless indifference").

While there is a great deal of confusion as to the exact meaning of these terms, all three imply a conscious or knowing disregard of an unreasonable and substantial risk of serious bodily harm to another. While the person may not wish to cause harm, he or she is aware of the potential for harm and proceeds anyway, indifferent to the consequences. Unlike negligence, which requires merely unreasonable behavior, recklessness requires a "*conscious* choice of a course of action, with knowledge or reason to know that it will create a serious danger to others."[39] As the conduct involves some level of conscious intent, punitive damages may be available. Also, most courts have held that a plaintiff's contributory negligence may not be used as a defense when the defendant has acted in a willful, wanton, or reckless manner.[40] Therefore, a plaintiff who has negligently contributed to his or her own injury may try to prove that the defendant's actions were willful, wanton, or reckless.

Because the courts have not been able to clearly define recklessness, it is decidedly difficult to know where negligence ends and recklessness begins, and in turn, where reckless behavior ends and intentional behavior begins. For example, if a golfer carelessly forgot to check to see if anyone was in the vicinity before taking a shot, that might be negligence. However, if that golfer had looked, seen a person in the line of sight, yelled a warning, and then taken the shot anyway before the person had a chance to move, some courts would find the behavior to have been reckless, but others would still see it as merely negligent. Finally, if the golfer was angry with another golfer and deliberately aimed his shot at the other player intending for the ball to hit her, then the golfer's actions would amount to either an intentional tort or recklessness. To establish an intentional tort, the plaintiff would have to prove the defendant intended for the ball to hit her. Otherwise, if it was proven that the defendant was merely trying to frighten her, but was indifferent as to whether the ball would hit her, the court will find the defendant was reckless.

Earlier in this chapter in discussing defamation, we saw one example of when courts apply a recklessness standard. When a public figure sues for defamation, there must be proof that the publisher of the statement acted in reckless disregard as to whether the statement was false or not. You will also see recklessness, and the other terms listed above, used in statutes that limit the liability of drivers who through their carelessness injure nonpaying passengers. The purpose behind these "guest statutes" is to protect drivers who voluntarily give transportation to nonpaying guests, unless the driver's conduct can be classified as at least reckless. Also, in some states, trespassers cannot sue for injuries unless the landowner acted in a willful, wanton, or reckless manner. One of the most interesting areas requiring the finding of at least reckless behavior is in the area of sport law.

As anyone who has ever seen or played in a sporting event knows, physical contact is an expected part of the game, and physical injury is always a possibility. Sometimes individual players engaged in vigorous competition go beyond what is expected and violate the rules of the game. Hence, we have yellow cards

---

[39]Schick v. Ferolito, 767 A.2d 962, 969 (N.J. 2001) (emphasis added).

[40]Restatement (Second) of Torts § 482(1) (1965) ("[A] plaintiff's contributory negligence does not bar recovery for harm caused by the defendant's reckless disregard for the plaintiff's safety.").

in soccer, the penalty box in hockey, and fouls in basketball.[41] But when a player exceeds the normal rules of play and injures another player, should the offending player suffer more than the sanction imposed by the rules of the game? Should the offending player also be held accountable in a court of law and be required to pay damages? If the answer is yes, the question becomes: on what basis should liability be found? Most courts have answered that question by finding that to be held accountable a player must act either intentionally or recklessly. A finding of mere negligence will not be enough to require the offending player to pay the injured player damages.

The majority of courts that limit liability to intentional or reckless behavior do so for two basic policy reasons. First, because some degree of physical contact is inherent in most sporting competitions, courts are concerned about the potential flood of litigation if participants could sue coparticipants for every injury received. Courts envision a world wherein "every punter with whom contact is made, every midfielder high sticked, every basketball player fouled, every batter struck by a pitch, and every hockey player tripped"[42] files a lawsuit. Second, the courts want to encourage vigorous participation by the athletes. They believe that the fear of litigation would dampen the athletes' competitive spirit, resulting in less vigorous play.

However, these policy reasons are also balanced by a concern for the safety of the players, so there must be some restraints on what can occur during an athletic competition. As one court has noted:

> The problem of imposing a duty of care on participants in a sports competition is a difficult one. Players, when they engage in sport, agree to undergo some physical contacts which could amount to assault and battery absent the players' consent. *Restatement (Second) of Torts § 50* comment b (1965). The courts are wary of imposing wide tort liability on sports participants, lest the law chill the vigor of athletic competition. Nevertheless, some of the restraints of civilization must accompany every athlete on to the playing field. [R]easonable controls should exist to protect the players and the game.[43]

These competing policy concerns have resulted in most courts stating that coparticipants can be found responsible for injuries they cause, but only if they were acting with the intent to harm or at least recklessly with a conscious decision to proceed despite the potential for causing harm.

Earlier in this chapter in the case of *Knight v. Jewett,* you saw how difficult it can be to prove that a participant intentionally harmed another participant. As you will recall, Ms. Knight was not able to maintain her claim for assault and battery because she was not able to prove that Mr. Jewitt intended to step on her finger. However, in her complaint, she had also alleged that his behavior toward her was negligent, that is, that his "rough play" amounted to unreasonable behavior. On further appeal, the California Supreme Court affirmed the dismissal of her battery claim and addressed her negligence claim. Note the standard of conduct the court thought should be applied to her case and the reasons the court advanced for denying her negligence claim.

---

[41]Jaworski v. Keirnan, 696 A.2d 332, 337 (Conn. 1997).

[42]Id. at 338.

[43]Gauvin v. Clark, 537 N.E.2d 94, 96 (Mass. 1989).

Knight v. Jewett
3 Cal. 4th 296, 834 P.2d 696, 11 Cal. Rptr. 2d 2 (1992)

. . . As a general rule, persons have a duty to use due care to avoid injury to others, and may be held liable if their careless conduct injures another person. Thus, for example, a property owner ordinarily is required to use due care to eliminate dangerous conditions on his or her property. In the sports setting, however, conditions or conduct that otherwise might be viewed as dangerous often are an integral part of the sport itself. Thus, although moguls on a ski run pose a risk of harm to skiers that might not exist were these configurations removed, the challenge and risks posed by the moguls are part of the sport of skiing, and a ski resort has no duty to eliminate them. In this respect, the nature of a sport is highly relevant in defining the duty of care owed by the particular defendant.

Although defendants generally have no legal duty to eliminate (or protect a plaintiff against) risks inherent in the sport itself, it is well established that defendants generally do have a duty to use due care not to increase the risks to a participant over and above those inherent in the sport. Thus, although a ski resort has no duty to remove moguls from a ski run, it clearly does have a duty to use due care to maintain its tow-ropes in a safe, working condition so as not to expose skiers to an increased risk of harm. The cases establish that the latter type of risk, posed by a ski resort's negligence, clearly is not a risk (inherent in the sport) that is assumed by a participant.

In some situations, however, the careless conduct of others is treated as an "inherent risk" of a sport, thus barring recovery by the plaintiff. For example, numerous cases recognize that in a game of baseball, a player generally cannot recover if he or she is hit and injured by a carelessly thrown ball, and that in a game of basketball, recovery is not permitted for an injury caused by a carelessly extended elbow. The divergent results of the foregoing cases lead naturally to the question how courts are to determine when careless conduct of another properly should be considered an "inherent risk" of the sport that (as a matter of law) is assumed by the injured participant. . . .

In the present case, defendant was a participant in the touch football game in which plaintiff was engaged at the time of her injury, and thus the question before us involves the circumstances under which a participant in such a sport may be held liable for an injury sustained by another participant.

The overwhelming majority of the cases, both within and outside California, that have addressed the issue of coparticipant liability in such a sport, have concluded that it is improper to hold a sports participant liable to a coparticipant for ordinary careless conduct committed during the sport—for example, for an injury resulting from a carelessly thrown ball or bat during a baseball game—and that liability properly may be imposed on a participant only when he or she intentionally injures another player or engages in reckless conduct that is totally outside the range of the ordinary activity involved in the sport. . . .

Accordingly, we conclude that a participant in an active sport breaches a legal duty of care to other participants—i.e., engages in conduct that properly may subject him or her to financial liability—only if the participant intentionally injures another player or engages in conduct that is so reckless as to be totally outside the range of the ordinary activity involved in the sport.[7]

As applied to the present case, the foregoing legal principle clearly supports the trial court's entry of summary judgment in favor of defendant.

---

[7][T]he limited duty of care applicable to coparticipants has been applied in situations involving a wide variety of active sports, ranging from baseball to ice hockey and skating. Because the touch football game at issue in this case clearly falls within the rationale of this rule, we have no occasion to decide whether a comparable limited duty of care appropriately should be applied to other less active sports, such as archery or golf. We note that because of the special danger to others posed by the sport of hunting, past cases generally have found the ordinary duty of care to be applicable to hunting accidents.

The declarations filed in support of and in opposition to the summary judgment motion establish that defendant was, at most, careless or negligent in knocking over plaintiff, stepping on her hand, and injuring her finger. Although plaintiff maintains that defendant's rough play as described in her declaration and the declaration of Andrea Starr properly can be characterized as "reckless," the conduct alleged in those declarations is not even closely comparable to the kind of conduct—conduct so reckless as to be totally outside the range of the ordinary activity involved in the sport—that is a prerequisite to the imposition of legal liability upon a participant in such a sport. . . .

The judgment of the Court of Appeal, upholding the summary judgment entered by the trial court, is affirmed.

CASE DISCUSSION QUESTIONS

1. Do you agree with the court that it is more appropriate to apply a recklessness rather than a negligence standard to injuries that occur as part of an athletic competition?

2. In footnote 7, the court notes that a different rule should be applied to some sports, such as archery. Why?

3. Do you agree with the court that Mr. Jewitt's actions were not so "totally outside the range of the ordinary activity involved in the sport" as to be considered reckless?

4. Do you think it would have mattered if Mr. Jewitt and Ms. Knight had agreed to a set of rules prior to the start of the game and then Mr. Jewitt had broken one of rules when he knocked down the plaintiff?

5. Do you think the same level of responsibility should apply no matter what the level of play? That is, do you think the courts should apply a different standard to recreational play, high school sports, college teams, and professional athletes?

6. Tom was golfing with a friend when he was hit in the eye by an unannounced mulligan (second shot). Do you think he should have to prove that the other golfer acted recklessly or only negligently? In other words, do you think that situation is analogous to or distinguishable from the *Knight* case?

7. On the same day the California Supreme Court decided *Knight v. Jewett*, it was faced with the following set of facts: while waterskiing backwards and barefoot on a river, the plaintiff was injured when his friend drove the boat too close to shore and the plaintiff hit a tree limb. How do you think the court decided? Why?

In summary, by their very nature athletic competitions involve physical contact between opposing players and even between players on the same team. Also, courts acknowledge that some degree of aggressiveness is essential to vigorous competition. Therefore, most courts have held that they will not impose liability based on mere negligence on the part of a player when that player causes injury to another player during an athletic competition. Instead, the player must have acted in an intentional or reckless manner. This promotes the dual policy concerns of limiting litigation and encouraging vigorous competition.

Remember that even in those situations where the plaintiff need only prove that the defendant was negligent, the plaintiff may still wish to introduce evidence that the defendant's actions went so far beyond negligence as to constitute reckless behavior. This is because at least some courts have found that while

Plaintiff's Prima Facie Case
1. The defendant must owe a duty to the plaintiff to act reasonably, and
2. the defendant must have breached that duty
3. causing (i.e., being both the cause in fact and the proximate cause)
4. the plaintiff harm.

Defenses
1. **Contributory negligence**
The plaintiff fails to use due care; traditionally, this has been a complete bar to the plaintiff's suit. Most states have abandoned contributory negligence and have adopted comparative negligence.

2. **Comparative negligence**
The plaintiff fails to use due care; the plaintiff's negligence is compared to the defendant's negligence, and damages are reduced accordingly.

3. **Assumption of the risk**
The plaintiff knowingly and voluntarily subjects himself or herself to danger; traditionally, this has been a complete bar to the plaintiff's suit. Today assumption of the risk has been eliminated in many states that have adopted comparative negligence.

4. **Immunity**
This complete bar to a lawsuit is based on policy considerations, such as preventing suits between family members and protecting charitable organizations.

Figure 7-3 Negligence Summarized

punitive damages should not be applied to the results of negligent behavior, they can be awarded in cases involving recklessness. Also, several courts have held that if the plaintiff can show that the defendant acted recklessly, the plaintiff's contributory negligence cannot be used as a defense.

In Figure 7-3 we have summarized our discussion of negligence law. In the next section we discuss the third main area of tort law, strict liability.

C. STRICT LIABILITY

Strict liability
Liability without having to prove fault.

Both negligence and intentional torts impose liability for improper behavior. In the former the injury is caused by carelessness, and in the latter it is intentional. In both cases the tortfeasor acts in an unreasonable manner and violates an established standard of care. When the concept of **strict liability** is applied, however, a person is held responsible for injuries that resulted from actions that were not necessarily unreasonable and that did not violate a standard of due care. In other words, it imposes liability even though the defendant is not at fault. Rather, the courts impose liability for the policy reason that, as between the defendant and the injured plaintiff, the defendant is in a better position to absorb the costs of the injury. The courts have applied the doctrine of strict liability in two situations: those involving ultrahazardous activities and products liability.

When persons engage in activities that are inherently dangerous, they should be responsible for any injuries that result, even though the activities may be carried out in the safest and most prudent way possible. Examples of areas in which strict liability has been imposed through the common law include the use of explosives, the building of dams, and the keeping of wild animals. In recent years the doctrine of strict liability has also been widely applied in product liability cases, in which the manufacturer is held liable for defects that occur in the product. A product is considered to be defective if it is unreasonably dangerous for use in the ordinary manner.

1. Ultrahazardous Activities

The Restatement of the Law of Torts, Second lists the six factors that courts review in determining whether a defendant should be held strictly liable when engaging in dangerous activities. Not all six factors have to be present. However, enough of the factors must be present for a court to feel justified in imposing strict liability—that is, liability even though the defendant did not intentionally or negligently cause the harm. The six factors listed in Section 520 are

(a) existence of a **high degree of risk of some harm** to the person, land, or chattels of others;
(b) likelihood that the **harm** that results from it **will be great;**
(c) **inability to eliminate the risk** by the exercise of reasonable care;
(d) extent to which the **activity is not a matter of common usage;**
(e) **inappropriateness** of the activity **to the place** where it is carried on; and
(f) extent to which its **value to the community is outweighed by its dangerous attributes.** (Emphasis added.)

Ultrahazardous Activities
Those activities that have an inherent risk of injury and therefore may result in strict liability.

The classic case for finding strict liability is the use of dynamite in blasting. The rationale for finding strict liability in such cases is that blasting as a business carries with it extreme risks that cannot be guarded against. Therefore, as between a for-profit company that chooses to engage in blasting and an innocent person harmed by the results of the blasting, the company should be held accountable, with the damages to be absorbed as part of the costs of doing business. Of course, any company engaging in such dangerous activities would be wise to purchase liability insurance.

In addition to such dangerous business activities as using or storing explosives, courts have frequently found the owners of wild animals strictly liable for injuries the animals cause. Applying the factors listed in the Restatement, you can see why keeping a lion, for example, in a backyard cage would lead to a finding of strict liability.

Products liability
The theory holding manufacturers and sellers liable for defective products when the defects make the products unreasonably dangerous.

2. Products Liability

When a product proves to be defective, an injured party can sue under any one of three theories: negligence, breach of warranty, or strict liability. (See Figure 7-4.) Which theory to use depends on the facts of the case and how the plaintiff's state has chosen to categorize products liability cases. Breach of warranty will be covered in the next chapter on contract remedies. Here we will discuss the tort theories of negligence and strict liability.

NETNOTE

The Consumer Product Safety Commission has a Web site where you can find information on recalls and unsafe products. Start at *www.cpsc.gov.*

There are three basic theories a plaintiff can use when bringing a products liability claim based on negligence: (1) a defect in the product caused by failing to use reasonable care in the manufacturing process; (2) a defect in the product caused by negligent design; and (3) negligent failure to warn. A classic case of bringing a negligence case based on proof of a manufacturing defect is *Mac-Pherson v. Buick Motor Co.*[44] The plaintiff's car had wooden wheel spokes, and one of the wheels was made of defective wood, causing the car to collapse, injuring the plaintiff. As noted above, the second basis for bringing a negligence claim would be proof of a design defect. For example, a hockey helmet with cutouts around the ears that allows penetration of a hockey puck is arguably defectively designed. Finally, a failure to warn of a danger known to the manufacturer but probably unknown to the user would form the basis for a negligence suit.

There are times, however, when a plaintiff cannot point to any one act of negligence. Nonetheless, the product was defective, and that defect caused an injury. In those cases the plaintiff might rely either on a warranty theory—the product failed to meet the buyer's expectations for a safe product—or on a tort strict liability theory. In the following case the court discusses the history of the development of products liability and why it thinks a tort as opposed to a contracts approach best meets the needs of consumers.

Caveat Emptor	Contract/Breach of Warranty	Negligence	Strict Liability
No liability	Liability unless disclaimed or lack of privity of contract	Liability if can prove unreasonable behavior	Liability if sold defective product that was unreasonably dangerous

Figure 7-4   History of Products Liability Law

---

[44]111 N.E. 1050 (N.Y.1916).

Doe v. Miles Lab., Inc.
675 F. Supp. 1466 (D. Md. 1987)

Norman P. RAMSEY, United States District Judge

A plague inflicts society and this Court is called upon to adjudicate the extent to which the effects will be visited upon its victims. The facts are tragic. In the autumn of 1983, plaintiff Jane Doe, who a week previous had given birth, sought emergency medical treatment for vaginal bleeding. During the course of treatment, the attending physician ordered the administration of 500 units of "Konyne," a blood-coagulation-factor concentrate produced by Cutter Laboratories, a division of Miles. Treatment appeared successful and plaintiff eventually was discharged.

Over the course of the months to follow, plaintiff suffered from a succession of ailments, ultimately being diagnosed as infected by the HTLV-III virus, and as having Acquired Immuno-Deficiency Syndrome-Related Complex (ARC), a predecessor of AIDS.... Defendant Miles... filed this motion for summary judgment on plaintiffs' counts for breach of warranties, for strict liability in tort, and for strict liability in tort—failure to warn; and further seeks summary judgment on the counts for loss of consortium and punitive damages to the extent they are derivative of the first three....

Products Liability Law

Defective products cause accidents that result in both economic losses and injuries either to persons or property. Allowing victims to recover for such losses was long a controversial issue. Indeed, the common law has followed a confusing and tortuous path in perceiving and remedying the situation.

Originally caveat emptor prevailed. Both English and early American courts found no liability on a seller's part—either in contract or in tort—toward anyone, either purchaser or bystander, for injuries caused by products....

It is not surprising the rule faded away. As societies shifting from agriculture to industry, more manufactured products entered the stream of commerce. Purchasers understandably expected products both to be what they were said to be and to perform in the manner predicted. As commerce expanded, courts propounded rules to protect people's expectations.

Arising as it did in the context of commerce, early products liability law adopted the concepts and parameters of contract law. Present in seedling form in *Chandelor v. Lopus,* the notion of warranties took root until it became widely recognized there could be either 1) express warranties resulting from representations or affirmations of fact about the characteristics of goods sold, or 2) implied warranties resulting simply from the act of selling where the seller was a merchant. Being based on conduct of the parties, either express or implied, such obligations are inherently contractual in nature, as compared to tort law which imposes obligations as a matter of policy independent of any express assumption on the part of a person....

Historically, contracts law never provided a credible basis for recovery for more than a few of the total numbers of persons injured in accidents. First, allowing warranties to be restricted limited the remedy. A manufacturer could contract out of liability by making disclaimers an express term of the contract. Second, the concept of privity severely restricted the class of persons who could recover. Consumers, for example, seldom buy directly from manufacturers. Instead, people usually buy products from intervening distributers or retailers, and courts seized upon this intervention as a reason for cutting off manufacturers' liability. Similarly, persons injured in on-the-job accidents faced equally bleak prospects of obtaining recovery from manufacturers of defective machinery and other equipment. Employees seldom purchase the tools they work with. Whenever manufacturers sold defective items to the employer, they were held to have no liability to the injured employee since he or she was not a party to the contract of sale....

Where contract law slammed the door, tort law served to pry it open a crack....

This law evolved dramatically when Judge Cardozo articulated negligence in products liability as we know it today. In *MacPherson v. Buick Motor Co.,* 217 N.Y. 382, 111 N.E. 1050 (1916), he [stated:]

If the nature of a thing is such that it is reasonably certain to place life and limb in peril when negligently made, it is then a thing of danger. Its nature gives warning of the consequences to be expected. If to the elements of danger there is added knowledge that the thing will be used by persons other than the purchaser, and used without new tests, then irrespective of contract, the manufacturer of this thing of danger is under a duty to make it carefully. . . . We have put aside the notion that the duty to safeguard life and limb, when the consequences of negligence may be foreseen, grew out of contract and nothing else. We have put the source of the obligation where it ought to be. We have put its source in the law.

Id. at 389-90, 111 N.E. at 1053. By 1966 the rule from *MacPherson v. Buick Motor Co.* had been universally recognized as the law in the United States. Thus manufacturers and vendors are held liable in tort for injury to consumers or ultimate users when found negligent.

Once liability in negligence became established, the concept of strict products liability gained favor as an alternative theory of recovery for injuries from defective products. It is commonly stated that there are three reasons for holding manufacturers and dealers strictly liable for personal or property injury caused by defective products. First, innocent victims should not be forced to bear the costs of accidents, which still occurs far too often, for even a negligence action may impose an evidentiary burden impossible to meet. Second, that strict liability promotes accident prevention, for the manufacturers are in a better position to ascertain and control the risks associated with their products. Third, that manufacturers are in a better position than victims to bear the costs, for they can distribute the losses across the many who purchase the product, whereas an individual victim, unless he or she is exceptionally well-to-do or heavily insured, will be driven into bankruptcy or into social welfare programs. . . .

[I]n *Greenman v. Yuba Power Products, Inc.*, 59 Cal. 2d 57, 27 Cal. Rptr. 697, 377 P.2d 897 (1963), [the court] inaugurated strict products liability in tort as an alternative theory of recovery. . . .

The *Greenman* court predicated liability on the idea a manufacturer "is strictly liable in tort when an article he places on the market, knowing that it is to be used without inspection for defects, proves to have a defect that causes injury to a human being." Id., 377 P.2d at 900. The court expressly moved away from an implied warranty theory of recovery, reasoning:

The abandonment of the requirement of a contract between [the plaintiff and the defendant], the recognition that the liability is not assumed by agreement but imposed by law [citations omitted], and the refusal to permit the manufacturer to define the scope of its own responsibility for defective products [citations omitted] make clear that the liability is not one governed by the law of contract warranties but by the law of strict liability in tort. Accordingly, rules defining and governing warranties that were developed to meet the needs of commercial transactions cannot properly be invoked to govern the manufacturers' liability to those injured by their defective products unless these rules also serve the purpose for which liability is imposed. Id. At 701, 377 P.2d at 901.

Shortly thereafter, the American Law Institute in 1965 in the Restatement (Second) of Torts included section 402A, which provides:

(1) One who sells any product in a defective condition unreasonably dangerous to the user or consumer or to his property is subject to liability for physical harm thereby caused to the ultimate user or consumer, or to his property, if (a) The seller is engaged in the business of selling such a product, and (b) It is expected to and does reach the user or consumer without substantial change in the condition in which it is sold. (2) The rule stated in subsection (1) applies although (a) The seller has exercised all possible care in the preparation and sale of his product, and (b) The user or consumer has not bought the product from or entered into any contractual relation with the seller.

. . . In 1976 the Maryland court explicitly adopted Section 402A's strict products liability in tort in *Phipps v. General Motors Corp.*, 278 Md. 337, 363 A.2d 955 (1976).

The court in *Phipps* iterated four essential elements for strict liability:

1) the product was in a defective condition at the time that it left the possession or control of the seller,
2) that it was unreasonably dangerous to the user or consumer,

3) that the defect was a cause of the injuries, and

4) that the product was expected to and did reach the consumer without substantial change in its condition.

Id. at 344, 363 A.2d at 958. The product had to be both "defective" and "unreasonably dangerous," with the latter described as "dangerous to an extent beyond which would be contemplated by the ordinary consumer who purchases it, with the ordinary knowledge common to the community as to its characteristics." Id., 363 A.2d at 959 (quoting Comment i to section 402A). Proof of both a "defective" and "unreasonably dangerous" product are required, for "the seller is not an insurer, as absolute liability is not imposed on the seller for any injury resulting from the use of his product." Id. at 352, 363 A.2d at 963. In essence the two characteristics create the legal cause requisite to liability. A plaintiff who cannot show that a product was both defective and unreasonably dangerous has failed to establish the basis for the defendant's liability.

Whatever the theory of recovery, whether negligence or strict liability, it is now clear that the test in products liability is the same. A plaintiff must show 1) the existence of a defect; 2) the attribution of the defect to the seller; and 3) a causal relation between the defect and the injury.

Jensen v. American Motors, 50 Md. App. 226, 234, 437 A.2d 242, 247 (1981).

Analysis

Defendant's motion for summary judgment leads the Court into ambiguous territory. Many of the issues raised are new. The Court is in a position common to *Erie* cases, namely being a federal court required to determine state law when the state courts have not directly addressed the issues. In such a case the federal court is obliged to view the matter as a state court would find the law, not necessarily as it would find the law to be. . . . [The court then went on to discuss whether policy considerations warranted exempting blood and blood products from strict liability in tort and decided they did not.]

Entrepreneurs by their nature are risk taking individuals. To the extent they need an incentive to engage in socially beneficial activities, the law already provides it in the form of a corporate shield on personal liability. To do as defendant argues, and exempt blood from strict liability would be to subsidize the product by forcing either victims or government through its social welfare programs to bear accident costs. . . .

Accordingly, the Court will deny defendant's motion for summary judgment on plaintiffs' claim for strict products liability. . . .

CASE DISCUSSION QUESTIONS

1. The court discusses a doctrine known as privity of contract. What does privity of contract mean, and why did the court see it as limiting the ability of plaintiffs to sue for defective products?

2. Why did the court think a tort-based approach to products liability was preferable to one based on contract and warranty law?

3. The court stated: "The argument is often made that strict products liability has the potential to bankrupt manufacturers. Such an argument misses the salutary economic role strict products liability plays. Understood properly, it can be seen that strict liability promotes a rational market place." How so?

As the court in *Doe v. Miles Laboratories, Inc.,* pointed out, a very influential development in the history of products liability law was the 1965 passage of Section 402A of the Restatement of the Law of Torts, Second. Under Section 402A a manufacturer or seller is liable if it sells a defective product that harms a consumer and that defect made the product unreasonably dangerous. Unlike other provisions of the Restatement, Section 402A was not really a restatement of existing law. Rather, it was the American Law Institute's vision of what the law should be. When it was passed, it had little support. Over the years that has changed, and today most states have adopted Section 402A.

In 1997 the American Law Institute finished a major redrafting of the Restatement of the Law of Torts, Third: Products Liability. The most notable way in which this new provision changes Section 402A is in requiring a plaintiff in a design defect case to prove that there was an alternative design that would have prevented the harm.

> A product . . . is defective in design when the foreseeable risks of harm posed by the product could have been reduced or avoided by the adoption of a reasonable alternative design by the seller . . . and the omission of the alternative design renders the product not reasonably safe.[45]

Largely because the courts see this as imposing an undue burden on plaintiffs and essentially converting strict liability into negligence, to date most courts have chosen not to accept the changes found in the Restatement, Third.

3. Defenses to Strict Liability Torts

Product misuse
When the product was not being used for its intended purpose or was being used in a dangerous manner; it is a defense to a products liability claim so long as the misuse was not foreseeable.

A plaintiff's contributory negligence is usually not considered a defense to strict liability; however, assumption of the risk and **product misuse** may be. For a manufacturer to assert the affirmative defense of product misuse, the manufacturer must prove that the product was not being used for its intended purpose or was being used in a dangerous manner that could not reasonably have been foreseen by the manufacturer. However, even if a plaintiff misuses a product, if that use is foreseeable, the manufacturer may be liable for a design defect. For example, assume a young child opened a stove door in order to step on it in an attempt to reach a shelf located above the stove. Although clearly a stove is not meant to be used as a stepping stool, a court might hold that this misuse was foreseeable and could have been avoided by a different design.

In Figure 7-5 on page 241 we have summarized the elements and defenses to strict liability. This figure covers strict liability both as it applies to ultra-hazardous activities and to product liability.

D. NEW TORTS

As you have seen, tort law is aspirational, striving to protect our interests in being free from unlawful intrusion into our privacy, reputation, and bodily integrity. As such, tort law is not a rigid doctrine but rather is ever changing to meet society's needs. In this section we will look at three developing areas of tort law. It is too soon to know whether any of these areas will become established, but they all illustrate the evolving nature of the law.

---

[45]Restatement (Third) of Products Liability § 2 (1997).

Prima Facie Case	Defenses
Ultrahazardous Activities (All six factors need not be present.) 1. Existence of a high degree of risk of some harm to the person, land, or chattels of others; 2. likelihood that the harm that results from it will be great; 3. inability to eliminate the risk by the exercise of reasonable care; 4. extent to which the activity is not a matter of common usage; 5. inappropriateness of the activity to the place where it is carried on; and 6. extent to which its value to the community is outweighed by its dangerous attributes.	1. Assumption of the risk
Product Liability (All of the following must be present.) 1. The product was in a defective condition at the time that it left the possession or control of the seller, 2. that it was unreasonably dangerous to the user or consumer, 3. that the defect was a cause of the injuries, and 4. that the product was expected to and did reach the consumer without substantial change in its condition.	1. Assumption of the risk 2. Unforseeable product misuse 3. Contributory negligence (in some states)

Figure 7-5   Summary of Strict Liability

1. Wrongful Life or Wrongful Birth

Wrongful life involves a child suing on the basis that but for someone's negligence the child never would have been born. Wrongful birth, on the other hand, involves parents suing over the birth of a child. In either case, these types of lawsuits raise the very fundamental question of whether a defendant should be liable for negligently causing the birth of a child. The courts have arrived at inconsistent answers to this question. These situations typically arise when a physician negligently failed to diagnose a pregnancy or negligently performed a sterilization procedure. One difficulty for the courts has been the problem of trying to weigh the costs of raising a child against the value of the life and the joy of parenthood. Another problem relates to the difficulty in assessing damages.

Courts frequently have simply allowed recovery for the costs of the failed medical procedure. On the other hand, when the child is born deformed, the courts are more willing to allow recovery for the costs associated with raising the child minus the costs associated with raising a healthy child.

2. Battered Woman's Syndrome

A new tort, recognized in only a few states, is the tort of battered woman's syndrome. Battered woman's syndrome is the result of a continuing pattern of abuse and violence. Typically, the cycle consists of three stages. The first stage involves minor physical or verbal abuse that escalates while the victim tries to mollify her abuser by remaining passive. Stage two is when the actual battering occurs. During the third stage, the abuser asks for forgiveness and promises never to abuse again. This period of relative calm then leads into the cycle beginning again. Victims often remain trapped in this cycle because they are ashamed or because they have the very realistic fear that reporting the behavior will only cause it to escalate.

When a plaintiff finally gains control of her situation and wishes to sue the abuser for the injuries she suffered, if she brings her claim under traditional battery or emotional distress theories, she may face dismissal under a statute of limitations defense. This is because it may have taken her longer than the statute of limitations allows, typically two years, to leave the relationship and develop the self-confidence needed to bring her claim. By instead bringing her claim under the theory of battered woman's syndrome, she may avoid the usual statute of limitations problems by arguing that the tort of battered woman's syndrome is a "continuing tort."

3. Drug Dealer Liability Act

Assume a baby is born already addicted to cocaine because of his mother's substance abuse while she was pregnant. Whom can the baby sue? Recalling the case of *Woods v. Lancet*, one possibility is that the baby could sue the person who supplied the drug or even the mother for negligence.

In addition, in a number of states there is now another possible defendant: anyone who sold or gave away cocaine to anyone (not necessarily the mother) in the same county and during the same time period that the mother used cocaine. Liability is based on a new statute, the Drug Dealer Liability Act, which has been adopted in at least fifteen states. Under that statute anyone who distributes an illegal drug can be sued by anyone harmed by that type of drug. The only limitations are that the distribution must have been in the same geographic area and during the same time period as the person who took the drugs. Obviously, such a statute has far-reaching consequences. At a backyard barbecue a businessman shares some marijuana with a friend. Two weeks later a teenager buys some marijuana on the street from an unknown dealer. The teenager is then injured in an automobile accident when he loses control due to his marijuana "high." That teenager could sue the businessman—someone he has never met—for his injuries. The difficulty, of course, would lie in locating potential defendants, such as the businessman, who have sufficient "deep pockets" to make such a lawsuit worthwhile.

Some have argued that the Drug Dealer Liability Act violates substantive due process in that it "shocks the conscience."[46] Others think that such a suit

---

[46]Dam, Injured Parties Can Sue Any Drug Dealer, 95 L.W.U.S.A. 869 (Sept. 11, 1995).

might violate double-jeopardy protections if the suit is brought by the government against someone who has already been convicted of drug dealing.

Discussion Questions

9. In most states, people can sue for loss of companionship of a spouse or a child who dies as a result of an intentional tort. Most states, however, treat the loss of a pet as the loss of personal property and will only award the value of the pet and not the pain and suffering caused by the death of the animal.[47] Advocates for a change in the law argue that dogs, cats, and other family pets should not be lumped with inanimate personal property, such as purses, furniture, or articles of clothing. Do you think more states should recognize a new tort to fully compensate owners for the loss of their pets?

10. Should tort law be an ever-expanding concept, or should there be some limits put on liability? Why? If the latter, what should those limits be?

11. Some argue that there is a litigation explosion; that instead of taking responsibility for their own actions, people are resorting in increasing numbers to the legal system for relief. Do you agree? Why? If you do agree, what should be done about it?

E. REMEDIES

As you have seen from reading the cases in this chapter, the most common form of remedy that a plaintiff seeks in a tort action is the awarding of some form of damages. From Chapter 3 you will recall that there are basically three types of damage awards: compensatory, punitive, and nominal. In addition to or instead of damages, the court might issue an **injunction**. An injunction is an order to the defendant ordering the defendant to do a specific act or to cease doing a specific act.

Compensatory damages (sometimes referred to as **actual damages**) are awarded to compensate the plaintiff for the harm done to him or her. In a tort action involving harm to a person, that might mean the cost of medical bills, lost time from work, and pain and suffering.

Compensatory damages can be further divided into general damages and special damages. **General damages** are those damages that you would naturally expect to occur given the type of harm suffered. For example, if Tom intentionally hit Sam's arm, thereby breaking it, Tom should expect to have to pay for Sam's pain and suffering. **Special damages** (sometimes called **consequential damages**) are damages that also flow naturally from the injury, but they may vary depending on the special circumstances of the case. They include the cost of repairing or replacing the damaged property, paying any medical bills, and replacing plaintiff's income lost while unable to work. For example, if, unbeknown to Tom, Sam was a major league pitcher and due to his injury he could no longer pitch, Sam could recover his future lost wages as special damages.

Unlike compensatory damages, which are designed to pay plaintiffs for harm done to them, **punitive damages** (also called **exemplary damages**) serve the

---

[47]Tresa Baldas, Bid to Create New Tort Over Pets Fails, For Now, Nat'l L.J. May 29, 2006, at 6.

dual functions of punishing and deterring tortfeasors. Because their purpose is to punish and deter, typically punitive damages are awarded only for intentional torts and only when the court determines that the defendant deserves an additional punishment beyond just compensating the plaintiff for the harm done to him or her. One study determined that plaintiffs are awarded punitive damages in only 6 percent of cases.[48]

Once the decision has been made to award punitive damages, courts often struggle with the appropriate ratio between those damages and the compensatory damages. For example, if a plaintiff were awarded $10,000 in compensatory damages, would adequate punishment be meted out with punitive damages that were twice, ten times, or even a hundred times the compensatory amount? The courts have never set an exact formula. However, the United States Supreme Court has held that under the Constitution's due process protections, a defendant must "receive fair notice not only of the conduct that will subject him to punishment, but also of the severity of the penalty that a state may impose."[49]

Therefore, if a punitive award is so large that the defendant could not have been expected to be on notice that he could be subjected to such a severe punishment, a court must set it aside as excessive. To help courts with this process, the Supreme Court developed three "guideposts" to analyze the appropriateness of the size of the punitive award:

1. the degree of reprehensibility of the defendant's action;
2. the ratio of punitive to compensatory damages, and
3. a comparison of the punitive award and the civil or criminal sanctions that could be imposed for similar conduct.

Using these guides, in *BMW v. Gore,* the Supreme Court reversed a $2 million punitive award. A BMW owner claimed that BMW had intentionally defrauded him. When the car he had ordered was shipped to the United States, it was damaged by acid rain. Instead of informing him of the damage, BMW simply repainted the car. Nine months later the owner found out that his car had been repainted and sued BMW. The trial court determined that his actual damages were only $4,000 (the decreased value of his car). After applying the three guideposts, the Supreme Court stated that $2 million in punitive damages was a "grossly excessive award," setting it aside as it "transcend[ed] the constitutional limit."[50]

Most recently, the Supreme Court applied the three guideposts in a case where an insurance company was ordered to pay $1 million in compensatory damages and $145 million in punitive damages. The case originated when Mr. Curtis Campbell caused an automobile accident. He was sued, and his insurance carrier, State Farm, refused settlement offers from the plaintiffs. The offers were within Campbell's policy limits of $50,000. Because they refused to settle, the case went to trial. The jury found against Mr. Campbell and awarded damages of $185,000. Campbell sued State Farm. The jury found that State Farm knew that if the case went to trial, it was likely to result in a verdict over

---

[48]Blum, Study Finds Punitives Are Small, Rare, Nat'l L.J., July 1, 1996, at A6.
[49]BMW v. Gore, 517 U.S. 559, 574 (1996).
[50]Id. at 585.

the policy limits and so had acted in bad faith when it refused to settle. In reviewing this award of damages, the Supreme Court relied heavily on the first guidepost, noting that "while State Farm's handling of the claims against the Campbells merits no praise," State Farm's actions were not so reprehensible as to justify the large amount of punitive damages in this case.[51] As to the second guidepost, the Court noted:

> [I]n practice, few awards exceeding a single-digit ratio between punitive and compensatory damages, to a significant degree, will satisfy due process. In *Haslip*, in upholding a punitive damages award, we concluded that an award of more than four times the amount of compensatory damages might be close to the line of constitutional impropriety. We cited that 4-to-1 ratio again in *Gore*. While these ratios are not binding, they are instructive. They demonstrate what should be obvious: Single-digit multipliers are more likely to comport with due process, while still achieving the State's goals of deterrence and retribution, than awards with ratios in range of 500 to 1, [as found in *Gore*] or, in this case, of 145 to 1.[52]

The Court spent little time on the third guidepost, simply stating that a relevant civil sanction of a $10,000 fine for fraud was "dwarfed" by the $145 million punitive damages award.[53]

At trial, the Campbells introduced evidence that State Farm's decision was due not to an isolated mistake in judgment but rather was part of a nationwide scheme to maximize profits by capping payouts on claims. This was a significant factor in the state court's awarding such a large punitive award. The Supreme Court rejected this argument, stating that "a defendant should be punished for the conduct that harmed the plaintiff, not for being an unsavory individual or business. Due process does not permit courts, in the calculation of punitive damages, to adjudicate the merits of other parties' hypothetical claims against a defendant."[54] Critics of the Supreme Court's approach argue that this raises the same issue we mentioned earlier in this chapter in our discussion of Carol Burnett and her suit against the National Enquirer. That is, if the ratio of punitive to compensatory damages is set at too low a level, there is the danger that punitive damages will cease to serve their deterrence function. Businesses may determine that a certain course of action will produce more profits than will be offset by any punitive damage award. Where, then, is the incentive for the business to choose a different and more socially responsible course of action?

Both *BMW v. Gore* and *State Farm* involved economic harm. In fact, in *BMW v. Gore,* the plaintiff suffered minimal damages: the difference in value between a new BMW and a new BMW that had been repainted. In *State Farm,* the plaintiff suffered greater economic harm as well as emotional distress. However, neither of these cases involved conduct that endangered anyone's physical health or safety. Therefore, it was unclear whether the Court would be as willing to set aside punitive damage awards in cases involving personal injury.

In 2007, the Court was faced for the first time with a personal injury case involving punitive damages. In an Oregon state court, a cigarette smoker's widow

---

[51]State Farm Automobile Ins. Co. v. Campbell, 538 U.S. 408 (2003).

[52]Id. at 426.

[53]Id. at 429.

[54]Id. at 422-423.

had sued a cigarette manufacturer for negligence and deceit for the smoking-related lung cancer death of her husband. During the trial, the plaintiff introduced evidence of the large numbers of smokers who had been harmed by the manufacturer's actions. The jury awarded the plaintiff $821,000 in compensatory damages and $79.5 million in punitive damages. On appeal, the Supreme Court was faced with two issues: (1) whether the cigarette manufacturer had been unconstitutionally punished for causing harm to nonparty victims, and (2) whether the punitive damages were excessive. The Court answered the first question in the affirmative. The Court stated that a jury may consider evidence of actual harm to nonparties as part of its reprehensibility determination (the first guidepost), but it may not "use a punitive damages verdict to punish a defendant directly on account of harms it is alleged to have visited on non-parties."[55] The Court declined to answer the second question as to whether the punitive damages were excessive. Instead, it remanded the case to the Oregon Supreme Court to determine whether there should be a new trial or a change in the level of punitive damages awarded.[56] Therefore, we still do not have a definite answer as to whether the Court will apply a different standard regarding the appropriate ratio of compensatory to punitive damages in a personal injury case.

Most recently in another case involving economic harm, the Supreme Court overturned a $2.5 billion punitive damage award in a federal maritime law case involving the 1989 Exxon Valdez Alaskan oil spill. In 1989 an Exxon supertanker had grounded on a reef in Alaska's Prince William Sound, spilling millions of gallons of oil, destroying the livelihood of thousands of commercial fishermen and inflicting tremendous environmental damage. Exxon argued that the punitive damage award exceeded the "bounds justified by the punitive damages goal of deterring reckless (or worse) behavior and the consequently heightened threat of harm."[57] After reviewing empirical data on jury awards, the Court concluded that "a 1:1 ratio, which is above the median award, is a fair upper limit" for punitive awards in cases involving maritime law and reckless, as opposed to intentional, behavior.[58]

Finally, **nominal damages** are awarded when a right has been violated but the plaintiff cannot prove any monetary harm. For example, a trespasser may have caused no harm to the land, but the landowner would still be entitled to a nominal award.

In recent years the topic of tort reform has often been in the news. Particularly in the area of medical malpractice, higher insurance costs and a perceived increase in the amount and number of damage awards have caused concern. As a consequence, some states have passed legislation to limit the amount of damages that can be awarded. In some instances that limit applies to the total award, but in others only to punitive damages or to noneconomic damages. Noneconomic damages are compensatory damages that deal with harm such as pain and suffering, as opposed to economic damages, such as lost wages and medical costs. In some states these so-called caps have been challenged and found to be unconstitutional. However, in other states these caps

---

[55]Philip Morris v. Williams, 127 S. Ct. 1057, 1064 (2007).

[56]Id. at 1065.

[57]Exxon Shipping Co. v. Baker, 128 S. Ct. 2605, 2619-2620 (2008).

[58]Id. at 2633.

have withstood constitutional challenge, or the state has amended its constitution to provide for the legitimacy of such caps. Opponents of caps suggest that they cause the most harm to those most injured (and hence logically those with the most damages that would be above the cap) and that a better approach is through insurance reform.

DISCUSSION QUESTIONS

12. Some commentators argue that the quotation from *State Farm* cited above indicates that the Supreme Court will look most favorably on punitive damage awards that are four times that of the compensatory award. Do you agree?

13. Do you think it is fairer to defendants to apply "guideposts" such as the Supreme Court has been using or a simple ratio, such as mandating that in nonpersonal injury cases punitive damage awards cannot exceed nine times the compensatory award? Would such a rule satisfy society's need to deter future bad conduct?

14. Typically, punitive damages are awarded to the plaintiff because it was the plaintiff who brought the lawsuit. However, punitive damages are designed to punish the defendant rather than compensate the victim. Some have argued, therefore, that punitive damages should be paid to the state (society as a whole) rather than to the individual plaintiff. Indeed, a few states have passed laws that split punitive damage awards between the plaintiff and the state. Alaska, Missouri, and Utah split awards equally between the plaintiff and the state; Oregon takes 60 percent of the awards; Georgia, Indiana, and Iowa take 75 percent; and Illinois leaves the allocation up to the discretion of the judge.[59] In Ohio, the state supreme court on its own initiative recently allocated almost two-thirds of a $30 million punitive damages award to a cancer research fund the court established.[60] What do you think of these various approaches?

SUMMARY

A tort is a private wrong that causes harm to a person or property. Torts are generally classified as involving intentional acts, negligence, or strict liability. Intentional torts occur whenever someone intends an action that results in harm. Examples include assault and battery, false imprisonment, defamation, invasion of privacy, intentional infliction of emotional distress, and trespass. Negligence involves a breach of duty that causes harm. Cause includes both actual cause and proximate cause. Strict liability includes both ultrahazardous activities and products liability, where an unreasonably dangerous defective product is sold. Finally, in a limited number of situations, such as those involving contact sports, the courts will apply a reckless standard. Recklessness involves a conscious decision to proceed despite a substantial and unjustifiable risk that harm will result.

Tort law is constantly evolving. The courts are still developing new torts to cover changing societal views as to what should be protected. Examples include the torts of wrongful life or birth and battered woman's syndrome.

---

[59]Hechler, California Eyes Share of Punitives, Nat'l L.J., Vol. 26, No. 38 (May 24, 2004).
[60]Dardinger v. Anthem Blue Cross & Blue Shield, 781 N.E.2d 121 (Ohio 2002).

Finally, in bringing a tort action a plaintiff is generally seeking either an injunction or damages. Damages can take the form of a compensatory, punitive, or nominal award.

||| CRITICAL THINKING EXERCISES

1. Martha Smith went to a K-Mart store at about 7:30 PM on September 8 to purchase some diapers and several cans of motor oil. She took her small child along to enable her to purchase the correct size diapers, carrying the child in an infant seat which she had purchased at K-Mart two or three weeks previously. A large K-Mart price tag was still attached to the infant seat.

Martha purchased the diapers and oil, and some children's clothes. She was in a hurry to leave because it was then 8:00 PM, her child's feeding time, and she rushed through the checkout lane. She paid for the diapers, oil, and clothing. Just after leaving the store she heard someone ask her to stop. She turned around and saw a K-Mart security guard, who asked, "Would you please come back into the store?" Martha replied, "What for?" The security guard pulled out a store badge, showed it to her, and said that if she would just come back into the store, he would like to talk to her about it.

When Martha hesitated, the security guard grabbed her by the arm and led her back into the store, stopping just inside the doors. The guard then told Martha that one of the K-Mart employees had informed him that she saw Martha steal the car seat. Martha denied that she had stolen the seat and explained that she had purchased the seat previously. She demanded to see the person who accused her of stealing the seat. The security guard said that it would take a while to find the employee. Martha asked if they could wait in a more private place, but the guard said that they could not.

After approximately twenty minutes, the employee was found. The employee stated that she saw Martha steal the infant seat by taking it off a table and putting her baby in it. Martha pointed out to the security guard that the seat had cat hairs, food crumbs, and milk stains on it. The guard then said, "I'm really sorry; there's been a terrible mistake. You can go." Martha looked at the clock as she left. The time was 8:30 PM.

The following statute, ch. 203, § 99, applies to the situation.

> A merchant or merchant's adult employee who has probable cause for believing that a person has stolen store merchandise may detain such person in a reasonable manner for a reasonable length of time.

If Martha sues K-Mart for false imprisonment, do you think she would win her case, or do you think K-Mart has a valid defense? Why?

2. Review the situation of Mrs. Day presented at the beginning of the chapter. What torts do you think Mr. Day committed?

3. Prosenjit Podar killed Tatiana Tarasoff. Two months earlier Prosenjit had told Dr. Lawrence Moore, a psychologist, that he intended to kill Tatiana. Dr. Moore did not warn Tatiana or her parents of Prosenjit's intention. What policy considerations would argue against finding the psychologist liable? How do you think an attorney representing Tatiana's parents would reply to those arguments?

4. The defendant company entered a float in a parade. As the float traveled down the street, employees threw candy to the crowd. Children running to collect the candy injured a spectator. Develop an argument for why the spectator should be allowed to sue the company.

5. A grocery store customer was mugged on a sidewalk adjacent to a shopping center. The mugging occurred immediately after the customer left the store. The sidewalk was owned not by the grocery store but by the shopping center. The grocery store knew of numerous similar muggings on the sidewalk. The store employees used the sidewalk to carry bags to customers' cars, and its lease provided that the store could hold sidewalk sales there. Analyze whether the grocery store should be held liable for the customer's injuries.

6. A young woman, Melissa, returned from a solo bicycling trip on Cape Cod to find that her car would not start. A young man, Michael Gentile, lent her his cell phone so that she could call her parents. Her father, who was a member of AAA, called AAA and asked that a tow truck go to the location of his daughter's disabled car. Two hours later the tow truck appeared. The driver asked Melissa where she wanted her car towed but did not offer to give her a ride. Michael offered to give her a lift to her mother's house. She accepted. Somewhere along the way Michael raped and killed her. The parents have sued AAA for negligence. AAA has filed a motion to dismiss. How do you think the court ruled? Why?

7. Every year Camp Good Times holds a hike to the top of Mount Snow or to the top of Barton Hill. Of the two hikes the one up Mount Snow is a bit more arduous, but either can be accomplished in under an hour. This past year the campers, who ranged in age from seven to twelve, voted to hike up Mount Snow. The fifty campers and two camp counselors made it to the top of the hill in about half an hour with no problems. On the way back down, however, eight-year-old Timmy tripped over a large moss-covered log lying across the path. As a result of his fall he suffered a broken leg. His parents now want to know whether they can successfully sue the camp for Timmy's injury. Please evaluate their claim based on *Sauer v. Hebrew Institute of Long Island, Inc.* (page 215).

8. Two crime victims were killed, having been shot. The families wanted to sue the handgun manufacturer under the theory that manufacturers of handguns negligently marketed them in such a way as to create an underground market, making it easy to obtain the guns. However, the plaintiffs were not able to identify which specific manufacturer made the handguns used in the shootings. Should they be allowed to pursue their lawsuit and, if so, against whom?

9. An alarm company delayed calling the fire department. By the time the firefighters arrived, the fire had advanced to such a stage that one of the firefighters was killed. The firefighter's widow sued the alarm company, alleging its negligent delay in calling in the fire resulted in her husband's death. How do you think the court decided? Why?

10. Assume you are a legislator and want to draft a statute dealing with social host liability. How would you fashion such a rule? For example, would you limit liability to those cases

    a. where minors are involved?

    b. where the host knows the guest is intoxicated?

    c. where the host actually serves the alcohol?

How would you avoid the concern that finding liability in some cases would potentially lead to unlimited liability for social hosts?

11. Do you think a social host should be liable for accidents caused by drivers who obtained alcohol from the social host? Why? For example, consider the following facts. Margaret Davis gave her daughter, a high school student, permission to hold a party. Davis did not keep alcoholic beverages in her home, and there were none on the night of the party. Before the party began, Davis left. During the unchaperoned party a seventeen-year-old guest obtained beer brought to the party by another guest. While driving home intoxicated, the guest lost control of his car and injured Ruth Langemann. Should Langemann be allowed to sue Davis for her injuries?

12. In *McGuiggan v. New England Telephone & Telegraph Co.*, the Massachusetts Supreme Court established a test for when social hosts will be held responsible for harm that comes to one of their guests. Please review the standard set by that court as given on page 223. Then think about the following hypothetical:

> Seventeen-year-old Sally held a party. She had some friends buy two kegs of beer and bring them to the party. She paid for the kegs and was then partially reimbursed by the other guests. At some point, four men whom she had not invited appeared at the party. They were visibly intoxicated and while at the party helped themselves to Sally's beer. Shortly after the uninvited guests arrived, Tom, one of Sally's friends, told her he was leaving. She asked him to stay because she was apprehensive about the four uninvited men. Tom stayed and later was "sucker punched" by one of those uninvited guests. Tom has sued Sally for his injuries. Sally's attorney filed a motion to dismiss.

How do you think the court ruled? Why?

13. Mr. Alack joined a local health club. He signed a two-page, single-spaced contract that included the following language:

> Member assumes full responsibility for any injuries, damages or losses and does hereby fully and forever release and discharge [the health club] from any and all claims, demands, damages, rights of action, or causes of action, present or future . . . resulting from or arising out of the Member's . . . use or intended use of said gymnasium or the facilities and equipment thereof.

One day while he was exercising, the handle of a rowing machine disengaged from the weight cable and smashed into Mr. Alack's mouth. It was discovered that the machine's handle was not connected with the necessary clevis pin and that the health club did not require periodic inspections of its equipment. How would you argue that the release would not bar Mr. Alack from suing the health club for its negligent failure to maintain the rowing machine?

14. Before taking part in a horseback riding tour at the Loon Mountain Equestrian Center, Ms. Wright signed the following release:

I understand and am aware that horseback riding is a HAZARDOUS ACTIVITY. . . . I therefore release Loon Mountain Recreation Corporation . . . FROM ANY AND ALL LIABILITY FOR DAMAGES AND PERSONAL INJURY TO MYSELF . . . RESULTING FROM THE NEGLIGENCE OF LOON MOUNTAIN RECREATION CORPORATION TO INCLUDE NEGLIGENCE IN SELECTION, ADJUSTMENT OR ANY MAINTENANCE OF ANY HORSE.

While on the tour, the guide's horse kicked Ms. Wright in the leg. Ms. Wright sued for negligence, arguing that the tour guide had failed to control the horse after it had given signs it was about to "act out." How would you argue that the release should not bar Ms. Wright from suing the tour company?

15. First review the *Irwin* case beginning on page 228. Then think about this hypothetical.

Jason was a tenth grader at Dartmouth High School, a Massachusetts public school. One day last April three "youths" who did not attend the school had a violent altercation at the school with two of Jason's classmates. Later that day the three youths returned to the school, proceeded to a second-floor classroom, and stabbed Jason to death.

Jason's mother has sued the school for negligence, alleging that it failed to maintain adequate security and failed to protect her son in the presence of a known threat. The school has filed a motion to dismiss on two grounds: first, that they are protected by the discretionary function exception to the Massachusetts Tort Claims Act and second, that the attack was unforeseeable.

How do you think the court ruled? Why?

16. An amateur soccer game was played between high school–aged players. Julian Nabozny was a goalie. David Barnhill was a forward for the opposing team. David was known for being a very rough player, having acquired more penalties than any other player on the team. Rather than cautioning David to play a clean game, David's coach urged all his players to play as hard as they could and to "go for the kill."

During the game David kicked Julian in the head while Julian was in possession of the ball. Contact with a goaltender while he is in possession of the ball is a violation of FIFA (International Association Football Federation—soccer's international governing body) rules, which governed the contest.

When Julian's dad saw David kick his son in the head, he jumped out of his chair, rushed onto the field, and hit David in the chin with his fist, breaking David's jaw.

Another parent, Mike Bishop, also rushed onto the field. Afraid that Julian might be hurt further, he scooped him up and carried him off the field. Unfortunately, when David had kicked Julian, he had broken his neck. When Mike picked him up, the movement caused compression in Julian's spinal cord, leaving him permanently paralyzed from the waist down.

    a. Julian wants to sue David, the other player. In his complaint, which tort theory is Julian's attorney most likely to allege and what will he have to prove for Julian to be successful?

    b. Julian also wants to sue the coach. In his complaint, which tort theory is Julian's attorney most likely to allege and what will he have to prove for Julian to be successful?

c. Finally, Julian wants to sue the parent who "helped" him. In his complaint, which tort theory is Julian's attorney most likely to allege and what will he have to prove for Julian to be successful?

d. For the court to allow David to recover against Julian's dad, on what tort theory will David's attorney rely?

REVIEW QUESTIONS

Pages 187 through 195

1. How can the same set of facts result in both a tort and a crime? Will every tort also create criminal liability?
2. How can a tort be distinguished from a contract action?
3. What are the elements of assault? Of battery?
4. How can there be an assault and no battery? A battery without an assault?
5. Review the situation of Mrs. Day presented at the beginning of the chapter. Do you think she has a valid claim for either assault or battery? Why?

Pages 195 through 198

6. What are the elements of false imprisonment?
7. When does a shopkeeper have a valid defense to a detained person's allegation of false imprisonment?

Pages 198 through 201

8. What are the elements of libel? The defenses?
9. In *New York Times v. Sullivan,* what limitations did the Supreme Court put on the ability of public figures to sue the press?
10. Assume Robin Barker dictates a letter to her secretary. The letter is addressed to Ms. Wanda Jones. In the letter Ms. Barker tells Ms. Jones that she thinks Ms. Jones is a thief. The secretary types and mails the letters to Ms. Jones. Can Ms. Jones sue for defamation? What element is arguably missing?
11. A grocery store employee followed a customer to the parking lot and accused her of having meat in her purse. The customer opened her purse and showed that she did not have any meat, and the employee left. Several passersby heard the remarks, but the plaintiff could not identify any of them. Should the customer be barred from proceeding with a defamation suit? Why?

Pages 201 through 206

12. How do the torts of defamation and invasion of privacy differ?
13. What must a plaintiff prove to win a case of intentional infliction of emotional distress?

Pages 206 through 213

14. What are the four basic elements of a negligence claim?
15. Do you think the result in the *Cordas* case would have been different if Mrs. Cordas and her two children had been in the taxicab rather than standing on the sidewalk? Why?

Pages 214 through 216

16. Explain the doctrine of res ipsa loquitur.
17. When might the court find that a defendant was negligent per se?

Pages 216 through 224

18. What is the difference between "but for" causation and proximate cause?

Pages 224 through 229

19. Describe the three basic affirmative defenses to negligence. How do they differ from each other?
20. A state court judge approved a mother's petition to have her "somewhat retarded" daughter sterilized. The daughter was told that she was to have her appendix removed. Later the daughter married and found out that she had been sterilized. She sued the judge. How do you think the court resolved the case?
21. A public high school required parents to sign a release-of-liability form before allowing their children to participate in interscholastic athletics. The parents objected to having to sign the form and went to court, requesting that the school district be enjoined from requiring the release. How do you think the court decided the issue?
22. State building codes set forth requirements for safe buildings. If a building inspector fails in his duty to carefully inspect a building, do you think a purchaser of such premises would have a cause of action for buying a building that was developed in violation of the governmental requirements? Why?

Pages 229 through 234

23. How is recklessness defined? How does it differ both from intentional conduct and negligence?
24. In what areas of tort law are you most likely to see the courts applying a recklessness standard? Why?

Pages 234 through 243

25. Describe the three theories that a plaintiff can use to sue a manufacturer when harmed by that manufacturer's product.
26. A woman keeps a pit bull dog as a pet. One day the neighbor children accidentally throw a Frisbee into her yard. In attempting to retrieve the Frisbee one of the children is severely bitten by the dog. Should the dog's owner be held strictly liable? Why?
27. Manuel Sanchez began smoking at the age of ten. Over his lifetime he smoked several different brands of cigarettes. At the age of fifty-three he was diagnosed with throat cancer and died within six months. His widow sued nine different cigarette manufacturers on the theory of strict liability. To win her case, what would Mrs. Sanchez have to prove? Do you think she was successful?
28. Five-year-old Daphne took a disposable lighter from her mother's purse that was stored on the top shelf of a closet in a bedroom in her grandparents' home. While playing with the lighter, she started a fire that severely burned her two-year-old brother, Ruben. While the lighter manufacturer produced lighters both with and without child safety mechanisms, this lighter did not have one. The children's mother sued the manufacturer of the lighter. How would you argue the manufacturer should be held liable for the boy's injury? How do you think the lawyers for the manufacturer would respond?

Pages 243 through 247

29. What are the three basic types of damages that a plaintiff can recover in a tort action, and what is the purpose of each?
30. What is the difference between general and special damages?
31. What limits has the United States Supreme Court placed on the ability of a plaintiff to recover for punitive damages?

Chapter 8

Contract Law

A contract has, strictly speaking, nothing to do with the personal, or individual, intent of the parties. . . . If . . . it were proved by twenty bishops that either party, when he used the words, intended something else than the usual meaning which the law imposes upon them, he would still be held.
Judge Learned Hand

INTRODUCTION

Contracts are involved in almost every aspect of our lives, from day-to-day commercial transactions to corporate mergers—from purchasing and financing a home to insuring one's home, automobile, life, or health. A contract is nothing more than an agreement, oral or written, that can be enforced in court. Contract law sets out the basic elements that must be present for an agreement to be considered legally enforceable. It also spells out when the court will excuse one of the parties for not living up to his or her side of the agreement. In sum, contract law reflects society's values regarding what promises we think should be kept and what excuses we will allow.

You will discover that contract law is very rule bound. That is, to become an expert in contract law, you must master a vast array of technical rules. However, do not let yourself feel overwhelmed by the seemingly endless rules and exceptions to those rules. What is most important is that you come to understand the basic concepts that lie behind contract law.

A. THE UNIFORM COMMERCIAL CODE (UCC)

Contract law has strong common-law roots, and in areas that do not deal with the business world, the common-law rules still govern. However, if a contract involves a business setting, then you may also have to consult legislation, in the form of the **Uniform Commercial Code (UCC)**. The UCC is a series of model statutory provisions drafted by prominent legal scholars. It was developed with the intent that states would voluntarily incorporate these provisions into their own statutes, thus providing a uniform set of legal principles that would facilitate commercial transactions among persons in different states.

Although all states, as well as the District of Columbia, have adopted the UCC entirely or in part, it is not a federal law. That would require its enactment by Congress. While the UCC was created by a group of learned scholars in the hopes of establishing uniformity for businesses that deal across state lines, the terms of the UCC are valid only if they have been adopted by the state. In addition, while most states have adopted the UCC as it was originally written, each state has the option of changing the terms. Therefore, when dealing with the UCC in a specific state be sure to check that state's precise wording.

The UCC is divided into eleven articles (Figure 8-1). The four articles that are most relevant to contract law are Articles 1, 2, 2A, and 9. Article 1 sets forth general provisions, such as definitions that apply to the entire UCC. Article 2 deals with the sale of goods, and Article 9 deals with secured transactions, a method whereby a creditor can be assured that if the debtor fails to repay the debt, then the creditor will be able to obtain specific property as an alternative form of payment. Therefore, while the UCC applies to some contract situations, it does not apply to all. For example, the UCC does not apply to real estate or service contracts. The discussion in this chapter is based on the law of contracts as developed by the common law. However, wherever Article 2 of the UCC has made a significant change to the common law, we will also discuss that change. Article 2A on leases is a new provision. To see whether it has been adopted in your state, you will need to check your state statutes. We will discuss Article 9 in Chapter 10, Laws Affecting Business.

Article 1 sets forth the basic principles that underlie the entire UCC.

- Article 1 states that the UCC is to be liberally construed in order to best fulfill its underlying purposes to "simplify, clarify and modernize the law governing commercial transactions," to "permit the continued expansion of commercial practices through custom, usage and agreement of the parties," and "to make uniform the law among the various jurisdictions." UCC § 1-102(2).
- The parties are almost always free to set their own terms, even if they are at variance with the UCC's requirements. UCC § 1-102(3).
- Unless displaced by a particular part of the UCC, the common-law rules of contract still apply. UCC § 1-103. Therefore, unless there is a conflict between the common law and the UCC, both apply, for example, to contracts for the sale of goods.
- Under the UCC everyone is under an obligation to act in good faith, defined as honesty in fact. UCC § 1-203.

Uniform Commercial Code (UCC)
Originally drafted by the National Conference of Commissioners on Uniform State Law, it governs commercial transactions and has been adopted by all states, entirely or in part.

Figure 8-1 The Uniform Commercial Code

Article 1	General Provisions
Article 2	Sales
Article 2A	Leases [New]
Article 3	Commercial Paper
Article 4	Bank Deposits and Collections
Article 5	Letters of Credit
Article 6	Bulk Transfers
Article 7	Warehouse Receipts, Bills of Lading, & Other Documents of Title
Article 8	Investment Securities
Article 9	Secured Transactions
Article 10	Effective Date and Repealer

Article 2 applies to sales of goods. A *sale* is defined as "the passing of title from the seller to the buyer for a price." UCC § 2-106(1). Goods are "all things (including specially manufactured goods) which are movable . . . other than the money in which the price is to be paid, investment securities (Article 8) and things in action. 'Goods' also includes the unborn young of animals and growing crops and other identified things attached to realty as described in the section on goods to be severed from realty (Section 2-107)." UCC § 2-105(1). When you run across terms such as "things in action," first consult the definitions section to see whether the UCC has defined the term. If not, refer to a standard legal dictionary. In this case a thing in action, also known as a chose in action, means a right to sue.

If the situation does not involve a contract for the sale of goods, then Article 2 of the UCC does not apply at all. Therefore, it does not apply, for example, to employment or service contracts. One area of confusion is the mixed services/goods situation. For example, assume you go to a beauty parlor to have your hair dyed. Are you there to purchase the services of the beautician or to purchase the dye? In those situations the court will try to determine which element predominates —the service or the sale of the goods. Only if the court perceives the transaction as being principally for the sale of goods will it apply the UCC.

As the UCC was specially developed to make the commercial world more uniform and efficient, there are special rules that apply only to merchants. For example, a merchant's obligation of good faith includes "honesty in fact and the observance of reasonable commercial standards of fair dealing in the trade." UCC § 2-103(b). Therefore, merchants are expected not only to deal honestly but also to be aware of the normal business practices for their trade.

A merchant is someone who

1. deals in the goods that are the subject of the contract, or
2. "holds himself out as having knowledge or skill peculiar to the practices or goods involved" in the contract, or
3. who employs someone who has such knowledge and skill. Under this last standard the employee's knowledge and skill are then attributed to the employer. UCC § 2-104(1).

Notice how broad this definition is. Normally we would all think of the person referred to in the first definition as a merchant. However, under the second definition even someone with a great deal of knowledge in an area, such as a law professor who as a hobby also happens to be a knowledgeable collector of antiques, could be declared a merchant when dealing in the sale or purchase of antiques. Finally, notice under the third definition that a person will also be considered a merchant if that person employs someone who meets the second definition.

NETNOTE

The Uniform Commercial Code as revised through 2001 can be found on the Internet at *www.law.cornell.edu/ucc/ucc.table.html.*

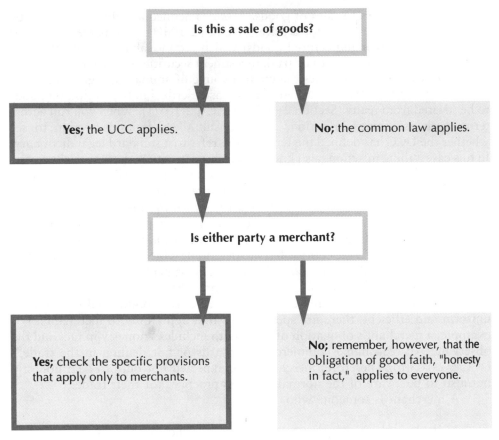

Figure 8-2   Does Article 2 of the UCC Apply?

Therefore, in summary, whenever you are faced with a contract situation, first ask yourself, Does this contract deal with the sale of goods? If the answer is yes, then ask whether either or both of the parties can be classified as a merchant. If yes, then be sure to check the special provisions that apply only to merchants. Finally, keep in mind the UCC's overall commitment to ensuring that all parties act in good faith and in such a way as to promote the expansion of commerce. See Figure 8-2.

B. TYPES OF CONTRACTS

As you may recall from Chapter 3, for a contract to be valid there must be an offer, an acceptance of the offer, and consideration; that is, something of value must be exchanged. However, before proceeding with our discussion of the elements of a binding contract, we need to mention the various ways in which courts classify contracts. Contracts can be either bilateral or unilateral; either express or implied in fact; either formal or informal; either executed or executory; and valid, void, voidable, or unenforceable. Each of these categories contains mutually exclusive terms. For example, a contract is always either bilateral or unilateral, always either express or implied in fact, and so forth.

A **bilateral contract** is one where a promise is exchanged for a promise. In a **unilateral contract** a promise is exchanged for an act. For example, I say to you, "I promise to pay you $5 if you will promise to mow my lawn." If you reply, "O.K., for $5 I promise to mow your lawn," then we have formed a bilateral contract. However, if I say, "I promise to pay you $5 if you will mow my lawn," I have made an offer for a unilateral contract. I promise to pay in return for your act of mowing the lawn. This may seem like a lot of quibbling over a difference that should not matter, but it can matter if both parties do not fully perform. In the first case we have a completed contract: an offer, an acceptance, and something of value to be exchanged. Both parties are bound to perform. In the second situation, however, we only have an offer. Acceptance cannot come except by doing the act of mowing. The question is, Does simply starting the act of mowing create an acceptance, or must the entire job be completed before the acceptance is finalized? For example, if you begin mowing my lawn, am I free to take back my offer, or do we at that point have a binding contract? The traditional view is that we do not. I am free to withdraw my offer at any time up until the act is completed. Because of the obvious unfairness of that approach, the more modern view states that once substantial performance has begun, the contract is binding. The obvious question is, What constitutes substantial performance? That must be determined on a case-by-case basis.

Contracts can also be express or implied in fact. **Express contracts** are formed through words, either oral or written. **Implied-in-fact contracts** are formed through conduct. For example, if you say to Susan, "I would like to sell you my watch for $10," and Susan says, "I accept," through your words you have formed an express contract. On the other hand, assume you go to the college bookstore. There is a long line at the cash register, and you are late for class. You grab a candy bar, wave it at the cash register clerk, and put 50 cents on the counter. The clerk nods and picks up the 50 cents. No words were spoken, but by your acts and those of the clerk you have formed an implied-in-fact contract.

Third, contracts can be either **formal** or **informal**. For most contracts today there are no special formalities that must be followed. Therefore, most contracts are classified as informal. There are a few exceptions, however. Certain contracts, such as those that transfer real estate, still require certain formalities. Other formal contracts include those under seal; a recognizance, which is an acknowledgment in court that a person will pay or act; negotiable instruments, such as a check; and letters of credit. All other contracts are classified as informal.

Once the parties have exchanged binding promises, a contract has been formed. Until it is fully performed, it is considered to be **executory**. Once both sides have fully performed, it is said that the contract has been **executed**. Be careful here. *Executed* also has another meaning in contract law: that a contract has been signed.

Finally, most contracts are classified as **valid**, having all the essential elements needed for a binding agreement. If a court finds, however, that the contract is for an illegal purpose, it will be declared **void.** In certain circumstances, if one of the parties was under a disability, such as being a minor, when he or she signed it, the court will say that the contract is **voidable** at the option of that party. Finally, there are times when two parties have entered into a perfectly valid contract, but because of a procedural error, such as the passage of the

Figure 8-3   Contract Classifications

Bilateral	or	Unilateral	and				
Express	or	Implied in fact	and				
Formal	or	Informal	and				
Executory	or	Executed	and				
Valid	or	Void	or	Voidable	or	Unenforceable

statute of limitations or the failure to put the contract in writing, the court will say the contract is **unenforceable**. Each of these possible contract classifications is summarized in Figure 8-3.

DISCUSSION QUESTION

1. We all enter into contracts every day. Think back over the past week, and list all the contracts that you have entered into.

C. THE ELEMENTS OF A BINDING CONTRACT

A contract can be either oral or written, but in order to be considered valid, each of its three key elements must be present:

1. an offer must be made,
2. an acceptance must be given, and
3. something of value must be exchanged (consideration).

Some writers list only two elements: an agreement and consideration. In such formulations an agreement is defined as both an offer and an acceptance, and consideration is defined as the exchange of something of value.

It is important to clearly distinguish a contract from a gift. A gift may also involve an offer (someone offers to give you something), an acceptance (you respond that you would like the gift), and the passage of something of value (the gift itself is delivered). The difference is that in a gift situation the consideration is one-sided. Only one of the parties receives something of value. On the other hand, in a contract situation, each party gives up something of value. Because of this difference, a contract is completed and binding on both parties once the parties have reached their agreement. However, a gift is not completed until the thing of value is actually delivered. This difference becomes important if one of the parties tries to take back a promise. In a contract situation the taking back of the promise creates a right in the other party to sue for breach of contract. In a gift situation, prior to delivery of the gift, the giver is free to take back the promise with no legal consequences. Consider the situation described in the following fact scenario.

Case 7: Who Owns the Watch?

Sally, a college student, had often told her friend Jill how much she admired Jill's Mickey Mouse watch. Last Monday, as the two were walking to class, Sally noticed that Jill was wearing a different watch and asked Jill about it. Jill replied that at her birthday party yesterday her boyfriend gave her this new watch. "In that case," Sally inquired, "would you be interested in selling your Mickey Mouse watch to me?" Jill replied, "I paid $200 for it, but because we are friends, I will sell it to you for $100 and will bring the watch with me tomorrow." Sally said, "Great, it's a deal." Unnoticed by Sally and Jill, Mike had overheard the conversation. "Wait," Mike said. "I have always wanted a Mickey Mouse watch. I will give you $150 for the watch." Jill thought about it for a moment and then turned to Sally and said, "Gosh, I'm sorry, Sally, but I'm afraid that unless you can match Mike's offer, I will have to sell the watch to him." Sally replied that she could not raise her offer. Mike, feeling a bit guilty, told Sally that on Tuesday when he got the Mickey Mouse watch, he would no longer need his current watch and would give it to Sally. The next day Jill sold her watch to Mike. Mike, however, had a change of heart and refused to give his old watch to Sally. Sally is understandably upset by the turn of events. Does she have any legal rights against either Jill or Mike?

Sometimes in analyzing contract situations it is helpful to diagram them. The arrow indicates something of value passing from one party to the other.

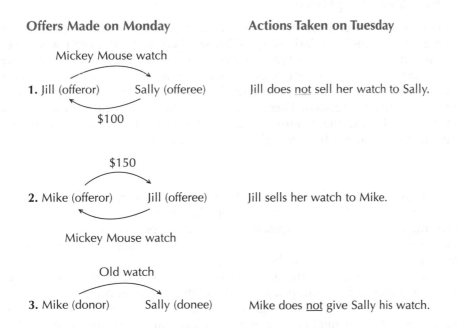

Offers Made on Monday

Mickey Mouse watch

1. Jill (offeror)   Sally (offeree)

$100

Actions Taken on Tuesday

Jill does <u>not</u> sell her watch to Sally.

$150

2. Mike (offeror)   Jill (offeree)

Jill sells her watch to Mike.

Mickey Mouse watch

Old watch

3. Mike (donor)   Sally (donee)

Mike does <u>not</u> give Sally his watch.

Looking at the first situation between Sally and Jill we see there was an agreement to exchange something of value. Recall that to form a binding contract, there must be an agreement to sell (Jill said she would sell the watch for $100 [an offer] and Sally said, "I agree" [an acceptance]); also, something of value must be exchanged (Sally was going to give $100 in return for the Mickey Mouse watch). Therefore, Sally and Jill had a binding contract. By selling the watch to someone else Jill is in breach of contract. Sally is entitled to the benefit of her bargain. However, it is unlikely that the court would order Jill to sell the watch to Sally. Such an order for specific performance occurs only when the item is unique. Instead Sally would be entitled to money damages. In this case she can purchase a similar watch, and if it costs more than the $100 she had agreed to spend, she can recover that difference.

The second situation illustrates a fully executed contract. Mike made an offer, Jill accepted, and they agreed to exchange something of value. A binding contract was formed. Then, when they fulfilled their promises, the contract was fully executed.

In the third situation, involving Sally and Mike, there was no contract. Sally did not agree to exchange anything with Mike. Mike simply offered to give Sally his old watch. For a gift to be complete, however, delivery must occur. Because Mike never handed Sally the watch, there was no completed gift, and Sally has no rights to Mike's watch.

The courts treat these situations so differently because in a contract negotiation both parties give up something of value. In the second situation, however, the transaction is one-sided. Because gift givers receive nothing in return, they should be allowed time to reconsider up until actual delivery. The delivery then provides proof that there was intent for a gift to occur.

1. Offer and Acceptance

In order for a valid contract to be formed, there must be mutual agreement to create a legally binding relationship. Whether there is a valid offer and acceptance is determined by the objective theory of contract. An objective theory means that the parties' intent is determined by whether an outside observer could discern a serious intent to be bound. A subjective theory would ask what the parties actually intended. Therefore, the objective theory calls for a review of what was said, how the offeror acted, and the circumstances, rather than of what the parties claim they were thinking at the time.

a. Offer

An offer is a promise to do something—for example, to sell a product or provide a service—that is conditioned on the other party's promising to do something in return—for example, to pay money or provide some other type of goods or services. The offer sets the parameters of the agreement and gives the other party the power to bind them to a contract.

Sometimes it may be difficult, however, to determine whether a statement really was an offer. For example, it could merely have been an expression of an intention to enter into further negotiations. In other circumstances a person making the statement might argue that the alleged offer was intended as a joke rather than as a serious offer. In all situations, for an offer to be valid, it must be obvious to an outside observer that the offeror meant to be bound.

In addition, the terms of the offer must be sufficiently definite such that a court can fashion a remedy. To be definite, the offer must contain at least the following four items:

1. the parties,
2. the subject matter of the contract,
3. the price, and
4. the time for performance.

When the time for performance is very important to the parties, as in the case of the sale of perishable fruit, then the time for performance may be stated along with the phrase "time is of the essence."

Finally, and perhaps obviously, the offer must be communicated to the offeree. Usually, this last requirement does not present any problems except in the case of rewards. Some courts have held that if a person fulfills the terms of a reward—for example, returning a lost dog to its owner—without knowing beforehand of the reward, that person cannot claim the reward, as it was never communicated to him or her.

(1) Statements of intent and preliminary negotiations

Problems can arise if the offeror uses words that indicate an intention to begin negotiations but no intention to be bound. For example, assume Sam says, "I am thinking of selling my car. What would you give me for it?" If John replies, "I will give you $750 for it," Sam has made only a statement of intent, not an offer. John's reply is the offer, and it is up to Sam whether he wants to accept or not. When an offeror asks, "Will you buy?" or says, "I plan to sell," this also gives rise to the inference that the offeror was only beginning the process of negotiation but was not yet ready to be bound by the statements.

(2) Terms definite

The courts require that the basic contract terms be definite not only as a basis on which they can fashion a remedy but also as evidence that a bargain was truly struck. For example, assume Sam says, "I want to sell my car," and John replies, "Done!" There is no contract. How can either Sam or John be bound if neither knows the price? Similarly, ads are usually not viewed as offers because their terms are too indefinite to constitute an offer. The following case, however, presents an interesting exception to that rule. As you read the case, look for what differentiated this ad from the usual ad.

Lefkowitz v. Great Minneapolis Surplus Store, Inc.
251 Minn. 188, 86 N.W.2d 689 (1957)

This case grows out of the alleged refusal of the defendant to sell to the plaintiff a certain fur piece which it had offered for sale in a newspaper advertisement. It appears from the record that on April 6, 1956, the defendant published the following advertisement in a Minneapolis newspaper:

"Saturday 9 A.M. sharp
3 Brand New
Fur Coats
Worth to $100.00
First Come
First Served
$1 Each"

On April 13, the defendant again published an advertisement in the same newspaper as follows:

"Saturday 9 A.M.
2 Brand New Pastel
Mink 3-Skin Scarfs
Selling for $89.50
Out they go
Saturday.
Each $1.00
1 Black Lapin Stole
Beautiful,
worth $139.50 $1.00
First Come
First Served"

The record supports the findings of the court that on each of the Saturdays following the publication of the above-described ads the plaintiff was the first to present himself at the appropriate counter in the defendant's store and on each occasion demanded the coat and the stole so advertised and indicated his readiness to pay the sale price of $1. On both occasions, the defendant refused to sell the merchandise to the plaintiff, stating on the first occasion that by a "house rule" the offer was intended for women only and sales would not be made to men, and on the second visit that plaintiff knew defendant's house rules.

The trial court properly disallowed plaintiff's claim for the value of the fur coats since the value of these articles was speculative and uncertain. The only evidence of value was the advertisement itself to the effect that the coats were "Worth to $100.00," how much less being speculative especially in view of the price for which they were offered for sale. With reference to the offer of the defendant on April 13, 1956, to sell the "1 Black Lapin Stole . . . worth $139.50 . . . " the trial court held that the value of this article was established and granted judgment in favor of the plaintiff for that amount less the $1 quoted purchase price.

1. The defendant contends that a newspaper advertisement offering items of merchandise for sale at a named price is a "unilateral offer" which

may be withdrawn without notice. He relies upon authorities which hold that . . . such advertisements are not offers which become contracts as soon as any person to whose notice they may come signifies his acceptance. . . . Such advertisements have been construed as an invitation for an offer of sale on the terms stated, which offer, when received, may be accepted or rejected and which therefore does not become a contract of sale until accepted by the seller; and until a contract has been so made, the seller may modify or revoke such prices or terms. . . .

The test of whether a binding obligation may originate in advertisements addressed to the general public is "whether the facts show that some performance was promised in positive terms in return for something requested." 1 Williston, Contracts (Rev. ed.) § 27.

The authorities above cited emphasize that, where the offer is clear, definite, and explicit, and leaves nothing open for negotiation, it constitutes an offer, acceptance of which will complete the contract. . . .

Whether in any individual instance a newspaper advertisement is an offer rather than an invitation to make an offer depends on the legal intention of the parties and the surrounding circumstances. We are of the view on the facts before us that the offer by the defendant of the sale of the Lapin fur was clear, definite, and explicit, and left nothing open for negotiation. The plaintiff having successfully managed to be the first one to appear at the seller's place of business to be served, as requested by the advertisement, and having offered the stated purchase price of the article, he was entitled to performance on the part of the defendant. We think the trial court was correct in holding that there was in the conduct of the parties a sufficient mutuality of obligation to constitute a contract of sale.

2. The defendant contends that the offer was modified by a "house rule" to the effect that only women were qualified to receive the bargains advertised. The advertisement contained no such restriction. This objection may be disposed of briefly by stating that, while an advertiser has the right at any time before acceptance to modify his offer, he does not have the right, after acceptance, to impose new or arbitrary conditions not contained in the published offer.

Affirmed.

CASE DISCUSSION QUESTIONS

1. Why did the court hold that in this case there was a binding contract for the black lapin stole?

2. Why was there no binding contract for the fur coats?

3. On the plaintiff's first visit the store informed him of its "house rule" limiting the offer to women. Why didn't the court find that term to be part of the second offer?

The *Lefkowitz* case is an example of an ad that fulfilled all the requirements for a valid contract by including the four basic terms: (1) the parties; (2) the subject matter of the contract, especially quantity; (3) the price; and (4) the time for performance. Traditionally, when any of these terms is missing, the courts have refused to find a binding contract. For example, assume Sara states to Judy, "I would like to purchase some TVs from you," and Judy says, "Agreed." If Judy then sells Sara only two TVs, a court would have no basis for deciding if Judy has breached their agreement. "Some TVs" is simply too indefinite.

The UCC has made some major changes in this area of the law. Under the UCC a contract can be formed even if there are missing terms. The missing terms are supplied by the UCC itself. For example, a missing price term becomes a reasonable price. UCC § 2-305(1). If time and place of payment are left out, payment is due at the time and place where the buyer is to receive the goods. UCC § 2-310(a). If the delivery term is left open, it is to be the seller's place of business. UCC § 2-308(a). However, if too many terms are missing, this may show that the parties were still only in the preliminary negotiation stage. In that situation the court will not force a contract on the parties. In addition, quantity must always be included in the contract. Therefore, in the example given above even the UCC could not help Sara. With the quantity term missing there is no way of knowing whether Judy was in breach.

There is one exception when a missing quantity term is not fatal: requirements and output contracts. When a buyer agrees to buy all of a commodity that he requires from a specific seller or a seller agrees to sell all of her output to a particular buyer, a requirements or an output contract has been created. UCC § 2-306(1). Even though the quantity is not stated in the contract, it can be determined by the court. A **requirements contract** means the buyer's actual requirements, not just what it ordered, and an **output contract** means the seller's actual output. Therefore, the quantity is based on an objective standard, enforceable by the court.

Requirements contract
A contract in which one party agrees to buy all its requirements for a particular product from the other party.

Output contract
A contract in which one party agrees to deliver its entire output of a particular product to the other party.

(3) Termination of an offer

An offer can be terminated in one of three ways: by the offeror's actions, by the offeree's actions, or by operation of law. See Figure 8-4 on page 266. First, normally the offeror can revoke the offer by words or acts if done before acceptance. In some cases this notice of revocation can be indirect, such as by selling the item to a third party. A revocation terminates the offer as soon as the offeree learns of it.

An exception is the **option contract**. In an option contract the potential buyer gives the seller consideration, usually money, to keep the offer open for a

Option contract
A contract in which the buyer gives the seller consideration to keep the offer open for a stated period of time.

■ By offeror's revocation
Unless option con-
tract or merchant's
firm offer
■ By offeree's rejection
or counteroffer
■ By operation of law

Figure 8-4   Termination
of an Offer

Merchant's firm offer
An offer made by a
merchant in a signed
writing that assures the
buyer the offer will
remain open for a
specific period of time. It
does not require
consideration to be
binding.

Mirror image rule
The requirement that the
acceptance exactly
mirror the offer or
the acceptance will
be viewed as a
counteroffer.

stated time period. This creates a separate contract between the potential buyer and seller. The buyer gives the seller consideration for keeping the offer open. If during that time period the seller sells the product to someone else, then the seller is in breach of contract.

In addition to the option contract, the UCC provides for a **merchant's firm offer**. A merchant can make an offer that is irrevocable for a reasonable time, even without the requirement of additional consideration. For such a firm offer to occur, the following requirements have to be met:

1. The offer has to be made by a merchant
2. in a signed writing
3. that assures the buyer that the offer will remain open for a specific period of time or, if no time is stated, for a reasonable time.

If these requirements are met, then the merchant must keep the offer open even though the buyer has not paid any consideration for the arrangement. UCC § 2-205.

Second, the offeree can terminate the offer by rejecting it or by changing the terms of the bargain by attempting to add new or different terms. Instead of an acceptance, such an attempt to vary the terms is seen as a rejection of the offer and a counteroffer. This allows the original offeror the chance to accept or reject it. This requirement that the acceptance completely agree with the terms of the offer is known as the **mirror image rule**. That rule and its exceptions under the UCC are discussed more fully in the next section on Acceptance.

Third, offers can be terminated by operation of law. By operation of law we simply mean that certain events will make it impossible for the offeree to accept the offer. These include lapse of time, destruction of the subject matter, death of one of the parties, and supervening illegality. As to lapse of time, frequently the offer includes a specific timeframe within which the other party must reach a decision about accepting or rejecting the offer. If the other party has not accepted it by that date, then it is automatically withdrawn. If no specific time limit is established, then it is assumed to be valid for a reasonable period of time. As you would expect, that phrase is open to interpretation and will vary depending on the circumstances. For example, if Sam offers to sell John his car in a face-to-face meeting, a reasonable time might last only until the end of that meeting. However, if Sam and John live in different states and Sam makes his offer by mailing John a letter, then a reasonable time might be at least as long as it would take John to receive the letter and mail his reply.

b. Acceptance

Once an offer is made, it is up to the other party to accept, reject, or propose a counteroffer. Earlier we saw that in a bilateral contract situation the offer invites acceptance by the offeree giving a return promise and that in a unilateral contract the offer invites acceptance only by the offeree doing the act itself. In commercial dealings, however, if the offeror indicates that either a promise to act or the action itself will suffice, then when either the promise is made or a substantial start is made on the act, the contract is formed. The UCC explicitly states that an offer can be accepted either by sending notification of such acceptance or by performing the act requested. If Alice offers to pay Bruce $10 for Bruce's bicycle, Bruce's acceptance can take the form of making a telephone call stating that he will sell her the bicycle or by delivering the bicycle to her. UCC § 2-206(b).

If the offeree decides to accept, then the mirror image rule requires that the acceptance exactly mirror the offer. The offeree cannot add new terms or vary the original terms. If he or she attempts to do so, then the acceptance becomes a counteroffer. A counteroffer takes away the power of the offeree to then accept the original offer. For example, if Johns states, "I accept; please send a written contract," then there is an acceptance. However, if John says, "I accept if you send a written contract," then there is no acceptance because John has added an additional term to the contract. A mere inquiry as to the possibility of changing the terms usually will not be seen as a counteroffer. Here again, the exact language used can be determinative of whether there was a counteroffer. If Sam offers to sell John his guitar for $200 and John replies, "I will give you $150 for the guitar," that is a counteroffer. If, however, John replies, "Would you consider $150?" that will probably not be seen as a counteroffer, and if Sam says no, John still has the power to accept the original offer.

The UCC has made some major changes to this mirror image rule. Basically the UCC states that if the parties intend to make a contract, then the use of additional or different terms in the acceptance will not prevent the contract from being formed. This provision recognizes that often the parties will assume they have made a contract and will act on that assumption even if the offer and acceptance do not match in every detail. It was also included in response to what is known as the "battle of the forms." In commercial dealings it is usual for both buyers and sellers to use their own preprinted forms, with blanks left to fill in the essential terms, such as quantity and price. These forms also often include a great deal of boilerplate language regarding other terms, such as whether in the case of a dispute the matter is to be sent to arbitration. However, because this provision essentially states that a contract will be found, even though the parties disagree as to some of the terms, it has given the courts some difficult problems of interpretation. Generally, the new terms are viewed as suggestions for addition to the contract. Between merchants they become a part of a contract unless the original offer limited acceptance to its terms, the new terms "materially alter" the contract, or the offeror objects to the terms. However, there will be no contract if the acceptance states that the offeror must agree to the new terms. UCC § 2-207. Because this provision has proven to be very difficult to interpret and apply, it was revised in 2003. However, to date, no state has adopted the revised version.

c. Quasi-Contract

Quasi means "as if." Therefore, a **quasi-contract** is not a real contract, but the situation is treated "as if" there was one. Usually, a quasi-contract situation arises when there is no agreement, but in order to avoid unjust enrichment, the court orders the party that benefited to pay. For example, in an emergency, an injured party might not be able to ask for assistance. Therefore, there could be no agreement between the injured person and the doctor. However, once the doctor gives medical aid, it would be unjust to let the patient benefit without

Quasi-contract
Although no contract was formed, the courts will fashion an equitable remedy to avoid unjust enrichment.

compensating the doctor. This is an example of a court using its equitable powers to do what it views as fair in order to avoid allowing one side to be unjustly enriched.

DISCUSSION QUESTION

2. Much of contract law is based on the theory of freedom of contract; that is, the parties are free to create their own contract terms as they, and not the court, choose. How can you reconcile the courts' equitable power to find a quasi-contract when no contract exists with the notion of freedom of contract?

2. Consideration

Consideration
Anything of value; it must be present for a valid contract to exist, and each side must give consideration.

Consideration must be present for a valid contract to exist. Each party must give something of value as part of the bargain. It can be money, services, goods, or anything else that is a benefit to one party or a detriment to the other. The key is that something of real value has to be exchanged by both parties. In other words, a contract must be distinguished from a gift. When a person promises to give something without expecting to receive anything in return, that promise does not constitute an enforceable contract.

At times it may appear as though something of value has been exchanged when in actuality it has not. For example, if someone promises to hire you and pay you "what you are worth," the phrase is so vague as to make the promise illusory. In addition, if someone makes a promise because he or she feels morally obligated to do so but receives nothing else in return, there is no consideration. For example, assume Julie is friends with Martha. Martha feels ill but does not have a doctor. Julie takes Martha to her doctor. Once Martha is cured, she refuses to pay the doctor bill. Julie may feel morally obligated to pay the bill because she took Martha to the doctor, but she is under no contractual obligation to do so.

Also, past consideration will not support a contract. Assume I volunteer to take care of your cat while you are away on vacation. When you return, if you are very pleased with the job I have done and offer to pay me for my services, no contract has been formed. I have already done my job, and there is no new consideration for me to give in return for your promise. Finally, if someone is under a preexisting duty to act, performing that duty cannot serve as the consideration for a new contract. If your house is on fire and you offer a firefighter $2,000 to put out the fire, you will be under no obligation to pay the money. The firefighter is already under a preexisting duty to put out the fire.

a. Detriment to Promisee or Benefit to Promisor

Both parties must exchange something of value to ensure that the promise is not illusory and that it was bargained for. Whatever is exchanged has to be detrimental to the party giving it up *or* beneficial to the party receiving it. It need not be both. In the following case ask yourself whether the uncle meant to give his nephew a gift or to be bound to a contractual arrangement.

Hamer v. Sidway
124 N.Y. 538, 27 N.E. 256 (1891)

SYLLABUS:

The plaintiff presented a claim to the executor of William E. Story, Sr., for $5,000 and interest from the 6th day of February, 1875. . . . The claim being rejected by the executor, this action was brought. It appears that William E. Story, Sr., was the uncle of William E. Story, 2d; that at the celebration of the golden wedding of Samuel Story and wife, father and mother of William E. Story, Sr., on the 20th day of March, 1869, in the presence of the family and invited guests he promised his nephew that if he would refrain from drinking, using tobacco, swearing and playing cards or billiards for money until he became twenty-one years of age he would pay him a sum of $5,000. The nephew assented thereto and fully performed the conditions inducing the promise. When the nephew arrived at the age of twenty-one years and on the 31st day of January, 1875, he wrote to his uncle informing him that he had performed his part of the agreement and had thereby become entitled to the sum of $5,000. The uncle received the letter and a few days later and on the sixth of February, he wrote and mailed to his nephew the following letter:

"Buffalo, Feb. 6, 1875." W.E. Story, Jr.:

"Dear Nephew—Your letter of the 31st ult. came to hand all right, saying that you had lived up to the promise made to me several years ago. I have no doubt but you have, for which you shall have five thousand dollars as I promised you. I had the money in the bank the day you was 21 years old that I intend for you, and you shall have the money certain. Now, Willie I do not intend to interfere with this money in any way till I think you are capable of taking care of it and the sooner that time comes the better it will please me. I would hate very much to have you start out in some adventure that you thought all right and lose this money in one year. The first five thousand dollars that I got together cost me a heap of hard work. . . . This money you have earned much easier than I did besides acquiring good habits at the same time and you are quite welcome to the money; hope you will make good use of it. . . . To-day is the seventeenth day that I have not been out of my room, and have had the doctor as many days. Am a little better today; think I will get out next week. You need not mention to father, as he always worries about small matters.

Truly Yours,

"W.E. STORY.

"P.S.—You can consider this money on interest."

The nephew received the letter and thereafter consented that the money should remain with his uncle in accordance with the terms and conditions of the letters. The uncle died on the 29th day of January, 1887, without having paid over to his nephew any portion of the said $5,000 and interest.

OPINION: The question which provoked the most discussion by counsel on this appeal, and which lies at the foundation of plaintiff's asserted right of recovery, is whether by virtue of a contract defendant's testator William E. Story became indebted to his nephew William E. Story, 2d, on his twenty-first birthday in the sum of five thousand dollars. . . .

The defendant contends that the contract was without consideration to support it, and, therefore, invalid. He asserts that the promise by refraining from the use of liquor and tobacco was not harmed but benefited; that that which he did was best for him to do independently of his uncle's promise, and insists that it follows that unless the promisor was benefited, the contract was without consideration. A contention, which if well founded, would seem to leave open for controversy in many cases whether that which the promisee did or omitted to do was, in fact, of such benefit to him as to leave no consideration to support the enforcement of the promisor's agreement. Such a rule could not be tolerated, and is without foundation in the law. The Exchequer Chamber, in 1875, defined consideration as follows: "A valuable consideration in the sense of the law may consist either in some right, interest, profit or benefit accruing to the one party, or some forbearance, detriment, loss or responsibility given, suffered or undertaken by the other." Courts "will not ask whether the thing which forms the consideration does in fact benefit the promisee or a third party, or is of any substantial value to anyone. It is enough that something is promised, done, forborne or suffered by the party to whom the promise is made as consideration for the promise made to him." (Anon's Prin. of Con. 63.) . . .

Pollock, in his work on contracts, page 166, after citing the definition given by the Exchequer Chamber already quoted, says: "The second branch of this judicial description is really the most important one. Consideration means not so much that one party is profiting as that the other abandons some legal right in the present or limits his legal freedom of action in the future as an inducement for the promise of the first."

Now, applying this rule to the facts before us, the promisee used tobacco, occasionally drank

liquor, and he had a legal right to do so. That right he abandoned for a period of years upon the strength of the promise of the testator that for such forbearance he would give him $5,000. We need not speculate on the effort which may have been required to give up the use of those stimulants. It is sufficient that he restricted his lawful freedom of action within certain prescribed limits upon the faith of his uncle's agreement, and now having fully performed the conditions imposed, it is of no moment whether such performance actually proved a benefit to the promisor, and the court will not inquire into it, but were it a proper subject of inquiry, we see nothing in this record that would permit a determination that the uncle was not benefited in a legal sense. . . .

The order appealed from should be reversed and the judgment of the Special Term affirmed, with costs payable out of the estate.

CASE DISCUSSION QUESTIONS

1. Why didn't the court simply view the uncle's offer to pay his nephew $5,000 as a gift?

2. If the court had decided it was a gift instead of a contract situation, how would that have changed the result?

b. Problems with Consideration

Generally, the court will not look into the adequacy of the consideration. Simply put, the court does not care if you made a poor bargain. The philosophy behind freedom of contract is that you are free to make any bargain you like, even a bad one. In addition, if people could sue to get out of their contractual obligations every time it turned out they had made a poor bargain, the courts would be flooded with lawsuits. Finally, the security of being able to rely on contractual performance would be gone.

Traditionally, courts would look at the adequacy of the consideration only if it was so inadequate as to raise a question, first, as to whether some factor such as undue influence or duress was affecting one of the parties or, second, as to whether the situation was actually one of a gift masquerading as a contract. In recent years the courts have also questioned the adequacy of the consideration in those situations where the parties are of very uneven bargaining power, and the bargain is so unfair as to "shock the conscience." For example, if a poor, illiterate person were to purchase a $300 freezer, agreeing to pay 24 monthly installments of $50 each, the seller would net a $900 profit (24 × $50 = $1,200 − $300 = $900). The court might declare this an **unconscionable contract** and refuse to enforce it.

The normal rule, however, is that a court will not invalidate a contract because one party turns out to have made a bad bargain. Nor will the court allow the parties to renegotiate the terms of the contract, unless there is new consideration

Unconscionable contract
A contract formed between parties of very unequal bargaining power where the terms are so unfair as to "shock the conscience."

given on both sides, because of the preexisting duty rule mentioned earlier. Parties typically want to renegotiate the terms of their contract when unforeseen difficulties arise before the contract is completed. The first hurdle is to convince the court that the unforeseen difficulties were truly unforeseen rather than the normal types of risks that should have been part of the original contract negotiations. Even if the other party agrees to a change in the terms of the contract, it is often unclear why that party agreed. It is possible that that party also thought the changes in circumstances were unforeseeable and justified the change. However, it is also possible that that party had no choice and was effectively being "held up" by the party wanting the change. For example, assume Harry hired William to build his house. Halfway through shingling the roof William refused to continue work unless Harry agreed to increase the price by $5,000. A major storm was approaching, and if the roof was not finished that day, the house would be severely damaged. Assume Harry agreed to the increase but then later refused to pay it. The court would have to determine whether the storm was an unforeseen circumstance necessitating extra work on William's part and thereby justifying the increase or whether it was just the sort of circumstance that William should have foreseen. If the latter is true, then he was already under a duty to finish the house at the agreed-on price, and the homeowner would not be required to pay the additional $5,000. In the following case, the court took the very firm position that there can be no change in a contract without new consideration.

Alaska Packers' Association v. Domenico
117 F. 99 (9th Cir. 1902)

Ross, Circuit Judge. . . . On March 26, 1900, at the city and county of San Francisco, the libelants entered into a written contract with the appellant, whereby they agreed to go from San Francisco to Pyramid Harbor, Alaska, and return, on board such vessel as might be designated by the appellant, and to work for the appellant during the fishing season of 1900, at Pyramid Harbor, as sailors and fishermen, agreeing to do "regular ship's duty, both up and down, discharging and loading; and to do any other work whatsoever when requested to do so by the captain or agent of the Alaska Packers' Association." By the terms of this agreement, the appellant was to pay each of the libelants $50 for the season, and two cents for each red salmon in the catching of which he took part.

On the 15th day of April, 1900, 21 of the libelants signed shipping articles by which they shipped as seaman on the Two Brothers, a vessel chartered by the appellant for the voyage between San Francisco and Pyramid Harbor, and also bound themselves to perform the same work for the appellant provided for by the previous contract of March 26th; the appellant agreeing to pay them therefore the sum of $60 for the season, and two cents each for each red salmon in the catching of which they should respectively take part. Under these contracts, the libelants sailed on board the Two Brothers for Pyramid Harbor, where the appellant had about $150,000 invested in a salmon cannery. The libelants arrived there early in April of the year mentioned, and began to unload the vessel and fit up the cannery. A few days thereafter, to wit, May 19th, they stopped work in a body, and demanded of the company's superintendent there in charge $100 for services in operating the vessel to and from Pyramid Harbor, instead of the sums stipulated for in and by the contracts; stating that unless they were paid this additional wage they would stop work entirely, and return to San Francisco. The evidence showed, and the court below found, that it was impossible for the appellant to get other men to take the places of the libelants, the place being remote, the season short and just opening; so that, after endeavoring for several days without success to induce the libelants to proceed with their work in accordance with their contracts, the company's superintendent, on the 22nd day of May, so far yielded to their demands as to instruct his clerk to copy the contracts executed in San Francisco, including the words "Alaska Packers' Association" at the end, substituting, for the $50 and $60 payments, respectively, of those contracts, the sum of $100, which document, so prepared, was signed by the libelants. . . .

The real questions in the case as brought here are questions of law, and, in the view that we take of the case, it will be necessary to consider but one of those. Assuming that the appellant's superintendent at Pyramid Harbor was authorized to make the alleged contract of May 22nd, and that he executed it on behalf of the appellant, was it supported by a sufficient consideration? From the foregoing statement of the case, it will have been seen that the libelants agreed in writing, for certain stated compensation, to render their services to the appellant in remote waters where the season for conducting fishing operations is extremely short, and in which enterprise the appellant had a large amount of money invested; and, after having entered upon the discharge of their contract, and at a time when it was impossible for the appellant to secure other men in their places, the libelants, without any valid cause, absolutely refused to continue the services they were under contract to perform unless the appellant would consent to pay them more money. Consent to such a demand, under such circumstances, if given, was, in our opinion, without consideration, for the reason that it was based solely upon the libelants' agreement to render the exact services, and none other, that they were already under contract to render. The case shows that they willfully and arbitrarily broke that obligation. . . . The circumstances of the present case bring it, we think, directly within the sound and just observations of the supreme court of Minnesota in the case of *King v. Railway Co.*, 61 Minn. 482, 63 N.W. 1105:

> No astute reasoning can change the plain fact that the party who refuses to perform, and thereby coerces a promise from the other party to the contract to pay him an increased compensation for doing that which he is legally bound to do, takes an unjustifiable advantage of the necessities of the other party. Surely it would be a travesty on justice to hold that the party so making the promise for extra pay was estopped from asserting that the promise was without consideration. A party cannot lay the foundation of an estoppel by his own wrong, where the promise is simply a repetition of a subsisting legal promise. There can be no consideration for the promise of the other party, and there is no warrant for inferring that the parties have voluntarily rescinded or modified their contract. The promise cannot be legally enforced, although the other party has completed his contract in reliance upon it.

. . . It results from the views above expressed that the judgment must be reversed, and the cause remanded, with directions to the court below to enter judgment for the respondent, with costs. It is so ordered.

CASE DISCUSSION QUESTIONS

1. What does this court say is the rule about allowing a modification of a contract with no new consideration? Why does the court think that is the only just result?

2. How do you reconcile this decision with the notion of freedom of contract? That is, shouldn't the parties be free to change the terms of their contract at any time?

3. Can you think of any circumstances when it would be fair to allow the parties to modify their contract without new consideration?

Note: Once again the UCC has changed one of the common-law rules. Under the UCC, merchants can modify a contract with no new consideration being given. UCC § 2-209(1).

c. Promissory Estoppel

Sometimes people rely on promises to their detriment, but they cannot sue for breach of contract because while promises were made, they were not definite enough to amount to consideration. Nonetheless, some courts think it would be unfair not to compensate the person who relied on the promise. In that situation the promisor is estopped, or prevented, from revoking his promise. This is known as **promissory estoppel** or detrimental reliance. For the courts to find a case of promissory estoppel,

Promissory estoppel
Occurs when the courts allow detrimental reliance to substitute for consideration.

1. a promise must be made with the intent to induce action,
2. it must do so, and
3. the court must believe that it would be unjust not to enforce the promise.

Assume an elderly relative induces you to give up your job in order to care for her with the promise of being remembered in her will. Her promise would not fulfill the requirements of valid consideration, as her promise of remembering you in her will is too indefinite to be enforceable. If, however, you give up your job and care for your relative for a number of years, the court might view your detrimental reliance on her promise as a substitute for consideration and enforce her promise to pay.

The Wisconsin Supreme Court was one of the first to adopt the theory of promissory estoppel as an alternative to a breach of contract action. In the case of *Hoffman v. Red Owl Stores, Inc.,*[1] Mr. Hoffman and his wife engaged in extensive negotiations with agents of the Red Owl grocery store chain in an attempt to obtain a Red Owl franchise, only to "have the rug pulled out from under them." The agents had originally promised the Hoffmans that for $18,000 they could establish a store. The figure was then changed to $24,100. Relying on further promises that the deal was about to go through and at the urging of the Red Owl representatives, Mr. Hoffman sold his own grocery store to raise the necessary money. While waiting to be placed in his new store, he began working the night shift at a local bakery. Finally, the Red Owl representatives said it would take $34,000 to close the deal. At that point Mr. Hoffman informed them that he could not afford to go through with the proposal. Mr. Hoffman then sued Red Owl for the damages he had incurred in relying on the promises of its representatives.

Because the negotiations had never gotten far enough for the parties to establish the precise terms of the contract, such as the size, layout, and design of the store, Mr. Hoffman was not able to sue on a breach of contract theory. He also could not sue for fraud. There was no evidence that the Red Owl representatives intended to misrepresent the facts. Relying instead on the doctrine of promissory estoppel, the court stated that each of the following questions must be answered in the affirmative:

(1) Was the promise one which the promisor should reasonably expect to induce action or forbearance of a definite and substantial character on the part of the promisee?
(2) Did the promise induce such action or forbearance?
(3) Can injustice be avoided only by enforcement of the promise?[2]

---

[1] 133 N.W.2d 267 (Wis. 1965).
[2] Id. at 275.

The court noted that the first two questions are issues of fact for the jury to decide. The third question, however, involves a policy decision that must be made by the court. In the Hoffmans' case the court concluded that "injustice would result here if plaintiffs were not granted some relief because of the failure of defendants to keep their promises which induced plaintiffs to act to their detriment."[3]

D. CONTRACT INTERPRETATION

Sometimes, even though it is clear that there is an offer, acceptance, and consideration, thus creating a valid contract, the parties disagree about the legal effect of the contract's terms. This is often due to the innate ambiguity of the English language. When such differences in interpretation arise, the parties may turn to the courts for assistance.

When asked to interpret ambiguous language, the courts generally follow many of the same guidelines that they use to interpret statutory language. A court usually begins by trying to give the words their plain or common-sense meaning. When that is not possible, the court will try to see if the meaning of the words can be deciphered from the parties' intent as expressed in the contract. The court may also apply commonly accepted definitions from the relevant industry or business. Finally, the court may interpret the language so as to favor the party who did not draft the contract.

E. DEFENSES TO A VALID CONTRACT

In addition to offer, acceptance, and consideration, you will sometimes hear that contractual capacity, legality, and genuineness of assent are necessary elements for a valid contract to be formed. While this is true, in this text we will treat these last three elements as defenses. Generally, it is assumed that those elements are present so the plaintiff has no obligation to allege their existence in the complaint. Rather it is incumbent on the defendant to raise their absence in the answer. First, the defendant can argue that one or both of the parties lacked contractual capacity. Second, the defendant can contend that the contract should not be enforced because it is illegal or because it violates public policy. Third, the defendant can assert that there was no true genuineness of assent because of fraud, mistake, or undue influence. Fourth, the defendant may argue that he or she owes nothing on a contract for sale because the product was defective in violation of the seller's warranties. Finally, at times the defendant may be able to show that the proper format was not followed, as, for example, with some contracts that must be in writing.

1. Lack of Contractual Capacity

The parties to a contract can be either people or corporations. However, an individual may be considered incapable of contracting if that person is a child, is mentally retarded or mentally ill, or is under the influence of drugs or alcohol.

---

[3]Id.

a. Minors

If one of the parties is a minor, the contract may be **voidable**. Therefore, the terms of the contract are enforceable against the adult party to the contract but not against the minor party. Under the common law one had to be at least twenty-one years old in order to enter into binding contracts, but today many states have established a lower age limit.

Minors can **disaffirm** a contract and thereby avoid any contractual liability at any time during their minority or for a reasonable time thereafter. If the contract involves the sale of goods, in a majority of states the minor must return the goods, but the minor does not have to fulfill the terms of the contract, even if the goods are damaged. In a minority of states the minor must act so as to return the other party to his or her position prior to the contract. Even if a minor misrepresents his or her age, in a majority of states the minor can still disaffirm the contract. The one exception is that minors are liable for **necessaries**. Although they can disaffirm the contract, they must pay the reasonable value of the goods or services they received. Housing, food, and clothing are commonly classified as necessaries. However, what is "necessary" can vary with the circumstances. For example, in one case a court held that a lease for an apartment was not necessary because the minor tenants were able to return home to their parents at any time.[4]

Once minors reach the age of majority, they can ratify the contract, thereby binding themselves to the terms of the contract. This can occur by the minor expressly stating that he or she wishes to be bound, by the minor's conduct, or by operation of law after a reasonable time has passed once the minor is of age.

This next case graphically illustrates how dangerous it can be for an adult to deal with minors.

Voidable
A valid contract that can be set aside at the option of one of the parties.

Disaffirm
The ability to take back one's contractual obligations.

Necessaries
Normally food, clothing, shelter, and medical treatment.

Quality Motors, Inc. v. Hays
216 Ark. 264, 225 S.W.2d 326 (1949)

DUNAWAY, J.

Johnny M. Hays, by his next friend, Dr. D. J. Hays, brought this suit to disaffirm his purchase of a Pontiac automobile and recover the purchase price of $1,750 from defendant Quality Motors, Inc.

On January 21, 1949, Johnny Hays, a minor sixteen years old, went to the Quality Motors, Inc., to inspect and test a Pontiac car. When E. C. Buttry, salesman for Quality Motors, raised the question of Johnny's age, he was told that Johnny's father in New York had sent him the money to buy the car. The salesman then refused to sell unless the purchase was made by an adult. Johnny left the salesman and returned shortly with Harry R. Williams, a young man twenty-three years of age, whom he met that day for the first time. Johnny then gave to Quality Motors, Inc., a cashier's check on the Citizens Bank of Jonesboro, in the sum of $1,800 which was made payable to him, in payment for the car. A bill of sale was made to Harry Williams. The salesman then recommended a Notary Public who could prepare the necessary papers for transferring title to the car to Johnny, and drove the two boys to town for this purpose. Williams did transfer title, and the Pontiac was delivered by the salesman to Johnny at Arkansas State College, where Dr. Hays, Johnny's father, was a teacher.

---
[4]Webster Street Partnership, Ltd. v. Sheridan, 368 N.W.2d 439 (Neb. 1985).

When Dr. Hays learned of his son's purchase he called E. C. Perkins, one of the owners of Quality Motors, Inc., on the night of January 25, 1949. Perkins knew nothing of the transaction and suggested that Dr. Hays call the motor company the next morning. On the morning of January 26, Dr. Hays talked to the salesman who had handled the transaction, and asked that defendant company take the car back. This the defendant refused to do. No physical tender of the car was made; Johnny had it out of town. The car was returned to Jonesboro on January 26, when Dr. Hays had his son arrested; it was then stored in a hangar at Arkansas State College. On January 27 Dr. Hays again called Quality Motors, Inc., and was informed the car would not be taken back. He then went to the office of his attorney where he once more called Quality Motors, Inc., and was told by W. E. Ebbert, one of the owners, that they would not accept the car and return the consideration for its purchase, but would try to sell it for him if they could. . . .

On February 12, 1949, while Dr. Hays was out of town, Johnny found the car keys and bill of sale and took the car to Kentucky where his grandmother lived.

On March 21, he returned to Jonesboro and asked Quality Motors for an estimate on repairs to the car which had been in a wreck. On this occasion he had an extended conversation with Buttry and Ebbert, who tried to persuade him to leave the car there and not go back to Kentucky as he told them he planned to do at once. At this time Quality Motors was still refusing to accept the car and return the purchase price. The suggestion was that the car be left with them for repairs "until this thing is settled." Johnny made a telephone call to his mother and immediately departed for Kentucky where the car was in a second and more serious wreck. At the time of trial the car was in Kentucky, subject to a repair bill for $557, and an attachment for $125, and not in running condition.

The special chancellor ordered the plaintiff to return the car within seven days and withheld final decree until this was done. When the wrecked car was returned, recovery of $1,750 from defendant was decreed. . . .

The law is well settled in Arkansas that an infant may disaffirm his contracts, except those made for necessaries, without being required to return the consideration received, except such part as may remain in specie in his hands.

We do not find any merit in appellant's contention that no proper tender of the car was made when appellee sought to disaffirm his purchase. The undisputed testimony shows that Dr. Hays and his attorney offered to return the car on several occasions, but were informed that appellant would not accept it. That it was not actually delivered to Quality Motors when the suit was filed is appellant's own fault. The law does not require that a tender be made under circumstances where it would be vain and useless.

Appellant's most serious contention is that the plaintiff is liable for damages to the car which occurred while he was driving over the country, after he had slipped the car from its storage place and while the suit to disaffirm was pending. In order to obtain any relief on this score, it must be shown that plaintiff was guilty of conversion in taking the automobile. Conversion is the exercise of dominion over property in violation of the rights of the owner or person entitled to possession. In advancing this argument appellant is in an inconsistent position.

. . . Until the court decreed return of the car and recovery of the consideration paid, plaintiff still had title to the car. One cannot be liable for conversion in taking his own property. . . .

Appellant knowingly and through a planned subterfuge sold an automobile to a minor. It then refused to take the car back. Even after the car was wrecked once, it was in appellant's place of business, and appellant was still resisting disaffirmance of the contract. The loss which appellant has suffered is the direct result of its own acts.

The decree is affirmed.

CASE DISCUSSION QUESTIONS

1. What does the court say is the general rule about the right of minors to disaffirm contracts?

2. What should this dealer have done differently in this case?

3. In general, how can merchants protect themselves in dealings with minors?

4. Some states simply require the return of the goods, no matter their condition. Others require that the adult be placed in the same position that he or she was in prior to the contract. Which approach do you think is better?

b. Intoxication

Intoxication is rarely used successfully to void a contract. The courts look with disfavor on this defense because the condition is self-inflicted. However, if the defendant can show the intoxication prevented him from understanding the import of his actions, a court might find that there was no meeting of the minds. In the next case notice how the defendant tried to raise two defenses: that he was intoxicated and that he was only playing a joke on his friend.

Lucy v. Zehmer
196 Va. 493, 84 S.E.2d 516 (1954)

BUCHANAN, J., delivered the opinion of the court.

This suit was instituted by W.O. Lucy and J. C. Lucy, complainants, against A.H. Zehmer and Ida S. Zehmer, his wife, defendants, to have specific performance of a contract by which it was alleged the Zehmers had sold to W.O. Lucy a tract of land owned by A.H. Zehmer in Dinwiddie county containing 471.6 acres, more or less, known as the Ferguson farm, for $50,000. J.C. Lucy, the other complainant, is a brother of W.O. Lucy, to whom W.O. Lucy transferred a half interest in his alleged purchase. . . .

W.O. Lucy, a lumberman and farmer, thus testified in substance: He had known Zehmer for fifteen or twenty years and had been familiar with the Ferguson farm for ten years. Seven or eight years ago he had offered Zehmer $20,000 for the farm which Zehmer had accepted, but the agreement was verbal and Zehmer backed out. On the night of December 20, 1952, around eight o'clock, he took an employee to McKenney, where Zehmer lived and operated a restaurant, filling station and motor court. While there he decided to see Zehmer and again try to buy the Ferguson farm. He entered the restaurant and talked to Mrs. Zehmer until Zehmer came in. He asked Zehmer if he had sold the Ferguson farm. Zehmer replied that he had not. Lucy said, "I bet you wouldn't take $50,000.00 for that place." Zehmer replied, "Yes, I would too; you wouldn't give fifty." Lucy said he would and told Zehmer to write up an agreement to that effect. Zehmer took a restaurant check and wrote on the back of it, "I do hereby agree to sell to W.O. Lucy the Ferguson Farm for $50,000 complete." Lucy told him he had better change it to "We" because Mrs. Zehmer would have to sign it too. Zehmer then tore up what he had written, wrote the agreement quoted above and asked Mrs. Zehmer, who was at the other end of the counter ten or twelve feet away, to sign it. Mrs. Zehmer said she would for $50,000 and signed it. Zehmer brought it back and gave it to Lucy, who offered him $5 which Zehmer refused, saying, "You don't need to give me any money, you got the agreement there signed by both of us."

The discussion leading to the signing of the agreement, said Lucy, lasted thirty or forty minutes, during which Zehmer seemed to doubt that Lucy could raise $50,000. Lucy suggested the provision for having the title examined and Zehmer made the suggestion that he would sell it "complete, everything there," and stated that all he had on the farm was three heifers.

Lucy took a partly filled bottle of whiskey into the restaurant with him for the purpose of giving Zehmer a drink if he wanted it. Zehmer did, and he and Lucy had one or two drinks together. Lucy said that while he felt the drinks he took he was not intoxicated, and from the way Zehmer handled the transaction he did not think he was either. . . .

Mr. and Mrs. Zehmer were called by the complainants as adverse witnesses. Zehmer testified in substance as follows: . . .

On this Saturday night before Christmas it looked like everybody and his brother came by there to have a drink. He took a good many drinks during the afternoon and had a pint of his own. When he entered the restaurant around eight-thirty Lucy was there and he could see that he was "pretty high." He said to Lucy, "Boy, you got some good liquor, drinking, ain't you?" Lucy then offered him a drink. "I was already high as a Georgia pine, and didn't have any more better sense than to pour another great big slug out and gulp it down, and he took one too."

After they had talked a while Lucy asked whether he still had the Ferguson farm. He replied that he had not sold it and Lucy said, "I bet you wouldn't take $50,000.00 for it." Zehmer asked him if he would give $50,000 and Lucy said yes. Zehmer replied, "You haven't got $50,000 in cash." Lucy said he did and Zehmer replied that he did not believe it. They argued "pro and con for a long time," mainly about "whether he had $50,000 in cash that he could put up right then and buy that farm."

Finally, said Zehmer, Lucy told him if he didn't believe he had $50,000, "you sign that piece of paper here and say you will take $50,000.00 for the farm." He, Zehmer, "just grabbed the back off of a guest check there" and wrote on the back of it. At that point in his testimony Zehmer asked to see what he had written to "see if I recognize my own handwriting." He examined the paper and exclaimed, "Great balls of fire, I got 'Firgerson' for Ferguson. I have got satisfactory spelled wrong. I don't recognize that writing if I would see it, wouldn't know it was mine."

After Zehmer had, as he described it, "scribbled this thing off," Lucy said, "Get your wife to sign it." Zehmer walked over to where she was and she at first refused to sign but did so after he told her that he "was just needling him [Lucy], and didn't mean a thing in the world, that I was not selling the farm." Zehmer then "took it back over there . . . and I was still looking at the dern thing. I had the drink right there by my hand, and I reached over to get a drink, and he said, "Let me see it." He reached and picked it up, and when I looked back again he had it in his pocket and he dropped a five dollar bill over there, and he said, "Here is five dollars payment on it." . . . I said, "Hell no, that is beer and liquor talking. I am not going to sell you the farm. I have told you that too many times before." . . .

The defendants insist that the evidence was ample to support their contention that the writing sought to be enforced was prepared as a bluff or dare to force Lucy to admit that he did not have $50,000; that the whole matter was a joke; that the writing was not delivered to Lucy and no binding contract was ever made between the parties.

It is an unusual, if not bizarre, defense. When made to the writing admittedly prepared by one of the defendants and signed by both, clear evidence is required to sustain it.

In his testimony Zehmer claimed that he "was high as a Georgia pine," and that the transaction "was just a bunch of two doggoned drunks bluffing to see who could talk the biggest and say the most." That claim is inconsistent with his attempt to testify in great detail as to what was said and what was done. It is contradicted by other evidence as to the condition of both parties, and rendered of no weight by the testimony of his wife that when Lucy left the restaurant she suggested that Zehmer drive him home. The record is convincing that Zehmer was not intoxicated to the extent of being unable to comprehend the nature and consequences of the instrument he executed, and hence that instrument is not to be invalidated on that ground. It was in fact conceded by defendants' counsel in oral argument that under the evidence Zehmer was not too drunk to make a valid contract.

. . . The appearance of the contract, the fact that it was under discussion for forty minutes or more before it was signed; Lucy's objection to the first draft because it was written in the singular, and he wanted Mrs. Zehmer to sign it also; the rewriting to meet that objection and the signing by Mrs. Zehmer; the discussion of what was to be included in the sale, the provision for the examination of the title, the completeness of the instrument that was executed, the taking possession of it by Lucy with no request or suggestion by either of the defendants that he give it back, are facts which furnish persuasive evidence that the execution of the contract was a serious business transaction rather than a casual, jesting matter as defendants now contend. . . .

If it be assumed, contrary to what we think the evidence shows, that Zehmer was jesting about selling his farm to Lucy and that the transaction was intended by him to be a joke, nevertheless the evidence shows that Lucy did not so understand it but considered it to be a serious business transaction and the contract to be binding on the Zehmers as well as on himself. The very next day he arranged with his brother to put up half the money and take a half interest in the land.

The day after that he employed an attorney to examine the title. The next night, Tuesday, he was back at Zehmer's place and there Zehmer told him for the first time, Lucy said, that he wasn't going to sell and he told Zehmer, "You know you sold that place fair and square." After receiving the report from his attorney that the title was good he wrote to Zehmer that he was ready to close the deal.

Not only did Lucy actually believe, but also the evidence shows he was warranted in believing, that the contract represented a serious business transaction and a good faith sale and purchase of the farm.

In the field of contracts, as generally elsewhere, "We must look to the outward expression of a person as manifesting his intention rather than to his secret and unexpressed intention. 'The law imputes to a person an intention corresponding to the reasonable meaning of his words and acts.'" . . .

An agreement or mutual assent is of course essential to a valid contract but the law imputes to a person an intention corresponding to the reasonable meaning of his words and acts. If his words and acts, judged by a reasonable standard, manifest an intention to agree, it is immaterial what may be the real but unexpressed state of his mind.

So a person cannot set up that he was merely jesting when his conduct and words would warrant a reasonable person in believing that he intended a real agreement.

Whether the writing signed by the defendants and now sought to be enforced by the complainants was the result of a serious offer by Lucy and a serious acceptance by the defendants, or was a serious offer by Lucy and an acceptance in secret jest by the defendants, in either event it constituted a binding contract of sale between the parties. . . .

Reversed and remanded.

CASE DISCUSSION QUESTIONS

1. What did the court think was the appropriate test for determining whether there was a serious intent to be bound?

2. Specific performance is not an absolute right but rather a question of equity. Do you think it was "fair" to enforce this contract?

3. The court stated, "Seven or eight years ago [Lucy] had offered Zehmer $20,000 for the farm which Zehmer had accepted, but the agreement was verbal and Zehmer backed out." Why was Zehmer able to back out of that agreement but not this one?

c. Mental Incompetence

Void

A contract that is invalid even if it is not repudiated by either party.

Mental incompetence can cause a contract to be voidable, a situation analogous to that of minors. Also as is true with minors, the incompetent person nonetheless remains responsible for the reasonable value of necessaries. However, if someone has been adjudged mentally incompetent and the court has appointed a guardian to handle the incompetent's affairs, then that individual is without the capacity to make contracts. Instead of being merely voidable, any contract the incompetent individual tries to make is **void**. Only the guardian can enter into valid contracts.

2. Illegal Contracts and Those That Violate Public Policy

Contracts can be declared unenforceable if they are found to be either illegal or against public policy. A contract involves illegality if it calls for behavior that violates the criminal law, such as robbery, gambling, or prostitution. In addition, a contract will be seen as involving illegality if it violates a licensing statute that explicitly states that it is for the protection of the public, antitrust laws, or state usury laws. Contracts for an illegal purpose are void and cannot be enforced by either party. For example, usury laws regulate interest rates. A loan that imposes an interest charge that exceeds the legal limit is said to be usurious and therefore illegal.

Covenant not to compete

A promise not to compete within a given geographical area for a specific time period.

In addition, the courts hold that some contracts are unenforceable because they are contrary to public policy. For example, **covenants not to compete** by their very nature are against public policy in that they restrict the right of an individual to earn a living or they tend to decrease competition. However, they can also be a form of necessary business protection. For example, if a pharmaceutical company expends a great deal of time and money training a chemist, the company will want the chemist to sign a noncompetition clause, promising not to work for another pharmaceutical plant for a certain amount of time after leaving employment with the first company. The courts are generally willing to enforce that type of covenant so long as

1. it is tied to employment or to the sale of a business and
2. its terms call for a reasonable time and
3. a reasonable geographic area.

Adhesion contract

A contract formed where the weaker party has no realistic bargaining power. Typically a form contract is offered on a "take it or leave it" basis.

A second type of contract that the courts may refuse to enforce as being against public policy is an **adhesion contract**. As you will recall from our discussion of inadequate consideration, normally courts will adhere to the theory of freedom of contract and will not inquire into the fairness of the bargain. However, when a contract is formed between two parties of very unequal bargaining power and the contract is drafted by the party with the greater power and then presented to the other party, who has no opportunity to negotiate the terms, the court may view this as a contract of adhesion. The court may then hold that such a contract is unconscionable and refuse to enforce it. Generally, a contract is considered unconscionable if, in the context of general commercial practices and under the specific circumstances in which the contract was made, it is so one-sided as to be oppressive and grossly unfair. An example would be a sale to a low-income family who speaks little English where the contract is drawn up by the seller and includes a clause that disclaims all warranties that traditionally go with such a transaction.

While the UCC holds that the terms of a contract that are unconscionable cannot be enforced, it does not attempt to define unconscionability. UCC § 2-302. One must rely on court cases for specific application of the doctrine. The courts are more responsive to low-income consumers who raise this defense than they are to merchants who deal with other merchants.

Third, some contracts contain provisions that purport to release parties from all liability for their own negligence. These are known as **exculpatory clauses**. These clauses were discussed in Chapter 7, as they are frequently raised as a defense in negligence actions. As we discussed there, the courts generally disfavor such clauses and frequently refuse to enforce them.

Exculpatory clause
A provision that purports to waive liability.

Finally, society's changing mores, as well as advances in medical science, have presented some interesting dilemmas to the courts. For example, courts have recently been confronted with the issue of whether to enforce a surrogacy contract. They have also been asked to decide whether a contract regarding the "ownership" of frozen embryos should be enforced. The argument against enforcement is that such contracts are against public policy. We will discuss these and similar problems more fully in Chapter 11, which covers laws affecting the family.

3. Lack of Genuineness of Assent

As we have seen, normally the courts apply an objective reasonable person standard in interpreting whether an agreement was reached between the parties. However, a court will not enforce a contract if one of the parties can convince the court that there was no true "meeting of the minds" because of fraud, mistake, undue influence, or duress.

a. Fraud

In order to prove fraud, it must be demonstrated that the other party made intentional misrepresentations or intentional nondisclosures of material facts during the course of the negotiations. Therefore, the four requirements for a defense based on fraud are as follows:

1. an intent to deceive
2. regarding material facts and
3. justifiable reliance on the deception
4. that causes harm.

A successful defendant can recover damages or ask the contract be **rescinded**. In addition, fraud can be brought under a tort theory, thereby creating the possibility of also receiving a punitive damage award.

Rescission
The act of canceling the contract and returning the parties to the positions they were in prior to the contract having been formed.

For the reliance to be justified, it must be shown that the defendant did not know of the fraud and had no way to find out. Note that the misrepresentations must be material and that they must be made regarding a factual statement, not merely opinion or sales puffery. It is expected that the reasonable person engaged in contract negotiations will realize that she or he should not rely on opinions or on overblown sales statements that are obviously made simply as part of the sales pitch. However, in certain circumstances the opinion of an expert can be viewed as a fact when it is reasonable to rely on the opinion of an expert and the other party has no independent means of testing the statement's validity. The issue of whether a dance student was justified in relying on the statements of a dance instructor is presented in the following case.

Vokes v. Arthur Murray, Inc.
212 So. 2d 906 (Fla. Dist. Ct. App. 1968)

PIERCE, Judge. LILES, C.J., and MANN, J., concur.

. . . Defendant Arthur Murray, Inc., a corporation, authorizes the operation throughout the nation of dancing schools under the name of "Arthur Murray School of Dancing" through local franchised operators, one of whom was defendant J.P. Davenport whose dancing establishment was in Clearwater.

Plaintiff Mrs. Audrey E. Vokes, a widow of 51 years and without family, had a yen to be "an accomplished dancer" with the hopes of finding "new interest in life." So, on February 10, 1961, a dubious fate, with the assist of a motivated acquaintance, procured her to attend a "dance party" at Davenport's "School of Dancing" where she whiled away the pleasant hours, sometimes in a private room, absorbing his accomplished sales technique, during which her grace and poise were elaborated upon and her rosy future as "an excellent dancer" was painted for her in vivid and glowing colors. As an incident to this interlude, he sold her eight ½-hour dance lessons to be utilized within one calendar month therefrom, for the sum of $14.50 cash in hand paid, obviously a baited "come-on."

Thus she embarked upon an almost endless pursuit of the terpsichorean art during which, over a period of less than sixteen months, she was sold fourteen "dance courses" totalling in the aggregate 2302 hours of dancing lessons for a total cash outlay of $31,090.45, all at Davenport's dance emporium. . . .

These dance lesson contracts and the monetary consideration therefor of over $31,000 were procured from her by means and methods of Davenport and his associates which went beyond the unsavory, yet legally permissible, perimeter of "sales puffing" and intruded well into the forbidden area of undue influence, the suggestion of falsehood, the suppression of truth, and the free exercise of rational judgment, if what plaintiff alleged in her complaint was true. . . .

All the . . . sales promotions, illustrative of the entire fourteen separate contracts, were procured by defendant Davenport and Arthur Murray, Inc., by false representations to her that she was improving in her dancing ability, that she had excellent potential, that she was responding to instructions in dancing grace, and that they were developing her into a beautiful dancer, whereas in truth and in fact she did not develop in her dancing ability, she had no "dance aptitude," and in fact had difficulty in "hearing the musical beat." The complaint alleged that such representations to her "were in fact false and known by the defendant to be false and contrary to the plaintiff's true ability, the truth of plaintiff's ability being fully known to the defendants, but withheld from the plaintiff for the sole and specific intent to deceive and defraud the plaintiff and to induce her in the purchasing of additional hours of dance lessons." It was averred that the lessons were sold to her "in total disregard to the true physical, rhythm, and mental ability of the plaintiff." In other words, while she first exulted that she was entering the "spring of her life," she finally was awakened to the fact there was "spring" neither in her life nor in her feet.

The complaint prayed that the Court decree the dance contracts to be null and void and to be cancelled, that an accounting be had. . . . The Court held the complaint not to state a cause of action and dismissed it with prejudice. We disagree and reverse.

The material allegations of the complaint must, of course, be accepted as true for the purpose of testing its legal sufficiency. Defendants contend that contracts can only be rescinded for fraud or misrepresentation when the alleged misrepresentation is as to a material fact, rather than an opinion, prediction or expectation, and that the statements and representations set forth at length in the complaint were in the category of "trade puffing," within its legal orbit. It is true that "generally a misrepresentation, to be actionable, must be one of fact rather than of opinion." But this rule has significant qualifications, applicable here. It does not apply where there is a fiduciary relationship between the parties, or where there has been some artifice or trick employed by the representor, or where the parties do not in general deal at "arm's length" as we understand the phrase, or where the representee does not have equal opportunity to become apprised of the truth or falsity of the fact represented. ". . . A statement of a party having . . . superior knowledge may be regarded as a statement of fact although it would be considered as opinion if the parties were dealing on equal terms." . . .

Even in contractual situations where a party to a transaction owes no duty to disclose facts within his knowledge or to answer inquiries respecting such facts, the law is if he undertakes to do so he must disclose the whole truth. . . .

We repeat that where parties are dealing on a contractual basis at arm's length with no inequities or inherently unfair practices employed, the Courts will in general "leave the parties where they find themselves." But in the case sub judice, from the allegations of the unanswered complaint, we cannot say that enough of the accompanying ingredients, as mentioned in the foregoing authorities, were not present which otherwise would have barred the equitable arm of the Court to her. In our view, from the showing made in her complaint, plaintiff is entitled to her day in Court.

It accordingly follows that the order dismissing plaintiff's last amended complaint with prejudice should be and is reversed.

Reversed.

CASE DISCUSSION QUESTIONS

1. Why did the court categorize the dance studio's statements as "fact" rather than "opinion"?

2. Which facts do you think the court found particularly relevant in reaching that decision?

3. What do you think would have kept the statements of the dance studio in the realm of mere "sales puffing"?

b. Mistake

Mistakes about facts can sometimes form the basis for rescinding a contract. If the mistake is bilateral, then both parties had a different concept of what was to be included in the contract. Therefore, there never was a meeting of the minds, and the failed contract can be rescinded by either. The classic case that illustrates this principle took place in England in 1864. A buyer purchased a shipment of cotton from a seller, the cotton to be shipped on the *Peerless*. Unknown to either party, there were two ships named the *Peerless*, one to depart in October and one in December. The buyer was thinking of the ship destined to leave in October and the seller the other in December. Consequently, the seller did not ship the cotton until December. By that time the buyer no longer needed the cotton. The court held that because there never was a "meeting of the minds" as to which ship was intended, no contract had been formed and the buyer was not obligated to pay for the cotton.[5]

---

[5]Raffles v. Wichelhaus, 159 Eng. Rep. 375 (1864).

Usually, however, if the mistake is unilateral and only one party is mistaken, then both parties are bound. The only exceptions are if the other party knew or should have known of the mistake and if the mistake was the result of a mathematical error.

Keep in mind that we are talking only about factual mistakes. Mistakes as to the value of the subject matter can never be the basis for rescission. For example, assume Joan contracts to sell her diamond ring to Bertha. Both think the ring is worth about $500, and they set $500 as the contract price. Later Bertha has the ring appraised and is delighted to learn that it is actually worth $5,000. Joan cannot ask to have the contract rescinded on the grounds that she was mistaken as to the value of the diamond. On the other hand, if Joan had contracted to sell what she thought was a zirconium ring to Bertha and upon appraisal it turned out to be a diamond ring, some courts could see that as a mutual mistake as to a fact and allow the contract to be rescinded.

c. Undue Influence

Sometimes a party will try to avoid contractual obligations by arguing that undue influence was exerted by the other party. Generally, for a court to find undue influence there must first be a showing that a special relationship existed between the parties. Then, because of the special relationship, one party is in a position of trust and misuses that trust to influence the actions of another. Situations alleging undue influence are frequently brought by family members against caretakers of the elderly or ill.

d. Duress

A contract is also not valid if it was agreed to under duress rather than as a result of a truly voluntary action. The actions of the second party must be sufficient for the court to find that the first party was forced into the agreement. Duress is difficult to prove because the defendant must show that the pressure exerted was so great as to overwhelm his or her ability to make a free choice.

4. Breach of Warranty

Warranty
A guarantee, made by the seller or implied by law, regarding the character, quality, or title of the goods being sold.

Implied warranty of merchantability
An implied promise that the goods being sold will be usable for the purpose for which they were sold.

Among the most frequently contested issues is the nature of the warranties involved in commercial transactions. In this context a **warranty** is a statement or representation, made by the seller as part of the contract of sale or implied in law, regarding the character, quality, or title of the goods being sold. If such warranted facts later prove to be untrue, then the seller has an obligation to compensate the buyer for any losses incurred as a result of the misrepresentation.

Under the terms of the UCC any contract of sale automatically includes a warranty of title, an implied promise that the seller owns the goods being offered for sale and that they will be delivered free from any security interest, lien, or encumbrance. UCC § 2-312. If the seller is a merchant, then there is also an **implied warranty of merchantability,** an implied promise that the goods being sold will be usable for the purpose for which they were sold.

(1) Unless excluded or modified by section 2-316, a warranty that the goods shall be merchantable is implied in a contract for their sale if the seller is a merchant with

respect to goods of that kind. Under this section the serving for value of food or drink to be consumed either on the premises or elsewhere is a sale. (2) Goods to be merchantable must at least be such as . . . (c) are fit for the ordinary purposes for which such goods are used. UCC § 2-314.

This is a warranty regarding the fitness of the goods for the ordinary purpose for which these types of goods are used.

When a more specialized use of the goods is communicated to the seller during the course of negotiations, an **implied warranty of fitness** is also created. UCC § 2-315. This is a warranty regarding the fitness of the goods for that special purpose. For example, if you go to a hardware store and ask the clerk for electrical wiring and say nothing more, the wire will be warranted for its usual purpose of carrying household current. If instead you want the wire for outside use, you tell the clerk your special purpose, and you rely on the clerk's expertise in picking out the wire, then there will be an implied warranty of fitness for that particular purpose.

In addition to these implied warranties, a contract can create **express warranties**. UCC § 2-313. The term *warranty* or *guarantee* does not have to be used in order for a warranty to be created. However, the seller's conduct or statements must have been communicated to the buyer so that the warranty becomes part of the "basis of the bargain." UCC § 2-313(1). Express warranties can be created by an affirmation of fact or a promise made by the seller; a description of the goods being sold, including technical specifications and blueprints; or a sample or a model provided. A mere expression of opinion as to the value of an item is considered "puffing" and does not constitute a warranty.

As you can imagine, two of the most common issues that arise in trying to resolve whether an express warranty exists are (1) whether the statement or actions were part of the "basis of the bargain" and (2) whether a statement is an affirmation of fact or merely the seller's opinion. There is no clear definition of either. The UCC does not define "basis of the bargain," and the courts have reached differing conclusions. Some have held that it means the warranty terms must have been bargained for; others hold that the buyer must have relied on the warranties in deciding to make the purchase; still others state that the buyer need not show any reliance but must have been aware of the warranty at the time the sale was made.

> **Implied warranty of fitness**
> An implied promise that the goods being sold will satisfy a special purpose.

DISCUSSION QUESTION

3. In a highly publicized case in the District of Columbia, a patron of a dry-cleaning establishment sued the mom-and-pop owners for $54 million for having allegedly lost his pair of pants. The owners claimed they had performed alterations to expand the waist of the pants to the customer's specifications, but the customer claimed the pants they altered were not the ones that he had brought in. While the amount of damages being claimed was clearly outrageous, the case does raise an interesting legal question. What are the legal implications of posting a sign that reads "Satisfaction Guaranteed"? Does the posting of this type of sign create some sort of express warranty as to the service being offered? What standards should be used in determining what "satisfaction" means in this context?

Type of Warranty	Created by	Excluded by
Implied warranty of merchantability	the sale of goods by a merchant. The goods must be fit for their ordinary purpose.	language that includes the word *merchantability* or a disclaimer that includes the word *merchantability* or phrases such as "as is" or "with all faults." If in writing, it must be conspicuous.
Implied warranty of fitness	a seller ■ knowing the particular purpose the buyer has in mind *and* ■ being aware that the buyer is relying on the seller's expertise.	a writing that is conspicuous.
Express warranty	■ an affirmation of fact or a promise made by the seller, *or* a description of the goods being sold, including technical specifications and blueprints, *or* a sample or model *and* ■ that becomes a basis of the bargain.	words or conduct tending to limit or negate the warranty so long as such interpretation is reasonable.

Figure 8-5   Warranties Summarized

Warranties may be excluded or modified by disclaimers. UCC § 2-316. In many states, however, merchants are limited in their ability to exclude or modify the implied warranty of merchantability when the sale is to a consumer. For each type of warranty, Figure 8-5 summarizes how it is created and what actions a seller must take to exclude the warranty.

An interesting example of when implied warranties can be applied to food occurred in the following classic case.

Webster v. Blue Ship Tea Room, Inc.
347 Mass. 421, 198 N.E.2d 309 (1964)

REARDON, J. This is a case which by its nature evokes earnest study not only of the law but also of the culinary traditions of the Commonwealth which bear so heavily upon its outcome. It is an action to recover damages for personal injuries sustained by reason of a breach of implied warranty of food served by the defendant in its restaurant. . . .

On Saturday, April 15, 1959, about 1 P.M., the plaintiff, accompanied by her sister and her aunt, entered the Blue Ship Tea Room operated by the defendant. The group was seated at a table and supplied with menus.

This restaurant, which the plaintiff characterized as "quaint," was located in Boston "on the third floor of an old building on T Wharf which overlooks the ocean."

The plaintiff, who had been born and brought up in New England (a fact of some consequence), ordered clam chowder and crabmeat salad. Within a few minutes she received tidings to the effect that "there was no more clam chowder," whereupon she ordered a cup of fish chowder. Presently, there was set before her "a small bowl of fish chowder. . . . The chowder was milky in color and not clear. The haddock and potatoes were in chunks" (also a fact of consequence). . . . She ate about 3 or 4 spoonfuls then stopped. She looked at the spoonfuls as she was eating. She saw equal parts of liquid, potato and fish as she spooned it into her mouth. She did not see anything unusual about it. After 3 or 4 spoonfuls she was aware that something had lodged in her throat because she couldn't swallow and couldn't clear her throat by gulping and she could feel it. This misadventure led to two esophagoscopies at the Massachusetts General Hospital, in the second of which, on April 27, 1959, a fish bone was found and removed. The sequence of events produced injury to the plaintiff which was not insubstantial.

We must decide whether a fish bone lurking in a fish chowder, about the ingredients of which there is no other complaint, constitutes a breach of implied warranty under applicable provisions of the Uniform Commercial Code, the annotations to which are not helpful on this point. As the judge put it in his charge, "Was the fish chowder fit to be eaten and wholesome? . . . [N]obody is claiming that the fish itself wasn't wholesome. . . . But the bone of contention here—I don't mean that for a pun—but was this fish bone a foreign substance that made the fish chowder unwholesome or not fit to be eaten?" . . .

The defendant asserts . . . "[f]ish chowder, as it is served and enjoyed by New Englanders, is a hearty dish, originally designed to satisfy the appetites of our seamen and fishermen"; that "[t]his court knows well that we are not talking of some insipid broth as is customarily served to convalescents." We are asked to rule in such fashion that no chef is forced "to reduce the pieces of fish in the chowder to miniscule size in an effort to ascertain if they contained any pieces of bone." . . .

It is not too much to say that a person sitting down in New England to consume a good New England fish chowder embarks on a gustatory adventure which may entail the removal of some fish bones from his bowl as he proceeds. We are not inclined to tamper with age old recipes by any amendment reflecting the plaintiff's view of the effect of the Uniform Commercial Code upon them. We are aware of the heavy body of case law involving foreign substances in food, but we sense a strong distinction between them and those relative to unwholesomeness of the food itself. . . . In any event, we consider that the joys of life in New England include the ready availability of fresh fish chowder. We should be prepared to cope with the hazards of fish bones, the occasional presence of which in chowders is, it seems to us, to be anticipated, and which, in the light of a hallowed tradition, do not impair their fitness or merchantability. While we are buoyed up in this conclusion by *Shapiro v. Hotel Statler Corp.* 132 F. Supp. 891 (S.D. Cal.), in which the bone which afflicted the plaintiff appeared in "Hot Barquette of Seafood Mornay," we know that the United States District Court of Southern California, situated as are we upon a coast, might be expected to share our views. We are most impressed, however, by *Allen v. Grafton,* 170 Ohio St. 249, where in Ohio, the Midwest, in a case where the plaintiff was injured by a piece of oyster shell in an order of fried oysters, Mr. Justice Taft (now Chief Justice) in a majority opinion held that "the possible presence of a piece of oyster shell in or attached to an oyster is so well known to anyone who eats oysters that we can say as a matter of law that one who eats oysters can reasonably anticipate and guard against eating such a piece of shell. . . . " (P. 259.) Thus, while we sympathize with the plaintiff who has suffered a peculiarly New England injury, the order must be

Exceptions sustained. Judgment for the defendant.

CASE DISCUSSION QUESTIONS

1. Why did the court think Ms. Webster failed in her claim for breach of an implied warranty?

2. Why did it matter that the plaintiff was brought up in New England? Would the result have been different if she lived in the Midwest and this was her first trip to the East Coast?

3. Do you agree with the court that this is a different case from one in which the food is contaminated? Why?

5. Lack of Proper Format—Writing

A commonly held misunderstanding is that all contracts must be in writing to be enforceable. That is not so. In many situations an oral contract is perfectly valid. However, contractual disputes arise not just about whether a valid contract exists but also about what the terms of the contract actually require. Deciding these disputes is particularly difficult when the agreement was oral rather than set down in writing. When the dispute is reduced to one person's word against the other's, the courts find it difficult to determine who is telling the truth. Even though many oral contracts are legally enforceable, it is always wiser to put them in writing.

Statute of frauds

A statutory requirement that, in order to be enforceable, certain contracts must be in writing.

In addition to the fact that it simply makes sense to reduce any important contract to writing, all states have a statute known as the **statute of frauds,** which lists those contracts that must be in writing in order to be enforceable. The purpose of such statutes is to ensure that there will be reliable evidence of important or complex matters. The required writing does not have to be a formal contract, however. It can take the form of any writing—for example, a check or a memo—so long as it fully expresses the terms of the agreement. The writing can also be in multiple pieces, so long as it is clear the pieces were intended to constitute one agreement. A common example is a written offer and a separate written acceptance. Finally, the signature can be any authentication, even initials. Generally, the types of contracts that must be in writing fall into one of the following categories:

1. contracts involving land, including fixtures, and documents dealing with land, such as mortgages and leases;
2. contracts that cannot be performed in one year;
3. collateral contracts, those that involve a secondary as opposed to a primary obligation, unless the main purpose is to secure a personal benefit;

4. promises made in consideration of marriage, such as prenuptial agreements; and
5. contracts for the sale of goods valued at $500 or more.

Note the exact wording regarding the second type of contract—those that *cannot* be performed in one year. If it is possible, even though unlikely, that it can be performed in one year, then a writing is not necessary. For example, a contract for life could be performed in one year and so need not be in writing.

Article 2 of the UCC contains its own statute of frauds that applies to the sale of goods. UCC § 2-201. It requires something in writing if the price of the goods is $500 or more. (*Note:* A 2001 revision to the UCC increased the amount to $5,000, but to date, no state has made this change.)The writing needs to be signed only by "the party to be charged." For example, Tom calls Jim, offering to buy his television for $600, and Jim mails back his signed reply agreeing to the arrangement. If Jim fails to perform his end of the bargain, Tom can sue Jim, the party to be charged, because Jim signed the letter agreeing to the arrangement. However, Jim would not be allowed to sue Tom, as there is no writing containing Tom's signature.

The statute of frauds does allow for some exceptions. The first is part performance. For example, if John made a partial payment for some land, took possession of the land, and made improvements, then the court might see this as enough evidence of an intended contract to enforce it. Also, under the UCC a contract will be enforced to the extent payment or delivery was accepted. Admissions in pleadings or testimony will also bind the party as to the quantity admitted. Finally, the court may invoke the doctrine of promissory estoppel when there is justifiable reliance.

A written agreement usually contains an integration clause that merges all previous oral agreements into the new written document. Under **the parole evidence rule** a written contract cannot be modified or changed by prior oral agreements.

Parole evidence rule
An evidentiary rule that a written contract cannot be modified or changed by prior verbal agreements.

F. TERMINATION OF CONTRACTUAL DUTIES

A contract is typically discharged by performance. However, there are times when the parties may agree to end their agreement prior to complete performance. Also, at times a court may declare a party's obligations over when performance is impossible or commercially impracticable.

1. By Performance

Complete performance ends both parties' obligations. At times, however, a party will perform most but not all of the required duties. If the party **substantially performs,** that party is in breach of contract and is liable for damages caused by the breach. However, the other party is not relieved of his or her obligations. If, however, the failure to perform is seen as a **material breach,** it is a breach of contract that excuses the other party from any obligations. Whether the performance is so complete as to amount to only a minor breach or so insufficient as to constitute a material breach is often a difficult question. In the next case the court grapples with what to do when a construction contract is not fully performed.

Substantial performance
Although a breach of contract, performance of all the essential terms of the contract will entitle the breaching party to the contractual price minus any damages caused by the breach.

Material breach
Such a grave failure to fulfill the contractual terms that the other party is relieved of all contractual obligations.

Jacob & Youngs, Inc. v. Kent
230 N.Y. 239, 129 N.E. 889 (1921)

CARDOZO, J. The plaintiff built a country residence for the defendant at a cost of upwards of $77,000, and now sues to recover a balance of $3,483.46, remaining unpaid. The work of construction ceased in June, 1914, and the defendant then began to occupy the dwelling. There was no complaint of defective performance until March, 1915. One of the specifications for the plumbing work provides that "all wrought iron pipe must be well galvanized, lap welded pipe of the grade known as 'standard pipe' of Reading manufacture." The defendant learned in March, 1915, that some of the pipe, instead of being made in Reading, was the product of other factories. The plaintiff was accordingly directed by the architect to do the work anew. The plumbing was then encased within the walls except in a few places where it had to be exposed. Obedience to the order meant more than the substitution of other pipe. It meant the demolition at great expense of substantial parts of the completed structure. The plaintiff left the work untouched, and asked for a certificate that the final payment was due. Refusal of the certificate was followed by this suit.

The evidence sustains a finding that the omission of the prescribed brand of pipe was neither fraudulent nor willful. It was the result of the oversight and inattention of the plaintiff's subcontractor. Reading pipe is distinguished from Cohoes pipe and other brands only by the name of the manufacturer stamped upon it at intervals of between six and seven feet. Even the defendant's architect, though he inspected the pipe upon arrival, failed to notice the discrepancy. The plaintiff tried to show that the brands installed, though made by other manufacturers, were the same in quality, in appearance, in market value and in cost as the brand stated in the contract—that they were, indeed, the same thing, though manufactured in another place. The evidence was excluded, and a verdict directed for the defendant. The Appellate Division reversed, and granted a new trial.

We think the evidence, if admitted, would have supplied some basis for the inference that the defect was insignificant in its relation to the project. The courts never say that one who makes a contract fills the measure of his duty by less than full performance. They do say, however, that an omission, both trivial and innocent, will sometimes be atoned for by allowance of the resulting damage, and will not always be the breach of a condition to be followed by a forfeiture. . . .

Those who think more of symmetry and logic in the development of legal rules than of practical adaptation to the attainment of a just result will be troubled by a classification where the lines of division are so wavering and blurred. Something, doubtless, may be said on the score of consistency and certainty in favor of a stricter standard. The courts have balanced such considerations against those of equity and fairness, and found the latter to be the weightier. The decisions in this state commit us to the liberal view, which is making its way, nowadays, in jurisdictions slow to welcome it. Where the line is to be drawn between the important and the trivial cannot be settled by a formula. "In the nature of the case precise boundaries are impossible" (2 Williston on Contracts, sec. 841). The same omission may take on one aspect or another according to its setting. Substitution of equivalents may not have the same significance in fields of art on the one side and in those of mere utility on the other. Nowhere will change be tolerated, however, if it is so dominant or pervasive as in any real or substantial measure to frustrate the purpose of the contract. There is no general license to install whatever, in the builder's judgment, may be regarded as "just as good." The question is one of degree, to be answered, if there is doubt, by the triers of the facts, and, if the inferences are certain, by the judges of the law. We must weigh the purpose to be served, the desire to be gratified, the excuse for deviation from the letter, the cruelty of enforced adherence. Then only can we tell whether literal fulfillment is to be implied by law as a condition. This is not to say that the parties are not free by apt and certain words to effectuate a purpose that performance of every term shall be a condition of recovery. That question is not here. This is merely to say that the law will be slow to impute the purpose, in the silence of the parties, where the significance of the default is grievously out of proportion to the oppression of the forfeiture. The willful transgressor must accept the penalty of his transgression. For him there is no occasion to mitigate the rigor of implied conditions. The transgressor whose default is unintentional and trivial may hope for mercy if he will offer atonement for his wrong.

In the circumstances of this case, we think the measure of the allowance is not the cost of replacement, which would be great, but the difference in value, which would be either nominal or nothing. . . . It is true that in most cases the cost of replacement is the measure. The owner is entitled to the money which will permit him to complete, unless the cost of completion is grossly and unfairly out of proportion to the good to be attained. When that is true, the measure is the difference in value. . . . The rule that gives a remedy in cases of substantial performance with compensation for defects of trivial or inappreciable importance, has been developed by the courts as an instrument of justice. The measure of the allowance must be shaped to the same end.

The order should be affirmed, and judgment absolute directed in favor of the plaintiff upon the stipulation, with costs in all courts.

MᴄLᴀᴜɢʜʟɪɴ, J. (dissenting). I dissent. The plaintiff did not perform its contract. . . .

. . . The defendant had a right to contract for what he wanted. He had a right before making payment to get what the contract called for. It is no answer to this suggestion to say that the pipe put in was just as good as that made by the Reading Manufacturing Company, or that the difference in value between such pipe and the pipe made by the Reading Manufacturing Company would be either "nominal or nothing." Defendant contracted for pipe made by the Reading Manufacturing Company. What his reason was for requiring this kind of pipe is of no importance. He wanted that and was entitled to it. It may have been a mere whim on his part, but even so, he had a right to this kind of pipe, regardless of whether some other kind, according to the opinion of the contractor or experts, would have been "just as good, better, or done just as well." He agreed to pay only upon condition that the pipe installed were made by that company and he ought not to be compelled to pay unless that condition be performed. . . .

Cᴀsᴇ Dɪsᴄᴜssɪᴏɴ Qᴜᴇsᴛɪᴏɴs

1. Why did the court find for the plaintiff contractor?
2. The dissent essentially states that people have a right to get what they contract for. The majority does not see things in such black-and-white terms, saying, "We must weigh the purpose to be served, the desire to be gratified, the excuse for deviation from the letter, the cruelty of enforced adherence." Which view do you think best serves the needs of the contracting parties?
3. What could the owner have done to ensure that there would be no deviations from his specifications?
4. Would this case have had a different outcome if the contractor had deliberately substituted the pipe in order to save money? Why?

The issue of not performing to the letter of the contract is one area where the UCC, instead of liberalizing the rules, has tightened them. Under Section 2-601, the UCC states that failure in any respect to supply conforming goods means that the buyer is free to accept the goods, reject them, or accept part and reject part. This is known as the **perfect tender rule**. The only relief from this rule involves the following exceptions: (1) if the parties agree to overlook the lack of conformity; (2) if "cure" is possible—that is, if the time for performance has not

Perfect tender rule
The requirement that the goods delivered exactly meet the contractual specifications.

yet expired, the seller notifies the buyer of his intent to rectify the matter, and he then does so; and (3) in some cases of commercial impracticability.

If the goods cannot be returned without their perishing, they must be sold in order to minimize the seller's losses. UCC § 2-603. If substandard goods are accepted and retained, then the buyer can seek damages that amount to the difference between the value of the goods promised and the value of the goods received. UCC § 2-714.

2. By Agreement

Rescission
The act of canceling the contract and returning the parties to the positions they were in prior to the contract having been formed.

Novation
When a third party is substituted for one of the original parties.

Accord and satisfaction
The agreement and then the performance of something different than originally promised.

Contractual obligations can be ended by agreement through rescission, novation, or accord and satisfaction. **Rescission** involves an agreement by both parties to cancel the contract. Rescission is generally viewed as appropriate if the contract is still completely executory. If one side has performed, a rescission will not be enforced unless the other side gives consideration for the rescission.

In a **novation** a third party is substituted for one of the original parties. This creates a new contract and as such differs from assignments or delegations. Because it is a new contract, it must be supported by new consideration.

Finally, the parties may enter into an **accord and satisfaction.** An accord is an agreement to do something different than originally promised. The satisfaction is the performance of the accord. For example, if John owes Sally $4,000 and they agree that Sally will accept John's Rolex watch in payment instead, their agreement is the accord. If John gives Sally his watch, there is a satisfaction. If he does not, then Sally can still sue John for the $4,000.

3. When Performance Is Impossible

A party can assert the defense of impossibility of contractual performance. This occurs when one party either dies or becomes too sick to carry through with the contractual responsibilities. It also could occur when the object to be sold is destroyed or stolen before the agreed-on transfer takes place or when there is a change in the law that makes the contract illegal. A party that hopes to win under the defense of impossibility must show that the contract cannot be performed, not simply that the party cannot perform it. For example, assume Mariann, who lives in Hampshire County, Massachusetts, agrees to sell 200 bushels of the apples she grows that year to William for $10 a bushel. But a week before the harvest, a tornado destroys her entire crop. It is now impossible for her to complete the contract; she is discharged from her contractual obligations, and William is simply out of luck (and apples). However, assume instead that Mariann had agreed to sell 200 bushels of apples harvested that year from Hampshire County, Massachusetts, to William for $10 a bushel. Mariann had been planning on buying the apples from local farms for $8 a bushel, thereby insuring a profit for herself of $2 a bushel. However, that same tornado destroys all of her apples and the majority of the apples grown that year in Hampshire County, forcing up the price of apples to $40 a bushel. If she has to buy 200 bushels of apples at $40 a bushel and then resell them to William for $10, not only will she not make a profit, she will incur a huge loss. Mariann may want to claim that it is now impossible for her to perform the contract, but she will not succeed. It has become difficult, and expensive, but not impossible.

4. Due to Commercial Impracticability

As we saw from our discussion of consideration, freedom of contract allows parties to make and be held to a bad bargain. When circumstances change, leaving one party at a disadvantage, that party may ask to be excused from the contract under the doctrine of commercial impracticability. The argument is not that the contract is impossible to perform but rather that it has become too costly for one of the parties. If the change of circumstances should have been foreseen, then generally the courts will not supply any relief. For example, in one case a farm agreed to sell to a school district all the milk it required. During the course of the contract the price of raw milk increased by 23 percent. If the farm was required to abide by the terms of the contract, it would lose a substantial amount of money. The court held the farm to its contract, refusing to allow it to pass the increase on to the school district, because the rise in price was a foreseeable occurrence.[6]

G. THIRD-PARTY RIGHTS

There are three ways in which a person or corporation not a party to the contract can have a legal interest in enforcing part of the terms of that agreement. The most common of these is through the process of assignment. Third-party rights also arise through delegation and the creation of beneficiaries.

1. Assignment

An **assignment** occurs when one of the original parties to a contract transfers part or all of his or her interest to a third party. See Figure 8-6. For example, assume a consumer signs a sales contract with a furniture store. In the contract the consumer agrees to make certain monthly payments. The furniture store then assigns the right to receive those payments to a finance company, and in return the finance company gives the furniture store ready cash. The finance company now has a legal interest in receiving the monthly payments that the consumer agreed to pay to the store.

Assignment
The transfer by one of the original parties to the contract of part or all of his or her interest to a third party.

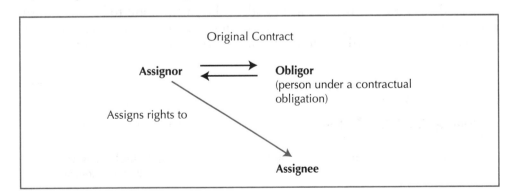

Figure 8-6   Assignment of a Contract

---

[6]Maple Farms, Inc. v. City School District of Elmira, 352 N.Y.S.2d 784 (Sup. Ct. 1974).

An assignment involves an assignor, an assignee, and an obligor. The assignee gets the same rights that the assignor had, but no more. The assignee is also subject to the same defenses as could have been raised against the assignor. Assignment is usually possible unless

1. the contract itself prohibits it,
2. the contract involves personal services, or
3. the assignment will materially alter the duties of the obligor.

Delegation
The transfer by one of the original parties to the contract of his or her obligations to a third party.

2. Delegation

Most duties can be delegated unless the contract prohibits it or the duty requires personal skill or special trust. The primary duty is not extinguished if the delegatee fails to perform. The original party remains obligated to fulfill the terms of the contract. See Figure 8-7.

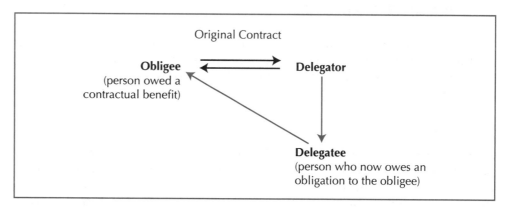

Figure 8-7   Delegation of Duties under a Contract

3. Third-Party Beneficiaries

Assignment and delegation happen after the contract is formed. However, if at the time the contract is formed one or both of the parties want to benefit a third party, then a third-party beneficiary relationship is created. There are two types of beneficiaries: intended (creditor or donee) and incidental. See Figure 8-8.

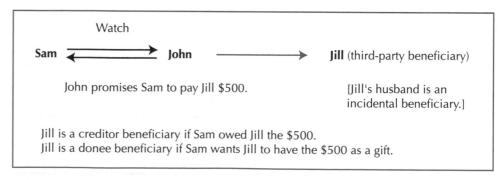

Figure 8-8   Third-Party Beneficiaries

a. Intended Beneficiaries

Contracts often contain provisions in which one of the parties agrees to provide some direct benefit to a third party, or beneficiary. For example, in purchasing a house the buyer might agree to assume the seller's current mortgage. In that case the mortgage lender is a third party that has been given a specific benefit under the terms of the contract; it is considered to be a creditor beneficiary. In a situation in which a father contracts with a bank to administer a trust fund for his children, those children would be considered donee beneficiaries.

If it is clear from the contract that the parties intended a third party to benefit, then that party is an intended beneficiary. Consider two further examples: If in return for Sam's watch John promises Sam to pay the $500 debt Sam owes to Jill, then Jill becomes a creditor beneficiary. If in return for Sam's car John promises Sam to give a $4,000 gift to Joan, then Joan is a donee beneficiary. In both cases the third party has a right to see that the contract terms are fulfilled, including the right to sue.

b. Incidental Beneficiaries

An incidental beneficiary is someone whom the original parties did not explicitly intend to benefit from the contract. An incidental beneficiary cannot enforce rights under the contract. For example, in the last example assume Bill is Joan's husband. If Joan plans on taking the two of them on a vacation with the $4,000, Bill will benefit, but if John fails to deliver the money, Bill has no right to enforce the contract.

H. DAMAGES

When one party fails to live up to the terms of a contract, a variety of remedies may be available to the other party. We have already discussed several actions that the parties can take on their own without court intervention: rescission, novation, and accord and satisfaction.

Alternatively, the nonbreaching party can go to court to seek monetary damages or specific performance. **Specific performance** is used in situations where there is no alternative comparable product available, such as a particular parcel of land or a rare piece of art. Under this remedy the injured party obtains a court order requiring the breaching party to fulfill the terms of the agreement. Specific performance is a wonderful remedy because the contracting party gets exactly what was contracted for. Also, there is no need to worry about collecting a judgment, the nonbreaching party need not expend time and effort to find another deal, and the actual performance may be more valuable than dollars. However, keep in mind that specific performance is possible only if dollars are inadequate. In addition, specific performance cannot be used to enforce personal service contracts. Not only would that constitute involuntary servitude, but it would impose an impossible task for the court due to the difficulty of monitoring the party's performance.

The purpose of monetary damages is to give the injured party the benefit of the bargain. Monetary damages can be classified as compensatory, consequential, incidental, nominal, or punitive. In addition, the injured party may be

Specific performance When money damages are inadequate, a court may use this equitable remedy and order the breaching party to perform his or her contractual obligations.

Mitigation of damages
The requirement that the nonbreaching party take reasonable steps to limit his or her damages.

required to take steps to lessen his or her loss. This is known as **mitigation of damages**.

Compensatory damages are awarded to compensate for the loss of the bargain. Their purpose is to place the injured party in the same position that party would have been in had the contract been performed. The classic case describing this form of damages is a 1929 New Hampshire case, known by law students everywhere as the "hairy hand" case.[7] In that case a father took his son to a doctor. The boy had burned his hand, leaving it scarred. The doctor promised to give the boy a "hundred percent perfect hand" by grafting a piece of skin taken from the boy's chest. Everything went well until a few years passed, and the boy entered puberty. When he did so, his hand began sprouting hair, leaving him with a hand uglier than when he had started. The court calculated the damages as the difference between a "perfect hand" and what the boy received, a hairy hand. Not included in the damage award was any pain the boy suffered from the operation or the cost of the operation. The boy would have had to undergo the pain and cost of the operation even if the operation had been successful. Therefore, to compensate the plaintiff for the pain and the cost of the operation, in addition to the difference in the hand, would give the plaintiff more than what was necessary to put him in the position he would have been in had the operation been successful.

In calculating compensatory damages, courts frequently use the following formula:

$$\text{Promised performance} - \text{actual performance} - \text{mitigation} + \text{expenses (incidental damages)}$$

For example, if John agrees with Bill to sell Bill his watch for $500, but Bill only pays $300, then John can sue Bill for $200. If Bill had paid nothing and simply reneged on the deal, then John could have sold the watch to someone else and could have recovered the difference between that price and the contract price, along with any expenses incurred in finding the new buyer (incidental damages).

On the other hand, if John refuses to sell the watch, then Bill has two options. First, he can try to find another watch. The UCC calls this finding of substitute goods *cover*. Then his damages are the cost of the substitute watch minus the contract price. For example, if Bill finds a similar watch but has to pay $700, then his damages are $200. Alternatively, he can decide to forgo a new watch. In that case his damages would be the difference between the market price and the contract price.

Cover
Finding substitute goods.

Consequential damages
Indirect damages that must be foreseeable to be recovered.

Consequential damages arise out of special circumstances that must be foreseeable to the other party. Typically this is handled by notifying the other party of any such circumstances. The classic case setting forth this rule is an English case from 1854.[8] The Hadley family ran a flour mill. Their crankshaft broke, and they gave it to Baxendale to deliver to a foundry for repair. Baxendale promised to deliver the shaft the next day. However, it was not delivered for several days. As a result, the mill was closed for those days. Despite the common practice, the Hadleys did not have an extra crankshaft. Because the

---

[7]Hawkins v. McGee, 146 A. 641 (N.H. 1929).
[8]Hadley v. Baxendale, 9 Exch. 341, 156 Eng. Rep. 14 (1854).

Hadleys had not notified Baxendale of that special circumstance, he could not be held liable for their lost profits.

Punitive damages are not allowed in contract actions. However, if the plaintiff can also bring a tort action—for example, for fraud—then punitives are possible. Finally, nominal damages are possible when there has been a breach but no provable damages.

In order to avoid having to litigate damages issues, some contracting parties put **liquidated damages clauses** in their contracts. Such clauses specify what will happen in case of breach. Such clauses are valid if two requirements are met. First, the amount of damages must be difficult or impossible to calculate. Second, the amount must bear a reasonable relationship to the true loss and not be seen as a penalty clause. Liquidated damages clauses are frequently found in university and major league coaching contracts. Should a coach leave before the end of the contract term, the damage to the school or team could go far beyond the costs of finding a replacement coach. For example, incalculable damages could include harm to alumni relations, loss of players who came to play for a particular coach, and a reduction in ticket sales.

Finally, when the parties imperfectly express themselves, sometimes the court will **reform the contract**. For example, assume a covenant not to compete is included in a sale of a business. While it is limited geographically to one county, its duration is for ten years. The court might reform the contract so that the duration is for a shorter period of time.

Liquidated damages clause
A contract provision that specifies what will happen in case of breach.

Contract reformation
An equitable remedy that allows the courts to "rewrite" contract provisions.

SUMMARY

A contract is an agreement that can be enforced in court. The basic elements of a contract are offer, acceptance, and consideration. Contracts can be classified as bilateral or unilateral; express or implied in fact; formal or informal; executory or executed; and valid, void, voidable, or unenforceable. The most common defenses are lack of contractual capacity, illegality, violation of public policy, lack of genuineness of assent, breach of warranty, and the statute of frauds. Third parties can attain contractual rights either through assignment or delegation or through being an intended beneficiary. A plaintiff bringing a contract action may be under a duty to mitigate damages and is usually seeking specific performance or compensatory or consequential damages.

While many contracts are still controlled by the common law, contracts for the sale of goods are generally governed by Article 2 of the Uniform Commercial Code (UCC). The UCC was drafted by a group of legal scholars with the hope of making commercial law more unified among the states. Most of the UCC's provisions apply to everyone, but some sections contain specific rules that apply to merchants only. Under the UCC everyone is under the obligation to act in good faith.

CRITICAL THINKING EXERCISES

1. Emma Johnson was the owner of two parcels of land. On March 27 Ms. Johnson's son-in-law, Edward Hicks, who was her agent to sell the property, wrote the following letter to James Mellen.

You will perhaps remember that we spent a pleasant visit on the breakwater at Nahant last summer. On that occasion either you or your brother-in-law expressed an interest in my Mother's property which is the Johnson cottage. . . . [Mother's] health is such that she will not be able to open the cottage this year. She has, therefore, decided that it will be best to place the property on the market; however, before turning it over to the real estate agents, I am writing to several people, including yourself, who have previously expressed an interest in the property. Our price is $7,500. This property consists of the lot and cottage on the south side of Willow Road, and also a very large plot on which a two-car garage is situated running from Willow Road clear through the block to the next street. Just how much property there is in this tract, I cannot tell you at the moment. . . . I will be interested in hearing from you further if you have any interest in this property, for as I said before, I am advising those who have asked for an opportunity to consider it. I might just add that the property would be available for immediate occupancy. By that I mean within such time as the present furnishings could be removed and title transferred.

On March 28 Mr. Hicks received a telegram from Mr. Mellon's brother-in-law that read:

We are interested in your offer. Will look at house tomorrow. Communicate with you first of week.

On the same day shortly after the telegram was received, Mr. Hicks telegraphed Mr. Mellon:

Have heard from three interested buyers tonight which means we must accept highest bid for Nahant property. Suggest you wire or phone us Elmsford N.Y. 7292 Saturday your best offer on cash basis.

Before this was received, Mr. Mellon telegraphed Mr. Hicks:

I accept your offer on Nahant cottage. Letter in mail.

When Mr. Hicks entered into a written contract to sell the property to someone else, Mr. Mellon sued to stop the sale from being completed.

   a. Do you think an offer was ever made? Why?
   b. Do you think Mr. Mellon's suit was successful? Why?

   2. UCC § 2-207 provides as follows:

   (1) A definite and seasonable expression of acceptance or a written confirmation which is sent within a reasonable time operates as an acceptance even though it states terms additional to or different from those offered or agreed upon, unless acceptance is expressly made conditional on assent to the additional or different terms.
   (2) The additional terms are to be construed as proposals for addition to the contract. Between merchants such terms become part of the contract unless:
      (a) the offer expressly limits acceptance to the terms of the offer;
      (b) they materially alter it; or
      (c) notification of objection to them has already been given or is given within a reasonable time after notice of them is received.

Please evaluate each of the following situations and determine whether a contract exists and, if so, what its terms are.

  a. Value City, a Georgia retailer, sends an order form to RCV, a Mississippi manufacturer, ordering 100 televisions at $200 each. On the back of the form in fine print is the following:

> Seller expressly warrants that the goods are fit for the ordinary purposes for which they are sold. Seller shall assume all costs of shipping.

RCV sends back an acknowledgment form. On the back of the form in small print is the following:

> All disputes arising out of the agreement must be submitted to binding arbitration.

  b. Value City, a Georgia retailer, sends an order form to RCV, a Mississippi manufacturer, ordering 100 televisions at $200 each. On the back of the form in fine print is the following:

> Seller shall assume all costs of shipping.

RCV sends back an acknowledgment form. On the back of the form in small print is the following:

> All goods are sold "as is" with no warranties of any kind.

  c. Value City, a Georgia retailer, sends an order form to RCV, a Mississippi manufacturer, ordering 100 televisions at $200 each. On the back of the form in fine print is the following:

> Seller expressly warrants that the goods are fit for the ordinary purposes for which they are sold. Seller shall assume all costs of shipping.

RCV sends back an acknowledgment form. On the back of the form in small print is the following:

> All goods are sold "as is" with no warranties of any kind.
> Buyer shall assume all costs of shipping.

  3. The 2005 hurricane season spawned a number of high-profile lawsuits over the interpretation of standard homeowners' insurance policies. Such policies are contracts between the insured homeowner and the insurance company to cover damage to the insured's house, home furnishings, and other types of listed property. These policies typically cover damage from high winds but exclude water damage. However, when hurricanes hit shore they usually combine high winds, heavy rain, and sometimes even tidal waves. Which of the following types of damage do you think should be considered wind damage?

  a. During the hurricane, a limb breaks off a tree and damages the roof of an insured's house.

b. During the hurricane, water came into an insured's house through windows that had been blown out by the hurricane's winds.

c. Rain from the hurricane caused a nearby river to overflow its banks, and flood waters covered the first-floor carpet.

d. Rain from the hurricane overwhelmed the local sewer system and caused water to back up into the insured's basement.

e. A beach house was knocked off its foundation by the tidal wave that accompanied the hurricane.

Now assume that a homeowner's policy explicitly excluded "water damage" and defined that term as "(1) flood, surface water, tsunami, seiche, overflow of a body of water, or spray from any of these, whether driven by wind or not; (2) water or sewage from outside the residence premise's plumbing system that enters through sewers or drains, or water which enters into and overflows from within a sump pump, sump pump well, or any other system designed to remove subsurface water which is drained from the foundation." Which, if any, of the types of damage listed above would be excluded from coverage under the terms of the policy?

4. Rogers Communications, a cable company, and Aliant Inc., a telecommunications company, signed a contract whereby Aliant agreed to let Rogers Communications string its cables on Aliant's poles for $9.60 a pole. The contract contained the following provision:

> This agreement shall be effective from the date it is made and shall continue in force for a period of five (5) years from the date it is made, and thereafter for successive five (5) year terms, unless and until terminated by one year prior notice by either party.

Rogers thought it had a solid deal for at least five years unless Aliant gave notice at least one year before the end of the five-year term that it wanted to terminate the contract. However, Aliant sent a termination notice just one year into the contract, offering to lease its poles for $28 a pole. The difference between the original $9.60 a pole and the $28 a pole came to $2.13 million over the course of the five years. Rogers sued. Who do you think won and why?

5. When the Panera Bread Co. bakery-café chain moved into the White City Shopping Center, it signed a lease containing a clause that prevents the center from renting to another "sandwich" shop. When the shopping center management later rented space to Jack in the Box, Inc. to open a Qdoba's Mexican Grill, Panera took the matter to court claiming that Qdoba's burritos, tacos, and quesadillas were sandwiches.

a. The key issue in this case involved interpretation of the term "sandwich," but that term was not defined in the lease. How do you think the judge should go about determining whether burritos, tacos, and quesadillas were sandwiches?

b. Based on your own common understanding of the term, how would you define a "sandwich"?

c. In what ways are burritos, tacos, and quesadillas like sandwiches? In what ways are they different?

d. How would you rule if you were the judge?

6. Janice Jones, along with her family, visited a Big Bill's Family Restaurant, a national chain. She was eating a piece of fried chicken when she bit into something that she thought was a worm. Naturally she became quite upset and has been unable to eat chicken since. Expert witnesses are likely to state that, instead of a worm, the object was actually either the chicken's aorta or its trachea, both of which would appear wormlike. Ms. Jones wants to know whether she can successfully sue the restaurant for breach of warranty. Please evaluate her claim based on *Webster v. Blue Ship Tea Room, Inc.* (page 287).

7. United Airlines posted on its Web site a fare of $49 round trip from New York City to Hong Kong. On the strength of that quote, 143 people purchased tickets. They were quite surprised when their credit cards were charged for the "real" fare, about 20 times what they had thought they had paid. It seems that for about an hour there was a bug in one of United's reservation computers that caused the low prices to be quoted on some flights to Asia. The customers want to know if they can force United to honor the quoted fare. Do you think a binding contract was formed, and if so, on what terms? Second, do you think United has any defense that it could raise? Finally, think about the ethical implications. Now that the customers know the posting was a mistake, should they voluntarily agree to pay the higher price?

8. Jonathan Shattuck thought he had a deal to buy a house for $1.825 million. Using e-mail, Shattuck and the seller had settled on the price. The last e-mail from the seller stated:

> Once we sign the P&S (purchase and sale agreement) we'd like to close ASAP. You may have your attorney send the P&S and deposit check for 10% of purchase price ($182,500) to my attorney. I'm looking forward to closing and seeing you as the owner of 5 Main Street, the prettiest spot in Marion village.

Before the buyer's attorney had a chance to draw up the purchase and sale agreement, the seller informed Shattuck that he was not going to follow through on the deal as he had another buyer who was willing to pay $1.96 million. His argument was that there was no signed writing binding him to the deal. How do you think the court decided? Why?

9. Sara Smith is a struggling young artist. Recently, however, she was "discovered" when an art dealer saw one of her paintings hanging in a local art gallery. The art dealer contracted with Sara to hold a major showing of her work in six months, on November 1. Under the contract Sara was to show no less than ten original paintings. In preparation for the show Sara contracted with Paint Masters, Inc., for four cases of her favorite oil paints to be shipped no later than July 1. Sara heard nothing more from Paint Masters, Inc., until September 1 when one case arrived. Sara attempted to find the same paint from other sources but was able to procure only one more case at $200 more than she had contracted to pay Paint Masters. Because of the delay in shipment, Sara was able to complete only six paintings and the show was canceled. Sara would like to sue Paint Masters, Inc., for the lost profits she would have received from her heightened recognition had the show gone as planned, for the money she had to spend on alternate paints, and for punitive damages to teach Paint Masters a lesson. Please evaluate Sara's situation.

10. Kate contracts with Bennett to buy 100 guitars at $300 each. Kate hopes to resell the guitars for $400 each. When the time for delivery arrives, Bennett refuses to deliver the guitars. Kate then spends $100 in phone calls trying to obtain an alternate supplier. Finally, she finds substitute guitars, but has to pay $350 each for them. She saved $50, however, because in her contract with Bennett she was going to have to pay the shipping. In her new contract, the seller paid the shipping. How much is Kate owed in compensatory damages?

‖‖‖ REVIEW QUESTIONS

Pages 255 through 260

1. How do the courts determine if the UCC governs a contract situation?
2. Why does it matter under the UCC whether one or both of the parties are merchants? Give at least two examples.
3. Describe each of the following contracts according to the categories listed in Figure 8-3.
   a. Carlos says to Mary, "Will you paint my house for $2,000?" Mary replies, "Yes, I would be happy to."
   b. Carlos says to Mary, "I will pay you $2,000 if you paint my house next week." The next week Mary begins to paint the house and gets about halfway done when severe weather forces her to wait until the next week to finish the job.
   c. Janet says to Jim, "I will sell you my car for $600." Later that day Jim sends Janet an e-mail saying, "I accept."
   d. Joan says to Bill, "I will give you $5,000 if you kill Robert." Bill kills Robert, but Joan refuses to give him the $5,000.
   e. Every Saturday Jimmy came to the Booths' home and mowed their lawn for $15. One Saturday Jimmy arrived while Mr. Booth was on the phone. Mr. Booth simply waved at Jimmy, who then mowed the lawn.

Pages 260 through 266

4. What are the three basic elements of a valid contract claim?
5. What is the objective view of contract law?
6. What are the four basic elements that every offer should contain?
7. Juan says to Jim, "I would like to sell my watch to you." Jim replies, "Great. I will be happy to give you a fair price for it." Has a contract been formed? Why?
8. Sally offers Tom a job, saying she will pay him "what he is worth." Tom accepts. Has a contract been formed? Why?
9. Janet says to Joan, "I am eager to sell my antique vase to you." Joan says, "Would you consider $400 for it?" Has a contract been formed? Why?
10. We Growum, a garden center, places the following advertisement in the Sunday paper.

Spring Planting Sale
Lilac bushes $20

Tuesday John goes to the garden center. All the lilac bushes have been sold. He sues for breach of contract. Will he succeed? Why?

11. Acme Lawn Care receives a call asking them to mow a lawn at 423 Main Street. Unfortunately the mowers misread the address as 432 Main Street. They arrive at that address, unload their mowers, and begin their work. Mr. Adams, the owner, is home

and sees what they are doing. He says nothing and lets them complete the job. When they finish and ask to be paid, he refuses. Would a court require Mr. Adams to pay and, if so, under what theory?

12. What are the three ways an offer can be terminated?
13. When may an offeror not revoke an offer?
14. What is the difference between an option contract and a merchant's firm offer?
15. What is the name of the rule that states that the acceptance must completely agree with the terms of the offer?
16. How has the UCC changed the mirror image rule?

Pages 266 through 274

17. An uncle offers his nephew $5,000 if the nephew promises not to smoke marijuana or use other illegal drugs during the next four years while he is away at college. Has a binding contract been formed? Why?
18. John volunteers to take care of Sam's pet rabbit while he is away on vacation. When Sam returns, he is very pleased with the good care John gave his rabbit and tells him that he is going to pay him $50. When John arrives the next day to receive his money, Sam says that he has changed his mind. Is Sam under a contractual obligation to pay John for the care of his rabbit? Why?
19. Anna Sacks was an employee of the Ajax Company for thirty-seven years. The president of the company told her that (in consideration for her outstanding service) when she retired, the company would pay her $200 per month for life. Two years later she retired and began receiving the payments. Shortly thereafter, the company was sold, and the new president refused to continue the payments, arguing that there had never been a valid contract between Ms. Sacks and the company. How do you think the court resolved the case?
20. Millie requested bids from three different contractors for a price to repair the roof on her house. The bids ranged from $5,000 to $20,000. Naturally, Millie accepted the $5,000 bid from We'gottcha Roofing. On a Monday We'gottcha began work by first removing all of the old shingles. The weather prediction was for rain by the end of the week. We'gottcha told Millie she had a choice. Either she could pay them a "bonus" of $15,000 and they would continue work on her roof, or they would have to take the rest of the week to finish other jobs they had started. Millie, afraid all of her household contents would be ruined if rain hit her "deshingled" roof, agreed to the extra money. Will Millie be required to pay the $15,000 bonus? Why?
21. Marvin began negotiations with the Big-W food chain to open a franchise store. The Big-W representative said that first Marvin would have to sell his bakery to raise the necessary money. Marvin was hesitant to do so, but based upon Big-W's representations that his selling the bakery was the only thing preventing them from finalizing the contract, Marvin did so. However, once he had sold the bakery, Big-W said they had found someone else and refused to sign a franchise contract with Marvin. If Marvin were to sue Big-W, would he win under a contract action? Why? Is there any alternative?

Pages 274 through 289

22. Name the six major defenses to a contract action.
23. Jim, who is sixteen years old, buys a stereo from Circuit Playground. Jim takes the stereo to the beach and ruins it when it becomes filled with sand. Jim takes it back to the store and demands the return of the money he paid for the stereo. Will the store have to refund his payment?
24. Mark and Bill are sitting at a bar drinking. They discuss the possibility of Mark selling Bill his watch for $50. Bill leaves, but Mark remains and continues to drink. Two hours later Bill calls Mark and offers him $5 for the watch. Now very

intoxicated, Mark mutters, "Whatever." The next day Mark has no memory of the phone call. Will the court enforce this arrangement? Why?

25. Sara offers to sell her car to Janet for $800. Janet thinks Sara means her 1978 VW Beetle and agrees. Sara was thinking of her 1970 VW van. Has a contract been formed? Why?

26. A law firm requires all new attorneys to sign an agreement that states that if they leave the firm for any reason, they will not work for another law firm or open their own practice within a fifty-mile radius for two years. How do you think the court would treat such an agreement? Why?

27. What is the difference between a warranty of merchantability and an implied warranty of fitness? How do both of those differ from an express warranty?

28. Joan offers to buy Bill's sailboat for $2,000. Bill agrees and asks Joan to put it in writing. Joan leaves an e-mail message for her secretary, stating that she wants him to draft a contract stating that she agrees to buy Bill's sailboat for $2,000. The next day Joan changes her mind. If Bill sues for breach of contract, will he succeed? Why?

Pages 289 through 295

29. What are the four ways in which the parties' contractual obligations can be discharged?

30. How does each of the following differ from the others—complete performance, substantial performance, and material failure to perform?

31. Jones contracted with Smith to log all the timber from his land between the months of September and December. Jones found he was not able to complete the work in the agreed time because his operations were slowed (a) by a local ordinance prohibiting logging during the hunting season, which occurred in September, and (2) by unusually heavy rains in the remaining months. Should Jones's lack of performance be excused? Why?

32. The city of Portage contracts with Get Going Builders to demolish a vacant building and replace it with a park. John Jakes is delighted, as his property is right across the street from the intended park. He envisions a significant increase in his property value. At the last minute the city decides to forgo the park in favor of increased pay for its firefighters. John is dismayed and wants to sue the city. Will he succeed in his suit? Why?

33. Martha contracts with Sam, a noted concert pianist, to take a series of ten music lessons. After the second lesson Sam is offered the opportunity to go on a world tour. He contacts William, a lesser known pianist, to take over his lessons. Martha is upset. Does she have any grounds to complain?

34. What is the difference between an assignment and a delegation?

35. What is the difference between assignments and delegations, on the one hand, and third-party beneficiary contracts, on the other?

Pages 295 through 297

36. When is specific performance an appropriate remedy?

37. What is cover?

38. What are consequential damages?

39. The city of Kalamazoo hired Good Builders, Inc., to build a new courthouse for $560,000. Good Builders had barely broken ground when the city notified them that it would not be able to pay for the building after all and asked Good Builders to stop all work. Good Builders refused, saying, "Hey, you guys signed a contract. We know our rights." At the time the city asked it to stop, Good Builders had expended $5,000 on materials, approximately $3,000 of which could have been returned at no loss to the company. By completing the project, however, Good Builders expended an additional $400,000. In a breach of contract action by Good Builders against the city, how much money do you think the court should award Good Builders? Why?

Chapter 9

Property and Estate Law

In no country in the world is the love of property more active and more anxious than in the United States.
Alexis de Tocqueville

INTRODUCTION

Property law affects everyone, as it governs ownership rights in both real and personal property. When you buy a home, rent an apartment, or sell a car, you are dealing with property law. Estate law determines how that property is distributed after death: either according to the terms of a will or, in the absence of a will, by following a statutory scheme. This chapter first covers the ownership, leasing, and sale of real and personal property. Then we discuss estate planning, including the importance of writing a will. The chapter ends with an overview of the probate process.

A. PROPERTY LAW

In its broadest sense the legal concept of **property** refers to any valuable right or interest that belongs to a person. Property is usually thought of as being a tangible object, such as a house or an automobile, which is "owned" by an individual, a corporation, or a government. However, the term also applies to the set of rights that specify how a tangible object is to be used. Examples include leases, easements, contractual rights, promissory notes, and even

Property
A tangible object or a right or ownership interest.

admission tickets to concerts or sporting events. There are also circumstances under which a person can have a "property interest" in a job, an idea, or a reputation.

There are two basic types of property: real property and personal property. **Real property,** also referred to as **real estate,** consists of land and whatever is growing on or built on that land. It includes not only the houses, garages, sheds, and other types of buildings that are on the land but also everything that is permanently attached to those buildings—such as light fixtures, plumbing fixtures, and built-in shelves. At times it can be difficult to determine whether something is "permanently" attached. For example, normally a room air conditioner is seen as personal property. However, if the window frame has been removed and the air conditioner bolted to the wall, it might be seen as "permanently" attached, and hence a fixture. When determining whether something should be considered a fixture, the courts look to the amount of damage that would be caused either to the item or to the underlying property if the item were to be removed from the premises. The courts will also take into account the intention of the parties. In addition, real estate includes the trees and plants growing on the land, as well as the rights to gas and minerals under the land and to the air space above it. In recent years the common law right to air space has been modified so as to not interfere with modern aviation.

Real property
Also known as *real estate;* land and items growing on or permanently attached to that land.

All property other than real property is classified as **personal property.** Personal property is sometimes referred to in the law as **chattel.** Personal property is often classified as being either tangible or intangible. **Tangible** property consists of goods that can be touched and moved, such as automobiles, jewelry, clothing, and television sets. **Intangible** property is personal property that cannot be touched, such as a stock certificate or a patent. While you can certainly touch the piece of paper that documents the stock ownership or the awarding of the patent, it is not the paper itself that has value.

Personal property
All property that is not real property.

The term **intellectual property** is used to cover intangible assets that are the product of someone's intellectual creation, such as inventions or the authorship of a book. Traditionally, land was the greatest measure of a person's wealth, but today intellectual property has become extremely important. With this new source of wealth have come new legal problems. For example, while it is usually quite clear if someone is illegally trespassing on your land, it is not always easy to know when someone is infringing on your rights to your intellectual property. To deal with this situation, the law has created various protections including trademarks, service marks, copyrights, and patents. **Trademarks** are terms, names, combinations of letters or numbers, and logos that identify particular products or services. Familiar examples include "Dodge," "IBM," and "V-8." **Service marks** are symbols that are used in connection with service-oriented businesses. The law gives the registered holders of these trademarks and service marks the right to control their use. **Copyrights** give authors, composers, and artists the right to control, with certain limitations related to "fair use," the use of their writings, musical performances, and artistic creations. A **patent** gives its owner the right to exclude others from making, using, or selling his or her invention.

Intellectual property
Intangible assets, such as trademarks, copyrights, and patents.

Property can change its nature from real to personal or, as noted above, from personal to real. For example, while oil is still in the ground, it is considered to be real property, but once it has been extracted from the ground and loaded on a tanker or sent down a pipeline, it becomes personal property. When trees are still in the forest, they are real property. When they are cut, they become personal property. It is not always easy to determine when this change occurs. For example, a mobile home on the sales lot is personal property. If it is moved to a mobile home park, has its tires removed, and is affixed to a foundation, it becomes real property. However, what if its tires are not removed and it is simply placed on the lot? Is it still personal property?

Determining whether property is real or personal can have important consequences, as the courts apply different rules to the different types of property. For example, the selling and leasing of personal property are covered by the general principles of contract law and the Uniform Commercial Code, discussed in Chapter 8. The selling and leasing of real estate will be covered below.

1. Ownership of Real Property

The nature of the rights and responsibilities of ownership varies with the type of ownership interest a person holds in the property. As Figure 9-1 illustrates, ownership of land can be categorized as being either a freehold estate or a leasehold estate. When the term **estate** is used as a means of classifying different types of ownership, it refers to an interest or a title in a parcel of real property. Be careful to avoid confusing this use of the term with the way *estate* is used in the probate context. There, it is used to refer to the total property, real and personal, that the decedent owned at the time of death.

A **freehold estate** is a right of title to real property that extends for life or some other indeterminate period of time. It involves what we ordinarily think of as "ownership" of a tract of land or a building. It is what you mean when you say that you own your house. A **leasehold estate**, on the other hand, gives a person certain "ownership rights" for a limited period of time, but the title to the property remains in the hands of the "owner." In everyday language these leasehold estates involve renting or leasing property.

The most common form of ownership is what is called a **fee simple absolute estate.** This is ownership that is free from any conditions or restrictions. A **conditional fee estate** is one in which the current owner retains ownership only as long as certain conditions are met. If those conditions are not met, the ownership reverts to the previous owner, the **grantor.** As an example, assume someone donates a piece of property to a charity but places conditions on how that property is to be used. If the charity fails to meet those conditions, the ownership of the property reverts to the person who made the gift or to his or her heirs.

A **life estate** gives the **life tenant** ownership that lasts only as long as that person, or some other named individual, lives. After the named person dies, the ownership reverts to the original owner or passes to a third party. An example might be a situation in which the wife of a second marriage is given a life estate to remain in a family home as long as she lives. Upon her death the ownership then reverts to the husband's estate or to his children from a previous marriage.

Ownership of property can be sole or shared, through either a joint tenancy or a tenancy in common. A **joint tenancy** occurs when a single estate of land is acquired by two or more persons who have equal rights in the use of that property during their respective lives. A **tenancy in common** is very similar in that it also involves two or more people who share use of the property. The ownership shares do not have to be equal, however, nor do they have to have

Estate
An interest in or a title to real property. (Note that this term has a different meaning when used in probate matters.)

Joint tenancy
Ownership by two or more persons who have equal rights in the use of that property. When a joint tenant dies, that person's share passes to the other joint tenant(s).

Tenancy in common
Ownership by two or more people. Ownership shares do not have to be equal, but each has an undivided interest in the property. When a tenant in common dies, that person's share passes either by will or by intestate statute.

Freehold Estates	Leasehold Estates
Fee simple absolute estate	Tenancy for a term (estate for years)
Conditional fee estate	Periodic tenancy
Life estate	Tenancy at will
	Tenancy at sufferance

Figure 9-1   Freehold versus Leasehold Estates

Tenancy by the entirety
A special type of joint tenancy applicable only to married couples.

been acquired at the same time. In addition, on death the ownership interest of a tenant in common passes to his or her heirs, while with a joint tenancy it passes to the co-owner(s). A **tenancy by the entirety** is a special type of joint tenancy applicable only to married couples. It is essentially a joint tenancy modified by the common-law theory that the husband and wife are one person. During their lifetimes neither the wife nor the husband can transfer the property without the other's consent. As with any joint tenancy, on the death of one of the spouses the other takes whole title to the exclusion of any other heirs. In some condominium arrangements the individual living units are individually owned or owned in joint tenancy, and the common halls, walks, parking lots, and garden areas are a form of tenancy in common.

The distinction between joint tenancy and tenancy in common is very important. While both represent ways to jointly own property, the part owner of property held as a tenancy in common can bequeath that share to whomever the owner pleases. However, the owner of property held in joint tenancy cannot choose to whom the property will pass on the owner's death. Even if the owner provides in a will that the property will pass to a named individual, it will nonetheless pass to the other joint tenant. In fact, you will often hear the term *joint tenancy* referred to as **joint tenancy with a right of survivorship.**

Restrictive covenant
A provision in a deed that prohibits specified uses of the property.

An owner's rights to use a piece of real estate can be limited by the existence of either a **restrictive covenant** or an **easement.** The former is a provision in a deed that prohibits specified uses of the property and commonly is added at the time a developer subdivides and improves the property before it is marketed for housing. Common provisions include requirements relating to minimum square footage, setback, and architectural styles. Others may prohibit the installation of satellite dishes in yards or the overnight parking of boats or recreational vehicles in driveways. These covenants are recorded in the county land records and become part of the title for all subsequent owners.

Given the close relationship between the value of an individual condominium unit and the condition and use of other units in the same building or complex, it is not surprising to find that condominium agreements often contain many restrictive covenants. Condominium developers trying to appeal to senior citizens have sometimes included covenants that prohibit young children from living in their units. Such restrictions have usually been upheld as a valid accommodation to the needs of older citizens for "peace and quiet." However, a court would probably not uphold the same restriction if applied to apartments or as part of a zoning plan, as it would violate fair housing laws, which prohibit age discrimination.

Historically, restrictive covenants were also used to exclude some racial and ethnic groups from living in certain areas. In *Shelly v. Kraemer,*[1] however, the U.S. Supreme Court ruled that such racially restrictive covenants could not be judicially enforced, and in *Jones v. Alfred H. Mayer Co.*[2] the Court interpreted the federal Civil Rights Act of 1866 as prohibiting racial discrimination in the purchasing and leasing of property. In addition, the federal Civil Rights Act of 1968 and many state and local open housing ordinances now prohibit such discrimination.

An **easement** is the right to use property owned by another for a limited purpose. Utility companies acquire easements that allow them to install and maintain electrical cables and gas pipes. Another common type of easement allows a neighbor to drive over a small section of someone else's lot in order to gain access to his or her own land.

Easement
A right to use property owned by another for a limited purpose.

DISCUSSION QUESTION

1. Should a condominium association that wishes to appeal to seniors be allowed to prohibit children from living in its units? What are the policy arguments for and against? How would you distinguish between children living in the unit versus those just visiting? Specifically, if you cannot discriminate on the basis of race, why should you be able to discriminate on the basis of age?

2. Rental of Real Property

A **lease** is an agreement in which the property owner, called either the **lessor** or the **landlord**, gives someone else, the **lessee** or the **tenant**, the right to use that property for a designated period of time. A **leasehold** is a parcel of real estate held under a lease. Look again at Figure 9-1. As you can see, leasehold estates can be classified as a tenancy for a term, a periodic tenancy, a tenancy at will, or a tenancy at sufferance.

With a **tenancy for a term**, also sometimes called an **estate for years**, the lease establishes a set period of time during which the lessee will have control and after which all rights revert to the lessor. With a **periodic tenancy** the rental periods are established at a set interval—for example, week to week, month to month, or year to year. At the end of each rental period the lease can be terminated with proper notice. However, if neither party gives such notice, then the lease automatically continues. When no time period is specified, it is called a **tenancy at will**, and either the lessee can leave or the lessor can reclaim the land at any time. The law in many states requires that the owner give thirty days' notice before reclaiming possession. This has the effect of converting a tenancy at will into a month-to-month periodic tenancy.

A **tenancy at sufferance** denotes a situation in which the person in possession of the land has no legal right to be there. An example of this would be homeless people occupying an abandoned building.

When real estate is leased, a landlord-tenant relationship is created between the lessor and the lessee. The common law favored landlords. The tenant

Lease
An agreement in which the property owner gives someone else the right to use that property for a designated period of time.

Lessor or landlord
The owner of the property being leased.

Lessee or tenant
The person with right of possession during the term of the lease.

---

[1] 344 U.S. 1 (1948).
[2] 392 U.S. 409 (1968).

Quiet enjoyment
The tenant's right to be free from interference from the landlord with respect to how the property is used.

Implied warranty of habitability
A requirement that property be fit for the purpose for which it is being rented. Owners are required to repair and maintain the premises at certain minimum levels.

Constructive eviction
An act by a landlord that makes the premises unfit or unsuitable for occupancy.

had to take the property in the condition it was in at the time that the lease was entered into, even if the tenant was not aware of defects at the time the lease was signed. The tenant also had to repair any damage resulting from natural disasters or the acts of other people, the tenant, or the tenant's family. The landlord's only obligation to the tenant was that of not interfering with the tenant's "quiet enjoyment" of the premises. **Quiet enjoyment** meant that the landlord could not interfere with the tenant's use of the property with respect to such things as what crops were planted or who was invited onto the property. The tenant's primary obligation was to pay the rent.

Over the years many state legislatures have enacted statutes that provide for a more equitable relationship between landlords and tenants. Such laws often require the owner to repair and maintain the premises at certain minimum levels. The plumbing and heating must work, the windows and the doors have to close, and so on. If an apartment is being rented as a residential unit, then it must come complete with running water, a working furnace, and other minimum living essentials. This requirement is present even if not written into the lease and is known as the **implied warranty of habitability**. It requires that the property be fit for the purpose for which it is being rented. These minimum standards are often equated with whatever is required in the local housing code.

A constructive eviction occurs when the landlord does something to deprive the tenant of quiet enjoyment of the land, such as shutting off the water or changing the locks. If the tenant is forced to abandon the property, then the tenant can rely on the constructive eviction as a defense to any further requirement to pay rent.

State laws also frequently regulate the handling of security deposits. A **security deposit** is an amount of money, usually equal to one month's rent, that is collected at the time the lease is signed and then held by the landlord to cover the cost of repairs that may be needed when the tenant moves out. Tenants are held responsible for any damage done to the property beyond what is considered to be "normal wear and tear." State laws often place limits on the amount of money that can be held as a security deposit, require the landlord to return the security deposit within a set amount of time after the tenant vacates, require the landlord to document the cost of repairs that are deducted from the deposit, and sometimes even require the payment of interest on the amount of money held.

Some states and cities have rent control statutes and ordinances that regulate the amount of rent that can be charged for existing apartments. In addition, most states have "open housing" laws that prohibit landlords from discriminating in terms of the types of tenants to whom they rent. As mentioned above in the context of restrictive covenants, while some restrictions are possible in relation to the sale of condominiums, such restrictions are usually not allowed with the rental of real estate. One area that has caused a great deal of controversy is the interpretation of state statutes that make it unlawful to discriminate on the basis of marital status. The courts are split on whether a landlord can refuse to rent to an unmarried couple. Even in states that have a fair housing statute prohibiting discrimination on the basis of marital status, some courts have allowed the discrimination under the theory that the denial was based on the couple's engaging in criminal conduct, "cohabiting," and not on their marital status.

Baiz v. Hoffius
222 Mich. App. 210, 564 N.W.2d 493 (1997)

CORRIGAN, P.J.

In these consolidated appeals, plaintiffs appeal by right the orders granting summary disposition to defendants in this fair housing action. We affirm.

Defendants John and Terry Hoffius, a married couple, rent residential property in Jackson, Michigan. In June 1993, plaintiffs Kristal McCready and Keith Kerr contacted defendants in response to defendants' advertisement about housing for rent. Defendants refused to rent to plaintiffs when they learned that McCready and Kerr were not married but intended to live in the same rental unit. Similarly, plaintiff Rose Baiz telephoned defendants in July 1993 about the property. Defendants also declined to rent to Baiz when they learned that she was not married to plaintiff Peter Perusse yet planned to live with him. Defendant John Hoffius told plaintiffs that unmarried cohabitation violated his religious beliefs.

Plaintiffs filed two separate complaints with the Jackson Fair Housing Commission. Testers from the Commission posed as potential renters and contacted defendants. Defendants did not ask the marital status of all the testers. Defendants, however, refused to permit unmarried testers to inspect the apartments, claiming that the units only were available to married couples. Defendants stated that they usually did not rent to unmarried couples.

Defendants moved for summary disposition on plaintiffs' complaints, arguing in part that plaintiffs failed to state a claim upon which relief could be granted because the Elliott-Larsen Civil Rights Act, MCL 37.2502(1); MSA 3.548 (502)(1), did not protect unmarried cohabitation. Defendants also argued that, if the Civil Rights Act protected unmarried cohabitation, it was unconstitutional because it would force defendants to violate their sincerely held religious beliefs against unmarried cohabitation.

The cases were heard separately, but decided similarly. Both circuit court judges opined that the cases involved statutory interpretation, and both declined to address the constitutional issues. The judges noted that the Civil Rights Act protected status, not conduct. They opined that unmarried cohabitation was unprotected conduct, not protected marital status. Accordingly, they determined that the Civil Rights Act did not protect unmarried cohabitation. We agree.

Plaintiffs first assert that defendants violated the Civil Rights Act by discriminating against them based on their marital status. Whether unmarried cohabitation enjoys protection from housing discrimination under the Civil Rights Act is an issue of first impression in this state. Cases from other jurisdictions reflect divergent opinions on this issue. For example, in *Smith v. Fair Employment & Housing Comm.*, 12 Cal. 4th 1143; 913 P.2d 909 (1996) *cert. pending,* the landlord presented arguments similar to those of defendants in this case. The California Supreme Court ruled that the California Fair Employment and Housing Act protected unmarried cohabitants against housing discrimination and rejected the landlord's argument that the unmarried tenants' sexual conduct, rather than their marital status, was at issue. Id. at 915-918. *See also Swanner v. Anchorage Equal Rights Comm.,* 874 P.2d 274, *cert. den.,* 115 S. Ct. 460 (1994); *Attorney General v. Desilets,* 418 Mass. 316; 636 N.E.2d 233 (1994), both of which held in accordance with Smith.

In contrast, the Supreme Court of Wisconsin decided that a landlord's refusal to rent to unmarried tenants was based on their conduct of living together and not on their marital status in *County of Dane v. Norman* 174 Wis. 2d 683; 497 N.W.2d 714, 717-718 (1993). The Minnesota Supreme Court considered that state's criminal fornication statute when deciding this same issue in *State by Cooper v. French,* 460 N.W.2d 2 (Minn. 1990). The Court concluded that the Minnesota Human Rights Act did not extend to protect unmarried, cohabitating couples in housing cases. Id. at 7. The Court added:

> Before abandoning fundamental values and institutions, we must pause and take stock of our present

social order: millions of drug abusers; rampant child abuse; a rising underclass without marketable job skills; children roaming the streets; children with only one parent or no parents at all; and children growing up with no one to guide them in developing any set of values. How can we expect anything else when the state itself contributes, by arguments of this kind, to further erosion of fundamental institutions that have formed the foundation of our civilization for centuries? [Id. at 11.]

Whether the Civil Rights Act protects unmarried cohabitants from housing discrimination raises questions of statutory interpretation. Statutory interpretation is a question of law, which we review de novo. When courts construe statutory meaning, their primary goal is to ascertain and give effect to legislative intent. This Court first considers the specific statutory language to determine the intent of the Legislature. The Legislature is presumed to intend the meaning that the statute plainly expresses. Judicial construction of a statute is not permitted where the plain and ordinary meaning of the language is clear.

MCL 37.2502(1); MSA 3.548(502)(1) provides in relevant part:

> (1) A person engaging in a real estate transaction, or a real estate broker or salesman, shall not on the basis of religion, race, color, national origin, age, sex, familial status, or marital status of a person or a person residing with that person:

> (a) Refuse to engage in a real estate transaction with a person.

The Civil Rights Act does not define the term "marital status." In defining a term, courts should attempt to give effect to the legislative intent. *Miller v. CA Muer Corp.*, 420 Mich. 355, 362; 362 N.W.2d 650 (1984). The Civil Rights Act's purpose is to prevent discrimination based on membership in certain classes and to "eliminate the effects of offensive or demeaning stereotypes, prejudices and biases." Id. at 363. "By including marital status as a protected class, the Legislature manifested its intent to prohibit discrimination based on whether a person is married." Id.

The public policy of this state, as reflected in our laws, favors the institution of marriage. . . .

When promulgating new laws, the Legislature is charged with the knowledge of existing laws on the same subject and is presumed to have considered the effect of new laws on existing laws. . . . Because the Legislature would not have intended the Civil Rights Act to insulate criminal conduct, cohabitation is not protected conduct under the act. . . . Although courts are to construe liberally remedial statutes, we decline to recognize the Civil Rights Act as preventing housing discrimination against unmarried couples and at the same time legitimizing criminal conduct.

Further, if two statutes lend themselves to a construction that avoids conflict, that construction should control. . . . Our construction avoids conflict between the Civil Rights Act and the criminal cohabitation statute. The Civil Rights Act prohibits discrimination against couples who enjoy marital status, but the act is not violated when a landlord refuses to rent to unmarried persons who will be engaging in criminal unmarried cohabitation.

When two acts relate to the same subject, courts presume against repeal of the former statute by implication. If possible, courts give effect to both acts. . . .

Plaintiffs have not met their heavy burden of demonstrating that the Legislature intended to repeal the criminal cohabitation statute. Had the Legislature intended to repeal the criminal cohabitation statute, it would have done so. . . . Making social policy is a job for the Legislature, not for this Court. Indeed, the appropriate branch for resolution of the moral issue presented is the legislative branch, which is well equipped to weigh these issues.

Plaintiffs next contend that society's need to provide equal access in housing outweighs defendants' religious beliefs that they should not rent to an unmarried couple. Neither trial court addressed this issue in its opinion; therefore, the issue is not preserved for review. Additionally, our Supreme Court has refused to reach constitutional claims that are unnecessary to the resolution of a case. We decline to review this unpreserved issue, and we will not reach the constitutional issue because it is unnecessary in deciding this matter.

Affirmed.

CASE DISCUSSION QUESTIONS

1. The court in *Baiz* quoted from *State of Minnesota v. French,* 460 N.W.2d 2 (Minn. 1990), for the general proposition that the state's requesting protection for unmarried couples in acquiring rental housing was the cause for much of society's problems. In that case, the dissent had this to say:

> Religious and moral values include not discriminating against others solely because of their color, sex, or whom they live with, avoiding unnecessary emotional suffering, showing tolerance for nontraditional lifestyles, and treating others as one would wish to be treated. . . . It may be difficult for some individuals to recognize invidious discrimination, but one must not lose sight of the continuing fight of minorities to be protected from a "probable majority" point of view. It was not long ago that blacks and women were widely viewed as second-class citizens. Discrimination usually comes in less obvious forms—such as against single parents, those with AIDS, homosexuals, the elderly, and those living together—but no less invidious forms. The majority, in effect, would have us return to the day of "separate but equal" where individuals such as French would be permitted to keep their neighborhoods free of "undesirables" and "nonbelievers." . . .
>
> Discriminating against unmarried individuals living with members of the opposite sex is neither the cause or the solution to societal woes. Id. at 17, 20.

Who do you think presents the better argument, and why?

2. What did the court state was the first step in statutory analysis?

3. Why did the court think that the refusal to rent to an unmarried couple did not violate the state's fair housing laws?

4. Why did the court refuse to discuss the issue of whether the landlord's religious beliefs justified the discrimination? This case has an interesting and somewhat puzzling continuing history.

The decision you just read was appealed to the Michigan Supreme Court. That court determined the landlords had violated the terms of the Civil Rights Act when they refused to rent to the unmarried couple, defining marital status as the presence or absence of marriage.[3] Then, even though the issue of the statute's constitutionality was not raised as an issue at the trial court nor addressed by the lower appellate court, Michigan's Supreme Court went on to hold that "defendants' religious freedom rights have not been violated. A compelling state interest in eradicating discrimination in real estate transactions justified the burden on their beliefs."[4] But then just a few months later, the court vacated the part of its decision where it had held that the Civil Rights Act did not violate the landlord's constitutional rights and remanded the case to the trial court for further consideration.[5]

State laws also determine the procedures landlords must use to retake possession of their property. Under the common law a landlord could forcibly **evict** a tenant who was in default of any term in the lease. The landlord or the landlord's agent could go in and literally throw the tenant and a tenant's personal

---

[3]McCready v. Hoffius, 586 N.W.2d 723, 729 (Mich. 1998).

[4]Id. at 730.

[5]McCready v. Hoffius, 593 N.W.2d 545 (Mich. 1999).

possessions out on the street. As a result of the hardship and the frequent violence such procedures brought about, most states now require that a landlord first give an appropriate eviction notice and then go to court to get local law enforcement agents, such as police or sheriff's deputies, to supervise the physical removal of the tenant and any possessions. In some states these eviction procedures are known as **forcible entry and detainer** or **unlawful detainer** actions. Note, however, that the phrase *forcible entry and detainer* can be confusing, as in some states such an action can be brought by anyone, including the tenant, who has been unlawfully deprived of rightful possession of the property.

In an eviction proceeding most state courts have held that an implied warranty of habitability defense can be used. Therefore, the landlord cannot evict a tenant for failure to pay rent if the landlord has failed to maintain the premises at minimum standards.

3. Transfer of Real Property

Real property can be transferred (1) through a sales transaction, (2) at the death of the owner, (3) as a gift, (4) through a seizure by a creditor, (5) through an eminent domain proceeding, or (6) by adverse possession.

a. Sale

In the typical residential real estate transaction, the seller either advertises the availability of the property or lists it for sale with a real estate agent. If a real estate agent is involved, the seller will sign a **listing agreement**, which spells out the nature of the services the agent will perform and how the agent will be compensated for those services.

The legal aspects of the sale start when the potential buyer makes an offer to purchase the property. Real estate agents usually carry standardized fill-in-the-blank offer forms, and the buyer's agent fills in the information regarding the description of the property, the amount of money being offered, a listing of the fixtures and appliances that are to be included, and the date of possession. The offer sheet also usually contains a number of clauses that make the offer contingent on the buyer's being able to obtain financing, often at a specified interest rate; the building's passing a termite inspection; and so forth. The buyer then turns over a specified sum of money to the real estate agent as **earnest money.** This money is applied to the purchase price at the time the sale is completed and may be forfeited if the buyer defaults prior to the completion of the sale. The seller, in turn, accepts the offer, rejects it, or proposes a counteroffer. To accept the offer, the seller simply signs the appropriate line on the offer sheet. A counteroffer usually consists of a lower asking price, somewhere between the buyer's offer and the original asking price.

While an offer and acceptance create a binding contract, one of the conditions of the offer sheet is frequently that a more formal contract be drawn up within a specified time. In a typical residential sale, this is the stage at which lawyers first become directly involved in the transaction. Real estate brokers and bar associations disagree about how much legal assistance real estate professionals should provide and how much of the work should be done by attorneys. Local practices differ based on the nature of the accommodations that have been worked out between the two groups.

While the buyer arranges for financing, the seller arranges for a title search, and sometimes title insurance. A **title search** is an examination of documents

Listing agreement
A document that spells out the nature of the services a real estate agent will perform with respect to selling real property and how the agent will be compensated for those services.

Earnest money
The money the buyer turns over to the real estate agent to be applied to the purchase price of property.

Title search
An examination of documents recording title to the property to ensure the owner has a clear title.

recording title to the property to ensure the owner has a clear title to the property. A **clear title**, also known as **marketable title**, is an ownership right that is free from encumbrances or other defects. An **encumbrance** is a lien or other type of security interest that signifies that some other party has a legitimate claim to the property as a means of satisfying debts of the current owner. Examples of encumbrances include mortgages, liens for unpaid taxes, and mechanic's liens. A **mechanic's lien** is a claim by a contractor or repair person who had done work on the house for which he or she has not been fully paid.

The buyer guarantees the title either by obtaining an up-to-date abstract or by purchasing title insurance. An **abstract** is a condensed history of the title, which includes the chain of ownership and a record of all liens, taxes, or other encumbrances that may impair the title. **Title insurance** is an insurance policy in which the insurer agrees to indemnify the purchaser or mortgage holder against any loss due to a defective title. If defects in the title are found and the seller is unwilling or unable to correct these defects, then the buyer can refuse to complete the transaction.

A **real estate closing** is a meeting at which the buyer and the seller and/or their representatives sign and deliver a variety of legal documents associated with the sale and transfer of the property. The most important part of the closing is the delivery of the deed. The **deed** is the legal document that formally conveys title to the property to the new owner. In most sales a **warranty deed** is used. With this type of deed, the seller, also known as the *grantor,* promises "clear title" to the property, one that has no encumbrances or other defects.

As part of a divorce settlement one spouse will often use a quitclaim deed to sign over his or her share of the real estate they held in joint ownership. With a **quitclaim deed** the grantor gives up any claims to the property without making any assertions about there being a clear title.

At the closing the buyer signs the mortgage documents, and the seller receives the proceeds of the sale. A **closing statement** is prepared to itemize and allocate all costs and moneys exchanged among the various parties, including financial institutions and real estate brokers. In many states, property taxes assessed for one year are not collected until the next year, and the new owner is responsible for paying taxes that were incurred by the previous owner. If this is the case, the seller will give the buyer a credit that corresponds to the amount of taxes still owed for the period preceding the sale. If the actual possession of the property does not correspond to the closing date, then credits are given to reflect the rent being paid by the seller to the buyer or by the buyer to the seller.

As an alternative to the standard sale process described above, real estate is sometimes sold through a **land contract.** In essence it is an installment sales contract. The buyer takes physical possession of the property and begins making monthly payments to the seller, which will be applied to the agreed-on sale price of the property. However, the seller retains legal title to the property until all the agreed-on installment payments have been made. If the buyer for some reason defaults in making the payments, the contract is broken, and the seller gets to keep title to the property, as well as any payments that were made during the course of the contract.

Clear title
Also known as **marketable title;** an ownership right that is free from encumbrances or other defects.

Abstract
A condensed history of the title, which includes the chain of ownership and a record of all liens, taxes, or other encumbrances that may impair the title.

Title insurance
Insurance against any loss due to a defective title.

Deed
The legal document that formally conveys title to the property to the new owner.

Warranty deed
A deed in which the seller promises clear title to the property.

Quitclaim deed
A deed in which the grantor gives up any claims to the property without making any assertions about there being a clear title.

Closing statement
An itemized allocation of all the costs and moneys exchanged among the various parties, including financial institutions and real estate brokers, when a property is sold.

Land contract
An installment contract for the sale of land.

b. Death of the Owner

Decedent
A person who died.

What happens to people's property when they die depends on the type of ownership they had and whether they had a will. If the property was held as a **joint tenancy**, then the **decedent's** share will pass automatically to the surviving joint owner(s). Such a transaction occurs independently of any provisions in the decedent's will, and the property is not considered to be part of her or his estate.

Devise
A gift of real estate that is given to someone through a will.

If property was owned individually or as a tenancy in common, then it will become part of the decedent's estate and will then be transferred according to the provisions of the will. A gift of real estate by will is called a **devise**. If the person died without a will, then the property will be distributed according to the special procedures set out in state statutes for those who do not leave a will. These procedures are explained in more detail in the section on estate planning below.

c. Gift

Property can also be transferred as a gift. The elements for a valid gift include an offer, an acceptance, and delivery. Wealthy parents might give a child a house as a wedding gift, or elderly parents might wish to transfer ownership of a vacation condo to their children before they die rather than having it become part of their estate. Such gifts are encouraged by the fact that federal tax laws allow gifts of less than a designated amount to be transferred tax free.

d. Seizure by a Creditor

Foreclosure
The process by which a creditor who holds a mortgage or some other form of a lien on real property can force the sale of that property in order to satisfy the debt to the mortgagee or lien holder.

Foreclosure is the process by which a creditor who holds a mortgage or some other form of a lien on real property can force the sale of that property in order to satisfy the debt to the mortgagee or lien holder. Many mortgages include **power of sale clauses**, authorizing private foreclosure sales that do not require court action.

Power of sale clause
A clause authorizing a private foreclosure sale that does not require court action.

Many states protect homeowners from creditors through what is known as a homestead exemption. As the name "homestead" suggests, usually the exemption only applies to a primary residence. The purpose of such laws is to protect not only the homeowner but also the homeowner's family so that creditors may not force a sale of their home in order to acquire assets to pay for the homeowner's debts. In some states, a homestead exemption is automatic as soon as the property is occupied and used as a home. In others, however, in order to gain the benefits of a homestead exemption, the homeowner must file a formal declaration, stating that the home is the declarant's principal dwelling. To find the requirements and benefits of a homestead exemption in any given state, you must research that state's statutes.

Eminent domain
The power of government to take private property for public purposes.

e. Eminent Domain

Just compensation
The amount of money the government must pay the owner of property it seizes through eminent domain.

Eminent domain is the power of government to take private property for a public use. Although the government does not need the owner's consent, it must provide the owner with **just compensation** for the property. If the government and the owner cannot agree on a "fair" price, then the courts must determine what constitutes fair market value for the property. These limitations—that the property must be taken for a public use and that the government must pay just compensation—are found in the U.S. Constitution. The Fifth Amendment states, "nor shall private property be taken for public use without just compensation." The Supreme Court has determined that this "taking clause" of the Fifth Amendment is also applicable to the states through the Fourteenth Amendment's due process clause.[6] In recent years controversies over eminent domain have centered around two issues: the use of zoning laws and what constitutes a "public use."

(1) Zoning laws

Zoning laws regulate the way in which property can be used, such as prohibiting the construction of a factory on land that is zoned residential. Other regulations require the owner to turn over a portion of the land as a condition of being granted a variance or special use permit. The issue in these cases usually revolves not around whether the government had the power to make the regulation but rather around whether compliance with the regulation amounted to a taking so that the owner would have to be compensated.

An example of the first type of restriction—when a zoning law regulates the way the property may be used—occurred in *Lucas v. South Carolina Coastal Council.*[7] In 1986 Mr. Lucas purchased two beachfront lots with the intention of building single-family houses. He paid $975,000 for the lots. Then in 1988, before he could start construction on the lots, the legislature enacted the Beachfront Management Act. The act prohibited Mr. Lucas from building any permanent structure on his land. He sued, contending that the act constituted a "taking" under the Fifth and Fourteenth Amendments that required payment of just compensation. The U.S. Supreme Court agreed.

The second type of zoning case—one dealing with a requirement that the owner dedicate a portion of the land for public purposes—was the focus of *Dolan v. City of Tigard.*[8] Florence Dolan, the owner of a plumbing and electric store, applied to the city for a permit to redevelop the site. The city agreed to give her the permit so long as she dedicated fifteen feet as a public greenway and an additional fifteen-foot strip as a pedestrian/bicycle pathway. The case eventually reached the U.S. Supreme Court. The Court first noted that the takings clause of the Fifth Amendment, applicable to the states through the Fourteenth Amendment, provides that the government cannot take land for public use without providing just compensation. On the other hand, the Court cited an earlier case for the proposition that

> "[g]overnment hardly could go on if to some extent values incident to property could not be diminished without paying for every such change in the general law." A land use regulation does not effect a taking if it "substantially advances legitimate state interests" and does not "deny an owner economically viable use of his land."[9]

The court next stated that it must determine whether there was an "essential nexus" between a "legitimate state interest" and the conditions that the city applied to Ms. Dolan's permit. The court stated that

---

[6]Chicago, B. & Q. R. R. v. Chicago, 166 U.S. 226, 241 (1897).
[7]505 U.S. 1003 (1992).
[8]512 U.S. 374 (1994).
[9]Id. at 384-385.

[un]doubtedly, the prevention of flooding along Fanno Creek and the reduction of traffic congestion in the Central Business District qualify as the type of legitimate public purposes we have upheld. It seems equally obvious that a nexus exists between preventing flooding along Fanno Creek and limiting development within the creek's 100-year floodplain. Petitioner proposes to double the size of her retail store and to pave her now-gravel parking lot, thereby expanding the impervious surface on the property and increasing the amount of stormwater run-off into Fanno Creek.

The same may be said for the city's attempt to reduce traffic congestion by providing for alternative means of transportation. In theory, a pedestrian/bicycle pathway provides a useful alternative means of transportation for workers and shoppers.[10]

However, that was not the end of the Court's decision. The second part of the analysis required a particularized look at the petitioner's case, specifically a determination of whether the "required dedication is related both in nature and extent to the impact of the proposed development."[11] The Court noted that "the city has never said why a public greenway, as opposed to a private one, was required in the interest of flood control."[12] The Court went on to explain the importance of the distinction. "The difference to petitioner, of course, is the loss of her ability to exclude others. As we have noted, this right to exclude others is 'one of the most essential sticks in the bundle of rights that we commonly characterized as property.'"[13] Similarly, the city had not demonstrated how the dedication of the pedestrian/bicycle pathway would offset the increased traffic demand caused by the increased size of Ms. Dolan's store. The Court concluded by stating that

[c]ities have long engaged in the commendable task of land use planning, made necessary by increasing urbanization particularly in metropolitan areas such as Portland. The city's goals of reducing flooding hazards and traffic congestion, and providing for public greenways, are laudable, but there are outer limits to how this may be done. "A strong public desire to improve the public condition [will not] warrant achieving the desire by a shorter cut than the constitutional way of paying for the change."[14]

The Court then remanded the case to the lower court for further proceedings consistent with its opinion.

To summarize, in this second type of zoning case, when the government places a zoning restriction on how a landowner may use a portion of his or her land, the government will not have to pay the landowner if the restriction advances legitimate state interests and does not deny the owner the economically viable use of the land. However, if the restriction does deny the owner an economically viable use of the land and there is no clear relationship between a legitimate state interest to be served by the restriction and the restriction itself, then the government will have to pay just compensation. The restriction then qualifies as a taking for which the government must pay.

---

[10]Id. at 387.

[11]Id. at 391.

[12]Id. at 392.

[13]Id. at 384.

[14]Id. at 396.

(2) Public use

Imagine buying a dilapidated house, having to hack away at weeds and brush just to reach the front door, and then working for months to restore and transform the house until it becomes a showpiece Victorian home. Then imagine opening the door one day to find a real estate agent on the front steps telling you that your house has been condemned. This is how Susette Kelo found out that the city of New London planned to take away and demolish her house so that it could lease her land and that of her neighbors to a private developer who was planning on building a luxury hotel, condominiums, offices, and shops. The city saw this as a way to revitalize an area of its waterfront district by creating more than 3,000 jobs and adding over $1 million annually in property tax revenue.

Ms. Kelo rejected the city's offer to demolish her home in return for "just compensation." As many homeowners would, probably she felt that no amount of money could pay her for the time and labor she had invested in creating her dream home. However, the legal argument she advanced was that the city was not taking her property for a public purpose, but rather was doing it for the benefit of a private developer. She was so determined to keep her home that she took her argument to court: first to the local trial court, then to the Connecticut Supreme Court, and finally to the U.S. Supreme Court.

It will help you in understanding the specifics of the city's and Ms. Kelo's arguments to first review the history of eminent domain. As indicated above, for a governmental taking to be constitutional, it must be for a "public use." Traditionally, "public use" meant a taking for a clearly governmental purpose, such as for a new public school, a new road, or a public park. Over time the definition of "public use" took on a broader meaning to also include a "public benefit" such as the elimination of urban blight. This definition was broadened even further in the landmark case of *Poletown Neighborhood Council v. Detroit*,[15] in which the Michigan Supreme court stated that "public use" could include the taking of property for private economic development. In that case, the court upheld the taking of private homes so that General Motors could build an assembly plant. The court stated, "The power of eminent domain is to be used in this instance primarily to accomplish the essential public purposes of alleviating unemployment and revitalizing the economic base of the community. The benefit to a private interest is merely incidental."[16] Therefore, the court held that a generalized economic benefit was sufficient to support the government's power to take private property.

Twenty-three years later, the Connecticut Supreme Court cited the *Poletown* opinion with approval in affirming the city of New London's decision to take private homes, including Ms. Kelo's, for the purpose of creating a revitalized waterfront area. The city did not argue that the area was blighted, but only that the land could be put to better economic use, thereby creating jobs and increasing tax revenues. Ironically, just four months later, the Michigan Supreme Court overruled *Poletown*. In overruling *Poletown*, the court described the debate as a "clash of two bedrock principles of our legal tradition: the sacrosanct right of individuals to dominion over their private property, on the

---

[15] 304 N.W.2d 455 (Mich. 1981).

[16] Id. at 459.

one hand and, on the other, the state's authority to condemn private property for the commonweal."[17]

From the very opening sentence of its *Kelo* decision, it was clear the Connecticut Supreme Court justices thought the use of eminent domain by the city of New London was constitutionally justified:

> The principle issue in this appeal is whether the *public use clauses of the federal* and state constitutions authorize the exercise of the eminent domain power in furtherance of a significant economic development plan that is projected to create in excess of 1000 jobs, to increase tax and other revenues, and to revitalize an economically distressed city, including its downtown and waterfront areas.[18]

The justices concluded that New London's taking of Ms. Kelo's property for economic development was an appropriate exercise of its eminent domain powers.

Having lost in both the trial and appellate courts in Connecticut, Ms. Kelo appealed to the U.S. Supreme Court. She and her supporters stated the issue quite differently:

> What protection does the Fifth Amendment's public use requirement provide for individuals whose property is being condemned, not to eliminate slums or blight, but for the sole purpose of "economic development" that will perhaps increase tax revenue and improve the local economy?[19]

During oral argument before the Supreme Court, Ms. Kelo's attorney began by stating:

> This case is about whether there are any limits on government's eminent domain power under the public use requirement of the Fifth Amendment. Every home, church or corner store would produce more tax revenue and jobs if it were a Costco, a shopping mall or a private office building. But if that's the justification for the use of eminent domain, then any city can take property anywhere within its borders for any private use that might make more money than what is there now.[20]

This was met by Justice Ginsburg's rejoinder:

> You are leaving out that New London was in a depressed economic condition, so this is distinguished from the case where the state has no particular reason for wanting this, but the critical fact on the city side, at least, is that this was a depressed community and they wanted to build it up, get more jobs. . . . [M]ore than tax revenue was at stake. The community had gone down and down and the town wanted to build it up.[21]

In one of the most controversial decisions of the 2004-2005 term, by a 5-4 vote, the Supreme Court upheld the town's seizure of Kelo's property on the

---

[17]County of Wayne v. Hathcock, 684 N.W.2d 765 (Mich. 2004).

[18]Kelo v. City of New London, 843 A.2d 500, 507 (Conn. 2004).

[19]Question presented as stated in the Amicus Curiae Brief of the Rutherford Institute in Support of Petitioners.

[20]Transcript of oral argument, Feb. 22, 2005.

[21]Id.

basis that a taking for economic development met the Constitution's requirement of a "public use," even when the land was being transferred to a private developer.[22]

The test is simply whether the city had a rational basis for believing the proposed economic development would benefit the public. Furthermore, such a public purpose should be broadly defined, reflecting the Court's longstanding policy of deference to state and local governmental decisions regarding local public need. Relying on prior decisions in which it had upheld condemnations for the purposes of slum clearance[23] and land redistribution,[24] the Court declared that this taking for economic development fell squarely within the traditional and long-accepted ideas of the reach of governmental power.

In a bitter dissent, Justice O'Connor argued that now there is nothing "to prevent the State from replacing any Motel 6 with a Ritz-Carlton, any home with a shopping mall, or any farm with a factory."[25] Dissenting separately, Justice Thomas warned that the harm stemming from this opinion will "fall disproportionately on poor communities."[26]

The decision created immediate outrage across the country. In the majority opinion of Kelo, the Court had noted that "[w]e emphasize that nothing in our opinion precludes any state from placing further restrictions on its exercise of the takings power. Indeed, many states already impose 'public use' requirements that are stricter than the federal baseline."[27] Within a year, more than half of the states responded to this opening and enacted legislation prohibiting the use of eminent domain for economic development purposes. Then in 2006, Ohio became the first state to have its highest court declare that a city could not take private property by eminent domain if its only justification was economic benefit.[28] In that case, a suburb of Cincinnati had wanted to take private property in order to build a $125 million project of offices and shops. The court held that under the public use requirement found in the Ohio constitution, economic development is not a sufficient reason to justify the taking of private property.[29] As to Kelo herself, she reached a settlement with the city whereby she was allowed to keep her home but was forced to move it to another location.

DISCUSSION QUESTION

2. Why should the government be able to take somebody's property without his or her consent? Give some examples of what you would view as legitimate uses of eminent domain.

---

[22]Kelo v. New London, 545 U.S. 469 (2005).

[23]Berman v. Parker, 348 U.S. 26 (1954).

[24]Hawaii Housing Authority v. Midkiff, 467 U.S. 229 (1984).

[25]Kelo, 545 U.S. at 503 (O'Connor, J., dissenting).

[26]Id. at 521 (Thomas, J., dissenting).

[27]Id. at 489.

[28]Norwood v. Horney, 853 N.E.2d 1115 (Ohio 2006).

[29]Id. at 1123.

f. Adverse Possession

Each night as Greg drove up his driveway, he paused to appreciate the lovely flowers he had planted alongside his fence, bordering his land. One night, however, he drove home to find the flowers dug up and the fence gone. After a few frantic calls he discovered that when he erected the fence, he had inadvertently placed it two feet over the property line and onto his neighbor's land. Does Greg have any legal recourse? The answer will depend on who owns the land—Greg or his neighbor. Even if the neighbor holds the deed to the property, it is possible for Greg to obtain real property rights through a process known as **adverse possession.** For someone to qualify for ownership in this manner, that person's use of someone else's property must be

Adverse possession
A transfer of real property rights that occurs after someone other than the owner has had actual, open, adverse, and exclusive use of the property for a statutorily determined number of years.

1. actual,
2. open,
3. adverse, and
4. exclusive

for a statutorily determined number of years, usually between five and twenty. If all these conditions are met, many states grant a right to assume legal control of that property. In this case Greg's use of the property was actual—he built a fence on the land. It was also open—anyone could view the fence. Adverse simply means that the use of the land interfered with that of the rightful owner. That element is also satisfied. Finally, because Greg placed a fence and not just flowers in the area, his use of the land was also exclusive. The only question that remains is whether in Greg's state he has used the land for the requisite number of years. If that element is also satisfied, then Greg and not his neighbor owns that strip of land. However, to ensure his claim, Greg should go to court and request that the court quiet title so that Greg, the adverse possessor, will have a marketable title to the land.

4. Transfer of Personal Property

Personal property changes hands in much the same way real property does. It can be sold, it can be given away, it can be seized for nonpayment of a debt, and it can become part of a person's estate. In addition, with personal property there is a distinction among lost, abandoned, and mislaid property. Property is classified as lost if the owner has involuntarily parted with it and does not know where to find it. On the other hand, if the owner deliberately placed it somewhere and then forgot where it had been placed, it is classified as mislaid rather than lost. It is considered abandoned property when the owner left it with no intention of coming back to reclaim it. If you find lost property, you acquire title that is good against everyone except the true owner. However, you may have to turn the property over to the police for a certain amount of time to ensure that the rightful owner does not return to claim it. On the other hand, if you find mislaid property, property that was inadvertently left behind, such as a ring next to a sink, then you acquire no ownership rights in it. Finally, if you find abandoned property, you become the owner.

Bailment
A temporary transfer of personal property to someone other than the owner for a specified purpose.

When personal property is only temporarily transferred to someone other than the owner for a specified purpose, a **bailment** occurs. For example, a bailment occurs when you take your clothes to be dry cleaned or your car to be repaired. A bailment also occurs when you contract with a moving company to move your furniture from one location to another. The owner is called the **bailor,** and the party taking temporary control of the property is called the **bailee.** The law imposes a duty on the bailee to exercise reasonable care toward the property while it is under the bailee's control.

B. ESTATE PLANNING

Estate planning is the analysis of a person's future financial needs and the development of strategies to meet those needs while the individual is alive, to expedite the probate process that follows death (see Section 4 below), and to avoid inheritance and estate taxes. In this context an **estate** is the total property of whatever kind, both real and personal, that a person owns at the time of his or her death. At the time of a person's death this property is distributed on the basis of the person's will and the terms of state laws with respect to such things as joint ownership rights, life insurance contracts, and probate laws.

1. Wills

A **will** is a legal expression of a person's wishes as to how his or her property should be distributed upon death. When someone dies without a valid will, that person is said to have died **intestate.** When this occurs, the person's property is distributed on the basis of guidelines laid down by the legislature of the state in which the deceased was domiciled (i.e., had his or her legal residence) at the time of death. Although these laws usually favor the spouse and the children, they may not correspond to how the deceased wanted to dispose of the estate. For this reason, as well as to take advantage of potential tax savings, it is generally desirable to have an up-to-date will.

In judging the validity of a will the courts focus on three factors: whether the testator was an adult, usually eighteen or older; his or her testamentary capacity; and whether the testator voluntarily executed the will. As to the second requirement of testamentary capacity, all that is required is that the testator know what he or she owns and what he or she wants to do with it, as well as knowing the "natural objects of the testator's bounty"—that is, the testator's spouse and other close relatives. The third requirement is intended to invalidate a will that the testator signed due to fraud or undue influence.

Consider the case of 86-year-old Ursula Lanning. Mrs. Lanning had ten children from a prior marriage to John Cathey and two children from her current marriage. When her first husband died, her older children petitioned for custody and they, not Mrs. Lanning, raised the youngest children.

Mr. and Mrs. Lanning received royalties for oil on property they owned and had combined assets of $2 million. In 1984, Mrs. Lanning had executed a will leaving the bulk of her estate to the two children of her second marriage. Each child of her first marriage (the Cathey children) would receive $1,000, and the rest of the estate would be divided equally between the two children of her second marriage (the Lanning children). In January 1996, Mrs. Lanning executed a new will that completely reversed the terms of her former will. The new will gave each of the Lanning children $1,000, and gave the remainder of

Bailor
The owner of the personal property that is being temporarily transferred as part of a bailment.

Bailee
The party taking temporary control of the personal property during a bailment.

Estate
The total property of whatever kind, both real and personal, that a person owns at the time of his or her death.

Will
The document used to express a person's wishes as to how his or her property should be distributed upon death.

Intestate
When a person dies without a valid will.

her $1 million estate in equal shares to the Cathey children. In April 1996, Mrs. Lanning had yet a third will drafted, and under it, all of Mrs. Lanning's children would share equally in the estate.

Following its appointment as conservator of the estate, Pioneer Bank moved to revoke the January 1996 will and to prevent the execution of the April 1996 will. The trial court determined that the January 1996 will was invalid and the petition to execute a new will should be denied because Mrs. Lanning lacked testamentary capacity. The Cathey children appealed.

Matter of Lanning
565 N.W.2d 794 (S.D. 1997)

[A]nyone over the age of 18 years who is of sound mind may make a will. We have defined "sound mind" for purposes of testamentary capacity as follows: One has a sound mind, for the purposes of making a will, if, without prompting, he is able "to comprehend the nature and extent of his property, the persons who are the natural objects of his bounty and the disposition that he desires to make of such property." Soundness of mind, for the purpose of executing a will, does not mean "that degree of intellectual vigor which one has in youth or that is usually enjoyed by one in perfect health." Mere physical weakness is not determinative of the soundness of mind, and it is not necessary that a person desiring to make a will "should have sufficient capacity to make contracts and do business generally nor to engage in complex and intricate business matters."

Testamentary capacity cannot be determined based on a single moment in time, but rather is based on consideration of the condition of the testator's mind a reasonable length of time before and after the making of the will.

Our review of the record supports the trial court's finding that Mrs. Lanning did not know the natural objects of her bounty. She could not, without prompting, name all 12 of the children born to her. The first time she was asked, by her own attorney at a January 19, 1996, hearing, Mrs. Lanning testified she thought she had six children born of the Cathey marriage. . . .

Mrs. Lanning also was unable to understand the nature and extent of her property. When asked about her assets, Mrs. Lanning testified she was "not right on top of this" and did not know "what everything is and where it's at." . . .

Mrs. Lanning's testimony regarding her disposition of property was conflicting. She testified she wanted to change her plan to be "fair" to all her children "alike." . . . Nevertheless, when asked if the petition disposed of her property as she wanted, she stated she hadn't made a decision on the disposal of her property yet. . . .

Based on the entire evidence, the trial court's finding of testamentary incapacity is not clearly erroneous. . . . We affirm.

CASE DISCUSSION QUESTIONS

1. What test did the court use to determine mental capacity to make a will?
2. Do you agree with the court's decision? Why or why not?

Testator/Testatrix
The person making a will to direct how his or her assets will be distributed at death.

Wills are classified as formal, informal, and nuncupative. A **formal will** is one that has been prepared on a word processor or typewriter and has been properly signed by the **testator** (the person making the will) and the required witnesses. (*Note:* In some states a female testator is known as a *testatrix*.) Will contests often revolve around arguments that the testator either was not competent or was unduly influenced. Should there be a will contest, the witnesses will be asked to testify as to whether the testator knew the extent of the testator's property and knew who the natural beneficiaries were. In addition, they will be asked to testify regarding whether the testator signed voluntarily, understood what was signed, knew it was a will, and asked the witnesses to sign.

A **holographic will**, or informal will, is one that was handwritten by the testator, without the witness signatures necessary for a formal will. Only about half the states recognize such wills as valid. A **nuncupative will** is an oral will. Few states recognize such wills, and those that recognize them do so only when the testator was in fear of imminent death and usually require at least two witnesses.

The standard will consists of a clause that identifies the testator, clauses making specific legacies or bequests, and signature clauses for the testator and witnesses. A gift of real estate in a will is called a **devise**, while a gift of personal property in a will is called a **bequest** or a **legacy**. The person named to receive the gift is called a **beneficiary**. The typical will also includes provisions for the payment of taxes and expenses, for funeral arrangements, and for the appointment of executors and guardians, as well as containing a simultaneous death clause. An **executor** (or **executrix**) is a person appointed by the testator to carry out the directions and requests in the will. A **guardian** is one who is given the responsibility of managing the affairs or property of a person who is incapable of administering his or her own affairs. For example, a guardian might be appointed to care for the decedent's minor children. A **simultaneous death clause** states that if a person named as a beneficiary in the will dies within a short period of time after the decedent dies, it will be assumed for purposes of the will that the person in question failed to survive the decedent. Such clauses are normally inserted for tax purposes. Without such a clause the estate of each decedent might be taxed as though each survived the other and hence inherited the property from the other. Therefore, estate taxes would have to be paid twice.

In some jurisdictions the courts will dispense with the need to call in witnesses to attest to the validity of a will if it contains a **self-proving clause.** Such a clause is actually a notarized affidavit, signed by the attesting witnesses. The clause simply states that the witnesses swear to the information that a probate court would need in order to admit the will to probate—that is, that the testator was at least eighteen years old, appeared to be of sound mind, and was not acting under any outside influence.

A testator can change a will with a codicil. The **codicil** has to be signed and witnessed like a will. Alternatively, the testator can destroy the old will and draft a new one.

2. Living Wills

A **living will** is not really a "will." It does not express a person's wishes as to how his or her property should be distributed upon death. Rather it is the expression of a person's wishes regarding the withholding or withdrawal of life-

Bequest
Also known as a legacy; a gift of personal property in a will.

Beneficiary
The person named in a will, insurance policy, or trust who receives a benefit.

Executor/Executrix
A person appointed by the testator to carry out the directions and requests in his or her will.

Self-proving clause
A notarized affidavit, signed by the attesting witnesses, that may eliminate the need to call witnesses during the probate process to attest to the validity of the will.

Codicil
A supplement or addition to a will that modifies, explains, or adds to its provisions.

Living will
Also known as a **medical directive**; a document expressing a person's wishes regarding the withholding or withdrawal of life-support equipment and other heroic measures to sustain life if the individual has an incurable or irreversible condition that will cause death.

support equipment and other heroic measures to sustain life if the individual has an incurable or irreversible condition that will cause death. These documents are also sometimes referred to as **medical directives.** Closely related are **health care proxies** and **durable powers of attorney,** in which individuals delegate legal authority to make medical or financial decisions for them if they are too incapacitated to make them themselves.

3. Trusts

Trust

A legal relationship in which one party holds property for the benefit of another.

Donor

Also known as a **grantor** or **settlor**; a person who creates a trust.

Trustee

The person appointed to administer a trust.

In order to avoid some aspects of probate and to minimize tax liabilities, modern estate planning often includes the creation of specialized trusts. A **trust** is a legal relationship in which one party holds property for the benefit of another. In this context the property is transferred to a trust fund, where it is to be used for the benefit of a designated person or persons rather than passing directly to them as part of the probate process. The person who creates the trust is called the **donor, grantor,** or **settlor.** The person appointed to administer the trust is the **trustee,** and the person who receives the benefits of the trust is the **beneficiary.**

The two types of trusts most commonly used in estate planning are inter vivos trusts and testamentary trusts. An **inter vivos trust** is one that is created before a person's death. *Inter vivos* is Latin for "among the living." A **living trust** is a commonly used type of inter vivos trust specifically designed to avoid probate. This type of trust allows a person, while still living, to benefit another. For example, parents might set up a trust that provides annual stipends to their children. Such inter vivos trusts can be either revocable or irrevocable. With a **revocable trust** the donor can change the beneficiaries and the terms, and even terminate the trust completely at any time and take back full ownership and control of the property. On the other hand, with an **irrevocable trust** the terms cannot be changed, and the donor cannot regain ownership or control of the property. A **testamentary trust** is created by a will and does not become effective until after the testator's death.

4. Probate Process

Probate

The process of court supervision over the distribution of a deceased person's property.

Administrator/ Administratrix

A person appointed by the court to carry out the directions and requests of someone's will.

Probate is the process of the court overseeing the distribution of property left by someone with a will or by someone who dies without a will. Jointly owned property does not have to go through probate, as it automatically passes to the joint owner. Also, unless the estate is named as the beneficiary, life insurance proceeds go directly to the named beneficiary.

The formal probate proceedings start with the filing of a petition in the probate court. This petition is usually accompanied by a certified copy of the death certificate and a will, if one exists. After payment of required fees, letters of testamentary are issued to give the **executor,** or a court-appointed **administrator** (or **administratrix**) if no executor is named in the will, the power to take control of the deceased's assets, pay the bills, and distribute the proceeds of the estate. Various inventories and other reports have to be filed with the court at several stages of this process. The probate process provides an opportunity for unsecured creditors of the decedent to submit claims for payment from the estate.

NETNOTE

The Uniform Probate Code has been adopted by eighteen states. You can access the text of the code as it has been adopted by each of those states by going to *www.law.cornell.edu/uniform/probate.html.*

a. Intestate Succession

The first step in the probate process is to determine whether the deceased had a will. As discussed earlier, if no will exists, the deceased is said to have died **intestate**, and the probate property will be distributed according to a series of rules established in state statutes. Most intestate laws give a set proportion of the estate to the surviving spouse, with the rest going to the children. If there are no children, the estate assets usually go first to the spouse, second to the decedent's parents, and then to brothers and sisters.

Heir is the generic term for someone entitled to inherit property left by the decedent. **Kindred** are those persons related to the decedent by blood. A relationship through blood is also known as **consanguinity.** Persons related by marriage are said to be related by **affinity.** A **lineal heir** is someone who is a grandparent, parent, child, grandchild, or great-grandchild of the decedent. **Descendants** or **issue** are those lineal heirs who descend from, or issue from, the decedent, such as children and grandchildren. A **collateral heir** is one who has the same ancestors but does not descend from the decedent. A brother or sister of the decedent would be a collateral heir. Figure 9-2 on page 328 illustrates these relationships.

If an heir is not alive at the time the assets are distributed, the dead heir's share passes to that person's heirs **per stirpes.** This is also known as the **right of representation.** For example, if a parent is dead, the children inherit the dead parent's share. Referring to Figure 9-2, assume the decedent's wife has predeceased him. If all three sons are still living, under most intestate statutes each son will receive one-third of the estate. If Son 1 has also predeceased his father, then his child, Grandchild A, will receive Son 1's one-third share. However, if Son 2 has predeceased his father, then Son 2's children, Grandchild B and Grandchild C, will only receive one-sixth each: their father's one-third, divided in half.

Adopted children have the same rights to inheritance as naturally born children. If there are no children, parents, siblings, aunts or uncles, nephews or nieces, or cousins, then the property reverts, or **escheats,** to the state.

b. Probating a Will

Although a will may exist, it may not be a valid will. There is always the possibility that the will in question may have been superseded by another will completed at a later date. The will may also be challenged on the grounds of **testamentary capacity.** Such a challenge argues that the testator was not of **sound mind.** In other words, the person lacked the required mental capacity to

Kindred
Also known as **consanguinity**; persons related to the decedent by blood.

Affinity
Persons related to the decedent by marriage.

Per stirpes
Also known as **right of representation**; a method of dividing an intestate estate whereby a person takes in place of the dead ancestor.

Escheat
A reversion of property to the state when there are no heirs.

Testamentary capacity
The mental capacity, also known as **sound mind,** whereby the testator understands the nature of his or her property and the identity of those most closely related to him or her.

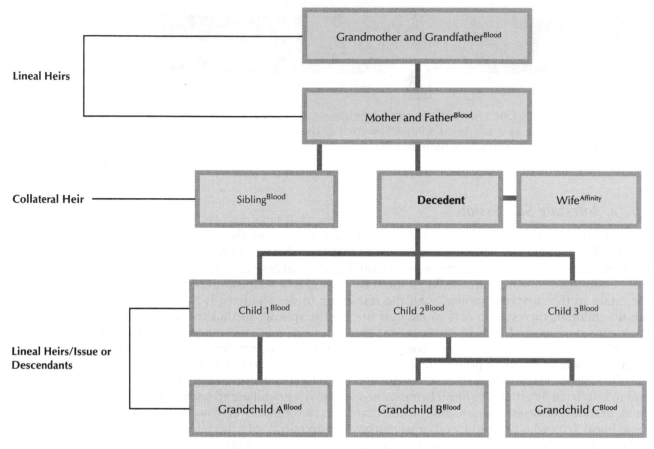

Figure 9-2   A Decedent's Intestate Heirs

understand the nature of his or her property or the identity of the people named in the will.

As indicated earlier, in order to protect against these types of claims, state laws usually require that the will be in writing, be signed by the testator, and be properly witnessed. In cases where the will is challenged, the attorney who drafted the will and the persons who witnessed it will be called on to testify as to the mental state of the testator at the time at which the will was signed.

In the following case there was a question as to whether the testator was suffering from undue influence. When Frank Till was eighty-three years old, he met Julie, the sixteen-year-old daughter of an old friend. Over the next four years the two became friends. Although Julie lived several hundred miles away from Frank, she frequently sent him letters and visited him while on vacation visiting her parents. In addition, when she learned that he was unhappy with his current nursing home, she helped him arrange to move to a new nursing home. She also drove him to an attorney when Frank wanted to cancel his power of attorney that he had given to one of his nephews and to change his will. On July 19, Frank prepared a new will that revoked his prior wills and gave the majority of his estate to Julie and her husband. When Frank died less than a month later, Frank's relatives, who were the sole beneficiaries under his prior will, contested the will, claiming it was a product of Julie's undue influence.

In the Matter of the Estate of Franklin J. Till
458 N.W.2d 521 (S.D. 1990)

This is an appeal from a will contest in which the circuit court held that the Last Will and Testament of the decedent, Frank Till (Frank), was a product of undue influence. As a result, the circuit court held this will to be invalid. We reverse. . . .

The first allegation of error raised by the executor regards the trial court's finding a confidential relationship existed between Julie and Frank. . . .

In the present case, the trial court not only found that Julie and Frank had a confidential relationship, but it also found that Julie actively participated in the preparation and execution of the will and that she unduly profited therefrom. As a result, the trial court further found that a presumption of undue influence had arisen in this case. Based upon our review of the entire evidence, we are firmly and definitely convinced that the trial court made a mistake in finding that a confidential relationship existed between Julie and Frank. Hence, Julie should not have been given the burden of going forward with the evidence to show she did not take advantage of her supposed dominant position. Also, a presumption of undue influence should not have arisen due to the absence of a confidential relationship between Julie and Frank. . . .

In prior cases in which we have been presented with the question of whether a confidential relationship existed between a testator and a beneficiary, we have looked to such factors as the amount of time that the beneficiary spent with the testator, whether the beneficiary handled many of the testator's personal or business affairs, and also whether the testator had ever sought the advice of the beneficiary. Although these are not the only factors that may be considered in determining if a confidential relationship exists between a testator and a beneficiary, they are nevertheless significant factors which demand consideration in the resolution of this issue.

Our review of the record reveals that none of the above-mentioned factors are present in this case. Julie spent very little time with Frank. . . . Julie never handled any of Frank's personal or financial affairs. Rather, Frank handled much of his own personal affairs and Robert [Frank's nephew] handled Frank's financial affairs. Finally, we note there is nothing in the record which indicates Frank ever sought the advice of Julie regarding any of his affairs. While Frank did give consideration to some of Julie's suggestions, Frank did not rely on Julie in any respect for advice.

Considering all of the aforementioned facts, we conclude there is not sufficient evidence to show that a confidential relationship existed between Julie and Frank. Hence, we conclude the trial court erred in finding a confidential relationship existed in this case. Furthermore, having reached this conclusion, we must also conclude the trial court erred in finding a presumption of undue influence had arisen in this case since in order to establish this presumption, one must first establish that a confidential relationship existed between the beneficiary and the testator.

Although we have concluded a presumption of undue influence had not been established in this case, this does not end our review in this particular case. The record reflects that the trial court also found that the will contestants had established, by a preponderance of the evidence, the four elements necessary to prove the existence of undue influence. These elements include: (1) decedent's susceptibility to undue influence; (2) opportunity to exert such influence and effect the wrongful purpose; (3) a disposition to do so for an improper purpose; and (4) a result clearly showing the effects of undue influence. . . .

We first address the trial court's finding that Frank was susceptible to the undue influence of Julie. The preponderance of the evidence in this case clearly indicates that Frank was not a person who was susceptible to undue influence. During the trial of this matter, several people who were acquainted with Frank, including two long-time friends, testified Frank was a very strong willed person. . . .

In finding that Frank was susceptible to the undue influence of Julie, the trial court emphasized that Frank was an old person who was in poor health. While it is true that Frank had some physical problems, there is no evidence that Frank was incapacitated to any significant extent as a result of these physical problems. . . .

Finally, the fact Frank was lonely at the nursing home with few relatives and friends to visit him was also listed as a factor indicating Frank's susceptibility to undue influence. This fact gives little support to the contention that Frank was susceptible to the undue influence of Julie, however, since Julie lived hundreds of miles away from Frank and obviously could not visit him on a regular basis. In fact, the finding that Frank was lonely and had few family and friends to visit him weighs more in the favor of upholding the will since Frank may very well have decided not to provide for those people who did not see fit to visit him. This is particularly true when one considers the undisputed fact that Frank was a strong-willed person. It is for these reasons that we hold, based upon an entire review of the evidence, that the preponderance of the evidence clearly does not support the conclusion that Frank was susceptible to the undue influence of Julie. Hence, we conclude the trial court was clearly erroneous in finding to the contrary. . . .

In resolving the issue of whether Julie had an opportunity to influence Frank it is important to note Julie lived hundreds of miles away from Frank. While it may have been true Frank was lonely and had few visitors, it is unlikely Julie could influence Frank by promising to keep him company since she lived so far away from Frank and since Frank did not like to use the telephone. Hence, Julie could not influence Frank by promising to visit him on a regular basis. . . .

We next address the issue of whether Julie had the disposition to exert undue influence upon Frank. The trial court held the preponderance of the evidence established that Julie did have such a disposition. Based upon our entire review of the record, we are firmly convinced the trial court erred in making this finding. The record clearly reveals Julie and Frank had a close relationship. Prior to Frank's death, Julie was accustomed to doing kind things for Frank including sending him letters and planning a birthday party for Frank. The record is devoid of any evidence which suggests that Julie ever tried to obtain any of Frank's property. In fact, the evidence points to the contrary. In assisting Frank to remove Robert as power of attorney, Julie sought to have the bank, not herself serve in that capacity. Nothing in the record reflects an attempt by Julie to obtain a power of attorney over Frank's property. If Julie did have a strong desire to gain control over Frank's property, it is likely she would have requested Frank to grant her a power of attorney. No such request was ever made. This strongly indicates that Julie did not have the disposition to exert undue influence upon Frank. . . .

Finally, we address the issue of whether, in the present case, there was a result clearly showing the effects of undue influence. . . . Prior to the 1988 will, the last will Frank had executed was in 1980. In the 1980 will, Frank left all of his estate to his relatives. What the trial court failed to note, however, was the fact that in 1980, Frank and Julie had not been acquainted with each other. Frank and Julie first became acquainted with each other in 1984 and thereafter developed what the trial court conceded was a close and loving relationship. Such a relationship is clearly revealed in the letters Frank and Julie sent to one another. Considering this strong relationship, it would be extremely unlikely for Frank not to provide for Julie after his death.

In the present case, there was an abundance of evidence showing Frank and Julie had a close and loving relationship. On the other hand, there was very little evidence, if any, which indicated Frank had a close and loving relationship with any of his collateral relatives. In fact, the greater weight of the evidence indicates Frank was upset with his relatives. It is undisputed that Frank's relatives placed him in a nursing home which he hated and considered as a "jail." Rather than making life more pleasant by frequent visits and contacts, Frank's relatives (at least in Frank's mind) ignored him. This is evidenced by the fact that Frank had to send Julie to Robert's house to recover several of his personal belongings and also some spending money. If Frank's relatives had paid more attention to Frank's needs and desires, Frank would not have had to make this request of Julie. . . .

Considering all of the above-mentioned facts, it is hardly surprising that Frank's "blood relatives" were excluded from the bulk of his estate. Also, considering the loving relationship that existed between Julie and Frank, it is not surprising that Frank decided to leave the bulk of his estate to Julie. . . .

As a final matter concerning the trial court's finding of undue influence, we note that in order for undue influence to exist, the influence "must be such as to destroy the free agency of the testator and substitute the will of the person exercising it for that of the testator." Considering the close relationship between Frank and Julie, it is extremely likely that Frank desired to provide for Julie to a significant extent after his death. This very likely was Frank's will or desire. Hence, if Julie did exercise influence over Frank, it is extremely unlikely that this amounted to undue influence since it is unlikely that Julie's will was substituted for that of Frank's insofar as Frank's last will and testament is concerned. This further supports the conclusion the trial court erred in finding Frank's last will was the product of undue influence.

From our examination of the entire record we are left with a firm and definite conviction the trial court erred in its findings of fact and conclusions of law. Accordingly, we reverse as to the denial of probate on the grounds of undue influence and we remand the matter to the court with instructions to admit the will to probate.

Judgment is reversed.

[Dissent omitted.]

CASE DISCUSSION QUESTIONS

1. The court noted that a presumption of undue influence arises if there was a confidential relationship between the testator and the beneficiary. What factors determine whether there was a confidential relationship? Did the court find such a relationship in this case? Why?

2. In the absence of proof of a confidential relationship, what are the four elements the court stated are necessary to prove the existence of undue influence?

3. The court concluded that there was no undue influence. Do you agree?

Because the probate process can require expensive fees and can delay the transfer and use of property in the estate, there has been a national movement to simplify the process, as well as to allow people with small estates to avoid it entirely. Some states exempt very small estates from this formal process and provide a simplified probate administration for intermediate-sized estates.

DISCUSSION QUESTION

3. Under what circumstances do you think people should be able to withdraw life-support equipment from someone who is in an irreversible coma? Should doctors be allowed to "help" a patient die by giving the patient a lethal dose of morphine or some other drug when the patient has an incurable disease, is in great pain, and wishes to end the misery? What should be done if that person is in a coma and did not have a formal living will but did tell a close relative that he or she did not wish to be kept alive in such a situation?

SUMMARY

Property law deals with ownership rights in real and personal property. Real property is land and anything permanently attached to land. Personal property is everything else. Property can be owned either individually or with others. Joint ownership that vests ownership rights upon death in the other co-owner(s) is known as joint tenancy with the right of survivorship. With a tenancy in common, the joint owner can pass his or her share to heirs at death. Real property can be transferred through sale, at the death of the owner, as a gift, through seizure by a creditor, by eminent domain, or through adverse possession.

Residential landlords are obligated to provide habitable living areas, and tenants can sue for constructive eviction if landlords fail to do so. Currently the states are divided as to whether their state open housing laws permit landlords to deny housing to cohabitating couples.

Estate planning involves the analysis of a person's future financial needs and of ways to ensure that the person's desires regarding distribution of assets will be accomplished after death. Wills and trusts are two of the most common estate-planning tools. If a person dies without a will, that person is said to have died intestate, and the property passes to the decedent's heirs according to that state's statutory intestacy scheme.

CRITICAL THINKING EXERCISES

1. Sam and Mary are planning to marry and build a home. With her own money Mary plans on purchasing a piece of property. She wants Sam's name to appear on the deed as a joint tenant. Do you think this is advisable?

2. For each of the following questions, assume the decedent died without a will and all the decedent's debts have been paid, as have all of his last sickness, funeral, and settlement of estate expenses. Base your answers on the following statutes:

Ch. 190, § 1 Spouse's share of property not disposed of by will
A surviving husband or wife shall be entitled to the following share in the spouse's real and personal property not disposed of by will:

(1) If the deceased leaves kindred and no issue, and the whole estate does not exceed two hundred thousand dollars in value, the surviving husband or wife shall take the whole thereof; otherwise such survivor shall take two hundred thousand dollars and one-half of the remaining personal and one-half of the remaining real property.

(2) If the deceased leaves issue, the survivor shall take one-half of the personal and one-half of the real property.

(3) If the deceased leaves no issue and no kindred, the survivor shall take the whole.

Ch. 190, § 2 Distribution of personal property
The personal property of the deceased shall be distributed in the proportions hereinafter prescribed for the descent of real property.

Ch. 190, § 3 Descent of real property

When a person dies seized of real property, it shall descend, subject to the rights of the husband or wife of the deceased, as follows:

(1) In equal shares to his children and to the issue of any deceased child by right of representation; and if there is no surviving child of the intestate then to all his other lineal descendants. If all such descendants are in the same degree of kindred to the intestate, they shall share the estate equally; otherwise, they shall take according to the right of representation.

(2) If he leaves no issue, in equal shares to his father and mother.

(3) If he leaves no issue and no mother, to his father.

(4) If he leaves no issue and no father, to his mother.

(5) If he leaves no issue and no father or mother, to his brothers and sisters and to the issue of any deceased brother or sister by right of representation; and if there is no surviving brother or sister of the intestate, to all the issue of his deceased brothers and sisters. If all such issue are in the same degree of kindred to the intestate, they shall share the estate equally; otherwise, according to the right of representation.

(6) If an intestate leaves no kindred and no widow or husband, his estate shall escheat to the commonwealth.

a. Juan died, leaving a wife, Carmen, whom he adored, and a brother, James, whom he hated and had not seen for the past thirty years. For each of the following, determine how much of Juan's estate Carmen will inherit and how much James will inherit.

(1) Juan leaves $180,000.

Wife Carmen:
Brother James:

(2) Juan leaves $500,000.

Wife Carmen:
Brother James:

(3) Juan leaves $500,000. Assume James had predeceased Juan but has a living child, James, Jr., whom Juan has never met.

Wife Carmen:
Nephew James, Jr.:

b. William died with an estate of $500,000. He left a wife, June, but no issue and no kindred. How much will June inherit?

c. Mary died with an estate of $500,000. She left a husband, John, and two living children, Rachel and Albert. How will the estate be divided among her husband and children?

Husband John:
Daughter Rachel:
Son Albert:

d. Roberto died with an estate of $500,000. He left a wife, Maria, and a living child, Bill, who has a child, Jill. His other child, Sam, predeceased him.

Sam has two living children, Tracy and Tim. How will the estate be divided among his wife, Maria; his child, Bill; his grandchild Jill; and his grandchildren Tracy and Tim?

Wife Maria:
Son Bill:
Grandchild Jill:
Grandchild Tracy:
Grandchild Tim:

e. Samantha died with an estate of $500,000. She left no husband and no children. They had all predeceased her. However, she did leave five grandchildren. Two of the grandchildren, Amy and Albert, are the children of her deceased son, Robert. The other three grandchildren, Bonnie, Brad, and Bennett, are the children of her deceased daughter, Emily. How will the estate be divided among the five grandchildren?

Grandchild Amy:
Grandchild Albert:
Grandchild Bonnie:
Grandchild Brad:
Grandchild Bennett:

||| REVIEW QUESTIONS

Pages 305 through 309

1. Define the two basic types of property.
2. Why is it important to know if property is classified as personal or real?
3. Describe the three basic types of freehold estates.
4. Why might it be important to know whether two friends shared ownership in a house as joint tenants or as tenants in common?
5. Describe two ways in which an owner's right to use his or her property may be limited by private arrangement.

Pages 309 through 323

6. Describe the four basic types of leasehold estates.
7. What is a constructive eviction, and how does it relate to the implied warranty of habitability?
8. What are land contracts? Can you envision any problems with their use? For example, do you think the terms of a standard land contract generally favor the buyer or the seller?
9. What is the purpose of the homestead exemption?
10. What is the purpose of zoning laws?
11. When can a zoning regulation be seen as a governmental "taking" such that the government must give the landowner just compensation?
12. According to the dictates of the Fifth Amendment, if a governmental body, such as a city, wants to take private property, what must it do and how have these requirements most recently been interpreted by the U.S. Supreme Court?

13. How does someone acquire property through adverse possession?
14. What is the distinction between lost and mislaid property? Why does it matter?

Pages 323-331
15. What does it mean to say someone died intestate?
16. Why is it not a good idea to die without a will?
17. Define each of the following:
    a. formal will
    b. holographic will
    c. nuncupative will
18. What is the purpose of a simultaneous death clause? Give an example of when such a clause would be relevant and why it would be important.
19. What is the purpose of a trust?
20. What types of property do not have to go through the probate process?

Chapter 10

Laws Affecting Business

*[Title VII of the Civil Rights Act of 1964] proscribes
not only overt discrimination but also practices that
are fair in form, but discriminatory in operation. . . .
[A]ny tests used must measure the person for the job
and not the person in the abstract.*
Chief Justice Burger, U.S. Supreme Court

INTRODUCTION

In Chapters 7 and 8, we presented the basic legal concepts of tort and contract
law. Those legal principles impact on a wide range of activities in both our
business and our personal lives. In this chapter we introduce more specialized
concepts, such as business formation, agency law, commercial paper, secured
transactions, and employment law, as they relate to common business activities.
Then, in the next chapter, we will focus on those specialized areas of the law
that have the greatest impact on our personal lives.

In this chapter, to help illustrate business law concepts, we will use the
experiences of an energetic group of entrepreneurs seeking the American dream
of owning their own business.

If the four friends decide to go into business together, there will be many
basic legal issues that they will have to confront. The first will be to decide what
form they would like their business to take. While they have at least four basic
forms from which to choose—**sole proprietorship, partnership, corporation,** and
limited liability company or **limited liability partnership**—each has its own
unique advantages and disadvantages. Second, they will probably need to secure

financing for their new business. In return, the creditor may ask for their written promise that they will repay the debt. Such a promise to pay is one form of **commercial paper.** Most suppliers and other creditors will want some additional guarantee that they will be repaid beyond the friends' simple promise that they will do so. Such a guarantee often takes the form of a **security interest;** that is, the debtor agrees to put up something as collateral that the creditor can then claim if the debtor fails to pay his or her debt. If the friends decide to share responsibility for running the business, they must also have a basic understanding of agency law. An **agent** is someone who has the power to act in place of another, known as the **principal.** Finally, unless they are able to run the business on their own, they will want to hire employees. The hiring and firing of employees raises a whole series of legal issues. We will concentrate on just two: at-will employment and federal discrimination law.

Case 8: The Four Friends

Four friends—Alice, Betty, Claire, and Dan—meet once a week to play bridge. During the course of one such meeting they began discussing the possibility of going into business together. Alice, who is thirty years old, is currently working as a baker for FreshStuff Bakeries, earning $22,000 a year. She loves her work but has long dreamed of opening her own bakery. She even has a name picked out—We BakeUm Fresh. Unfortunately she is a single parent raising two small children and does not feel she can afford to invest any of her approximately $5,000 in savings into such a business. Her friends, however, think that they may be able to help.

Betty, a sixty-two-year-old retired school teacher, just won $150,000 in the state lottery. In addition, she has $80,000 in retirement savings. Enjoying her retirement, she does not feel she would want anything to do with the day-to-day running of a business. However, assuming her money would not be at risk, she would be willing to invest up to $100,000 in the business.

Claire, a twenty-year-old college student, recently inherited a small two-story building, worth $50,000, in the downtown area that could easily house a bakery. She would be too busy with classes to help run the business, but she would be willing to let the others use her building to house the bakery.

Finally, Dan is twenty-five years old. He currently works odd jobs for a local landscaping company. However, he feels that he is a born salesperson and manager. Of the $10,000 he has in savings, he feels he could contribute up to $5,000 toward the business. He would love to quit his current job, at which he earns $19,000 a year, to serve as the bakery salesperson and manager.

A. THE FOUR BASIC BUSINESS FORMS

As indicated above, the first basic legal decision involved in the formation of a business is the legal form the business will take. Until recently the choices were limited to three basic business forms: sole proprietorship, partnership, or corporation. Starting in the mid-1990s, however, two new business forms emerged: the limited liability company and the limited liability partnership. These new forms are quite appealing to many businesses, as they provide some of the best benefits of both the partnership and the corporate form. Figure 10-1 summarizes the major features of each business type.

1. Sole Proprietorship

The sole proprietorship is the most common form of business organization. Approximately two-thirds of all businesses are sole proprietorships. However, while they account for the greatest number of businesses, as most are small businesses, their revenues do not begin to approach those produced by corporations.

There are several advantages to forming a business as a sole proprietorship. First, it is the simplest form to start and maintain, requiring a minimum of paperwork and expense. No forms have to be filed with any state agency unless the owner chooses to use a fictitious business name, such as "We BakeUm Fresh." In that case the owner may have to file a "doing business as" (DBA) certificate. Another primary advantage of the sole proprietorship is that the business's profits and losses are treated as personal profits and losses of the owner. Therefore, business profits are taxed as ordinary personal income, and the owner pays taxes on these business profits only once. In the corporate form of organization, on the other hand, the business's profits are taxed first at the corporate level and then again when they are distributed to the individual. Perhaps the major advantage, however, is that the owner retains complete control over the business operation.

The major disadvantage of the sole proprietorship is that all the owner's personal assets, regardless of whether they are related to the operation of the business, are available to satisfy business-incurred debts. For example, if the business is not able to pay its debts, in addition to seizing the assets of the business, creditors can take the business owner's home, automobiles, jewelry, or any other personal assets. Another disadvantage of this type of business operation is that the business dies with the owner. Finally, the owner of a sole proprietorship is often limited in funding to his or her own resources. One of the most common reasons for changing from a sole proprietorship to a partnership or corporate form is the need for additional capital to finance the business's expansion.

As the name implies, a sole proprietorship can have only one owner. In the hypothetical example we presented, only one of the four friends could be designated as the owner. They could not share ownership. (The remaining three could be either investors or employees or both, but they could not be owners.) If they want their business to have more than one owner, they will have to form a partnership, a corporation, or a limited liability company.

2. Partnership

Under the Uniform Partnership Act a partnership is defined as "an association of two or more persons to carry on as co-owners a business for profit." Notice that this provision requires that there be (1) two or more persons (2) who serve as co-owners and (3) run the business for profit. As with a sole proprietorship, partnership assets are only taxed once as personal income to the partners. However, a partnership must file an informational tax return with the Internal Revenue Service that indicates how the profits and losses were divided among the partners.

One of the major disadvantages to doing business as a partnership is that every partner assumes liability for the actions of every other partner. And as

Type of Business	Sole Proprietorship	Partnership	Corporation	Limited Liability Company	Limited Liability Partnership
Number of Owners	One	Two or more	One or more	Usually one or more	Two or more
Taxation	Single	Single	Double	Single	Single
Liability	Unlimited	Unlimited	Limited to capital contribution	Limited to capital contribution	Usually limited to capital contribution; sometimes liable for business debts and for own negligent acts
Ease of Formation	Very easy; nothing to file except "DBA" certificate if using fictitious name	Very easy; formed by partners' oral or written agreement; no filing required except for "DBA" certificate if using fictitious name (can also be established by partners' words or conduct—partnership by estoppel)	File articles of organization; pay annual fee; elect board of directors and officers; hold annual meetings; keep corporate records; use designation such as Corp. or Inc.	File certificate of organization; pay annual fee; use designation such as LLC	Register with the state; pay annual fee; use designation such as LLP
Managed by	Sole owner	Partners	Board of directors and officers	Manager (either an ower or a nonowner) or the owners	Usually the partners

Figure 10-1   A Comparison of the Basic Types of Businesses

with a sole partnership, personal assets can be taken to pay for business liabilities. Thus partners share in the liability for the actions of the partnership and for every other partner. This is known as **joint liability.** Usually, a plaintiff suing a partnership has the option of suing just the partnership, or the partnership and one or more selected partners, or just one of the partners. This is known as **joint and several liability.** For example, someone harmed by partner A's actions could sue the partnership, partner A and partner B, only partner A, or any combination of the above.

Some partnerships have both general and limited partners. This type of partnership is known as a **limited partnership.** The general partners (there must be at least one) have all the rights and liabilities of a normal partner within a **general partnership.** The limited partners, however, are only investors and do not actively participate in the management of the business. Therefore, their liability is limited to the extent of their investment in the partnership. In our example of the four friends both Betty and Claire might be interested in becoming limited partners, thereby limiting their liability to their investment. However, if they actually take part in making business decisions for the partnership, they forfeit their limited partner status.

A partnership can be created in one of three ways: by a written agreement, by an oral agreement, or by operation of law. While there is no requirement that a partnership agreement be in writing, by far the safest course is to use a written partnership agreement listing the rights and duties of each of the partners. Recall also that most states have a statute of frauds requiring any contract that cannot be performed in a year to be in writing.

If there is no written partnership agreement, then the provisions of the **Uniform Partnership Act (UPA)** will govern. The UPA has been adopted in all states except Louisiana. The UPA is a "gap filler." That is, its provisions control only if the partners have not covered a particular area in their written agreement. For example, if two people form a partnership, the UPA will assume they intend to share profits on a 50/50 basis. If the partners want the profits to be divided differently, they can provide for that so long as they explicitly state their intentions. It is obviously prudent to do so.

If two or more individuals through their actions of sharing control, profits, and losses act as though they are a partnership but have no written partnership agreement, it may be difficult to determine whether the parties intended to do business as partners. In those situations the court will frequently be called on to determine whether a partnership has been formed. There is no single requirement that determines whether a partnership exists. Rather, most courts have adopted a three-part test. They will look at the facts of each individual case to see whether there is

1. common ownership,
2. a sharing of the profits and losses, and
3. a shared right to management.

Consider, for example, a 1978 case from Michigan,[1] in which the court had to determine whether a surviving wife had worked with her now-deceased husband as a partner or as an employee. If Mrs. Miller could prove she and her husband were partners, she would be entitled to keep her half of the business, and only his half would have to be probated. However, if the business was found to be solely his, then the entire business would be subject to inheritance taxes.

In court she showed that in 1959 she met her future husband, Philip Miller. Mr. Miller asked her to marry him, to move to Jackson, and to help him run his nursery business. She agreed and gave up a well-paying job to move to Jackson. "Although Mr. Miller had been operating the business for some time, it was

Limited partnership
A partnership of at least one general partner and one or more limited partners. The limited partners' liability is limited to their investments so long as they do not participate in management decisions.

Uniform Partnership Act (UPA)
Known as a gap filler, the UPA comes into play only if terms are left out of a partnership agreement.

---

[1] Miller v. City Bank & Trust Co., 266 N.W.2d 687 (Mich. 1978).

close to failing at the time of their marriage. However, by 1974, the time of Mr. Miller's death, the business was prosperous."[2] Although she had not invested any money in the business, Mrs. Miller had acted as manager, keeping the books and hiring and firing employees. She and her husband also shared the profits 50/50. In addition, their business registration certificate said they were a partnership, and their checking account, vehicles, and equipment were in the partnership name. However, on their annual tax forms they listed the husband's occupation as sole proprietor and the wife's as housewife. Also, the husband's retirement fund listed him as owning a sole proprietorship.

Applying the traditional three-part test used to determine the existence of a partnership, the court found that the second element, sharing of profits, was not conclusive. The money given to the wife could be seen as wages or simply as her wifely due rather than as her partnership share. As to the third element, sharing the right of control, there was no evidence that she did anything other than what any trusted employee could do. Also, there was no written agreement to prove that she had the right to control the business. Therefore, the court concluded that a partnership had not been formed.

A partnership can also be created without any explicit agreement but rather by operation of a law, even when the parties involved do not want to form a partnership. While Mrs. Miller wanted to prove a partnership existed, in the following case a group of doctors tried to argue that they had not been working together as partners in order to escape liability for the malpractice of another doctor with whom they had worked.

Van Dyke v. Bixby
388 Mass. 665, N.E.2d 353 (1983)

The plaintiffs recovered judgments against the defendants solely on the theory that as partners of Richard E. Alt (Dr. Alt), a physician who died in 1975, they were liable for Dr. Alt's negligent treatment of the plaintiff Edwin S. Van Dyke (Van Dyke). In this appeal the defendants argue that the admissible evidence did not warrant a finding that a partnership existed. . . . We affirm the judgments and the order denying the defendants' motion for a new trial. . . .

1. We start with the question whether the jury were warranted in finding that the defendants were partners of Dr. Alt because, if not, they could not be held liable for his negligent conduct. The defendants concede, by implication, that, if certain challenged evidence was admissible, the jury would have been warranted in finding that a partnership involving Dr. Alt and the defendants existed between 1962 and the end of 1969. . . .

We turn our attention then to the defendants' challenges to the admission of evidence offered to show that The Johnson Clinic was a partnership from 1962 through 1969.[6] The judge

---

[6]The partnership was succeeded by a corporation on January 1, 1970. The judge instructed the jury not to consider the acts of Dr. Alt after January 1, 1970, on the issue of partnership. From the judge's charge, it is reasonably clear that the jury were informed that the defendants could be liable only for negligent acts or omissions of Dr. Alt during the time a partnership existed.

---

[2]Id. at 689.

properly admitted a certificate filed with the city clerk in Beverly in 1962 . . . stating that ten doctors, all of whom signed the certificate, were conducting a business in Beverly under the name THE JOHNSON CLINIC. Five of the defendants signed the certificate, as well as Dr. Peer P. Johnson and Dr. Alt. The certificate was relevant, although certainly not conclusive, on the question whether a partnership had been formed. A person conducting business under any title other than his real name, "whether individually or as a partnership," must file such a certificate.

The judge properly admitted, solely on the issue of the existence of a partnership, the endorsement page only of a professional liability insurance policy stating that the defendants and Dr. Alt were insured "individually and as co-partners dba [doing business as] Johnson Clinic." The fact that the defendants insured their liability as partners is some evidence that a partnership existed.

An October 31, 1969, billing statement of The Johnson Clinic was properly admitted. It showed that the defendants, Dr. Alt, and other physicians were associated with the clinic and stated that all checks should be made payable to The Johnson Clinic. It was relevant on the question whether the defendants were associated with Dr. Alt in the business at that time.

The statements of certain defendants in answers to interrogatories that they were partners and the testimony of two of those defendants that they were partners were admissible as tending to prove that they were partners. That evidence was admissible only against the defendant who made the statements. It was not binding on such a defendant, but it did show his state of mind concerning his relationship with Dr. Alt. Such questions do involve a legal conclusion. One might believe that he was a partner when, as a matter of law, he was not. The jury, therefore, must be made aware, as they were in this case through the judge's charge, that the partnership question must be determined on all the evidence.

2. There was evidence to warrant a finding that during the period when a partnership existed Dr. Alt was negligent in his treatment or failure to treat Van Dyke. . . . The jury could have found that Dr. Alt failed to remove the Penrose drain from Van Dyke after the 1969 operation. They could have found that, in his treatment of Van Dyke in 1969 after the drainage persisted, Dr. Alt failed to conform to accepted medical practice because he delayed taking substantial affirmative measures to investigate and to correct the cause of the condition. . . .

Order denying motion for a new trial affirmed.

Judgments affirmed.

CASE DISCUSSION QUESTIONS

1. Why was it crucial to the plaintiff's case to prove that Dr. Alt and the other doctors were working together as a partnership?

2. What evidence do you think was particularly relevant in answering that question?

As this case illustrates, if business owners give the appearance that they are partners, the courts may hold them liable for each other's actions, just as though they had intentionally formed a partnership. Sometimes this is referred to as **partnership by estoppel.** In other words, if the persons doing business together, through their words or conduct, lead others reasonably to believe that they are working as partners and others rely on that belief, a court may prevent (estop) the business owners from denying they are a partnership. Once a court finds a partnership by estoppel, the partners by estoppel are held liable for the actions of all the other partners.

Partnership by estoppel A partnership created by the words or actions of persons acting as though they were a partnership.

The death or withdrawal of any partner results in the dissolution of the partnership. However, the business entity often continues under a new restructured partnership agreement. The partnership can also end by the agreement of the partners.

3. Corporation

If our four friends are worried about assuming unlimited liability for their business actions, they may choose to form a corporation. A corporation can sue, be sued, own property, and make contracts in its own name. In a corporation, therefore, the investors have the advantage of being owners without having to assume any liability beyond the cost of their individual shares. While this limitation on liability may be important in the context of lawsuits, it may be somewhat illusionary when it comes to seeking credit because banks and other creditors often require shareholders in small corporations to provide personal guarantees to secure loans.

NETNOTE

The Electronic Data Gathering, Analysis, and Retrieval (EDGAR) system contains information that companies are required to file with the U.S. Securities and Exchange Commission (SEC). Two places to locate EDGAR filings are *www.sec .gov/edgarhp.htm* and *www.freeedgar.com*.

Another benefit of the corporate form is perpetual existence and transferability of shares. Unlike a partnership, it has a continuing life of its own that is not affected by the death of a stockholder or the exchange of shares of stock.

The major disadvantage of a corporation is the "double taxation" involved. The corporation's profits are taxed at the corporate level before dividends are distributed to shareholders. The shareholders then are taxed again on the dividends they receive. A **dividend** is a distribution of the corporate profit as ordered by the directors.

The primary document needed to form a corporation is the **articles of incorporation.** The articles of incorporation must include the legal name of the corporation, the purpose of the corporation, a list of the incorporators and directors, the name and address of a **registered agent** (the person designated to receive service of legal documents), and the share structure. Sometimes a business has its main place of business in one state but chooses to incorporate in another state. The articles of incorporation must be filed with the secretary of state for the state in which the corporation wishes to incorporate. Once a certificate of incorporation has been issued, the corporation must maintain certain types of records, file periodic reports to the appropriate state and federal agencies, and pay an annual fee. Its name must also include a designation such as Corp. or Inc. to alert those doing business with the company that it enjoys the benefits of corporate limited liability.

Most corporate capital comes from the sale of shares of stock to **shareholders.** Shareholders have no responsibility for the daily management of the corporation. They do, however, elect the board of directors. Also, they must approve fundamental changes, such as amending the articles of incorporation or agreeing to the sale of all of the corporation's assets. They receive a share of the corporation's profits when the board chooses to distribute some of those profits through dividends on its stock. The corporation can also borrow money when it needs capital.

The **board of directors** is responsible for the management of the corporation. The board stands in a **fiduciary** relationship to the corporation and to the shareholders. A fiduciary relationship is one in which a person in a position of trust is responsible for acting in the best interests of another party. In this case the board is responsible for doing what is best for the stockholders of the corporation. The board typically makes major policy and investment decisions, as well as appointing, supervising, and removing corporate officers.

The officers of the corporation are elected by the board and are responsible for executing the board's policies. They are also expected to provide leadership for the corporation. In addition, officers have a fiduciary duty to act in the best interests of the corporation and its shareholders. They can be held liable for their actions if they fail to live up to this obligation.

Some corporations are relatively small operations in which one person or the members of one family own all the stock. Such corporations are referred to as **close or closely held corporations.** The rights of shareholders of a closely held corporation usually are restricted with respect to the transfer of shares to others. Most larger corporations are publicly held, meaning that their stock is openly traded on the New York and American Stock Exchanges.

When a corporation incorporated in one state does business in another state, it is called a **foreign corporation.** In its own state it is referred to as a **domestic corporation.** A corporation formed in another country is known as an **alien corporation.**

Persons wishing to sue a corporation may try to "**pierce the corporate veil,**" that is, prove that the corporate form is really a sham and that the business should be treated as a sole proprietorship or partnership. This would mean that the personal assets of the owners could then be used to pay business debts. In order to pierce the corporate veil, the court would have to be convinced that it should set aside the normal protections offered by the corporate form. Factors that a court might look to in deciding whether to set aside the corporate form include situations in close corporations where the principal shareholder or shareholders did not follow the corporate formalities, such as by failing to issue stock, or commingled personal assets with corporate assets, such as by failing to set up a separate checking account for the corporation.

Piercing the corporate veil
When a court sets aside the unlimited liability protection normally given to corporate shareholders.

4. Limited Liability Company and Limited Liability Partnership

After reviewing the pros and cons of forming a sole proprietorship, a partnership, and a corporation, our four friends may wish to take advantage of one of

Limited liability company (LLC)
A new form of business ownership that gives small businesses the advantage of liability limited to the amount of the owner's investment along with single taxation.

the two new business forms, the **limited liability company (LLC)** and the **limited liability partnership (LLP)**, that are particularly attractive to small businesses. These forms are entirely creatures of statute and offer the best of two worlds—the limited liability that is afforded by the corporate form and the single taxation that occurs in a partnership. Because the statutes authorizing these new forms are of relatively recent origin (generally the early 1990s), there is very little case law as yet to guide us in understanding how the courts will view these new business forms.

The purpose of these new forms is to give a business the main advantage of the corporate form—limited liability—along with the main advantage of the partnership form—single taxation. The profits from the LLC or LLP are "passed through" to the members. Also, the limited liability protects the members from being sued for the negligent actions of their partners, but as is true with corporate limited liability, it cannot protect them from their own personal conduct.

Because limited liability companies and partnerships are creatures of statute, you must consult the statute in your individual state for the specific requirements for forming and running these business forms. Generally, most businesses appear to be following the route of becoming LLCs for two basic reasons. First, in most states the LLC form offers more liability protection. In an LLP the partners are protected from being personally liable for the wrongful acts of the other partners. However, in some states they remain liable for other business debts, such as rent or utilities. In an LLC personal liability is limited to the amount the person has invested in the company. Second, the LLC form avoids some of the disadvantages of having to use a partnership structure. For example, as you learned earlier, in a partnership each partner has authority to bind the business. With an LLC the business can provide that only some members have that authority and in fact may appoint a manager.

Usually, to become a limited liability company, a business must file articles of organization with the appropriate state office, such as the secretary of state, and pay an annual fee. The articles contain the name of the company, the period of its duration, the address, and the name and address of a statutory agent. The company name must include the words "Limited Liability Company," "Limited," or "Ltd." In addition, an operating agreement should set forth the basics of how the LLC will be run. Typical provisions would include information about how the LLC is to be managed; its purpose; the type and amount of contributions by each member, whether in cash, property, or service; how periodic allocations of income are to be made; transferability of a member's interest in the LLC; and when and how the LLC can dissolve.

Professional partnerships, such as law firms, appear to be gravitating more toward the LLP form. Because this form is essentially identical to a general partnership, except for obtaining the benefits of limited liability, law firms can easily make the change to a limited liability partnership with minimal disruption of the firm's internal workings. Typically, to attain LLP status, a business must register with the state and pay an annual fee. The partnership name must also add the LLP designation.

Today, all fifty states have adopted LLC and LLP statutes. However, one of the biggest disadvantages to operating as an LLC or LLP remains the uncertainty of how the LLC and LLP statutes will be applied and interpreted by the courts.

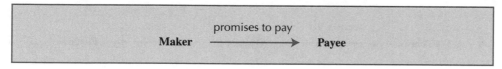

Figure 10-2   A Note

B. BORROWING MONEY

At some point most businesses will need to buy supplies or equipment on credit or to borrow cash. If a business writes a check to pay for new equipment or signs a promissory note promising to repay a loan, the law of **commercial paper** is involved. Whenever a supplier or creditor asks for a guarantee of repayment in the form of collateral, a **secured transaction** is created. Then if the debtor fails to repay the debt, the creditor can seize the collateral (the asset) that was used to secure the loan.

1. Commercial Paper

Commercial paper refers to a variety of instruments (written documents) used for making payments. Commercial paper has two basic functions: as a substitute for money and as a credit device. For example, if you pay for a new stereo with a check, you have just used a form of commercial paper (the check) to substitute for cash and to give yourself some free credit until the store cashes the check.

There are a lot of terms involved in how commercial paper is categorized. The important point is not to memorize all the terminology but to become familiar with it so that later, when you encounter your first client who has a legal problem involving commercial paper, you will be conversant with the basic terms. Commercial paper is categorized in the following ways:

1. as two- or three-party instruments,
2. as orders or promises to pay,
3. as bearer or order paper, and
4. as negotiable or nonnegotiable.

Therefore, the first way of categorizing commercial paper is by how many parties are involved. Notes only involve two parties. A **note** is a promise to pay money, whereby the **maker** signs the instrument promising to pay money to the **payee.** See Figure 10-2. These notes can be collectable either on a specific date in the future (time notes) or at any time the payee wishes to collect (demand notes). Installment notes establish a series of dates on which portions of the money are to be paid.

Three-party instruments include drafts and checks. A **draft** is a three-party instrument in which the **drawer** orders the **drawee,** usually a bank, to pay money to the **payee.** A **check** is a specialized form of a draft in which a bank depositor names a specific payee to whom funds are to be paid from the drawer's account. See Figure 10-3 on page 348.

Second, drafts and checks are classified as orders to pay, as each contains an order by the drawer to the drawee to pay money to the payee. Notes are promises to pay.

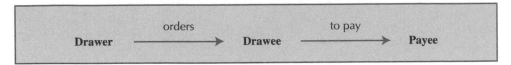

Figure 10-3   A Draft or Check. (For a check, the drawee is a bank.)

Negotiable instrument
Commercial paper that can be transferred by indorsement or delivery. It must meet the requirements of UCC § 3-104 to be negotiable. If it does not, a transferee cannot become a holder in due course but only gets the rights along with the liabilities of a contract assignee.

Third, instruments are also classified as being either **bearer paper** or **order paper**. Bearer paper will have written on its front a statement that it is payable to cash or payable to the bearer, or it will have a signature on the back, causing it to be indorsed in blank. An **indorsement in blank** occurs when an indorser simply signs his or her name and does not specify to whom the instrument is payable. Order paper states on its face "pay to the order of" a specific payee and has not been indorsed in blank on its back.

The fourth category, **negotiable** versus nonnegotiable, is the most essential category. Only if the paper is seen as negotiable can it be treated as a substitute for money. This is important because, as we mentioned above, one of the two main functions of commercial paper is as a substitute for cash. If the paper does not satisfy the requirements to be negotiable, that purpose has not been satisfied. Article 3 of the Uniform Commercial Code (UCC) spells out the requirements for an instrument to be negotiable. It must

1. be in writing,
2. be signed by the maker or drawer,
3. be an unconditional promise or order to pay,
4. state a specific sum of money,
5. be payable on demand or at a definite time, and
6. be payable to order or to bearer.

A person becomes a **holder** of a negotiable instrument that is bearer paper by proper delivery. If it is order paper, it must be properly delivered and have all necessary indorsements.

The reason all these steps are important is that if a note, check, or draft meets the requirements of negotiability, a holder can become a **holder in due course** and have the right not only to enforce the agreement but also to be exempt from some of the defenses that could have been asserted against the original payee. Under the UCC a person becomes a holder in due course only if that person receives the instrument under the following conditions. A holder in due course is someone

1. who gives value
2. in good faith (a subjective standard) and
3. without notice that the instrument is overdue or has been dishonored or has any claims against it or defenses to it (an objective standard).

Again, the main benefit of being a holder in due course, rather than a mere holder, is that a holder in due course takes the instrument free of most claims against payment. A holder, on the other hand, takes the instrument along with any defenses to its payment. Therefore, for commercial paper to truly work as a substitute for cash, it must be negotiable, and the person owning it must be a holder in due course. The steps by which commercial paper becomes negotiable and its owner becomes a holder in due course are outlined in Figure 10-4.

For example, assume a bakery owner signs a contract with a furniture store. The store gives the bakery owner a loan so that she can purchase new tables and chairs for her reception area. In return, the bakery owner promises to repay the loan on an installment basis. Later a finance company purchases that installment contract from the furniture store. The finance company becomes the holder in due course. Assume the furniture proves to be defective. If the store had not sold the installment contract, the bakery owner might have been able to stop paying on the loan to the furniture store by raising a defense of breach of warranty. However, the holder in due course doctrine prevents the bakery owner from being able to raise those defenses against the finance company. Therefore, even though the furniture is defective, the bakery owner will have to pay what it owes to the finance company. It can separately sue the furniture

Figure 10-4 How to Determine Whether a Holder in Due Course Has Been Created

Front of the Paper	Do you have a negotiable instrument? ■ in writing and ■ signed by maker or drawer and ■ unconditional promise or order and ■ sum certain in money and ■ payable on demand or at a definite time and ■ to order or bearer If any are missing ≠ a negotiable instrument—STOP. If all present, continue on.
Back of the Paper	Is the transfer proper? ■ bearer paper—transfer alone enough ■ order paper—transfer plus proper indorsements If transfer was not proper—STOP. If transfer was proper, continue on; you have a HOLDER.
What Happened	Did the holder do all of the following? ■ give value ■ in good faith ■ with no notice that the instrument is overdue or has been dishonored or that there is a defense or a claim to it. If all were not met—STOP. If all were met, you have a HOLDER IN DUE COURSE.
Type of Defense Being Raised	Is the defense a **personal defense,** such as a defense to a breach of contract claim? Then the holder in due course takes the instrument clear of that defense. Is the defense a **real defense,** such as forgery of the instrument? Then the defense is good even against the holder in due course.

store for breach of warranty, but the results of the lawsuit do not affect the bakery owner's obligation to pay the finance company.

2. Secured Transactions

Attachment
Gives the creditor rights against the debtor. The creditor must possess the collateral or have a signed security agreement, have given something of value, and the debtor must have rights in the collateral.

Perfection
Gives the creditor rights ahead of other creditors. The creditor must first be attached and then possess the collateral, or file a financing statement, or give money to purchase consumer goods.

Often a creditor will demand more than the mere promise to repay a debt. The creditor will want assurance that if the debtor fails to repay the debt, the creditor can take something of value from the debtor. Therefore, promises to repay a debt are often secured by a pledge of something of value, such as a house, an automobile, or a stock certificate, that the creditor can seize and sell if the debtor does not repay the loan. Such an arrangement is known as a **secured transaction** and is governed by Article 9 of the UCC.

A creditor who has obtained a security interest has two main concerns if a debtor defaults. First, the creditor wants to be able to obtain the secured collateral from the debtor. This is done through an **attachment.** Second, the creditor wants to have priority over other creditors who may also have rights to the same collateral. This is done through a process called **perfection.**

As to the first concern, for a creditor to have an enforceable security interest against the debtor, the following must be true:

1. the creditor must either possess the collateral or have a signed **security agreement,**
2. the creditor must have given something of value, and
3. the debtor must have rights in the collateral.

If all three requirements are satisfied, it is said that the security interest has attached. The creditor's first concern is satisfied. If the debtor fails to pay, the creditor can take the collateral from the debtor unless another creditor has a higher right to the collateral by having a perfected security interest.

For a creditor to establish priority over other creditors, the creditor must obtain a **perfected security interest** by taking additional steps. The requirements for perfection are

1. possessing the collateral, or
2. filing a **financing statement,** or
3. giving money to purchase consumer goods.

The purpose behind each of these three methods is to give third parties notice that the creditor has "first dibs" on the property. This gives the perfected creditor first rights to the collateral over other creditors.

Therefore, the difference between attachment and **perfection** is that with attachment the creditor has an enforceable security interest against the debtor. With perfection the creditor also has priority to the collateral over other creditors. See Figure 10-5.

A special type of perfected security interest, a **purchase money security interest,** arises when a seller gives credit to a debtor so that the debtor can purchase an item. For example, if a car dealership lets you purchase a car on credit, the dealership will have a purchase money security interest in the car you buy. Also, if another creditor, such as a bank, gives value to a debtor so that the debtor can purchase the item, a purchase money security interest is formed. This could occur in the prior example if you obtained your loan from a credit union

Attachment (must occur first)	Perfection (can occur only after attachment)
Notice to the debtor that the creditor has an interest in the goods: **1a.** actual possesion *or* **b.** a security agreement, signed by the debtor, describing the collateral *and* **2.** the creditor has received something of value *and* **3.** the debtor has rights in the collateral.	*Notice to third parties* that the creditor has an interest in the goods: **1a.** possession *or* **b.** a filed financing statement that was signed, describing the collateral, with addresses of the debtor and creditor *or* **c.** a purchase money security interest in consumer goods.

Figure 10-5 A Comparison of Attachment and Perfection

instead of the car dealership. The credit union would then have a purchase money security interest in your car. If you purchased the car for your own use, as opposed to that of your business, then the security interest would also be classified as a purchase money security interest in consumer goods. Purchase money security interests in *consumer* goods are automatically perfected without the necessity of filing a financing statement.

While those with a perfected security interest will prevail over those whose interest has only attached, even a creditor with a perfected security interest will lose to a **buyer in the ordinary course of business.** If this were not so, once a store took out a secured loan, everyone would stop shopping at that store. For example, assume Sears took out a secured loan in order to increase its inventory of refrigerators. Without the rule protecting the ordinary buyer, if Sears failed to pay back the debt, the bank could go after customers, trying to reclaim the refrigerators they had purchased from Sears.

In sum, keeping in mind the two purposes of obtaining a security interest, to get repaid and to be first in line for the security, the general order of priorities among creditors and buyers is as follows:

1. buyers in the ordinary course of business,
2. perfected purchase money security interests,
3. perfected security interests,
4. lien creditors (such as a trustee in bankruptcy),
5. unperfected security interests, and
6. general creditors.

Finally, a security interest can be retained in collateral even when the collateral changes in character or location. For example, there can be a security interest in proceeds or after-acquired property. This is known as a **floating lien.** Assume our four entrepreneurs introduced at the beginning of the chapter obtain a loan to purchase an oven for their bakery. In addition to getting a security interest in the oven, the creditor who loans the money for the oven's purchase can also acquire a security interest in the proceeds from the bakery sales and in property, such as a new refrigerator, that the bakery later acquires.

C. AGENCY LAW AND AN EMPLOYER'S RESPONSIBILITY FOR AN EMPLOYEE'S ACT

Returning to the hypothetical we introduced at the beginning of the chapter, unless Alice chooses to run her business as a sole proprietorship with no employees, she will need to worry about how her potential partners' or employees' actions can affect her business. If she and her friends decide to form a partnership, corporation, or limited liability company, each will be seen as an agent of the others and of the business. Therefore, the actions of one of them would affect all of them. Their employees may also be given agency powers. Finally, a business is always responsible for the negligent acts of its employees when the employees are acting within the scope of their duties.

1. Agency Law

Agent
Someone who has the power to act in the place of another.

Principal
A person who permits or directs another person to act on the principal's behalf.

Fiduciary duty
A legally imposed obligation to act in the best interests of the party to whom the duty is owed.

An **agent** is someone who has the power to act in the place of another. A **principal** is a person who permits or directs another person, the agent, to act on his or her behalf, subject to the principal's direction and control. When an agent is authorized to act in the principal's place, the acts of the agent become binding on the principal. For example, in a partnership each partner is an agent for the partnership. Therefore, each partner has the right to make decisions that will bind the partnership as a whole.

In a principal-agent relationship the agent owes a **fiduciary duty** to the principal. As explained earlier, a fiduciary duty is a legally imposed obligation to act in the best interests of the party to whom this duty is owed. Because of this fiduciary duty, agents owe their principals competent performance, notification of any important information (notice to the agent is considered to be notice to the principal, so the agent must keep the principal informed), loyalty, obedience, and an accounting of all moneys spent and earned. Therefore, agents must not place themselves in a conflict of interest situation and must exercise reasonable care, skill, and diligence in carrying out the principal's instructions. An agent who fails to fulfill these duties is liable for damages that result from this failure.

Ethics Alert

Many of the ethical requirements governing the attorney-client relationship are grounded in the fiduciary duties that any agent owes her or his principal. For example, the agent's duty of loyalty requires that the agent not represent two principals at the same time unless both know and consent to the representation. Similarly, an attorney cannot represent two clients if to do so would be against the best interests of either. An agent must keep all information confidential; an attorney must always respect the client's confidences. Finally, the agent's duty to give an accounting of all dollars received and paid is similar to the requirement that attorneys keep all client accounts separate and never commingle the client's and the firm's funds.

The principal, in turn, must cooperate with the agent and compensate the agent for losses incurred in the course of discharging the assigned duties. The principal must also pay the agreed-on fee for the agent's services.

2. Employees versus Independent Contractors

When a business—whether a sole proprietorship, partnership, corporation, or limited liability partnership—pays people to work for it, these individuals can be hired either as employees or as independent contractors. An **employee** is someone who works for another person or an organization in what the law has defined as an employer-employee relationship. In such a relationship the worker is typically paid an hourly wage or a monthly salary to perform a variety of tasks assigned by the employer, and the employer is responsible for withholding money for taxes and Social Security. Finally, the employer maintains control over both the task and how the task is to be performed.

An **independent contractor,** on the other hand, is someone who contracts to perform a specific service for a set fee. The employer does not withhold taxes or make contributions to retirement funds or health insurance for an independent contractor. Another difference is that contractors are usually expected to supply their own tools. Ultimately the employer dictates the task to be done, but the independent contractor determines how the task is to be performed.

The distinction between employees and independent contractors is important because the duties, responsibilities, and liabilities of the employer differ between the two classes of workers. The courts have developed various tests to help determine if an employer-employee or an employer–independent contractor relationship exists. While no one factor will be determinative, the courts look to who controls the details of the job, who owns the tools, who sets the hours, how the worker is paid, whether the worker receives training from the employer, whether the worker is engaged in a business different from the employer's, and how long the worker has been employed.

Figure 10-6 shows some of the important differences between employees and independent contractors.

Figure 10-6   The Employee versus the Independent Contractor

Employee	Independent Contractor
Can be agent of employer	Can be agent of employer
Employer responsible for negligent acts under doctrine of respondeat superior	Employer not responsible for negligent acts unless they involve ultrahazardous activities
Must be covered by worker's compensation, unemployment, etc.	Not covered by employer's worker's compensation, unemployment, etc.
Works for hire belong to employer	Works for hire belong to the independent contractor unless a writing gives rights to employer

3. Employees and Independent Contractors as Agents

If an employee's duties include dealing with third parties, the employee may be seen as an agent of the employer. Therefore, an employee's acts can bind the employer. An employer–independent contractor relationship may involve an agency relationship if the independent contractor is hired to act on the employer's behalf in making arrangements with third parties. For example, if you wish to sell your house, you will most likely hire a real estate agent. The agent will then negotiate on your behalf and can through his or her actions bind you to contracts formed with third parties. However, because you will have little control over how the agent performs the job, the real estate agent will not be seen as your employee. Therefore, either an employee or an independent contractor can be an agent, but not all employees and not all independent contractors are agents. Figure 10-7 illustrates the relationships between employees, independent contractors, and agents.

4. Employer's Liability for Acts of Employees

When someone is hurt by an employee's negligence, that person will often choose to sue the employer rather than or in addition to the employee because the employer has "deeper pockets"—that is, more resources to pay a large damage award. The extent to which an employer is held accountable for the acts of a worker depends on three factors. First, was the worker an employee or an independent contractor? Second, if the worker was an employee, did the employee act negligently? Third, at the time of the injury was the employee engaged in work of the type the employee was hired to perform? This last question requires an assessment of whether the employee was working within the "scope of employment" or, as the courts so quaintly put it, whether the employee was "on a frolic of the employee's own."

Respondeat superior
The tort theory that an employer can be sued for the negligent acts of its employees.

The employer-employee relationship follows common law principles that grew out of the master-servant relationship. Under the doctrine of **respondeat superior,** a Latin expression translated as "Let the master answer," a business may be sued for the negligent acts of one of its employees. On the other hand, an employer is generally not responsible for the negligent actions of an independent contractor unless the contractor is engaged in an ultrahazardous activity, such as dynamiting. In such a case the employer is still held liable because not to do so

Figure 10-7   Relationship between Employees, Independent Contractors, and Agents

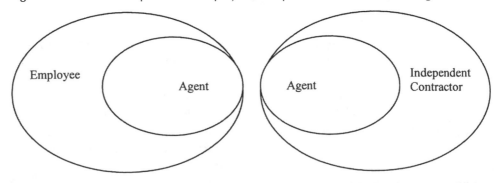

would encourage employers to hire independent contractors simply to avoid liability in admittedly dangerous situations.

Therefore, to find an employer responsible under the doctrine of respondeat superior, a plaintiff must prove that

1. a true employer-employee relationship existed,
2. the employee was legally responsible for the injury, and
3. at the time of the negligent action the employee was "working within the scope of his or her employment."

In order to establish that the employee was working within the "scope of employment," the plaintiff will have to show that the employee responsible for the injury was at that time engaged in work of the type he or she was hired to perform. If the employee was "on a frolic of his or her own," the employer is not responsible. For example, if Joe, a driver for Pizzas Are Us, negligently causes an accident while delivering a pizza, the company will be liable. However, if while returning from a delivery Joe decides to take an unauthorized side trip to visit his girlfriend and negligently injures someone, the company should not be held responsible for Joe's unauthorized side trip. In the following case the court acknowledges that it is much easier to state the rule than it is to apply it to the facts of a specific case.

O'Connor v. McDonald's Restaurants of California, Inc.
220 Cal. App. 3d 25, 269 Cal. Rptr. 101 (1990)

Plaintiff Martin K. O'Connor appeals summary judgment favoring defendants McDonald's Restaurants of California, Inc., and McDonald's Corporation (together McDonald's) on his complaint for damages for personal injuries on a theory of McDonald's vicarious liability for the negligence of its employee Evans. . . .

I
Facts

In reviewing the propriety of the summary judgment, we state the facts in the light most favorable to O'Connor.

From about 8 P.M. on August 12, 1982, until between 1 and 2 A.M. the next day, Evans and several McDonald's coworkers scoured the children's playground area of McDonald's San Ysidro restaurant. The special cleaning prepared the restaurant for inspection as part of McDonald's "spring-blitz" competition. Evans—who aspired to a managerial position—worked without pay in the cleanup party at McDonald's request. Evans's voluntary contribution of work and time is the type of extra effort leading to advancement in McDonald's organization.

After completing the cleanup, Evans and four fellow workers went to the house of McDonald's employee Duffer. Duffer had also participated in the evening's work. At Duffer's house, Evans and the others talked shop and socialized into the early hours of the morning. About 6:30 A.M., as Evans drove from Duffer's house toward his own home, his automobile collided with O'Connor's motorcycle.

II
Superior Court Proceedings

O'Connor filed a lawsuit for negligence against Evans, McDonald's and others. O'Connor complained of serious injuries resulting in permanent disability and the loss of his left leg below the knee. The suit claimed McDonald's was liable for negligence on a theory of respondeat superior.[1] . . .

III
Analysis

The central issue before us is of some antiquity. In 1834 Baron Parke addressed the issue: "The master is only liable where the servant is acting in the course of his employment. If he was going out of his way, against his master's implied commands, when driving on his master's business, he will make his master liable; but if he was going on a frolic of his own, without being at all on his master's business, the master will not be liable." *Joel v. Morison* (1834) 6 Car. & P. 501, 503, 172 Eng. Rep. 1338, 1339.

Unfortunately, as an academic commentator observed in 1923, "It is relatively simple to state that the master is responsible for his servant's torts only when the latter is engaged in the master's business, or doing the master's work, or acting within the scope of his employment; but to determine in a particular case whether the servant's act falls within or without the operation of the rule presents a more difficult task." . . .

Whether there has been a deviation so material as to constitute a complete departure by an employee from the course of his employment so as to release employer from liability for employee's negligence, is usually a question of fact. . . .

Here the evidence . . . raises triable issues on the factors bearing on whether Evans completely abandoned the special errand in favor of pursuing a personal objective.

A. Evans's Intent

. . . The record contains evidence McDonald's encourages its employees and aspiring managers to show greater dedication than simply working a shift and going home. O'Connor presented McDonald's operations and training manual and employee handbook to demonstrate McDonald's fosters employee initiative and involvement in problem solving. Such evidence could reasonably support a finding of "a direct and specific connection" between McDonald's business and the gathering at Duffer's because the gathering was consistent with the "family" spirit and teamwork emphasized by McDonald's in its communications with employees. Such evidence could also reasonably support a finding McDonald's emphasis on teamwork made a group discussion of McDonald's business at Duffer's house a foreseeable continuation of Evans's special errand. . . .

B. Nature, Time, and Place of Evans's Conduct

McDonald's contends the gathering at Duffer's house after normal business hours was an informal social function unconnected to Evans's special errand for his employer. However, O'Connor submitted evidence suggesting the gathering benefited McDonald's, occurred at Evans's fellow employee's house immediately after McDonald's place of business closed, consisted of continuation of employees' discussion about the spring blitz, and was inspired by the spirit of competition engendered by McDonald's. . . .

C. Work Evans Was Hired to Do

McDonald's contends the asserted managerial discussions at Duffer's house went beyond the scope of work Evans was hired to do. However, O'Connor introduced evidence suggesting Evans was in training to become a manager and was expected to show initiative in his work to be worthy of future promotion. Such evidence raises an inference Evans's participation in discussions at Duffer's house did not exceed the scope of his assigned work. . . .

F. Amount of Time Consumed in Personal Activity

McDonald's contends Evans stopped at Duffer's home for four hours on his own volition, for his own enjoyment and without McDonald's explicit direction or suggestion. However, O'Connor presented evidence showing much of the discussion at Duffer's home was related to Evans's employment at McDonald's. Such evidence raises a triable factual issue about the combination of personal entertainment and company business at Duffer's house. "Where the employee

---

[1] "Under the doctrine of respondeat superior, an employer is liable for the torts of his employees committed within the scope of their employment."

may be deemed to be pursuing a business errand and a personal objective simultaneously, he will still be acting within the scope of his employment."

G. Conclusion

The superior court found—and the parties here do not challenge—Evans's voluntary participation in the spring blitz until after midnight constituted a special errand on McDonald's behalf. The question here is whether the gathering at Duffer's to discuss the spring blitz and socialize constituted a complete departure from the special errand.

Because disputed factual questions and reasonable inferences preclude determination as a matter of law of the issue whether Evans completely abandoned his special errand, the court should have denied McDonald's motion for summary judgment.

The summary judgment is reversed.

CASE DISCUSSION QUESTIONS

1. What factors will be particularly important in determining whether an employee is "on a frolic of his or her own"?

2. Why did the court reverse summary judgment in this case? Does this mean the plaintiff will be able to hold McDonald's liable for his injury?

D. EMPLOYMENT LAW

Prior to the Industrial Revolution most workers in the United States were either self-employed or worked as part of a family unit. After the Civil War the percentage of people working for businesses grew rapidly, and the courts applied the concept of employment "at will" to allow employers to hire and fire employees without government interference. When Congress first tried to curb the use of child labor and set limits on the number of hours employees could be required to work, the U.S. Supreme Court struck down such legislation on the grounds that it violated the business owners' substantive due process right to "freedom of contract."

Although the doctrine of at-will employment still remains, the Supreme Court rejected the right to "freedom of contract" in a series of cases beginning in 1934. Today, with a few limited exceptions (usually based on the number of employees), most businesses in the United States are covered by federal and state statutes that limit the freedom of employers with regard to their employees' working conditions. For example, statutes set a minimum age at which someone is eligible to work, prohibit discrimination in hiring and promotion, establish minimum wages, establish overtime pay requirements, impose safety standards for the workplace, and establish procedures whereby workers can seek union representation and collective bargaining. Workers' compensation laws, unemployment insurance requirements, and regulations of employee benefit plans represent other areas of employment law. Public employers—local, state, and the federal government—are also constrained by constitutional restrictions, such as those imposed by the Fifth and Fourteenth Amendments' due process and equal protection clauses.

Employment law is a vast topic, and it would be impossible to even mention all of its aspects in an introductory text. Therefore, our approach in this section is much more limited. We will focus our discussion on contemporary judicial interpretations of the concept of employment at will and on several key federal antidiscrimination statutes.

1. Title VII: Discrimination Based on Race, Color, Religion, Sex, or National Origin

Until 1964 it was perfectly legal for private employers to discriminate against current and potential employees based on their race, sex, or national origin. Congress dramatically changed this with the passage of Title VII of the Civil Rights Act of 1964. With the passage of the Civil Rights Act, Congress hoped to stop all forms of discrimination, whether in voting, education, public accommodations, or employment.

a. Introduction to Title VII

Title VII of the Civil Rights Act of 1964 deals specifically with employment. It states that

> [i]t shall be an unlawful employment practice for an employer (1) to fail or refuse to hire or to discharge any individual, or otherwise to discriminate against any individual with respect to his compensation, terms, conditions, or privileges of employment, because of such individual's race, color, religion, sex, or national origin.[3]

NETNOTE

The EEOC home page is located at *www.eeoc.gov.*

In Title VII Congress also established the Equal Employment Opportunity Commission (EEOC) and delegated to it the task of developing regulations to more specifically delineate what is unlawful behavior. It also provided that persons who feel they have been discriminated against must first file claims with the EEOC, or a similar state agency, before taking their cases to court.

As you will recall from Chapter 2, the federal government is a government of limited powers. Congress can legislate only in those areas listed in the U.S. Constitution. One of those areas involves regulating interstate commerce. To ensure that it was acting within its constitutional powers, before the passage of the Civil Rights Act Congress held hearings during which numerous witnesses testified how commerce was being impeded by various segregation practices, including those that prevented some traveling salespersons from staying in local motels and eating in local restaurants.

In addition, to meet the argument that only those employers who have an effect on interstate commerce should be covered, Congress limited the definition of employer to those with twenty or more employees. Since then Congress has amended the statute to reduce that number to fifteen employees. Does that mean that employers with less than fifteen employees can still freely discriminate?

---

[3]42 U.S.C.S. § 2000e-2(a) (2008).

Perhaps. The answer depends on state law. Although Congress has prohibited discrimination by employers with fifteen or more employees, it has not pre-empted the field. States are free to legislate so long as their statutory scheme does not conflict with the federal prohibition. For example, in Massachusetts, employers of six or more employees may not discriminate on the basis of race, color, religious creed, national origin, sex, sexual orientation, or age.

In addition, in 1997 the U.S. Supreme Court ruled that "employee" includes any employee on the weekly payroll no matter how many days the employee actually worked in a given week. Therefore, under the federal statute an employer could have fifteen part-time employees and still be covered by Title VII.[4] Note, however, that Title VII covers only employees, not independent contractors. For example, in a Seventh Circuit decision the court held that a staff doctor could not sue his employing hospital, as he was an independent contractor and not an employee of the hospital.[5]

As originally proposed, Title VII would not have prohibited sex discrimination. However, a congressman from the South proposed an amendment from the floor to add sex to the list of protected categories. The legislative history recording the debate[6] on this amendment is an interesting study in politics. From the following brief excerpt see if you can divine why Congressman Smith proposed the amendment and why some congresswomen, whom you would think would favor it, instead were opposed to the amendment.

Mr. Smith of Virginia. Mr. Chairman, this amendment is offered . . . with our desire to prevent discrimination against another minority group, the women, but a very essential minority group, in the absence of which the majority group would not be here today. . . .

Mr. Cellar. Mr. Chairman, I heard with a great deal of interest the statement of the gentleman from Virginia that women are in the minority. Not in my house. I can say as a result of 49 years of experience . . . that I usually have the last two words, and those words are, "Yes, dear." . . . You know, the French have a phrase for it when they speak of women and men. When they speak the difference, they say "vive la difference."

I think the French are right.

Imagine the upheaval that would result from adoption of blanket language requiring total equality. Would male citizens be justified in insisting that women share with them the burdens of compulsory military service? What would become of traditional family relationships? What about alimony? Who would have the obligation of supporting whom? Would fathers rank equally with mothers in the right of custody to children? What would become of the crimes of rape and statutory rape? . . . Would the many State and local provisions regulating working conditions and hours of employment for women be struck down? . . .

Mrs. Griffiths. . . . Some people have suggested to me that labor opposes "no discrimination on account of sex" because they feel that through the years protective legislation has been built up to safeguard the health of women. Some protective legislation was to safeguard the health of women, but it should have safeguarded the health of men, also. Most of the so-called protective legislation has really been to protect men's rights in better paying jobs. . . .

---

[4]Walters v. Metropolitan Educational Enterprises, Inc., 519 U.S. 202 (1997).
[5]Alexander v. Rush North Shore Medical Center, 101 F.3d 487 (7th Cir. 1996).
[6]110 Cong. Rec. 2,577-2,584 (1964).

Mrs. George. . . . Protective legislation prevents, as my colleague from the State of Michigan just pointed out—prevents women from going into the higher salary brackets. Yes, it certainly does.

Women are protected—they cannot run an elevator late at night and that is when the pay is higher.

They cannot serve in restaurants and cabarets late at night—when the tips are higher—and the load, if you please, is lighter . . .

But what about the offices, gentlemen, that are cleaned every morning about 2 or 3 o'clock in the city of New York and the offices that are cleaned quite early here in Washington, D.C.? Does anybody worry about those women? I have never heard of anybody worrying about the women who do that work. . . .

The addition of that little, terrifying word "s-e-x" will not hurt this legislation in any way. In fact, it will improve it. It will make it comprehensive. It will make it logical. It will make it right.

Mrs. Green. . . . I wish to say first to the gentleman who offered this amendment and to others who by their applause I am sure are giving strong support to it that I, for one, welcome the conversion, because I remember when we were working on the equal pay bill that, if I correctly understand the mood of the House, those gentlemen of the House who are most strong in their support of women's rights this afternoon, probably gave us the most opposition when we considered the bill which would grant equal pay for equal work just a very few months ago. I say I welcome the conversion and hope it is of long duration. . . .

[A]s the author of the equal pay bill and as a member of the President's Commission on the Status of Women, I believe I have demonstrated my concern and my determination to advance women's opportunities in every reasonable way possible. But—I do not believe this is the time or place for this amendment.

Let me say first that I agree with many of the statements my women colleagues have made about the great amount of discrimination against women. . . . This is true when I am invited to a club in Washington as a guest to attend a conference, and when I arrive at the front door to attend that conference, solely because I am a woman, I have to go to the side door to gain admittance.

After I have said all of this Mr. Chairman, I honestly cannot support the amendment. For every discrimination that has been made against a woman in this country there has been 10 times as much discrimination against the Negro of this country. There has been 10 times maybe 100 times as much humiliation for the Negro woman, for the Negro man and for the Negro child. Yes: and for the Negro baby who is born into a world of discrimination. . . . [T]his bill is primarily for the purpose of ending discrimination against Negroes in voting and in public accommodations and in education and, yes, in employment. . . . As much as I hope the day will come when discrimination will be ended against women, I really and sincerely hope that this amendment will not be added to this bill. It will clutter up the bill and it may later—very well—be used to help destroy this section of the bill by some of the very people who today support it. And I hope that no other amendment will be added to this bill on sex or age or anything else, that would jeopardize our primary purpose in any way.

DISCUSSION QUESTIONS

1. What do you think Mr. Smith was trying to accomplish by amending the statute to include sex discrimination?

2. When courts are asked to interpret a statute, they often look to legislative history. Having just read an excerpt from the legislative history for Title VII, what can you extrapolate about the value of relying on legislative history?

3. In addition to the categories that Congress included in Title VII, can you think of any other categories that should be included to completely protect individuals from employment discrimination?

The end result was the passage of Mr. Smith's amendment, as well as of Title VII. Therefore, the category of sex discrimination was added to race, color, religion, and national origin discrimination. The precise meaning of "sex discrimination," however, was hotly debated for many years. For example, recall our discussion in Chapter 2 of the U.S. Supreme Court case of *Gilbert v. General Electric*. In that case the Court held that pregnancy discrimination did not come within the definition of sex discrimination under Title VII. In reaction to that decision Congress passed the Pregnancy Discrimination Act of 1978, which states that the phrase "because of sex" includes pregnancy, childbirth, and related medical conditions.[7] And it was not until 1998 that the United States Supreme Court decided that same-sex harassment qualified as prohibited sex discrimination under Title VII.[8]

Race, color, religion, sex, and national origin are known as **protected categories.** Title VII does not mean that an employer can never make an employment decision adverse to a member of a protected class. For example, an employer can refuse to hire an African American because that person lacks the skills required for the job, withhold a woman's promotion because of a bad attendance record, or fire a Muslim because that employee was caught embezzling company funds. The key is the reason behind the employer's actions. A negative action against a member of a protected class is unlawful only when the action was taken *because* that person is a member of a protected class.

The most difficult part of the typical employment discrimination case is the determination of the employer's true motivation behind the allegedly discriminatory action. While some employers may admit to discriminatory motives, most employers will claim that their decisions were based on legitimate considerations, such as educational credentials or work record. The sections that follow will identify the three major approaches the courts have taken to this problem.

b. The Three Theories of Discrimination

Title VII prohibits both intentional and unintentional discrimination. The U.S. Supreme Court has developed three theories to help plaintiffs prove these two types of discrimination: overt discrimination, disparate treatment, and disparate impact. The theories of overt discrimination and disparate treatment are used in cases of intentional discrimination. The disparate impact theory is used in cases of unintentional discrimination.

First, there are those rare cases of **overt discrimination,** where the employer openly refuses to treat all applicants or employees equally. The only defense to such an action is proof that sex, religion, or national origin is a requirement of the job. This is known as establishing a **bona fide occupational qualification (BFOQ).** Note that race can never be a bona fide job requirement.

Bona fide occupational qualification (BFOQ) A defense to an overt discrimination claim, alleging that the qualification is necessary to the essence of the business operation.

---

[7] 42 U.S.C.S § 2000e-(k) (2008).
[8] *Oncale v. Sundowner Offshore Services, Inc.*, 523 U.S. 75 (1998).

Disparate treatment
The legal theory applied when a rejected applicant claims the reason for rejection was based on a discriminatory intent but the employer alleges a nondiscriminatory reason.

Disparate impact
The legal theory applied when the use of a neutral standard has a disproportionate impact on one protected group.

The second type of case involves **disparate treatment**, where a rejected applicant or employee thinks the reason for the rejection is based on discrimination, but the employer alleges a nondiscriminatory reason. Here the main issue is one of proof; that is, the plaintiff must find a way to prove that the real reason for the rejection was discrimination.

Third, there are times when an employer uses a neutral standard, such as a requirement that all employees have a high school education, that nonetheless excludes a large number of one classification of potential employees. This type of case does not require any proof of discriminatory intent, but the plaintiff must show that the neutral standard has a disproportionate negative impact on one protected group. This last type of case is known as a **disparate impact** case.

(1) Overt intentional discrimination and the BFOQ defense

Sometimes an employer will state that it will hire only members of a particular sex, religion, or national origin. Because the discrimination is done openly, this is called overt discrimination. Title VII allows a limited exception for such overt discrimination when sex, national origin, or religion is "a bona fide occupational qualification reasonably necessary to the normal operation of that particular business or enterprise."[9] Notice how specific this provision is. First, it applies only to religion, sex, and national origin discrimination. Second, the occupational qualification must be "reasonably necessary" to the "normal operation" of that "particular" business. Figure 10-8 shows what the plaintiff in an overt discrimination case must prove and the requirements of the defendant's rebuttal.

A valid BFOQ defense would arise when an employer limits applicants for a locker room attendant's job to women if it is a women's locker room and to men if it is a men's locker room. The defense becomes more problematic when, for example, the owner of a Chinese restaurant argues that being Chinese is a valid BFOQ for working as a waiter in order to meet customer expectations. Similarly, an upscale restaurant might argue that its clientele expects to be assisted only by a male maître d'. Read the following landmark case to see how the U.S. Court of Appeals for the Fifth Circuit dealt with a similar argument.

Figure 10-8   Summary of the Order of Proof in Overt Discrimination Cases

1. Plaintiff's Prima Facie Case	Must prove overt discrimination against a member of a protected group
2. Defendant's Rebuttal	Must prove that discrimination is the result of a bona fide occupational qualification—that is, that the qualification is necessary to the essence of the business operation

---

[9]42 U.S.C.S. § 2000e(a) (2008).

Diaz v. Pan American World Airways, Inc.
442 F. 2d 385 (5th Cir. 1971)

TUTTLE, C.J.

This appeal presents the important question of whether Pan American Airlines' refusal to hire appellant and his class of males only on the basis of their sex violates § 703(a)(1) of Title VII of the 1964 Civil Rights Act. Because we feel that being a female is not a "bona fide occupational qualification" for the job of flight cabin attendant, appellee's refusal to hire appellant's class solely because of their sex, does constitute a violation of the Act.

The facts in this case are not in dispute. Celio Diaz applied for a job as flight cabin attendant with Pan American Airlines in 1967. He was rejected because Pan Am had a policy of restricting its hiring for that position to females. He then filed charges with the Equal Employment Opportunity Commission (EEOC) alleging that Pan Am had unlawfully discriminated against him on the grounds of sex. The Commission found probable cause to believe his charge, but was unable to resolve the matter through conciliation with Pan Am. Diaz next filed a class action in the United States District Court for the Southern District of Florida on behalf of himself and others similarly situated, alleging that Pan Am had violated Section 703 of the 1964 Civil Rights Act by refusing to employ him on the basis of his sex; he sought an injunction and damages.

Pan Am admitted that it had a policy of restricting its hiring for the cabin attendant position to females. Thus, both parties stipulated that the primary issue for the District Court was whether, for the job of flight cabin attendant, being a female is a "bona fide occupational qualification (hereafter BFOQ) reasonably necessary to the normal operation" of Pan American's business.

The trial court found that being a female was a BFOQ. Before discussing its findings in detail, however, it is necessary to set forth the framework within which we view this case.

Section 703(a) of the 1964 Civil Rights Act provides, in part:

(a) It shall be an unlawful employment practice for an employer—(1) to fail or refuse to hire or to discharge any individual, or otherwise to discriminate against any individual with respect to his compensation, terms, conditions, or privileges of employment, because of such individual's race, color, religion, sex or national origin. . . .

The scope of this section is qualified by § 703(e) which states:

(e) Notwithstanding any other provision of this subchapter,

(1) it shall not be an unlawful employment practice for an employer to hire and employ employees . . . on the basis of his religion, sex, or national origin in those certain instances where religion, sex, or national origin is a bona fide occupational qualification reasonably necessary to the normal operation of that particular business or enterprise. . . .

Since it has been admitted that appellee has discriminated on the basis of sex, the result in this case turns, in effect, on the construction given to this exception. . . .

In construing this provision, we feel . . . that it would be totally anomalous to do so in a manner that would, in effect, permit the exception to swallow the rule. Thus, we adopt the EEOC guidelines which state that "the Commission believes that the bona fide occupational qualification as to sex should be interpreted narrowly." 29 CFR 1604.1(a). Indeed, close scrutiny of the language of this exception compels this result. As one commentator has noted:

"The sentence contains several restrictive adjectives and phrases: it applies only 'in those certain instances' where there are 'bona fide' qualifications 'reasonably necessary' to the operation of that 'particular' enterprise. The care with which Congress has chosen the words to emphasize the function and to limit the scope of the exception indicates that it had no intention of opening the kind of enormous gap in the law which would exist if an employer could legitimately discriminate against a group solely because his employees, customers, or clients discriminated against that group.

Absent much more explicit language, such a broad exception should not be assumed for it would largely emasculate the act." 65 Mich. L. Rev. (1967).

Thus, it is with this orientation that we now examine the trial court's decision. Its conclusion was based upon (1) its view of Pan Am's history of the use of flight attendants; (2) passenger preference; (3) basic psychological reasons for the preference; and (4) the actualities of the hiring process.

Having reviewed the evidence submitted by Pan American regarding its own experience with both female and male cabin attendants it had hired over the years, the trial court found that Pan Am's current hiring policy was the result of a pragmatic process. . . . The performance of female attendants was better in the sense that they were superior in such non-mechanical aspects of the job as "providing reassurance to anxious passengers, giving courteous personalized service and, in general, making flights as pleasurable as possible within the limitations imposed by aircraft operations."

The trial court also found that Pan Am's passengers overwhelmingly preferred to be served by female stewardesses. Moreover, on the basis of the expert testimony of a psychiatrist, the court found that an airplane cabin represents a unique environment in which an air carrier is required to take account of the special psychological needs of its passengers. These psychological needs are better attended to by females. This is not to say that there are no males who would not have the necessary qualities to perform these non-mechanical functions, but the trial court found that the actualities of the hiring process would make it more difficult to find these few males. . . .

Because of the narrow reading we give to section 703(e), we do not feel that these findings justify the discrimination practiced by Pan Am.

We begin with the proposition that the use of the word "necessary" in section 703(e) requires that we apply a business necessity test, not a business convenience test. That is to say, discrimination based on sex is valid only when the essence of the business operation would be undermined by not hiring members of one sex exclusively.

The primary function of an airline is to transport passengers safely from one point to another. While a pleasant environment, enhanced by the obvious cosmetic effect that female stewardesses provide as well as, according to the finding of the trial court, their apparent ability to perform the non-mechanical functions of the job in a more effective manner than most men, may all be important, they are tangential to the essence of the business involved. No one has suggested that having male stewards will so seriously affect the operation of an airline as to jeopardize or even minimize its ability to provide safe transportation from one place to another. Indeed the record discloses that many airlines including Pan Am have utilized both men and women flight cabin attendants in the past and Pan Am, even at the time of this suit, has 283 male stewards employed on some of its foreign flights.

We do not mean to imply, of course, that Pan Am cannot take into consideration the ability of individuals to perform the non-mechanical functions of the job. What we hold is that because the non-mechanical aspects of the job of flight cabin attendant are not "reasonably necessary to the normal operation" of Pan Am's business, Pan Am cannot exclude all males simply because most males may not perform adequately. . . .

Appellees also argue, and the trial court found, that because of the actualities of the hiring process, "the best available initial test for determining whether a particular applicant for employment is likely to have the personality characteristics conducive to high-level performance of the flight attendant's job as currently defined is consequently the applicant's biological sex." Indeed, the trial court found that it was simply not practicable to find the few males that would perform properly.

We do not feel that this alone justifies discriminating against all males. Since, as stated above, the basis of exclusion is the ability to perform non-mechanical functions which we find to be tangential to what is "reasonably necessary" for the business involved, the exclusion of all males because this is the best way to select the kind of personnel Pan Am desires simply cannot be justified. Before sex discrimination can be practiced, it must not only be shown that it is impracticable to find the men that possess the abilities that most women possess, but that the abilities are necessary to the business, not merely tangential.

Similarly, we do not feel that the fact that Pan Am's passengers prefer female stewardesses should alter our judgment. On this subject, EEOC guidelines state that a BFOQ ought not be based on "the refusal to hire an individual because of the preferences of co-workers, the employer, clients or customers . . ." 29 CFR § 1604.1(iii).

As the Supreme Court stated in *Griggs v. Duke Power Co.*, 401 U.S. 424, 91 S. Ct. 849, 28 L. Ed. 2d 158 (1971), "the administration interpretation of the Act by the enforcing agency is entitled to great deference." . . . While we recognize that the public's expectation of finding one sex in a particular role may cause some initial difficulty, it would be totally anomalous if we were to allow the preferences and prejudices of the customers to determine whether the sex discrimination was valid. Indeed, it was, to a large extent, these very prejudices the Act was meant to overcome. Thus, we feel that customer preference may be taken into account only when it is based on the company's inability to perform the primary function or service it offers. . . .

The judgment is Reversed and the case is Remanded for proceedings not inconsistent with this opinion.

CASE DISCUSSION QUESTIONS

1. Why did the male plaintiff win his claim of sex discrimination?

2. In the district court trial, Pan Am introduced evidence of a survey that indicated 79 percent of all passengers, both men and women, preferred female stewardesses. What did the court of appeals have to say about an employer using such customer preferences to make hiring decisions?

3. During the trial Dr. Eric Berne, author of *Games People Play*, testified, trying to explain in psychological terms why most passengers prefer female attendants (stewardesses).

> Dr. Berne explained that the cabin of a modern airliner is, for passengers, a special and unique psychological environment ("sealed enclave"), characterized by the confinement of a number of people together in an enclosed and limited space, by their being subjected to the unusual physical experience of being levitated off the ground and transported through the atmosphere at high speed, by their being substantially out of touch with their accustomed world, and by their own inability to control events. That environment . . . creates three typical passenger emotional states . . . a sense of apprehension, . . . a sense of boredom . . . and . . . a feeling of excitement. . . . [F]emale stewardesses . . . would be better able to deal with each of these psychological states. . . . [P]assengers of both sexes would . . . respond better to the presence of females than males. He explained that many male passengers would subconsciously resent a male flight attendant perceived as more masculine than they, but respond negatively to a male flight attendant perceived as less masculine, whereas male passengers would generally feel themselves more masculine and thus more at ease in the presence of a young female attendant. He further explained that female passengers might consider personal overtures by male attendants as intrusive and inappropriate, while at the same time welcoming the attentions and conversation of another woman.[10]

How do you think this testimony should have been factored into the court's decision?

---

[10]*Diaz v. Pan American World Airways, Inc.*, 311 F. Supp. 559, 565-566 (S.D. Fla. 1970).

(2) Intentional discrimination—disparate treatment

In most cases of alleged discrimination the employer does not broadcast its intent to discriminate. Rather, the employer argues that its reasons are totally justified and nondiscriminatory. For example, the employer might argue that a decision to fire an employee was justified because the worker had a poor job performance rating. In this second type of employment discrimination case, known as **disparate treatment**, the plaintiff has the burden of proving that the decision was based on race, color, sex, religion, or national origin rather than on the alternative explanation offered by the employer.

For example, in the following case a laid-off worker applied for reinstatement. When his employer did not rehire him, he alleged it was due to his race. His employer argued, however, that its only reason for refusing to rehire him was his illegal labor union activities, which included, among other actions, being involved in a "stall in." The U.S. Supreme Court grappled with the issue of how such cases should be presented and proven and in the process laid down guidelines for future disparate treatment cases.

McDonnell Douglas Corp. v. Green
411 U.S. 729 (1973)

Certiorari to the United States Court of Appeals for the Eighth Circuit.

POWELL, J.

The case before us raises significant questions as to the proper order and nature of proof in actions under Title VII of the Civil Rights Act of 1964, 78 Stat. 253, 42 U.S.C. § 2000c et seq.

Petitioner, McDonnell Douglas Corp., is an aerospace and aircraft manufacturer head-quartered in St. Louis, Missouri, where it employs over 30,000 people. Respondent, a black citizen of St. Louis, worked for petitioner as a mechanic and laboratory technician from 1956 until August 28, 1964 when he was laid off in the course of a general reduction in petitioner's work force.

Respondent, a long-time activist in the civil rights movement, protested vigorously that his discharge and the general hiring practices of petitioner were racially motivated. As part of this protest, respondent and other members of the Congress on Racial Equality illegally stalled their cars on the main roads leading to petitioner's plant for the purpose of blocking access to it at the time of the morning shift change. The District Judge described the plan for, and respondent's participation in, the "stall-in" as follows:

"Five teams, each consisting of four cars would 'tie up' five main access roads into McDonnell at the time of the morning rush hour. The drivers of the cars were instructed to line up next to each other completely blocking the intersections or roads. The drivers were also instructed to stop their cars, turn off the engines, pull the emergency brake, raise all windows, lock the doors, and remain in their cars until the police arrived. The plan was to have the cars remain in position for one hour.

Acting under the 'stall in' plan, plaintiff [respondent in the present action] drove his car onto Brown Road, a McDonnell access road, at approximately 7:00 A.M., at the start of the morning rush hour. Plaintiff was aware of the traffic problems that would result. He stopped his car with the intent to block traffic. The police arrived shortly and requested plaintiff to move his car. He refused to move his car voluntarily. Plaintiff's car was towed away by the police, and he was arrested for obstructing traffic. Plaintiff pleaded guilty to the charge of obstructing traffic and was fined." 318 F. Supp. 846, 849. . . .

[O]n July 25, 1965, petitioner publicly advertised for qualified mechanics, respondent's trade, and respondent promptly applied for re-employment. Petitioner turned down respondent, basing its rejection on respondent's participation in the "stall-in." . . . Shortly thereafter, respondent filed a formal complaint with the Equal Employment Opportunity Commission. . . .

In order to clarify the standards governing the disposition of an action challenging employment discrimination, we granted certiorari, 409 U.S. 1036 (1972). . . .

In this case respondent, the complainant below, charges that he was denied employment "because of his involvement in civil rights activities" and "because of his race and color." Petitioner denied discrimination of any kind, asserting that its failure to re-employ respondent was based upon and justified by his participation in the unlawful conduct against it. Thus, the issue at the trial on remand is framed by those opposing factual contentions. . . .

The complainant in a Title VII trial must carry the initial burden under the statute of establishing a prima facie case of racial discrimination. This may be done by showing (i) that he belongs to a racial minority; (ii) that he applied and was qualified for a job for which the employer was seeking applicants; (iii) that, despite his qualifications, he was rejected; and (iv) that, after his rejection, the position remained open and the employer continued to seek applicants from persons of complainant's qualifications.[13] In the instant case, we agree with the Court of Appeals that respondent proved a prima facie case. 463 F.2d 337, 353. Petitioner sought mechanics, respondent's trade, and continued to do so after respondent's rejection. Petitioner, moreover, does not dispute respondent's qualifications and acknowledges that his past work performance in petitioner's employ was "satisfactory."

The burden then must shift to the employer to articulate some legitimate, nondiscriminatory reason for the employee's rejection. We need not attempt in the instant case to detail every matter which fairly could be recognized as a reasonable basis for a refusal to hire. Here petitioner has assigned respondent's participation in unlaw-ful conduct against it as the cause for his rejection. We think that this suffices to discharge petitioner's burden of proof at this stage and to meet respondent's prima facie case of discrimination. . . .

Nothing in Title VII compels an employer to absolve and rehire one who has engaged in such deliberate, unlawful activity against it.[17]

Petitioner's reason for rejection thus suffices to meet the prima facie case, but the inquiry must not end here. While Title VII does not, without more, compel rehiring of respondent, neither does it permit petitioner to use respondent's conduct as a pretext for the sort of discrimination prohibited by § 703(a)(1). On remand, respondent must . . . be afforded a fair opportunity to show that petitioner's stated reason for respondent's rejection was in fact pretext. Especially relevant to such a showing would be evidence that white employees involved in acts against petitioner of comparable seriousness to the "stall-in" were nevertheless retained or rehired. Petitioner may justifiably refuse to rehire one who was engaged in unlawful, disruptive acts against it, but only if this criterion is applied alike to members of all races.

Other evidence that may be relevant to any showing of pretext includes facts as to the petitioner's treatment of respondent during his prior term of employment; petitioner's reaction, if any, to respondent's legitimate civil rights activities; and petitioner's general policy and practice with respect to minority employment. On the latter point, statistics as to petitioner's employment policy and practice may be helpful to a determination of whether petitioner's refusal to rehire respondent in this case conformed to a general pattern of discrimination against blacks. . . . In short, on the retrial respondent must be given a full and fair opportunity to demonstrate by competent evidence that the presumptively valid reasons for his rejection were in fact a coverup for a racially discriminatory decision. . . .

The judgment is vacated and the cause is hereby remanded to the District Court for further proceedings consistent with this opinion.

So ordered.

---

[13]The facts necessarily will vary in Title VII cases, and the specification above of the prima facie proof required from respondent is not necessarily applicable in every respect to differing factual situations.

[17]The unlawful activity in this case was directed specifically against petitioner. We need not consider or decide here whether, or under what circumstances, unlawful activity not directed against the particular employer may be a legitimate justification for refusing to hire.

CASE DISCUSSION QUESTIONS

1. What do you think happened next in this case?

2. Why do you think the court established such an elaborate procedure for establishing the plaintiff's prima facie case?

3. How do you think the test proposed in this case could be modified to cover a case of a person denied a promotion?

As articulated in *McDonnell Douglas* and the cases that have followed it, the person bringing a disparate treatment case must first establish through the prima facie case that

1. he or she is a member of a protected class,
2. he or she applied and was qualified for the position,
3. his or her application was rejected, and
4. the employer continued to seek other applicants for the same position or filled the position with someone who was not within the protected class.

This four-part test can also be adjusted to fit firing and failure-to-promote cases.

Once the plaintiff has established this prima facie case, the employer has to articulate a valid reason for not hiring, for not promoting, or for firing the plaintiff. Note that this is a **burden of production** as opposed to a **burden of proof.** It means the employer will lose the case if it cannot come up with a reason that does not involve discrimination based on a protected class criterion, but it does not mean the defendant has the burden of proving that the reason offered is true. After this alternative reason is presented, the plaintiff has the burden of proving by a preponderance of the evidence that the employer's reason is really just a pretext and that the employer actually acted with a discriminatory intent. See Figure 10-9 on page 369.

Because the focus in a discriminatory treatment case remains on the actual intent of the defendant, any evidence that the employer was motivated by a discriminatory animus is relevant. For example, in one case involving a nationwide professional accounting firm,[11] a female senior manager became a candidate for partnership. When she failed to get the promotion, the rejected employee sued. Supporters of her candidacy described her as "an outstanding professional" with a "strong character, independence and integrity." However, those who denied her the promotion appeared to react negatively to her personality because she was a woman. Evidence that the Court looked at in making this determination included the fact that one of the partners suggested she "take a course at charm school." In addition, "[s]everal partners criticized her use of profanity; in response, one partner suggested that those partners object to her swearing only 'because it[']s a lady using foul language.' "[12] Finally, one of the partners, in advising the female candidate how to advance her candidacy, suggested that she should "walk more femininely, talk more femininely, dress more femininely, wear make-up, have her hair styled, and wear jewelry."[13] Such

Burden of production
The necessity to produce some evidence, but it need not be so strong as to convince the trier of fact of its truth.

Burden of proof
The necessity of proving the truth of the matter asserted.

---

[11]Price Waterhouse v. Hopkins, 490 U.S. 228 (1989).

[12]Id. at 235.

[13]Id.

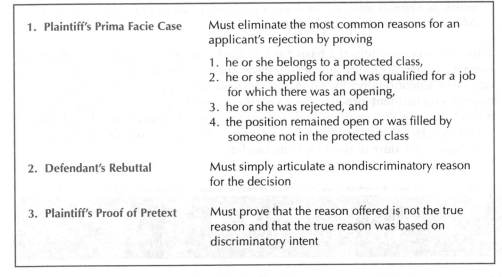

1. Plaintiff's Prima Facie Case	Must eliminate the most common reasons for an applicant's rejection by proving
	1. he or she belongs to a protected class,
	2. he or she applied for and was qualified for a job for which there was an opening,
	3. he or she was rejected, and
	4. the position remained open or was filled by someone not in the protected class
2. Defendant's Rebuttal	Must simply articulate a nondiscriminatory reason for the decision
3. Plaintiff's Proof of Pretext	Must prove that the reason offered is not the true reason and that the true reason was based on discriminatory intent

Figure 10-9 Three-Part McDonnell Douglas Analysis

"smoking gun" evidence can be used by the plaintiff to convince the court that any proffered nondiscriminatory reason for her rejection is really pretext.

With the passage of the Civil Rights Act of 1991 Congress made it easier for plaintiffs to win mixed-motive cases by amending Title VII to add this provision: "[A]n unlawful employment practice is established when the complaining party demonstrates that race, color, religion, sex, or national origin was a motivating factor for any employment practice, even though other factors also motivated the practice."[14]

(3) Unintentional discrimination—disparate impact

As we have seen, Title VII makes it unlawful for any employer

(1) to fail or refuse to hire or to discharge any individual, or otherwise to discriminate against any individual with respect to his compensation, terms, conditions, or privileges of employment, *because of* such individual's race, color, religion, sex, or national origin.[15]

Therefore, to intentionally discriminate against someone "because of" that person's membership in a protected class is to engage in unlawful discrimination. As we have seen, in such cases the plaintiff has the burden of proving the employer had the intent to discriminate. However, Title VII also makes it unlawful for an employer to

(2) limit, segregate, or classify his employees or applicants for employment in any way which would deprive or tend to deprive any individual of employment opportunities or

---

[14]Civil Rights Act of 1991, § 107(a), 42 U.S.C.S. § 2000e-2(m) (2008).
[15]42 U.S.C.S. § 2000e-2(a)(1) (2008) (emphasis added).

otherwise adversely affect his status as an employee, because of such individual's race, color, religion, sex, or national origin.[16]

This provision provides the basis for the third type of discrimination, **disparate impact.** Under disparate impact analysis there is no need to prove that the employer intentionally discriminated. Instead, the plaintiff must show that a neutral employment practice deprived the plaintiff of "employment opportunities" because the practice had a disproportionate impact on the plaintiff's protected class. This theory of discrimination was originally developed by the U.S. Supreme Court in the following landmark decision.

Griggs v. Duke Power Co.
401 U.S. 424 (1971)

BURGER, C.J., delivered the opinion of the Court, in which all members joined except BRENNAN, J., who took no part in the consideration or decision of the case.

We granted the writ in this case to resolve the question whether an employer is prohibited by the Civil Rights Act of 1964, Title VII, from requiring a high school education or passing of a standardized general intelligence test as a condition of employment in or transfer to jobs when (a) neither standard is shown to be significantly related to successful job performance, (b) both requirements operate to disqualify Negroes at a substantially higher rate than white applicants, and (c) the jobs in question formerly had been filled only by white employees as part of a long-standing practice of giving preference to whites.

The District Court found that prior to July 2, 1965, the effective date of the Civil Rights Act of 1964, the Company openly discriminated on the basis of race in the hiring and assigning of employees at its Dan River plant. The plant was organized into five operating departments. . . . Negroes were employed only in the Labor Department where the highest paying jobs paid less than the lowest paying jobs in the other four "operating" departments in which only whites were employed. Promotions were normally made within each department on the basis of job seniority. Transferees into a department usually began in the lowest position.

In 1955 the Company instituted a policy of requiring a high school education for initial assignment to any department except Labor, and for transfer from the Coal Handling to any "inside" department (Operations, Maintenance, or Laboratory). When the Company abandoned its policy of restricting Negroes to the Labor Department in 1965, completion of high school also was made a prerequisite to transfer from Labor to any other department. From the time the high school requirement was instituted to the time of trial, however, white employees hired before the time of the high school education requirement continued to perform satisfactorily and achieve promotions in the "operating" departments. Findings on this score are not challenged.

The Company added a further requirement for new employees on July 2, 1965, the date on which Title VII became effective. To qualify for placement in any but the Labor Department it became necessary to register satisfactory scores on two professionally prepared aptitude tests, as well as to have a high school education. Completion of high school alone continued to render employees eligible for transfer to the four desirable departments from which Negroes had been excluded if the incumbent had been employed prior to the

---

[16]42 U.S.C.S. § 2000e-2(a)(2) (2008).

time of the new requirement. In September 1965 the Company began to permit incumbent employees who lacked a high school education to qualify for transfer from Labor or Coal Handling to an "inside" job by passing two tests—the Wonderlic Personnel Test, which purports to measure general intelligence, and the Bennett Mechanical Comprehension Test. Neither was directed or intended to measure the ability to learn to perform a particular job or category of jobs. The requisite scores used for both initial hiring and transfer approximated the national median for high school graduates.[3] . . .

The objective of Congress in the enactment of Title VII is plain from the language of the statute. It was to achieve equality of employment opportunities and remove barriers that have operated in the past to favor an identifiable group of white employees over other employees. Under the Act, practices, procedures, or tests neutral on their face, and even neutral in terms of intent, cannot be maintained if they operate to "freeze" the status quo of prior discriminatory employment practices. . . .

Congress did not intend by Title VII, however, to guarantee a job to every person regardless of qualifications. In short, the Act does not command that any person be hired simply because he was formerly the subject of discrimination, or because he is a member of a minority group. Discriminatory preference for any group, minority or majority, is precisely and only what Congress has proscribed. What is required by Congress is the removal of artificial, arbitrary, and unnecessary barriers to employment when the barriers operate invidiously to discriminate on the basis of racial or other impermissible classification. Congress has now provided that tests or criteria for employment or promotion may not provide equality of opportunity merely in the sense of the fabled offer of milk to the stork and the fox. On the contrary, Congress has now required that the posture and condition of the job-seeker be taken into account. It has—to resort again to the fable—provided that the vessel in which the milk is proffered be one all seekers can use. The Act proscribes not only overt discrimination but also practices that are fair in form, but discriminatory in operation. The touchstone is business necessity. If an employment practice which operates to exclude Negroes cannot be shown to be related to job performance, the practice is prohibited.

On the record before us, neither the high school completion requirement nor the general intelligence test is shown to bear a demonstrable relationship to successful performance of the jobs for which it was used. Both were adopted, as the Court of Appeals noted, without meaningful study of their relationship to job-performance ability. Rather, a vice president of the Company testified, the requirements were instituted on the Company's judgment that they generally would improve the overall quality of the work force.

The evidence, however, shows that employees who have not completed high school or taken the tests have continued to perform satisfactorily and make progress in departments for which the high school and test criteria are now used. The promotion record of present employees who would not be able to meet the new criteria thus suggests the possibility that the requirements may not be needed even for the limited purpose of preserving the avowed policy of advancement within the Company. . . .

The Court of Appeals held that the Company had adopted the diploma and test requirements without any "intention to discriminate against Negro employees." 420 F.2d at 1232. We do not suggest that either the District Court or the Court of Appeals erred in examining the employer's intent; but good intent or absence of discriminatory intent does not redeem employment procedures or testing mechanisms that operate as "built-in headwinds" for minority groups and are unrelated to measuring job capability. . . .

The Company contends that its general intelligence tests are specifically permitted by § 703(h) of the Act. That section authorizes the use of

---

[3]The test standards are thus more stringent than high school requirement, since they would screen out approximately half of all high school graduates.

"any professionally developed ability test" that is not "designed, intended or used to discriminate because of race. . . . " (Emphasis added.) . . .

Nothing in the Act precludes the use of testing or measuring procedures; obviously they are useful. What Congress has forbidden is giving these devices and mechanisms controlling force unless they are demonstrably a reasonable measure of job performance. Congress has not com-manded that the less qualified be preferred over the better qualified simply because of minority origins. Far from disparaging job qualifications as such, Congress has made such qualifications the controlling factor, so that race, religion, nationality, and sex become irrelevant. What Congress has commanded is that any tests used must measure the person for the job and not the person in the abstract.

CASE DISCUSSION QUESTIONS

1. What did the U.S. Supreme Court understand to be the objective of Title VII? That is, precisely what does it proscribe, and what does it require?

2. Do you think the *Griggs* decision is a fair reading of the statute? Should an employer be found in violation of an antidiscrimination statute when there is no proof of prejudice or biased motive?

3. What does "business necessity" mean, and what is its role in the order of proof discussed in this case?

4. Did the employer prove business necessity? Why?

5. In footnote 6 the *Griggs* Court noted that "[i]n North Carolina, 1960 census statistics show that, while 34% of white males had completed high school, only 12% of Negro males had done so. . . . Similarly, with respect to standardized tests, the EEOC in one case found that use of a battery of tests, including the Wonderlic and Bennett tests used by the Company in the instant case, resulted in 58% of whites passing the tests, as compared with only 6% of the blacks." What do you make of these statistics?

Following *Griggs* the courts have grappled with many situations involving disparate impact. To prove such a case, the plaintiff must first show that the employer's facially neutral practices have a disproportionately discriminatory impact on a protected class. To prove the disproportionate impact, the plaintiff frequently will resort to statistics to show the disparity between the numbers of available workers belonging to that classification versus those actually able to qualify for employment under the employer's neutral test. The burden is then shifted to the employer to prove that the practice was necessary for its business operation. If it does so, then the plaintiff has the opportunity to prove that an alternative practice would also accomplish the employer's purposes but without the negative discriminatory impact. See Figure 10-10. In the Civil Rights Act of 1991 Congress codified the concepts of "business necessity" and "job related" as they had been developed in *Griggs*.

DISCUSSION QUESTION

4. One day a Fox invited a Stork to dinner and, being disposed to divert himself at the expense of this guest, provided nothing for the entertainment but some thin soup in a shallow dish. This the Fox lapped up very readily, while the Stork, unable to gain a mouthful with her long narrow bill, was as hungry at the

1. Plaintiff's Prima Facie Case	Must prove that the facially neutral practice disproportionately discriminates against a protected class (often demonstrated through statistics)
2. Defendant's Rebuttal	Must prove business necessity—that is, that the practice "bears a demonstrable relationship to successful performance of the jobs for which it was used"
3. Plaintiff's Proof of a Nondiscriminatory Alternative	Must prove that an equally useful but less discriminatory alternative exists that could be used by the employer.

Figure 10-10   Summary of the Order of Proof in Disparate Impact Cases

end of dinner as at the beginning. The Fox meanwhile professed his regret at seeing his guest eat so sparingly and feared that the dish was not seasoned to her liking. The Stork said little but begged that the Fox would do her the honor of returning her visit. Accordingly, he agreed to dine with her on the following day. He arrived true to his appointment, and the dinner was ordered. But when it was served up, he found to his dismay that it was contained in a narrow-necked vessel, down which the Stork readily thrust her long neck and bill, while the Fox was obliged to content himself with licking the neck of the jar.

Is this fable about disparate treatment or disparate impact? Why?

c. Sexual Harassment

Title VII prohibits discrimination based on sex. Therefore, absent a BFOQ, an employer cannot make employment decisions based on the gender of the employee. But what if the employer sexually harasses an employee by repeatedly making unwelcome sexual advances?

Until the mid-1980s it was unclear whether Title VII's prohibition against sex discrimination prohibited such "sexual harassment." Then in *Meritor Savings Bank v. Vinson*[17] the U.S. Supreme Court held that, even in the absence of a tangible job loss (such as a failure to receive a raise), an employee can maintain an action for unlawful sex discrimination if the employer creates a hostile or abusive work environment. The Court cited an Eleventh Circuit opinion with approval:

Sexual harassment which creates a hostile or offensive environment for members of one sex is every bit the arbitrary barrier to sexual equality at the workplace that racial harassment is to racial equality. Surely, a requirement that a man or woman run a gauntlet of sexual abuse in return for the privilege of being allowed to work and make a living can be as damaging and disconcerting as the harshest of racial epithets.[18]

---

[17] 477 U.S. 57 (1986).
[18] Id. at 67 citing Henson v. Dundee, 682 F.2d 897, 902 (11th Cir. 1982).

As a result of *Meritor Savings Bank v. Vinson,* and subsequent cases, it is clear that Title VII prohibits both **quid pro quo sexual harassment** and the creation of an **intimidating, hostile, or offensive work environment.** The EEOC guidelines detail each of these two forms of discrimination. Quid pro quo situations involve an exchange of sexual favors for employment benefits. For example, this type of situation would occur if an employee were passed by for a promotion because she refused to have sex with her supervisor. Sexual harassment can also consist of

> [u]nwelcome sexual advances, requests for sexual favors, and other verbal or physical conduct of a sexual nature . . . [that have] the purpose or effect of unreasonably interfering with an individual's work performance or creating an intimidating, hostile, or offensive working environment.[19]

In 1993 the U.S. Supreme Court held that it is not necessary for the victim in a hostile work environment case to prove it seriously harmed his or her psychological well-being.[20] It is enough that "a reasonable person" would find it to be hostile or abusive and that the victim perceived the environment to be abusive. The Court noted that "Title VII comes into play before the harassing conduct leads to a nervous breakdown."[21]

Also, as noted earlier in this chapter, in 1998 the U.S. Supreme Court held that same-sex sexual harassment is actionable under Title VII so long as there is a proven connection between the sexual harassment and gender discrimination; that is, the plaintiff must still be able to prove the harassment was "because of" the person's gender.[22] The Court noted that while same-sex harassment was not the "primary evil" Congress hoped to eliminate through Title VII, it was a "reasonably comparable evil."[23]

However, there are still many unanswered questions in the area of sexual harassment, such as how to distinguish between voluntary sexual activity and "unwelcome" sexual advances. Also, from whose point of view should a court judge whether a "hostile or offensive environment" was created? The U.S. Court of Appeals for the Ninth Circuit tackled this question and determined that the appropriate standard was that of a "reasonable woman" rather than that of a "reasonable person." The case involved co-workers Kerry Ellison and Sterling Gray. Sterling repeatedly asked Kerry to go out with him. When she refused, he started sending her notes, such as this one:

> I cried over you last night and I'm totally drained today. I have never been in such constant term oil [sic]. Thank you for talking with me. I could not stand your hatred for another day.[24]

---

[19]29 C.F.R. § 1604.11 (2008).

[20]Harris v. Forklift Systems, 510 U.S. 17 (1993).

[21]Id. at 22.

[22]Oncale v. Sundowner Offshore Services, Inc., 523 U.S. 75 (1998).

[23]Id. at 79.

[24]Ellison v. Brady, 924 F.2d 872, 874 (9th Cir. 1991).

The notes then escalated into multiple-page letters.

> I know that you are worth knowing with or without sex. . . . Leaving aside the hassles and disasters of recent weeks. I have enjoyed you so much over these past few months. Watching you. Experiencing you from O so far away. Admiring your style and élan. . . . Don't you think it odd that two people who have never even talked together, alone, are striking off such intense sparks. . . . I will [write] another letter in the near future.[25]

Kerry became increasingly frightened. The question for the court was whether Sterling's actions had become so severe or pervasive as to create an abusive working environment. The court applied a "reasonable woman's" point of view and found that he had, whether consciously or not, created a hostile work environment.

> We realize that there is a broad range of viewpoints among women as a group, but we believe that many women share common concerns which men do not necessarily share. For example, because women are disproportionately victims of rape and sexual assault, women have a stronger incentive to be concerned with sexual behavior. Women who are victims of mild forms of sexual harassment may understandably worry whether a harasser's conduct is merely a prelude to violent sexual assault. Men, who are rarely victims of sexual assault, may view sexual conduct in a vacuum without a full appreciation of the social setting or the underlying threat of violence that a woman may perceive.[26]

The court acknowledged that applying this standard might sometimes mean classifying conduct as unlawful when the sexual harasser does not even realize he is creating a hostile working environment. However, the court noted that "Title VII is not a fault-based tort scheme. 'Title VII is aimed at the consequences or effects of an employment practice and not at the . . . motivation' of co-workers or employers."[27]

DISCUSSION QUESTIONS

5. Do you agree that in cases of sexual or racial harassment the correct test is whether a reasonable person of that sex or race would have been offended?

6. Do you think it is appropriate to classify conduct as unlawful sexual harassment even when the harasser does not realize his conduct is creating a hostile work environment?

d. Affirmative Action

Affirmative action raises very fundamental and controversial questions about what constitutes equality and fairness. Many disagree as to whether

---

[25]Id.

[26]Id. at 879.

[27]Id. at 880; *see also* McGinest v. GTE Serv. Corp., 360 F.3d 1103 (9th Cir. 2004) (allegations of a racially hostile workplace must be assessed from the perspective of a reasonable person belonging to the racial or ethnic group of the plaintiff).

employers should take factors such as race and sex into consideration in hiring and promotions in order to achieve a more diverse workforce that more closely approximates the balance of these groups in society.

In addition to a basic disagreement as to the value of affirmative action, there is much confusion in this area as to what people believe affirmative action entails. Many use the term very loosely to mean a quota system or any other preferential treatment accorded to otherwise unqualified applicants. However, this reflects a basic misunderstanding of the law. Permissible affirmative-action plans cannot involve quotas or preferences for unqualified applicants over qualified applicants. In fact, any type of quota system is illegal, unless mandated as part of a court order[28] based on an employer's own past discriminatory action. A valid affirmative action only allows an employer to use race or gender as a "plus factor" when choosing between two equally qualified applicants.

While opponents contend that affirmative action

- unfairly "punishes" today's white males for the actions of previous generations,
- puts racial minorities and women under a cloud of suspicion as to their value by sending a message that members of the protected group cannot make it on their own, and
- violates Title VII and the Constitution by discriminating on the basis of race or sex,

proponents of affirmative action counter by advancing a variety of philosophical and practical business rationales. They believe affirmative action

- gives role models to minority children and young women,
- allows businesses to successfully compete in our culturally diverse society, and
- makes up for effects of past discrimination.

As to the last point raised, one year after Title VII was enacted President Lyndon Johnson forcefully argued the need to make up for the effects of past discrimination. In a speech to the graduating class at Howard University he elaborated on how simply prohibiting discrimination is not enough and why there is a need for affirmative action:

> You do not wipe away the scars of centuries by saying: Now you are free to go where you want, and do as you desire, and choose the leaders you please.
>
> You do not take a person who, for years, has been hobbled by chains and liberate him, bring him up to the starting line of a race and then say, "you are free to compete with all the others," and still justly believe that you have been completely fair.
>
> Thus it is not enough just to open the gates of opportunity. All our citizens must have the ability to walk through those gates.[29]

---

[28]Title VII directs courts to "order such affirmative action as may be appropriate." 42 U.S.C.S. § 20003-5(g)(1) (2008).

[29]Public Papers of the Presidents of the United States: Lyndon B. Johnson, 1965. Volume II, entry 301, pp. 635-640. Washington, D.C.: Government Printing Office, 1966. Later that year, President Johnson

In 1978 the U.S. Supreme Court heard the first challenge to an affirmative-action plan. In the landmark decision of *Regents of the University of California v. Bakke,* the Court held that race cannot be used as a sole determinate in decision making.[30] However, race could be deemed a "plus" and factored in with other characteristics. While that case involved admissions into a medical school, the Court's reasoning set the stage for how the courts resolved further challenges to affirmative-action plans in both the education and the employment sectors.

One year later, in *United Steelworkers of America v. Weber,*[31] the U.S. Supreme Court considered the extent to which Title VII prohibited the use of racial criteria in a "voluntary" affirmative-action plan. The Court acknowledged that a literal reading of Title VII might lead to the conclusion that employers could never voluntarily make decisions based on race. However, the Court ruled that a special training program Kaiser Aluminum had created did not violate Title VII. The Court held that prohibiting all voluntary race-conscious employment decisions would be contrary to the legislation's purpose of increasing employment opportunities.[32]

However, not all race-conscious decisions, even in the name of affirmative action, are permissible. To determine if a plan is permissible under Title VII, the Court developed a two-pronged test. First, the plan must be "designed to eliminate conspicuous racial imbalance in traditionally segregated job categories."[33] The Court noted the historic exclusion of blacks from craft positions and that Kaiser's training program was specifically designed to remedy this history of discrimination. Second, the plan must "not unnecessarily trammel the interests of the white employees."[34] Not only were no employees terminated, but all employees were given the opportunity to learn new job skills through the plan's training program. While 50 percent of the positions were reserved for minority candidates, the other 50 percent were open to white workers, thereby giving them a job benefit that they would not have had but for the plan. Finally, the plan was designed to be temporary and would cease once racial imbalance was eliminated.

Eight years later, in *Johnson v. Transportation Agency of Santa Clara County,*[35] the Supreme Court applied *Weber*'s two-pronged test and upheld a highway department's affirmative-action program to promote women into management positions. At the time the employer adopted its voluntary affirmative-action plan, of the 238 workers in its "skilled craft" positions, none were women. A skilled craft position opened, and there were twelve applicants. Nine were interviewed and scored based on the interview. Seven of the applicants scored a 70 or higher, the lowest score an applicant could receive to be

---

issued Executive Order 11246, which requires that most employers who have contracts with the federal government take affirmative steps to ensure equal opportunity in employment, without regard to race, color, religion, sex, or national origin.

[30]438 U.S. 265 (1978).

[31]444 U.S. 193 (1979).

[32]Id. at 203.

[33]Id. at 209.

[34]Id. at 208.

[35]480 U.S. 616 (1987).

deemed qualified. Two men received a 75. A woman scored 73. The agency's director did not perceive the two-point difference as significant when viewed in light of the total work history of the three top applicants. Using gender as one of the factors considered, he offered the position to the female applicant, Johnson.

Applying the two-pronged test it had developed in *Weber,* the Court found that the plan was justified. First, there was a manifest imbalance of females in the workplace, and second, the plan did not unduly trammel the rights of nonminorities or men. The Court noted that the rejected male applicant had "no absolute entitlement to the road dispatcher position. Seven of the applicants were classified as qualified and eligible, and the Agency Director was authorized to promote any of the seven. Thus, denial of the promotion unsettled no legitimate, firmly rooted expectation on the part of petitioner."[36]

As exemplified in the *Weber* and *Johnson* cases, in the employment law context involving private employers, challenges to an affirmative-action plan have arisen most often when a white male has lost an employment opportunity and has sued under Title IV, alleging so-called reverse discrimination. The Court has stated that when an affirmative-action plan is challenged, the proper approach is to follow the analytical framework set forth in *McDonald Douglas Corp. v. Green,* 411 U.S. 792 (1973). Once a plaintiff establishes a prima facie case that race or sex has been taken into account in an employer's employment decision, the burden shifts to the employer to articulate a nondiscriminatory rationale for the decision. The existence of an affirmative-action plan provides such a rationale. If such a plan is articulated as the basis for the employer's decision, the burden shifts to the plaintiff to prove that the employer's justification is pretextual and the plan is invalid.[37]

The last time the U.S. Supreme Court addressed the issue of affirmative action and Title VII was the 1987 *Johnson* decision. One of the issues left unresolved by *Johnson,* as well as *Weber,* was whether an employer could justify creating an affirmative-action plan based on a reason other than remedying past discrimination, such as a desire to encourage a more diverse workplace. A recent Supreme Court case dealing with law school admissions suggests such a possibility. In that case the Court held that a desire for a racially diverse student body served a compelling governmental interest.[38] To date, however, the Court has not addressed whether a desire for racial diversity in the workplace can be used as a justification for affirmative action.

In summary, many people use the term *affirmative action* very loosely to refer to any type of preferential treatment based on race or gender. That is not how the courts have interpreted affirmative action. A valid affirmative-action plan must be designed to remedy past discrimination, and the plan must not unduly override the rights of other employees. First, the employer must determine if there is an imbalance in the employer's workforce as compared to the relevant labor market in "traditionally segregated job categories." Next, to ensure that the plan does not "unnecessarily trammel" the rights of other

---

[36]Id. at 638.

[37]Johnson, 480 U.S. at 626.

[38]Grutter v. Bollinger, 539 U.S. 306 (2003).

Affirmative-action plans analyzed using the *Weber* two-step approach

Step 1 Is there a valid rationale for the plan?
> To remedy past discrimination on the part of the employer or society evidenced by an imbalance in the employer's workforce as compared to the relevant labor market in "traditionally segregated job categories"

Step 2 Is the plan reasonable?

> Cannot trammel the rights of other employees or applicants
>
> - all employees receiving preferential treatment must be qualified
> - race or sex can be a "plus" factor only
> - there can be no absolute bar to other employees' advancement
> - plan must be temporary

Figure 10-11 Analysis of Affirmative-Action Plans under Title VII

individuals, any applicant who receives preferential treatment must be qualified for the job. While race or gender may be used as a "plus" factor, there can be no absolute bar to employment based on race or gender. For example, courts are more inclined to support affirmative-action plans that involve hiring than ones that involve layoffs, because no particular candidate is entitled to any particular job, whereas layoffs are imposed on specific individuals. Finally, the plan must be temporary to remedy past discrimination, not permanent in order to maintain a diverse workforce. Figure 10-11 summarizes how courts evaluate affirmative-action plans under Title VII.

Title VII applies to both private and public employers, but public employers must also obey the constraints of the equal protection clause of the Fourteenth Amendment (state and local governmental employers) and the due process clause of the Fifth Amendment (federal governmental employers). Therefore, public employers may have to defend their affirmative-action plans on both constitutional and statutory grounds. When undergoing a constitutional challenge to an affirmative-action plan involving race, the Court applies a standard known as strict scrutiny. Under that standard a public employer can justify its use of a race-conscious plan only for the very strongest of reasons. The plan must "serve a compelling governmental interest, and . . . be narrowly tailored to further that interest."[39] While it is not clear what will satisfy the strict scrutiny standard, the Court has held that a desire to remedy general societal discrimination is not sufficient.[40] This is in contrast to its decisions under Title VII, where it has found

---

[39]Adarand Constructors, Inc. v. Pena, 515 U.S. 200, 235 (1995).

[40]Wygant v. Jackson Bd. of Educ., 476 U.S. 267, 276 (1986) ("Societal discrimination, without more, is too amorphous a basis for imposing a racially classified remedy").

plans permissible even if there is no showing that the employers themselves were responsible for past discrimination.[41]

DISCUSSION QUESTIONS

7. Do you think President Johnson's statement—"[I]t is not enough just to open the gates of opportunity. All our citizens must have the ability to walk through those gates"—still provides a valid rationale for affirmative action?

8. Should affirmative-action plans be used only to remedy past discrimination, or should employers be allowed to use them to create a diverse workforce, even absent any evidence of past discrimination? For example, what if a car dealership located in a minority neighborhood could show that it would sell more cars if it had a more diverse sales force? Should the dealership be allowed to treat race as a necessary job requirement? Would your answer be different if the employer was a city, and it was looking to hire new police officers whose main duties would require them to spend time in a minority neighborhood where in the past white police officers had been attacked?

e. Damage Awards and Other Relief under Title VII

Until 1991 a plaintiff prevailing in a Title VII case was entitled to a court order enjoining the employer from engaging in unlawful employment practices and requiring affirmative action as appropriate, including reinstatement or hiring with or without back pay and other equitable relief. Congress amended Title VII in the Civil Rights Act of 1991 so that in cases of intentional discrimination the complaining party may also recover compensatory and punitive damages. Punitive damages are possible if the plaintiff can show that the employer acted "with malice or reckless indifference" to his or her federally protected rights. Compensatory damages can include "future pecuniary losses, emotional pain, suffering, inconvenience, mental anguish, loss of enjoyment of life, and other nonpecuniary losses."[42] However, damages are limited based on the size of the employer, from $50,000 for the smallest employers to $300,000 for those with over 500 employees.

Claims must be filed with the EEOC either 180 or 300 days, depending on the state, after the alleged unlawful employment practice has occurred. Compared to other statutes of limitations for common-law tort and contract claims, this is a very short period of time. Congress apparently chose to balance the new burden placed on employers with the guarantee that employees would have to act quickly to maintain any claim of discrimination.

As with all types of statutes of limitations, it is frequently necessary to determine when the plaintiff became aware of the alleged violation. Take for example the situation of Lilly Ledbetter, who learned through an anonymous tip that years ago a former supervisor had set her salary rate significantly below that of her fellow male employees. Because of that discriminatory decision, every

---

[41]Weber, 444 U.S. at 212 ("[T]he Court considers a job category to be 'traditionally segregated' when there has been a *societal* history of purposeful exclusion of blacks from the job category") (emphasis added).

[42]42 U.S.C.S. § 1981a (2008).

paycheck since then had remained below that of her fellow male workers. Within 180 days of learning of this discrimination, Ms. Ledbetter filed a claim with the EEOC. When the case was brought to the federal district court, the jury found that she had been the victim of intentional sex discrimination and the judge awarded her $223,776 in back pay, $4,662 in compensatory damages, and more than $3 million in punitive damages. But then the court of appeals reversed on the grounds that she had not met the statutory time limit for filing her claim.

The U.S. Supreme Court affirmed that reversal in the 2007 case of *Ledbetter v. Goodyear Tire.*[43] Because the discriminatory acts that had resulted in smaller paychecks over the years had all occurred long before she filed her claim, the Court ruled that they were barred by the statute of limitations. The dissent argued that in determining when the 180 days begins, pay discrimination cases should be judged differently from those where there is an obvious, discrete act, such as a firing or a failure to promote. Essentially, the majority claimed it was simply reading the "plain meaning" of the statute in denying the plaintiff relief. The dissent argued that the statute should be read in light of its remedial purpose and not given a "cramped interpretation."[44]

Justice Ginsberg ended her dissent by prophetically declaring that "the Legislature may act to correct this Court's parsimonious reading of Title VII."[45] Within a month of the Court's decision, the House of Representatives had introduced and soon passed an amendment to Title VII, clarifying that the time for filing compensation claims begins either when the original discriminatory act occurs or at any time an individual is "affected by application of a discriminatory compensation decision or other practice, including each time wages, benefits, or other compensation is paid, resulting in whole or in part from such a decision or other practice."[46] The bill received its final passage through congress in early January 2009 and soon after his inauguration, President Obama signed the bill into law, thereby nullifying the 2007 Supreme Court decision. This action illustrates the basic concept we introduced in Chapter 2, that when interpreting a statute, the courts are simply making their best guess as to the legislative intent. If they guess wrong, the legislature (in this case, Congress) is free to amend the statute. The Ledbetter decision now signifies the third time that the Supreme Court has "guessed" wrong about Congress's intentions as to Title VII, resulting in a congressional amendment to the statute.

2. ADEA: Age Discrimination

In 1967 Congress passed the Age Discrimination in Employment Act (ADEA).[47] This act prohibits employers from discriminating against persons aged forty or older because of their age. While the protected classes found under Title VII are generally described by immutable characteristics, such as race or sex, everyone will move into the protected age category. In fact, according to the Bureau of

---

[43]127 S. Ct. 2162 (2007)

[44]Id. at 2188.

[45]Id.

[46]H.R. 2831: Lilly Ledbetter Fair Pay Act of 2007, 110th Congress (as passed by House July 31, 2007).

[47]42 U.S.C.S. § 623 (2008).

Labor Statistics, over half of the labor force will be over the age of forty by the year 2012.[48]

As with other forms of discrimination, enforcement of the ADEA involves proof problems. In case of alleged disparate treatment employees can use a modified version of the *McDonnell Douglas* four-part analysis:

1. the plaintiff belongs to the protected class of persons forty years of age or older,
2. the plaintiff applied for a job for which the plaintiff was qualified,
3. the plaintiff was rejected, and
4. the position remained open or was filled by someone substantially younger than the plaintiff.

Note that the fourth part of this test has been modified from requiring "someone not in the protected class" to "someone substantially younger than the plaintiff." Without this change, if the person who replaces the plaintiff is younger than the plaintiff but is also from the protected age group, the plaintiff would be left without a cause of action. The U.S. Supreme Court was faced with that situation in *O'Connor v. Consolidated Coin Caterers Corp.*[49] The Court was called on to decide if the ADEA was violated when the Consolidated Coin Caterers Corporation fired a fifty-six-year-old middle manager and then gave his job to a forty-year-old. The company argued that by replacing one protected class individual with another, it had not violated the law. The Court, however, rejected this argument and ruled that the law had been violated because the evidence showed that O'Connor had been fired because of his age.

> Or to put the point more concretely, there can be no greater inference of age discrimination (as opposed to "40 or over" discrimination) when a 40 year-old is replaced by a 39 year-old than when a 56 year-old is replaced by a 40 year-old. Because it lacks probative value, the fact that an ADEA plaintiff was replaced by someone outside the protected class is not a proper element of the *McDonnell Douglas* prima facie case.[50]

Therefore, the Court concluded that age discrimination can be more reliably indicated by a showing that the replacement is substantially younger than by a showing that the replacement is not a member of the protected class.

> Because the ADEA prohibits discrimination on the basis of age and not class membership, the fact that a replacement is substantially younger than the plaintiff is a far more reliable indicator of age discrimination than is the fact that the plaintiff was replaced by someone outside the protected class.[51]

This statement would seem to indicate that the replacement worker must be substantially younger than the plaintiff. However, the Tenth Circuit has ruled that all that is necessary is proof that age was the motivating factor. The court

---

[48]See U.S. Department of Labor Bureau of Labor Statistics, Employment Projections at *www.bls.gov/emplab2002-08.htm* (last modified 2/11/04).

[49]517 U.S. 308 (1996).

[50]Id. at 312.

[51]Id.

found that a fifty-seven-year-old replaced by a fifty-two-year-old could win an age discrimination case where he had direct proof that the reasons given for his firing were pretextual.[52]

Recently, the U.S. Supreme Court also removed the uncertainty that had existed as to whether the ADEA's prohibition against age discrimination prohibits employers from favoring older employees over younger employees. In *General Dynamics Land Systems, Inc. v. Cline,*[53] the Court confronted that issue. General Dynamics and the union representing the employees reached a collective bargaining agreement that eliminated the company's obligation to provide health benefits to subsequently retired employees. However, an exception was made for current workers who were at least fifty years old. Cline and other employees who were at least forty years old (and thus protected by the ADEA) but less than fifty years old (and therefore not entitled to the benefits) claimed that the agreement discriminated against them because of their age and hence violated the ADEA.

The Court disagreed. "We see the text, structure, purpose, and history of the ADEA, along with its relationship to other federal statutes, as showing that the statute does not mean to stop an employer from favoring an older employee over a younger one."[54] Therefore, the collective bargaining agreement favoring the older workers was not unlawful discrimination.

Finally, while it was clear that an older worker could bring a claim for disparate treatment under the ADEA, for many years there had been a split in the circuits regarding whether they could bring a claim using the disparate impact theory. For example, when seeking to decrease operating expenses, employers often choose to reduce the number of highest-paid workers. As increased pay and longevity at work tend to run together, such work reductions raise the issue of disparate impact. The circuits were split on whether the ADEA allowed for such claims based on disparate impact, with at least three circuits expressly permitting such claims and five expressly prohibiting them.

In 2005, the Supreme Court resolved this issue by finding that the ADEA does allow for claims based on disparate impact. In *Smith v. City of Jackson,*[55] the city of Jackson decided to give all police officers a raise, but to give proportionately more money to those police officers with less than five years' service in an attempt to bring starting salaries up to the regional average. The older police officers sued, alleging that the policy had a disparate impact, because under the policy most of the older officers would get a smaller percentage raise than the younger officers.

As you know, under Title VII, plaintiffs in a disparate impact case must prove that a facially neutral plan or practice has the effect of disproportionately impacting a protected group of employees, such as women or minorities. Because the ADEA's language outlawing discrimination mirrors that of Title VII,[56] in *Smith v. City of Jackson* the Supreme Court held that the older police officers could bring a claim under the disparate impact theory of discrimination. Once

---

[52]Greene v. Safeway Stores, Inc., 98 F.3d 554 (10th Cir. 1996).

[53]540 U.S. 581 (2004).

[54]Id. at 601.

[55]544 U.S. 228 (2005).

[56]ADEA § 4(a)(2) substitutes "age" for "race, color, religion, sex, or national origin."

Title VII plaintiffs have shown that the employer's practice has a disparate impact, the employer can justify its use only by proving business necessity, that is, that there is no alternative means that could accomplish the same goal with a less discriminatory effect. Under the ADEA, however, the Court held that employers only need to show that their practice is reasonable—that it advances some reasonable business purpose. This is because, unlike Title VII, the ADEA has what is known as the RFOA provision—if an employer can advance a "reasonable factor other than age" in support of its policy, it has a valid defense even if it cannot show that the practice is a business necessity.

Applying this provision, the Supreme Court held that

> the disparate impact is attributable to the City's decision to give raises based on seniority and position. Reliance on seniority and rank is unquestionably reasonable given the City's goal of raising employees' salaries to match those in surrounding communities. . . . [T]he city's decision to grant a larger raise to lower echelon employees for the purpose of bringing salaries in line with that of surrounding police forces was a decision based on "reasonable factors other than age" that responded to the City's legitimate goal of retaining police officers.
>
> While there may be other reasonable ways for the City to achieve its goals, the one selected was not unreasonable. Unlike the business necessity test, which asks whether there are other ways for the employer to achieve its goals that do not result in a disparate impact on a protected class, the reasonableness inquiry includes no such requirement.[57]

Having found that the city had met its burden of defending its actions, the Court affirmed dismissal of the case. As a result of this decision, it is now clear that older workers may bring a discrimination lawsuit based on the theory of disparate impact.

In the latest development regarding disparate impact litigation and the ADEA, the Supreme Court recently clarified that it is the employer who bears the burden of proof that its decision was based on a reasonable factor other than age.[58] In *Meacham v. Knolls Atomic Power Laboratory* thirty-one employees had been laid off as result of an involuntary reduction in force, thirty of whom were over the age of forty. There were a number of factors that the employer used to determine who should be laid off, including "flexibility" and possession of "critical" skills. The employees argued that the use of such subjective factors had the effect of eliminating older workers. A jury agreed and awarded the employees a total of $6 million. On appeal, the Second Circuit reversed, holding that the employees had the burden of proving that reasonable factors other than age were *not* the basis for the employer's decision. Because the court thought the employees had not carried the burden of proving that the employers' non-age factors were unreasonable, it found for the employer. In reversing, the Supreme Court held that an employer defending a disparate-impact claim under the ADEA bears both the burden of production and the burden of persuasion for the affirmative defense of "reasonable factors other than age" (RFOA).

---

[57]Smith, 544 U.S. at 242–43.

[58]Meacham v. Knolls Atomic Power Laboratory, 123 S. Ct. 2395 (2008).

In answer to the concerns of business groups that this decision would induce employers to alter business practices simply to avoid being sued, Justice Souter responded:

> [T]here is no denying that putting employers to the work of persuading fact-finders that their choices are reasonable makes it harder and costlier to defend than if employers merely bore the burden of production; nor do we doubt that this will sometimes affect the way employers do business with their employees. But at the end of the day, *amici*'s concerns have to be directed at Congress, which set the balance where it is, by both creating the RFOA exemption and writing it in the orthodox format of an affirmative defense. We have to read it the way Congress wrote it.[59]

NETNOTE

The U.S. Department of Justice maintains information on the Americans with Disabilities Act at *www.usdoj.gov/crt/ada/adahom1.htm*. Another good source of information is the Americans with Disabilities Act Document Center, found at *www. jan.wvu.edu/links/adalinks.htm*.

3. ADA: Disability Discrimination

In 1990 Congress enacted the Americans with Disabilities Act (ADA).[60] As is true under Title VII this act applies to employers with fifteen or more employees. An employer cannot discriminate against a qualified individual with a disability if reasonable accommodations are possible.

A **disability** is defined as a physical or mental impairment that substantially limits a major life activity. An individual with a disability is someone who

- has such an impairment, or
- has a history or record of such an impairment, or
- is regarded as having an impairment.

A **qualified individual with a disability** is an individual with a disability who can perform the essential job functions. Examples of conditions that the courts have found to qualify as disabilities include cancer, heart disease, paraplegia, morbid obesity, and alcoholism. Note, however, that while an employer could not refuse to hire nor fire an employee for being an alcoholic, the employer could fire an employee for drinking while at work. Finally, the employer is only required to make a **reasonable accommodation.** An accommodation is not considered reasonable if it would create an undue hardship for the employer. In such

---

[59]Id. at 2407.
[60]42 U.S.C.S. § 12101 (2008).

situations the employer is excused from compliance. Examples of reasonable accommodations might include providing flexible working hours or installing a ramp to make an office wheelchair accessible. Cases in this area tend to focus on three issues: (1) defining "disability," (2) determining what constitutes essential job functions, and (3) resolving what is required by way of a reasonable accommodation without creating an undue hardship.

As to what constitutes a disability, if the plaintiff has a condition that can be corrected with medication, glasses, or other corrective devices, he or she is not disabled.[61] In *Sutton v. United Air Lines, Inc.,* the plaintiffs applied for positions as airline pilots. They both wore glasses. Without their glasses their eyesight was 20/200. With the glasses their eyesight was corrected to 20/20. The airline had a policy of requiring 20/100 or better of uncorrected visual acuity and refused to hire the plaintiffs. When they sued, the Supreme Court held that they could not proceed with their lawsuit, as they were not "disabled" within the meaning of the statute.[62] Following this decision there was concern that the Supreme Court's interpretation of the word "disabled" would leave many employees without the protections afforded by the ADA. In response, in 2007 legislation was introduced in Congress to amend the ADA to prohibit courts from considering mitigating measures such as medication or medical devices in determining whether a person is disabled. At the time this text went to print, the bill had passed the House but had not yet been enacted into law. Should the statute be amended in this manner, then in the future, plaintiffs using corrective devices, such as glasses or hearing aids, would fit within the ADA's definition of "disabled."

An additional requirement is that the disability must affect a "major life activity." Therefore, when analyzing whether a particular person is disabled, the courts focus on the abilities of the individual rather than solely on the condition. Because every individual is affected differently, the same condition may affect a "major life activity" in one person but not in another. Also, as you can imagine, the phrase "major life activity" is itself open to interpretation. Recently, the Supreme Court determined that a woman suffering from carpal tunnel syndrome was not suffering from a disability within the meaning of the ADA.[63] While the pain she experienced prevented her from performing the precise tasks required of her job—holding her arms over her head for long periods of time—it did not prevent her from carrying on such normal daily activities as brushing her teeth, washing her face, bathing, tending her flower garden, and doing laundry. Therefore, while her carpal tunnel syndrome prevented her from performing her job, it did not qualify her as a "disabled individual" under the statute. To so qualify, a permanent or long-term condition must severely restrict the person's

---

[61]Sutton v. United Air Lines, Inc., 527 U.S. 471 (1999).

[62]While this case defines what qualifies as a disability under the ADA, a federal statute, many states have similar statutes protecting their disabled citizens. Not all state courts have similarly interpreted their state statutes to disallow coverage, but have rather analyzed the disability in its uncorrected state. *See, e.g.,* Dahill v. Police Dept. of Boston, 748 N.E.2d 956, 962 (Mass. 2001) ("Determining [disability] with reference to mitigation measures might produce anomalous results. . . . Two individuals with the same hearing impairment might be treated differently under the statute because one can afford a hearing aid and one cannot").

[63]Toyota v. Williams, 534 U.S. 184 (2002).

ability to do tasks central to most people's daily lives, rather than simply making them unable to perform tasks associated with a specific job.[64]

As to the second issue, determining what constitutes essential job functions, employees must be able to show that although they are disabled, they can perform all essential functions. For example, being in a wheelchair would not prevent someone from performing all the essential job functions of an accountant. Some areas are not as clear-cut, however, such as regular job attendance, which is usually seen as an essential job function. The courts are divided on whether absenteeism disqualifies a claimant under the statute if the claimant can show that the absenteeism is due to a disability.

The third issue, what qualifies as a "reasonable" accommodation without creating an undue hardship, is something that the courts have been grappling with on a case-by-case basis. These cases are very fact based, as the courts attempt to determine whether a particular accommodation will involve significant difficulty or expense. For example, while employers normally might not be required to pay for employee parking, one court said that the reasonableness of such a determination could only be made after a full analysis of the employer's geographic location and financial resources.[65]

4. Limitations on Employee Lawsuits against State and Local Governmental Employers

As is true with enforcing anyone's rights, employees who have been discriminated against need to be able to bring the discrimination to the attention of the appropriate officials, and those officials have to take proper actions to sanction those responsible for the violations. Statutes covering discrimination by private employers provide for filing complaints with governmental agencies and the courts. Public employees often face additional challenges when it comes to getting their complaints addressed.

The first hurdle involves the Eleventh Amendment, which makes the states immune from "any suit in law or equity, commenced or prosecuted . . . by Citizens of any Foreign State." While this wording appears to prohibit only those suits brought by citizens of another state, the U.S. Supreme Court has determined that it also applies to any suit brought by a state's own citizens unless the state consents to the suit. This, in turn, creates problems when aggrieved state workers want to sue their state employer for alleged violations of Title VII, the ADEA, the ADA, or other federal statutes that prohibit unlawful employment discrimination.

Such suits are authorized, however, if two conditions are met. First, the court must find that when Congress wrote the legislation, Congress's intent to authorize such suits was made clear. Second, as you will recall from our earlier discussion of federal legislative power, Congress can only legitimately enact statutes if it does so pursuant to a specific constitutional provision. The courts have determined that in the case of statutes prohibiting discrimination, in appropriate situations Congress does have this power under the Fourteenth

---

[64]Id. at 198.

[65]Lyons v. Legal Aid Soc'y, 68 F.3d 1512 (2d Cir. 1995).

Amendment's § 5 enforcement powers. Therefore, the second step is to ensure that Congress was validly exercising that power.

While the Supreme Court has long held that Congress was empowered under § 5 of the Fourteenth Amendment to hold state employers accountable under Title VII,[66] the Court's application of this two-part test has had varying results in relation to other statutes. In 2001 in *Board of Trustees of University of Alabama v. Garrett*,[67] the Court ruled that disabled state employees could not use the federal courts to sue their employers for money damages under Title I of the ADA. However, just two years later, the Court ruled in *Nevada Department of Human Resources v. Hibbs*[68] that state employees could sue state employers for money damages in federal court for violations of the Family and Medical Leave Act (FMLA). This act allows eligible employees to take up to twelve work weeks of unpaid leave because of the birth of a child, to care for such child, upon placement of a child with the employee for adoption or foster care, in order to care for a close family member suffering from a serious health condition, or because the employee is suffering from a serious health condition.[69] The Court found that Congress's purpose in passing the statute was to protect the right to be free from gender-based discrimination in the workplace. "The text of the act makes this clear. Congress found that, 'due to the nature of the roles of men and women in our society, the primary responsibility for family caretaking often falls on women, and such responsibility affects the working lives of women more than it affects the working lives of men.' 29 U.S.C. § 2601(a)(5)."[70] The Court distinguished *Hibbs* from *Garrett* by saying that *Garrett* involved discrimination against the disabled, a classification that is not subjected to the heightened scrutiny required in cases of sex discrimination, such as that found in *Hibbs*.[71] And in 2004 they ruled in *Tennessee v. Lane*[72] that private individuals could sue states under Title II of the ADA when the suit concerned access to a county courthouse. The Court found that the interest being challenged here, like the one in *Hibbs*, was deserving of heightened judicial scrutiny as it involved the right of access to the courts.[73]

5. Retaliation

Fear of retaliation is another factor that often affects the enforcement of anti-discrimination laws. If victims of discrimination are afraid to register formal complaints and if fellow workers are afraid to provide corroborating evidence, the discriminatory practices will go unchallenged and will continue to harm other employees.

The Supreme Court has repeatedly emphasized the importance of protecting employees from retaliation. For example, in *Burlington Northern &*

---

[66]Fitzpatrick v. Bitzer, 427 U.S. 445 (1976).

[67]531 U.S. 356 (2001).

[68]538 U.S. 721 (2003).

[69]29 U.S.C.S. § 2612 (2008).

[70]*Hibbs*, at 728, n. 2.

[71]Id. at 733.

[72]541 U.S. 509 (2004).

[73]Id. at 522.

Santa Fe Railway Co. v. White, the Supreme Court started with the premise that "Title VII's anti-retaliation provision forbids employer actions that 'discriminate against' an employee (or job applicant) because he has 'opposed' a practice that Title VII forbids or has 'made a charge, testified, assisted, or participated in' a Title VII 'investigation, proceeding, or hearing'"[74] and concluded that this prohibition against retaliation extends beyond actions taken at the workplace.[75] They cited as an example a case where an employer was found liable when it retaliated by filing false criminal charges.[76] Most recently the Court held that a federal employee who had sued for age discrimination could recover for harm caused by the employer's retaliatory actions, even though the section of the ADEA dealing with federal employers does not explicitly prohibit retaliation.[77]

6. Common Law Approaches: At-Will Employment

As mentioned at the beginning of this chapter, most employees work on an at-will basis. That is, they have not signed formal contracts with their employers governing their employment relationships, and they are not working in companies that have unions to protect the rights of employees. Therefore, they are free to leave work at any time, and likewise their employers are allowed to fire them at any time so long as the reasons for the dismissal do not violate any federal or state statutes, such as the antidiscrimination statutes covered above.

Under traditional interpretations of the at-will doctrine, employers have been free to fire their employees for a good reason, a bad reason, or no reason at all so long as that reason does not conflict with specific statutes to the contrary. For example, if an employee reports late for work, the employer is free to fire that employee, even if this is the first instance of that employee's arriving late. Employees thus had no protection from arbitrary and even unreasonable employer actions.

However, in recent years some courts have begun to give at-will employees more protection. In some cases where employers have established employee handbooks that spell out various personnel procedures, the courts have generally required those employers to follow their own rules. In addition, a few courts have stated that employers owe employees an implied covenant to act in good faith. Finally, many courts have found a public policy exception that prevents an employer from firing an employee when the employer's actions are seen as harming not only the employee but also society as a whole. Examples include an employer firing an employee for asserting a legally guaranteed right, such as applying for worker's compensation; for doing what the law requires, such as reporting for jury duty; and for refusing to do an unlawful act, such as committing perjury.

At-will employment is another area of the law that is rapidly changing. You should expect to see the rights of employers to freely fire at-will employees come under increased judicial scrutiny in the coming years.

---

[74]548 U.S. 53, 59 (2006).

[75]Id. at 62.

[76]Id. at 64.

[77]Gomez-Perez v. Potter, 128 S. Ct. 1931 (2008).

SUMMARY

Businesses must be concerned with many areas of the law, including business formation, agency, commercial paper, secured transactions, and employment discrimination. One of the first decisions a business makes relates to its business form: whether it be a sole proprietorship, partnership, corporation, or limited liability company. When a company borrows money, commercial paper is involved. The business may also have to guarantee repayment by supplying collateral, thereby creating a secured transaction.

Any employer who hires employees must be aware of agency law. Generally, an agent is someone who has the power to act in the place of another. If an employee/agent acts within the scope of his or her responsibilities, the employer can be held liable for the agent's actions.

Finally, employment law is dominated by federal statutes, including Title VII of the Civil Rights Act of 1964, prohibiting discrimination based on race, color, religion, sex, or national origin; the Age Discrimination in Employment Act (ADEA), prohibiting discrimination based on age; and the Americans with Disabilities Act (ADA), prohibiting discrimination based on disability. If the case is not one of overt discrimination, the plaintiff can usually bring a discrimination claim under a theory of either disparate treatment or disparate impact.

CRITICAL THINKING EXERCISES

1. Reread the opening chapter scenario. What do you think would be the advantages and disadvantages of each of the four major business forms in light of the needs of Alice and her friends? Be sure to take into account the special life situation of each person and how that would impact that person's choice of business form.

2. For each of the following situations, determine what happens when the method of payment changes from cash, to the assignment of a contract, to a promissory note.

    a. Buyer pays Seller $600 in cash for 1,000 calculators. Seller then takes the $600 and uses it to pay for a cruise.
    If the calculators prove to be defective and the seller is insolvent, who loses, the buyer or the third party who accepted $600 from the seller?

    b. Buyer signs a contract with Seller promising to pay $600 for 1,000 calculators on or before 6/6/08. Seller then assigns the contract to the owner of a travel agency in payment for a cruise.
    If the calculators prove to be defective and the seller is insolvent, who loses, the buyer or the third party who accepted the assigned contract rights from the buyer?

    c. Buyer signs a note promising to pay Seller $600 for 1,000 calculators on or before 6/6/08. Seller then delivers the note to the owner of a travel agency in payment for a cruise.
    If the calculators prove to be defective and the seller is insolvent, who loses if the note is a negotiable instrument? Who loses if the note is not a negotiable instrument? Why?

3. For each of the following, base your analysis on the case of *O'Connor v. McDonald's Restaurants of California, Inc.*, beginning on page 355 of the text.

    a. At the request of his employer, Bob worked late one night and missed the last bus home. No one was left at work except for Bob, and not being able to figure out any other way to get home, Bob borrowed his employer's truck. The next morning, while driving to work, he was in an automobile accident, injuring Martha. Martha wants to sue Bob's employer. Do you think her lawsuit will be successful? Why or why not?

    b. Jill was a traveling salesperson. During the day she drove one of her employer's cars. If at the end of the day she happened to be in the vicinity of her house, she could keep the car overnight. One morning while driving her employer's car to work, she was in an automobile accident and injured Billy. Billy wants to sue Jill's employer. Do you think his lawsuit will be successful? Now consider the following: As Jill left her house that morning, she was juggling her keys, coffee, and purse. Afraid she might spill her coffee, she placed her purse on the roof, forgot she had done so, and drove off. When she realized what she had done, she immediately did a U-turn so that she could retrace her route to search for her purse. It was while she was making the U-turn that she had the accident. Do these additional facts change your answer? Why or why not?

    c. Jim worked for Pest-Be-Gone. All Pest-Be-Gone employees wear a distinctive green uniform and name tags. Martha, a homeowner, had hired Pest-Be-Gone to come to her house to spray for termites. When Jim arrived, she let him into her home so that he could perform the extermination. Jim locked her in her bedroom and raped her. Martha has sued Pest-Be-Gone for negligence. Do you think her lawsuit will be successful? Why or why not?

    d. As part of a goodwill campaign, James Manufacturing entered a team in a citywide golf league. It recruited players from among its employees, provided them with uniforms and equipment, and paid their expenses. During the tournament, one of the employees negligently hooked a golf ball that struck and injured Sally. Sally wants to sue James Manufacturing. Do you think her lawsuit will be successful? Why or why not?

    e. Brown Bakery allows its employees to play baseball in a field behind the bakery during their lunch hour. During one game, the pitcher threw a ball that hit Sam in the face. The pitcher admitted after the game that he meant to hit Sam, a notorious home run hitter, so he could walk him. Sam sued Brown Bakery. Do you think his lawsuit will be successful? Why or why not?

4. Johnson Controls, Inc., manufactures batteries. In the process, lead is a primary ingredient. Because the company was afraid that exposure to lead could lead to harm to any fetus carried by a female employee, the company excluded women who were pregnant or "capable of bearing children" from jobs that exposed them to lead. When a group of women challenged this policy, the company argued that it was a BFOQ. How do you think the court resolved this issue?

5. Dianne Rawlinson sought employment with the Alabama Board of Corrections as a correctional officer. Alabama had established minimum height and weight requirements of 120 pounds and 5 feet 2 inches for all correctional officers. These combined requirements excluded 41.13 percent of the female population and less than 1 percent of the male population. Ms. Rawlinson was refused employment because she failed to meet the minimum 120-pound weight requirement. The prison argued that the requirements were necessary because they have a relationship to strength. Ms. Rawlinson filed a charge of discrimination with the EEOC. While her claim was pending, the Alabama Board of Corrections adopted another regulation prohibiting female correctional officers in any maximum-security institution housing men. In those prisons the inmate living area was divided into large dormitories with communal showers and toilets that are open to the dormitories and hallways. The main duty of correctional officers in such a setting is to maintain security. Because of inadequate staff and facilities, no attempt was made in the four maximum-security male prisons to segregate inmates according to their offenses or levels of dangerousness, leading to what some described as a "jungle atmosphere." Ms. Rawlinson then amended her charge to also challenge this regulation. Do you think Ms. Rawlinson was successful on either claim? Think about the arguments Ms. Rawlinson would advance as well as any defenses the employer would raise.

6. Judith Smith was a unit director at a facility for the mentally retarded. Ms. Smith's six-month rating was "outstanding." She came in conflict, however, with the superintendent over an issue regarding the reorganization of the facility. The superintendent wanted to centralize all power within his office. Ms. Smith and the other unit directors thought it would be in the best interest of the patients and staff to also give them an opportunity to participate in policy decisions. The superintendent refused to consider that option. The unit directors then wrote a letter critical of the superintendent. Shortly thereafter Ms. Smith was fired. Ms. Smith sued, alleging that her dismissal was against public policy. Do you think a court would agree?

7. A hospital administrator promoted a fifty-two-year-old "fishing buddy" because he wanted to help his friend. A better qualified younger black woman sued, saying that her rights under Title VII had been violated. Do you think the hospital has engaged in unlawful discrimination?

‖ REVIEW QUESTIONS

Pages 337 through 346
1. What are the four basic forms of business organizations, and what are the main advantages and disadvantages of each?
2. What is the most common reason for changing from a sole proprietorship to a partnership or a corporation?
3. Name the ways by which a general partnership can be terminated.
4. What are the essential elements that the court looks for in trying to determine whether a partnership exists?

5. What types of information are contained in a business's articles of incorporation?
6. List the general responsibilities of a corporate board of directors.
7. Why might forming a limited liability company be preferable to forming either a partnership or a corporation?

Pages 347 through 352

8. Name the requirements for an instrument to be negotiable.
9. What must be satisfied for someone to be a holder in due course?
10. What are the two basic functions of commercial paper?
11. How does one become a holder of a negotiable instrument?
12. In a secured transaction, what is the difference between attachment and perfection?
13. Name the requirements that a creditor must meet in order to have an enforceable security interest against a debtor (to have the interest attach).
14. How can a creditor perfect a security interest?
15. What are the two main concerns of a creditor if a debtor defaults?
16. Define a *floating lien*, and give an example.
17. Define a *purchase money security interest*.
18. What is the main benefit of being a holder in due course rather than a mere holder?
19. List the following creditors in order of priority, starting with those that have the highest level of priority: general creditors, perfected security interest holders, unperfected security interest holders, buyers in the ordinary course of business, lien creditors, and perfected purchase money security interest holders.

Pages 352 through 357

20. What are the four basic duties that a principal owes an agent?
21. What are the basic duties that an agent owes a principal?
22. Name two of the factors a court will look to in trying to determine if an employer-employee or an employer–independent contractor relationship exists.
23. Give two examples of why it would matter whether a relationship is one of employer-employee or one of employer–independent contractor.
24. When will an employer be held responsible for an employee's act?

Pages 357 through 389

25. What is a bona fide occupational qualification (BFOQ)? What role does it play in a Title VII litigation?
26. In a Title VII case alleging discriminatory treatment, how does the plaintiff prove the prima facie case? What must the defendant do in response? What must the plaintiff do to rebut the defendant's response?
27. In a Title VII case alleging discriminatory impact, how does the plaintiff prove the prima facie case? What must the defendant do in response? What must the plaintiff do to rebut the defendant's response?
28. After *Griggs,* can employers use tests to evaluate people for hiring and promotion purposes? Why?
29. When must an employer have an affirmative-action plan?
30. When may an employer adopt a voluntary affirmative-action plan?
31. How does the presentation of an age discrimination case differ from that of one under Title VII?
32. Under the ADA who is a qualified individual?
33. What are the three main issues that arise when litigating cases under the [Americans with Disabilities Act] ADA?
34. What are the limits on employees suing state and local governmental employers?
35. What is employment at will?
36. Name two exceptions to the employment at-will doctrine.

Chapter 11

Family Law

Children are our most valuable national resource.
President Herbert Hoover

INTRODUCTION

This chapter presents an introduction to the basic legal principles of what is commonly called **family law.** The first section will cover the legal aspects of marriage and divorce. It will include a discussion of what marriage is, the requirements for a valid marriage, and how the marital bond can be dissolved. The second section will explore the legal aspects of the parent-child relationship, including problems related to adoption and paternity. It will also cover parental rights and responsibilities and problems related to the enforcement of those rights and responsibilities.

Family law
The area of the law that covers marriage, divorce, and parent-child relationships.

Family law is one of the most dynamic areas of the law. The very notion of what constitutes a family has become a politically and emotionally charged issue. No longer can we limit our definition of a family to a unit made up of a husband, a wife, and children. Today a family might mean an unmarried mother and her children; a single father and his children; a mother, her children, and a stepfather; or a mother, her child, and her female companion. Legislatures and courts are struggling to update the law in this area as our societal views on these issues change.

Family law also illustrates the inability of the courts to solve basic social problems. The breakdown of the traditional family, advances in medical science, and changing societal mores are all pressing the courts with increasingly complex issues that can be only imperfectly resolved within the legal arena. Family law decisions go to the very heart of what we feel is important. For example, should the best interests of the child or the rights of a natural parent govern the outcome of a custody dispute? Should the courts enforce a contract whereby a woman agrees to serve as a surrogate parent? Should couples who choose to live together without getting married receive the same legal benefits as do married couples? These are just a few of the issues that we will grapple with in this chapter on family law.

Because family law is dominated by state statutes and the court decisions interpreting those statutes, there is a great deal of variation from one state to the next. However, while state law is the principal source of family law, recently the federal government has enacted legislation in certain areas of family law, such as those laws assisting states with the collection of child support and trying to prevent divorced or separated parents from kidnapping their own children and taking them across state lines.

Most aspects of family law—governing who can be married, how marriages take place, the property rights of marital partners, how marriages are dissolved, how children are adopted—are part of the civil law. However, criminal statutes cover some aspects of family law, such as child and spousal abuse.

As is true of any law, the laws that state and federal legislatures develop governing family relationships must conform to the restrictions of state constitutions, as well as the U.S. Constitution. For example, laws regulating who may marry and those concerning parental rights have at times been challenged on the grounds that they violate either the due process or the equal protection guarantees of the Fourteenth Amendment.

A. MARRIAGE

Marriage has traditionally been defined as a legally recognized union in which a man and a woman form a family unit and take on special legal rights and obligations. In states such as Pennsylvania, where the marriage statute does not actually define marriage, the courts have relied on common-law cases and standard dictionary definitions in order to conclude that marriage is "the legal union of one man and one woman as husband and wife."[1] Later in this chapter we will examine recent court opinions, legislation, and proposed constitutional amendments related to same-sex marriages and civil unions.

Solemnized marriage
A marriage in which the couple has obtained the proper marriage license from a local government official and has then taken marriage vows before either a recognized member of the clergy or a judge and a designated number of witnesses.

In addition to being members of the opposite sex, state regulations have traditionally required persons applying for a marriage license to be over a minimum age (usually eighteen), not be too closely related by blood to their spouses, and be "of sound mind" (i.e., mentally capable of giving consent). Minors of a certain age are often allowed to marry if they have the consent of their parents or guardians. While a requirement for some sort of health certificate or blood test for sexually transmitted diseases was becoming less common, with the increased public concern over AIDS, the pendulum may be swinging back toward more premarital testing requirements.

The legal system recognizes two forms of marriage. In the first and most common type, known as a **solemnized marriage,** the parties first apply for and receive an official marriage license from a local governmental official. Usually

---

[1] See DeSanto v. Barnsley, 476 A.2d 952, 954 (Pa. Super. Ct. 1984) (quoting Black's Law Dictionary).

after a brief waiting period, they then have their commitment solemnized by saying their vows either through a religious ceremony presided over by a recognized member of the clergy or a civil ceremony presided over by a judge. The marriage becomes official once the license is signed and filed with the appropriate governmental office.

The second type of marriage is much less common and is referred to as **common-law marriage.** It is one in which the parties have mutually agreed to enter into a relationship in which they accept all the duties and responsibilities that correspond to those of a marital relationship and have openly cohabitated together but have never obtained a marriage license or had their marriage solemnized by someone who is legally authorized to do so. Most states no longer recognize the validity of such common-law marriages unless the couple established their common-law marital relationship in one of the few states that still formally recognize common-law marriages and then moved into the state.

Common-law marriage
A marriage that has not been solemnized but in which the couple has mutually agreed to enter into a relationship in which they accept all the duties and responsibilities that correspond to those of marriage.

DISCUSSION QUESTIONS

1. The following section from the Illinois Marriage and Dissolution of Marriage Act illustrates the types of prohibitions that appear in many state statutes:

750 Ill. Comp. Stat. 5/212
(a) The following marriages are prohibited:
    (1) a marriage entered into prior to the dissolution of an earlier marriage of one of the parties;
    (2) a marriage between an ancestor and a descendant or between a brother and a sister, whether the relationship is by the half or the whole blood or by adoption;
    (3) a marriage between an uncle and a niece or between an aunt and a nephew, whether the relationship is by the half or the whole blood;
    (4) a marriage between cousins of the first degree; however, a marriage between first cousins is not prohibited if:
        (i) both parties are 50 years of age or older; or
        (ii) either party, at the time of application for a marriage license, presents for filing with the county clerk of the county in which the marriage is to be solemnized, a certificate signed by a licensed physician stating the party to the proposed marriage is permanently and irreversibly sterile;
    (5) a marriage between 2 individuals of the same sex.

What do you think is the legislative purpose behind each of these provisions? With which ones do you agree or disagree?

2. List as many valid reasons as you can for why states require a marriage license.

3. As part of the legal requirements for getting married many states require a waiting period between the time the license is issued and the time the actual marriage can take place. Do you think states should impose these types of waiting periods? If yes, why and how long should they be? If no, why not?

4. As part of the legal requirements for getting a marriage license some states require a blood test for such things as sexually transmitted diseases or AIDS. Would you support such requirements? Why?

1. Consequences of Marriage

In the romantic haze that surrounds courtship and marriage a couple may not fully realize all the legal consequences that flow from their decisions to marry. Under our common-law traditions marriage was viewed as a contract in which a man and woman relinquished their former independence to merge themselves into a new joint enterprise. For example, married persons have a legal obligation to support each other not only during the marriage but often even after a divorce. Property purchased by one spouse may be seen as marital property, in which both have rights. Through a legal right known as a **forced share,** each of the married partners is given a statutory right to inherit from the other, even if the other spouse seeks to prevent it. One spouse may also be immune from being sued by the other spouse for torts committed against the first spouse. There are also many legal benefits to being married that are not given to nonmarital partners. For example, if a spouse is injured, the other spouse may recover loss of consortium damages. Marriage partners normally qualify for employer and governmental benefits not available to nonmarried couples. They also have the right to be taxed as a marital unit. Finally, both partners generally may not be forced to testify against each other.

As with other areas of family law, the liabilities and benefits of marriage are constantly being altered. For example, many states now allow one spouse to sue the other for tortious injuries. Also, in what may start a trend, the Alaska Supreme Court recently held that a state statute prohibiting discrimination based on "marital status" means that employers must give cohabiting partners the same health insurance benefits offered to employee spouses.[2]

Of course, choosing to live together instead of getting married also has legal consequences. In the famous case of *Marvin v. Marvin*[3] a woman who had lived with the actor Lee Marvin for six years sought enforcement of an oral agreement regarding the division of their property when they separated. The court held that the agreement was a valid, enforceable contract so long as it was not based solely on immoral consideration.

2. Same-Sex Marriages and Civil Unions

Starting in the 1990s gay and lesbian groups began seeking legal recognition of and legal rights for "committed relationships" between partners of the same sex. Advocates for same-sex marriage usually focus on the need for equal treatment of all citizens, thereby allowing same-sex couples to enjoy all the traditional privileges accorded married persons. They emphasize practical concerns such as inheritance rights, child custody situations, and employee and government

---

[2]University of Alaska v. Tumeo, 933 P.2d 1147 (Alaska 1997).
[3]557 P.2d 106 (Cal. 1976).

benefits for partners. At the symbolic level gays and lesbians stress the importance of receiving the legal recognition that their committed relationships are equal to those of opposite-sex partners.

Opponents of same-sex marriage rely on arguments that relate principally to religious values and to the traditional notion that the purpose of marriage is procreation. They argue that God has ordained that a marriage can only consist of one man and one woman and that official recognition of same-sex partnerships threatens the stability of traditional families. Further, they contend that homosexual couples could use contractual law to resolve problems involving issues such as inheritances, child custody, and visitation rights.

The first significant court challenge to the traditional view of marriage as being limited to opposite-sex partners occurred in Hawaii in 1990, when two women applied for a marriage license. When their application was denied, they went to the courts, seeking a judicial declaration that Hawaii's statute limiting marriage to men and women was unconstitutional sex discrimination. They based their argument on the Hawaii constitution, which, unlike the U.S. Constitution, specifically prohibits discrimination based on sex. The Hawaii Supreme Court held that the statute was unconstitutional unless at trial the state could prove that the statute furthered compelling state interests.[4]

In 1996 the trial court ruled that the state had failed to present compelling reasons why the public interest in the well-being of children and families would be adversely affected by same-sex marriages. The court noted that expert witnesses for both sides testified that it was the nurturing ability of the parents, rather than their sexual orientation, that determined whether they would make good parents. The quality of parenting that a child received was more important than a biological connection or the gender of the parent. The trial court entered judgment in favor of the plaintiffs, ruling that the statute limiting marriage to opposite-sex couples was unconstitutional, as it violated the Hawaii state constitution's equal protection clause.

While the case was again on appeal to Hawaii's supreme court, the Hawaii legislature worked on a proposed amendment to the state constitution that would give the legislature the power to limit marriage to opposite-sex couples. After that amendment was ratified in November 1999, the Hawaii Supreme Court ruled that in light of this change to the Hawaii constitution, the statute limiting marriage to opposite-sex couples was now constitutional and the court dismissed the plaintiff's case.[5]

Eleven days later, in an unrelated case, the Vermont Supreme Court held that the common benefits clause of the Vermont constitution required the state to give same-sex couples the same benefits and protections that opposite-sex couples receive from marriage under Vermont law. The court noted that under the Vermont Constitution legislative classifications must "reasonably relate to a legitimate public purpose," and Vermont's marriage statute failed that test. It was not reasonably related to safeguarding the interests of children

---

[4]Baehr v. Lewin, 853 P.2d 44 (Haw. 1993).
[5]Baehr v. Miike, 92 Haw. 634, 994 P.2d 566 (table) (1999).

and was inconsistent with public policy against discrimination based on sexual orientation.

After deciding that same-sex couples were being denied their common rights and benefits, the court left it to the legislature to choose between allowing same-sex marriages or creating a parallel domestic partnership system that would provide legal benefits equivalent to those that married couples enjoyed.[6] The legislature reacted by passing a "civil union" statute. In April 2000 the Vermont governor signed the law, making Vermont the first state to grant same-sex couples the benefits of marriage, such as preferential tax status, the ability to make medical decisions for each other should one of the parties become incapacitated, and the ability to inherit under state statutes.

While the Hawaii courts and legislature were debating the constitutionality of denying same-sex couples the right to marry, the U.S. Congress passed the Defense of Marriage Act. This federal law declared first, that states do not have to recognize same-sex marriages created in another state,[7] and second, that at the federal level "the word 'marriage' means only a legal union between one man and one woman as husband and wife, and the word 'spouse' refers only to a person of the opposite sex who is a husband or a wife."[8]

Three years after Vermont settled on the solution of civil unions, Massachusetts surprised the rest of the nation when its highest appellate court found that under the Massachusetts constitution, the state could not deny the benefits of marriage to two individuals of the same sex who wish to marry. When the state legislature then asked for the court's advisory opinion on a statute that would instead allow for same-sex civil unions, the court specifically rejected that approach, stating that "[t]he history of our nation has demonstrated that separate is seldom, if ever, equal."[9]

Opinions of the Justices to the Senate, Supreme Judicial Court of Massachusetts
440 Mass. 1201, 802 N.E.2d 565 (2004)

To the Honorable the Senate of the Commonwealth of Massachusetts:

The undersigned Justices of the Supreme Judicial Court respectfully submit their answers to the question set forth in an order adopted by the Senate. . . . The order indicates that there is pending before the General Court a bill, Senate No. 2175, entitled "An Act relative to civil unions." . . . [T]he bill . . . provides for the establishment of "civil unions" for same-sex "spouses," provided the individuals meet certain qualifications described in the bill.

The order indicates that grave doubt exists as to the constitutionality of the bill if enacted into law and requests the opinions of the Justices on the following "important question of law":

Does Senate No. 2175, which prohibits same-sex couples from entering into marriage but allows them to form civil unions with all 'benefits, protections, rights and responsibilities' of marriage,

---

[6]Baker v. State, 744 A.2d 864, 867 (Vt. 1999).

[7]28 U.S.C.S. § 1738C (2008).

[8]1 U.S.C.S. § 7 (2008).

[9]Opinions of the Justices to the Senate, 802 N.E.2d 565 (Mass. 2004).

comply with the equal protection and due process requirements of the Constitution of the Commonwealth and articles 1, 6, 7, 10, 12 and 16 of the Declaration of Rights?[2] . . .

1. *Background of the proposed legislation.* In *Goodridge v. Department of Pub. Health,* 440 Mass. 309, 798 N.E.2d 941 (2003) *(Goodridge),* the court considered the constitutional question "whether the Commonwealth may use its formidable regulatory authority to bar same-sex couples from civil marriage. . . ." *Id.* at 312-313. The court concluded that it may not do so, determining that the Commonwealth had failed to articulate a rational basis for denying civil marriage to same-sex couples. The court stated that the Massachusetts Constitution "affirms the dignity and equality of all individuals" and "forbids the creation of second-class citizens." *Id.* at 312. The court concluded that in "limiting the protections, benefits, and obligations of civil marriage to opposite-sex couples," the marriage licensing law "violates the basic premises of individual liberty and equality under law protected by the Massachusetts Constitution." *Id.* at 342.

In so concluding, the court enumerated some of the concrete tangible benefits that flow from civil marriage, including, but not limited to, rights in property, probate, tax, and evidence law that are conferred on married couples. *Id.* at 322-325. The court also noted that "intangible benefits flow from marriage," *id.* at 322, intangibles that are important components of marriage as a "civil right." *Id.* at 325. The court stated that "marriage also bestows enormous private and social advantages on those who choose to marry . . . [and] is at once a deeply personal commitment to another human being and a highly public celebration of the ideals of mutuality, companionship, intimacy, fidelity, and family." *Id.* at 322. "Because it fulfils yearnings for security, safe haven, and connection that express our common humanity, civil marriage is an esteemed institution, and the decision whether and whom to marry is among life's momentous acts of self-definition." *Id.* Therefore, without the right to choose to marry, same-sex couples are not only denied full protection of the

laws, but are "excluded from the full range of human experience." *Id.* at 326.

The court stated that the denial of civil marital status "works a deep and scarring hardship on a very real segment of the community for no rational reason." *Id.* at 341. These omnipresent hardships include, but are by no means limited to, the absence of predictable rules of child support and property division, and even uncertainty concerning whether one will be allowed to visit one's sick child or one's partner in a hospital . . . All of these stem from the status of same-sex couples and their children as "outliers to the marriage laws." *Id.* . . . .

In response to the plaintiffs' specific request for relief, the court preserved the marriage licensing statute, but refined the common-law definition of civil marriage to mean "the voluntary union of two persons as spouses, to the exclusion of all others." *Id.* at 343. . . .

2. *Provisions of the bill* . . . The proposed law states that "spouses" in a civil union shall be "joined in it with a legal status equivalent to marriage." Senate No. 2175, § 5. The bill expressly maintains that "marriage" is reserved exclusively for opposite-sex couples by providing that "persons eligible to form a civil union with each other under this chapter shall not be eligible to enter into a marriage with each other under chapter 207." *Id.* Notwithstanding, the proposed law purports to make the institution of a "civil union" parallel to the institution of civil "marriage." For example, the bill provides that "spouses in a civil union shall have all the same benefits, protections, rights and responsibilities under law as are granted to spouses in a marriage." In addition, terms that denote spousal relationships, such as "husband," "wife," "family," and "next of kin," are to be interpreted to include spouses in a civil union "as those terms are used in any law." The bill goes on to enumerate a nonexclusive list of the legal benefits that will adhere to spouses in a civil union, including property rights, joint State income tax filing, evidentiary rights, rights to veteran benefits and group insurance, and the right to the issuance of a "civil union" license, identical to a marriage license under G.L. c. 207, "as if a civil union was a marriage."

---

[2]*Article I of the Massachusetts Declaration of Rights* . . . provides: . . . "Equality under the law shall not be denied or abridged because of sex, race, color, creed or national origin."

3. *Analysis.* . . . We have now been asked to render an advisory opinion on Senate No. 2175, which creates a new legal status, "civil union," that is purportedly equal to "marriage," yet separate from it. The constitutional difficulty of the proposed civil union bill is evident in its stated purpose to "preserve the traditional, historic nature and meaning of the institution of civil marriage." . . . We recognize the efforts of the Senate to draft a bill in conformity with the *Goodridge* opinion. Yet the bill, as we read it, does nothing to "preserve" the civil marriage law, only its constitutional infirmity. This is not a matter of social policy but of constitutional interpretation. As the court concluded in *Goodridge,* the traditional, historic nature and meaning of civil marriage in Massachusetts is as a wholly secular and dynamic legal institution, the governmental aim of which is to encourage stable adult relationships for the good of the individual and of the community, especially its children. The very nature and purpose of civil marriage, the court concluded, renders unconstitutional any attempt to ban all same-sex couples, as same-sex couples, from entering into civil marriage.

. . . Because the proposed law by its express terms forbids same-sex couples entry into civil marriage, it continues to relegate same-sex couples to a different status. The holding in *Goodridge,* by which we are bound, is that group classifications based on unsupportable distinctions, such as that embodied in the proposed bill, are invalid under the Massachusetts Constitution. The history of our nation has demonstrated that separate is seldom, if ever, equal.

In *Goodridge,* the court acknowledged, as we do here, that "many people hold deep-seated religious, moral, and ethical convictions that marriage should be limited to the union of one man and one woman, and that homosexual conduct is immoral. Many hold equally strong religious, moral, and ethical convictions that same-sex couples are entitled to be married, and that homosexual persons should be treated no differently than their heterosexual neighbors." *Id.* at 312. The court stated then, and we reaffirm, that the State may not interfere with these convictions, or with the decision of any religion to refuse to perform religious marriages of same-sex couples. These matters of belief and conviction are properly outside the reach of judicial review or government interference. But

neither may the government, under the guise of protecting "traditional" values, even if they be the traditional values of the majority, enshrine in law an invidious discrimination that our Constitution, "as a charter of governance for every person properly within its reach," forbids.

The bill's absolute prohibition of the use of the word "marriage" by "spouses" who are the same sex is more than semantic. The dissimilitude between the terms "civil marriage" and "civil union" is not innocuous; it is a considered choice of language that reflects a demonstrable assigning of same-sex, largely homosexual, couples to second-class status. The denomination of this difference . . . as merely a "squabble over the name to be used" so clearly misses the point that further discussion appears to be useless. If . . . the proponents of the bill believe that no message is conveyed by eschewing the word "marriage" and replacing it with "civil union" for same-sex "spouses," we doubt that the attempt to circumvent the court's decision in *Goodridge* would be so purposeful. For no rational reason the marriage laws of the Commonwealth discriminate against a defined class; no amount of tinkering with language will eradicate that stain. The bill would have the effect of maintaining and fostering a stigma of exclusion that the Constitution prohibits. It would deny to same-sex "spouses" only a status that is specially recognized in society and has significant social and other advantages. The Massachusetts Constitution, as was explained in the *Goodridge* opinion, does not permit such invidious discrimination, no matter how well intentioned. . . .

We are well aware that current Federal law prohibits recognition by the Federal government of the validity of same-sex marriages legally entered into in any State, and that it permits other States to refuse to recognize the validity of such marriages. The argument . . . that . . . society will still accord a lesser status to those marriages is irrelevant. Courts define what is constitutionally permissible, and the Massachusetts Constitution does not permit this type of labeling. That there may remain personal residual prejudice against same-sex couples is a proposition all too familiar to other disadvantaged groups. That such prejudice exists is not a reason to insist on less than the Constitution requires. . . . Indeed, we would do a grave disservice to every Massachusetts resident, and to our constitutional duty to interpret the law, to conclude that the strong protection of individual rights guaranteed by the Massachusetts Constitution should not be available to their fullest extent in the Commonwealth because those rights may not be acknowledged elsewhere. We do not resolve, nor would we attempt to, the consequences of our holding in other jurisdictions. But, as the court held in *Goodridge,* under our Federal system of dual sovereignty, and subject to the minimum requirements of the Fourteenth Amendment to the United States Constitution, "each State is free to address difficult issues of individual liberty in the manner its own Constitution demands." *Id.* at 341.

4. *Conclusion.* We are of the opinion that Senate No. 2175 violates the equal protection and due process requirements of the Constitution of the Commonwealth and the Massachusetts Declaration of Rights. . . .

The answer to the question is "No."

CASE DISCUSSION QUESTIONS

1. According to the court, what tangible and intangible benefits flow from marriage? What hardships are created by denying same-sex couples the right to marry?

2. How does the Massachusetts Constitution's equal protection provision differ from the U.S. Constitution's Fourteenth Amendment protections?

3. In what ways did the statutory proposal for civil unions differ from marriage?

4. Why do the justices who wrote this opinion think there is more involved than just "a squabble over the name to be used"?

5. Do you agree that the decision to allow same-sex marriages should be only a matter of constitutional interpretation and not a matter of social policy?

6. How does the court respond to the argument that Massachusetts's same-sex marriages may not be recognized in other states or by the federal government?

7. Unlike the Massachusetts Supreme Judicial Court, the U.S. Supreme Court does not give advisory opinions. What do you think are the advantages and disadvantages of this type of action?

Since 2005, five other states (California, Connecticut, New Hampshire, New Jersey, and Oregon) have followed Vermont's path of creating a process by which the state government formally recognizes what is either called a "civil union" or a "domestic partnership." While these civil union and domestic partnership laws may give same-sex couples most of the legal rights that married people enjoy, society and the law still view their relationship as being different from a marriage.

In 2008, the supreme courts of California and Connecticut joined Massachusetts in ruling that same-sex couples have the constitutional right to marry. The California Supreme Court went further than had the Massachusetts court by finding that discrimination on the basis of sexual orientation is equivalent to race and sex discrimination and therefore cannot form the basis for withholding legal rights.[10] The Connecticut court ruled that the state statutory prohibition against same-sex marriage violated rights to substantive due process and equal protection under their state constitution.[11]

---

[10] In re Marriage Cases, 43 Cal.4th 757, 183 P.3d 384 (2008).

[11] Kerrigan v. Commissioner of Public Health, 957 A.2d 407 (Conn. 2008).

In California, shortly after the court decision allowing same-sex marriages, voters passed Proposition 8, amending the state Constitution to restrict the definition of marriage to a union between a man and a woman. At the time this text went to print, the validity of Proposition 8 was being challenged in court on the basis that a simple majority vote cannot deprive a minority group of its constitutional rights.

As discussed on pages 181 of Chapter 6, Constitutional Law, because of these variations in law among the states and between some states and the federal government, the federal Defense of Marriage Act has created a situation where same-sex married couples may receive all of the benefits of marriage within their own states but may not be recognized as married by other states nor be able to file a joint federal income tax return or collect some types of Social Security and other federal benefits. These situations will most certainly lead to a challenge to the constitutionality of the Defense of Marriage Act based on the Full Faith and Credit clause in Article IV, Section 1, of the U.S. Constitution. This provision states: "Full Faith and Credit shall be given in each State to the public Acts, Records, and judicial Proceedings of every other State." In addition, such federal legislation treads heavily in the field of family law, an area that traditionally has been reserved for individual state regulation.

Same-sex marriages and civil unions are likely to remain hot political and emotional topics for some time to come. Some have argued that the U.S. Constitution should be amended to define and protect marriage as a "union of man and woman as husband and wife." Others contend that this is an area of law that should be left completely to the states. As of the writing of this edition, more than half of the states have passed constitutional amendments that bar the recognition of same-sex marriage, and some of these provisions also prohibit the legal recognition of same-sex civil unions and domestic partnerships. Kentucky and Michigan have even gone so far as to revoke employee benefits that had previously been extended to domestic partners of public employees.

Internationally, the first country to recognize same-sex marriages was the Netherlands in 2001. In Belgium, same-sex marriages have been allowed since 2003. In 2005, Spain and then Canada passed legislation giving full marriage rights to same-sex couples. Figure 11-1 on page 405 summarizes the history of same-sex unions worldwide.

DISCUSSION QUESTIONS

5. Traditionally, states have defined not only marriage but also the rights and responsibilities that accompany marriage. The proposed federal constitutional amendment would alter that. It reads:

> Marriage in the United States shall consist only of the union of a man and a woman. Neither this Constitution or the *constitution of any State*, nor *state* or federal *law,* shall be construed to require that marital status or the legal incidents thereof be conferred upon unmarried couples or groups. (Emphasis added.)

Do you think this is an area of the law that should be controlled by the federal government or left to the individual states? Why?

6. Until 1967 Virginia had an antimiscegenation law, prohibiting interracial marriage. An interracial couple was convicted of violating the statute and

1989	Denmark legalizes "registered partnerships"
1996	Passage of the federal Defense of Marriage Act
2000	Vermont approves civil unions
2001	Netherlands creates full civil marriage rights
2003	Belgium allows for same-sex marriages; President Bush proposes the Federal Marriage Amendment (FMA) to amend the U.S. Constitution to define marriage as between a man and a woman
2004	Massachusetts becomes first state to legalize same-sex marriages
2005	California amends its domestic partnership legislation to give same-sex couples the same rights and responsibilities as spouses; Connecticut becomes the second state to approve same-sex civil unions; Spain and Canada legalize same-sex marriage
2007	New Jersey became the third state to offer civil unions
2008	New Hampshire approves civil unions; Oregon authorizes domestic partnerships; California and Connecticut legalize same-sex marriages; California's voters amend their state constitution to prohibit same-sex marriage.

Figure 11-1 History of Same-Sex Unions

given a one-year jail sentence. The sentence was suspended but only on the condition that the couple leave Virginia and not return for twenty-five years. The couple appealed their conviction. In *Loving v. Virginia,* 388 U.S. 1 (1967), the U.S. Supreme Court held that Virginia's statute violated the due process clause of the Fourteenth Amendment. Marriage is a fundamental right that states cannot regulate absent a compelling state interest. Should the Supreme Court be asked to decide whether statutes prohibiting same-sex marriages are unconstitutional, the *Loving* decision might form a basis for arguing by analogy that statutes banning same-sex marriages are unconstitutional. Do you think the two situations are analogous? If you were arguing for preserving the statutes prohibiting same-sex marriage, how would you distinguish the *Loving* decision?

7. Every state has laws against polygamy—that is, having more than one husband or wife at a time. What do you think are the arguments for and against allowing a man to have more than one wife at a time or a woman to have more than one husband at a time? Are such laws a form of religious discrimination against Mormons and Islamics, who have traditionally allowed men to have more than one wife?

8. M.T., a transsexual, was born a male but had the mental and emotional reactions of a female. She underwent surgery to become female. In a state that bans same-sex marriages, do you think she would be able to obtain a marriage license to marry a man? Explain the basis for your answer.

3. Premarital Agreements

Premarital agreements, also known as **prenuptial** or **antenuptial agreements,** are becoming increasingly popular. Their basic purpose is to set forth the financial arrangements should one of the parties die or the marriage end in divorce. Premarital agreements are becoming especially common in situations involving second marriages in which the spouses have children from a previous marriage. Usually, the focus of such agreements is financial considerations. For example, a

Prenuptial agreement
Also known as an **antenuptial agreement;** a document that prospective spouses sign prior to marriage regarding financial and other arrangements should the marriage end.

premarital agreement would be used when a couple in their sixties marries and wishes to ensure that the property they bring with them to the marriage will be passed on to their children rather than to the surviving spouse. Such an agreement in this type of situation can put to rest the children's concerns that the parent's new spouse will cut them out of their inheritance.

Traditionally, the courts saw such agreements as encouraging divorce, and therefore they found such contracts to be void as against public policy. Today, however, most courts will enforce these agreements if the standard contract requirements were met. First, in most states to satisfy the statute of frauds, premarital agreements must be in writing. Second, there must be an offer, an acceptance, and consideration. Usually, the agreement to marry satisfies the consideration requirement.

The extent to which a court will enforce premarital agreements regarding matters other than financial arrangements depends on the nature of the specific provision. For example, although courts will generally enforce reasonable provisions relating to the distribution of property, they will not enforce provisions relating to third parties, such as those dealing with child custody.

Normal contract defenses are also available. For example, if the agreement was not based on full disclosure of all financial assets or was the result of undue influence, the courts might see it as against public policy and either modify its provisions or refuse to enforce it. Also, as noted above, the courts view some provisions, especially those trying to predetermine the rights of children, as against public policy and hence unenforceable. An example would be a provision that states that the custodial spouse will not seek child support if the couple divorces.

DISCUSSION QUESTION

9. The prenuptial agreement between a Catholic woman and a Jewish man stated that any children born of the marriage would be raised in the Jewish faith. After the couple divorced, the wife was given custody of the children. The father went to court, seeking to have the prenuptial agreement enforced. How do you think the court responded?

4. Consequences of Broken Engagements

Anti-heart-balm statute
A law that prohibits lawsuits for such things as breach of a promise of marriage, alienation of affection, and seduction of a person over the legal age of consent.

Under common law the victim of a broken engagement could sue for an array of tort and contractual damages for mental and emotional suffering, damage to reputation, humiliation, embarrassment, and even "loss of worldly advantage." However, most states have adopted "**anti-heart-balm**" statutes, which prohibit lawsuits for such things as breach of a promise of marriage, alienation of affection, and seduction of a person over the legal age of consent.

Nevertheless, issues ranging from the return of the engagement ring to disposition of joint property may still find their way to the courts when wedding plans fall through. Such conflicts are illustrated in the following case. Note that this suit is not barred by the New Jersey anti-heart-balm statute because it is a suit to recover conditional gifts, not an action for damages for breach of a contract to marry.

Aronow v. Silver
223 N.J. Super. 344, 538 A.2d 851 (1987)

Option by Judge HAINES

Philip Aronow, plaintiff, and Elizabeth Silver, defendant, were engaged to be married. The engagement was a stormy one. Problems arose involving the parties themselves and their relatives. On three occasions, Elizabeth cancelled the engagement and returned the engagement ring, only to recant. Finally, with the marriage ceremony a few days away, the engagement was broken irretrievably. Each party, in this resulting litigation, faults the other. Each claims the engagement ring, certain shares of stock and a jointly-owned condominium. . . .

A. The Law Concerning Engagement Rings

The majority rule in this country concerning the disposition of engagement rings is a fault rule: the party who unjustifiably breaks the engagement loses the ring. The minority rule rejects fault. . . . New Jersey courts have considered the question in only four published opinions, with split results. This court, not bound by any of those opinions, joins the minority.

Our earliest case is *Sloin v. Lavine*, 11 N.J. Misc. 899 (Sup. Ct. 1933), in which the court, citing the law of foreign jurisdictions, said:

> So we have on the merits the simple case of an engagement ring and engagement broken and ring not returned. The decisions are not numerous, but we follow those holding what we deem the correct rule, viz., that such a gift is impliedly conditional, and must be returned, particularly when the engagement is broken by the donee, as the court was entitled to find in this case.

Sloin's implication that the person who breaks the engagement loses the ring was rejected by Judge (later Justice) Sullivan in *Albanese v. Indelicato*, 25 N.J. Misc. 144 (D. Ct. 1947). The decision involved ownership of an engagement ring and a dinner ring. The court said:

> As far as the engagement ring is concerned, the defendant had no right to keep it. An engagement ring is a symbol or pledge of the coming marriage and signifies that the one who wears it is engaged to marry the man who gave it to her. If the engagement is broken off the ring should be returned since it is a conditional gift. True, no express condition was imposed but the law implies a condition because of the symbolic significance of the ring. It does not matter who broke the engagement. A person may have the best reasons in the world for so doing. The important thing is that the gift was conditional and the condition was not fulfilled.
>
> The giving of the dinner ring is an entirely different proposition. True, it was given after the parties became engaged. No doubt plaintiff would not have given the ring to defendant if they had not been engaged. The dinner ring though, has no symbolic meaning and is only a token of the love and affection which plaintiff bore for the defendant. Many gifts are made for reasons that sour with the passage of time. Under the law though, there is no consideration required for a gift and it is absolute once made unless a condition is imposed. There was no express condition here and the law will not imply one as in the case of the engagement ring since the dinner ring has no symbolic meaning attached to it. Defendant was under no obligation to return the dinner ring. . . .

The fault rule is sexist and archaic, a too-long enduring reminder of the times when even the law discriminated against women. The history is traced in 24 A.L.R.2d at 582–586. In ancient Rome the rule was fault. When the woman broke the engagement, however, she was required not only to return the ring, but also its value, as a penalty. No penalty attached when the breach was the man's. In England, women were oppressed by the rigidly stratified social order of the day. They worked as servants or, if not of the servant class, were dependent on their relatives. The fact that men were in short supply, marriage above one's station rare and travel difficult abbreviated betrothal prospects for women. Marriages were arranged. Women's lifetime choices were limited to a marriage or a nunnery. Spinsterhood was a centuries-long personal tragedy. Men, because it was a man's world, were much more likely than women to break engagements. When one did, he left behind a woman of tainted reputation and ruined prospects. The law, in a de minimis gesture, gave her the engagement ring, as a consolation prize. When the man was jilted, a seldom thing, justice required the ring's return to him. Thus, the rule of life was the rule of law—both saw women as inferiors.

To accept the ancient rule of law is to ignore our constitutional insistence upon the equality of women, to further the unfortunate reality that society still discriminates. That reality is one which courts must not promote. Our obligation is to enforce the law, which bars discrimination. By doing so we move reality in the right direction.

The majority rule, even without its constitutional infirmity, will not withstand elementary scrutiny. Its foundation is fault, and fault, in an engagement setting, cannot be ascertained.

What fact justifies the breaking of an engagement? The absence of a sense of humor? Differing musical tastes? Differing political views? The painfully learned fact is that marriages are made on earth, not in heaven. They must be approached with intelligent care and should not happen without a decent assurance of success. When either party lacks that assurance, for whatever reason, the engagement should be broken. No justification is needed. Either party may act. Fault, impossible to fix, does not count. . . .

Philip's gift of a ring to Elizabeth was conditioned upon marriage. When the promise of marriage was not kept, regardless of fault, the condition was not fulfilled and the ring must be returned to him. . . .

C. The Stock Purchases

During their engagement, the parties, in anticipation of their marriage, purchased stock with Philip's money upon the understanding that the stock certificate was to be placed in joint names. The broker, however, had the certificate issued in Elizabeth's name only. She sold it without Philip's knowledge after the engagement was broken and kept the proceeds. Other stock previously owned by Elizabeth was placed in joint names. That stock has not been sold. Quite clearly, these stock arrangements were conditioned upon marriage. When the engagement was broken, the stocks should have been returned to the parties who donated them. Philip's stock should not have been sold and Elizabeth must pay the proceeds of the sale to him. Philip is directed to transfer his interest in the jointly-held stock to Elizabeth.

CASE DISCUSSION QUESTIONS

1. The *Silver* court refused to apply a "fault standard." Do you think it should matter who was at fault for breaking off the engagement? Why?

2. In the cited case of *Albanese v. Indelicato,* why did the court treat the diamond ring and the engagement ring differently? The *Silver* court did not apply different standards to the engagement ring and stock. Can you reconcile these seemingly different approaches? Do you think one approach reaches a fairer result?

3. Elizabeth's parents also sued, seeking recovery of various wedding expenses paid by them. Do you think they should be able to recover? Why?

Annulment
A legal (or religious) judgment that a valid marriage never existed.

Divorce
Also called **dissolution;** a legal judgment that dissolves a marriage.

5. Termination of the Marital Relationship

Once the state has recognized a couple as being married, they will continue to be treated as married persons until one of the spouses dies or a court grants either an **annulment** or a **divorce.** The latter is sometimes referred to as **dissolution.** The major difference between an annulment and a divorce is that an annulment can be granted only for causes that existed at the time the marriage took place, whereas divorces are based on causes that occurred before or during the marriage.

a. Annulment

An annulment proceeding has the effect of rescinding the marriage and returning the parties to the status they had before the marriage took place. Therefore, if an annulment is granted, it is, from the legal perspective, as if the marriage had never taken place. Because the marriage never existed, normally there are no continuing matrimonial obligations, such as a duty to pay support or attorney's fees. On the other hand, a divorce or dissolution ends but does not erase the existence of the marital relationship. Although the parties are no longer married to each other, it does not necessarily cancel legal obligations that arose out of the marriage. One exception to this difference between annulment and marriage relates to children born during the marriage. Under the common law, children born during a marriage later annulled were considered illegitimate. Many state statutes have changed this, at least as to **voidable marriages.** However, if it was a **void marriage,** some states still consider the children to be illegitimate.

Recall the contract law distinction between void and voidable. A void contract is a legal nullity, even without court intervention. A voidable contract remains valid unless one of the parties takes steps to void it through legal proceedings. Similarly, marriages are considered void in certain situations, as when they involve incest or bigamy. A voidable marriage, on the other hand, is one where the marriage remains valid until a court has determined that it should be voided.

The grounds for voiding a marriage that are typically listed in state statutes include such things as the following:

1. One of the parties to the marriage lacked capacity to consent to the marriage because of being either mentally incapacitated or under the influence of alcohol, drugs, or other incapacitating substances.
2. One of the parties lacks the physical capacity to consummate the marriage, and the other party did not know of the incapacity.
3. One of the parties was under the prescribed age for marriage and did not have a parent's or guardian's consent.
4. The parties are too closely related to each other—for example, siblings or first cousins.
5. One of the parties was induced to enter into the marriage by force, duress, or fraud.

Most of the criteria listed in these statutes are fairly straightforward and relatively objective, but the language in the last provision relating to **fraud** often leads to difficult and controversial cases. For example, courts in some states have ruled that it is appropriate to annul a marriage on the grounds that the woman falsely represented herself as being pregnant or was pregnant but lied about who the father was. On the other hand, it has also been ruled that false representations as to being a virgin at the time of marriage do not constitute a basis for granting an annulment. Another interesting line of cases involves fraudulent representations regarding one's wealth and ability to support and

Voidable marriage
A marriage that was valid when it was entered into and that remains valid until either party obtains a court order dissolving it.

Void marriage
A marriage that is invalid from its inception and that does not require court action for the parties to be free of any marital obligations.

Fraud
A false representation of facts or intentional perversion of the truth to induce someone to take some action or give up something of value.

maintain a certain lifestyle after the marriage. In such situations the courts have generally adopted a "buyer beware" attitude and have not recognized such representations as being the basis for granting an annulment. An example of a situation that would be the basis for an annulment based on fraud would be one where a spouse made promises of love, devotion, and living together in a normal marital relationship and then fled with the other spouse's bank account a few days after the wedding.

Keep in mind that there is a difference between legal annulments and religious ones. The two are completely separate processes, and clients must take additional steps to attain a religious annulment.

DISCUSSION QUESTION

10. Most statutes require the parties to be "mentally competent" in order to marry, but what does that mean? Should someone who has a mental or genetic disability, such as Down's syndrome, be allowed to marry? Should a court annul a marriage if the parties later allege they were so intoxicated at the time of the ceremony that they did not realize the significance of their actions?

NETNOTE

You can find various uniform laws governing the family, such as the Uniform Child Custody Jurisdiction Act, the Uniform Interstate Family Support Act, the Uniform Premarital Agreement Act, and the Uniform Marriage and Divorce Act at *www.law.cornell.edu/uniform/vol9.html.*

b. Divorce/Dissolution

Traditionally, marriage meant that the norm was for spouses to be together for life, and divorce was seen as the exception. Therefore, the spouse wishing a divorce had to convince the court that there were extraordinary reasons justifying that request. Those reasons, called grounds, included such behavior as adultery and desertion. Today, every state also allows a divorce based on "**no fault.**" Rather than having to assess blame for the breakup, either party can end the marriage, with or without the consent of the partner. Either spouse can simply file a petition for dissolution. The parties merely must allege that the marriage has suffered an irretrievable breakdown, with no hope for reconciliation. In some states the parties must also allege that they are living separate and apart.

The "costs" of divorce are many. First, when couples seek a divorce, they relinquish to the state the power to make major life decisions for them. State courts can oversee a divorced family's financial arrangements in ways not permitted for intact families. For example, normally a court will not interfere with an intact family's decision as to whether to send a child to college. However,

No-fault divorce
A form of divorce that allows a couple to end their marital relationship without having to assess blame for the breakup.

during divorce proceedings child support orders can include a requirement that the parents pay for their child's college education. In *LeClair v. LeClair*[12] the court stated that it could enforce such an order because the state had an interest in promoting higher education and in protecting children of divorce.

In addition, divorce can have severe economic consequences. This is especially true for women. The money that may have been insufficient to maintain one household is now being asked to maintain two homes. Studies have consistently shown that in the first year after divorce the standard of living for men increases anywhere from 17 to 43 percent, while that for women and children decreases by 29 to 73 percent.[13] Finally, for many divorcing parents the greatest cost is the loss of daily contact with their children.

(1) Divorce procedures

Whichever method is used, there are basic divorce procedures that must be followed. First, the grounds, even under no fault, must exist to end the marriage. Then the party wishing a divorce must file a petition or complaint, requesting the divorce and including the reasons why one should be granted. Most states require the petition to include the following information:

1. the age, occupation, and residence of each party;
2. the length of time each party has resided in the state;
3. the date of the marriage and the place at which it was registered;
4. the names, ages, and addresses of all living children of the marriage and whether the wife is pregnant;
5. any arrangements as to support, custody, and visitation of the children and maintenance of a spouse; and
6. the relief sought.

If the petitioner wants to proceed on a fault basis, then there will also be an identification of the grounds. Exhibit 11-1 on pp. 413 provides an example of a no-fault petition.

As you can see from the sample petition, usually other documents, such as affidavits, must be filed along with the petition. Once the petition is filed with the court, the opposing party must be notified. This can be accomplished as in other civil suits through service of process. If the other spouse cannot be found, then an alternative method of notification must be used, such as publication in a newspaper. When both parties are agreeable to the divorce, the defendant may willingly appear in court without the need for formal service of process.

The other party can indicate he or she does not want to contest the divorce or can countersue. Then both sides may engage in discovery.

Many states incorporate alternative dispute resolution mechanisms into the decisions regarding distribution of property and child custody and support. Mediation is becoming increasingly common, on either a voluntary or a court-ordered

---

[12]624 A.2d 1350 (N.H. 1993).

[13]Lenore Weitzman, The Divorce Revolution: The Unexpected Social and Economic Consequences for Women and Children in America xii (1995); Joseph I. Lieberman, Child Support in America: Practical Advice for Negotiating and Collecting a Fair Settlement 11 (1988), cited in J. Shoshanna Ehrlic, Family Law for Paralegals 181 (1997).

[FACE SIDE OF FORM]

Commonwealth of Massachusetts
The Trial Court
Probate and Family Court Department

_____ Division   Docket No. _____

Joint Petition For Divorce Under M.G.L. Ch. 208, Sec. 1A

_____ and _____
Petitioner   Petitioner

of _____   of _____
(Street and No.)   (Street and No.)

_____   _____
(City or Town) (State) (Zip)   (City or Town) (State) (Zip)

1. Now come the Husband and Wife in a joint petition for divorce pursuant to Massachusetts General Laws, Chapter 208, Sec. 1A.

2. The parties were lawfully married at _____ on _____ and last lived together at _____ on _____ 19___.

3. The minor child _____ of this marriage and date(s) of birth is/are:

   _____   _____

   _____   _____

4. The parties certify that no previous action for divorce, annulment, affirmation of marriage, separate support, desertion, living apart for justifiable cause, or custody of child _____ has been brought by either party against the other except _____.

5. On or about _____, 19___, an irretrievable breakdown of the marriage under M.G.L. Ch. 208, Sec. 1A occurred and continues to exist.

6. Wherefore, the parties pray that the Court:
   [ ] grant a divorce on the ground of irretrievable breakdown
   [ ] approve the separation agreement executed by the parties
   [ ] incorporate and merge said agreement executed by the parties
   [ ] incorporate but not merge said agreement, which shall survive and remain as an independent contract
   [ ] allow Wife to resume her former name _____
   [ ] _____

Date _____

_____   _____
SIGNATURE OF WIFE OR ATTORNEY   SIGNATURE OF HUSBAND OR ATTORNEY

_____   _____
(Print address if not pro se)   (Print address if not pro se)

_____   _____
Tel. No. (   ) _____   Tel. No. (   ) _____
B.B.O. # _____   B.B.O. # _____

CJ-D 101A (6/90)

Exhibit 11-1 Joint Petition for Divorce   _(continues)_

[BACK SIDE OF FORM]

Joint Petition For Divorce Under M.G.L. Ch. 208, Sec. 1A

For Wife:

_____

Address _____

_____

Tel. No. (   ) _____

For Husband:

_____

Address _____

_____

Tel. No. (   ) _____

Docket No. _____

Filed _____ 19__

Agreement Approved _____ 19__

Judgment _____ 19__

Documents filed:

Marriage Certificate	[ ]
Wife's Financial Statement	[ ]
Husband's Financial Statement	[ ]
Separation Agreement	[ ]
Affidavit of Irretrievable Breakdown	[ ]
Affidavit Disclosing Care or Custody Proceedings	[ ]
Child Support Guidelines Worksheet	[ ]

Exhibit 11-1   Joint Petition for Divorce *(concluded)*

basis, especially if minor children are involved. The philosophy behind mediation is that it can create a win-win atmosphere as opposed to the courtroom mentality of winner take all. In addition, it allows the participants to have a sense of ownership in the decision, as they craft it themselves, rather than allowing a judge to impose it on them.

After the filing of the petition, the court will hold a hearing to deal with such matters as temporary child custody; child and spousal support; who remains in the house and who leaves; liability for home mortgages, car payments, and credit card bills; and orders protecting existing joint assets. In cases where there have been allegations of domestic abuse, there may also be a hearing on the issuance of a **temporary restraining order (TRO)**, sometimes also called a **protection order,** to keep one spouse away from the other spouse, the children, and the home. Although these are labeled temporary orders, do not be fooled. If the proceedings drag on for any length of time, when it is finally time to frame the permanent orders, it may prove very difficult to change the "temporary" arrangements.

In an effort to help parents appreciate the needs of their children during the divorce process, some states are starting to mandate parent education programs for all divorcing parents. A certificate of attendance must be submitted to the court prior to a hearing on the merits of the case.

At any point in this process a **settlement agreement** can be reached and submitted to the court. The most important aspect of divorce is the separation agreement, as it sets out the rights and obligations of the parties, including the custody and support arrangements for the children, the distribution of **marital**

Temporary restraining order (TRO)
A court order of limited duration designed to maintain the status quo pending further court action at a later date.

Protection order
A court order issued in domestic violence and abuse cases to keep one spouse away from the other, the children, or the home.

Settlement agreement
A document that contains the arrangements agreed on by the parties to a dispute.

Marital property
Property that is subject to court distribution upon termination of the marriage.

Alimony
Also known as **maintenance** or **support;** financial support and other forms of assistance required to supply the "necessities" of life.

Collaborative divorce
A nonadversarial process whereby the divorcing couple hires a team of professionals to help them reach a mutually satisfactory agreement.

property, and **alimony (maintenance).** In most cases these negotiations eventually lead to agreements that are then formalized in the final court decree. In those instances in which the parties cannot reach agreement, a trial is held at which witnesses testify to such things as the spouses' fitness as parents, how and when various financial assets were obtained, the fair market value of various assets, and the nature of the children's or spouses' future financial needs. This is often a poor solution, as all major decisions as to custody, alimony, property division, and child support will be taken away from the parties and left for the judge to decide. The judge then renders a decision on the basis of this evidence and issues the final divorce decree and related orders. The court retains jurisdiction in matters of child and spousal support, and at a later date the parties may come back to seek a modification of the original order based on such things as a change in marital status, a significant change in income, or a child's unanticipated needs.

As mentioned above, many state courts now incorporate alternative dispute resolution mechanisms, principally mediation, into the divorce process. A new alternative to traditional ADR techniques that attempts, so far as possible, to minimize the court's involvement in the divorce process is known as **collaborative law** or **collaborative divorce.** In 1990 a Minnesota attorney was tired of seeing the damage that the divorce process often produced. He started telling his clients that he would represent them but only so long as they agreed to settle out of court. If the negotiations broke down, and they had to resort to litigation, then they would have to find another attorney. From that beginning has sprung the nationwide movement known as collaborative law or collaborative divorce.

Collaborative divorce is similar to mediation in that all of the parties seek a win-win resolution rather than a battle based on individual interests. However, it differs in that a mediator is a neutral who cannot represent either of the parties. In a collaborative divorce, typically each partner has an attorney who advocates for his or her client. Further, what makes collaborative divorce truly unique is that all four parties—the divorcing couple and both attorneys—sign a participation agreement. That agreement contains a number of standard provisions, such as promises to show respect for all participants and not to hide any information. The most important provision is that the attorneys will not litigate the case. If the collaborative process does not succeed, then the attorneys must withdraw and the parties must retain new counsel. Obviously, this means it is not only in the parties' but also in the attorneys' best interest to work toward a negotiated result.

The collaborative model is based on a team approach. First, the two parties and the attorneys meet frequently as a group in joint sessions to try to determine what is in the best interests of the divorcing couple as well as any children. Second, the parties agree to jointly hire experts to help them with the process. This can include a financial specialist, a divorce coach (to help with communication skills), and a child specialist if there are children involved. Because the couple shares experts, they save the cost of hiring two of each type of expert and are better able to reach agreement on key financial and other matters. Only when a mutually beneficial understanding is reached, does the court become involved, as the recipient of the couple's written agreement.

(2) Property settlements

When a marriage ends, decisions need to be made regarding how jointly owned property will be divided. Such decisions relate not only to major assets, such as a home, but also to such specifics as who gets the living room sofa or the good china. In fact, some of the most hotly contested property fights relate to who gets "custody" of the family pet. Because only jointly owned property is subject to distribution, the first task is to determine which property is joint and which is separate.

Traditionally, there were three methods the courts used to determine what qualifies as marital property: by who holds title, by community property law, or through equitable distribution. Only the last two methods are still in use. Under a **community property** statute everything acquired during the marriage, with the exception of gifts or inheritances, is owned 50/50. Property acquired prior to the marriage is separate property, but it can lose its status if it is commingled. For example, if money acquired before the marriage is placed in a joint bank account, it loses its separate identity. At the time of divorce each spouse retains his or her share of separate property, but all property classified as community property is divided 50/50.

In noncommunity property states, courts follow the **doctrine of equitable distribution** and award a "marital interest" in any property that was acquired during the marriage through the efforts of both spouses. This acknowledges the contributions of both spouses, whether that contribution be financial or through a spouse's work in the home, regardless of whose name is on the legal title. Typically a statute will provide that the judge must look at several factors, including the length of the marriage, the age and health of the spouses, and their ability to make a living. While this process may also result in a 50/50 division, under the theory of equitable distribution such an equal split is not mandated.

Where the specific piece of property, such as a house, cannot be literally split between the parties, the court can either require that it be sold with a distribution of the profits or that a portion of its assessed value be given to the other spouse, either in cash or through some other item of equal value.

In addition to the types of property that you would normally view as being available for distribution, the courts have recently been faced with the necessity of deciding whether such items as frozen embryos, personal injury awards, pension plans, and professional degrees qualify as marital property. One of the first cases discussing frozen embryos was *Davis v. Davis.*[14] Mrs. Davis was unable to carry a pregnancy to term. She and her husband turned to a new medical technique, in vitro fertilization, for help. The doctors removed eggs from Mrs. Davis and fertilized them in vitro. Two were unsuccessfully implanted, and seven were frozen for future use. When the Davises decided to divorce, the embryos' fate was called in question. Mrs. Davis wanted to donate the frozen embryos to a childless couple. The husband did not want to become a parent. The court held that the father's right not to procreate won out over the wife's desire to donate the embryos.

Once the spouse has a vested interest in either a personal injury award or a pension plan, most states will view it as a divisible marital asset. However, the courts have come to varying conclusions as to how they should classify professional degrees. At one end of the spectrum, some courts do not factor it into a property or alimony agreement. Others view it as valuable marital property that must be valued and divided. Somewhere in between, other courts do not view it

Community property states
States that classify all property acquired by either the husband or the wife during the marriage, with the exception of gifts or inheritance, as marital property to be equally distributed between the spouses at the time of the divorce.

Doctrine of equitable distribution
A system for distributing property acquired during a marriage on the basis of such factors as the contributions of the spouses, the length of the marriage, the age and health of the spouses, and their ability to make a living.

---

[14] 842 S.W.2d 588 (Tenn. 1992).

as property but do award the party without the degree reimbursement for the time and money expended in assisting the other spouse in attaining the degree. Finally, some courts simply take it into account when calculating possible future earning power and alimony awards. The following case illustrates the difficulty in determining whether a professional degree should qualify as a marital asset.

Woodworth v. Woodworth
126 Mich. App. 258, 337 N.W.2d 332 (1983)

BURNS, J.

The parties were married on June 27, 1970, after plaintiff had graduated from Central Michigan University with a bachelor's degree in secondary education and defendant had graduated from Lansing Community College with an associate degree. They then moved to Jonesville, where plaintiff worked as a teacher and coach for the high school and defendant worked as a nursery school teacher in Hillsdale. In the fall of 1973, they sold their house, quit their jobs, and moved to Detroit, where plaintiff attended Wayne State Law School. Three years later, they moved to Lansing where plaintiff took and passed the bar exam and accepted a job as a research attorney with the Court of Appeals. Plaintiff is now a partner in a Lansing law firm.

The basic issue in this case is whether or not plaintiff's law degree is marital property subject to distribution. The trial court held that it was, valued it at $20,000, and awarded this amount to defendant in payments of $2,000 over ten years. Plaintiff contends that his law degree is not such a marital asset. We disagree.

The facts reveal that plaintiff's law degree was the end product of a concerted family effort. Both parties planned their family life around the effort to attain plaintiff's degree. Toward this end, the family divided the daily tasks encountered in living. While the law degree did not pre-empt all other facets of their lives, it did become the main focus and goal of their activities. Plaintiff left his job in Jonesville and the family relocated to Detroit so that plaintiff could attend law school. In Detroit, defendant sought and obtained full-time employment to support the family.

We conclude, therefore, that plaintiff's law degree was the result of mutual sacrifice and effort by both plaintiff and defendant. While

plaintiff studied and attended classes, defendant carried her share of the burden as well as sharing vicariously in the stress of the experience known as the "paper chase."

We believe that fairness dictates that the spouse who did not earn an advanced degree be compensated whenever the advanced degree is the product of such concerted family investment. The degree holder has expended great effort to obtain the degree not only for himself or herself, but also to benefit the family as a whole. The other spouse has shared in this effort and contributed in other ways as well, not merely as a gift to the student spouse nor merely to share individually in the benefits but to help the marital unit as a whole. . . .

[W]e also agree that divorce courts cannot recompense expectations. However, we are not talking about an expectation here. Defendant is not asking us to compensate for a failed expectation that her husband would become a wealthy lawyer and subsequently support her for the rest of her life. Instead, she is merely seeking her share of the fruits of a degree which she helped him earn. We fail to see the difference between compensating for a degree which she helped him earn and compensating her for a house in his name which her earnings helped him buy.

The third argument against including an advanced degree as marital property is that its valuation is too speculative. . . .

However, future earnings due to an advanced degree are not "too speculative." While a degree holder spouse might change professions, earn less than projected at trial, or even die, courts have proved adept at measuring future earnings in such contexts as personal injury, wrongful death, and workers' compensation actions. In fact, pain and suffering, professional goodwill and mental distress, within these general legal issues, have similar valuation "problems." . . .

The last argument is that these matters are best considered when awarding alimony rather than when distributing the property. . . . However, alimony is basically for the other spouse's support. . . . The considerations for whether or not a spouse is entitled to support are different than for dividing the marital property. *McLain v. McLain*, 108 Mich. App. 166; 310 N.W.2d 316 (1981), listed 11 factors that the trial judge is to consider in determining whether or not to award alimony. Some of these deal with the parties'

financial condition and their ability to support themselves. If the spouse has already supported the other spouse through graduate school, he or she is quite possibly already presently capable of supporting him or herself. Furthermore, MCL 552.13; MSA 25.93 gives the trial court discretion to end alimony if the spouse receiving it remarries. We do not believe that the trial judge should be allowed to deprive the spouse who does not have an advanced degree of the fruits of the marriage and award it all to the other spouse merely because he or she has remarried. Such a situation would necessarily cause that spouse to think twice about remarrying. . . .

CASE DISCUSSION QUESTIONS

1. In deciding how much to compensate the wife, the *Woodworth* court stated that there were two basic methods. The award could be a percentage share of the present value of the future earnings attributable to the law degree, or the award could be limited to the amount of money the wife actually contributed to the cost of earning the degree. Which formulation do you prefer? Why? The court chose the first method. What problems do you foresee this created in this and future cases?

2. The court noted that some courts have held that

[a]n education degree, such as an M.B.A., is simply not encompassed by the broad views of the concept of "property." It does not have an exchange value or any objective transferable value on an open market. It is personal to the holder. It terminates on death of the holder and is not inheritable. It cannot be assigned, sold, transferred, conveyed, or pledged. An advanced degree is a cumulative product of many years of previous education, combined with diligence and hard work. It may not be acquired by the mere expenditure of money. It is simply an intellectual achievement that may potentially assist in the future acquisition of property. In our view, it has none of the attributes of property in the usual sense of that term.[15]

Should the outcome of this and similar cases be determined by whether an education degree is "property"? On what other factors might the court base its decision?

(3) Alimony/maintenance agreements

Alimony, also referred to as **maintenance** or **support,** was traditionally awarded to the wife, who had stayed at home and raised the children, while the husband was working outside the home to provide the income needed to support the family's needs. The primary rationale for alimony was that the divorced wife needed continued support from the former husband because she either lacked the skills and/or experience to support herself after the divorce or should

---

[15]Id. at 334.

not be expected to have to go to work outside the home. In its 1979 decision in *Orr v. Orr*[16] the U.S. Supreme Court ruled that gender-based alimony violated the equal protection clause of the Fourteenth Amendment and that the court must decide solely on the basis of the educational backgrounds and job opportunities of both spouses.

In determining alimony the court looks to many of the same factors that are used in equitable property division. Also, the court may take into account the lifestyle to which the parties have become accustomed.

The trend in recent years has been to award rehabilitative or limited-term support rather than a permanent alimony for an indefinite time period. In many cases the nonworking spouse will be given support for a specific amount of time to return to school and reestablish job skills. After that period has expired, the spouse has to provide for his or her own support.

Alimony can also be paid in one lump sum rather than over time. Psychologically a lump sum payment may allow the parties to "get on with their lives." However, there might be severe tax consequences for the recipient, who might have to pay taxes on the entire amount when received.

(4) Custody, visitation, and child support

Child custody and visitation rights often become two of the most contentious and difficult issues to deal with in a divorce case. Ideally the divorcing couple puts their own selfish interests aside and works with a professional mediator to arrive at an arrangement that is in the best long-term interests of the children. All too often, however, the issues of custody and visitation are decided in an atmosphere of acrimony and retribution. Sometimes those ill feelings can even lead to false charges of child abuse. Nothing can compare to the emotional trauma felt by everyone involved in a contested child custody dispute.

(a) Custody   Custody can be either legal or physical, and it can be either sole or joint. Traditionally, it was common for the mother to get sole legal and physical custody. The trend today is toward joint legal custody, regardless of who has physical custody.

Physical custody
The child lives with and has day-to-day activities supervised by the designated parent or guardian.

Legal custody
The designated parent or guardian has authority to make legal decisions for the child relating to such matters as health care and education.

Physical custody determines with whom the child will live and who will supervise the child's day-to-day activities. **Legal custody** relates to who will have authority to make legal decisions for the child relating to such things as health care and education. If one party to the divorce is given **sole custody,** that parent has both physical and legal custody of the child until either the child reaches the age of majority or the court decides that it is in the best interests of the child to change this custody arrangement. **Joint legal custody** allows both parents to have an equal say in making major decisions—for example, decisions regarding the education of the child. Joint physical custody is also possible, allowing the child to spend a significant amount of time with each parent. When parents live in different states, they often have **split custody,** whereby one parent has both physical and legal custody during the school year and then the other parent gets both physical and legal custody during designated vacation periods. The term **split** or **divided custody** can also refer to those rare situations when the court

---

[16]440 U.S. 268 (1979).

separates the children so that each parent is awarded custody of one or more of the children.

If the parents cannot agree on a mutually acceptable custody arrangement, the court holds a hearing at which interested parties give testimony regarding the child's needs and the fitness of each parent. The court should consider the wishes of the parents and the child; the child's adjustment to his or her home, school, and community; and the mental and physical health of all involved. The court may appoint a **guardian ad litem,** usually an attorney or a social worker, to speak for the interests of the child.

(b) Visitation In addition to determining which parent will be given custody of any children, the court must determine the extent to which the noncustodial parent can visit the child. Normally, when physical custody is given to one parent, the noncustodial parent is given visitation rights and ordered to pay support. However, the right to visit is not tied directly to the obligation to support. Therefore, if the custodial parent wrongfully denies the other parent access to the children, that does not relieve the noncustodial parent of the obligation to provide support. Likewise, if the support payments are late, that does not give the custodial parent the right to deny visitation. The appropriate response in either case is to return to court and ask for a court-ordered remedy. This is often a difficult concept for divorced couples to grasp, as evidenced by the following case.

Carroll v. Carroll
593 So. 2d 1131 (Fla. Dist. Ct. App. 1972)

PARKER, Judge.

Jane Carroll, the former wife of Ira Carroll, Sr., appeals a supplemental final judgment which temporarily suspended child support based upon her sixteen-year-old son, Hunter Carroll, refusing to visit his father, Mr. Carroll. Although we sympathize with a trial judge dealing with an almost impossible situation, we reverse that portion of the judgment suspending the father's child support obligation, concluding that the noncustodial parent's child support obligation does not cease upon the child refusing to visit the noncustodial parent.

A review of this court file reflects that for six years following a final judgment of dissolution of marriage, there has been bitter strife between Mr. and Mrs. Carroll over Mr. Carroll's rights of visitation with their three children. Two things happened to involve this court. The first was that the parties' sixteen-year-old child filed a motion through his mother's attorney to have the trial judge terminate the requirement that he visit his father. The trial court granted the son's motion. The next thing to occur was the trial court, on its own motion, terminated Mr. Carroll's child support obligation for that child on a temporary basis until visitation was reinstituted.

We recognize the dilemma of the trial judge and quote from his order denying Mrs. Carroll's motion for rehearing:

> The Former Wife's position is that the Court erred in tying a child support obligation to a visitation issue. Ordinarily, the Former Wife would be correct, and as a general rule it is clear that both Chapter 61 and the apposite case law provide that child support cannot be conditioned upon visitation. However, the instant case defies, in many ways, the general rule.

> It would serve no useful purpose, except for appellate review, to expend the labor necessary to fully lay out the post judgment etiology of this case. The file speaks for itself. By the time the temporary visitation order was entered in the fall

of last year, the parties and the child in question had reached a point justifying not only a temporary cessation of visitation, but also support for that child. Hunter Carroll and his father had become adversaries in about every sense of the word. They had escalated their enmity to the point of a physical confrontation. Hunter referred to his father as "Mr. Carroll," and indicated no respect whatsoever for him. Hunter actively resisted visitation with his father and in fact was the movant himself in the motion to terminate visitation. Hunter Carroll is a very sophisticated, bright, articulate sixteen year old boy who has, as he so forcefully points out, reached an age of discretion which all but insures that if he doesn't want to have meaningful visitation, it simply will not occur. He believes he has been driven to this emotional juncture by his father's behavior; the father believes his son's attitude is a by-product of the poisonous relationship between him and his former wife who is the custodial parent. Whatever the truth, it appears to the Court that where a child of sufficient maturity and intellect and discretion moves to terminate visitation, and where the motion is granted, this conduct justifies the suspension of support on a temporary basis. Of course support will be automatically and immediately re-instated once visitation recommences.

We first note that this record contains no findings by the trial judge that Mrs. Carroll orchestrated her son's motion to terminate visitation. We do not have to address today what this court's position would be if that were the case. Although Mr. Carroll feels strongly that the wife and maternal grandparents have caused these problems, the trial judge made no such findings. Florida Statutes do provide a remedy for a noncustodial parent who is denied his or her visitation rights by the custodial parent.

Both natural parents share a duty to support a minor child, even though the trial court, under section 61.13(1)(a), may order either or both parents to pay child support upon dissolution of the marriage. Thus if this animosity had developed between the father and child while the parents were still married, the father still would have a duty of support of his family, including Hunter.

This court has recognized that ordinarily, if a parent supports his child, he has the right to visit the child. However, this court has further recognized that there are instances where a former spouse has a duty of support when visitation would not be advisable for various "sociological, psychiatric and other reasons." . . .

[W]e are unwilling to say that conduct by a child, not shown to be orchestrated by one of the parents, should relieve a parent of his or her duty to support the child. This seems to punish only the other parent's ability to pay for that child's needs.

The all too familiar tragedy in this case is, as stated by the guardian ad litem, that "this appears to be a classic case of parental strife affecting the dependent children; the children are always the losers." Instead of two parents working with one another and their child to deal with his concerns regarding visitation, we have instead the young man employing an attorney to file motions which require court resolution. And throughout this scenario, quality time between a child and his father is being lost which can never be replaced. The parents also should consider the effect this may have upon the other children.

While fully understanding the trial court's attempt to do equity in this case, we reverse and remand with directions for the trial court to order the payment of all of the suspended child support payments.

CASE DISCUSSION QUESTIONS

1. Do you agree with the *Carroll* court's decision in this case? Why?

2. Should the court have considered the needs of the two other children in reaching its decision?

3. Do you think the court would have reached a different result if it had found that Mrs. Carroll had "orchestrated" her son's decision to terminate visitation? Most courts will not relieve a parent of his or her obligation to supply child support solely on the basis that the custodial parent had denied that parent his or her court-ordered visitation rights. Do you agree with this? Why should the

noncustodial parent have to continue to pay child support if he or she is being denied visitation rights?

(c) Custody and visitation rights of others   Until recently the only party with standing to request custody or visitation rights after divorce was the noncustodial parent. Today, however, in some cases courts have expanded those rights to encompass unwed fathers, grandparents, stepparents, and gay and lesbian partners.

(i) Unwed fathers   In contradistinction to the legal protections offered unwed mothers, with regard to unwed fathers the U.S. Supreme Court has stated that the "mere existence of a biological link" is not enough to merit protection. For example, an unwed father who has not participated in the rearing of his child or given any financial support is not entitled to a hearing before his child can be adopted by the stepfather.[17] However, if an unwed father has demonstrated a full commitment to parental responsibilities, then his desire for personal contact with his child will acquire substantial protection under the due process clause of the Fourteenth Amendment. For example, where the father had lived with the mother and his children off and on for eighteen years, the unwed father was entitled to a hearing before the state could take his children from him.[18]

(ii) Grandparents   Traditionally, grandparents had no legal rights to visitation. In recent years, however, the courts have been more willing to grant visitation rights if the children are no longer living in an intact home with both parents and if it can be shown to be in the best interests of the children.

By 1999 a majority of the states had enacted legislation allowing third parties, such as grandparents, to petition for visitation, at least in situations where the parental unit was no longer intact due to divorce, separation, or death. In *Troxel v. Granville*[19] the U.S. Supreme Court was asked to rule on the constitutionality of a Washington State statute that allowed any third party to petition for visitation if it was in the "best interests" of the child. The Supreme Court held that the Constitution protects the interest of parents in the care, custody, and control of their children and that the Washington statute unconstitutionally infringed on that right. The Court noted that the statute was "breathtakingly broad" in that it allowed *any* person (with no requirement that the person have established a substantial relationship to the child) to petition the court for visitation at *any* time (with no requirement that the parent first be deemed unfit, that evidence be introduced showing that the child would be adversely affected by the lack of visitation, or that the parent first have unreasonably denied visitation). Under the statute a trial court had the power to grant visitation rights if the court determined it was in the best interests of the child. The Court was troubled by all of these statutory provisions as well as the lack of according at least a rebuttable presumption of validity to the parent's decision regarding visitation. Although the Court invalidated the Washington statute, it limited its decision to the specifics of that statute and declined to address the validity of the statutes enacted by the other forty-nine states. Nor did the Court

---

[17]Lehr v. Robertson, 463 U.S. 248 (1983).

[18]Stanley v. Illinois, 405 U.S. 645 (1972).

[19]530 U.S. 57 (2000).

clearly delineate what the Washington legislature would need to do to amend the statute to cure its constitutional problems. Therefore, because the Court did not lay down any clear guidelines, we should expect to see a great deal of litigation in which parents challenge the validity of the other state statutes that grant grandparents and others the right to petition for visitation.

(iii) Stepparents   When divorced parents remarry, their children often form very strong "parental" bonds with the new stepparent. However, if stepparents do not take the necessary steps to adopt the child of the new spouse, they may have no visitation rights if they divorce or their spouse dies. Sometimes visitation is allowed if the court determines that the person has become a "de facto parent" through prolonged contact and care for the child. However, it is not safe to rely on this exception, as evidenced by a 1997 Vermont case. In *Titchenal v. Dexter,*[20] the court held that even though a woman was a "de facto parent" to a child she had raised with her lesbian partner, she had no visitation rights. The court stated that allowing such visitation rights raised the potential danger that parents would be forced to defend against visitation claims by anyone who had formed a strong bond with the child. The court stated that if the "de facto parent" wanted to preserve her rights, the proper approach would have been to adopt the child. However, adoption is not always a viable option. For example, in *In re EWB Applying for Adoption*[21] a stepfather was denied the right to adopt his wife's daughter even though he was "an ideal father figure" and the girl only occasionally saw her natural father, who owed unpaid child support. The court determined that it was in the best interest of the child to have "the best of both worlds" and denied the adoption request.[22]

In an unusual case an Oregon court granted custody to a stepfather. In *Fenimore v. Smith,*[23] a twelve-year-old girl was present when her mother died of heart failure. Experts testified that the girl suffered great guilt because she felt the mother died as a result of being upset over an argument between her and her half-sister. In addition, the girl did not administer CPR and called her father rather than dialing 911. In those circumstances the court ruled it would be an additional loss for the girl to be taken away from her stepfather and half-sister. However, other courts have held the opposite, stating that unless the biological parent has abused or neglected the child, the award of custody must be to the natural parent. For example, in the case of *In re A.R.A.*[24] the parents, Tracy and Bill, were married for six years. During that time A.R.A. was born. When she was nineteen months old, they divorced, and Tracy was given custody. A year later Tracy married Patrick, and they had a son. Then Tracy died in a plane crash. In her will, Tracy named Patrick A.R.A.'s guardian. When Bill came to pick up A.R.A., Patrick refused. The trial court determined that there was a close relationship between Patrick and A.R.A., that she was attached to her half-brother, that Patrick's parenting skills were better than Bill's, and that A.R.A. would be adversely affected by changing schools and homes. The court awarded custody to Patrick. The Montana Supreme Court reversed. It stated that the

---

[20]693 A.2d 682 (Vt. 1997).

[21]441 So. 2d 478 (La. App. 1983).

[22]Id. at 483.

[23]930 P.2d 892 (Or. App. 1997).

[24]919 P.2d 388 (Mont. 1996).

"best interest of the child" test can be used only after a showing of dependency or abuse and neglect by the natural parent. Because there was no such showing here, the natural parent should be awarded custody.[25]

(iv) Gay and lesbian partners   The rights of homosexual parents constitute an emerging issue in family law. Traditionally, a homosexual parent had difficulty being awarded custody, as the court often thought that the parent's choice of lifestyle would have a bad influence on the child. As recently as 1996, a headline in the National Law Journal could proclaim: "Mom's a Lesbian, Dad's a Killer. Judge: She's Unfit." The article reported how a Florida judge, looking at the following facts, found the mother unfit. An eleven-year-old daughter had been living with her mother for the past five years, ever since her parents' separation. When the mother went to court seeking past-due child support, her ex-husband responded by suing for custody. He had served eight years in jail for killing his first wife and was currently living with his fourth wife. Because the mother was living with a female partner, the judge sent the daughter to live with the father. The judge noted that the daughter should be "given the opportunity and the option to live in a non-lesbian world."[26]

In another well-publicized case the Virginia Supreme Court upheld a trial court's decision to allow a grandmother to seek custody of her grandson on the grounds that her daughter was a lesbian. The court noted that "living daily under conditions stemming from active lesbianism practiced in the home may impose a burden upon a child by reason of the 'social condemnation' attached to such an arrangement, which will inevitably afflict [sic] the child's relationships with its 'peers and with the community at large.' "[27]

At the other end of the spectrum, many courts hold that, absent evidence that the child is being harmed, a parent's sexual orientation should not be a significant factor in custody cases. For example, in *Bezio v. Patenaude*[28] the court noted that "[b]oth parties introduced evidence to the effect that a mother's sexual preference per se is irrelevant to a consideration of her parental skills."[29] The court went on to hold that the "state may not deprive parents of custody of their children 'simply because their household fails to meet the ideals approved by the community' . . . [or] simply because the parents embrace ideologies or pursue life-styles at odds with the average."[30]

Additional problems are created when a same-sex couple marries or enters into a civil union, chooses to bring a child into that union, and then later separates. Matters become even more difficult if one of the former partners moves to a state that does not recognize same-sex marriage or civil unions. Such was the case of Janet and Lisa. Janet and Lisa lived in Virginia, a state that does not recognize same-sex unions. In 2000 they traveled to Vermont to enter into a civil union. They then returned to Virginia where they decided to have a child through Lisa undergoing artificial insemination. Their daughter was born in 2002 and later that year they moved to Vermont for approximately a year

---

[25]Id. at 392.

[26]Nat'l L.J., Feb. 12, 1996, at A9.

[27]Bottoms v. Bottoms, 457 S.E.2d 102, 108 (Va. 1995).

[28]410 N.E.2d 1207 (Mass. 1980).

[29]Id. at 1215.

[30]Id.

before ending their relationship. Lisa returned with the child to Virginia. She then began legal proceedings in a Vermont family court to dissolve her civil union and to award her custody of their child. The Vermont court entered an order awarding Janet visitation rights.

Unhappy with that decision, Lisa petitioned the Virginia court to declare her the sole parent and to deny Janet any parental rights. The Virginia court found that Virginia's Affirmation of Marriage Act, which states that same-sex unions from other states are void in all respects in Virginia, meant that Janet had no legal rights. Meanwhile, Vermont's Supreme Court ruled that the Vermont family court, and not Virginia's courts, had jurisdiction over the case and that Janet had all the parental rights of any parent whose child is born into a marriage.[31] What could have turned into a major jurisdictional fight between the courts of Vermont and Virginia ended when the Virginia Court of Appeals accepted the Vermont ruling and the power of the Vermont courts to resolve the matter.[32] Meanwhile, Janet had gone for more than two years without seeing her daughter. It appears that in order to ensure that both same-sex parents retain parental rights after a separation, the nonbirth parent should take the additional precaution of adopting any children conceived during the union.

Child support
Money that the noncustodial parent contributes to assist the custodial parent in paying for a child's food, shelter, clothing, medical care, and education.

(d) Child support   The level of **child support** that the noncustodial parent will be required to contribute is another frequently contentious aspect of divorce proceedings. These determinations require a careful balancing of such factors as the parents' income and standard of living, the child's age, and the child's health and educational needs. The courts retain jurisdiction over this aspect of the divorce decree and often modify the support order based on changes in a parent's job status or remarriage.

Every state has guidelines to help the courts determine how much the child support payments should be. Exhibit 11-2 on page 425 shows the 2006 guidelines for Massachusetts. These are only guidelines, and the court has discretion to either increase or decrease these amounts based on a number of factors.

As you can see, payments are dependent on the income of the parents and the number of children. These guidelines assume traditional custody and visitation arrangements. They do not apply when the parents share physical custody or have split custody—that is, when each parent has physical custody of one or more children. They also do not apply if the combined gross income of the parents exceeds $100,000.

Garnishment
A process through which a court can require an employer to withhold money from an employee's wages and turn this money over to the party to whom a debt is owed.

One of the biggest problems with child support is collecting it. The problem of "deadbeat dads" has been widely publicized in recent years and has resulted in significant legislation at both the state and the national levels. In most states the custodial parent can attach the wages of the delinquent parent. Through a process called **garnishment** a court can require an employer to withhold money from an employee's wages and turn this money over to the party to which a debt is owed. Some states assist in the collection of child support by requiring that the payments be made directly to the local clerk of the court.

If the parent with a child support obligation moves to another state, two uniform laws come into play: the Uniform Reciprocal Enforcement of Support

---

[31]Miller-Jenkins v. Miller-Jenkins. 912 A.2d 951 (Vt. 2006).

[32]Miller-Jenkins v. Miller-Jenkins, 637 S.E.2d 330 (Va. 2006).

The basic child support obligation, based on the income of the noncustodial parent, is as follows:

Gross Weekly Income	Monthly Payment per Number of Children		
	1	2	3
$0–$100	Discretion of the court, but not less than $80 per month		
$101–$280	21%	24%	27%
$281–$750	$59 + 23% (% refers to all dollars over $280)	$67 + 28%	$76 + 31%
$751–max.	$167 + 25% (% refers to all dollars over $750)	$199 + 30%	$222 + 33%

Exhibit 11-2   Massachusetts Child Support Guidelines

Act (URESA), adopted by all fifty states, and the Uniform Interstate Family Support Act (UIFSA), adopted by approximately half the states. Both allow an order for support issued in one state to be enforced in another state. A major difference in the two laws is whether the enforcing state is allowed to modify the original support order. Under URESA it can; under UIFSA it cannot. The federal Child Support Recovery Act of 1992[33] authorizes **extradition**—that is, the return of delinquent parents for criminal prosecution—in states that make willful failure to pay child support a crime.

Extradition
The transportation of an individual from one state to another so that person can be tried on criminal charges.

DISCUSSION QUESTIONS

11. A husband and wife decided to try in vitro fertilization. They signed an agreement that provided that, in the event of their separation, the wife could use the embryos. The procedure was successful, and the wife gave birth to twins. When the couple separated, the wife sought "custody" of the remaining frozen embryos. The father objected. How do you think the court ruled?

12. In settling custody issues the courts are supposed to use a "best interest of the child" standard. To what extent do you think it is appropriate for the courts to take into consideration such things as a parent's gender, age, or religion? In determining custody, how much, if any, consideration should be given to the fact that one of the parents smokes and would therefore be exposing the child to secondhand smoke? What if the new partner of one of the parents is of a different race than the child? What if one of the parents openly lives with his or her new homosexual partner?

13. To what extent should children at various ages be permitted to help determine which parents should have custody?

14. What should the court do if a child refuses to visit the noncustodial parent? In the case of *In re Marriage of Marshall*, 663 N.E.2d 1113 (Ill. App. 1996), nine-year-old Rachel and thirteen-year-old Heidi flatly refused to visit

---

[33]18 U.S.C.S. § 228 (2008).

their father. The court "found both Rachel and Heidi to be in direct civil contempt. The court 'grounded' Rachel, and ordered that she not leave her mother's home. Rachel could not watch television or have friends over to the house, but she could read and do crafts. The court ordered [the mother] to enforce these measures. The court placed Heidi in a juvenile detention facility until she agreed to go to North Carolina. The judge indicated that the girls' conduct arose from the efforts of adults to manipulate the system." Id. at 1119. Do you agree that such sanctions are appropriate? What other remedies do you think the court could have pursued?

15. Which of the following two provisions for child visitation do you prefer? Do you think your answer might vary depending on the couple involved? Why?

- The parties shall determine visitation schedules between them. At a minimum the husband will see the children at least two weekends a month and one day or early evening during the week.
- The husband will have visitation with the three children every other weekend, commencing at 6:00 PM on Friday evening, when he will pick up the children at the wife's home. He will return them at 6:00 PM on Sunday evening.

B. THE PARENT-CHILD RELATIONSHIP

Having discussed the legal nature of the marital relationship, we now turn to a second major area of family law—the relationship between parents and their children. In this section we will cover the procedure for establishing paternity, adoption, surrogacy, parental rights, child neglect and abuse, and the status of minors.

1. Establishing the Relationship

In most cases the parent-child relationship is legally established at the point at which the names of the mother and father are recorded on a child's birth certificate, either at the time of birth or later through an adoption proceeding. While there have always been situations in which the identity of the father has not been clear, because of current advances in the scientific methods for treating infertility, both legal (as opposed to biological) paternity and legal maternity may be difficult to establish. For example, in the case of an anonymous sperm donor, state statutes cut off all rights of the donor and vest paternity in the married husband. However, if an unmarried woman has knowledge of a sperm donor's identity, then the donor may later be in a position to assert paternity rights. Another difficult situation occurs when an infertility clinic artificially combines a man's sperm with a woman's egg and then implants that fertilized egg into the womb of a second woman. The result is a genetic mother and a gestational mother. In this section we will discuss how parental rights are established through paternity actions, adoption, sperm or egg donation, and surrogacy arrangements.

a. Paternity Actions

The need to establish paternity usually arises when the mother wishes her child to receive court-ordered support payment from the alleged father. As one aspect of recent attempts at "welfare reform," many states have become much more aggressive at identifying fathers of children born out of wedlock. Regulations in some states require the mother to name the child's father as a condition of qualifying for welfare benefits. The government itself then takes the lead in filing petitions to establish paternity that require the alleged father to submit to blood tests and to pay child support if found to have fathered the child.

An increasingly common occurrence is the case of a presumptive father who voluntarily desires to establish paternity in order to gain custody or visitation rights. For unwed fathers who wish to voluntarily assert their paternity, some states have established a putative fathers' registry. Signing the registry ensures that the father will be notified before any court determination regarding adoption of the child.

When a man wishes to establish himself as a child's father and he was not wedded to the mother at the time of birth, he may run into a presumption that a husband who was living with his wife at the time of the birth is the father of the child. Such presumptions sometimes can be overcome if evidence shows the husband is impotent or sterile or if a blood test shows the child could not be his. However, some courts treat this presumption as a conclusive presumption and will not allow paternity to be established even through DNA testing.

An example of a court allowing the father to overcome such a presumption in favor of the husband is the case of *Comino v. Kelley*.[34] In that case the evidence established that although the child's mother, Stephanie Kelley, was legally married to Jeffrey Moyer, the marriage had been a mutually convenient "business relationship" that involved living in separate bedrooms. When Kelley became pregnant after having had intercourse with Paul Comino, she told him that he was the father, and prior to the birth she moved into Comino's home. Comino attended at least one Lamaze childbirth class with Kelley, was present at the birth, and was identified as the father on the birth certificate. After the birth Kelley, Comino, and the baby all returned to Comino's house, and birth announcements were sent identifying him as the father. More than two years later, Kelley moved out of Comino's home. When she threatened to restrict his access to the child, Comino went to court to formally establish his parental relationship and to obtain joint physical and legal custody. Kelley, in turn, asserted that "as a matter of law" Moyer was presumed to be the child's father because she had been married to him at the time the child was conceived.

In ruling in Comino's favor, the California appellate court found that Comino's fatherhood was established by another section of the California Code that provides a presumption for paternity when a man "receives the child into his home and openly holds out the child as his natural child."[35] The court ruled, in effect, that this statutory presumption took precedence over the one on which Kelley relied.

---

[34]25 Cal. App. 4th 678 (1994).
[35]Id. at 685.

DISCUSSION QUESTIONS

16. Do you agree with a policy that denies welfare assistance to a child because the mother refuses to cooperate with authorities in identifying the child's father?

17. A fifteen-year-old girl was raped and found herself pregnant. She decided not to have an abortion but to give the child up for adoption. The rapist, however, had other plans. He threatened to assert his paternity rights by signing the state's putative fathers' registry unless the girl dropped the charges against him. What actions do you think a state can take to protect the rights of unwed fathers, while preventing such abuses of the system?

18. Do you think the courts should continue to follow the conclusive presumption that a child born of married parents is their child?

b. Adoption

Adoption is the legal process by which someone other than a child's natural parent assumes the legal rights and responsibilities as a parent for the child. The new adoptive parent literally takes the place of the child's natural parent. Therefore, before the new parent-child relationship can be established, either the child's natural parent must voluntarily relinquish his or her parental rights, or a court of competent jurisdiction must terminate such rights. For example, if a woman remarries and her new husband wishes to adopt her child from her previous marriage, he cannot do so until the child's natural father either voluntarily gives up his parental rights or has them terminated by a court.

Although they are still few and far between, there have been some cases in which a child has sought to "divorce" his or her parents so that the child could be adopted by someone else. One such highly publicized case occurred in 1992 in Florida, where a state circuit court in Orlando allowed Gregory Kingsley to terminate the parental rights of his natural parents so that he could be adopted by the foster parents with whom he had been living. There is also a process for adult adoptions, which allows one adult to adopt another adult as a son or daughter. Such an adoption requires the consent of both parties and is designed to establish certain rights under the probate laws. The remainder of this section will focus on the more common occurrence of infant adoption.

Agency adoption
An adoption in which a licensed agency assumes responsibility for screening adoptive parents and matching them with available children.

Most states have different procedures and rules for agency adoptions and independent adoptions. Many **agency adoptions** involve children born out of wedlock to parents who do not feel they are prepared to accept the responsibilities of parenthood. Licensed agencies assume responsibility for these children, providing temporary foster care, and screen individuals and couples who wish to adopt. An **independent adoption** is one that involves a private agreement between the birth parents and the adoptive parents. Such adoptions still require investigations by approval agencies and formal actions by the courts.

Independent adoption
An adoption that involves a private agreement between the birth parents and the adoptive parents.

Some states have adopted formal criteria that are to be used in selecting among potential adoptive parents. In California, for example, the first choice is a relative. If that is not possible or is not in the child's best interest, the foster parents as well as others can be considered. In making that determination the religious background of the child may be taken into account. However, the agency may not delay or deny the placement "on the basis of the race, color, or national origin of the adoptive parent or the child involved."[36] When a match is made, the new parent or parents are given temporary custody of the child for a trial period, during which the agency monitors the new parents' care of the child. During this time a social worker or other official conducts a home study to determine whether they are fit to adopt.

Before an adoption can be finalized, the birth parents must sign a document agreeing to give up their parental rights. Usually, this release cannot be signed prior to the baby's birth. Once it is signed, however, normally the birth parents cannot take back their relinquishment of parental rights unless they can show their consent was obtained by fraud. After the birth parents have released their parental rights and the adoptive parents are deemed fit, the adoptive parents must go to court to have the adoption finalized. Therefore, the child can live with the adoptive parents for a lengthy period before the adoption is finalized by the court.

DISCUSSION QUESTIONS

19. Do you agree with the placement criteria included in the California statute discussed above? What is the justification for matching the child's religious background with those of the adoptive parents? Should that factor take precedence over the economic and lifestyle advantages that an alternative placement might have?

20. Should children be allowed to "divorce" their parents so that they can be adopted by others?

The importance of obtaining and documenting the consent of the child's natural parents to an adoption is illustrated in a highly controversial Illinois Supreme Court decision, the "Baby Richard" case, excerpted below.

In re Petition of John Doe and Jane Doe, Husband and Wife, to Adopt Baby Boy Janikova
159 Ill. 2d 347, 638 N.E.2d 181 (1994)

Justice HEIPLE delivered the opinion of the court:

John and Jane Doe filed a petition to adopt a newborn baby boy. The baby's biological mother, Daniella Janikova, executed a consent to have the baby adopted four days after his birth without informing his biological father, Otakar Kirchner, to whom she was not yet married.

The mother told the father that the baby had died, and he did not find out otherwise until 57 days after the birth. The trial court ruled that the father's consent was unnecessary because he did not show sufficient interest in the

child during the first 30 days of the child's life. The appellate court affirmed with one justice dissenting. We granted leave to appeal and now reverse.

Otakar and Daniella began living together in the fall of 1989, and Daniella became pregnant in June of 1990. For the first eight months of her pregnancy, Otakar provided for all of her expenses.

In late January 1991, Otakar went to his native Czechoslovakia to attend to his gravely ill grandmother for two weeks. During this time,

---

[36]Cal. Fam. Code §§ 8708-8709 (2008).

Daniella received a phone call from Otakar's aunt saying that Otakar had resumed a former romantic relationship with another woman.

Because of this unsettling news, Daniella left their shared apartment, refused to talk with Otakar on his return, and gave birth to the child at a different hospital than where they had originally planned. She gave her consent to the adoption of the child by the Does, telling them and their attorney that she knew who the father was but would not furnish his name. Daniella and her uncle warded off Otakar's persistent inquiries about the child by telling him that the child had died shortly after birth.

Otakar found out that the child was still alive and had been placed for adoption 57 days after the child was born. He then began the instant proceedings by filing an appearance contesting the Does' adoption of his son. As already noted, the trial court ruled that Otakar was an unfit parent under section 1 of the Adoption Act because he had not shown a reasonable degree of interest in the child within the first 30 days of his life. Therefore, the father's consent was unnecessary under section 8 of the Act.

The finding that the father had not shown a reasonable degree of interest in the child is not supported by the evidence. In fact, he made various attempts to locate the child, all of which were either frustrated or blocked by the actions of the mother. Further, the mother was aided by the attorney for the adoptive parents, who failed to make any effort to ascertain the name or address of the father despite the fact that the mother indicated she knew who he was. Under the circumstances, the father had no opportunity discharge any familial duty.

In the opinion below, the appellate court, wholly missing the threshold issue in this case, dwelt on the best interests of the child. Since, however, the father's parental interest was improperly terminated, there was no occasion to reach the factor of the child's best interests. That point should never have been reached and need never have been discussed.

Unfortunately, over three years have elapsed since the birth of the baby who is the subject of these proceedings. To the extent that it is relevant to assign fault in this case, the fault here lies initially with the mother, who fraudulently tried deprive the father of his rights, and secondly, with the adoptive parents and their attorney, who

proceeded with the adoption when they knew that a real father was out there who had been denied knowledge of his baby's existence.

When the father entered his appearance in the adoption proceedings 57 days after the baby's birth and demanded his rights as a father, the petitioners should have relinquished the baby at that time. It was their decision to prolong this litigation through a lengthy, and ultimately fruitless, appeal.

The adoption laws of Illinois are neither complex nor difficult of application. Those laws intentionally place the burden of proof on the adoptive parents in establishing both the relinquishment and/or unfitness of the natural parents and, coincidentally, the fitness and the right to adopt of the adoptive parents. In addition, Illinois law requires a good-faith effort to notify the natural parents of the adoption proceedings. These laws are designed to protect natural parents in their preemptive rights to their own children wholly apart from any consideration of the so-called best interests of the child. If it were otherwise, few parents would be secure in the custody of their own children. If best interests of the child were a sufficient qualification to determine child custody, anyone with superior income, intelligence, education, etc., might challenge and deprive the parents of their right to their own children. The law is otherwise and was not complied with in this case.

Accordingly, we reverse. . . .

Justice HEIPLE, writing in support of the denial of rehearing: . . .

I have been a judge for over 23 years. In that time, I have seldom before worked on a case that involved the spread of so much misinformation, nor one which dealt with as straightforward an application of law to fact. . . .

As for the child, age three, it is to be expected that there would be an initial shock, even a longing for a time in the absence of the persons whom he had viewed as parents. This trauma will be overcome, however, as it is every day across this land by children who suddenly find their parents separated by divorce or lost to them through death. It will not be an insurmountable trauma for a three-year-old child to be returned, at last, to his natural parents who want to raise him as their own. It will work itself out in the fullness of time. As for the adoptive parents, they will have to live with their pain and the knowledge that they wrongfully deprived a father of his child past the child's third birthday. They and their lawyer brought it on themselves.

This much is clear. Adoptive parents who comply with the law may feel secure in their adoptions. Natural parents may feel secure in their right to raise their own children. If there is a tragedy in this case, as has been suggested, then that tragedy is the wrongful breakup of a natural family and the keeping of a child by strangers without right. We must remember that the purpose of an adoption is to provide a home for a child, not a child for a home.

CASE DISCUSSION QUESTIONS

1. The trial court stated: "Fortunately, the time has long past when children in our society were considered the property of their parents. . . . [W]e start with the premise that Richard is not a piece of property with property rights belonging to either his biological or adoptive parents. Richard 'belongs' to no one but himself. . . . A child's best interest is not part of an equation. It is not to be balanced against any other interest." Obviously, the Illinois Supreme Court disagreed. Articulate the standard adopted by the Illinois Supreme Court. Which standard, that of the trial court or that of the Illinois Supreme Court, produces the more just result? Just to whom?

2. The Illinois Supreme Court's decision in the "Baby Richard" case brought on a great deal of negative media coverage, including Chicago Tribune columns by Bob Greene entitled "Damn Them All," "The Sloppiness of Justice Heiple," and "Supreme Injustice for a Little Boy." Following Greene's columns the governor publicly backed legislation designed to change the court's decision. Do you think this is the type of decision that should be left to the courts, or could it be better handled through legislation? Why?

3. If you were drafting a statute to cover the type of situation that occurred in this case, what balance would you strike between the parents' rights to their natural-born children and the rights of adoptive parents? In drafting your statute, consider the proper balance between the natural parents' rights to keep their children and the "best interest of the child."

4. In January 1997 it was reported that Otakar Kirchner had moved out of his home, leaving custody of Baby Richard to his birth mother. Does this have any impact on your view as to whether the court reached a just decision in this case?

(1) Adoption records

Once a child is adopted, the original birth certificate is placed in the court records, and a new birth certificate is issued with the names of the adoptive parents. Those records are then sealed to protect the privacy of all the parties. In recent years many adults who were adopted as children have sought access to such records to learn the identity of their natural parents. In response to this "desire to know," some states have developed a registry system whereby adopted children and birth parents can let a state agency know they desire to be reunited. If both sides contact the agency, then the agency will facilitate such a reunion. In addition, records may be opened if the adoptee can show a compelling medical need. However, in the absence of such a procedure or a medical need the courts have been reluctant to open adoption records, as evidenced in the following case.

In re Roger B
84 Ill. 2d 323, 418 N.E.2d 751, 49 Ill. Dec. 731 (1981)

Mr. Justice MORAN delivered the opinion of the court.

The circuit court of Cook County dismissed the amended petition of plaintiff, Roger B., which sought a judgment declaring section 18 of the Adoption Act (Section) (Ill. Rev. Stat. 1977, ch.40, par. 1522) unconstitutional. That statute places adoption records and original birth records under seal. The appellate court, in a two-to-one decision, affirmed. . . .

The facts are uncontradicted. Plaintiff, who was born in 1949, filed an amended petition in the circuit court, asserting that his status as an adult adoptee who had feelings of inadequacy and uncertainty as to his background permitted access to his adoption records. Alternatively, plaintiff alleged that the Section is unconstitutional. At the hearing, plaintiff testified that he had been searching for his biological family for three years. Plaintiff regarded himself as "emotionally, physically, and financially comfortable." He testified that his search was not based on any psychiatric or medical need. Rather, the search emanated from plaintiff's desire to know "information which pertains to [him] as a person." . . .

Plaintiff contends that the right to know his own identity is a fundamental right. He argues that the Section infringes upon his right without serving a compelling State interest, thereby violating the equal protection clause of the Federal Constitution. Plaintiff maintains that the right to determine one's natural identity finds its basis under one's right to privacy. He relies on several Supreme Court cases involving familial relationships, rights of family privacy, and freedom to marry and reproduce: *Roe v. Wade* (1973), (woman's right to terminate her pregnancy); *Eisenstadt v. Baird* (1972), (matters involving contraception); *Loving v. Virginia* (1967), (freedom to marry); *Prince v. Massachusetts* (1944), (matters involving child rearing); Skinner v. *Oklahoma ex rel. Williamson* (1942), (the right to procreate).

These cases concern the most intimate areas of personal and marital privacy. The Supreme Court has been very hesitant in expanding the list of fundamental rights. . . . Several courts, however, have found that the right asserted here is not a fundamental right. . . .

Inasmuch as a fundamental right is not involved, the statute will be upheld if it is not arbitrary and bears a rational relationship to a legitimate State objective. . . .

Section 18 and its related statutes represent a considered legislative judgment that confidentiality promotes the integrity of the adoption process. Confidentiality is needed to protect the right to privacy of the natural parent. The natural parents, having determined it is in the best interest of themselves and the child, have placed the child for adoption. This process is done not merely with the expectation of anonymity, but also with the statutory assurance that his or her identity as the child's parent will be shielded from public disclosure. Quite conceivably, the natural parents have established a new family unit with the expectation of confidentiality concerning the adoption that occurred several years earlier. . . . These interests of the natural parents do not cease when the adoptee reaches adulthood. . . .

The statute, by providing for release of adoption records only upon issuance of a court order, does no more than allow the court to balance the interests of all the parties and make a determination based on the facts and circumstances of each individual case.

We find the statute to be rationally related to the legitimate legislative purpose of protecting the adoption process. Consequently, the Section does not unconstitutionally infringe upon an adoptee's right to discover his own identity. . . .

In this case, plaintiff's attempt to have his adoption records released did not result from any physical or psychological medical need. It arose from plaintiff's desire to discover his natural identity. Further, the record does not show that the natural parents have ever waived their privacy right by consenting to divulgence of the information. We find that the trial court did not abuse its discretion in concluding that plaintiff's desire to obtain release of the records should not prevail over the potential infringement of the rights of other parties. Accordingly, the judgment of the appellate court is affirmed.

CASE DISCUSSION QUESTIONS

1. Do you agree with the Illinois Supreme Court's ruling? Why? What do you think the proper balance should be between the adopted child's interest in knowing about his or her parents and the natural parents' interest in protecting their privacy?

2. What, if any, types of medical conditions justify giving a child or a child's guardians access to sealed adoption records?

In recent years a few states have changed this traditional approach by enacting laws allowing adult adoptees access to their birth records. Such laws have created an emotional debate. On the one side are the adoptees who feel they have an absolute right to find out "who they are and where they came from." On the other side are the birth parents who wish to remain anonymous and who do not want to be contacted by the children they gave up for adoption. While birth parents have attempted to have such laws invalidated on the grounds that they violate their right to privacy, to date no court has done so.

(2) Tort of wrongful adoption

Although adoption is a lifelong commitment from which the parents cannot escape, recently several states have developed a new tort of wrongful adoption. For example, in the case of *Mohr v. Commonwealth*[37] the court held that an adoption agency must notify the prospective parents of information that would enable them to make a knowledgeable decision about whether to adopt the child. In that case the social worker had not told the parents that the birth mother was hospitalized for schizophrenia and that the child had been diagnosed with mental retardation. While this would not form the basis for revoking the adoption, it would provide grounds for the recovery of resulting medical and educational expenses. States vary as to whether they require an act of intentional fraud on the part of the agency or whether negligent failure to disclose will suffice.

c. Assisted Reproduction

While sperm donation and artificial insemination have been available for many years, thanks to advances in medicine, those yearning for a child have found new ways to conceive: through egg donation and surrogacy arrangements. All of these methods have spawned a host of legal issues.

---

[37]653 N.E.2d 1104 (Mass. 1995).

(1) Sperm Donation

Traditionally, an anonymous sperm donor acquired neither parental rights nor obligations. Absent a written agreement to the contrary, in some states this remains true even when the donor is known to the woman receiving the sperm. For example, recently a Kansas man was asked by an unmarried female friend to donate his sperm so that she could have a child. He agreed with the understanding that he would act as the father. However, they never put their agreement in writing, and when the woman petitioned the court the day after her twins were born, he found that he was without any parental rights.[38] This is because the state in which he lived, Kansas, had enacted a statute providing that absent a written agreement, sperm donors have no parental rights. However, most states do not have any provisions covering situations such as this, where the donor is known to the mother, and so the law varies greatly from state to state. In fact, in some states a sperm donor doing a "favor" for a friend may later find himself obligated to provide child support.

(2) Egg Donation

As indicated above, the courts are divided as to how to resolve a dispute between a genetic mother (the egg donor) and the gestational mother (the woman who carries the child to term). In an interesting variation of this problem, recently the Tennessee Supreme Court was faced with a dispute between a genetic father and a gestational mother. The unmarried couple had conceived and given birth to triplets following an egg implantation from an anonymous donor. When the couple's relationship deteriorated, the mother sought custody and child support. The father argued that she did not qualify as a parent as she had no genetic connection to the children and asked for sole custody. The court found that the woman was the children's legal mother, but it took pains to point out that the case did not involve a controversy between a genetic donor and a gestational carrier or between a gestational surrogate and a genetically unrelated but intended mother.[39]

(3) Surrogacy Contracts

Surrogacy contract
A document in which a woman agrees to conceive and give birth to a child, deliver the child to its natural father, and terminate her parental rights so the father's wife can become its adoptive mother.

A **surrogacy contract** is one in which a woman agrees to conceive a child, usually through artificial insemination; deliver the child to its natural father after birth; and then terminate her parental rights so the father's wife can become its adoptive mother. Such surrogacy agreements are typically used by couples who wish to have a baby that is genetically related to the husband in situations where the mother is infertile or medically unable to give birth. Opponents argue that such surrogacy agreements amount to "baby selling" and that they exploit women.

The "Baby M" case in New Jersey drew national attention to this issue in the mid-1980s. William Stern entered into a surrogacy contract in which Mary Beth Whitehead agreed to be artificially inseminated with Mr. Stern's sperm, to carry any resulting pregnancy to term, to turn the baby over to Mr. Stern after birth, and to terminate her maternal rights so that Mrs. Stern could then adopt

---

[38]In re K.M.H., 169 P.3d 1025 (Kan. 2007).

[39]In re C.K.G., 173 S.W.3d 714 (Tenn. 2005).

the child. In return, Mr. Stern agreed to pay Ms. Whitehead $10,000 after the child was delivered to him. After an uneventful pregnancy, a baby girl was born on March 27, 1986, and turned over to the Sterns three days later. However, after having left the baby at the Sterns, Ms. Whitehead returned later in the evening and begged to be able to keep her for an additional week. The Sterns gave permission for her to keep the baby for one more week because Ms. Whitehead appeared so depressed that they feared she might commit suicide. But at the end of this extra week Ms. Whitehead not only refused to turn the baby back over to the Sterns but also fled with the baby to Florida. When the Sterns discovered Ms. Whitehead's location, they started legal actions to carry out the terms of the surrogacy contract.

In the Matter of Baby M 109 N.J. 396, 537 A.2d 1227 (1988)

WILENTZ, C.J.

We invalidate the surrogacy contract because it conflicts with the law and public policy of this State. While we recognize the depth of the yearning of infertile couples to have their own children, we find the payment of money to a "surrogate" mother illegal, perhaps criminal, and potentially degrading to women. Although in this case we grant custody to the natural father, the evidence having clearly proved such custody to be in the best interests of the infant, we void both the termination of the surrogate mother's parental rights and the adoption of the child by the wife/stepparent. We thus restore the "surrogate" as the mother of the child. We remand the issue of the natural mother's visitation rights to the trial court, since that issue was not reached below and the record before us is not sufficient to permit us to decide it de novo. . . .

. . . The contract's basic premise, that the natural parents can decide in advance of birth which one is to have custody of the child, bears no relationship to the settled law that the child's best interests shall determine custody. . . .

The surrogacy contract guarantees permanent separation of the child from one of its natural parents. Our policy, however, has long been that to the extent possible, children should remain with and be brought up by both of their natural parents. . . . A child, instead of starting off its life with as much peace and security as possible, finds itself immediately in a tug-of-war between contending mother and father.[9] . . .

Under the contract, the natural mother is irrevocably committed before she knows the strength of her bond with her child. She never makes a totally voluntary, informed decision, for quite clearly any decision prior to the baby's birth is, in the most important sense, uninformed, and any decision after that, compelled by a preexisting contractual commitment, the threat of a lawsuit, and the inducement of a $10,000 payment, is less than totally voluntary. Her interests are of little concern to those who controlled this transaction. . . .

Worst of all, however, is the contract's total disregard of the best interests of the child. There is not the slightest suggestion that any inquiry will be made at any time to determine the fitness of the Sterns as custodial parents, of Mrs. Stern as an adoptive parent, their superiority to Mrs. Whitehead, or the effect on the child of not living with her natural mother.

---

[9]The impact on the natural parents, Mr. Stern and Mrs. Whitehead, is severe and traumatic. The depths of their conflict about Baby M, about custody, visitation, about the goodness or badness in which each tried to persuade the other to give up the child. The potential adverse consequences of surrogacy are poignantly captured here—Mrs. Whitehead threatening to kill herself and the baby, Mr. Stern begging her not to, each blaming the other. The dashed hopes of the Sterns, the agony of Mrs. Whitehead, their suffering, their hatred—all were caused by the unraveling of this arrangement.

This is the sale of a child, or, at the very least, the sale of a mother's right to her child, the only mitigating factor being that one of the purchasers is the father. Almost every evil that prompted the prohibition on the payment of money in connection with adoptions exists here. . . .

In the scheme contemplated by the surrogacy contract in this case, a middle man, propelled by profit, promotes the sale. Whatever idealism may have motivated any of the participants, the profit motive predominates, permeates, and ultimately governs the transaction. The demand for children is great and the supply small. The availability of contraception, abortion, and the greater willingness of single mothers to bring up their children has led to a shortage of babies offered for adoption. . . .

Intimated, but disputed, is the assertion that surrogacy will be used for the benefit of the rich at the expense of the poor. In response it is noted that the Sterns are not rich and the Whiteheads not poor. Nevertheless, it is clear to that surrogate mothers will be as proportionately numerous among those women in the top twenty percent income bracket as among those in the bottom twenty percent. Put differently, we doubt that infertile couples in the low-income bracket will find upper income surrogates. . . .

The point is made that Mrs. Whitehead agreed to the surrogacy arrangement, supposedly fully understanding the consequences. Putting aside the issue of how compelling her need for money may have been, and how significant her understanding of the consequences, we suggest that her consent is irrelevant. There are, in a civilized society, some things that money cannot buy. In America, we decided long ago that merely because conduct purchased by money was "voluntary" did not mean that it was good or beyond regulation and prohibition. Employers can no longer buy labor at the lowest price they can bargain for, even though that labor is "voluntary," or buy women's labor for less money than paid to men for the same job,

or purchase the agreement of children to perform oppressive labor, or purchase the agreement of workers to subject themselves to unsafe or unhealthful working conditions. There are, in short, values that society deems more important than granting to wealth whatever it can buy, be it labor, love, or life. Whether this principle recommends prohibition of surrogacy, which presumably sometimes results in great satisfaction to all of the parties, is not for us to say. We note here only that, under existing law, the fact that Mrs. Whitehead "agreed" to the arrangement is not dispositive.

The long-term effects of surrogacy contracts are not known, but feared—the impact on the child who learns her life was bought, that she is the offspring of someone who gave birth to her only to obtain money; the impact on the natural mother as the full weight of her isolation is felt along with the full reality of the sale of her body and her child; the impact on the natural father and adoptive mother once they realize the consequences of their conduct. . . .

Beyond that is the potential degradation of some women that may result from this arrangement. In many cases, of course, surrogacy may bring satisfaction, not only to the infertile couple, but to the surrogate mother herself. The fact, however, that many women may not perceive surrogacy negatively but rather see it as an opportunity does not diminish its potential for devastation to other women. . . .

We have found that our present laws do not permit the surrogacy contract used in this case. Nowhere, however, do we find any legal prohibition against surrogacy when the surrogate mother volunteers, without any payment, to act as a surrogate and is given the right to change her mind and to assert her parental rights. Moreover, the Legislature remains free to deal with this most sensitive issue as it sees fit, subject only to constitutional constraints. . . .

The judgment is affirmed in part, reversed in part, and remanded for further proceedings consistent with this opinion.

CASE DISCUSSION QUESTIONS

1. Opponents of surrogacy contracts argue that they should be outlawed because they amount to baby selling. Defenders of surrogacy contracts claim such contracts do not involve the purchase of a baby—they merely provide compensation to the surrogate mother for her time and expenses. With which position do you agree? Did the judges in the "Baby M" case treat this as a case about the "sale of a child"?

2. Opponents of surrogacy contracts also argue that they should be outlawed because they exploit women. Defenders counter that they are not exploitive because the women who agree to be surrogate mothers do so voluntarily and wish to help other women have babies of their own. Whose arguments do you find most persuasive and why? What kind of protections, if any, could be built into surrogacy contracts to prevent exploitation?

3. Why did the court think the surrogate mother's consent to the arrangement was irrelevant?

4. If you lived in New Jersey and wanted the court to uphold a surrogacy arrangement like the one in this case, what avenues would be open to you to change the law? Under what circumstances would the court enforce a surrogacy arrangement? How should the surrogacy contract be drafted to be enforceable?

DISCUSSION QUESTION

21. Do you think the law should treat anonymous and known sperm donors the same?

2. Parental Rights, Responsibilities, and Liabilities

Parents have traditionally been given a great deal of discretion with respect to how they raise their children. Although they are required to provide an education, they can choose public schools, private schools, or in some states "home schooling." Parents can also decide the religious tradition and value structure in which they wish to raise their children. And short of crossing the line into child abuse, they can determine how they wish to discipline their children.

Under the common law, parents are normally not liable for their child's negligent acts unless the injury was caused by the parents' own negligent failure to properly supervise the child. In addition, if a child intentionally harms someone, the parent can be held responsible only if the parent was negligent in supervising the child's activities. Section 316 of the Restatement of the Law of Torts, Second describes a duty to exercise reasonable care to control one's minor children to prevent them from intentionally harming others. However, the comments point out that a parent is only responsible for a child's conduct insofar as the parent had the ability to control it.

In derogation of the common law, some states have statutes making parents strictly liable for the intentional torts of their children. However, when only property is damaged, there is often a liability cap, usually set to a relatively low amount of no more than a few thousand dollars.

3. Child Neglect and Abuse

The state imposes responsibilities on parents to provide food, shelter, medical care, and other basic needs for their children. It also prohibits parents from physically or mentally abusing their children. Unfortunately, there are often differences of opinion as to when one crosses the line between a parent's right to discipline a child and the state's right to protect that child from abuse.

As a society we have been reluctant to criminalize family law issues for several reasons. First, the courts are already struggling to manage their caseloads and are naturally cautious about adding to them by criminalizing family law issues. Second, law enforcement personnel have often been hesitant to arrest those who abuse family members. This is due both to a concern that an arrest will escalate the tension and to an awareness that frequently the victim will later refuse to prosecute, thereby eliminating any possibility that the abuser can be convicted. Third, what constitutes child neglect or abuse is colored by time and culture. For example, corporal punishment has been viewed with varying degrees of approval over time and across cultures. Fourth, as a society we are torn by the conflict between our belief that parents should have the right to raise their children as they see fit and our desire to protect those children. For example, if a parent's refusal to allow his or her child to receive needed medical treatment is based on strongly held religious views, should the state be allowed to interfere with that decision?

Child neglect
The negligent failure to provide a child with the necessaries of life.

Generally, **child neglect** can be defined as the negligent failure to provide a child with necessaries, such as food, clothing, shelter, and education. **Child abuse** involves intentional misconduct. However, in specific cases it is often difficult to determine where neglect stops and abuse begins. For example, the failure to feed a child breakfast occasionally might be seen as neglect. The failure to feed a child breakfast every day might be seen as abuse.

Child abuse
Intentional harm to a child's physical or mental well-being.

Evidence of abuse or neglect triggers state intervention, which can begin a multiyear process of trying to meet the needs of both the child and the parents. Normally, the state first becomes aware of a potential neglect or abuse situation when someone reports suspicions of child neglect or abuse. Every state requires that those in a position of trust or authority with regard to children, such as teachers and doctors, report any suspected abuse. Because the state has the power to protect its citizens, including its children, it has the right to investigate such reports. Usually, the first step is to try to get voluntary compliance. If that is not possible, the investigating agency may request court-ordered physical examinations of the child, visits to the home, and a general psychological evaluation of the family. During this process the court may appoint a **guardian ad litem** to represent the child. If the end result of the investigation is a determination that the child is in danger, the court may remove the child from the home and place the child in foster care. The final and most drastic remedy is termination of parental rights.

Guardian ad litem
Someone appointed by the court to speak for the interests of a child.

Clear and convincing
An evidentiary standard that requires more than a preponderance of the evidence but less than beyond a reasonable doubt.

A state must have **"clear and convincing"** evidence before parental rights can be terminated. A clear and convincing standard is something more than a preponderance of the evidence (used in most civil suits) but less than beyond a reasonable doubt (used in criminal cases).

Child advocates argue that this standard is too difficult to meet, thereby allowing children to remain with abusive or neglectful parents. Those representing parents, however, argue that, short of incarceration or death, there is no harsher penalty that the state can impose than removing children from a parent's care. Therefore, they argue the standard is not efficiently stringent to protect parental rights.

NETNOTE

Concerned over making decisions about abused and neglected children's lives without sufficient information, a Seattle judge conceived the idea of using trained community volunteers to speak for the best interests of these children in court. So successful was this Seattle program that soon judges across the country began utilizing citizen advocates. This program is now known as CASA, Court Appointed Special Advocates. To learn more about CASA and how to train as a volunteer, go to its national Web site at *www.nationalcasa.org*.

Evidence of the lack of parental fitness can result from direct actions of the parent, as well as from a parent's refusal to act to protect a child. For example, when a mother did nothing to protect her child from the abuse of her third husband (the child was found naked in a filthy motel room with multiple bruises and cigarette burns), the court involuntarily terminated her rights.[40]

DISCUSSION QUESTIONS

22. To what extent should child abuse protection laws apply to the actions of pregnant women? Should the fact that a pregnant woman smokes or drinks alcoholic beverages be treated as child abuse?

23. When deciding whether to terminate parental rights, some argue that a "clear and convincing" standard gives abused children too little protection. They would advocate a "preponderance of the evidence" standard. On the other hand, parent advocates argue that termination of parental rights is such a final determination that parents should be judged unfit only if the court can find them so "beyond a reasonable doubt." Which standard do you think best balances the needs of the children and of the parents?

24. Recently a New York judge ordered a couple to abstain from procreating until they could prove they can take care of their children. The mother had four children between 1998 and 2003. As newborns, all four babies tested positive for cocaine and were placed in foster care. The judge ruled the woman could not be a mother again until she could prove that she could care for the children she already had. A representative of the American Civil Liberties Union argued that this ruling was inconsistent with fundamental principles of privacy and autonomy. What do you think about the judge's ruling? Can you think of other approaches to the problems presented by pregnant women suffering from drug addiction and poverty?

---

[40]In the Interest of B.R.S., 402 S.E.2d 281 (Ga. App. 1991).

4. Legal Status of Minors

Minor
A child who is under the age of legal competence.

From the time they are born until they reach the age of majority (eighteen in most states), children are classified as **minors.** Being classified as a minor has both its benefits and its detriments. Although they have legal rights, minors must rely on their parents or other guardians to act on their behalf in enforcing those rights. For example, minors cannot file lawsuits on their own.

Also, minors have more limited rights than do adults in regard to making major life decisions, such as whether to obtain an abortion. A minor who wants an abortion may be required to get the consent of a parent or the authorization of a trial court judge.

As we discussed in Chapter 8, Contract Law, one of the benefits of being a minor is that when he or she enters into a contract, it is considered to be "voidable." The minor may either enforce the terms of the contract or "disaffirm" it within a reasonable time period. In some states this has been modified so that contracts for necessaries may be enforced, at least as to their reasonable value. Also, some states have developed special laws to change this principle as it applies to contracts for things such as artistic performances and sports as long as the contract has court approval.

If a minor commits a crime, the case is ordinarily handled by a special juvenile court system, which is designed to be less punitive and more focused on rehabilitation. However, if the crime is a violent felony, in some states the minor is automatically transferred to the regular court system and is tried as an adult. In other states the judge holds a transfer hearing to determine whether the child should be treated as an adult.

Once minors have reached the age of majority, they are no longer legally subject to parental authority. They become adults and at that point trade in the special protections and liabilities they had as minors for the full set of legal rights and responsibilities given to adults.

Emancipated minor
Someone who is still under the legal age of adulthood but who has nevertheless been released from parental authority and given the legal rights of an adult.

An **emancipated minor** is someone who is still under the legal age of adulthood but who has nevertheless been released from parental authority and given the legal rights of an adult. Such emancipated status is usually given when a minor has entered into a valid marriage or is on active duty in the armed services. It can also be given at the discretion of the courts in situations where the minor is living independently, physically and financially, from his or her parents.

SUMMARY

Marriage, traditionally viewed as the union of a man and woman, is categorized as either a solemnized or a common-law marriage. If the proper grounds exist, either type of marriage can be ended through annulment or divorce. An annulment is usually granted because of factors, such as fraud, that existed before the couple was married. A divorce can be based either on grounds or on no fault. Under no-fault divorce neither party is blamed for the divorce. As part of the divorce process the parties must reach agreement as to property division, alimony, child custody, child support, and child visitation rights. Once the parties enter into a settlement agreement, the court can finalize the divorce. If the parties are unable to agree, the case proceeds to trial.

A rapidly changing area of family law relates to child visitation and custody rights for persons other than the natural parents. In recent years grandparents, stepparents, and gay and lesbian partners have all received more receptive hearings from the courts than they have in the past.

Finally, family law deals with many issues relating to the parent-child relationship, including establishing the relationship through paternity actions, adoption, or surrogacy and defining parental rights and liabilities. In this latter category, child neglect and abuse have received national attention as the legal system continues to struggle with these concerns.

CRITICAL THINKING EXERCISES

1. A prenuptial agreement stated that the wife could not share in her husband's property. During the early years of their marriage the couple kept their businesses and bank accounts separate. Eventually, however, the wife left her job to work full-time for no pay in the pro shop at her husband's golf course. When the golf course ran into financial troubles, she cashed in her retirement plan and took out a loan to keep the business going. Now the couple has divorced, and the wife wants "her share" of the husband's golf course. What do you think the court decided?

2. Before the honeymoon was even over, Ashley Jones realized that her new husband had a major drinking problem. When he refused to seek help for his drinking problem or look for a job, she sought to have the marriage annulled. If you were the judge, would you grant her an annulment? Why?

3. Brian LeClair lives in Tucson, Arizona. In early 2006 he bought a small home for $50,000, $45,000 of which he financed through a mortgage. Later that year, Brian met Monica, and they married within the week. Brian was later to regret his quick decision.

Shortly after they were married, Brian discovered that Monica liked to shop. In fact, she entered the marriage with approximately $5,000 in credit card bills. During their marriage this pattern persisted, with Monica on average charging $500 per month for clothes and jewelry for herself. Brian and Monica each deposited their earnings in a joint checking account, and each paid half of the monthly mortgage payments.

When Brian's father died in 2007, he left Brian 100 shares of stock, valued at $10 per share. Brian, knowing little about investments, asked Monica to handle his stock for him. She did so, and through careful buying and selling Brian now owns 150 shares of stock, valued at $15 a share. Brian's father also left Brian his mother's wedding ring, which as part of his father's estate was valued at $1,000. A jeweler recently appraised it at $1,500. Finally, his father left him $5,000, which he deposited into his and Monica's joint banking account.

In 2008 Monica stated that she was tired of living in Brian's tiny house and wanted to buy some land so that they could build a new, larger home. Brian was against the purchase both because of the cost and because of the rumors the land was about to be rezoned industrial. Monica went ahead anyway and took out a

$20,000 loan from Commercial Savings to purchase the land. Brian did not sign the loan papers. The deed, however, lists them as joint owners. When the rumors proved to be true, the value of the land plummeted to $2,000.

Last week Monica informed Brian that she was tired of being married and that she needed some "space." When Brian got home from work the next day, he found that she was gone. Later that day when he opened the mail, he found a letter from Commercial Savings notifying him that the remaining amount of the loan ($18,000) was due immediately, as Monica had not made any payments in the last year. Also, there was a letter from the credit card company showing Monica's total balance of $12,000. As far as Brian could tell, at least $4,000 was money she had charged before they were married.

Brian has come to your firm because he is thinking of initiating divorce proceedings against Monica. He realizes, however, that Arizona is a community property state and is concerned, first, that he may be liable for what he considers to be Monica's debts and, second, that she may claim some of his property should be categorized as community property, thereby allowing her to take one half. Your boss wants you to research (1) whether Brian is liable for either the Commercial Savings loan or Monica's credit card bills, (2) which assets would qualify as community assets and hence be available to satisfy a community debt if the court were to find him liable, and (3) which remaining assets Monica might be able to claim belong one-half to her as her share of community property.

The contested assets include the stock valued at $2,250, the house (with a mortgage of $40,000 and a resale value of $60,000), the diamond ring valued at $1,500, the land worth $2,000, and $10,000 in their joint checking account. As to the latter, Brian claims that $5,000 is from his inheritance, $4,000 came from money he earned, and the remaining $1,000 came from Monica's earnings. In doing your research, you found the following Arizona statutes:

> *Chapter 25-211*   All property acquired by either husband or wife during the marriage, except that which is acquired by gift, devise or descent, is the community property of the husband and wife.
>
> *Chapter 25-213*   All property . . . of each spouse, owned by such spouse before marriage . . . is the separate property of such spouse.
>
> *Chapter 25-214 C.*   Either spouse separately may acquire, manage, control or dispose of community property, or bind the community. . . .
>
> *Chapter 25-215 A.*   The separate property of a spouse shall not be liable for the separate debts or obligations of the other spouse. . . .
>
> *Chapter 25-215 D.*   [E]ither spouse may contract debts and otherwise act for the benefit of the community. In an action on such a debt or obligation the spouse shall be sued jointly and the debt or obligation shall be satisfied: first, from the community property, and second, from the separate property of the spouse contracting the debt or obligation.

4. Michael and Bonnie were married. The couple separated, and Michael began living with Donna. Bonnie filed for divorce. On February 10 a hearing was held to end the marriage, but because Bonnie's attorney sent Michael a notice with the wrong date, a new hearing date was set. In the meantime Michael and Donna won a $2.2 million jackpot in the Arizona state lottery. At the rescheduled hearing Bonnie claimed an interest in one-half of the winnings. Should the

judge award it to her? *Note:* Arizona is a community property state. Would your answer be different if it was not?

5. As a favor to Joan, Bill agreed to donate his sperm so that she and her female partner could have a child. The baby was born in 1990. Over the years, as the three adults were friends, Bill frequently visited them and when he did so, often brought gifts for their child, Sam, and signed the cards as "Daddy." In 1993 the mother, partner, and child moved out of state to Oregon. Over the next fifteen years Bill talked with Sam about seven times. Sam is now eighteen and his mother has petitioned the court asking that Bill provide child support until Sam reaches the age of twenty-one (the statutory age in Oregon for the termination of child support). How do you think the court should rule?

6. Mark and Chris Cooley were unable to have children because Chris had undergone a hysterectomy. They decided to enter into a surrogacy arrangement whereby a zygote formed of the gametes of the husband and the wife would be implanted in the uterus of Anna Johnson. Therefore, Mark and Chris were the natural parents of the child, and Anna served as the host surrogate. Anna was a co-worker of Chris's and had volunteered to serve as the surrogate. In return for agreeing to act as surrogate, the Cooleys agreed to reimburse Anna for her medical expenses and any loss of wages for the time she had to take off from work, both during and after the pregnancy. In return, Anna agreed to relinquish all parental rights to the child. Shortly before she was to give birth, Anna announced that she would not go through with the agreement unless the Cooleys gave her an additional $20,000. The Cooleys responded with a lawsuit asking that they be declared the parents of the unborn child. Evaluate the arguments both for and against having the court rule in favor of the Cooleys. Base your arguments on *In the Matter of Baby M,* as well as on any additional policy considerations that you think should matter to the court.

7. Jane and John Doe entered into an arrangement with a surrogate mother. The result of that arrangement was the birth of a girl. Since birth she has lived with Jane and John Doe. However, there was never any legal termination of the parental rights by the surrogate mother and her husband. Jane and John Doe are now divorcing. The girl is thirteen years old. Through blood-testing John Doe was determined to be the natural father. The surrogate mother, not Jane Doe, is the natural mother. Both Jane and John Doe are seeking custody or, in the alternative, visitation rights. How do you think the court should rule?

REVIEW QUESTIONS

Pages 395 through 408
1. What are some of the legal benefits of marriage?
2. What is the difference between solemnized and common-law marriages?
3. What requirements does the state usually impose before allowing a couple to marry?
4. How does a civil union differ from marriage?
5. According to the text, how many states have legalized same-sex marriage? Same-sex civil unions?

6. How does California's domestic partnership statute differ from both marriage and civil unions?
7. What is the purpose of a prenuptial agreement? What restrictions are placed on the enforceability of such agreements?

Pages 408 through 418

8. What is the difference between void and voidable marriages?
9. How does an annulment differ from a divorce?
10. What are some of the "costs" of divorce?
11. Describe the basic procedural steps involved in obtaining a divorce.
12. How do courts determine what qualifies as marital property and how it should be divided at divorce?
13. When dividing marital property, how have the courts handled professional degrees?

Pages 418 through 426

14. What is the difference between physical custody and legal custody?
15. Is the right to visitation directly tied to the obligation to provide support payments? Why?
16. How are the courts handling the requests of nonparents for visitation and custody?

Pages 426 through 440

17. What must happen to the natural parents' rights before a child can be freed for adoption?
18. Why are adoption records normally sealed? Are there any exceptions?
19. What is a surrogacy contract? What factors would tend to make such a contract enforceable? Unenforceable?
20. When are parents responsible for the negligent acts of their children? When are they liable for the intentional torts of their children?
21. What is the difference between child neglect and child abuse?
22. Describe the normal procedure that is followed when child neglect or abuse is suspected.
23. In what ways does the law favor the rights of minors? In what ways are minors legally disadvantaged?
24. Who is an emancipated minor?

Chapter 12

Criminal Law and Procedure

The real significance of crime is in its being a breach of faith with the community of mankind.
Joseph Conrad

INTRODUCTION

Almost any time you turn on your television you can see someone's interpretation of how our criminal justice system works, or fails to work. Real-life court cases intertwine in the public's mind with fictitious courtroom battles, and this sends mixed messages. It seems that more people question the criminal justice system than believe in it, and they raise fundamental questions: How far should police go to capture suspected criminals and to construct cases against them? Can defense attorneys and prosecutors protect the rights of criminal defendants and still respond to the needs of crime victims? How can criminal defense attorneys represent defendants who they know are guilty? Is it really better to let ten guilty people go free than to have one innocent person sent to jail? Are some innocent persons being sent to jail in spite of all our system's due process guarantees? Hardly any aspect of our legal system is as dynamic as the study of crime and criminals. Reacting to the fears and concerns of society, this field of law changes rapidly.

Criminal law defines for society what behaviors are illegal and determines how lawbreakers should be punished. As you read this chapter, keep in mind our earlier discussions of the differences between criminal and civil law. Also remember that while some behavior might be considered morally or ethically wrong, it is not a crime unless the law makes it a crime. Therefore, no act is a

Crime
An activity that has been prohibited by the legislature as violating a duty owed to society and hence prosecutable, with the possibility of resulting incarceration or the payment of a fine.

Rules of criminal procedure
Federal and state rules that regulate how criminal proceedings are conducted.

crime unless the legislature has written a statute explicitly prohibiting that behavior. This principle is expressed by the Latin maxim *nullum crimen, nulla poena sine lege* ("there can be no crime and no punishment without the law").

Criminal procedure dictates the methods the criminal justice system must follow to achieve the goal of protecting all society, even alleged criminals, from unjust prosecutions. As you will recall, one method for ensuring this is to require the prosecution to prove each element of the crime beyond a reasonable doubt. The federal and state **rules of criminal procedure** govern everything from investigation and arrest through sentencing and appeals. The federal and state **rules of evidence** regulate what types of evidence can be used in the trial and how it must be presented.

NETNOTE

The FBI maintains a Web site at *www.fbi.gov,* where you can find a great deal of information, including the Ten Most Wanted list.

A. SUBSTANTIVE CRIMINAL LAW

In this section we will explore the origins of criminal law and how it is currently classified. We will also take a closer look at a concept we introduced in Chapter 3, the required elements of mens rea and actus reus. Finally, we will highlight some of the more common defenses to criminal activity, such as the insanity defense.

1. Common-Law Heritage and Model Penal Code

We inherited our system of criminal laws from many sources. The earliest influences came from religious origins. The Hebrews, the Greeks, the Romans, and the Catholics of the Middle Ages all contributed toward our understanding of what was "right" and "wrong," "moral" and "immoral," "legal" and "criminal." Our most significant contributors by far, however, were the English, who, influenced by all these prior lawmakers, developed the system of common law that defined and classified crimes, defenses, and punishments. Over the years our American legislative bodies have clarified and added to these common-law crimes and enacted them into systems of formal criminal statutes on both the state and the federal levels.

By putting our criminal laws in statutory form, we provide all citizens with written notice as to what behaviors may result in prosecution and punishment. This notice helps contribute to **due process** as it is guaranteed to all citizens through the Fifth and Fourteenth Amendments to the U.S. Constitution.

Due process
Fifth and Fourteenth Amendments guarantee that notice and a hearing must be provided before depriving someone of property or liberty.

Amendment V

No person shall be . . . deprived of life, liberty, or property, without due process of law . . .

> ## Amendment XIV
>
> [N]or shall any State deprive any person of life, liberty, or property, without due process of law. . . .

Although the principles of due process require the federal government and each of the states to set out their criminal laws in written form, there is no requirement for uniformity among the states. Thus, while lotteries or casino gambling may be legal in some states, they may be illegal in others.

In 1956 the American Law Institute assembled a group of law professors and practicing lawyers to attempt to rectify this problem and simplify American criminal law by creating a **Model Penal Code and Commentaries**, which would be adopted in all fifty-one jurisdictions. However, this hoped-for uniformity was never achieved. While many of the provisions of the Model Penal Code have been adopted and incorporated into the laws of various states, the Code itself has not led to a uniform set of criminal laws in all states. Significant variations continue to exist among the state criminal codes.

Model Penal Code and Commentaries
The American Law Institute's proposal for a uniform set of criminal laws; not the law unless adopted by a state's legislature.

DISCUSSION QUESTIONS

1. Think back to the last movie or television program you watched about the criminal justice system. Was the system portrayed in a realistic light? How would you describe the portrayal of the attorneys' behavior, both prosecutors and defense attorneys? If the system did not work in that instance, who was portrayed as being at fault? Do you agree?

2. What would you say to a friend who comments on your desire to work for a defense firm by stating, "But why would you want to do that? Defense attorneys are just hired guns."

3. A Victims' Rights Amendment to the U.S. Constitution was introduced in Congress that would give victims the right to be present at court and parole proceedings, to be heard at sentencing, and to be notified about the release or escape of a defendant or prisoner. Would you support such an amendment? Some 450 law professors submitted a letter saying the amendment would hamper prosecutions by placing new burdens on law enforcement agencies. What do you think would be the basis for reaching such a conclusion?

2. Classification of Crimes

Crimes are classified in a number of ways. They are commonly classified on the basis of the severity of the punishment, the type of harm done to the victim, and whether they involve federal, state, or local law.

a. Severity of Punishment

One way that crimes are classified is according to the severity of the punishment the defendant faces upon conviction. Offenses that are considered to be serious crimes, such as murder, rape, armed robbery, and aggravated assault, are classified as **felonies** and call for the severest sanctions. Less serious

Felony
A serious crime, usually carrying a prison sentence of one or more years.

Misdemeanor
A minor crime not amounting to a felony, usually punishable by a fine or a jail sentence of less than a year.

offenses, such as disorderly conduct, shoplifting, and trespassing, are categorized as **misdemeanors**. Sometimes the same basic activity, such as drug possession, can be either a felony or a misdemeanor, depending on the drug and the quantity involved. For example, while possession of a single marijuana cigarette might be only a misdemeanor, possession of a large quantity of heroin would certainly qualify as a felony. Legislators determine whether a given act is to be considered a felony or a misdemeanor at the time they enact the statute making it a crime.

Felonies generally involve a punishment that can include a year or more in a state prison. Some felonies are also classified as **capital crimes**, those for which a death sentence, or capital punishment, can be imposed. The crimes for which the death penalty is typically authorized include multiple murders, murder of a police officer, murder of a child, and murder perpetrated during a rape or kidnapping. The penalty for a misdemeanor is usually less than one year in a county jail or some alternate form of punishment, such as a fine, probation, or restitution. While these types of crimes are not considered serious, they have a serious impact on the judicial system in terms of the time and other resources it takes to process these crimes.

Capital crime
A crime for which the death sentence can be imposed.

Legislatures often subdivide felonies and misdemeanors into different classes with different ranges of imprisonment. For example, most states have divided murder into murder in the first degree, often carrying a maximum life sentence, and murder in the second degree, carrying a lesser sentence. The Model Penal Code also divides felonies into first-, second-, and third-degree felonies, with punishment linked to the degree. The MPC classifies all forms of murder as a felony of the first degree. Misdemeanors are sometimes also subdivided into classes that reflect greater or lesser degrees of punishment.

Although the state criminal code usually can be divided neatly into felonies and misdemeanors, there are some other types of quasi–criminal law situations of which you need to be aware. For example, traffic laws are usually codified in a different part of the state's statutes, and violations of these laws do not carry the same stigma as do violations of the criminal law. Nevertheless, the judicial proceedings used to enforce these traffic laws are criminal in nature. The state prosecutes offenders who, in turn, must be found guilty beyond a reasonable doubt. Some juvenile proceedings are also criminal in nature. Local ordinances covering matters like garbage disposal and barking dogs are also enforced through quasi-criminal proceedings. Violations of these types of administrative regulations and ordinances that involve only fines are often simply referred to as violations rather than as crimes.

b. Type of Harm

The criminal codes of most states further classify crimes according to the type of harm caused to society. The more severe the harm, the more serious the crime. Offenses involving physical harm to a person are considered more serious than offenses involving damage to someone's property. Figure 12-1 illustrates how some of the more familiar crimes fit within the major harm-based classifications. They include harm to the person, harm to property and home, harm to society's health and safety, and crimes against the government itself.

Homicide
The killing of one human being by another.

Offenses against the person include various types of homicides, kidnapping, and acts involving the infliction of bodily harm. A **homicide** is the killing

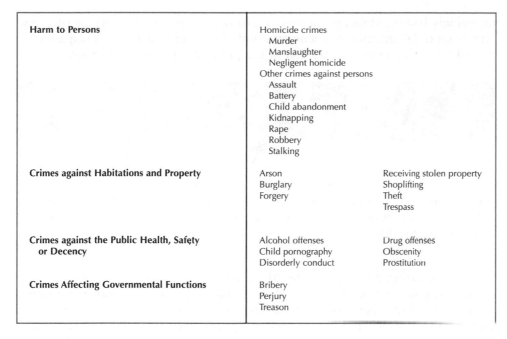

Harm to Persons	Homicide crimes	
	Murder	
	Manslaughter	
	Negligent homicide	
	Other crimes against persons	
	Assault	
	Battery	
	Child abandonment	
	Kidnapping	
	Rape	
	Robbery	
	Stalking	
Crimes against Habitations and Property	Arson	Receiving stolen property
	Burglary	Shoplifting
	Forgery	Theft
		Trespass
Crimes against the Public Health, Safety or Decency	Alcohol offenses	Drug offenses
	Child pornography	Obscenity
	Disorderly conduct	Prostitution
Crimes Affecting Governmental Functions	Bribery	
	Perjury	
	Treason	

Figure 12-1   Classifications of Crime Based on Harm

of one human being by another. As we will discuss further later in this chapter, the circumstances under which the killing takes place and what the defendant was thinking at the time of the killing determine whether it was a first-degree murder, manslaughter, negligent homicide, or not a crime at all. Criminal assault and battery are similar to the torts of the same names. As you will recall, a **battery** is a wrongful physical contact with a person that entails some injury or offensive touching. An **assault** is conduct that places another person in reasonable apprehension of receiving a battery. **Kidnapping** is similar to the tort of false imprisonment in that it involves unlawful confinement. However, in most states asportation, or movement of the victim, must also occur. How much movement is required is often an issue in cases involving charges of criminal kidnapping. **Robbery** is a theft of personal property in circumstances that involve either the infliction of serious bodily injury or the threat of such injury. **Stalking** is a relatively new crime. It is committed when a person intentionally or knowingly engages in a course of conduct that causes a reasonable person to fear the imminent physical injury or death of himself or herself or of a member of that person's family.

Crimes against habitations and property involve harm to or the taking of another's property without consent. **Arson** is the malicious burning of the house or property of another. Despite frequent misuse of the term, **burglary** is not synonymous with theft. Burglary involves breaking into and entering a building with the intent of committing a felony. That felony could be theft, but it also could be some other felony, such as rape. **Theft**, also known as **larceny**, is the act of "stealing"—that is, taking property without the owner's consent. To be found guilty of **receiving stolen property**, the state must prove that the property was stolen, that the defendant knew the property was stolen, and that the defendant knowingly had the stolen property in his or her possession. **Forgery** involves the alteration or falsification of documents with the intent to defraud. **Trespass** is an unauthorized intrusion or invasion of the premises or land of another.

NETNOTE

The U.S. Department of Justice maintains statistics about crimes and victims at *www.ojp.usdoj.gov/bjs,* as does the University of Michigan through its National Archive of Criminal Justice Data (NACJD) project at *www.icpsr.umich.edu/ NACJD/archive.html.*

Crimes affecting the public health, safety, and decency cover a wide variety of crimes, ranging from alcohol and drug abuse to obscenity and prostitution. This is one of the most controversial areas of the criminal law. As "victimless crimes," many of the laws in this category are criticized for interfering with basic civil liberties. Offenses covering alcohol and drugs include the possession, use, and sale of these substances. Some drugs are totally outlawed, while others can be sold or possessed only when prescribed by a licensed physician. Alcohol regulation can range from the establishment of a minimum drinking age to complete prohibition. **Prostitution** involves participation, or offering to participate, in sexual activity for a fee, and **obscenity** regulations restrict the availability of sexually explicit books, magazines, movies, videos, and live performances.

Crimes affecting governmental functions include bribery, perjury, and treason. Historically, **bribery** involved offering something of value to a public official that, if accepted, would cause that public official to act in such a way as to violate the public trust. Today there is also commercial bribery. **Perjury** involves knowingly making a false statement while under oath. Finally, **treason** consists of either attempting to overthrow the government or betraying the government to a foreign power.

c. Federal or State Law

Criminal law can also be classified according to its source. Most criminal behavior is defined by state statutes; the federal criminal law tends to focus on interstate activities. Nevertheless, there are numerous situations in which a single act could be prosecuted as either a federal or a state crime, or both. One notorious example is that of Terry Nichols, who was tried twice, first in federal court and then in state court, for his role in the 2000 bombing of a federal building in Oklahoma City. In federal court he was tried and convicted of conspiring to build a weapon of mass destruction and of involuntary manslaughter, resulting in a sentence of life without parole. Dissatisfied with this result, the state of Oklahoma then put him on trial for first-degree murder and asked for a death sentence. While Nichols was convicted in state court, the jury was unable to decide on a sentence. The judge ordered Nichols to serve 161 consecutive life terms without the possibility of parole.

Another way in which state criminal activity can also be seen as a federal crime is through a federal statute known as **RICO**. In the early 1970s the federal government enacted the Racketeer Influenced and Corrupt Organizations Act, also known as RICO, to help stop the spread of organized crime in the United States.

RICO
The federal Racketeer Influenced and Corrupt Organizations Act.

For a RICO conviction, the United States must prove that the defendant obtained or received money from a pattern of racketeering and invested it in enterprises (business activities) that had an effect on interstate commerce. A defendant convicted under RICO can be forced to pay stiff penalties, which could include up to three times the damages, called treble damages, and forfeiture. While a **fine,** or money payment, is intended to make the defendant pay financially for the crime committed, a **forfeiture** allows the government to take additional money and property from the defendant. The government may take any property connected to the commission of the crime. This could include real property, such as land on which illegal drugs were grown; personal property, such as a boat on which there was illegal gambling; and any money or items found to have been connected to the criminal activity, such as a defendant's bank accounts and jewelry.

Forfeiture
The loss of money or property as a result of committing a criminal act.

3. Elements of the Crime

In order for a crime to take place, someone with a "guilty intent" (mens rea) must commit a "guilty act" (actus reus) that causes specified harmful results.

a. Actus Reus

The Model Penal Code and every criminal statute in every jurisdiction require the defendant to do some act to be found guilty of a crime. This act, referred to as the **actus reus** of the crime, must be voluntary. The act in itself need not do any harm. For example, just possessing some substances, such as an illegal drug, may be a sufficient action to satisfy the actus reus.

Actus reus
Bad act.

Consider the following crimes from the Illinois Criminal Code.

720 Ill. Comp. Stat. 5/18-1 Robbery

(a) A person commits robbery when he or she takes property, except a motor vehicle covered by Section 18-3 or 18-4, from the person or presence of another by the use of force or by threatening the imminent use of force.

720 Ill. Comp. Stat. 5/18-2 Armed Robbery

(a) A person commits armed robbery when he or she violates Section 18-1 while he or she carries on or about his or her person or is otherwise armed with a dangerous weapon.

Therefore, to be found guilty of robbery in the state of Illinois, a defendant must

1. take property, except a motor vehicle,
2. from the person or presence of another

3. by the use of force *or*

4. by threatening the imminent use of force.

A prosecutor must prove all portions of the statute (1, 2, and either 3 or 4) before the defendant may be found guilty. These individual portions, referred to as the elements, include the actus reus of this crime—the taking of property. A defendant would be found not guilty if the prosecutor failed to prove any part or element of the statute or if the finder of fact had a reasonable doubt about any part of the prosecutor's proof. The more serious offense of armed robbery shares all of the elements of the robbery statute plus the added action or element of

5. carrying on or about his or her person or otherwise being armed with a dangerous weapon.

Lesser included offense
A crime whose elements are contained within a more serious crime. Theft is a lesser included offense of robbery.

Because all the robbery elements are contained in the armed robbery statute, robbery is called a **lesser included offense** of armed robbery. Typically, a defendant may be charged with both crimes, but if found guilty of the more serious offense, the lesser included offense usually will be dismissed.

Inchoate crimes
Attempted crimes.

Sometimes the criminal is prevented from completing the crime. Therefore, because there is no required actus reus, the defendant cannot be charged with having committed that crime. Such attempts, however, can form the basis for a separate conviction. Such attempts are classified as **inchoate crimes**. To be found guilty of an attempt, the state must prove the defendant intended to commit the crime. To satisfy the actus reus requirement, the state also must prove that the defendant did some overt act in furtherance of that intent that went beyond mere preparation. For example, the Model Penal Code lists several acts that indicate an intent to commit the crime, such as "possession of materials to be employed in the commission of the crime, which are specially designed for such unlawful use or which can serve no lawful purpose of the actor under the circumstances."[1]

Solicitation
Encouraging someone to commit a crime.

Conspiracy
An agreement to commit an unlawful act.

Two other inchoate crimes are solicitation and conspiracy. **Solicitation** involves requesting or encouraging someone to commit a crime. For example, if a wife encourages her boyfriend to kill her husband, she could be found guilty of the crime of solicitation. **Conspiracy** involves an agreement between two or more persons to commit an unlawful act. The state must show that they intended to enter into an agreement and that they had the specific intent to commit some crime. Unlike an attempt, where mere preparation is not enough of an overt act to satisfy the actus reus requirement, in many states preparation is sufficient to prove conspiracy. In others the defendants must take substantial overt steps to be found guilty.

Mens rea
Bad intent.

b. Mens Rea

The **mens rea**, the nature of a person's intent, is also a critical factor in the definition of most crimes. The difference between innocently bumping into someone on a crowded street and the commission of the crime of battery depends for the most part on the state of mind of the person who initiated the

---

[1]Model Penal Code § 5.01(2)(c).

contact. In order for the act to be considered a crime, there has to be evidence of a "guilty mind."

Under the common law, intent was divided between general and specific intent. If the defendant intended to act only, without regard to causing the results of the act, then the defendant had **general intent**. If the defendant did the act *and* intended to cause the harm that resulted from the act, then the defendant possessed **specific intent**. For example, as mentioned earlier, most states divide murder into first- and second-degree murder. To be found guilty of first-degree murder, most state statutes require that the defendant's actions be "willful, deliberate, and premeditated." As such, first-degree murder is a specific intent crime. That is, the defendant must not only intend to do the act, such as shooting a gun, but also intend that the victim die. States differ as to whether willfulness (also referred to as malice aforethought), deliberation, and premeditation are synonymous, or whether they refer to three separate elements. While some courts have held that one or more of the terms are synonymous, others separately define *willfulness* as the specific intent to kill, *premeditation* as having enough time to plan, and *deliberation* as carrying out that plan with a cool head.

In the following case the court grappled with a new issue: whether someone diagnosed as infected with the human immunodeficiency virus (HIV) had the specific intent to kill when he raped his robbery victims. Over the space of four days, Dwight Smallwood and an accomplice separately robbed and raped three women at gunpoint. At the time Smallwood raped the women, he knew that he was HIV-positive and that he must practice "safe sex" in order to avoid transmitting the virus. Smallwood pled guilty to attempted first-degree rape and robbery with a deadly weapon. The Maryland trial court also convicted Smallwood on three counts of attempted second-degree murder. Maryland's intermediate appellate court found that there was sufficient evidence for the trial court to conclude that Smallwood had intended to kill his victims and upheld the convictions. The following case is how the issue was resolved by Maryland's highest court.

General intent
An intention to act without regard to the results of the act.

Specific intent
An intention to act and to cause a specific result.

Smallwood v. State
343 Md. 97, 680 A.2d 512 (1996)

MURPHY, J.

. . . Smallwood asserts that the trial court lacked sufficient evidence to support its conclusion that Smallwood intended to kill his three victims. Smallwood argues that the fact that he engaged in unprotected sexual intercourse, even though he knew that he carried HIV, is insufficient to infer an intent to kill. The most that can reasonably be inferred, Smallwood contends, is that he is guilty of recklessly endangering his victims by exposing them to the risk that they would become infected themselves. The State disagrees, arguing that the

facts of this case are sufficient to infer an intent to kill. The State likens Smallwood's HIV-positive status to a deadly weapon and argues that engaging in unprotected sex when one is knowingly infected with HIV is equivalent to firing a loaded firearm at that person . . . .

As we have previously stated, "the required intent in the crimes of assault with intent to murder and attempted murder is the specific intent to murder, i.e., the specific intent to kill under circumstances that would not legally justify or excuse the killing or mitigate it to manslaughter."

State v. Earp, 319 Md. 156, 167, 571 A.2d 1227 (1990). Smallwood . . . was properly found guilty of attempted murder and assault with intent to murder only if there was sufficient evidence from which the trier of fact could reasonably have concluded that Smallwood possessed a specific intent to kill at the time he assaulted each of the three women . . . .

An intent to kill may be proved by circumstantial evidence. "Since intent is subjective and, without the cooperation of the accused, cannot be directly and objectively proven, its presence must be shown by established facts which permit a proper inference of its existence." *Earp, supra,* 319 Md. at 167 (quoting *Davis v. State,* 204 Md. 44, 51, 102 A.2d 816 (1954)). Therefore, the trier of fact may infer the existence of the required intent from surrounding circumstances such as "the accused's acts, conduct and words." *State v. Raines,* 326 Md. 582, 591, 606 A.2d 265 (1992). As we have repeatedly stated, "under the proper circumstances, an intent to kill may be inferred from the use of a deadly weapon directed at a vital part of the human body." *Raines, supra,* 326 Md. at 591.

In *Raines, supra,* we upheld the use of such an inference. In that case, Raines and a friend were traveling on a highway when the defendant fired a pistol into the driver's side window of a tractor trailer in an adjacent lane. The shot killed the driver of the tractor trailer, and Raines was convicted of first degree murder. The evidence in the case showed that Raines shot at the driver's window of the truck, knowing that the truck driver was immediately behind the window. We concluded that "Raines's actions in directing the gun at the window, and therefore at the driver's head on the other side of the window, permitted an inference that Raines shot the gun with the intent to kill." *Id.* at 592-93.

The State argues that our analysis in *Raines* rested upon two elements: (1) Raines knew that his weapon was deadly, and (2) Raines knew that he was firing it at someone's head. The State argues that Smallwood similarly knew that HIV infection ultimately leads to death, and that he knew that he would be exposing his victims to the risk of HIV transmission by engaging in unprotected sex with them. Therefore, the State argues, a permissible inference can be drawn that Small-

wood intended to kill each of his three victims. The State's analysis, however, ignores several factors.

First, we must consider the magnitude of the risk to which the victim is knowingly exposed . . . . Before an intent to kill may be inferred based solely upon the defendant's exposure of a victim to a risk of death, it must be shown that the victim's death would have been a natural and probable result of the defendant's conduct . . . . When a deadly weapon has been fired at a vital part of a victim's body, the risk of killing the victim is so high that it becomes reasonable to assume that the defendant intended the victim to die as a natural and probable consequence of the defendant's actions.

Death by AIDS is clearly one natural possible consequence of exposing someone to a risk of HIV infection, even on a single occasion. It is less clear that death by AIDS from that single exposure is a sufficiently probable result to provide the sole support for an inference that the person causing the exposure intended to kill the person who was exposed. [T]he State has presented no evidence from which it can reasonably be concluded that death by AIDS is a probable result of Smallwood's actions to the same extent that death is the probable result of firing a deadly weapon at a vital part of someone's body. Without such evidence, it cannot fairly be concluded that death by AIDS was sufficiently probable to support an inference that Smallwood intended to kill his victims in the absence of other evidence indicative of an intent to kill.

In this case, we find no additional evidence from which to infer an intent to kill. Smallwood's actions are wholly explained by an intent to commit rape and armed robbery, the crimes for which he has already pled guilty . . . . As one commentator noted, . . . "because virus transmission occurs simultaneously with the act of rape, that act alone would not provide evidence of intent to transmit the virus. Some additional evidence, such as an explicit statement, would be necessary to demonstrate the actor's specific intent." Note, Criminal Liability for Transmission of AIDS: Some Evidentiary Problems, 10 Crim. Just. J. 69, 78 (1994). Smallwood's knowledge of his HIV-infected status provides the only evidence in this case supporting a conclusion that he intended anything beyond the rapes and robberies for which he has been convicted.

The cases cited by the State demonstrate the sort of additional evidence needed to support an inference that Smallwood intended to kill his victims. The defendants in these cases have either made explicit statements demonstrating an intent to infect their victims or have taken specific actions demonstrating such an intent and tending to exclude other possible intents . . . .

In *State v. Caine,* 652 So. 2d 611 (La. App.), a conviction for attempted second degree murder was upheld where the defendant had jabbed a used syringe into a victim's arm while shouting "I'll give you AIDS." *Id.* at 616. The defendant in *Weeks v. State,* 834 S.W.2d 559 (Tex. App. 1992), made similar statements, and was convicted of attempted murder after he spat on a prison guard. In that case, the defendant knew that he was HIV-positive, and the appellate court found that "the record reflects that [Weeks] thought he could kill the guard by spitting his HIV-infected saliva at him." *Id.* at 562 . . . .

The evidence in *State v. Haines,* 545 N.E.2d 834 (Ind. App. 1989), contained both statements by the defendant demonstrating intent and actions solely explainable as attempts to spread HIV. There, the defendant's convictions for attempted murder were upheld where the defendant slashed his wrists and sprayed blood from them on a police officer and two paramedics, splashing blood in their faces and eyes. Haines attempted to scratch and bite them and attempted to force blood-soaked objects into their faces. During this altercation, the defendant told the officer that he should be left to die because he had AIDS, that he wanted to "give it to him," and that he would "use his wounds" to spray the officer with blood . . . .

In contrast with these cases, the State in this case would allow the trier of fact to infer an intent to kill based solely upon the fact that Smallwood exposed his victims to the risk that they might contract HIV. Without evidence showing that such a result is sufficiently probable to support this inference, we conclude that Smallwood's convictions for attempted murder . . . must be reversed.

JUDGMENTS FOR ATTEMPTED MURDER IN THE SECOND DEGREE REVERSED.

CASE DISCUSSION QUESTIONS

1. In general, what must the state prove to show attempted murder?

2. Why did the court believe the defendant's convictions for attempted murder should be reversed? Do you agree, or do you think his actions were sufficient to show that he had the specific intent required for an attempted murder conviction?

The Model Penal Code abandoned the use of general and specific intent. Instead, it divides intent into four categories that illustrate the defendant's state of mind: purposeful, knowing, reckless, and negligent.

When the defendant's acts are **purposeful,** they are specifically intended by the defendant. Notice the old standard of specific intent included here. The defendant must desire to cause the harm that resulted from the actions taken. For example, the defendant shoots a gun with the intent to harm one particular person. This is the highest level of intent, and when found, the defendant usually pays the highest price. If the judge or jury finds that the defendant acted **knowingly,** they determine that the defendant knew or had reason to know that harm would be caused by the actions taken even if the specific harm was not the objective of the defendant. For example, a defendant who shoots a gun into a crowded room would know that the action would cause harm (knowingly) even though the defendant was unaware that the action would harm one particular victim (purposeful).

Purposeful
Intending to cause a specific harm.

Knowingly
Not intending to cause a specific harm but being aware that such harm would be caused.

Under the Model Penal Code, for a defendant to act knowingly, he or she need not literally "know" that a certain result will occur. For example, in *United States v. Jewell*[2] the issue was whether the defendant "knowingly" concealed marijuana in a secret compartment between his trunk and rear seat. It was undisputed that the defendant knew of the secret compartment and that something was inside. There was also evidence that the defendant had taken steps to avoid any actual positive knowledge of the contents of the secret compartment. The court stated that the term *knowingly* "includes a mental state in which the defendant is aware that the fact in question is highly probable but consciously avoids enlightenment."[3] Actual knowledge is not necessary. If that were not so, those who transport drugs could always avoid conviction by simply testifying that they did not "know" what they were carrying.

Recklessness
Disregarding a substantial and unjustifiable risk that harm will result.

A defendant is said to have acted **recklessly** when he or she disregards a substantial and unjustifiable risk that harm will result from that action. For example, the defendant shoots a gun into the air while walking through a park at night, and the bullet strikes a person sitting on a bench. The defendant's intent is said to be **negligent** when he or she simply fails to be aware of that substantial and unjustifiable risk. For example, negligence could be found if, when cleaning a gun, a defendant forgets to check the bullet chamber, accidentally pulls the trigger, and shoots someone.

Negligence
The failure to act reasonably under the circumstances.

Compare how the Model Penal Code treats the various forms of homicide. Notice how the same act, the death of another human being, can result in different crimes based on the intent of the defendant.

Definitions of Specific Crimes

Offenses Involving Danger to the Person
Article 210. Criminal Homicide

Section 210.1   Criminal Homicide
(1) A person is guilty of criminal homicide if he purposely, knowingly, recklessly or negligently causes the death of another human being.
(2) Criminal homicide is murder, manslaughter or negligent homicide.

Section 210.2   Murder
(1) Except as provided in Section 210.3(1)(b), criminal homicide constitutes murder when
      (a) it is committed purposely or knowingly; or
      (b) it is committed recklessly under circumstances manifesting extreme indifference to the value of human life. Such recklessness and indifference are presumed if the actor is engaged or is an accomplice in the commission of, or an attempt to commit, or flight after committing or attempting to commit robbery, rape or deviate sexual intercourse by force or threat of force, arson, burglary, kidnapping or felonious escape.

Section 210.3   Manslaughter
(1) Criminal homicide constitutes manslaughter when:
      (a) it is committed recklessly; or
      (b) a homicide which would otherwise be murder is committed under the influence of extreme mental or emotional disturbance for which there is

---

[2] 532 F.2d 697 (9th Cir. 1976).
[3] Id. at 704.

reasonable explanation or excuse. The reasonableness of such explanation or excuse shall be determined from the viewpoint of a person in the actor's situation under the circumstances as he believes them to be.

(2) Manslaughter is a felony of the second degree.

Section 210.4   Negligent Homicide

(1) Criminal homicide constitutes negligent homicide when it is committed negligently.

(2) Negligent homicide is a felony of the third degree.

Section 210.5   Causing or Aiding Suicide

(1) A person may be convicted of criminal homicide for causing another to commit suicide only if he purposely causes such suicide by force, duress or deception.

(2) A person who purposely aids or solicits another to commit suicide is guilty of a felony of the second degree if his conduct causes such suicide or an attempted suicide, and otherwise of a misdemeanor.

As mentioned above, not all states have chosen to follow the Model Penal Code, and that is certainly true of its classification of mental states into the four categories of purposeful, knowing, reckless, and negligent. For example, instead of defining murder as a homicide committed purposely or knowingly, states often define first-degree murder as a homicide done willfully with premeditation, deliberation, and malice; and second-degree murder as an intentional killing that was not premeditated. Frequently, they also deviate from the Model Penal Code's definition of manslaughter and instead categorize it as either voluntary or involuntary. Voluntary manslaughter is usually defined as an intentional killing that is partially excused either by extenuating circumstances, such as provocation, or by the defendant's raising what is known as an imperfect defense. For example, if the defendant committed homicide believing he or she was acting in self-defense when in reality there was no imminent danger, then the mistaken belief as to the existence of a threat may serve to reduce the charge from murder to manslaughter. For involuntary manslaughter, the defendant must not have intended to cause the death but must have done so by acting recklessly. In sum, it is important to check the specific language of the statutes in your state, so that you can see precisely how the degree of culpability varies depending on the defendant's mental state.

As you might suspect, without a direct statement from the defendant that explains what he or she was thinking at the time of the incident, proving mental state is a difficult task. However, as we saw in *Smallwood v. State*, the law assumes that people know the probable consequences of their acts. A person who strikes another may be presumed to have intended the infliction of harm in that such a result naturally flows from hitting another. Also, during a criminal trial the judge or the jury is allowed to draw **inferences**. After looking at the facts of the case presented during the trial, including any statements and actions of the defendant and other prosecution or defense witnesses, the jury is allowed to reach a conclusion about the defendant's intent and to draw an inference about the defendant's state of mind, as well as what most likely occurred. For example, in *Commonwealth v. Gilbert*[4] a man was charged with having murdered his roommate by beating her with his cane. He told the police that she had died

Inference
A conclusion reached based on the facts given.

---

[4] 673 N.E.2d 46 (Mass. 1996).

from an overdose of painkillers. Based on the testimony that the victim had been beaten, that there were no traces of any painkillers found during the autopsy, that the victim and the defendant had been having difficulties, and that the defendant was the only individual in the apartment at the time of the victim's death, the court held that it was reasonable for the jury to conclude he had deliberately premeditated his roommate's death and hence was guilty of first-degree murder.

4. Parties to the Crime

Principal
The person who commits the crime.

When more than one person commits a crime, the perpetrators may be classified as principals, accomplices, or accessories. The person who commits a criminal act is a **principal** in the first degree. A principal in the second degree, also referred to as an **accomplice**, assists the principal in the first degree during the commission of the crime. That person could literally be standing next to the principal in the first degree or be waiting close by, for example, in a getaway car. An **accessory** is someone who assisted in the preparation of the crime but was not present during the crime. An accessory can also be referred to as an accomplice. The MPC defines accomplice in the context of when a person should be held accountable for the conduct of another:

Accomplice
Also known as a **principal in the second degree**; a person who assists the principal with the crime or with the preparation of the crime.

> **Section 2.06 Liability for Conduct of Another; Complicity**
> (2) A person is legally accountable for the conduct of another person when: . . .
>   (c) he is an accomplice of such other person in the commission of the offense.
> (3) A person is an accomplice of another person in the commission of an offense if:
>   (a) with the purpose of promoting or facilitating the commission of the offense, he
>   (i) solicits such other person to commit it; or
>   (ii) aids or agrees or attempts to aid such other person in planning or committing it; or
>   (iii) having a legal duty to prevent the commission of the offense, fails to make proper effort so to do. . . .
> (6) Unless otherwise provided by the Code or by the law defining the offense, a person is not an accomplice in an offense committed by another person if: . . .
>   (c) he terminates his complicity prior to the commission of the offense and
>   (i) wholly deprives it of effectiveness in the commission of the offense; or
>   (ii) gives timely warning to the law enforcement authorities or otherwise makes proper effort to prevent the commission of the offense.

Finally, an **accessory after the fact** is someone who aided the principal after the commission of the crime. When it comes to punishment, principals of any degree and accomplices are all treated the same. Accessories after the fact are not punished as severely as are principals and accomplices.

5. Defenses

Although most people accused of crimes eventually agree to plead guilty to either the crime with which they were originally charged or to some lesser offense, many still go to court, asserting either that they did not do whatever it is they are accused of doing or that their actions were justified under the law.

If believed by the judge or jury, some defenses are **complete defenses** to a crime, and the defendant will be found not guilty. **Partial defenses** may reduce a crime to a lesser included offense.

In this section we will briefly discuss the alibi defense, status defenses (including infancy, insanity, and intoxication), duress and necessity, entrapment, reactive defenses, statutes of limitations, and constitutional defenses.

a. Alibi Defense

An **alibi defense** is one in which the defense attempts to show that the defendant could not have committed the crime because the defendant was in a specified place at a specific time that would make it impossible for him or her to have committed the crime. For example, if four witnesses testify that they were playing poker with the defendant at a home on the east side of town, then the defendant could not have been the person who robbed a liquor store on the west side of town at that time.

b. Ignorance or Mistake

We have all heard that ignorance of the law is no excuse. Generally, that is true. On the other hand, ignorance or mistake as to facts can form the basis for a defense if it can be shown that the defendant's ignorance or mistake negated the requisite mens rea. For example, if you left a classroom with a classmate's textbook, thinking it was your own, you would be mistaken as to the fact of ownership. Therefore, you could not be prosecuted for theft, as you did not have the required mens rea, the intent to steal the property of another.

The Model Penal Code places the following conditions on the use of the defense of ignorance or mistake:

Section 2.04   Ignorance or Mistake
    (1) Ignorance or mistake as to the matter of fact or law is a defense if:
        (a) the ignorance or mistake negatives the purpose, knowledge, belief, recklessness or negligence required to establish a material element of the offense. . . .
    (3) A belief that conduct does not legally constitute an offense is a defense to a prosecution for that offense based upon such conduct when:
        (a) the statute or other enactment defining the offense is not known to the actor and has not been published or otherwise reasonably made available prior to the conduct alleged; or
        (b) he acts in reasonable reliance upon an official statement of the law, afterward determined to be invalid or erroneous. . . .

c. Status: Infancy, Insanity, and Intoxication

The defenses in this group all involve excusing people from the criminal consequences of their actions because their status or condition renders them incapable of formulating the required element of mens rea.

Under the common law, children under the age of seven were conclusively presumed to be incapable of forming criminal intent, while there was a rebuttable presumption that those between the ages of seven and fourteen were not capable of forming such intent. The juvenile court system was created to provide a noncriminal alternative for processing juveniles who are accused of acts that are considered crimes if they are committed by adults. In recent years, however,

Complete defense
A defense that, if proven, relieves the defendant of all criminal responsibility.

Partial defense
A defense that reduces a crime to a lesser included offense.

Alibi defense
A defense requiring proof that the defendant could not have been at the scene of the crime.

especially with the increase in violent, gang-related crimes, there has been a movement to waive juvenile court jurisdiction and apply adult standards to the prosecution of these juvenile offenders.

Insanity defense
A defense requiring proof that the defendant was not mentally responsible.

As noted above, the **insanity defense** is based on the assertion that the defendant was incapable of formulating the required element of mens rea. In addition, many people believe that it is not appropriate to punish someone for actions over which the individual had no control. While most jurisdictions have the insanity defense available to criminal defendants, there is disagreement among the states and the federal circuits about the standard that should be used to determine insanity. The three alternative standards are the M'Naghten test, the irresistible impulse test, and the Model Penal Code Substantial Capacity test. These tests are summarized in Figure 12-2.

M'Naghten test
A test that provides that the defendant is not guilty due to insanity if, at the time of the killing, the defendant suffered from a defect or disease of the mind and could not understand whether the act was right or wrong.

The oldest of the standards, the **M'Naghten test**, originated in the 1840s in an English case where Daniel M'Naghten was tried for killing the secretary to the prime minister of England. M'Naghten mistook the secretary for the prime minister, whom M'Naghten thought to be engaged in a plot to kill him. The court found M'Naghten not guilty due to insanity because, at the time of the killing, he suffered from a defect or disease of the mind and could not understand whether the act was right or wrong. This test, or standard, is commonly known as either the M'Naghten test (sometimes also spelled McNaughten, M'Naughten, and M'Naughton) or the "right from wrong" test.

Under this test a defendant is not considered guilty of the crime if, at the time of committing the actus reus, the defendant was suffering from a defect or disease of the mind and could not understand whether the act was right or wrong. However, the court did not define what constituted a disease or defect of the mind.

Figure 12-2   Insanity Tests

M'Naghten or "Right from Wrong" Test

"[T]o establish insanity sufficient to relieve the defendant of guilt, it must be proved that, at the time of the commission of the act, the defendant was laboring under such a defect of reason, from disease of the mind as not to know the nature and quality of the act he was doing, or if he did know it, that he did not know that what he was doing was wrong." *M'Naghten's Case,* 8 Eng. Rep. 718, 722 (1843).

Irresistible Impulse Test

One is not guilty by reason of insanity if it is determined that the defendant has a mental disease that kept the defendant from controlling his or her conduct.

Substantial Capacity Test (Model Penal Code)

(1) A person is not responsible for criminal conduct if at the time of such conduct, as a result of mental disease or defect, he or she lacks substantial capacity to appreciate the criminality (wrongfulness) of his or her conduct or to conform that conduct to the requirements of law.

(2) The terms *mental disease* and *mental defect* do not include an abnormality manifested only by repeated criminal or otherwise antisocial conduct.

Under the M'Naghten test a defendant will be found sane if he or she knew that a certain action was wrong but could not stop from taking that action. Therefore, some jurisdictions use both the M'Naghten standard and a variation of what is commonly known as the **irresistible impulse test**. With this test the focus is on the defendant's ability to control his or her own actions. If a mental disease robs the individual of control over his or her conduct, the person is not guilty by reason of insanity.

The drafters of the American Law Institute's Model Penal Code developed a third test, which combines elements of the other two. This ALI test is known as the **substantial capacity test**. It requires that the defendant "appreciate," rather than "know," the wrongfulness of his or her actions. Under the two options provided in this test, defendants can lack either the ability to understand that their acts were wrong or the ability to control their behavior. Although the complete Model Penal Code has not been widely adopted, this section has been accepted as the test for insanity in a majority of jurisdictions.

The following case illustrates the role of both jurors and psychiatrists in determining insanity. In this appellate court opinion Justice Schauer explains why the court upholds a jury finding that the defendant was sane even though four psychiatrists testified at the trial that he suffered from "schizophrenia" and was therefore insane at the time he murdered his mother.

Irresistible impulse test
A test that provides that the defendant is not guilty due to insanity if, at the time of the killing, the defendant could not control his or her actions.

Substantial capacity test
Part of the Model Penal Code; a test that provides that the defendant is not guilty due to insanity if, at the time of the killing, the defendant lacked either the ability to understand that the act was wrong or the ability to control the behavior.

People v. Wolff
61 Cal. 2d 795, 394 P.2d 959, 40 Cal. Rptr. 271 (1964)

SCHAUER, Justice.

Defendant appeals from a judgment imposing a sentence of life imprisonment (with recommendation that he be placed in a hospital for the criminally insane) after he pleaded not guilty by reason of insanity to a charge of murder, the jury found that he was legally sane at the time of the commission of the offense, and the court determined the killing to be murder in the first degree . . . .

The defendant, a 15-year-old boy at the time of the crime, was charged with the murder of his mother. The juvenile court found him to be "not a fit subject for consideration" under the Juvenile Court Law, and remanded him to the superior court for further proceedings in the criminal action . . . .

The California M'Naughton Rule

On the issue of insanity the jury were instructed in terms of the California rule; i.e., the so-called M'Naughton rule as that rule has been developed by statute and decision in California . . . .

"The test of sanity is this: First, did the defendant have sufficient mental capacity to know *and understand* what he was doing, and second, did he know *and understand* that it was wrong *and a violation of the rights of another*? To be sane and thus responsible to the law for the act committed, the defendant must be able to know *and understand* the nature and quality of his act *and* to distinguish between right and wrong at the time of the commission of the offense." (Italics added.) . . .

The Sufficiency of the Evidence of Sanity

Turning now to defendant's more specific contentions, it is first urged that "As a matter of law, [defendant] was legally insane at the time of the commission of the offense." In support of this proposition defendant stresses the fact that each of the four psychiatrists who testified at the trial stated (1) that in his medical opinion defendant suffers from a permanent form of one of the group of mental disorders generically known as "schizophrenia" and (2) that defendant was also legally insane at the time he murdered his mother . . . .

However impressive this seeming unanimity of expert opinion may at first appear, . . . our inquiry on this just as on other factual issues is necessarily limited at the appellate level to a determination whether there is substantial evidence in the record to support the jury's verdict of sanity . . . under the law of this state . . . .

Conduct of Defendant as Evidence of Legal Sanity

[T]here was evidence that in the year preceding the commission of the crime defendant "spent a lot of time thinking about sex." He made a list of the names and addresses of seven girls in his community whom he did not know personally but whom he planned to anesthetize and then either rape or photograph nude. One night about three weeks before the murder he took a container of ether and attempted to enter the home of one of these girls through the chimney, but he became wedged in and had to be rescued. In the ensuing weeks defendant apparently deliberated on ways and means of accomplishing his objective and decided that he would have to bring the girls to his house to achieve his sexual purposes, and that it would therefore be necessary to get his mother (and possibly his brother) out of the way first.

The attack on defendant's mother took place on Monday, May 15, 1961. On the preceding Friday or Saturday defendant obtained an axe handle from the family garage and hid it under the mattress of his bed. At about 10 P.M. on Sunday he took the axe handle from its hiding place and approached his mother from behind, raising the weapon to strike her. She sensed his presence and asked him what he was doing; he answered that it was "nothing," and returned to his room and hid the handle under his mattress again. The following morning defendant . . . ate the breakfast that his mother prepared, then went to his room and obtained the axe handle from under the mattress. He returned to the kitchen, approached his mother from behind and struck her on the back of the head. She turned around screaming and he struck her several more blows. They fell to the floor, fighting. She called out her neighbor's name and defendant began choking her. She bit him on the hand and crawled away. He got up to turn off the water running in the sink, and she fled through the dining room. He gave chase, caught her in the front room, and choked her to death with his hands. Defendant then took off his shirt and hung it by the fire, washed the blood off his face and hands, read a few lines from a Bible or prayer book lying upon the dining room table, and walked down to the police station to turn himself in. Defendant told the desk officer, "I have something I wish to report . . . . I just killed my mother with an axe handle." The officer testified that defendant spoke in a quiet voice and that "His conversation was quite coherent in what he was saying and he answered everything I asked him right to a T."

Defendant's counsel repeatedly characterizes as "bizarre" defendant's plan to rape or photograph nude the seven girls on his list. Certainly in common parlance it may be termed "bizarre"; likewise to a mature person of good morals, it would appear highly unreasonable. But many a youth has committed—or planned—acts which were bizarre and unreasonable. This defendant was immature and lacked experience and judgment in sexual matters. But it does not follow therefrom that the jury were precluded as a matter of law from finding defendant legally sane at the time of the murder. From the evidence set forth hereinabove the jury could infer that defendant had a motive for his actions (gratification of his sexual desires), that he planned the attack on his mother for some time (obtaining the axe handle from the garage several days in advance; abortive attempt to strike his mother with it on the evening before the crime), that he knew that what he was doing was wrong (initial concealment of the handle underneath his mattress; excuse offered when his mother saw him with the weapon on the evening before the crime; renewed concealment of the handle under the mattress), that he persisted in the fatal attack (pursuit of his fleeing mother into the front room; actual infliction of death by strangling rather than bludgeoning), that he was conscious of having committed a crime (prompt surrender to the police), and that he was calm and coherent (testimony of desk officer and others) . . . .

It is contended that the foregoing evidence of defendant's conduct and declarations is equally consistent with the type of mental illness (i.e., a form of "schizophrenia") from which, according to the psychiatric witnesses, defendant is said to be suffering. But this consistency establishes only that defendant is suffering from the diagnosed mental illness—a point that the prosecution readily concedes; it does not compel the conclusion that on the very different issue of legal sanity the evidence is insufficient as a matter of law to support the verdict. To hold otherwise would be in effect to substitute a trial by "experts" for a trial by jury, for it would require that the jurors accept the psychiatric testimony as conclusive on an issue—the legal sanity of the defendant—which under our present law is exclusively within the province of the trier of fact to determine . . . .

[T]he evidence adequately supports the jury's verdict . . . .

CASE DISCUSSION QUESTIONS

1. Why did the *Wolff* court refuse to accept the testimony of the experts regarding the defendant's sanity? Do you agree that there should be a difference between the legal and the medical definitions of insanity? Why?

2. Do you think the result would have been different in this case if the court had been following the standard for insanity set out in the Model Penal Code?

As the *Wolff* case illustrates, insanity is not an easy defense to prove, particularly in those states that apply the M'Naghten test. While *Wolff* was decided over forty years ago, the M'Naghten test is still used in over half of the states. It also remains difficult for defendants to use the defense successfully, as demonstrated in the recent and highly publicized Texas case of Andrea Yates. Yates confessed to drowning her five children in a bathtub because she heard voices telling her to kill her children in order to "save them from Satan."[5] Both the prosecution and defense agreed Yates was mentally ill but disagreed as to whether she was aware that what she was doing was wrong. In a three-week-long trial the defense called as witnesses psychiatrists, relatives, and friends to testify that Yates suffered from severe post-partum depression. The prosecution countered by arguing that Yates's prompt action in reporting the drowning to the police established that she did know what she had done was wrong. The jury members apparently agreed with the prosecution that Yates was not legally insane. They convicted Yates of murder, and she was sentenced to life in prison. Following her sentencing, Yates was sent to a prison psychiatric ward to receive treatment for her mental illness.

It is also possible that the jury found her guilty not because they thought she was sane when she drowned her children, but because they were afraid that a "not guilty by reason of insanity" verdict would have resulted in her being released from state custody. What the jury did not know, because by Texas statute[6] they could not be told, is that even a "not guilty by reason of insanity" verdict would most likely have resulted in her immediate involuntary commitment to a mental institution. Although a successful insanity defense results in a "not guilty" verdict, relieving the defendant from any criminal responsibility, the defendant is most often not set free but is instead civilly committed to a

---

[5] *Jury to Decide Yates' Sentence*, USA Today, March 14, 2002, p. 3A.

[6] Tex. Code Crim. Proc., art. 46.03(1)(e) ("The court, the attorney for the state, or the attorney for the defendant may not inform a juror . . . of the consequences to the defendant if a verdict of not guilty by reason of insanity is returned.").

mental health facility for treatment. According to the American Psychiatric Association, "studies show that persons found not guilty by reason of insanity, on average, are held at least as long as—and often longer than—persons found guilty and sent to prison for similar crimes."[7]

Another misconception about the insanity defense relates to its frequency of use. Murder cases in which the insanity defense is raised receive a great deal of publicity, misleadingly giving the impression that the defense is frequently used by defendants trying to escape liability for their actions. In reality, however, studies have shown that defendants allege insanity in less than 1 percent of all criminal cases. Of those cases, less than half involve murder charges. In addition, even when the insanity defense is raised, it proves to be successful in only one out of four cases. To put this in concrete terms, out of every 1,000 criminal cases, the insanity defense is raised in approximately nine and is successful in two.[8] Further, in a majority of the cases in which insanity was raised and used successfully, it was as the result of an agreement between the prosecution and defense. The insanity defense is raised so rarely because of the difficulty of proof and because of the uncertainty as to the consequences if it is successful. While a finding of guilt will result in a fixed sentence, a finding of not guilty by reason of insanity can result in defendants being committed for an indefinite term, potentially for life, until they are deemed to no longer be a threat to themselves or society. In fact, Daniel M'Naghten's trial in 1843, which resulted in the creation of the M'Naghten test, also resulted in his commitment to a mental institution, where he remained until his death.[9]

In recent years some states have adopted a "guilty, but mentally ill" verdict either as a replacement for or as a supplement to "not guilty by reason of insanity." The defendant who receives this verdict is considered guilty and sentenced to a prison term, often without receiving any medical treatment. Because of this, the American Psychiatric Association has stated its opposition to using the "guilty, but mentally ill" plea as either a substitute for, or supplement to, the insanity defense.

Even if a defendant was sane at the time the crime was committed, he or she can be considered legally incompetent at the time of trial. If a defendant cannot understand the legal process or assist in his or her own defense by, for example, talking about the case with the attorney or testifying meaningfully at trial, the defendant may not be tried and therefore may not be found guilty.

Intoxication defense
A defense requiring proof that the defendant was not able to form the requisite mens rea due to intoxication.

The third defense of this type is the **intoxication defense**. In some jurisdictions and under some circumstances, being under the influence of drugs or alcohol is considered a valid defense. Here the argument is that the intoxicating substance interfered with the defendant's ability to form the required mens rea. Although intoxication cannot be used as a defense for charges involving reckless behavior (such as drunk driving or criminal damage to property), it can generally be used as a defense for crimes requiring a specific intent, such as murder.

---

[7]American Psychiatric Association, The Insanity Defense, *www.psych.org/publicinfo/insanity.cfm* (last updated 9/03).

[8]For a full discussion of this issue, see Grant H. Morris, Placed in Purgatory: Conditional Release of Insanity Acquittees, 39 Ariz. L. Rev. 1061 (1997).

[9]Id. at 1062.

Discussion Questions

4. If children engage in criminal behavior, how old do you think they should be before being treated the same as adult criminals? Do you think that answer should change based on the crime committed?

5. Why do you think we have not been able to settle on one definition of legal insanity?

6. Do you think anyone should ever be found not guilty on the basis of insanity? If so, under what circumstances?

d. Duress and Necessity

Because one of the fundamental principles of criminal law is that criminal behavior must be the result of a voluntary act, the law recognizes both duress and necessity as legitimate defenses. If a defendant can establish that the criminal act was committed because he or she was forced to carry it out, that individual is not held accountable for the criminal act.

Section 2.09 of the Model Penal Code defines duress as coercion through "the use of, or a threat to use, unlawful force against his person or the person of another, which a person of reasonable firmness in his situation would have been unable to resist." Therefore, if someone held a gun to your head and forced you to commit a criminal act, you would be entitled to use the defense of **duress**.

Duress
A defense requiring proof that force or a threat of force was used to cause a person to commit a criminal act.

To assert this defense, you must prove that you reasonably believed that you were threatened with your death, the death of another person, or serious injury to yourself or others unless you committed the crime. In a highly publicized case in the mid-seventies Patty Hearst, the daughter of a millionaire newspaper publisher, was placed on trial for bank robbery. Approximately a year before the robbery took place she had been kidnapped by a radical group calling itself the Symbionese Liberation Army. When members of this same group robbed a bank, Ms. Hearst appeared to be a willing participant. At her trial, attorney F. Lee Bailey argued that Ms. Hearst had been "brainwashed" by her Symbionese Liberation Army kidnappers and had been coerced into participating in the robbery. The state countered with evidence that showed that Ms. Hearst had passed up opportunities to flee and call police and argued that this showed she was a willing participant who was acting voluntarily. The jury agreed with the prosecution and convicted her of armed robbery.

The **necessity** defense is similar to the duress defense except the force is exerted by nature rather than by another person. For example, you may be forced to trespass across a neighbor's yard to escape a fire in your home. In addition, this defense may be used in a more general way to exonerate otherwise criminal conduct when a person believes that such conduct is necessary to avoid a greater injury. An example would be where a motorist chooses to crash an automobile into a building in order to avoid hitting a child who runs into the street.

Necessity
A defense requiring proof that the defendant was forced to take an action to avoid a greater harm.

e. Entrapment

The defense of **entrapment** arises when a defendant believes that he or she was tricked or led to commit a crime by a law enforcement agency when the defendant would not have committed the crime without the government's enticement. It is not entrapment if the government agents provide a person with

Entrapment
A defense requiring proof that the defendant would not have committed the crime but for police trickery.

the opportunity to commit a crime that he or she was already contemplating. The key is whether the defendant had a predisposition to commit the crime before the government agents contacted the person.

f. Reactive Defenses

Self-defense
The justified use of force to protect oneself or others.

This category includes defenses such as self-defense and the use of force in law enforcement. As to **self-defense**, individuals are allowed to use force in defending themselves or others and in defending their dwellings and other property. There is significant variation among the states as to the amount of force that can be used and the circumstances under which one is required to retreat when that is a viable option.

Deadly force
A force that would cause serious bodily injury or death.

Generally, however, this right to use force is valid only as long as the following conditions are met. First, the person claiming self-defense must not have been the initiator of the violence. Second, the threat of bodily harm must be immediate. Third, once the threatening party ceases the threatening behavior, the right to self-defense disappears. Fourth, the amount of force used must be no more than is reasonably necessary to repel the attack. **Deadly force**, a force that would cause serious bodily injury or death, can be used only when the danger faced includes fear of serious bodily injury or death.

In the mid-1980s a man named Bernhard Goetz made headlines when he took out a gun and shot four youths who had been attempting to rob him while on a subway in New York City. In the following excerpts from an appellate court decision in this case, the court reviews the facts of the case and the New York law on self-defense.

People v. Goetz
68 N.Y.2d 96, 497 N.E.2d 41, 506 N.Y.S.2d 18 (1986)

Chief Judge WACHTLER

A Grand Jury has indicted defendant on attempted murder, assault, and other charges for having shot and wounded four youths on a New York City subway train after one or two of the youths approached him and asked for $5. The lower courts, concluding that the prosecutor's charge to the Grand Jury on the defense of justification was erroneous, have dismissed the attempted murder, assault and weapons possession charges. We now reverse and reinstate all counts of the indictment.

I . . . .

On Saturday afternoon, December 22, 1984, Troy Canty, Darryl Cabey, James Ramseur, and Barry Allen boarded an IRT express subway train in The Bronx and headed south toward lower Manhattan. The four youths rode together in the rear portion of the seventh car of the train. Two of the four, Ramseur and Cabey, had screwdrivers inside their coats, which they said were to be used to break into the coin boxes of video machines.

Defendant Bernhard Goetz boarded this subway train at 14th Street in Manhattan and sat down on a bench towards the rear section of the same car occupied by the four youths. Goetz was carrying an unlicensed .38 caliber pistol loaded with five rounds of ammunition in a waistband holster. The train left the 14th Street station and headed towards Chambers Street . . . .

According to Goetz's statement, the first contact he had with the four youths came when Canty, sitting or lying on the bench across from him, asked "how are you," to which he replied "fine." Shortly thereafter, Canty, followed by one of the other youths, walked over to the defendant and stood to his left, while the other two youths remained to his right, in the corner of the subway car. Canty then said "give me five dollars." Goetz stated that he knew from the smile on Canty's face that they wanted to "play with me." Although he was certain that none of the youths had a gun, he had a fear, based on prior experiences, of being "maimed." Goetz then established "a pattern of fire," deciding specifically to fire from left to right. His stated intention at that point was to "murder [the four youths], to hurt them, to make them suffer as much as possible." When Canty again requested money, Goetz stood up, drew his weapon, and began firing, aiming for the center of the body of each of the four. Goetz recalled that the first two he shot "tried to run through the crowd [but] they had nowhere to run." Goetz then turned to his right to "go after the other two." One of these two "tried to run through the wall of the train, but . . . he had nowhere to go." The other youth (Cabey) "tried pretending that he wasn't with [the others]" by standing still, holding on to one of the subway hand straps, and not looking at Goetz. Goetz nonetheless fired his fourth shot at him. He then ran back to the first two youths to make sure they had been "taken care of." Seeing that they had both been shot, he spun back to check on the latter two. Goetz noticed that the youth who had been standing still was now sitting on a bench and seemed unhurt. As Goetz told the police, "I said '[you] seem to be all right, here's another,'" and he then fired the shot which severed Cabey's spinal cord. Goetz added that "if I was a little more under self-control . . . I would have put the barrel against his forehead and fired." He also admitted that "if I had had more [bullets], I would have shot them again, and again, and again." . . .

III.

Penal Law article 35 recognizes the defense of justification, which "permits the use of force under certain circumstances." One such set of circumstances pertains to the use of force in defense of a person, encompassing both self-defense and defense of a third person. Penal Law § 35.15(1) sets forth the general principles governing all such uses of force: "[a] person may . . . use physical force upon another person when and to the extent he *reasonably believes* such to be necessary to defend himself or a third person from what he *reasonably believes* to be the use or imminent use of unlawful physical force by such other person" (emphasis added).

Section 35.15(2) sets forth further limitations on these general principles with respect to the use of "deadly physical force": "A person may not use deadly physical force upon another person under circumstances specified in subdivision one unless (a) He *reasonably believes* that such other person is using or about to use deadly physical force . . . or (b) He *reasonably believes* that such other person is committing or attempting to commit a kidnapping, forcible rape, forcible sodomy or robbery" (emphasis added).

Because the evidence before the second Grand Jury included statements by Goetz that he acted to protect himself from being maimed or to avert a robbery, the prosecutor . . . properly instructed the grand jurors to consider whether the use of deadly physical force was justified to prevent either serious physical injury or a robbery, and, in doing so, to separately analyze the defense with respect to each of the charges . . . .

As expressed repeatedly in the Appellate Division's plurality opinion, because section 35.15 uses the term "he reasonably believes," the appropriate test, according to that court, is whether a defendant's beliefs and reactions were "reasonable to him." Under that reading of the statute, a jury which believed a defendant's testimony that he felt that his own actions were warranted and were reasonable would have to acquit him, regardless of what anyone else in defendant's situation might have concluded. Such an interpretation defies the ordinary meaning and significance of the term "reasonably" in a statute, and misconstrues the clear intent of the Legislature, in enacting section 35.15, to retain an objective element as part of any provision authorizing the use of deadly physical force.

Penal statutes in New York have long codified the right recognized at common law to use deadly physical force, under appropriate circumstances, in self-defense. These provisions have never required that an actor's belief as to the intention of another person to inflict serious injury be correct in order for the use of deadly force to be justified, but they have uniformly required that the belief comport with an objective notion of reasonableness . . . .

In 1961 the Legislature established a Commission to undertake a complete revision of the Penal Law and the Criminal Code. The impetus for the decision to update the Penal Law came in part from the drafting of the Model Penal Code by the American Law Institute, as well as from the fact that the existing law was poorly organized and in many aspects antiquated . . . . While using the Model Penal Code provisions on justification as general guidelines, however, the drafters of the new Penal Law did not simply adopt them verbatim.

The provisions of the Model Penal Code with respect to the use of deadly force in self-defense reflect the position of its drafters that any culpability which arises from a mistaken belief in the need to use such force should be no greater than the culpability such a mistake would give rise to if it were made with respect to an element of a crime. Accordingly, under Model Penal Code § 3.04(2)(b), a defendant charged with murder (or attempted murder) need only show that he "[*believed*] that [the use of deadly force] was necessary to protect himself against death, serious bodily injury, kidnapping or [forcible] sexual intercourse" to prevail on a self-defense claim (emphasis added). If the defendant's belief was wrong, and was recklessly, or negligently formed, however, he may be convicted of the type of homicide charge requiring only a reckless or negligent, as the case may be, criminal intent . . . .

New York did not follow the Model Penal Code's equation of a mistake as to the need to use deadly force with a mistake negating an element of a crime, choosing instead to use a single statutory section which would provide either a complete defense or no defense at all to a defendant charged with any crime involving the use of deadly force. The drafters of the new Penal Law adopted in large part the structure and content of Model Penal Code § 3.04, but, crucially, inserted the word "reasonably" before "believes." . . .

We cannot lightly impute to the Legislature an intent to fundamentally alter the principles of justification to allow the perpetrator of a serious crime to go free simply because that person believed his actions were reasonable and necessary to prevent some perceived harm. To completely exonerate such an individual, no matter how aberrational or bizarre his thought patterns, would allow citizens to set their own standards for the permissible use of force. It would also allow a legally competent defendant suffering from delusions to kill or perform acts of violence with impunity, contrary to fundamental principles of justice and criminal law.

We can only conclude that the Legislature retained a reasonableness requirement to avoid giving a license for such actions . . . .

Goetz also argues that the introduction of an objective element will preclude a jury from considering factors such as the prior experiences of a given actor and thus, require it to make a determination of "reasonableness" without regard to the actual circumstances of a particular incident. This argument, however, falsely presupposes that an objective standard means that the background and other relevant characteristics of a particular actor must be ignored. To the contrary, we have frequently noted that a determination of reasonableness must be based on the "circumstances" facing a defendant or his "situation." Such terms encompass more than the physical movements of the potential assailant. As just discussed, these terms include any relevant knowledge the defendant had about that person. They also necessarily bring in the physical attributes of all persons involved, including the defendant. Furthermore, the defendant's circumstances encompass any prior experiences he had which could provide a reasonable basis for a belief that another person's intentions were to injure or rob him or that the use of deadly force was necessary under the circumstances . . . .

Accordingly, the order of the Appellate Division should be reversed, and the dismissed counts of the indictment reinstated.

CASE DISCUSSION QUESTIONS

1. The *Goetz* case gives an excellent example of how critical the choice can be as to which standard, objective or subjective, to apply. First, define each standard, and then discuss which standard you think should be applied to similar situations in the future.

2. How does the New York penal law differ from the Model Penal Code on the use of deadly force in self-defense? Which do you think is the better approach?

3. After nearly eight weeks of trial, Goetz was acquitted of attempted murder but convicted of illegal gun possession. If you could read the jurors' minds, what do you think was a determining factor in their verdict?

This right to defend oneself does not extend to all people at all times. In fact, it does not even extend to all people who find themselves in dangerous positions. Most jurisdictions include a **retreat exception** to the right to self-defense. This doctrine of retreat generally requires a person in danger to get away from the danger, or give up possessions, before resorting to the use of deadly force. If the victim can avoid danger but chooses instead to use deadly force, that victim may be prosecuted for any crime committed. Potential victims need not retreat if they are in their own homes or if retreating would create additional danger for them. Potential victims using nondeadly force need not retreat.

Retreat exception
The rule that in order to claim self-defense there must have been no possibility of retreat.

In most jurisdictions the rights and requirements of self-defense can also be applied to a person's right to protect another person. The defense of others permits you to use reasonable force to protect another person if you believe that the threat of bodily harm is immediate and that the amount of force used is reasonable.

You may also act against another person in defense of property. Rarely can deadly force be applied to protect property. Generally, we value human life over property even when the human life in question is trying to steal property. However, the right to self-defense extends inside the home, and deadly force is still permitted if the home intruder is attempting to do great bodily harm.

One recent change to the self-defense rule in a few jurisdictions is the addition of the **battered woman's or spouse's syndrome**. This defense allows a person who has been the victim of repeated attacks the right to self-defense even when there may not be immediate danger at the exact moment that the right to self-defense is exercised. Experts believe that, especially for battered women, the fear of immediate harm extends beyond individual episodes of violence and becomes a part of everyday life. Based on that theory, fear of immediate harm is always present. However, not all states have been willing to accept this defense, as the woman's actions usually are not taken in the face of "imminent" death or great bodily harm. The effects of the battered woman's syndrome may be used, however, to reduce the charge from murder to manslaughter.

Battered woman's or spouse's syndrome
A syndrome of being the victim of repeated attacks; self-defense is sometimes allowed to the victim, even when the victim is not in immediate danger.

Finally, it should be noted that law enforcement and military personnel are given special exemptions from the law to take actions that are required as part of their official duties. Soldiers killing enemy soldiers in battle and police officers killing an escaping felon fall under the category of justifiable homicide.

g. Statutes of Limitations and Speedy Trial Acts

Many crimes, like civil actions, are covered by statutes of limitations. Under these statutes the government cannot prosecute an individual after a designated number of years have passed since either the date of the crime or the discovery of the crime. However, there are some crimes, such as murder, for which there usually is no time limit on when charges may be brought.

The Speedy Trial Act of 1974[10] requires that defendants in federal court be brought to trial within 100 days of their being charged with a crime. Many state legislatures have also set down specific time limits. While defendants usually can waive these time limits if added time is needed to prepare for the trial, prosecutors cannot claim the same privilege. Speedy trial statutes may require that the charges be dismissed if defendants are not brought to trial within a given number of days. Therefore, as is true with statutes of limitations, failure to comply with these dates can become a basis for having the charges dismissed.

h. Constitutional Defenses

The U.S. Constitution provides a variety of defenses. For example, the Fifth Amendment protects a defendant from being tried twice for the same crime. In addition, criminal convictions can sometimes be challenged on the grounds that the statute on which the conviction was based was unconstitutional. If a statute is found to be unconstitutional, a defendant cannot be legally convicted or punished for violating it.

Double jeopardy
A constitutional protection against being tried twice for the same crime.

The Fifth Amendment provides that "no person shall be subject for the same offense to be twice up in jeopardy of life or limb." The U.S. Supreme Court has held that this protection against **double jeopardy** applies to both federal and state prosecutions.[11] Generally, "jeopardy" attaches once a jury has been selected. If the trial concludes with either a conviction or acquittal, a defendant cannot be tried again for the same offense. However, if the trial ends in a mistrial, for example, because of a hung jury, the double jeopardy clause will not prevent the state from prosecuting the defendant in a second trial. This protection against double jeopardy also does not apply if the same action constitutes two different criminal offenses. For example, an act that is prosecuted as a homicide in state court may also be prosecuted as a violation of civil rights in federal court. Furthermore, double jeopardy does not prevent a civil action for damages based on the same set of facts presented in a criminal prosecution. Finally, if the defendant successfully appeals a conviction, the appellate court may remand the case for a new trial without violating the double jeopardy clause.

Void for vagueness
A reason for invalidating a statute where a reasonable person could not determine a statute's meaning.

Vague or overbroad criminal statutes can be challenged under the due process clauses of the Fifth and Fourteenth Amendments. The **void for vagueness** concept is based on the principle that a statute must be written in such a way that a person of average intelligence has notice as to what is or is not prohibited by the law. Consider, for example, a Texas stalking statute that made it illegal to engage in conduct that is "reasonably likely to harass, annoy, alarm, abuse,

---

[10]18 U.S.C.S. § 3161 (2008).
[11]Brown v. Ohio, 432 U.S. 161, 164 (1977) (double jeopardy clause of the Fifth Amendment applicable to the states through the Fourteenth Amendment).

torment, or embarrass" someone. Because terms such as "annoy," "alarm," and "embarrass" are ambiguous and susceptible to different meanings, the highest Texas criminal appellate court struck down the statute on the basis that it was unconstitutionally vague on its face.[12]

Overbreadth is closely related to the concept of vagueness. The courts require criminal statutes to be narrowly drawn so as to prohibit only those things the government has a right to prohibit. For example, as in the Texas statute mentioned above, whenever terms such as "annoy" are used, there is the potential for them to be interpreted in such a way as to infringe on protected speech. Therefore, the statute could also have been challenged on the grounds that it covered protected lawful activity as well as criminal activity.

Criminal statutes can also be challenged on the basis that they violate the defendant's First Amendment rights of freedom of religion or freedom of speech. When freedom of religion is used as a basis for challenging a statute, the government must show the law in question is neutral on its face and of general applicability. If this standard is met, the statute is valid even though it may have the incidental effect of burdening a particular religious practice.[13] For example, the U.S. Supreme Court upheld the constitutionality of a statute prohibiting polygamy, even though the Mormon defendant argued that polygamous marriage was part of his religion.[14] However, the Court invalidated a city ordinance prohibiting the ritual sacrifice of animals on the grounds that it was neither neutral on its face nor of general applicability.[15] It was not neutral because it was directed at a specific religious group, the Santerias, and it was not of general applicability because it only applied to the killing of animals in the context of a religious service. If the city had been motivated by legitimate public health concerns, the ordinance would have been applicable to all situations in which animals are killed.

The First Amendment protection of freedom of speech can also form the basis for a constitutional challenge. The concept of **content neutrality** plays a critical role in First Amendment cases. For example, in *Texas v. Johnson*,[16] the Supreme Court determined that the state of Texas could not punish someone for symbolic speech, in that case the burning of an American flag, simply because they disagreed with the message being sent. Similarly, the government cannot grant or deny a permit for a rally or parade on the basis of which political party is sponsoring the event. The Court held that the Village of Skokie could not prevent a neo-Nazi group from marching in its town even though their presence would be offensive to the 60 percent of its residents who were Jewish, 10 percent of whom were survivors of the Holocaust.[17]

Content neutrality also plays a role in the Court's treatment of **hate crime** laws. Hate crimes are offenses that are motivated by a hatred of a specific group or category of people, such as racial or religious minorities or homosexuals. In analyzing these types of laws, one needs to distinguish between those prohibiting

Overbreadth
A reason for invalidating a statute where it covers both protected and criminal activity.

Content neutrality
Laws may not limit free expression on the basis of whether the speech's content supports or opposes any particular position.

Hate crime
Crime where the selection of the victim is based on that person's membership in a protected category, such as race, sex, or sexual orientation.

---

[12]Long v. State, 931 S.W.2d 285 (Tex. 1996).

[13]Employment Div. v. Smith, 494 U.S. 872 (1990).

[14]Reynolds v. United States, 98 U.S. 611 (1878).

[15]Church of the Lukumi Balbalu Aye Inc. v. Hialeah, 508 U.S. 520 (1993).

[16]411 U.S. 397 (1989).

[17]National Socialist Party v. Skokie, 432 U.S. 43 (1977).

Hate speech
Speech directed at a particular group or classification of people that involves expressions of hate or intimidation.

certain types of "**hate speech**" and those that enhance the punishment of another underlying crime.

The contrast between these two approaches can be seen in two recent Supreme Court cases. In a case dealing with a form of "hate speech," the Court was asked to consider whether a state statute that outlawed cross burning unconstitutionally infringed on protected symbolic speech. The Court held that cross burning by itself could be protected speech. However, if the intent behind the cross burning was to intimidate, the state could constitutionally criminalize that behavior.[18] Therefore, the Court reversed the conviction of a man who had led a Ku Klux Klan rally during which a cross was burned but affirmed that the state could prosecute those who used a cross burning to intimidate, as was done by two men who placed a burning cross in the yard of an African American family.

In contrast to "hate speech" laws, the penalty enhancement statutes simply provide for stiffer penalties in situations where the defendant has been found guilty of another crime, such as robbery, but it is proven that the defendant selected the specific victim because of that person's race, religion, or other specified factors. The Supreme Court upheld the validity of such a statute in *Wisconsin v. Mitchell*.[19]

NETNOTE

To learn more about hate crimes, visit *www.tolerance.org*, a Web site project supported by the Southern Poverty Law Center. There you can click on a link to take a self-assessment on bias, and you can find information about the Laramie Project, a play and later an HBO film, based on the murder of a young gay man in Laramie, Wyoming. The American Anti-Defamation League has also posted an article on hate crimes on its Web site at *www.adl.org/99hatecrime/intro.asp*.

Several young black men attacked a white youth, beating him so badly that he was in a coma for four days. Just before they assaulted him, one of the defendants yelled, "There goes a white boy. Go get him." The defendants admitted that they had chosen the victim because he was white. Under Wisconsin law, the penalty for battery is increased from two years to seven years if the defendant "intentionally selects the person against whom the crime . . . is committed . . . because of the race, religion, color, disability, sexual orientation, national origin or ancestry of that person."[20] In upholding the constitutionality of the statute, the Justices reasoned that it was appropriate for the statute to single out for enhancement bias-inspired conduct "because this conduct is thought to inflict greater individual and societal harm. . . . Bias-motivated

---

[18]Virginia v. Black, 538 U.S. 343 (2003).
[19]509 U.S. 476 (1993).
[20]Wis. Stat. § 939.645(1)(b) (2008).

crimes are more likely to provoke retaliatory crimes, inflict distinct emotional harms on their victims, and incite community unrest."[21]

DISCUSSION QUESTIONS

7. In *Mitchell*, the Court also rejected an argument that the statute was overbroad. The Court stated that the suggestion that the statute would have a "chilling effect" on free speech was "attenuated and unlikely." Do you agree?

8. While virtually all states have some form of hate crime statute, according to the FBI the number of hate crimes is on the increase. Do you think this serves as evidence that hate crime statutes do not really work?

9. Some have argued against the adoption of hate crime statutes on several grounds, including the difficulty of proving that the crime was motivated by hate. In addition, they contend that it is the crime itself, not the motive, that should form the basis of punishment, arguing that a person is just as dead if a murder is committed in the course of a robbery gone wrong as during a race riot. How would you answer such critics?

NETNOTE

To read about recent developments and issues involving criminal justice, go to the American Civil Liberties Union Web site at *www.aclu.org/CriminalJustice/ CriminalJusticeMain.cfm.*

6. Dynamic Change

State legislatures frequently revise our complex system of crimes, defenses, and punishments as they react to specific incidents in our society, such as a particularly gruesome episode of crime or changes in societal opinions about a particular crime. In some instances, such as the nonmedicinal use of alcohol and the use of birth control, statutes have been changed to decriminalize conduct. More often we have added new crimes to cover new concerns.

The most frequent change in criminal statutes, however, usually involves the penalties. As society continues to be afraid of the consequences of crime, many think that if the penalties get stiffer, the incidents of crime may decrease. For example, in Massachusetts several years ago a person who was convicted of driving an automobile while intoxicated only had to pay a fine of not more than $25, no matter how many such offenses that person had committed. In response to the public's growing concern about alcohol-related traffic accidents, the legislature significantly increased the penalties associated with drunk driving. Now, even for a first offense, the defendant who is arrested for operating a

---

[21]Mitchell, 509 U.S. at 487-488.

motor vehicle under the influence of an alcoholic beverage may face a driver's education program, loss of his or her driver's license for a specified number of days, probation for up to one year, and a fine in excess of $1,500. Subsequent offenses may include a more lengthy, or permanent, loss of license and jail time.

B. CRIMINAL PROCEDURE

Whereas **criminal law** defines for society what behaviors are illegal and determines how lawbreakers should be punished, **criminal procedure** specifies the rules and procedures governing the manner in which alleged criminals are prosecuted and punished. In addition to moving cases through the criminal justice system as smoothly and efficiently as possible, the rules of criminal procedure are also designed to protect the rights of the accused and ensure a just result. They cover the actions of law enforcement, the court system, defense attorneys and prosecutors, and the guidelines by which convicted criminals are sentenced.

Even though approximately 95 percent of criminal prosecutions occur in state courts, the U.S. Constitution has a significant impact on how all prosecutions are conducted because the Fourteenth Amendment due process clause has been interpreted as having made most of the provisions of the Bill of Rights applicable to the states. See pages 153–155 in the chapter on Constitutional Law.

Figure 12-3 provides an overview of the stages in a criminal prosecution. Be warned, however, that the details of criminal procedure vary greatly among jurisdictions. For example, only about half the states have a grand jury system. Also, especially for misdemeanors, the stages may be accelerated or even combined. The only mandated uniformity is the U.S. Supreme Court requirement that a probable cause hearing be held within forty-eight hours after a person is arrested without a warrant.[22] Also, the figure assumes that the process continues until there is either a guilty plea or a trial. However, the charges can be dropped at any time. For example, the prosecutor might decide that there is insufficient evidence to file an information, or the grand jury might refuse to indict.

1. Investigation of the Crime

The criminal process usually begins when a law enforcement officer (such as a police officer, a sheriff, an FBI agent, or a state trooper) learns that a crime has been committed or is about to be committed. Either the officer personally observes the crime being committed, or the officer is sent to investigate a crime that either the victim or a witness has reported. A good example of the former would be a situation in which a police officer observes an automobile being driven in a dangerous and erratic manner, pulls the car over, and observes that the driver appears to be drunk. The incident described below provides an example of the situation in which the police learn of the crime from the victim.

---

[22]County of Riverside v. McLaughlin, 500 U.S. 44 (1991).

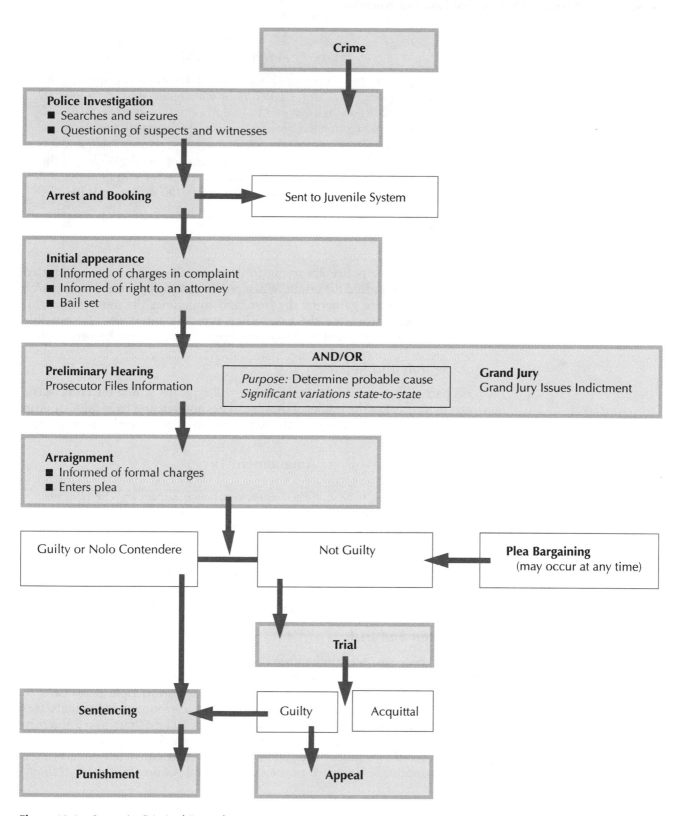

Figure 12-3 Stages in Criminal Procedure

> ## Stage I: *People v. Grant*
>
> When Stephen Joseph returned home about 10:00 PM on April 30, he discovered that the window of his porch door was broken and someone had taken his stereo, VCR, and television. Mr. Joseph called the police.
>
> The police took information from Mr. Joseph, and they searched the scene for additional clues. The next-door neighbor, Pat Baker, remembered seeing a van parked in Mr. Joseph's driveway earlier in the evening. According to the neighbor, the van had *Grant's Audiovisual Equipment* written on the side. She saw two men in dark clothes standing at the end of the driveway. When the police finished at the scene, they left the Joseph home.

At this stage the police are trying to determine if a crime was committed and, if so, who committed the crime. When police investigate a crime and search a crime scene, they are gathering the first, and sometimes the most important, information needed to solve the case. They typically interview any possible witnesses and collect physical evidence that might be linked to the perpetrator.

a. Search and Seizure

As part of their investigation the police will typically search the crime scene and seize evidence. For the results of those searches and seizures to be admissible in court, the police must comply with the requirements of the Fourth Amendment.

Amendment IV

The right of the people to be secure in their persons, houses, papers, and effects, against unreasonable searches and seizures, shall not be violated, and no Warrants shall issue, but upon probable cause, supported by Oath or affirmation, and particularly describing the place to be searched, and the persons or things to be seized.

As you can see, the Fourth Amendment requires that all searches and seizures be "reasonable." There are literally thousands of cases in which the courts have interpreted whether certain types of searches or seizures were "reasonable."

(1) Stop and frisk

Stop and frisk
The right of the police to detain an individual for a brief period of time and to search the outside of the person's clothing if the police have a reasonable suspicion that the individual has committed or is about to commit a crime.

If the police suspect criminal behavior, they are entitled to **stop** (detain) an individual for a brief period of time, to ask a few questions, and to **frisk** (pat down the outside of a suspect's clothes). The origin of this right dates back to 1963, when an Ohio police officer thought that a group of individuals was hanging around a street corner to plan a "stick-up." The officer asked the men to identify themselves. Then the officer patted down the men's clothing. The officer uncovered two guns. After one of the men was convicted of carrying a concealed weapon, he appealed to the U.S. Supreme Court. In *Terry v. Ohio*[23]

---

[23]392 U.S. 1 (1968).

the Supreme Court declared that the officer's stop and frisk was a search and seizure covered by the Fourth Amendment of the Constitution, giving the people the right "to be secure in their persons, houses, papers and effects, against unreasonable searches and seizures." However, because the intrusion into the person's privacy was slight, there was no Fourth Amendment violation.

But as suggested above, the police cannot stop and frisk any individual they want at any time they want. An individual may be stopped only when the officer has a **reasonable suspicion** that the individual has committed, is in the process of committing, or is about to commit a crime. According to *Terry*, that reasonable suspicion must be based on "specific and articulable facts which, taken together with rational inferences from those facts, reasonably warrant that intrusion."[24]

Reasonable suspicion
A suspicion based on specific facts; less than probable cause.

If such a reasonable suspicion exists, however, the police can stop, "frisk," and ask individuals to identify themselves. But what if those individuals do not wish to identify themselves? A decade after the *Terry* decision, the Court held that if the police officer was not involved in a lawful "Terry stop," that is, if the police officer did not have reasonable suspicion of criminal activity, and the individuals refused to identify themselves, the police officer could not arrest them for remaining silent.[25] But what if the police officer was engaged in a lawful "Terry stop"? It was only recently, in *Hiibel v. Nevada*,[26] that the Supreme Court answered that question.

A Nevada police officer was investigating a possible assault. He asked a rancher he suspected of having committed the crime to identify himself. The rancher refused, and he was arrested. The police officer was responding to a call reporting that a man had assaulted a woman. The officer found the defendant standing outside a parked truck, the truck matched the description that the police had been given, and a woman was inside the truck. On these facts, the Court concluded that the officer had reasonable suspicion to stop the defendant and to ask him to identify himself.[27] When the defendant did not do so, the police were justified in arresting him.[28] Therefore, in states such as Nevada that have "stop and identify" statutes, police officers may detain persons under suspicious circumstances, ask them to identify themselves, and arrest them if they refuse to do so, without violating their Fourth Amendment rights. The Court also noted that asking an individual to reveal his or her name does not violate the Fifth Amendment right against self-incrimination.[29]

Again, before making a "Terry stop," keep in mind that an officer cannot simply guess that an individual is a suspect. The officer must be able to tell the court about the facts that led to the suspicion. Consider what happened next in *People v. Grant*.

---

[24] Id. at 21.

[25] Brown v. Texas, 443 U.S. 47 (1979).

[26] 542 U.S. 177 (2004).

[27] Id. at 2457.

[28] Id. at 2460.

[29] Id. at 2461.

> ## Stage II: *People v. Grant*
>
> As the police were returning to the station to file a report, they noticed two men in dark clothes walking about ten blocks from the Joseph home. The police turned on their cruiser lights and pulled up behind the men. After briefly questioning the men and patting down their clothes to make sure that they did not carry any weapons, the police determined that these men were late-night joggers and not related to the crime.

Because of the information the police had gathered, they would argue they had reasonable suspicion that the men might be involved in the crime. First, the neighbor's description of the men matched their appearances. Second, they were two in number. Finally, they wore dark clothes, and they were in the neighborhood of the crime late at night.

The court will also look at the circumstances of the stop. The length of time that the officers detain the suspect cannot be long. The longer the period of time is, the closer the court will look at the intrusiveness of the search. The court will also look at the number and the type of questions the police ask. If the questions become detailed or the officers begin to accuse the suspect of committing a crime, then the court may consider the stop too intrusive.

The court will also look carefully at the circumstances of a frisk. Because the purpose of the frisk is to protect the officers and to aid in the detection and prevention of crime, the officers may frisk the suspect only if the officers, in their experience, believe that the suspect is carrying a weapon. The frisk may take place outside the suspect's clothes. The officers are not allowed to search the inside clothing or pockets of the suspect. If a motorist is stopped, the officer may pat down the areas within the suspect's immediate control, such as the car's seat.

(2) Arrest

Arrest
Occurs when the police restrain a person's freedom and charge the person with a crime.

Probable cause
Not susceptible to a precise definition; a belief based on specific facts that a crime has been or is about to be committed; more than a reasonable suspicion.

By definition, persons are considered to be under **arrest** when their freedom is restrained by law enforcement officers and they are in the process of being charged with a crime. Based on current interpretations of the Fourth Amendment, the act of placing someone under arrest is viewed as a seizure of the person. Therefore, law enforcement officers are either required to have an **arrest warrant** or be able to prove independently that there is **probable cause** to believe the person committed a crime. This probable cause is a higher standard than "reasonable suspicion." To determine probable cause, the police can rely on their knowledge of the suspect and information provided by witnesses and victims. In the above example a stop and frisk was probably justified. There was not enough evidence, however, to establish probable cause for a full body search or an arrest.

Due to the greater degree of privacy that one has in one's home, police are generally required to have an arrest warrant when the arrest is taking place in one's residence. An exception exists in situations in which the police are in "hot pursuit" of a suspect.

When making an arrest, police are allowed to use "reasonable force." This means, for example, that they cannot purposely bang the arrested person's head on the top of the car door when placing him or her in their squad car, but they can tackle someone who is trying to run away. State laws differ as to the circumstances under which law enforcement personnel can use "deadly force" to effectuate an arrest.

In recent years the topic of high-speed auto chases has garnered a great deal of attention, with CNN and other television news outlets broadcasting them live from helicopters flying overhead. The U.S. Supreme Court recently spoke to this issue in *Scott v. Harris*, where they ruled that it was not unreasonable for a deputy sheriff to have ended a high-speed chase by applying his "push bumper" to the rear of the fleeing vehicle.[30]

(3) Searches and seizures of evidence

Searches of a suspect's home, business, or automobile and seizures of property from those locations are crucial law enforcement tools. Through legal searches and seizures, officers may uncover items that are illegal on their face, such as illegal drugs or weapons. Officers may also locate the fruits of crime, such as stolen property, or the instruments of crime, such as burglary tools, weapons, and plans.

Because the Fourth Amendment protects only against unreasonable searches, the court must first determine whether the police activity constituted a search. To determine whether a search has taken place, the court evaluates the defendant's expectation of privacy. Some areas, such as a suspect's bedroom closet and the inside of a suspect's refrigerator, are private places where the suspect expects people will enter only by the suspect's invitation. Other areas, such as the license plate of a suspect's automobile and the outside stairs of a suspect's home, are less private. The suspect expects that these areas will be seen by anyone passing by. Therefore, it is not a "search" to write down a speeding car's license plate number. Entering the private places in the suspect's life, however, constitutes a search for which the police must show probable cause.

Searches and seizures, if supported by probable cause, may be conducted with or without warrants. A **warrant** is the court's prior permission for the officers to search and seize. However, because the suspect's right to privacy is so important, the courts prefer that officers search with a warrant. The officers must show probable cause to the court that the items they seek are located where the officers intend to search. Read Stage III of *People v. Grant*.

Warrant
A court's prior permission for the police to search and seize.

Stage III: People v. Grant

After some investigation the officers determined that Bruce Grant is the owner of Grant's Audiovisual Equipment. By checking with the motor vehicle department the police also discovered that the vehicle was registered to Bruce Grant, age forty-two. The business is located at 17 Hastings Street. When they checked Mr. Grant's record, they discovered that he had twice been convicted of stealing audiovisual equipment and selling the stolen goods.

The officers wanted to search the business premises to look for Mr. Joseph's missing goods. They wanted to be able to take those goods, and any other stolen goods, from Mr. Grant's place of business to be used against him at a trial.

---

[30]127 S. Ct. 1769 (2007).

The officers went to court and told the judge what their investigation has produced. They told the judge exactly what they wanted to search (Grant's place of business and the inside of the van), and they told the judge exactly what they expected to find there (Mr. Joseph's stolen items). The judge determined that there was probable cause and issued the warrant to search.

The officers must show that they are looking for specific items and are not just going on a hunt to find something incriminating. The officers must show probable cause to believe that the items they seek are connected to criminal activity. In our case it would probably not be appropriate for the officers to simply ask the court for a warrant to search for TV sets because the business could have several TVs for sale that are not the products of the crime. The officers should list the specific brands, models, model numbers if they are known, and any other specific characteristics of the stolen items. Where the police are looking for illegal drugs, however, they need not be as specific. They can indicate on the warrant that they are looking for heroin because there is no legal heroin that can be found by mistake. The officers should also be as specific as possible about the location, noting street address, apartment number, or level. This not only makes the officers' probable cause stronger but also assists the officers who execute the warrant.

Execute
To perform.

The search warrant must be **executed**—that is, the search must actually be carried out—within a specific period of time. The officers must announce themselves as police officers and execute the warrant during the daytime unless the warrant specifically allows other arrangements. They must inventory and describe in writing all the items they seize, and usually they must give the suspect a receipt.

No-knock warrant
A warrant that allows the police to enter without announcing their presence in advance.

Under special conditions the courts will sometimes issue **no-knock warrants**, which allow the police to enter at night without announcing their presence in advance. In order to receive one of these special search warrants, the police must convince the judge that evidence is likely to be destroyed or that the police administering the warrant will be in danger.

Plain view doctrine
Without the need for a warrant, the police may seize objects that are openly visible.

One exception to the warrant requirement is the **plain view doctrine**. Because the Fourth Amendment is designed to protect one's privacy, it is reasoned that police have the right to seize contraband items or evidence of a crime when they see such items "in plain view." Therefore, when an officer looks in the driver's window of a car that has been stopped for a minor traffic offense, that police officer can seize a partially filled beer can she observes sitting on the automobile's front seat. Note, however, that the police must have adequate justification to pull the car over. In a recent case, the U.S. Supreme Court determined that not only does a traffic stop entail the seizure of the driver, but also of any passengers. Therefore, passengers, as well as the driver, can challenge the constitutionality of any such stop.[31]

But what if the driver stops at a police "checkpoint" rather than being stopped for a traffic violation? It depends on the purpose for the stop. If the checkpoint was established for the specific purpose of finding evidence of illegal drugs and the police did not have either probable cause or a reasonable

---

[31]Brendlin v. California, 127 S. Ct. 2400 (2007).

suspicion to stop any given driver, then such a stop is illegal.[32] Any evidence of criminal activity that the police found could not be used in court. On the other hand, if the police established the checkpoint for a valid purpose, then the stop might be legal. In *Illinois v. Lidster*,[33] police officers stopped motorists in an attempt to obtain information concerning a hit-and-run accident that had occurred nearby. They only stopped each vehicle for 10 to 15 seconds, asked the occupants whether they had seen anything happen there the previous weekend, and handed each driver a flyer requesting information about the accident. As one driver approached the checkpoint, his van swerved, nearly hitting an officer. The officer smelled alcohol on the driver's breath. After failing a sobriety test, the driver was arrested and later convicted for driving under the influence of alcohol. To determine the reasonableness of the checkpoint, the Court relied on three factors it had used in the past to determine whether a stop is constitutional: (1) the reason for the stop; (2) the degree to which it advances the public interest; and (3) the severity of the interference with individual liberty.[34] Applying the first two criteria, the Court characterized this investigation into a recent death as grave and, given the timing and location, found that it advanced the public interest in investigating a possible crime. Most important to the Court, however, was the third criterion. The Court held that the stop "interfered only minimally with the liberty of the sort the Fourth Amendment seeks to protect."[35] Therefore, the checkpoint was constitutional, and the driver's conviction was affirmed.

In addition to the "plain view" exception, there are several other situations in which the police are not required to obtain a warrant prior to conducting a search. Figure 12-4 on page 482 lists the various **exigent circumstances** that allow for warrantless searches, the rationales behind them, and how they would affect the search in our case.

If one of the exigent circumstances applies to our case, then the officers may enter and search for or seize items from Grant's Audiovisual Equipment without a warrant. If the defendant objects to the search, the court will look carefully at the search by considering the totality of the circumstances—that is, all the facts that the officers and the defendant believe are true. The court will then decide whether the search was valid and whether the information found because of the search can be used against the defendant.

Exigent circumstances Generally, an emergency situation that allows a search to proceed without a warrant.

DISCUSSION QUESTIONS

10. Which of the following areas do you think should be considered "private" and therefore require a warrant to be searched?
   a. your bedroom in your parents' home
   b. your garage
   c. your office at work
   d. your school locker
   e. your garbage that you have placed at your roadside curb

---

[32]Indianapolis v. Edmond, 531 U.S. 32 (2000).

[33]540 U.S. 419 (2004).

[34]Id. at 427.

[35]Id.

Exigent Circumstance	Rationale	Impact on Our Case
Plain view	The suspect leaves the item where it can be seen. The officers may not touch or move the item for a better view.	If the officers can see the Joseph equipment by looking into the windows of the shop, they may enter and seize it.
Consent	The suspect voluntarily invites the officers into the premises or lets the officers search his or her person. The suspect consents to the scope of the search, and the officers cannot exceed the scope.	If Mr. Grant allows the officers to search, they can seize anything they have probable cause to believe is related to the crime. Mr. Grant can limit their search to an area of any size and can demand that they stop searching at any time.
Third-party consent	If a person shares access and control of a location with the suspect, that person may give consent for the suspect.	If Mr. Grant has a partner who shares access to and control of the business, the partner can consent to the search.
Emergency (plain view items only)	The officers enter a premises to answer a call for help or to assist an emergency vehicle, such as an ambulance.	If Mr. Grant calls for help or suffers another emergency, the police cannot be expected to ignore illegal items in plain view.
Preservation of evidence	When evidence might be destroyed if the officers wait for the court to issue a warrant, they may act without one.	If the officers see Mr. Grant taking the Joseph equipment apart or otherwise destroying it, they can seize it.
Hot pursuit	When officers are chasing a suspect, they do not have to stop the chase when the suspect enters a building. They should enter, secure the location, and then get a warrant before searching.	If Mr. Grant runs from the scene of the crime with the police chasing him, the police can follow him into the store and arrest him but should not search until they get a warrant.
Incident to lawful arrest (vehicles and persons)	When a suspect is arrested, the officers need not get a warrant before searching the suspect's person or impounding and doing an inventory of the suspect's vehicle so that evidence is not destroyed or lost and the officers' lives are not endangered. The officers probably cannot search a locked glove box or trunk without a warrant.	If Mr. Grant is arrested and booked for a crime, the officers do not have to get a warrant before emptying his pockets.
Prisoners	Safety and security outweigh the privacy interests of prisoners. The Fourth Amendment does not apply to prisoners.	If Mr. Grant is in prison, his person and his room can be searched and items can be seized.

Figure 12-4   Exigent Circumstances Justifying Warrantless Searches

11. For each of the following, determine if you believe marijuana could be lawfully seized if its discovery was based on the following:
   a. Using a helicopter, the police fly over your fenced backyard and see it growing in pots on your back patio.
   b. Standing across the street from your house, the police use binoculars and see it growing inside your sunroom.
   c. Aiming a thermal-imaging device at your house, the police find suspicious "hot spots," indicating the probable presence of marijuana growing within your home.
   d. Using a police dog that has been specially trained to smell marijuana and other illegal drugs, the dog "points" to your briefcase, when
      i. you are walking down the street.
      ii. you are walking through an airport.
      iii. your briefcase is located in the locked trunk of your car, and you have been stopped for speeding 6 miles per hour over the limit on a major highway.

b. Questioning Suspects

As previously noted, police officers usually investigate criminal activity by questioning victims and witnesses. As is well illustrated on TV shows, the interrogation of the leading suspects is one of the most glamorous parts of the investigation. In many cases the suspects will reveal information that can then be used against them in a trial. In some cases they even confess. If the suspects did not commit the crime, they may be able to help the officers refocus their investigation.

Stage IV: People v. Grant

When the search warrant was executed, the police found the stolen items in an unlocked cabinet in the rear of the store. The officers seized the equipment, gave Mr. Grant a receipt for the items they seized, and filed a report with the court. The police officers then asked Mr. Grant to come to the station to talk to them about the equipment. Mr. Grant rode along with them in the back seat of one of the patrol cars.

On the ride to the station one of the officers asked Mr. Grant where he had been on the evening of April 30. He replied that he and his cousin had gone to a movie. The officer then asked him what movie they had seen and what time it had started. Mr. Grant said they had gone to an 8 o'clock showing of *Star Wars*. Next the officer asked him where he had gotten the electronic equipment that they had seized from his store. He replied that he had taken it as a trade-in as part of a sale of a big-screen TV.

When they arrived at the police station, the officers took Mr. Grant into an interrogation room and read him his Miranda rights. He responded that he did not want to talk to them unless he had an attorney present. When they gave him a telephone so he could call his attorney, he told them he wanted a court-appointed attorney because he could not afford to hire one on his own.

Both the Fifth and Sixth Amendments to the Constitution are relevant to interrogation situations. The Fifth Amendment prohibits law enforcement agents from forcing defendants to give testimonial evidence that would tend to incriminate them. Note that this applies only to testimonial evidence and does not protect a suspect from having to take a breathalyzer test, to be fingerprinted, or to provide a handwriting sample. The Sixth Amendment guarantees a right to be represented by an attorney.

Amendment V

No person shall . . . be compelled in any criminal case to be a witness against himself. . . .

Amendment VI

In all criminal prosecutions, the accused shall enjoy the right to . . . have the assistance of counsel for his defense.

Miranda warnings
The requirement that defendants be notified of their rights to remain silent and to have an attorney present prior to being questioned by the police.

In the landmark cases of *Escobedo v. Illinois*[36] and *Miranda v. Arizona*,[37] the U.S. Supreme Court ruled that the privilege against self-incrimination and the right to assistance of counsel apply to the interrogation stage, as well as to the trial. The Court reasoned that the right to counsel at trial would not benefit the defendant if the defendant had already confessed before meeting with an attorney and that the presence of an attorney during an interrogation would help to ensure that any statements given would be truly voluntary rather than coerced. The famous **Miranda warnings** are designed to notify defendants of their rights and to explain those rights in language they will understand.

Miranda Warnings

Prior to custodial interrogation, the suspect must be told of these rights:

1. The right to remain silent.
2. That anything said can be used against the suspect in a court of law.
3. The right to the presence of an attorney.
4. That if the suspect cannot afford an attorney, one will be appointed prior to any questioning.[38]

---

[36]378 U.S. 478 (1964).
[37]384 U.S. 436 (1966).
[38]Id. at 479.

Once these *Miranda* warnings are given, the police cannot interrogate the suspect further unless he or she waives these rights.

Although the *Miranda* warnings are now firmly entrenched in our criminal justice system, at the time it was announced, the *Miranda* decision was quite controversial. Prior to *Miranda*, courts had judged the admissibility of a suspect's confession under a voluntariness test. Under that approach, the voluntary nature of a confession and hence its admissibility as evidence of guilt was judged based on all of the circumstances, rather than being subject to exclusion solely because the suspect was not advised of his or her rights. Two years after *Miranda* was decided, Congress enacted a law that was intended to nullify the *Miranda* decision and to return the requirement to the voluntariness test that prevailed prior to *Miranda*. This federal statute was largely ignored until the late 1990s, when the United States Court of Appeals for the Fourth Circuit held that *Miranda* was not required by the Constitution. Thus Congress had the power by statute to have the final say on the question of the admissibility of confessions. According to the Fourth Circuit, the totality-of-the-circumstances test outlined in the statute, and not the *Miranda* warnings, were to be used by courts to determine the voluntary nature and hence admissibility of confessions. The Supreme Court disagreed. In *Dickerson v. United States*, the Court held that "*Miranda*, being a constitutional decision of this Court, may not be in effect overruled by an Act of Congress."[39] Therefore, *Miranda*, and not the federal statute, continues to govern the admissibility of statements made during custodial interrogations in both state and federal courts.

In the *People v. Grant* case we have been discussing, the police read Mr. Grant his *Miranda* rights before they began questioning him at the police station. However, they questioned him in the car about his activities on the night of the burglary before they informed him of his *Miranda* rights. Did this questioning in the car constitute an interrogation, and were the police required to have read the *Miranda* rights before they questioned him in the car?

The answer depends on the definition of a **custodial interrogation**. Suspects are in police **custody** when they feel that their freedom has been deprived in a significant way. It does not matter whether the suspects have been arrested (formally charged with a crime), although an arrest might indicate that the suspects are not free to leave. When suspects are in police custody and are questioned by the police, it is difficult, and maybe even frightening, for them to say, "No, thank you," to police questions. Therefore, before beginning this custodial interrogation (questioning of suspects when they feel that their liberty has been deprived), the police are *required* to tell the suspects about their rights. However, what constitutes "interrogation" is not always clear, as you can see from reading the following U.S. Supreme Court opinion.

Custodial interrogation
Questioning that occurs after a defendant has been deprived of his or her freedom in a significant way.

Custody
Occurs when the defendant has been deprived of freedom in a significant way.

---

[39]*Dickerson v. United States*, 530 U.S. 428 (2000).

Rhode Island v. Innis
446 U.S. 291 (1980)

Mr. Justice STEWART delivered the opinion of the Court.

In *Miranda v. Arizona*, 384 U.S. 436, 474, the Court held that, once a defendant in custody asks to speak with a lawyer, all interrogation must cease until a lawyer is present. The issue in this case is whether the respondent was "interrogated" in violation of the standards promulgated in the *Miranda* opinion.

I

On the night of January 12, 1975, John Mulvaney, a Providence, R.I., taxicab driver, disappeared after being dispatched to pick up a customer. His body was discovered four days later buried in a shallow grave in Coventry, R.I. He had died from a shotgun blast aimed at the back of his head.

On January 17, 1975, shortly after midnight, the Providence police received a telephone call from Gerald Aubin, also a taxicab driver, who reported that he had just been robbed by a man wielding a sawed-off shotgun. Aubin further reported that he had dropped off his assailant near Rhode Island College in a section of Providence known as Mount Pleasant. While at the Providence police station waiting to give a statement, Aubin noticed a picture of his assailant on a bulletin board. Aubin so informed one of the police officers present. The officer prepared a photo array, and again Aubin identified a picture of the same person. That person was the respondent. Shortly thereafter, the Providence police began a search of the Mount Pleasant area.

At approximately 4:30 A.M. on the same date, Patrolman Lovell, while cruising the streets of Mount Pleasant in a patrol car, spotted the respondent standing in the street facing him. When Patrolman Lovell stopped his car, the respondent walked towards it. Patrolman Lovell then arrested the respondent, who was unarmed, and advised him of his so-called *Miranda* rights. While the two men waited in the patrol car for other police officers to arrive, Patrolman Lovell did not converse with the respondent other than to respond to the latter's request for a cigarette. Within minutes, Sergeant Sears arrived at the scene of the arrest, and he also gave the respondent the *Miranda* warnings. Immediately thereafter, Captain Leyden and other police officers arrived. Captain Leyden advised the respondent of his *Miranda* rights. The respondent stated that he understood those rights and wanted to speak with a lawyer. Captain Leyden then directed that the respondent be placed in a "caged wagon," a four-door police car with a wire screen mesh between the front and rear seats, and be driven to the central police station. Three officers, Patrolmen Gleckman, Williams, and McKenna, were assigned to accompany the respondent to the central station. They placed the respondent in the vehicle and shut the doors. Captain Leyden then instructed the officers not to question the respondent or intimidate or coerce him in any way. The three officers then entered the vehicle, and it departed.

While en route to the central station, Patrolman Gleckman initiated a conversation with Patrolman McKenna concerning the missing shotgun. As Patrolman Gleckman later testified:

> At this point, I was talking back and forth with Patrolman McKenna stating that I frequent this area while on patrol and [that because a school for handicapped children is located nearby,] there's a lot of handicapped children running around in this area, and God forbid one of them might find a weapon with shells and they might hurt themselves. App. 43-44.

Patrolman McKenna apparently shared his fellow officer's concern:

> A. I more or less concurred with him [Gleckman] that it was a safety factor and that we should, you know, continue to search for the weapon and try to find it. Id., at 53.

While Patrolman Williams said nothing, he overheard the conversation between the two officers:

> A. "He [Gleckman] said it would be too bad if the little—I believe he said a girl—would pick up the gun, maybe kill herself." Id., at 59.

The respondent then interrupted the conversation, stating that the officers should turn the car around so he could show them where the gun was located. At this point, Patrolman McKenna radioed back to Captain Leyden that they were returning to the scene of the arrest, and that the respondent would inform them of the location of the gun. At the time the respondent indicated that the officers should turn back, they had traveled no more than a mile, a trip encompassing only a few minutes.

The police vehicle then returned to the scene of the arrest where a search for the shotgun was in progress. There, Captain Leyden again advised the respondent of his *Miranda* rights. The respondent replied that he understood those rights but that he "wanted to get the gun out of the way because of the kids in the area in the school." The respondent then led the police to a nearby field, where he pointed out the shotgun under some rocks by the side of the road.

On March 20, 1975, a grand jury returned an indictment charging the respondent with the kidnapping, robbery, and murder of John Mulvaney. Before trial, the respondent moved to suppress the shotgun and the statements he had made to the police regarding it . . . . [T]he trial court sustained the admissibility of the shotgun and testimony related to its discovery. That evidence was later introduced at the respondent's trial, and the jury returned a verdict of guilty on all counts.

On appeal, the Rhode Island Supreme Court, in a 3-2 decision, set aside the respondent's conviction . . . .

II

. . . In the present case, the parties are in agreement that the respondent was fully informed of his *Miranda* rights and that he invoked his *Miranda* right to counsel when he told Captain Leyden that he wished to consult with a lawyer. It is also uncontested that the respondent was "in custody" while being transported to the police station.

The issue, therefore, is whether the respondent was "interrogated" by the police officers in violation of the respondent's undisputed right under *Miranda* to remain silent until he had consulted with a lawyer. In resolving this issue, we first define the term "interrogation" under *Miranda* before turning to a consideration of the facts of this case.

The starting point for defining "interrogation" in this context is, of course, the Court's *Miranda* opinion. There the Court observed that "[by] custodial interrogation, we mean *questioning* initiated by law enforcement officers after a person has been taken into custody or otherwise deprived of his freedom of action in any significant way." Id., at 444 (emphasis added). This passage and other references throughout the opinion to "questioning" might suggest that the *Miranda* rules were to apply only to those police interrogation practices that involve express questioning of a defendant while in custody.

We do not, however, construe the *Miranda* opinion so narrowly. The concern of the Court in *Miranda* was that the "interrogation environment" created by the interplay of interrogation and custody would "subjugate the individual to the will of his examiner" and thereby undermine the privilege against compulsory self-incrimination . . . .

This is not to say, however, that all statements obtained by the police after a person has been taken into custody are to be considered the product of interrogation. As the Court in *Miranda* noted:

> Confessions remain a proper element in law enforcement. Any statement given freely and voluntarily without any compelling influences is, of course, admissible in evidence. The fundamental import of the privilege while an individual is in custody is not whether he is allowed to talk to the police without the benefit of warnings and counsel, but whether he can be interrogated . . . . Volunteered statements of any kind are not barred by the Fifth Amendment and their admissibility is not affected by our holding today.

It is clear therefore that the special procedural safeguards outlined in *Miranda* are required not where a suspect is simply taken into custody, but rather where a suspect in custody is subjected to interrogation. "Interrogation," as conceptualized in the *Miranda* opinion, must reflect a measure of compulsion above and beyond that inherent in custody itself . . . .

We conclude that the *Miranda* safeguards come into play whenever a person in custody is subjected to either express questioning or its functional equivalent. That is to say, the term "interrogation" under *Miranda* refers not only to express questioning, but also to any words or actions on the part of the police (other than those normally attendant to arrest and custody) that the police should know are reasonably likely to elicit an incriminating response from the suspect. The latter portion of this definition focuses primarily upon the perceptions of the suspect, rather than the intent of the police. This focus reflects the fact that the *Miranda* safeguards were designed to vest a suspect in custody with an added measure of protection against coercive police practices, without regard to objective proof of the underlying intent of the police . . . .

Turning to the facts of the present case, we conclude that the respondent was not "interrogated" within the meaning of *Miranda*. It is undisputed that the first prong of the definition of "interrogation" was not satisfied, for the conversation between Patrolmen Gleckman and McKenna included no express questioning of the respondent. Rather, that conversation was, at least in form, nothing more than a dialogue between the two officers to which no response from the respondent was invited.

Moreover, it cannot be fairly concluded that the respondent was subjected to the "functional equivalent" of questioning. It cannot be said, in short, that Patrolmen Gleckman and McKenna should have known that their conversation was reasonably likely to elicit an incriminating response from the respondent . . . . Given the fact that the entire conversation appears to have consisted of no more than a few offhand remarks, we cannot say that the officers should have known that it was reasonably likely that Innis would so respond . . . . It is our view, therefore, that the respondent was not subjected by the police to words or actions that the police should have known were reasonably likely to elicit an incriminating response from him . . . .

For the reasons stated, the judgment of the Supreme Court of Rhode Island is vacated, and the case is remanded to that court for further proceedings not inconsistent with this opinion.

Mr. Justice MARSHALL, with whom Mr. Justice BRENNAN joins, dissenting.

I am substantially in agreement with the Court's definition of "interrogation" within the meaning of *Miranda v. Arizona*, 384 U.S. 436 (1966) . . . . Thus the Court requires an objective inquiry into the likely effect of police conduct on a typical individual, taking into account any special susceptibility of the suspect to certain kinds of pressure of which the police know or have reason to know.

I am utterly at a loss, however, to understand how this objective standard as applied to the facts before us can rationally lead to the conclusion that there was no interrogation. Innis was arrested at 4:30 A.M., handcuffed, searched, advised of his rights, and placed in the back seat of a patrol car. Within a short time he had been twice more advised of his rights and driven away in a four-door sedan with three police officers. Two officers sat in the front seat and one sat beside Innis in the back seat. Since the car traveled no more than a mile before Innis agreed to point out the location of the murder weapon, Officer Gleckman must have begun almost immediately to talk about the search for the shotgun.

The Court attempts to characterize Gleckman's statements as "no more than a few offhand remarks" which could not reasonably have been expected to elicit a response. Ante, at 303. If the statements had been addressed to respondent, it would be impossible to draw such a conclusion. The simple message of the "talking back and forth" between Gleckman and McKenna was that they had to find the shotgun to avert a child's death.

One can scarcely imagine a stronger appeal to the conscience of a suspect—any suspect—than the assertion that if the weapon is not found an innocent person will be hurt or killed. And not just any innocent person, but an innocent child—a little girl—a helpless, handicapped little girl on her way to school. The notion that such an appeal could not be expected to have any effect unless the suspect were known to have some special interest in handicapped children verges on the ludicrous. As a matter of fact, the appeal to a suspect to confess for the sake of others, to "display some evidence of decency and honor," is a classic interrogation technique.

Gleckman's remarks would obviously have constituted interrogation if they had been explicitly directed to respondent, and the result should not be different because they were nominally addressed to McKenna. This is not a case where police officers speaking among themselves are accidentally overheard by a suspect. These officers were "talking back and forth" in close quarters with the handcuffed suspect, traveling past the very place where they believed the weapon was located. They knew respondent would hear and attend to their conversation, and they are chargeable with knowledge of and responsibility for the pressures to speak which they created . . . .

CASE DISCUSSION QUESTIONS

1. How did the *Innis* court define interrogation?
2. Applying that definition of interrogation, why did the Court believe the officers' remarks were not a form of interrogation? Do you agree with the Court's decision?

Although suspects have the right not to answer questions during custodial interrogation, this does not mean that they have to remain silent. Suspects may waive their *Miranda* rights as long as they do so voluntarily, knowingly, and intelligently. To determine whether a suspect waived his or her rights, the court will look carefully at all the circumstances. The court will consider the educational level of the suspect, language barriers, the existence of a mental condition or impairments, addictions to alcohol or illegal substances, the suspect's prior court experiences, the duration and intensity of the questioning period, and any other facts brought to the court's attention. The prosecution has the burden of proving that the defendant made a proper waiver. A signed *Miranda* card and evidence of the defendant's waiver of rights should be part of the defendant's file. The defense team should have access to these records so that motions to suppress can be considered. Police departments can be compelled to give this information to the defense team.

To avoid confusion about whether a suspect received *Miranda* warnings or about whether there were proper waivers of the suspect's rights, law enforcement agencies usually require defendants to sign a card that lists the suspect's rights and asks the defendant questions, such as these:

1. Do you understand these rights as they have been explained to you?
2. Understanding these rights, do you wish to speak to me now?
3. Please sign this card indicating that you understand the above information.

In addition to the *Miranda* cards, many police departments videotape or tape-record the suspects as they receive their rights and consider waiving their rights. Then, if the suspects later claim that they did not receive their rights or that they did not understand the waiver of their rights, the police have documentation to show to the court.

Once a suspect decides to remain silent, the police cannot continue the questioning and must give the suspect an opportunity to communicate with an attorney. The police cannot try to continue questioning at a later time unless an attorney is present. A suspect can waive his or her *Miranda* rights at a later interrogation.

Juvenile suspects are also entitled to be given their *Miranda* rights. In addition to a right to speak to an attorney, juvenile suspects are given the right to talk to an interested adult, such as a parent or guardian, before deciding to waive their rights. Because of their age, or in some circumstances because of their lack of experience with the criminal justice system, juveniles may need extra help making such important decisions. Just as parents or guardians may help juveniles with other life decisions, the court recognizes that a juvenile needs the extra protection that talking to a trusted adult may provide.

Because Mr. Grant told police that he did not wish to be questioned without his lawyer being present and because he indicated that he could not afford to hire a lawyer, the police must withhold any further questioning until they can arrange to have a public defender present or have the court appoint counsel.

2. The Court System

A suspect's involvement with the court system begins with the initial appearance and then continues through a series of stages, eventually leading to either a guilty or a not guilty plea. If a guilty plea is entered, the case moves into the sentencing phase. If a not guilty plea is entered, the case is scheduled for trial. Finally, in some situations either the defendant or the prosecution may appeal the results of a court proceeding.

a. Formal Charges, Initial Appearances, and Bail

The formal process of charging someone with a crime begins by notifying the person that he or she is being placed under arrest. How a defendant actually discovers that he or she must answer to criminal charges depends on the circumstances of the case. In some cases, especially when the crime is a misdemeanor, the defendant may be notified by mail to appear at court to answer criminal charges. When the defendant is caught in the act or shortly thereafter, he or she may be arrested on the spot without a warrant. Otherwise, officers must obtain a warrant for arrest.

Booking
The process after arrest that includes taking the defendant's personal information, giving the defendant an opportunity to read and sign a *Miranda* card, and allowing the defendant the opportunity to use a telephone.

Normally, a defendant who is arrested is brought to the police facility and booked. The **booking process** usually includes taking the defendant's personal information, giving the defendant an opportunity to read and sign a *Miranda* card, and allowing the defendant the opportunity to use a telephone. Additionally, the police may take photographs, or "mug shots," of the defendant for identification purposes. The police may also require the defendant to be fingerprinted. Fingerprints may then be compared to fingerprints found at the scene of the crime or saved to be compared to prints found at future crime scenes. The defendant is then searched, and his or her belongings are inventoried and stored by the police.

Bail
Money or something else of value that is held by the government to ensure the defendant's appearance in court.

Some defendants are released by the police after the booking process is completed. They are usually given the date of their first court appearances and instructed that they must appear at court or risk a court default. Other defendants may give the police a fee and promise to appear as instructed to face criminal charges. The process of giving money and promising to appear as instructed is called **posting bail**. Usually, when the case is over, the court will return the bail money to the defendants. Persons can also be released prior to the trial date on a **personal recognizance bond,** by which defendants personally promise to appear in court when instructed to do so. These defendants are indebted to pay a specified amount if they fail to fulfill the conditions of the bond. In many states one's driver's license is accepted in lieu of a cash bail for most traffic offenses. Other defendants may be held in the police facility until the next possible court session, when they are delivered by the police into the custody of the court.

Personal recognizance bond
A defendant's personal promise to appear in court.

Stage V: People v. Grant

On the basis of the witness's testimony about seeing the Grant's Audiovisual Equipment van and the evidence seized from Mr. Grant's store, the police were convinced that Mr. Grant had burglarized Stephen Joseph's home. They therefore informed him that he was under arrest and began the process of fingerprinting and booking him.

The following morning he was taken to court to have bail set and to determine if he was qualified to have a public defender appointed. At this initial appearance the judge told Mr. Grant of the charges being brought against him, set bail at $5,000, and denied his request for a public defender because he appeared to have enough assets in his business to be able to afford to hire his own attorney.

His case was then bound over to the grand jury to determine if there was sufficient evidence to proceed to trial.

After an individual has been placed in custody, the law requires that he or she be brought before a judge or magistrate without unnecessary delay. At this initial appearance the defendant must be told of the charges being brought against him or her, be advised of the right to counsel, and have bail set. In some states the amount of bail is preset for minor offenses, and the accused can post bail at the police station prior to this initial appearance.

At the initial appearance a defendant who cannot afford the services of a private attorney will usually have either a public defender or a member of the private bar appointed to provide representation. Most courts have developed local guidelines that take into consideration the income and assets of the defendant, as well as the nature of the offense. In *Scott v. Illinois*[40] the U.S. Supreme Court ruled that attorneys do not have to be provided in all misdemeanor cases but that indigent defendants cannot be given jail sentences unless they either were provided with counsel or waived their right to such representation.

b. Preliminary Hearings and Grand Juries

A defendant in a felony case cannot be put through the ordeal of a trial solely on the authority of the prosecutor. The evidence must be tested independently to determine whether sufficient probable cause exists to justify placing the individual on trial. This independent testing of the evidence often occurs through a preliminary hearing or the use of the grand jury.

---

[40]440 U.S. 367 (1979).

Grand jury
A group of people, usually twenty-three, whose function is to determine if probable cause exists to believe that a crime has been committed and that the defendant committed it.

The Fifth Amendment to the U.S. Constitution requires that "[n]o person shall be held to answer for a capital, or otherwise infamous crime, unless on a presentment or indictment of a Grand Jury. . . . " Although this applies only to federal cases, about half the states require the use of a **grand jury**. Other states allow the prosecutor the option of using or not using a grand jury; some do not use grand juries at all.

Historically, grand juries were seen as a protection against arbitrary governmental prosecutions. Today, however, there are many who advocate abolition of the grand jury system. Critics point out that the government, in the form of the prosecutors, has too much control over the proceedings. It is the prosecutor who presents witnesses and evidence. The defendant is not even allowed to attend, and the proceedings are kept secret. Generally, the use of grand juries does appear to be declining. The federal government and most states that do use grand juries follow the common-law format of having twenty-three persons serve during a term and requiring at least twelve votes for an **indictment**.

Indictment
A grand jury's written accusation that a given individual has committed a crime.

As an aside, the grand jury also can serve as an investigative arm of the government and can be especially useful when it comes to investigating organized crime or corruption in the government's own bureaucracy. The Watergate grand jury is probably the most famous example of a grand jury used for such investigations. The ability to subpoena and give immunity to key witnesses makes the grand jury an effective weapon in the hands of a well-trained prosecutor. When the grand jury takes on this type of investigative role, its investigations frequently include people who are not yet under arrest. If the grand jury decides that those people should be brought to trial, arrest warrants are issued on the basis of the grand jury's indictment. Defendants arrested in this manner go directly from the initial appearance stage to the arraignment.

In sum, the main function of a preliminary hearing or a grand jury proceeding is to review the government's case to determine whether there is enough evidence to justify holding the defendant for trial. If a grand jury is used and the decision is to proceed, an indictment is issued. If the same decision is reached after a preliminary hearing, the prosecutor files an **information**.

Information
A prosecutor's written accusation that a given individual has committed a crime.

Finally, not all states require either a preliminary hearing or a grand jury indictment. In some instances, especially for misdemeanors, after the initial court appearance the prosecutor can simply file the information.

Stage VI: People v. Grant

Two weeks later the grand jury heard testimony from the police officers who had taken the report of what had been stolen from Mr. Joseph's home and had interviewed the witness about seeing the Grant's Audiovisual Equipment truck there. It also heard from the officer who was involved in executing the search warrant and had heard Mr. Grant say that he had been watching *Star Wars* at the local theater that night. In addition to describing the goods they had seized, the officer reported that when he checked with the local theaters, he discovered that none had been showing *Star Wars* on April 30. The grand jury never heard any testimony from Mr. Grant.

The grand jury then followed the prosecuting attorney's suggestion and indicted Bruce Grant for possession of stolen property, selling stolen property, and larceny.

c. Arraignments, the Exclusionary Rule, and Pretrial Motions

At the **arraignment** the court informs the defendant of the charges contained in the indictment or the information. The judge then asks the defendant to answer the charges by pleading guilty or not guilty. If the defendant wishes to plead guilty, the judge must speak with the defendant to be sure that he or she understands the nature of the charge, the minimum and maximum sentences prescribed by law, and that by entering a guilty plea he or she waives the right to have a trial and to confront and cross-examine witnesses. The prosecution usually reads the facts of the case, and the defendant agrees that the facts are true. If the court determines that the defendant is aware of the guilty plea and is voluntarily pleading guilty, usually the court will ask the prosecution to recommend the sentence. The judge may either pronounce the sentence at that time or set a specific time for a sentencing hearing at some later date.

Sometimes the prosecution and the defense negotiate the defendant's punishment. This negotiation is called **plea bargaining**. In plea bargaining the defendant may agree to plead guilty to the crime, or to a lesser included offense of the crime, in exchange for the prosecution's recommendation for a lighter sentence. The judge may consider the results of the plea bargain but is not required to accept it. If the defendant enters a not guilty plea, a tentative date is set for the trial based on whether the defendant requests a jury trial or a bench trial.

Defendants usually have a third option at arraignment. They may plead **nolo contendere**. This Latin phrase means "no contest." A defendant neither admits nor denies the charges. He or she simply agrees that if the case went to trial, the prosecution would have sufficient evidence to prove its case beyond a reasonable doubt. This plea is not considered an admission of guilt and so cannot be used later against the defendant at a civil trial. However, for purposes of the arraignment the case proceeds as though the defendant had pleaded guilty.

Arraignment
A criminal proceeding at which the court informs the defendant of the charges being brought against him or her and the defendant enters a plea.

Plea bargaining
A process whereby the prosecutor and the defendant's attorney agree for the defendant to plead guilty in exchange for the prosecutor's promise to charge him or her with a lesser offense, drop some additional charges, or request a lesser sentence.

Nolo contendere
A defendant's plea meaning that the defendant neither admits nor denies the charges.

Stage VII: People v. Grant

Mr. Grant was released from custody after posting his bond, and he arrived at his arraignment with a private attorney he had hired. The judge informed him that he had been charged with possessing stolen property, selling stolen property, and committing larceny. Following his attorney's advice Mr. Grant pleaded not guilty and demanded a jury trial. The judge accepted his plea and assigned the case to the next jury calendar.

At this point Mr. Grant's attorney filed a motion to require the state to turn over police notes regarding interviews with witnesses. She also moved to suppress the statements her client had made in the back of the police car about his activities on the night of the crime.

As in civil proceedings, the parties in a criminal case have an opportunity to use various discovery devices to avoid "trial by ambush." Although the particulars vary from one jurisdiction to another, the defense generally has a right to discover all the evidence that the prosecution intends to use at trial, including such things as the names, addresses, and statements of persons that the prosecution intends to call as witnesses; transcripts of any electronic surveillance; and physical evidence, such as a gun, a knife, illegal drugs, or the results of scientific tests. In addition to turning over **inculpatory evidence**, which suggests the defendant's guilt, the prosecution is required to produce **exculpatory evidence**, which suggests that the defendant did not commit the crime. If the prosecution refuses to provide discovery to the defense, the defense team may file motions to compel the evidence and ask the court to force the prosecution to supply the evidence. The prosecution, in turn, has a right to have the defendant appear in line-ups, give handwriting samples, provide names and addresses of people who will be called as defense witnesses, and provide results of laboratory and medical reports to be used as evidence.

Inculpatory evidence
Evidence that suggests the defendant's guilt.

Exculpatory evidence
Evidence that suggests the defendant's innocence.

The most common pretrial motions relate to facilitating the discovery process and preventing certain types of evidence from being used at the trial. Figure 12-5 on pages 498–499 lists the motions you are most likely to encounter. Note, however, that not all of these are available in every jurisdiction. You need to check local court rules to determine the availability and format of specific motions. The federal and state rules of criminal procedure typically require that motions be accompanied by a memorandum of law, analyzing how the courts have decided similar motions in past cases and arguing how the motions should be decided in this case.

Because criteria for presenting and proving each motion depend on the jurisdiction, not all of these motions are available to every defendant and prosecutor in every jurisdiction. Other pretrial motions may also be available.

The format and requirements for each motion, such as the requirement to file a memorandum of law to accompany the motion, will also depend on the jurisdiction. Remember, nothing in the table of typical motions, or in this chapter, takes the place of your research in your own jurisdiction.

Motion to suppress
A request that the court prohibit the use of certain evidence at the trial.

Exclusionary rule
A rule that states that evidence obtained in violation of an individual's constitutional rights cannot be used against that individual in a criminal trial.

Because these pretrial motions are designed to significantly influence the course of the case, defending against pretrial motions is a crucial job. Carefully dissect the factual analysis, legal research, and legal reasoning of your opponent's motion and, if applicable, the supporting memoranda of law. Do not take any detail or citation for granted.

DISCUSSION QUESTION

12. How do you reconcile the purpose behind a motion for a view with the traditional belief that jurors are supposed to base their decision solely on what they hear and see in the courtroom?

Fruit of the poisonous tree doctrine
Evidence that is derived from an illegal search or interrogation is inadmissible.

A **motion to suppress**, the first type of motion listed in Figure 12-5, is a request to have the court prohibit the use of certain evidence at the trial. Motions to suppress are based on what is known as the exclusionary rule. Under the terms of the **exclusionary rule**, evidence that has been obtained in violation of an individual's constitutional rights cannot be used against that individual in a criminal trial. Furthermore, the **fruit of the poisonous tree doctrine** holds that evidence that is spawned by or directly derived from an illegal search or illegal interrogation is inadmissible against the defendant by virtue of being tainted by the original illegality. If the tree (the primary evidence) has been poisoned from the illegal search, then all the fruit (collateral or additional evidence) must also be suppressed. The application of this doctrine does not invalidate the arrest or prevent the defendant from being convicted on the basis of independent evidence. Nor does it prohibit officers from later conducting legal searches and gathering additional evidence as long as that evidence was gathered without the aid of knowledge gained from the tainted evidence that was suppressed.

The exclusionary rule, which remains one of the most controversial aspects of constitutional law, applies to state as well as federal court cases. The exclusionary rule, as applied to the states, was established in the following landmark case.

It may be considered legal malpractice *not* to file a motion to suppress evidence when that motion has a probability for success. Anytime there is a search, the defense attorney should carefully evaluate the file to determine whether these motions are required.

Ethics Alert

Mapp v. Ohio
367 U.S. 643 (1961)

Mr. Justice CLARK delivered the opinion of the Court.

Appellant stands convicted of knowingly having had in her possession and under her control certain lewd and lascivious books, pictures, and photographs in violation of § 2905.34 of Ohio's Revised Code. As officially stated in the syllabus to its opinion, the Supreme Court of Ohio found that her conviction was valid though "based primarily upon the introduction in evidence of lewd and lascivious books and pictures unlawfully seized during an unlawful search of defendant's home . . . ."

On May 23, 1957, three Cleveland police officers arrived at appellant's residence in that city pursuant to information that "a person [was] hiding out in the home, who was wanted for questioning in connection with a recent bombing." . . . Miss Mapp and her daughter by a for-

mer marriage lived on the top floor of the two-family dwelling . . . . . When Miss Mapp did not come to the door immediately, at least one of the several doors to the house was forcibly opened and the policemen gained admittance . . . . It appears that Miss Mapp was halfway down the stairs from the upper floor to the front door when the officers, in this highhanded manner, broke into the hall . . . . Running rough-shod over appellant, a policeman "grabbed" her, "twisted [her] hand," and she "yelled [and] pleaded with him" because "it was hurting." Appellant, in handcuffs, was then forcibly taken upstairs to her bedroom where the officers searched a dresser, a chest of drawers, a closet and some suitcases. They also looked into a photo album and through personal papers belonging to the appellant. The search spread to the rest of the second floor including the child's bedroom, the living room, the kitchen and a dinette. The basement of the building and a trunk found therein were also searched. The obscene materials for possession of which she was ultimately convicted were discovered in the course of that widespread search.

At the trial no search warrant was produced by the prosecution, nor was the failure to produce one explained or accounted for . . . .

The State says that even if the search were made without authority, or otherwise unreasonably, it is not prevented from using the unconstitutionally seized evidence at trial, citing *Wolf v. Colorado*, 338 U.S. 25 (1949), in which this Court did indeed hold "that in a prosecution in a State court for a State crime the Fourteenth Amendment does not forbid the admission of evidence obtained by an unreasonable search and seizure." At p. 33. On this appeal, of which we have noted probable jurisdiction, it is urged once again that we review that holding.

I.

[T]his Court, in *Weeks v. United States*, 232 U.S. 383 (1914), stated that

the Fourth Amendment . . . put the courts of the United States and Federal officials, in the exercise of their power and authority, under limitations and restraints [and] . . . forever secure[d] the people, their persons, houses, papers and effects against all unreasonable searches and seizures under the guise of law . . . and the duty of giving to it force and effect is obligatory upon all entrusted under our Federal system with the enforcement of the laws.

Specifically dealing with the use of the evidence unconstitutionally seized, the Court concluded:

If letters and private documents can thus be seized and held and used in evidence against a citizen accused of an offense, the protection of the Fourth Amendment declaring his right to be secure against such searches and seizures is of no value, and, so far as those thus placed are concerned, might as well be stricken from the Constitution. The efforts of the courts and their officials to bring the guilty to punishment, praiseworthy as they are, are not to be aided by the sacrifice of those great principles established by years of endeavor and suffering which have resulted in their embodiment in the fundamental law of the land.

Finally, the Court in that case clearly stated that use of the seized evidence involved "a denial of the constitutional rights of the accused." At p. 398. Thus, in the year 1914, in the *Weeks* case, this Court "for the first time" held that "in a federal prosecution the Fourth Amendment barred the use of evidence secured through an illegal search and seizure." . . .

IV.

Since the Fourth Amendment's right of privacy has been declared enforceable against the States through the Due Process Clause of the Fourteenth, it is enforceable against them by the same sanction of exclusion as is used against the Federal Government. Were it otherwise, then just as without the *Weeks* rule the assurance against unreasonable federal searches and seizures would be "a form of words," valueless and undeserving of mention in a perpetual charter of inestimable human liberties, so too, without that rule the freedom from state invasions of privacy would be so ephemeral and so neatly severed from its conceptual nexus with the freedom from all brutish means of coercing evidence as not to merit this Court's high regard as a freedom "implicit in the concept of ordered liberty." . . .

Moreover, our holding that the exclusionary rule is an essential part of both the Fourth and Fourteenth Amendments is not only the logical dictate of prior cases, but it also makes very good sense. There is no war between the Constitution and common sense. Presently, a federal prosecutor may make no use of evidence illegally seized, but a State's attorney across the street may, although he supposedly is operating under the enforceable prohibitions of the same Amendment. Thus the State, by admitting evidence unlawfully seized, serves to encourage disobedience to the Federal Constitution which it is bound to uphold . . . .

There are those who say, as did Justice (then Judge) Cardozo, that under our constitutional exclusionary doctrine "the criminal is to go free because the constable has blundered." In some cases this will undoubtedly be the result. But, as was said in *Elkins*, "there is another consideration—the imperative of judicial integrity." 364 U.S. at 222. The criminal goes free, if he must, but it is the law that sets him free. Nothing can destroy a government more quickly than its failure to observe its own laws, or worse, its disregard of the charter of its own existence. As Mr. Justice Brandeis, dissenting, said in *Olmstead v. United States*, 277 U.S. 438, 485 (1928): "Our Government is the potent, the omnipresent teacher. For good or for ill, it teaches the whole people by its example . . . . If the Government becomes a lawbreaker, it breeds contempt for law; it invites every man to become a law unto himself; it invites anarchy." . . .

Twenty-three years later in *United States v. Leon*[41] the U.S. Supreme Court curtailed its broad holding in *Mapp*. That case involved the admissibility of drugs seized by police after executing a search warrant. Leon's defense attorney filed a motion to suppress the drugs based on the theory that the affidavit on which the warrant was based was insufficient to establish the probable cause needed to justify its issuance. The trial judge found that the affidavit had been insufficient but that the officer who filed it had done so in good faith. Therefore, he rejected the motion to suppress the evidence. The Supreme Court agreed, noting that "substantial social costs [have been] exacted by the exclusionary rule."[42] The Court held that evidence obtained by officers "acting in reasonable reliance on a search warrant issued by a detached and neutral magistrate but ultimately found to be unsupported by probable cause"[43] should not be excluded from the prosecution's case.

CASE DISCUSSION QUESTIONS

1. According to the Supreme Court, what is the main justification for the exclusionary rule?
2. What negative consequences arise out of application of the exclusionary rule?
3. What problems would be created by having one set of rules for the federal courts and a separate set of rules for the state courts?
4. The dissenting justices in *Leon* saw that decision as a step toward the destruction of the Fourth Amendment. They wrote that "[t]he right to be free from the initial invasion of privacy and the right of exclusion are coordinate components of the central embracing right to be free from unreasonable searches and seizures."[44] Do you agree?

Typical of the manner in which the United States Supreme Court has been chipping away at many of the most famous precedents of the Warren Court era, a recent Roberts Court ruling held that the Fourth Amendment did not require the exclusion of evidence that was obtained in a search that violated Michigan's "knock-and-announce" rule. Writing for the majority, Justice Scalia stated that:

Whether that preliminary misstep had occurred *or not*, the police would have executed the warrant they had obtained, and would have discovered the gun and drugs inside the

---

[41]468 U.S. 897 (1984).
[42]Id. at 907.
[43]Id.
[44]Id. at 935.

Type of Motion	Goal	Rationale
Motion to suppress	To eliminate all or some of the evidence against the defendant	Without evidence, the state cannot meet its burden of proof. Evidence obtained during an illegal search and seizure, or other improper behavior, may be suppressed.
Motion to dismiss	To dismiss all or some of the charges against the defendant	The best way for the defense team to win is to get the case (or at least a few charges) dismissed before subjecting the defendant to the dangers of trial.
Motion to compel	To force the opposition to provide evidence that has been refused	There is no more trial by ambush. The prosecution must disclose inculpatory *and* exculpatory evidence.
Motion to sever	To try multiple defendants at separate trials	If several defendants are tried together, they may be deprived of certain defenses that point to another defendant as more culpable, and the jury may be overwhelmed and confused about what evidence pertains to each defendant. Through this motion the court attempts to eliminate undue prejudice.
Motion to bifurcate	To isolate the charges against a defendant and try each charge at a separate trial	If the jury would be misled by alternative charges, the defendant would benefit by defending against one charge at a time. Prejudice and unfairness are considered proper grounds under most circumstances.
Motion for a bill of particulars	To force the prosecution to provide specific information regarding the case	The defense team is entitled to know the details of the case with as much specificity as possible.
Motion to sequester witnesses	To keep witnesses out of the court-room until after they testify	The testimony of one witness or the questioning tactics used by the attorneys may influence the testimony of witnesses yet to testify. Keeping witnesses outside the courtroom may help keep their testimony pure.

Figure 12-5 Typical Pretrial Motions

Type of Motion	Goal	Rationale
Motion to recuse	To remove a particular judge from a case	If a judge knows a victim or defendant in a case, publicly voices an opinion about the outcome of the case, or otherwise has a conflict of interest, the judge should step down, and another judge should proceed.
Motion for funds	To allow indigent defendants access to funds from the state	An indigent defendant has the same legal needs for trial preparation as a wealthy defendant. Money may be made available through the court for expert witnesses, scientific tests, or other investigatory needs.
Motion for change of venue	To achieve an impartial jury panel through a request for a change of the location for trial	Sometimes a defendant cannot get a fair trial in the location where the crime was committed. Pretrial publicity or local prejudice may inhibit justice.
Motion to continue	To change the date of trial, usually to postpone to a later date	The parties may require more time to prepare or to allow witnesses to travel to the trial. Attorneys, witnesses, or the defendant could fall ill. When the trial cannot proceed as scheduled, this motion should be filed. Motions of this type, if not abused, are usually allowed.
Motion in limine	To make evidentiary and trial decisions prior to the beginning of trial	Some decisions, such as the order of witnesses, the scope of examination or cross-examination, and the admission of certain documents, may be decided by the parties prior to the start of trial. This speeds up the trial process and avoids bickering in front of the jury.
Motion for a view	To let the jury visit the scene of the crime	A viewing can give the jury members a better understanding of the crime scene than they could otherwise gain from witness testimony alone.

house. . . . What the knock-and-announce rule has never protected . . . is one's interest in preventing the government from seeing or taking evidence described in a warrant. Since the interests that *were* violated in this case have nothing to do with the seizure of the evidence, the exclusionary rule is inapplicable.[45]

d. Plea Bargaining

Stage VIII: People v. Grant

After several continuances had pushed back the original court date, the judge announced that he would tolerate no further delays in the case and that both attorneys needed to be ready to begin the trial on January 10. Shortly before Christmas Mr. Grant's attorney called the assistant prosecutor that had been assigned to the case to discuss the terms of a possible plea bargain.

The prosecutor offered to drop the larceny charges if Mr. Grant would plead guilty to possession of stolen property. Mr. Grant's attorney then proceeded to inquire as to what the prosecutor would recommend for jail time if her client accepted this offer. When the prosecutor said five years, she countered with one year. The prosecutor then laughed and said that his absolute minimum offer was four years. She responded that she would discuss the offer with her client but that she doubted he would accept. When she discussed the matter with Mr. Grant, he told her he would rather take his chances with a trial.

Plea bargaining was mentioned briefly above in the context of arraignment. However, a plea bargain can happen at any time in the process. Ninety percent of criminal cases never reach trial, as they are settled through a plea bargain. The defendant agrees to plead guilty to a criminal charge in exchange for a reduction in the charges or the sentence. The incentives offered by the government can include reducing the severity of the charge (for example, the prosecutor can settle for a guilty plea on a robbery charge where the original charge was for the more serious offense of armed robbery), dropping related counts (for example, an original indictment may include three counts of burglary, but the prosecutor may agree to drop two of them in return for a guilty plea to the third), and recommending the minimum sentence or even a suspended sentence rather than going for the maximum authorized by the law.

Prosecutors are willing to make these types of bargains for a variety of reasons. Because most prosecutors' offices are understaffed and overworked, plea bargaining provides a way to more efficiently manage their workloads and produce high conviction rates. Many prosecutors are willing to settle for a sure conviction on the record with at least some jail time for the defendant rather than risking an uncertain conviction for the sake of longer jail time. In *Santobello v. New York*[46] the U.S. Supreme Court spoke of the benefits of encouraging plea bargaining in a case in which the government tried to change the terms of a bargain after the defendant had entered a guilty plea. The Court

---

[45]Hudson v. Michigan, 547 U.S. 586, 594 (2006).
[46]404 U.S. 257 (1971).

stated that this was improper. Once a deal has been struck and the defendant has entered a guilty plea, the state cannot change the terms of the agreement.

e. The Right to a Jury Trial

The Sixth Amendment to the U.S. Constitution creates a right to trial by an impartial jury in federal criminal cases. The due process clause of the Fourteenth Amendment applies the right to a trial by jury to defendants in state criminal actions who face possible incarceration of six months or more.[47]

The U.S. Constitution requires that criminal juries at the federal level consist of twelve members and that their verdicts be unanimous. The U.S. Supreme Court has ruled that six-member juries are permissible at the state level,[48] as are less-than-unanimous verdicts.[49] It is left to the states to select which of these options they wish to use.

One of the most frequently misunderstood principles of the jury system is the concept of being tried before a jury of one's peers. This does not mean that the jury must consist of a group of people who are similar to the defendant. Rather, the jury simply must be broadly representative of the community in which the trial takes place.

If the defendant waives the right to a jury trial, a bench trial is held, in which the judge serves as the fact finder, as well as the presiding officer.

f. Trial Procedures

There are few, but very important, differences between civil and criminal trials. The major difference is that the prosecutor in a criminal case must bear the burden of a higher standard of proof, beyond a reasonable doubt, as opposed to preponderance of the evidence. The defense is not required to put the defendant, or any other witnesses, on the stand. If the defendant chooses not to testify, the prosecution cannot comment or otherwise draw attention to it during any part of the trial.

The prosecution goes first, presenting all the information necessary to meet its burden of proof beyond a reasonable doubt. Through witnesses and the introduction of evidence the prosecution attempts to prove each element of each charge. With cross-examination of the prosecution's witnesses, the defense attempts to discredit their testimony.

When the prosecution has completed its case, it "rests." At that time, in most jurisdictions, the defense may make a **motion to require a finding of not guilty** for some or all of the charges. Outside of the hearing of the jury the defense may argue that the prosecution failed to meet its burden and that the court should remove the case from the jury by finding the defendant not guilty. The judge looks at the evidence presented and evaluates it in the light most favorable to the prosecution. If the judge grants this defense motion, the defendant can be found not guilty of the individual charges or the entire case. There is no penalty if the judge does not allow this motion. The jury returns and simply resumes hearing the case.

Motion to require a finding of not guilty
The defense's request that the court find the prosecution failed to meet its burden and that it remove the case from the jury by finding the defendant not guilty.

---

[47]Baldwin v. New York, 399 U.S. 66 (1970).
[48]Williams v. Florida, 399 U.S. 78 (1970).
[49]Apodaca v. Oregon, 406 U.S. 404 (1972).

As mentioned above, the defense is not required to put witnesses on the stand. If the defense calls witnesses, the defense examines and the prosecution cross-examines each witness, again with an eye toward credibility.

Once the defense has rested its case, the defense may renew the motion for a required finding of not guilty. This time the judge looks at the motion in the light most favorable to the defendant. If the motion is allowed, the case never goes to the jury for a verdict. If the motion is denied, the court process begins again. The attorneys deliver their closing arguments to the jury, and the judge informs the jurors of the law that they need to know to make their decision, which is called **charging the jury**. Once they are charged and sworn to do their duty, the jury members are released from the courtroom to deliberate. They may bring any items entered into evidence into the jury room with them to help them decide, and they can come back into the courtroom to ask questions.

Nothing can describe the waiting period while the jury is deliberating. It is too late to change anything, too soon to know whether your strategy worked. Many attorneys spend this time discussing possible outcomes with their clients or evaluating their trial performances. There is no set length of time that a jury can deliberate and no special process that a jury must follow. If the defendant is found not guilty, the case is over. If the defendant is found guilty, then the case moves into the sentencing phase.

Charging the jury
The judge informs the jurors of the law they need to know to make their decision.

DISCUSSION QUESTION

13. Criminals are guaranteed a jury of their peers. If you were on trial for a criminal offense, what factors would you consider when trying to select a jury of your peers? Is there really such a thing?

3. Sentencing and Punishment

Most state statutes establish a minimum and a maximum sentence for each crime. Often there are significant differences between these minimums and maximums. For example, under the Model Penal Code, the sentence for murder can range from one year to life imprisonment. When the legislators determine the range of punishments applicable to each criminal offense, they are motivated by the belief that punishment is the most effective way to enforce criminal laws and to stop crime.

a. Theories of Punishment

There are at least five theories of punishment that help explain what society hopes to gain from punishing criminal offenders. They are summarized in Figure 12-6.

General and specific deterrence are both designed to prevent future crime by convincing would-be criminals that any benefits they might get from carrying out criminal acts will be outweighed by the punishments they will receive. The difference between general and specific deterrence is that specific deterrence applies to the person who has already committed a crime, while general deterrence is directed at others who might be tempted to commit a similar crime.

Theory of Punishment	Rationale
Specific deterrence	The perpetrator of a crime is punished so that *this individual* will not commit other crimes.
General deterrence	The perpetrator of a crime is punished so that *other* individuals will not commit this or other crimes.
Incapacitation	The perpetrator of a crime is isolated in a prison so that *this individual* will not be able to commit any crimes during the length of the incarceration.
Rehabilitation	The perpetrator of a crime is given treatment so that *this individual* will have no need or desire to commit crimes in the future.
Retribution	The perpetrator of a crime is punished to exact revenge on behalf of the victim or the victim's family.

Figure 12-6   Theories of Punishment

Both versions of deterrence theory rely on the assumption that would-be criminals will consciously weigh the benefits of committing crimes against the punishments they will receive if they are caught. Critics point out that criminals often act on emotion rather than reason and that they usually believe they will not be caught.

Incapacitation of criminals keeps individuals who commit crimes separated from society and limits their opportunities to commit further crimes. Criminals who are incarcerated or executed are not deterred from committing crimes; they are simply denied the opportunity to commit criminal acts. Instead of incarceration, criminals who are not citizens of the United States may be deported back to their countries of origin.

Rehabilitation involves efforts to reduce crime by changing the perpetrator of a crime so that he or she will have no need or desire to commit crimes in the future. Programs designed to rehabilitate criminals usually include education and job skill development that will help these persons become productive members of society who do not need to turn to crime for financial support. They may also include psychological counseling to help the criminals understand the difference between right and wrong and to appreciate the harm their crimes produce. Through the successful completion of these retraining and reshaping programs, it is hoped that criminals will alter the patterns of their behavior and return to society without further episodes of criminal activity.

Retribution is based on society's desire for revenge. Many people wish to have the government enforce the Biblical admonition that punishment should involve "an eye for an eye, a tooth for a tooth." The theory is that it is better to have the government administer retribution than to leave it up to the victims to seek their own vengeance, thereby starting a cycle of retaliation involving friends and relatives.

b. Sentencing Procedures

With the exception of capital punishment cases, where statutes frequently give the defendant the option of having the jury decide if the death penalty should be imposed, the jury usually has no role to play in the sentencing process. Once the jury has found the defendant guilty of a specified crime, the judge is responsible for determining what the sentence will be. Because criminal codes usually provide a broad range of options between a minimum and a maximum sentence, judges are given a great deal of discretion to fashion a penalty that best fits the particular facts of the case. Under the Model Penal Code, for example, the sentence for murder can range from one year to life imprisonment. Furthermore, judges often have the power to sentence defendants to **probation**, to give them a conditional discharge, or to suspend their sentences altogether.

After a guilty verdict has been returned, the judge usually holds a special sentencing hearing, in which evidence can be presented "in aggravation and mitigation." At such a hearing both the prosecution and the defense have an opportunity to present evidence that was not relevant to whether the defendant committed the crime but is relevant to the nature of the punishment that is to be imposed. The judge also receives a presentence report, which reviews the defendant's criminal record, work record, family background, and other factors considered relevant in determining the appropriate punishment. In some states, "victims' rights laws" provide for "victim impact statements" in which the victim of the crime describes how it negatively affected his or her life and the lives of family members.

c. Sentencing Guidelines

While the broad ranges between minimum and maximum sentences give judges discretion to personalize the sentence, in the past they sometimes led to very great disparities in the sentences received by individuals who had committed similar crimes. Such disparities raise equity and potential discrimination concerns and have led the federal government and some state governments to create sentencing guidelines. These guidelines reduce the discretion given to trial judges by specifying narrower ranges of prison terms based on such factors as prior criminal record, the amount of illegal drugs sold or possessed, and the degree of harm to the victim.

The U.S. Supreme Court first addressed the constitutionality of these types of sentencing guidelines in 2004. Ralph Blakely had pled guilty to kidnapping his estranged wife. Washington's statutory maximum sentence for second-degree kidnapping is ten years, but the state's statutory sentencing guidelines set a presumptive range of 49 to 53 months. At sentencing, the judge imposed a 90-month sentence after finding that Blakely had acted with deliberate cruelty. The Court held that Blakely's sentence was imposed in a manner inconsistent with the Sixth Amendment right to a jury trial because the guidelines allowed the judge to increase the length of the sentence based on facts the defendant had not admitted and that had not been proven beyond a reasonable doubt to a jury.[50] In *Cunningham v. California*, the Court invalidated California's determinate

---

[50]Blakely v. Washington, 542 U.S. 296 (2004).

sentencing law because it exposed the defendant to a sentence in excess of the statutory maximum a jury could impose.[51]

While the *Blakely* decision involved state sentencing guidelines, the rationale for the Court's decision cast doubt upon the validity of the **federal sentencing guidelines**. That doubt was addressed one year later in *United States v. Booker*.[52] The Court ruled the federal sentencing guidelines were unconstitutional to the extent that they forced judges to increase prison time based on facts that had not been determined by the jury. Following *Booker*, the guidelines are no longer mandatory, but judges must still consult them to help impose sentences that "reflect the seriousness of the offense, promote respect for the law, provide just punishment, afford adequate deterrence, protect the public, and effectively provide the defendant with needed educational or vocational training and medical care."[53]

In 2006, an official federal study on the impact of *Booker* reported a wide variation in the way that district court judges modified their sentencing practices after the decision was announced.[54] The study found that while a majority of federal defendants continued to be sentenced in conformity with the sentencing guidelines, the average length of the sentences being given increased after *Booker*.[55] One of the most troubling findings was that black offenders are associated with sentences 4.9 percent longer than white offenders.[56]

In 2007, the Supreme Court returned two more decisions dealing with the now-advisory federal sentencing guidelines. In *Kimbrough v. United States*, the Court ruled that judges were not bound by federal sentencing guidelines that punished crack-cocaine crimes more harshly than similar crimes involving powdered cocaine.[57] Three months later, the U.S. Sentencing Commission amended its guidelines to retroactively reduce the penalties for crack-cocaine crimes.

In *Gall v. United States*, the Court considered how much deference should be given under the "abuse of discretions standard." The defendant had been a second-year college student at the University of Iowa when he joined an ongoing enterprise distributing a controlled substance popularly known as "ecstasy." A month or two later he stopped using ecstasy and withdrew from the conspiracy. He had not sold illegal drugs of any kind since then and had, in the words of the district court, "self-rehabilitated." After graduating from the University of Iowa in 2002, he obtained a job in the construction industry and later became a master carpenter. Federal drug agents learned of his earlier involvement with ecstasy and brought charges against him. He entered into a plea agreement. The presentence report recommended a sentencing range of 30 to 37 months of imprisonment, but the District Judge sentenced Gall to probation for a term of 36 months. The court of appeals reversed and remanded for resentencing. The

---

[51]Cunningham v. California, 127 S. Ct. 856 (2007).

[52]543 U.S. 220.

[53]Id. at 260.

[54]United States Sentencing Commission, Final Report on the Impact of United States v. Booker on Federal Sentencing, iv (March 2006).

[55]Id. at vi.

[56]Id. at viii.

[57]128 S. Ct. 558 (2007).

Supreme Court ruled, however, that the court of appeals should have given due deference to the district court's reasoned and reasonable sentencing decision.[58]

d. Habitual Offender Statutes

Criminals who continue to commit crimes after their first offense are called recidivists. In an attempt to attack the problem of recidivism, approximately half of the states, as well as the federal government, have enacted "three strikes" or habitual offender statutes. Typically, these statutes mandate required prison sentences for third-time offenders. As these statutes remove a great deal of the sentencing discretion from the hands of judges, some believe that they can create unfair results in individual cases. For example, a man in California was sentenced to twenty-five years to life under the state's three strikes law. His crime? Attempting to steal three golf clubs, worth $399 apiece. He challenged the length of his sentence, arguing that the Eighth Amendment's prohibition against cruel and unusual punishment required greater proportionality between the crime and the punishment. In a 5 to 4 decision, the U.S. Supreme Court disagreed, declaring that such three strikes provisions do not violate the Eighth Amendment.[59]

NETNOTE

The Southern Center for Human Rights represents defendants facing the death penalty. To read about their work in that and other areas of criminal law, go to *www.schr.org*.

e. Capital Punishment

The federal system as well as the majority of states allow for the death penalty. Such capital punishment raises one of the most controversial issues in our criminal justice system, especially when it is applied to defendants who because of their youth or mental disabilities are arguably less culpable. As recently as 1989 the Supreme Court concluded that there was no constitutional prohibition against executing juveniles as young as sixteen or the mentally retarded. However, in 2002 the Court changed its position regarding the mentally retarded when it considered a case involving a defendant who had an IQ of only 59. The Court held that mental retardation diminishes personal culpability. It also noted that the impairments of mentally retarded offenders make it less defensible to impose the death penalty as retribution and less likely that the death penalty will have a real deterrent effect.[60] Stating that a national consensus had formed against executing the mentally retarded, the Court held that such executions are excessive and violate the Eighth Amendment's prohibition

---

[58]128 S. Ct. 586 (2007).
[59]Ewing v. California, 538 U.S. 11 (2003).
[60]Atkins v. Virginia, 536 U.S. 304, 318-20 (2002).

against cruel and unusual punishment.[61] Three years later, when it was confronted with a case involving a seventeen-year-old convicted murderer,[62] the Court reaffirmed its reliance on the concept of an evolving standard of decency to guide its decisions as to which punishments are so disproportionate as to be cruel and unusual. As recounted by the Court, the facts were as follows:

> At the age of 17, when he was still a junior in high school, Christopher Simmons, the respondent here, committed murder. About nine months later, after he had turned 18, he was tried and sentenced to death. There is little doubt that Simmons was the instigator of the crime. Before its commission Simmons said he wanted to murder someone. In chilling, callous terms he talked about his plan, discussing it for the most part with two friends, Charles Benjamin and John Tessmer, then aged 15 and 16 respectively. Simmons proposed to commit burglary and murder by breaking and entering, tying up a victim, and throwing the victim off a bridge. Simmons assured his friends they could "get away with it" because they were minors.
>
> [O]n the night of the murder, . . . Simmons and Benjamin entered the home of the victim, Shirley Crook, after reaching through an open window and unlocking the back door. Simmons turned on a hallway light. Awakened, Mrs. Crook called out, "Who's there?" In response Simmons entered Mrs. Crook's bedroom, where he recognized her from a previous car accident involving them both. Simmons later admitted this confirmed his resolve to murder her.
>
> Using duct tape to cover her eyes and mouth and bind her hands, the two perpetrators put Mrs. Crook in her minivan and drove to a state park. They reinforced the bindings, covered her head with a towel, and walked her to a railroad trestle spanning the Meramec River. There they tied her hands and feet together with electrical wire, wrapped her whole face in duct tape and threw her from the bridge, drowning her in the waters below.
>
> By the afternoon of September 9, Steven Crook had returned home from an overnight trip, found his bedroom in disarray, and reported his wife missing. On the same afternoon fishermen recovered the victim's body from the river. Simmons, meanwhile, was bragging about the killing, telling friends he had killed a woman "because the bitch seen my face."

The Court started with the premise that the Constitution must be read in light of society's evolving sense of decency. As objective evidence of that evolution, the Court cited the statistic that thirty states prohibit the juvenile death penalty. The Justices also noted that the United States is the only country that continues to sanction the death penalty for juveniles. Also significant was that as compared to adults, juveniles under the age of eighteen are immature with an underdeveloped sense of responsibility, are more vulnerable to outside influences, including peer pressure, and have personality traits more transitory than adults. Therefore, as it had found in respect to the mentally retarded, the Court determined that the death penalty as applied to juveniles does not serve either purpose of retribution or of deterrence.[63] This reasoning led the Court to hold that the Constitution forbids the imposition of the death penalty on offenders who are under the age of eighteen when their crimes are committed.[64]

---

[61]Id. at 321.
[62]Roper v. Simmons, 125 S. Ct. 1183 (2005).
[63]Id. at 571-72.
[64]Id. at 578.

A second major issue involves the nature of the crime committed. While the death penalty has generally been reserved for crimes of homicide and treason, it was historically applied to crimes ranging from rape to stealing horses. In recent years many states have limited its application to situations involving multiple murders, murders involving special classes of victims—such as children, government officials, etc.—or murders involving torture. In 2008, the Supreme Court issued a 5-4 decision holding that it was a violation of the Eighth amendment to execute someone for the rape of a child when the child victim did not die.[65]

There are also constitutional questions about the manner in which a death sentence is carried out. In recent years there has been a trend toward using a lethal injection of drugs to bring about the convicted criminal's death because it was perceived to be more "humane" than using an electric chair or gas chamber. However, many opponents of capital punishment argued that rather than bringing about a swift, painless death, these injections amounted to cruel and unusual punishment because they caused extreme pain before bringing about death. Nonetheless, in *Braze v. Rees,* seven Supreme Court justices voted to uphold a three-drug, lethal-injection protocol used by Kentucky for carrying out its executions.[66]

DISCUSSION QUESTIONS

14. How might you respond to your neighbor who says the judicial system is "falling apart" because of plea bargaining?

15. "It is better that ten guilty men go free than one innocent man be convicted" is an often-quoted legal expression. Do you agree or disagree?

16. Discuss the manner in which the death penalty serves each of the major theories of punishment. Do you support or oppose the use of capital punishment? Why?

17. In death penalty cases, a troubling dilemma is created by the need to select jurors who are willing to impose the death penalty without at the same time creating a jury that is predisposed toward doing so. Indeed, the Supreme Court in *Witherspoon v. Illinois*, 391 U.S. 510, 521 (1968), noted that the systematic removal of those opposed to the death penalty can lead to a jury "uncommonly willing to condemn a man to die." How do you think the courts should balance the needs of the state to have a jury that is able to apply capital punishment with that of the defendant to have a jury not unduly inclined toward doing so?

18. How much discretion should the judge have in sentencing? Why?

19. On November 4, Leandro Andrade stole five videotapes worth $84.70 from a Kmart store. Fourteen days later, Andrade entered a different Kmart store and placed four videotapes worth $68.84 in the rear waistband of his pants. (The tapes included "Batman Forever" and "Cinderella.") The police arrested Andrade for these crimes. At trial, Andrade was found guilty of two counts of petty theft. The jury also made a special finding that he had previously been convicted of three counts of first-degree residential burglary. (One case involved

---

[65]Kennedy v. Louisiana, 128 S. Ct. 2641 (2008).
[66]128 S. Ct. 1520 (2008).

his attempt to steal a bicycle.) Each of his petty theft convictions for stealing the videotapes triggered a separate application of the three-strikes law. Therefore, the judge sentenced him to two consecutive terms of twenty-five years to life, with no chance for parole. Does it seem as though his punishment was proportionate to his crime? How would you argue that his case is similar to or different from the *Ewing* case discussed on page 506.

4. Appeal

As with parties who want to pursue civil appeals, a criminal defendant who wishes to appeal a conviction must file the appropriate posttrial motions, usually accompanied by a notice of appeal. There is a specified time during which an appeal may be filed. Because the Supreme Court has determined that this is a jurisdictional requirement, the courts are without power to hear an appeal filed beyond the deadline.[67]

The Fifth Amendment protection against double jeopardy prohibits the state from trying a defendant more than once for the same crime and prevents the government from appealing an acquittal. It does not prevent a prosecutor from appealing the dismissal of a case on technical grounds or from appealing a lower appellate court ruling to a higher court.

5. Writ of Habeas Corpus

The **writ of habeas corpus** ensures that someone imprisoned has the right to question the reason for the detention. This right dates back to the English common law and the signing of the Magna Carta in 1215. Translated from Latin as "you have the body," a writ of habeas corpus is used to gain the release of someone who is being unlawfully imprisoned. It is a court order to produce the person detained, so that a neutral judge can determine if there is a lawful basis for the incarceration. Without such a protection, there would be nothing to prevent a person's imprisonment for indefinite periods of time when there was, in fact, no legal reason for the incarceration.

Writ of habeas corpus
A court order to produce the person detained; designed to give a neutral judge an opportunity to review the charges, to ensure there is a lawful basis for the incarceration.

The right to habeas corpus relief can be found in Article 1, Section 9 of the Constitution: "The privilege of the Writ of Habeas Corpus shall not be suspended, unless when in Cases of Rebellion or Invasion the public Safety may require it." It is a right that has rarely been suspended. However, in recent years Congress has curtailed its use; first in 1996 in relation to appeals by death row inmates, and then in 2005 and 2006 through legislation aimed at limiting the rights of alleged terrorists.

Following the September 11, 2001, terrorist attacks, the Bush administration began holding suspected terrorists in military prisons within the United States and at Guantanamo Bay, Cuba. Lawyers representing these detainees filed habeas corpus actions in the federal court to challenge these incarcerations. The Bush administration took the position that the federal courts lacked jurisdiction because he had, by executive order, authorized indefinite detention.

---

[67]Bowles v. Russell, 127 S. Ct. 2360 (2007). The defendant's counsel had relied on the district court's wrongly calculated date as the filing deadline and so had filed two days late. The dissent argued in vain that "it is intolerable for the judicial system to treat people this way, and there is not even a technical justification for condoning this bait and switch." Id. at 2367.

Several issues were raised by these cases, including whether the writ of habeas corpus could be denied to a group of people classified as "enemy combatants" when the country was not engaged in a traditional war against soldiers from another sovereign country. And should different rules be applied to citizen and noncitizen detainees? Finally, could the right to habeas corpus be suspended without a specific finding that such a suspension was required for the public's safety?

The U.S. Supreme Court first addressed this controversy in 2006, in *Hamdan v. Rumsfeld*.[68] The Court ruled that a noncitizen detainee who was being held at Guantanamo Bay, Cuba, could not be tried by a military commission because the commission lacked statutory authorization. Following that decision, Congress enacted legislation authorizing special military commissions to conduct terrorist trials. The legislation included a provision that denied federal courts jurisdiction to hear detainees' habeas corpus petitions.

Then, in 2008, the Supreme Court ruled in *Boumediene v. Bush* that because the right to habeas corpus proceedings is guaranteed by the Constitution, Congress lacked authority to authorize its suspension.[69] In response to the government's concerns about the dangers that would be presented by granting habeas corpus rights to the detainees, Justice Kennedy, writing for the majority, stated, "The laws and Constitution are designed to survive, and remain in force, in extraordinary times."[70]

SUMMARY

Criminal law defines what behaviors are illegal and what punishments convicted defendants are to receive. Criminal procedure governs how the criminal process works.

Crimes can generally be divided into felonies, crimes that usually involve punishment by incarceration for a year or more, and misdemeanors. For any crime, the government must prove that the defendant had the requisite mens rea while committing the actus reus. Common defenses include alibi, ignorance or mistake, infancy, insanity, intoxication, duress, necessity, entrapment, self-defense, and defense of others. In addition, a defendant may challenge a prosecution on the basis of a statute of limitations or the Constitution.

The rules governing criminal procedure begin with the criminal investigation and continue in force through trial and any possible appeal. The Fourth Amendment requires that all searches and seizures be reasonable. The court-crafted exclusionary rule provides that any evidence unlawfully seized may not be used in court against the defendant. The Fifth Amendment protects defendants against self-incrimination, and the Sixth Amendment guarantees a right to an attorney. While every defendant has a right to a trial, most cases end through a negotiated plea bargain.

If a trial does occur, the prosecution bears the burden of proving guilt beyond a reasonable doubt. The defense attorney is not required to put the defendant, or any other witnesses, on the stand. If the defendant chooses not to testify, the prosecution cannot comment or otherwise draw attention to the defendant's silence.

---

[68]548 U.S. 557.
[69]128 S. Ct. 2229 (2008).
[70]Id. at 2277.

If the jury finds the defendant guilty, the judge is usually responsible for determining what the sentence will be. Most state statutes give the judge a broad range of discretion between a minimum and a maximum sentence for the crime. In recent years, however, this discretion has been severely curtailed through the enactment of sentencing guidelines.

If a criminal defendant wishes to appeal a conviction, he or she may do so. The Fifth Amendment protection against double jeopardy prohibits the state from trying a defendant twice for the same crime and prevents the government from appealing an acquittal. It does not, however, prevent a prosecutor from appealing the dismissal of a case on technical grounds or from appealing a lower appellate court ruling to a higher court.

CRITICAL THINKING EXERCISES

1. Review the robbery and armed robbery statutes from the Illinois Criminal Code on page 451 of the text. What crimes were committed under the following circumstances?
   a. Martin waited until the bartender turned her head. Then he slipped $10 from the cash register into his pocket.
   b. Kamil broke the lock on the kickstand and stole a bicycle while the owner was in the grocery store.
   c. David drove his car slightly behind a woman walking on the side of the road. When she stopped for the light, David reached out of the car window and grabbed her purse. The set of knives that David just won while playing bingo was on the front passenger seat of the car.
   d. After everyone left the party, Rosie took a fur coat that had been left behind, hid it in a shopping bag, left the apartment, and pushed the doorman as she left the building.

2. Apply the Model Penal Code, Article 210, Criminal Homicide, to each of the following situations. What crimes, if any, have been committed?
   a. Sam, a hired assassin, pulls out a gun and points it at Mary's head. He pulls the trigger, the bullet strikes Mary in the temple, and she is killed instantly.
   b. Janet, to protest what she views as the increasing decadence of modern society, leaves a bomb in an empty adult movie theater. Later that night the bomb goes off and kills the janitor, who was there cleaning the theater.
   c. Rita accompanies John while he robs a store owner at gunpoint. The gun goes off, and the owner is killed by the gunshot.
   d. Five boys are playing a game of "chicken" in which they pass a partially loaded gun (one of the six chambers contains a live bullet) around the circle. Each player takes a turn spinning the cylinder, pointing the gun at his head, and pulling the trigger. When Dan takes his turn, the gun goes off, and he dies instantly.
   e. Marjorie owned a 130-lb. dog. On more than thirty occasions the dog had lunged, snapped, and growled at people or physically attacked other dogs. One day, in the hallway of her apartment building, the dog broke away from her, and attacked and killed a neighbor. Marjorie did not call 911 for help, never asked after the

attack about the victim's condition, and returned to the scene of the attack, not to assist the dying victim, but to find her keys.

3. Jimmy Jones and his best friend, Bobby Smith, are both twenty-year-old high school dropouts. They have held several part-time jobs in the past but are currently unemployed.

Last Saturday night Jimmy and Bobby, along with their friend Doris, were restless with nothing to do. Bobby then had a brainstorm, and what started out as a frolic has since ended in a nightmare for Jimmy.

For "fun" and money the three decided to hold up the local convenience store. Doris volunteered the information that the only person on duty at that time of night would be an elderly gentleman who would give them no trouble. Shortly before leaving for the store Doris had a change of heart and told the other two that she would not be coming along.

Neither Jimmy nor Bobby owns a gun. Unbeknown to Jimmy, Bobby decided to take along his kid brother's very realistic looking water pistol. When they got to the store, no customers were present. Jimmy and Bobby went up to the counter and demanded that the clerk hand over the money in the cash register. When the clerk simply stared at them, Bobby pulled out the water pistol, which had been concealed under his jacket. He said, "Hand over the money, old man, or I'll spray you with acid." Actually, the gun only had water in it. The clerk, who was an elderly, overweight man, began to perspire and shake. He placed the money on the counter. Then he suddenly clutched his chest and fell to the floor. Bobby grabbed the money and ran from the store.

Although very frightened by the turn of events Jimmy decided to stay and try to help the clerk. He called the police, telling them to send an ambulance right away. When the police arrived, Jimmy turned himself in. Unfortunately, on his way to the hospital the store clerk died.

    a. With what crimes do you think Bobby could be charged?

    b. What would be the major weaknesses in the prosecution's case?

    c. Do you think Doris could be convicted of any crimes? If so, which ones?

    d. What about Jimmy?

4. Apply the Model Penal Code, Article 210, Criminal Homicide, to the following situations. Have any homicide crimes been committed?

Last summer Willie Albano stabbed and killed Roberto Basso during an argument outside a convenience store. Willie was apprehended by police only ten minutes later and one block away from the scene. A knife, the alleged murder weapon, was recovered at the scene and only the defendant's fingerprints were on it.

Two months later the victim's parents, Peter and Maria Basso, and their only other child, Michael, attended a pretrial hearing. At the hearing the Bassos discovered that the police department had lost the knife, and the judge agreed to dismiss all charges against Willie Albano. The defendant turned toward the family and smiled. He slowly walked toward the Bassos, leaned over them, and said, "Too bad. Better luck next time—after I kill your other son." To Michael he said, "Watch out, buddy. You're next."

    a. Mr. Basso jumped from his courtroom seat and grabbed the defendant's neck with a force so great that they both fell to the floor. A few seconds later Willie Albano was dead from a broken neck and other injuries inflicted by Mr. Basso.

b. After Willie's comments Mr. Basso walked next to Willie out of the courtroom. Once outside the building Mr. Basso grabbed Willie by the neck and strangled him.

c. Mr. Basso stayed in his seat as Willie walked past. When Willie exited the courtroom, Mr. Basso was waiting with a loaded pistol he had stolen from an unsuspecting guard. He aimed the gun at Willie but shot and killed the prosecutor, who was standing near Willie.

d. Mr. Basso waited in his seat until Willie left the courthouse, and then he brought his family home. The next day he purchased a rifle from the local sporting goods store. Later that day he waited outside Willie's apartment, and when Willie returned, Mr. Basso called out, "You'll never touch anyone in my family again." He then pulled the trigger and killed Willie.

e. Three days after the hearing Mr. Basso waited with his shotgun outside Willie's apartment for several hours. While he was waiting, Mr. Basso drank six cans of beer and two small bottles of whisky. Finally giving up on his plan, Mr. Basso sped away from the apartment. He failed to notice a stop sign and killed a pedestrian with his car. The pedestrian was Willie Albano.

f. Mr. Basso arrived at Willie's apartment and forced his way inside. While he held a gun to Willie's head, Willie slit his own wrists with a kitchen knife. Willie died from those wounds six hours later.

5. Apply each of the three tests for insanity to determine whether this defendant might succeed with an insanity defense.

Emanuel Jones had been on medication for several years to stop the voices he heard in his head. He recently stopped taking his medication because it made him feel sleepy. Five days ago, during a visit with his best friend, Sam, Emanuel became angry and confused. He attacked Sam with a golf club and chased him from room to room as he tried to escape. He hit Sam several times with the golf club, and Sam died as the result of the wounds he sustained.

a. Emanuel walked out of the house and stopped at a nearby restaurant for a hamburger. When the waiter asked him how Sam was, Emanuel replied that he thought Sam was at home sleeping.

b. Before leaving the house Emanuel put the golf club and his bloody clothes in the bath tub and filled the tub with water. He changed his clothes and ran home.

c. When the police questioned Emanuel the next day and asked him about Sam, he replied, "I killed him. He'll be back tomorrow."

d. When the police questioned Emanuel the next day and asked him about Sam, he replied, "I killed him. I tried to stop, but he just kept laughing at me."

e. Several weeks after the incident and his return to his medication Emanuel expressed great grief and guilt over the death of Sam.

6. Using the standard discussed in this chapter, did custodial interrogation take place during the following incidents?

  a. A suspect ran up to the police officer and cried, "Help! I killed him. I killed him. I didn't mean to do it!"

  b. An officer walked up to a group of boys hanging around a street corner and said, "Hey, guys. What are you doing here?"

  c. While at the police station the suspect explained how he stole the car from the parking lot down the street.

  d. As an officer asked questions, the suspect wrote answers on a piece of paper.

  e. In the case scenario being used in this chapter the police questioned Bruce Grant on the ride to the police station.

 7. Suppose someone fired a bullet through the floor of an apartment into the apartment below. The police entered the shooter's apartment looking for the shooter, for other weapons, and possibly for victims. While they were in the apartment, the police discovered weapons and a stocking cap. The police also noticed stereo equipment and, suspecting it was stolen, recorded the serial numbers. In order to read all the numbers, the police moved some of the equipment. When the police headquarters notified the police that the equipment was stolen, the police officers seized it.

  a. If you were arguing on the side of the defense, what arguments would you make to convince the court to suppress the evidence?

  b. If you were arguing for the prosecution, what arguments would you make to convince the court that the search was legal?

  c. Which side has the most persuasive arguments?

||| REVIEW QUESTIONS

Pages 445 through 451

1. Why is "[n]o behavior a crime unless the law makes it a crime"?
2. Who has the burden of proving a criminal case? Why is the standard of proof not the same in criminal and civil cases?
3. What is the Model Penal Code? What was the intent of its drafters? Has that intent been accomplished?
4. What are the differences between felonies and misdemeanors?

Pages 451 through 458

5. What is the actus reus of a crime? What is the mens rea of a crime?
6. How do you determine whether one crime is a lesser included offense of another crime?
7. What is an inchoate crime?
8. What is the difference between general intent and specific intent?
9. Define and describe the categories of intent used by the Model Penal Code.
10. Who is the principal of a crime? What is the difference between the principal and the accessory to a crime?

Pages 458 through 474

11. What defense(s) might be available to the following individuals?
  a. The Elliots complained to the police that the son of their next-door neighbor broke their garage windows with rocks. They wanted him arrested. The police went next

door to arrest the boy, and they discovered that he is seven years old. They arrested him and brought him to the police station. He was charged with destroying the Elliots' property.

   b. Marcus was arrested for the murder of his cousin Michael. At the time that Michael was killed Marcus claimed that he was on a business trip 300 miles away.

   c. Every day on the way to school Rosa pushed Carmen to the ground and stole her lunch. On Tuesday Carmen hid behind a car on the way to school, and when she saw Rosa walking toward her, she jumped out and hit her. Rosa pushed Carmen to the ground and walked away without taking her lunch.

   d. As Paula walked toward her car after work, she was confronted by Terry, who pointed a realistic toy gun at Paula and demanded that Paula hand over her wallet. Paula took a gun out of her purse and shot and killed Terry.

   e. After his car was forced off the road, Patrick tried to stop the bleeding on his wife's face. When she passed out, Patrick ran to a nearby home, jumped over the fence, and banged on the front door. When the occupants would not let him in, Patrick broke a window of the house, climbed through, and ran toward the telephone. The homeowner grabbed a rifle and shot Patrick in the back.

   f. During a grocery store robbery a thief held a gun to a customer's head and demanded that he put all the money from the store safe into a bag, which he did. When the police arrived, they arrested the customer for robbery.

   g. During the last five years of their marriage David beat his wife, Mary, so severely that she was hospitalized four times. About six months after the last beating Mary stabbed David to death while he was sleeping. She was arrested for murder.

   h. Officer Kaplan responded to an emergency call for a store robbery in progress. When the masked thief shot at the officer, Officer Kaplan shot and killed the thief. The man's family wanted Officer Kaplan charged with murder.

12. What is the difference between a complete defense and a partial defense?
13. Describe the various tests that have been developed to determine whether a defendant was insane at the time he or she committed the crime.
14. What are the possible results of successfully proving an insanity defense?
15. What is the difference between the duress and the necessity defenses?
16. What does a defendant have to show to prove entrapment?
17. When can a potential victim use deadly force to protect himself or herself?
18. What is the retreat exception to the self-defense doctrine?
19. What problems arise with using battered woman's syndrome as the basis for a self-defense argument?
20. What protections are afforded by the double jeopardy clause?
21. When might a statute be challenged for vagueness? For overbreadth?
22. What must the government show when a statute is questioned as violating the defendant's First Amendment right of freedom of religion?
23. What are the two different approaches that states might take to legislate against hate crimes?
24. On what basis might a defendant challenge his conviction under a hate crimes statute?

Pages 474 through 483
25. What is a stop-and-frisk search?
26. What is the difference between reasonable suspicion and probable cause? Why does it matter?
27. Why does the court consider the suspect's expectation of privacy when evaluating a search?
28. What is a warrant?
29. List some specific facts that must be included when police officers apply for a warrant to search a suspect's home.

30. What is a no-knock warrant?
31. What exigent circumstances may allow the police to search without a warrant?

Pages 483 through 490

32. What are the *Miranda* warnings, when are the police required to give them, and under what circumstances might a defendant waive them?
33. What extra protection do juveniles usually get when they are given their *Miranda* rights?

Pages 490 through 500

34. What might a defendant expect to occur during booking?
35. What is the exclusionary rule?
36. How do motions to suppress affect the prosecution's case against defendants?
37. What are the differences between a guilty plea and a plea of nolo contendere?
38. If you worked for the prosecution, would you consider the following items to be potentially inculpatory or exculpatory? Could this evidence be potentially inculpatory *and* exculpatory?
    a. the fingerprints of a second person on the murder weapon
    b. a statement that the defendant gave to the police shortly after the arrest disclosing the location of the missing body
    c. samples of hair and skin found at the scene of the crime
39. If the following facts are true, what pretrial motions might you file on behalf of the defendants?
    a. All the local papers have reported that the judge on the case used to be married to the victim.
    b. Each of the two defendants claims that the other defendant was the sole assassin.
    c. The defendant, who was represented by a public defender, needs to conduct an independent drug evaluation, especially since the defendant alleged the green, leafy substance was oregano bought to add spice to spaghetti sauce.
    d. Four of the seven witnesses prepared to testify at trial are related by blood or marriage.
    e. The police stopped the defendant for speeding and then proceeded to search the glove compartment, in which they found a bag of heroin.

Pages 500 through 510

40. Describe the basic steps that occur in a criminal trial.
41. Why is there no requirement that the defendant take the stand?
42. What is the purpose of charging the jury?
43. What are the theories of punishment? Which theory or theories do you think are the most effective in eliminating crime in society?
44. Why is it not double jeopardy for the prosecutor to appeal an intermediate-appellate-level decision?
45. What are the Federal Sentencing Guidelines, and are they mandatory or only advisory?
46. What is the purpose of "three strikes" or habitual offender statutes?
47. What constitutional limitations are there on the state's right to execute a convicted felon?

Chapter 13

Ethical Dilemmas Facing Attorneys

Virtually all difficult ethical problems arise from conflict between a lawyer's responsibilities to clients, to the legal system and to the lawyer's own interest in remaining an ethical person.
Model Rules of Professional Conduct, Preamble, Comment 9 (2003)

INTRODUCTION

Legal decisions often involve ethical and moral choices. You have already encountered several examples in the early chapters of this text: Should the law support a system whereby couples who cannot have children of their own pay a surrogate mother; should spouses be able to sue each other for tortious injuries that occur while they are married; should the court recognize the rights of an unborn child? These and other legal decisions involve a balance between conflicting goals and values in the search to reach the just or ethical result. In this chapter we will focus on the particular ethical dilemmas that are presented to attorneys in their role as advocates for their clients.

As advocates, attorneys sometimes find themselves confronted with situations in which they are torn between their loyalty to their client, their role as a member of the legal system, and their own sense of morality. For example, consider the following true story.

Attorney Belge, along with his colleague Frank Armani, was appointed to represent a criminal defendant charged with murder. In the course of their conversations, the client revealed that not only had he committed the murder but three others as well. The attorneys went to the location where his client had said one of the bodies was buried and found the corpse of a young girl, Alicia Hauck. For six months, neither attorney reported their gruesome discovery despite repeated frantic pleas by Alicia's parents for any information they might have that would let them know if their daughter was still alive. Finally, the truth was revealed in court when the attorneys used the information to try and mount an insanity defense for their client. The townspeople were outraged. How could these attorneys, members of this small community, have kept silent so long, while the parents agonized over whether their little girl was dead or alive?[1]

Stories like this raise complex issues that do not have simple solutions. Did Belge and Armani act appropriately? Should they have notified the police or at least the parents either directly or through an anonymous telephone call? What harm would have been done if they had notified either the police or the parents? Before you answer these questions, you need to learn more about the principles and assumptions that underlie our adversary system, the ethical rules that govern attorney behavior, and the nature of the attorney-client relationship. We will then return to the *Belge* case and the tension created by the need to keep client confidences when doing so can cause harm to others. We will also examine two other areas that raise ethical dilemmas: conflict of interest and access to justice. Conflict of interest issues arise when attorneys find themselves with divided loyalties. This can occur when attorneys try to represent two clients with differing interests or when an attorney's personal loyalties jeopardize his or her ability to give impartial representation. We end the chapter with a discussion of access to justice issues, including the need to represent unpopular clients and to ensure that those with limited resources receive representation.

A. THE ADVERSARIAL SYSTEM

In Chapter 4 we saw how our courts are organized to discover the facts underlying a case and then to interpret and apply the law to those facts. In Chapter 5 we learned about the variety of things lawyers do in preparing cases for trial. The legal system described in those chapters is known as an "adversarial system" because it places lawyers in an adversarial relationship and then relies on them to present all of the relevant facts and arguments needed for a neutral judge or jury to reach a proper decision.

To better understand our adversarial system, we need to contrast it with the "inquisitorial system" used in many European nations where judges are active participants in the search for truth rather than neutral arbitrators. It is judges, rather than lawyers, who determine who will be called as witnesses, and it is the judges who ask most of the questions of the witnesses. Lawyers are present in the courtroom to assist the judge, and the lawyers' duty to the litigants is clearly secondary to their duty to the court.

---

[1]For a fascinating discussion of the events that led up to this case, *see* Richard Zitrin & Carol M. Langford, The Moral Compass of the American Lawyer (Ballantine Publishing Group 1999).

The primary criticism of the inquisitorial system is that it puts too much power in the hands of judges, thereby creating an imbalance of power between the individual and the government. Our adversary system is thought to better serve the needs of the individual litigants because it places greater emphasis on the lawyer's responsibility to serve the client's interests and limits the judge's role to that of a neutral arbitrator of the rules.

A constitutional basis for our adversary system can be found in the Bill of Rights. The adoption of the Sixth Amendment guarantee of the right to counsel recognizes the importance placed on the role of lawyers in our adversarial legal system. The Fourth Amendment prohibition against unreasonable searches and seizures and the Fifth Amendment privilege against self-incrimination demonstrate that due process rights take precedence over the government's search for the truth. Although the use of these rights may result in allowing some guilty persons to go free, they help ensure the innocent are not unjustly convicted.

Critics of the adversary system argue that it places too much reliance on the quality of the lawyers handling the case. It assumes that the lawyers will use skillful examinations of witnesses and well-researched arguments about the interpretation of the law to present the strongest possible case for their clients. However, if a lawyer is poorly prepared or lacks certain key skills, justice is not necessarily done, and the client will suffer for the lawyers' inadequacies.

DISCUSSION QUESTIONS

1. Approximately 90 percent of all criminal cases scheduled for trial are instead resolved through plea bargaining. In a plea bargain, the two sides work together to reach a compromise. Does this undermine the very notion that ours is an adversarial system?

2. It is often said that the function of the adversarial system is to find the truth. How is it then that courts frequently block access to information that would assist in that search for truth? For example, courts routinely exclude evidence if the police officers used unconstitutional means to acquire it, and they do not require spouses to testify against each other.

B. REGULATION OF ATTORNEYS

Historically, state supreme courts have claimed the power to determine who can or cannot "practice law." Typically they establish specialized boards or agencies to administer bar exams, investigate the character and fitness of applicants, review complaints against attorneys, and discipline those who violate their rules of professional conduct. But while each state is responsible for establishing its own rules of professional conduct, the content of these rules generally follows model rules promulgated by the American Bar Association. In 1908 the American Bar Association adopted the first set of rules dealing directly with attorney behavior. Entitled the Canons of Ethics, this document contained suggestions for what attorneys should do. It was almost sixty years (1969) before the ABA produced a more detailed document, the **Model Code of Professional Responsibility**, that for the first time told lawyers what they must do or be in danger of being disciplined through reprimand, suspension, or loss of their license to practice law. Then came a series of incidents, including the Watergate scandal of the Nixon presidency,

Model Code of Professional Responsibility
An older set of standards governing attorney ethics developed by the American Bar Association.

NETNOTE

You can locate the ABA Model Rules of Professional Conduct at *www.abanet.org/cpr/mrpc/mrpc_toc.html.*

Model Rules of Professional Conduct
A set of ethical rules developed by the American Bar Association in the 1980s. The Model Rules have been adopted by more than half the states.

that increased the public's sensitivity to the issue of attorneys and ethics. Working quickly, it took the ABA only a little more than eleven years to produce an entirely new set of rules, the **Model Rules of Professional Conduct**. Adopted in 1983, these rules have been amended many times, most recently in 2003 as a result of an ABA initiative known as Ethics 2000.

While most states have adopted some version of the Model Rules of Professional Conduct, a few states still follow the Model Code of Professional Responsibility. Therefore, as you read this text, keep in mind that in any given state attorneys in that state may be subject to any one of the following:

1. the Model Code of Professional Responsibility;
2. the Model Rules of Professional Conduct (pre-2003 version);
3. the Model Rules of Professional Conduct (as revised in 2003); or
4. a state's individual variation on any of the above three.

With so many different approaches in existence, you may well ask how can any of these sets of rules claim to guide attorneys as to ethical behavior? One answer is that neither the Code nor the Rules are actually ethical codes based on moral values but rather are simply rules to govern attorney behavior. This possibility is even reflected in the change in their name from the Canon of *Ethics* to the Code of *Professional Responsibility* and the Rules of *Professional Conduct*. That is, these rules are not meant to offer attorneys moral guidance but rather to set forth a strict set of rules that attorneys must follow at peril of losing their license to practice law. Arguably, when they study these rules in law school, law students are not really studying a code of ethics but rather a series of rules governing behavior, violation of which could result in disbarment. Therefore, when confronted with what might be seen as an ethical dilemma, attorneys may not immediately ask "what is right?" but rather "what does the rule say I have to do?"[2] Perhaps it should not be surprising, therefore, that at least in the public's view, at times lawyers do engage in immoral behavior.

The drafters of the Model Rules had as one of their goals the creation of more definitive answers than could be found in the older Model Code. Theoretically, lawyers would be able to find specific guidance in order to avoid

---

[2]American Bar Association, Section on Tort Trial & Insurance Practice, Leonard Bucklin, Ethics in a Time of Historical Change, available at *www.edicta.org/NeoethicsBucklin/Neoethics04 history.htm* (last visited July 10, 2004).

disciplinary sanctions. However, as we will see later, the Model Rules are often ambiguous and offer less than complete instructions on how to behave in difficult situations. Even on their own terms, the Model Rules cannot be seen simply as a set of proscriptions. Rule 2.1 provides that in "rendering advice, a lawyer may refer not only to law but to other considerations such as moral, economic, social and political factors, that may be relevant to the client's situation." Even more telling is this statement from Comment 7 of the Preamble: "Many of a lawyer's professional responsibilities are prescribed in the Rules. . . . However, a lawyer is also guided by personal conscience and the approbation of professional peers."

For an attorney mired in an ethical dilemma, this acknowledgment—that at times attorneys may have to look to their own consciences rather than at the exact rules—does not provide much assistance. Also, it appears that the very purpose of a set of rules—to make it easy for attorneys to know the right thing to do—is completely undercut if there is a general acknowledgment that the rules will not provide for an efficacious result in many situations. We will see this tension between following the rules versus doing "the right thing" throughout our discussions in this chapter.

In sum, probably it should not surprise us that following any set of rules will not always provide attorneys with the best answer in any individual situation. After all, rules are simply society's best guess as to what is the most appropriate behavior most of the time. Because by its nature a set of rules is designed to apply to the usual situation, the rules cannot provide answers for the unusual. For the unusual, attorneys are thrown back onto their individual senses of morality, having to make individual choices in situations where the rule no longer "works." In the next section, we will explore some of these difficult situations in the context of the rules regarding attorney-client confidentiality and conflict of interest. Later in the chapter, we will discuss the impact these regulations have on the availability of legal services.

DISCUSSION QUESTIONS

3. On a basic level, do you think attorneys have to face ethical dilemmas that are fundamentally different from those faced by other professionals, such as physicians or accountants?

4. In the popular media, attorneys are often referred to as "hired guns." We have also all heard the lawyer jokes: "How do you know when a lawyer is lying? His lips are moving." Why do you think there is this negative perception of lawyers and what they do? Do you think it is a fair characterization?

5. What do you think of the statement "At times following the rules may not lead to the best moral response and indeed may produce an amoral or even immoral response"?

C. THE ATTORNEY-CLIENT RELATIONSHIP

The attorney-client relationship is critical to the successful operation of the adversary system of justice. To fulfill this critical role, the lawyer must be able to obtain confidential information about the client's situation and must not have any interests that might conflict with those of the client.

1. Confidentiality

Confidentiality
The ethical rule prohibiting attorneys and paralegals from disclosing information regarding a client or a client's case.

While there is little empirical data to support the claim, it is generally assumed that without the assurance of **confidentiality**, many clients would be reluctant to reveal potentially embarrassing or incriminating information to their attorneys. There is also the assumption that only if an attorney knows of a client's planned bad acts can the attorney have the opportunity to try to talk the client out of proceeding with those acts. Because of these concerns, there is a general rule prohibiting attorneys from revealing client confidences. Except in very rare situations, an attorney can never mention any aspect of a client's case to those outside the law firm. In fact, the very presence of the client in the firm must be kept confidential. This confidentiality covers any information that clients tell their attorneys as well as any information that attorneys learn from a third party, such as witnesses or an investigator. The prohibition against revealing client confidences applies to potential clients, clients, and prior clients. It even remains in effect after the client's death.[3]

Attorney-client privilege
A rule of evidence that prevents an attorney or a paralegal from being compelled to testify about confidential client information.

Confidentiality is also protected by the doctrine of "attorney-client privilege." The **attorney-client privilege** is a rule of evidence that prevents an attorney from being compelled by a court to reveal confidential information unless certain conditions are satisfied. Therefore, the rule on attorney-client privilege governs when a court can order an attorney to testify, despite the fact that otherwise the attorney would be required to keep the information confidential. It is similar to the concept of spousal privilege, which prohibits the use of a spouse's statement against the other spouse. The attorney-client privilege also protects the attorney's work product from being subpoenaed. This protected work product includes private memoranda, written statements of witnesses, and mental impressions, conclusions, or legal strategies related to litigation.

For the attorney-client privilege to apply, the client, while seeking legal advice, must speak directly to an attorney or his or her employee, with no unnecessary third parties present. This is more restrictive than the ethical rule protecting client confidences. The ethical rule applies no matter how the attorney acquired the confidential information, so long as it was during the course of the representation. The rules regarding client confidentiality have always been very broad, requiring that the attorney keep secret almost all information learned from any source during the course of representation. The evidentiary rule of attorney-client privilege is much narrower because it keeps out testimony during trials—the purpose of which is to reveal as much information as possible to the court in its search for the truth.

Figure 13-1 summarizes the differences between the attorney-client privilege and the ethical rules regarding confidentiality. As you can see from Figure 13-1, the attorney-client privilege does not cover as many situations as do the ethical rules regarding confidentiality. The ethical rules generally cover any confidence regarding the client, no matter the source. Therefore, an attorney cannot voluntarily repeat that information without the client's consent. However,

---

[3]Swidler v. U.S., 524 U.S. 399 (1998), discussing whether communications made by White House counsel Vincent Foster, Jr., and his lawyer, James Hamilton, made nine days before Foster's suicide, remained confidential. The Court determined the communications were still protected by the attorney-client privilege.

Ethical Rule Regarding Confidentiality	Attorney-Client Privilege
Under the Model Code applies to ■ confidences and secrets ■ learned from any source ■ regarding anything and ■ made anywhere *Under the Model Rules applies to* ■ information ■ relating to representation of the client	Applies to ■ a client statement ■ to an attorney or a paralegal ■ made while seeking legal advice and ■ given in confidence (no unnecessary persons present)
Result: If all the conditions are present, the attorney or paralegal may not voluntarily reveal the information (but may be compelled to testify unless statements also satisfy criteria for the attorney-client privilege).	*Result:* If any of these four conditions is missing, the attorney or paralegal can be compelled to testify.

Figure 13-1   A Comparison of the Ethical Rule Regarding Confidentiality and the Attorney-Client Privilege

a court could require the attorney to testify regarding that information unless it also meets the four-part test for satisfying the attorney-client privilege:

1. The *client* made a statement
2. to the attorney
3. while seeking legal advice and
4. no unnecessary persons were present.

Therefore, you can think of information covered by the attorney-client privilege as a subset of all confidential information. See Figure 13-2.

With this background information on client confidentiality and the attorney-client privilege, think back to the situation mentioned at the beginning of this chapter. Attorneys Belge and Armani chose not to report their knowledge of the death of Alicia Hauck or the location of her body because they believed that they would be violating the confidentiality of attorney-client communications. Did they do the right thing, or should the obligation to maintain client confidentiality take a back seat to other, more important societal needs?

More than a hundred years ago, Lord Broughham, while representing Queen Caroline in a divorce trial that threatened to end the reign of King George IV, declared:

> [A]n advocate . . . knows but one person in all the world, and that person is the client. To save that client by all means and expedients, and at all hazards and costs to other persons, and among them, to himself, is his first and only duty; *and in performing*

Figure 13-2   Attorney-Client Privilege: A Subset of Confidentiality

Confidences

Attorney-client privilege

this duty he must not regard the alarm, the torments, the destruction which he may bring upon others.[4]

On the other hand, Rule 1.6 of the Model Rules of Professional Conduct, which has been adopted in most states, specifically authorizes attorneys to reveal confidential information about their clients in specified situations, such as statements that a lawyer reasonably believes are necessary "to prevent the client from committing a criminal act that the lawyer believes is likely to result in imminent death or substantial bodily harm."

Before returning to our discussion of the situation involving attorneys Belge and Armani, we will explore this most controversial exception to the rule requiring attorneys to keep their client confidences.

a. Harm to Others Involving Death or Substantial Bodily Harm

It is important to note that this exemption from client confidentiality applies only to *future* crimes that may be committed *by the client*. Therefore, if the client reveals past criminal conduct, the attorney may not reveal it. If the client reveals he or she is planning a criminal act, the attorney may, but is not required to, reveal the planned crime. In only a few states an attorney may reveal a confidence in those situations where the criminal activity is over, but there is the potential for ongoing harm. One area of disagreement relates to the nature of the crime that would warrant revealing a client confidence. Should the exemption apply to any crime or only to a criminal act "that the lawyer believes is likely to result in *imminent death or substantial bodily harm*"?

In addition, the exemption allows for confidences to be revealed only when it is the client who is planning the criminal activity. For example, if Mrs. Smith was to tell her attorney that her husband was so upset with the course of her litigation that he was planning to kill the opposing attorney, under the ethical rules in effect in most states, Mrs. Smith's attorney could not breach that confidence. Only a few states would allow the attorney to breach the client's confidence in situations such as that involving Mrs. Smith's husband—that is, when persons other than the client plan the criminal acts, and those plans are discovered by the attorney through a conversation with the client.

As a result of the Ethics 2000 initiative, the ABA amended its Model Rules. An attorney may now reveal information to "prevent reasonably certain death or substantial bodily harm."[5] There is no longer a requirement that the actor be

---

[4] 2 Trial of Queen Caroline 83 (1879) (emphasis added).

[5] The full text of proposed Rule 1.6(b) reads:

> A lawyer may reveal information relating to the representation of a client to the extent the lawyer reasonably believes necessary:
>
> (1) to prevent reasonably certain death or substantial bodily harm;
>
> (2) to prevent the client from committing a crime or fraud that is reasonably certain to result in substantial injury to the financial interests or property of another and in furtherance of which the client has used or is using the lawyer's services;
>
> (3) to prevent, mitigate or rectify substantial injury to the financial interests or property of another that is reasonably certain to result or has resulted from the client's commission of a crime or fraud in furtherance of which the client has used the lawyer's services;
>
> (4) to secure legal advice about the lawyer's compliance with these Rules;

the client, that the harm be imminent, or that there be planned future criminal behavior. According to the comments this means that the rules recognize

> the overriding value of life and physical integrity. . . . Thus, a lawyer who knows that a client has accidentally discharged toxic waste into a town's water supply may reveal this information to the authorities if there is a present and substantial risk that a person who drinks the water will contract a life-threatening or debilitating disease and the lawyer's disclosure is necessary to eliminate the threat or reduce the number of victims.[6]

In a very few states the rules differ significantly from either version of the Model Rules. For example, in some the verb "may reveal" has been changed to "shall reveal." In those states, attorneys are given no option but instead must report their client's planned criminal activities. In others, attorneys are also allowed to reveal a confidence to prevent the incarceration or execution of an innocent person.

DISCUSSION QUESTION

6. Do you think that clients will seriously be dissuaded from revealing confidences if they know that their attorney may be allowed to reveal that information after the client's death?

b. Harm to Others Not Involving Death or Substantial Bodily Harm

With these rules in mind, let us return to the situation facing attorneys Belge and Armani. After the townspeople found out that the attorneys had kept quiet for months about the location of the girl's body, their outrage put pressure on the local district attorney to prosecute the men for their inaction. The problem was in finding a law that the attorneys had violated. Remarkably, the district attorney did not charge Belge and Armani with obstruction of justice or being accessories after the fact. Instead, the indictment was based on two little-known statutes: one that requires a decent burial be accorded the dead and the other that anyone knowing that a person died without medical attendance must report that death to the proper authorities. The grand jury indicted one of the attorneys, Francis Belge. Prior to trial, his attorney brought a motion seeking dismissal of the indictment. The following is the trial court's decision regarding whether or not the charges against attorney Belge should be dropped.

---

(5) to establish a claim or defense on behalf of the lawyer in a controversy between the lawyer and the client, to establish a defense to a criminal charge or civil claim against the lawyer based upon conduct in which the client was involved, or to respond to allegations in any proceeding concerning the lawyer's representation of the client; or

(6) to comply with other law or a court order.

[6]Model Rules of Professional Conduct, Rule 1.6, Comment 6 (2003).

New York v. Belge
County Court of New York, Onondaga County
83 Misc. 2d 186, 372 N.Y.S.2d 798 (1975)

GALE, J.

In the summer of 1973 Robert F. Garrow, Jr., stood charged in Hamilton County with the crime of murder. The defendant was assigned two attorneys, Frank H. Armani and Francis R. Belge. A defense of insanity had been interposed by counsel for Mr. Garrow. During the course of the discussions between Garrow and his two counsel, three other murders were admitted by Garrow, one being in Onondaga County. On or about September of 1973 Mr. Belge conducted his own investigation based upon what his client had told him and with the assistance of a friend the location of the body of Alicia Hauck was found in Oakwood Cemetery in Syracuse. Mr. Belge personally inspected the body and was satisfied, presumably, that this was the Alicia Hauck that his client had told him that he murdered.

This discovery was not disclosed to the authorities, but became public during the trial of Mr. Garrow in June of 1974, when to affirmatively establish the defense of insanity, these three other murders were brought before the jury by the defense in the Hamilton County trial. Public indignation reached the fever pitch. . . . [T]he District Attorney of Onondaga County . . . caused the Grand Jury of Onondaga County, then sitting, to conduct a thorough investigation. As a result of this investigation . . . Indictment No. 75-55 was returned as against Francis R. Belge, Esq., accusing him of having violated subdivision 1 of *section 4200 of the Public Health Law,* which, in essence, requires that a decent burial be accorded the dead, and *section 4143 of the Public Health Law,* which, in essence, requires anyone knowing of the death of a person without medical attendance, to report the same to the proper authorities. Defense counsel moves for a dismissal of the indictment on the grounds that a confidential, privileged communication existed between him and Mr. Garrow, which should excuse the attorney from making full disclosure to the authorities.

The National Association of Criminal Defense Lawyers, as *amicus curiae (Times Pub. Co. v Williams, 222 So. 2d 470, 475* [Fla]), succinctly state the issue in the following language: If this indictment stands, "The attorney-client privilege will be effectively destroyed. No defendant will be able to freely discuss the facts of his case with his attorney. No attorney will be able to listen to those facts without being faced with the Hobson's choice of violating the law or violating his professional code of Ethics."

Initially in England the practice of law was not recognized as a profession, and certainly some people are skeptics today. However, the practice of learned and capable men appearing before the court on behalf of a friend or an acquaintance became more and more demanding. Consequently, the King granted a privilege to certain of these men to engage in such practice. There had to be rules governing their duties. These came to be known as "Canons." The King has, in this country, been substituted by a democracy, but the "Canons" are with us today, having been honed and refined over the years to meet the changes of time. Most are constantly being studied and revamped by the American Bar Association and by the bar associations of the various States. While they are, for the most part, general by definition, they can be brought to bear in a particular situation. Among those is the following . . . : "Confidential communications between an attorney and his client are privileged from disclosure . . . as a rule of necessity in the administration of justice."

In the most recent issue of the New York State Bar Journal (June, 1975) there is an article by Jack B. Weinstein, entitled "Educating Ethical Lawyers." In a subcaption to this article is the following language which is pertinent: "The most difficult ethical dilemmas result from the frequent conflicts between the obligation to one's client and those to the legal system and to society. It is in this area that legal education has its greatest responsibility, and can have its greatest effects." In the course of his article Mr. Weinstein states that there are three major types of pressure facing a practicing lawyer. He uses the following language to describe these: "First, there are those that originate in the attorney's search for his own well-being. Second, pressures arise from the attorney's obligation to his client. Third, the lawyer has certain obligations to the courts, the legal system, and society in general."

Our system of criminal justice is an adversary system and the interests of the State are not absolute, or even paramount. "The dignity of the individual is respected to the point that even when the citizen is known by the state to have committed a heinous offense, the individual is nevertheless accorded such rights as counsel, trial by jury, due process, and the privilege against self incrimination."

A trial is in part a search for truth, but it is only partly a search for truth. The mantle of innocence is flung over the defendant to such an extent that he is safeguarded by rules of evidence which frequently keep out absolute truth, much to the chagrin of juries. Nevertheless, this has been a part of our system since our laws were taken from the laws of England and over these many years has been found to best protect a balance between the rights of the individual and the rights of society.

The concept of the right to counsel has again been with us for a long time, but . . . [t]he effectiveness of counsel is only as great as the confidentiality of its client-attorney relationship. If the lawyer cannot get all the facts about the case, he can only give his client half of a defense. This, of necessity, involves the client telling his attorney everything remotely connected with the crime.

Apparently, in the instant case, after analyzing all the evidence, and after hearing of the bizarre episodes in the life of their client, they decided that the only possibility of salvation was in a defense of insanity. For the client to disclose not only everything about this particular crime but also everything about other crimes which might have a bearing upon his defense, requires the strictest confidence in, and on the part of, the attorney. . . .

The following language [is] from the brief of the *amicus curiae* . . . : "The client's Fifth Amendment rights cannot be violated by his attorney. . . . Because the discovery of the body of Alicia Hauck would have presented 'a significant link in a chain of evidence tending to establish his guilt,' Garrow was constitutionally exempt from any statutory requirement to disclose the location of the body. And Attorney Belge, as Garrow's attorney, was not only equally exempt, but under a positive stricture precluding such disclosure. Garrow, although constitutionally privileged against a requirement of compulsory disclosure, was free to make such a revelation if he chose to do so. Attorney Belge was affirmatively required to with hold disclosure. The criminal defendant's self incrimination rights become completely nugatory if compulsory disclosure can be exacted through his attorney."

. . . In the case at bar we must weigh the importance of the general privilege of confidentiality in the performance of the defendant's duties as an attorney, against the inroads of such a privilege on the fair administration of criminal justice as well as the heart tearing that went on in the victim's family by reason of their uncertainty as to the whereabouts of Alicia Hauck. In this type situation the court must balance the rights of the individual against the rights of society as a whole. There is no question but Attorney Belge's failure to bring to the attention of the authorities the whereabouts of Alicia Hauck when he first verified it, prevented bringing Garrow to the immediate bar of justice for this particular murder. This was in a sense, obstruction of justice. This duty, I am sure, loomed large in the mind of Attorney Belge. However, against this was the Fifth Amendment right of his client, Garrow, not to incriminate himself. If the Grand Jury had returned an indictment charging Mr. Belge with obstruction of justice under a proper statute, the work of this court would have been much more difficult than it is.

There must always be a conflict between the obstruction of the administration of criminal justice and the preservation of the right against self-incrimination which permeates the mind of the attorney as the alter ego of his client. But that is not the situation before this court. We have the Fifth Amendment right, derived from the Constitution, on the one hand, as against the trivia of a pseudo-criminal statute on the other, which has seldom been brought into play. Clearly the latter is completely out of focus when placed alongside the client-attorney privilege. . . .

It is the decision of this court that Francis R. Belge conducted himself as an officer of the court with all the zeal at his command to protect the constitutional rights of his client. Both on the grounds of a privileged communication and in the interests of justice the indictment is dismissed.

CASE DISCUSSION QUESTIONS

1. What do you think the court meant when it said that a "trial is in part a search for truth, but it is only partly a search for truth"?

2. Ultimately, why did the court find that the indictment against attorney Belge should be dismissed?

3. Do you think the result would have been the same if attorney Belge had been charged with obstruction of justice?

Because New York follows the Model Code, which provides that the only time an attorney can reveal a client confidence is to prevent a crime, attorney Belge would have been violating the attorney's code of ethics if he had revealed the girl's location. After the town learned what the lawyers knew and when they knew it, one of the lawyers made the following statement: "I caused pain, I prolonged their pain. What can you say . . . How do you . . . Nothing I could say would justify it in their minds. You couldn't justify it to me."[7] Even the lawyers in the case were troubled by having to follow what they considered to be binding ethical rules. If New York adopts the newly proposed Model Rule revisions, an attorney in a situation identical to the one in which attorney Belge found himself still would not be able to act.

But however much pain attorney Belge's actions caused him and others, no life was at stake. What if a client's past actions create the possibility for future harm of a more serious nature? That is what we will discuss in the next section.

DISCUSSION QUESTIONS

7. The common justification for having such strict limits on when an attorney can reveal client confidences is because without such restrictions, clients would be afraid to give their attorneys the complete story. Do you think this is really true? Given the complexities of the legal system and hence the need for an attorney to help others through it, do you think a client would risk not getting adequate representation by not being forthcoming to the attorney?

8. What do you make of the fact that in every jurisdiction the confidentiality rules do not apply where the litigation is between a lawyer and the client and the issue is the attorney's fees?

c. Substantial Bodily Harm or Death Due to Past Actions

Some have argued that the *Belge* case does not really present a clear conflict between the attorneys' duty of maintaining client confidences and

---

[7]Zitrin & Langford, supra, at 19.

preventing harm to others because in *Belge,* the crime had already been committed and could not be undone. Nothing attorney Belge could have done would have prevented further harm except perhaps to shorten the time of the parents' not knowing of their daughter's death. But who is to say learning of her death several months later caused them any more harm than the time they spent with some hope she was still alive. A more striking conflict was presented by a case that arose in Minnesota.

> Late in the day of August 24, 1956, in Brandon, Minnesota, two cars approached each other on country roads. One car, driven by John Zimmerman, age nineteen, was traveling west; the second car, driven by Florian Ledermann, age fifteen, was heading south toward the intersection. There were no stop signs at the crossing, and sight of approaching traffic was obscured by the mature corn in the surrounding fields. The cars collided, resulting in the deaths of two young persons, one from each car, and serious injury to nine of the ten other persons involved in the accident.[8]

David Spaulding, who was twenty years old at the time and considered a minor under Minnesota law, was a passenger in a car driven by John Zimmerman. He was injured in the collision with the car driven by Florian Ledermann. Theodore Spaulding, David's father, sued on behalf of his son for the injuries David sustained. During the discovery phase of the lawsuit David was examined by his own physician as well as an orthopedic specialist, both of whom found David had suffered severe, but not life-threatening, injuries.

On the eve of settlement, the defendants' attorneys learned for the first time that David was also suffering from a life-threatening medical condition caused by the car accident. The information came from one of the defendant's doctors who had also examined David. In a report to the defendants' attorneys, the doctor wrote:

> The one feature of the case which bothers me more than any other part of the case is the fact that this boy of 20 years of age has an aneurysm, which means a dilatation of the aorta and the arch of the aorta. . . . Of course an aneurysm or dilatation of the aorta in a boy of this age is a serious matter as far as his life. This aneurysm may dilate further and it might rupture with further dilatation and this would cause his death.

---

[8]Roger C. Cramton & Lori P. Knowles, Professional Secrecy and Its Exceptions: Spaulding v. Zimmerman Revisited, 83 Minn. L. Rev. 63, 63 (Nov. 1998).

The defendants were poised to settle the case. Obviously, the doctor's report contained critical information that David and his physicians needed to have him properly treated. But if the defendants' attorneys revealed this information to the plaintiffs, they could count on seeing the projected amount of the settlement multiplied many times over. The defendants' attorneys decided not to share this information with David, David's father, or David's attorneys. Without this piece of information, the parties reached a pretrial settlement of $6,500.

Because David was a minor, the parties had to submit the settlement to the court for its approval, which it gave. Two years later, before entering the army reserve, David was given a physical examination. During that examination, his family physician for the first time discovered the aorta aneurysm that had been caused by the automobile accident and that was threatening David's life. David underwent immediate surgery that repaired the aneurysm but left David with permanent severe speech loss. Shortly thereafter David petitioned the court to set aside the settlement so that he could recover additional compensation. The trial court set aside the settlement, and the defendants appealed. In the following case the supreme court of Minnesota discussed whether the settlement should have been set aside. After the court's decision in this case, David entered into a new settlement with the defendants for a larger but undisclosed amount.

Spaulding v. Zimmerman
263 Minn. 346, 116 N.W.2d 704 (1962)

GALLAGHER, J.

... On appeal defendants contend that the court was without jurisdiction to vacate the settlement ... because (1) no mutual mistake of fact was involved; [and] (2) no duty rested upon them to disclose information to plaintiff which they could assume had been disclosed to him by his own physicians. ...

The case was called for trial on March 4, 1957. ... On the following day an agreement for settlement was reached wherein, in consideration of the payment of $6,500, David and his father agreed to settle in full for all claims arising out of the accident. ... Richard S. Roberts, counsel for David, thereafter presented to the court a petition for approval of the settlement. ... Attached to the petition were affidavits of David's physicians, Drs. James H. Cain and Paul S. Blake. ... At no time was there information disclosed to the court that David was then suffering from an aorta aneurysm which may have been the result of the accident. Based upon the petition for settlement and such affidavits of Drs. Cain and Blake, the court on May 8, 1957, made its order approving the settlement.

Early in 1959, David was required by the army reserve, of which he was a member, to have a physical checkup. For this, he again engaged the services of Dr. Cain. In this checkup, the latter discovered the aorta aneurysm. He then reexamined the X rays which had been taken shortly after the accident and at this time discovered that they disclosed the beginning of the process which produced the aneurysm. He promptly sent David to Dr. Jerome Grismer for an examination and opinion. The latter confirmed the finding of the aorta aneurysm and recommended immediate surgery therefor. This was performed by him at Mount Sinai Hospital in Minneapolis on March 10, 1959.

Shortly thereafter, David, having attained his majority, instituted the present action for additional damages due to the more serious injuries including the aorta aneurysm which he alleges proximately resulted from the accident. As indicated above, the prior order for settlement was vacated. In a memorandum made a part of the order vacating the settlement, the court stated: ...

"The mistake concerning the existence of the aneurysm was not mutual. For reasons which do not appear, plaintiff's doctor failed to ascertain its existence. By reason of the failure of plaintiff's counsel to use available rules of discovery, plaintiff's doctor and all his representatives did not learn that defendants and their agents knew of its existence and possible serious consequences. Except for the character of the concealment in the light of plaintiff's minority, the Court would, I believe, be justified in denying plaintiff's motion to vacate, leaving him to whatever questionable remedy he may have against his doctor and against his lawyer.

"That defendants' counsel concealed the knowledge they had is not disputed. . . . There is no doubt of the good faith of both defendants' counsel. There is no doubt that during the course of the negotiations, when the parties were in an adversary relationship, no rule required or duty rested upon defendants or their representatives to disclose this knowledge. However, once the agreement to settle was reached, it is difficult to characterize the parties' relationship as adverse. At this point all parties were interested in securing Court approval. . . .

"When the adversary nature of the negotiations concluded in a settlement, the procedure took on the posture of a joint application to the Court, at least so far as the facts upon which the Court could and must approve settlement is [sic] concerned. It is here that the true nature of the concealment appears, and defendants' failure to act affirmatively, after having been given a copy of the application for approval, can only be defendants' decision to take a calculated risk that the settlement would be final. . . .

"To hold that the concealment was not of such character as to result in an unconscionable advantage over plaintiff's ignorance or mistake, would be to penalize innocence and incompetence and reward less than full performance of an officer of the Court's duty to make full disclosure to the Court when applying for approval in minor settlement proceedings." . . .

2. From the foregoing it is clear that in the instant case the court did not abuse its discretion in setting aside the settlement which it had approved on plaintiff's behalf while he was still a minor. It is undisputed that neither he nor his counsel nor his medical attendants were aware that at the time settlement was made he was suffering from an aorta aneurysm which may have resulted from the accident. The seriousness of this disability is indicated by Dr. Hannah's report indicating the imminent danger of death therefrom. This was known by counsel for both defendants but was not disclosed to the court at the time it was petitioned to approve the settlement. While no canon of ethics or legal obligation may have required them to inform plaintiff or his counsel with respect thereto, or to advise the court therein, it did become obvious to them at the time that the settlement then made did not contemplate or take into consideration the disability described. This fact opened the way for the court to later exercise its discretion in vacating the settlement. . . .

Affirmed.

CASE DISCUSSION QUESTIONS

1. Why did the Minnesota Supreme Court agree that the trial court could set aside the settlement? Do you think the result would have been the same if the settlement had involved an adult plaintiff rather than a child? Should it matter?

2. Did the court view the attorney's decision not to reveal the extent of David's injury as a violation of an ethical obligation or rather as a strategic move that in this case simply did not work out?

3. Do you think the court should have tackled head on the ethical and moral issues involved in choosing to keep a client's confidence over saving a child's life?

4. David Spaulding was represented by a young, inexperienced attorney. Perhaps the attorney was not aware that he was entitled to ask for a copy of the

defendant doctor's examination. Or perhaps he just thought it would duplicate the information his own doctors had found. Or perhaps in the rush to settle the case, he simply forgot to ask for a copy. No matter the answer, should the system develop better protections for clients against the inexperience or incompetence of their attorneys?

5. It appears in this case that the defendants' attorneys never even consulted with the defendants about what they wanted to do but rather just assumed they would not want the information revealed. Should the attorneys have made such an assumption?

6. Assuming the attorneys had discussed with their clients the decision regarding whether to reveal this information, and the clients had said they did not wish to have the information revealed, what options would the attorneys have had?

7. Consider whether you think your answer to number 6 would change under the newly revised Model Rules. Do you think the defense attorney would have an ethical obligation to reveal the injury? Would you change your answer if David had been suffering from an inoperable tumor rather than a correctable, but life-threatening condition?

d. Revelation of a Client's Plan to Cause Substantial Bodily Harm or Death

In both the *Belge* and *Spaulding* cases, neither the Model Code nor the Model Rules, prior to the 2003 revision, would permit disclosure of the confidential information. When, however, a client directly tells his attorney that he is planning on killing someone or causing substantial bodily harm, both the Model Code and the Model Rules would allow but not mandate that the attorney reveal this information. Assuming for the moment that the attorney does tell the police of a client's plans and thereby saves a life, can that information then be used in court against the client? If the answer is yes, would knowledge of such potential use of the information further discourage attorneys from revealing the information?

Specifically, in situations where attorneys may reveal a confidence without breaking the code of ethics, what impact does that have on the attorney-client privilege? If an attorney makes the decision to reveal a client's plan to harm another person, can that information be used against the client later in court? If so, it seems that very few attorneys would be willing to reveal a confidence, even to save a life.

In a case from Massachusetts, the Supreme Judicial Court discussed the intersection between the ethical rules of client confidentiality and the evidentiary rule of attorney-client privilege. In that case,[9] Joseph Tyree met with attorney Purcell, a legal services attorney. Mr. Tyree was seeking advice about being evicted. He was about to lose his apartment because he had been fired as the maintenance man for his apartment complex. In the course of the conversation, the client told the attorney he planned to burn down the building. After thinking long and hard, the attorney reported this information to the police. When they investigated, they found gas cans and fuses in Tyree's apartment. Also all of the fire detectors had been disabled. At Tyree's trial for arson, the prosecution

---

[9]Purcell v. District Attorney for the Suffolk District, 676 N.E.2d 436 (Mass. 1997).

called attorney Purcell to testify. Purcell invoked the attorney-client privilege, and the judge agreed he did not have to testify. The jury was unable to reach a verdict, and the judge was forced to call a mistrial. At the second trial, a different judge ordered Purcell to testify, and when he refused, the judge determined Purcell was not protected by the attorney-client privilege and held him in contempt for refusing to testify. Purcell appealed to the Massachusetts Supreme Judicial Court, the highest appellate court in Massachusetts. That court determined that he should not have to testify, concluding "lawyers will be reluctant to come forward if they know that the information that they disclose may lead to adverse consequences to their clients."[10]

Three years later, the Ohio Supreme Court was confronted with a similar case. Attorney Helmick was representing a defendant in a capital murder trial. While he was preparing for trial, one of his investigators gave him a letter written by his client that the investigator had gotten from the client's mother. The letter contained death threats. After consulting with the state ethics committee, attorney Helmick revealed the contents of the letter to the police and then filed a motion to withdraw as defense counsel. The district attorney served attorney Helmick with a subpoena ordering him to produce the letter in his former client's murder trial. Helmick refused, and he was found in contempt of court. In the following case, the Supreme Court of Ohio discusses whether attorney Helmick can be required to turn over the letter to the prosecution.

In re Original Grand Jury Investigation
89 Ohio St. 3d 544, 2000 Ohio 170, 733 N.E.2d 1135 (2000)

SWEENEY, SR., J. The issue presented in this case is whether an attorney can be compelled to disclose to the grand jury a letter written by a client and discovered by an investigator that contains evidence of a possible crime or whether the Ohio Code of Professional Responsibility prohibits such disclosure. . . .

DR 4-101(B) states, "Except when permitted under DR 4-101(C), a lawyer shall not knowingly . . . reveal a confidence or secret of a client."

We must first determine whether the letter sought falls within the definition of a client "secret." Unlike "confidence," which is limited to information an attorney obtains directly from his or her client, the term "secret" is defined in broad terms. Therefore, a client secret includes information obtained from third-party sources, including

"information obtained by a lawyer from witnesses, by personal investigation, or by an investigation of an agent of the lawyer, disclosure of which would be embarrassing or harmful to the client." . . .

[W]e find that the letter falls within the definition of a client "secret," since it was obtained in the professional attorney-client relationship, by appellant's agent (the investigator), and since it contains detrimental information detailing a possible crime committed by appellant's former client.

Although the letter is a client secret, this does not necessarily mean that disclosure of the letter is absolutely prohibited. An attorney may disclose a client secret if one of the four listed exceptions in DR 4-101(C) applies.

Appellant concedes that DR 4-101(C)(3) permits him to "reveal . . . the intention of his

[10]Id. at 440.

client to commit a crime and the information necessary to prevent the crime." . . .

We agree with appellant that he was authorized by DR 4-101(C)(3) when he chose to reveal the intent of his client to commit a crime. . . . However, the fact that he revealed this information does not answer the question whether he is obligated to produce the letter itself. Thus, the question that remains is whether appellant is required to relinquish the letter itself and present it to the grand jury. We find that the exception found in DR 4-102(C)(2) governs disposition of this issue.

DR 4-101(C)(2) provides that an attorney may reveal "confidences or secrets when permitted under Disciplinary Rules or required by law or court order." . . .

The exception of DR 4-101(C)(2) for disclosures required by law has been applied in the context of mandating that attorneys relinquish evidence and instrumentalities of crime to law-enforcement agencies. Thus, the rule has emerged that, despite any confidentiality concerns, a criminal defense attorney must produce real evidence obtained from his or her client or from a third-party source. . . . *State v. Green (La.1986), 493 So. 2d 1178* (holding that the attorney had an obligation to relinquish client's gun, an instrumentality of a crime, to authorities). In essence, the confidentiality rules do not give an attorney the right to withhold evidence.

Appellant contends, however, that there are strong policy reasons against mandating disclosure. Appellant believes that mandatory disclosure will discourage attorneys from reporting possible threats made by their clients and will therefore run contrary to the intent of the code, which is to prevent crimes from occurring. Appellant cites the Massachusetts decision of *Purcell v. Dist. Atty. for Suffolk Dist. (1997), 424 Mass. 109, 676 N.E.2d 436*, which highlights these concerns.

In *Purcell*, an attorney informed police about his client's intention to commit arson. The trial court ordered the attorney to testify about the conversation he had with his client concerning his client's intention to commit this crime, and the state defended the order on the basis of the crime-fraud exception to the attorney-client privilege.

The Massachusetts Supreme Court vacated the trial court's order and held that the attorney did not have to testify against his client. In so holding, the court noted:

"We must be cautious in permitting the use of client communications that a lawyer has revealed only because of a threat to others. Lawyers will be reluctant to come forward if they know that the information that they disclose may lead to adverse consequences to their clients. A practice of the use of such disclosures might prompt a lawyer to warn a client in advance that the disclosure of certain information may not be held in confidence, thereby chilling free discourse between lawyer and client and reducing the prospect that the lawyer will learn of a serious threat to the well-being of others."

Although these may be valid concerns, we find that the *Purcell* decision is distinguishable from the instant case, and that the policy reasons cited in *Purcell* have less validity here. *Purcell* involved direct communications between an attorney and client. The issue in that case was whether the attorney was required to testify against his client. In this case, the attorney-client privilege is not at issue. Nor is appellant being asked to testify against his former client. Instead, the instant case revolves around whether a physical piece of evidence must be relinquished to the grand jury. While we recognize the importance of maintaining a client's confidences and secrets and understand that an attorney may have concerns in turning over incriminating evidence against his or her client, we do not believe that these concerns should override the public interest in maintaining public safety and promoting the administration of justice by prosecuting individuals for their alleged criminal activity.

Since the letter sought in this case contains evidence of a possible crime, we find that the letter must be turned over to the grand jury. Accordingly, we hold that where an attorney receives physical evidence from a third party relating to a possible crime committed by his or her client, the attorney is obligated to relinquish that evidence to law-enforcement authorities and must comply with a subpoena issued to that effect. . . .

Judgment affirmed.

CASE DISCUSSION QUESTIONS

1. On what basis did the court decide that the attorney should turn over the client's letter?

2. The dissent argued that the reasoning in *Purcell* should have been followed and that the court's failure to do so will mean "attorneys and their clients will be less likely to discuss potential crimes, which will decrease the likelihood that the crimes can be prevented."[11] Do you agree? Why or why not?

Arguably, under the current rules governing attorney-client privilege, the information the Ohio attorney received was not privileged, and he could be forced to testify. After all, he did not receive the letter directly from his client. But should that be the rule? Should the outcome turn on from whom the attorney got the information—the investigator or directly from the client—or simply on whether the information was discovered as part of the attorney's representation? So long as the ethical rule regarding revealing confidences is discretionary, would it not better serve the interests of society (and certainly the victim) if the rule was that any confidences revealed would not lead to admissible evidence against the accused?

e. Responding to Client Perjury

One of the most difficult ethical challenges attorneys face involves balancing a client's confidentiality interests against the attorney's responsibility to be truthful to the court. While attorneys must act as the zealous advocates of their clients, they also owe a duty of candor toward the court. Rule 3.3(a)(4) of the Model Rules states, "A lawyer shall not knowingly offer evidence that the lawyer *knows* to be false. If a lawyer has offered material evidence and comes to know of its falsity, the lawyer shall take reasonable remedial measures." However, Rule 3.3(c) states, "A lawyer may refuse to offer evidence that the lawyer *reasonably believes* is false.

Note that the rule makes a distinction between testimony the attorney "knows" will be false and testimony the attorney "reasonably believes" will be false. If the attorney knows the testimony will be false, he cannot present it, and if it has already been given, he must take reasonable remedial measures. If, however, the attorney simply believes it is or will be false, it is at the discretion of the attorney whether or not to present the evidence.[12]

There is often ambiguity over what is or is not truthful testimony. Was President Clinton testifying falsely when he said he and Monica Lewinsky were never alone? There were always other persons present somewhere in the White House even if no one else was present in the same room as they were. The problem is that people may give different definitions to the same word. By giving uncommon definitions to common words, the statements may be technically true but misleading.

---

[11]733 N.E.2d at 1141.

[12]Under the revised Rules this has been modified to read, "A lawyer may refuse to offer evidence, *other than the testimony of a defendant in a criminal matter,* that the lawyer reasonably believes is false." (Emphasis added.)

Consider the following exchange that occurred during a bankruptcy hearing. The questioner was trying to determine if Mr. Bronston in the past or currently had any personal accounts in Swiss banks.

Q. Do you have any bank accounts in Swiss banks, Mr. Bronston?
A. No, sir.
Q. Have you ever?
A. The company had an account there for about six months, in Zurich.

Mr. Bronston's last answer, while truthful, was incomplete. For five years he had a Swiss bank account. He was charged with perjury based on the "theory that in order to mislead his questioner, [he] answered the second question with literal truthfulness but unresponsively addressed his answer to the company's assets and not to his own—thereby implying that he had no personal Swiss bank account at the relevant time."[13] The court reversed his conviction, finding that he could not be found guilty of perjury for giving a nonresponsive answer. The court distinguished this from the situation where a witness has visited a store fifty times in a given day and when asked how many times she entered the store, replied "five." While technically true (she did enter five times, and ten times, etc.), such a responsive answer would do nothing to alert the questioner to probe further.

In our adversarial system, cross-examination is supposed to be used to ferret out the truth if a witness is evasive or misleading. That is not possible, however, when the answer is given in such a way, as in the example of the answer of having entered five times, that the questioner will not be alerted that only a partial answer has been given.

Assuming, however, that the attorney "knows" that the statements a witness plans to make will be "false," the rules clearly state that the attorney must refuse to offer the testimony. When that witness is a criminal defendant, the defense attorney is faced with what Monroe Freedman termed "the defense lawyer's trilema."[14] A lawyer in this situation must balance three separate and sometimes conflicting responsibilities:

- To best represent the client's interests, the lawyer must discover all relevant facts about the case.
- The lawyer must keep in strictest confidence all disclosures made by the client in the course of their professional relationship.
- As an "officer of the court," the lawyer must not knowingly present false evidence.

The ideal ethical solution is for the lawyer to talk the client out of presenting perjured testimony. The attorney can point out the dangers of lying: the potential of being charged with the additional crime of perjury and the consequences if the defendant's statement is proved to be false in court. But what if the client insists on going ahead with the perjured testimony? Can the attorney threaten to withdraw from the case without violating the client's Sixth Amendment right to assistance of counsel? The U.S. Supreme Court addressed this issue in *Nix v. Whiteside*.

---

[13]Bronston v. United States, 409 U.S. 352, 355 (1973).

[14]*See* Monroe Freedman, Lawyers' Ethics in an Adversary System (Bobbs-Merrill Company 1975).

Nix v. Whiteside
475 U.S. 157 (1986)

BURGER, J.

We granted certiorari to decide whether the Sixth Amendment right of a criminal defendant to assistance of counsel is violated when an attorney refuses to cooperate with the defendant in presenting perjured testimony at his trial.

Whiteside and two others went to one Calvin Love's apartment late [at] night, seeking marihuana. Love was in bed when Whiteside and his companions arrived; an argument between Whiteside and Love over the marihuana ensued. At one point, Love directed his girlfriend to get his "piece," and at another point got up, then returned to his bed. According to Whiteside's testimony, Love then started to reach under his pillow and moved toward Whiteside. Whiteside stabbed Love in the chest, inflicting a fatal wound.

Whiteside was charged with murder, and when counsel was appointed he objected to the lawyer initially appointed, claiming that he felt uncomfortable with a lawyer who had formerly been a prosecutor. Gary L. Robinson was then appointed and immediately began an investigation. Whiteside gave him a statement that he had stabbed Love as the latter "was pulling a pistol from underneath the pillow on the bed." Upon questioning by Robinson, however, Whiteside indicated that he had not actually seen a gun, but that he was convinced that Love had a gun. No pistol was found on the premises; shortly after the police search following the stabbing, which had revealed no weapon, the victim's family had removed all of the victim's possessions from the apartment. Robinson interviewed Whiteside's companions who were present during the stabbing, and none had seen a gun during the incident. Robinson advised Whiteside that the existence of a gun was not necessary to establish the claim of self-defense, and that only a reasonable belief that the victim had a gun nearby was necessary even though no gun was actually present.

Until shortly before trial, Whiteside consistently stated to Robinson that he had not actually seen a gun, but that he was convinced that Love had a gun in his hand. About a week before trial, during preparation for direct examination, Whiteside for the first time told Robinson and his associate Donna Paulsen that he had seen something "metallic" in Love's hand. When asked about this, Whiteside responded:

> [In] Howard Cook's case there was a gun. If I don't say I saw a gun, I'm dead.

Robinson told Whiteside that such testimony would be perjury and repeated that it was not necessary to prove that a gun was available but only that Whiteside reasonably believed that he was in danger. On Whiteside's insisting that he would testify that he saw "something metallic" Robinson told him, according to Robinson's testimony:

> [We] could not allow him to [testify falsely] because that would be perjury, and as officers of the court we would be suborning perjury if we allowed him to do it; . . . I advised him that if he did do that it would be my duty to advise the Court of what he was doing and that I felt he was committing perjury. . . .

Robinson also indicated he would seek to withdraw from the representation if Whiteside insisted on committing perjury.

Whiteside testified in his own defense at trial and stated that he "knew" that Love had a gun and that he believed Love was reaching for a gun and he had acted swiftly in self-defense. On cross-examination, he admitted that he had not actually seen a gun in Love's hand. Robinson presented evidence that Love had been seen with a sawed-off shotgun on other occasions, that the police search of the apartment may have been careless, and that the victim's family had removed everything from the apartment shortly after the crime. Robinson presented this evidence to show a basis for Whiteside's asserted fear that Love had a gun.

The jury returned a verdict of second-degree murder. . . .

[W]e [have] recognized counsel's duty of loyalty and his "overarching duty to advocate the defendant's cause." Plainly, that duty is limited to legitimate, lawful conduct compatible with the very nature of a trial as a search for truth. Although counsel must take all reasonable lawful means to attain the objectives of the client, counsel is precluded from taking steps or in any way assisting the client in presenting false evidence or otherwise violating the law. . . .

It is universally agreed that at a minimum the attorney's first duty when confronted with a proposal for perjurious testimony is to attempt to dissuade the client from the unlawful course of conduct. A statement directly in point is found in the commentary to the Model Rules of Professional Conduct under the heading "False Evidence":

"When false evidence is offered by the client, however, a conflict may arise between the lawyer's duty to keep the client's revelations confidential and the duty of candor to the court. Upon ascertaining that material evidence is false, the lawyer *should seek to persuade the client that the evidence should not be offered* or, if it has been offered, that its false character should immediately be disclosed." Model Rules of Professional Conduct, Rule 3.3, Comment (1983) (emphasis added).

The commentary thus also suggests that an attorney's revelation of his client's perjury to the court is a professionally responsible and acceptable response to the conduct of a client who has actually given perjured testimony. Similarly, the Model Rules . . . expressly permit withdrawal from representation as an appropriate response of an attorney when the client threatens to commit perjury. . . . The essence of the brief *amicus* of the American Bar Association reviewing practices long accepted by ethical lawyers is that under no circumstance may a lawyer either advocate or passively tolerate a client's giving false testimony. This, of course, is consistent with the governance of trial conduct in what we have long called "a search for truth." The suggestion sometimes made that "a lawyer must believe his client, not judge him" in no sense means a lawyer can honorably be a party to or in any way give aid to presenting known perjury.

Considering Robinson's representation of respondent in light of these accepted norms of professional conduct, we discern no failure to adhere to reasonable professional standards that would in any sense make out a deprivation of the Sixth Amendment right to counsel. Whether Robinson's conduct is seen as a successful attempt to dissuade his client from committing the crime of perjury, or whether seen as a "threat" to withdraw from representation and disclose the illegal scheme, Robinson's representation of Whiteside falls well within accepted standards of professional conduct. . . .

Nothing counsel did in any way undermined Whiteside's claim that he believed the victim was reaching for a gun. . . . We see this as a case in which the attorney successfully dissuaded the client from committing the crime of perjury. . . .

Robinson's admonitions to his client can in no sense be said to have forced respondent into an *impermissible* choice between his right to counsel and his right to testify as he proposed for there was no *permissible* choice to testify falsely. For defense counsel to take steps to persuade a criminal defendant to testify truthfully, or to withdraw, deprives the defendant of neither his right to counsel nor the right to testify truthfully. In *United States v. Havens,* we made clear that "when defendants testify, they must testify truthfully or suffer the consequences." When an accused proposes to resort to perjury or to produce false evidence, one consequence is the risk of withdrawal of counsel.

. . . An attorney's duty of confidentiality, which totally covers the client's admission of guilt, does not extend to a client's announced plans to engage in future criminal conduct. In short, the responsibility of an ethical lawyer, as an officer of the court and a key component of a system of justice, dedicated to a search for truth, is essentially the same whether the client announces an intention to bribe or threaten witnesses or jurors or to commit or procure perjury. No system of justice worthy of the name can tolerate a lesser standard. . . .

[Authors' Note: The Court affirmed the District Court's denial of a habeas corpus petition, meaning that the defendant had no valid grounds for contesting his conviction.]

STEVENS, J., concurring in the judgment.

Justice Holmes taught us that a word is but the skin of a living thought. A "fact" may also have a life of its own. From the perspective of an appellate judge, after a case has been tried and the evidence has been sifted by another judge, a particular fact may be as clear and certain as a piece of crystal or a small diamond. A trial lawyer, however, must often deal with mixtures of sand and clay. Even a pebble that seems clear enough at first glance may take on a different hue in a handful of gravel.

As we view this case, it appears perfectly clear that respondent intended to commit perjury, that his lawyer knew it, and that the lawyer had a duty—both to the court and to his client, for perjured testimony can ruin an otherwise meritorious case—to take extreme measures to prevent the perjury from occurring. The lawyer was successful and, from our unanimous and remote perspective, it is now pellucidly clear that the client suffered no "legally cognizable prejudice."

Nevertheless, beneath the surface of this case there are areas of uncertainty that cannot be resolved today. A lawyer's certainty that a change in his client's recollection is a harbinger of intended perjury . . . should be tempered by the realization that, after reflection, the most honest witness may recall (or sincerely believe he recalls) details that he previously overlooked. . . . Thus, one can be convinced—as I am—that this lawyer's actions were a proper way to provide his client with effective representation without confronting the much more difficult questions of what a lawyer must, should, or may do after his client has given testimony that the lawyer does not believe. . . .

CASE DISCUSSION QUESTIONS

1. The court assumes, without really discussing, that Robinson "knew" Whiteside was going to commit perjury. Given the nature of memory and how a person's recollections can change over time, is it fair to say that Robinson "knew" that Whiteside was lying when he said he had seen something metallic?

2. What guidance does this case provide for other attorneys confronted with a client who recalls events one way shortly after first meeting with the attorney and then differently right before trial?

3. Why did Justice Stevens concur?

Because the absolute prohibition against offering testimony only applies when the attorney *knows* the client is lying, several commentators have suggested that attorneys often work very hard to "not know." The classic literary presentation of this approach occurred in Robert Traver's *Anatomy of a Murder* in the famous scene where the defense attorney meets with a client who has been arrested for murder. The attorney first describes the elements of an insanity defense and then asks for the client's version of the events.

While some lawyers may indeed coach their clients or tell them that they do not want to know "if they did it," these lawyers are not fulfilling their duty to know all the facts and as a result they may fail to provide the most effective defense. For example, while a client charged with murder may indeed have "done it" by stabbing the victim to death, telling all of the facts may reveal information that could lead to a valid self-defense argument.

In situations in which a lawyer is concerned about a client's committing perjury, some state courts allow the attorney to call the client to testify in a narrative fashion. Rather than having the client respond to specific questions posed by the attorney, the attorney simply asks the client to give an account of what happened. While the attorney cannot ask any follow-up questions, the prosecuting attorney conducts a regular cross-examination. Additionally, the defense attorney may not refer to the client's false testimony during closing argument. The obvious problem with this procedure is that it signals the judge and the opposing attorney, and possibly the jury, that the client is lying.

Another option is for the lawyer to withdraw from the case when the client insists on going ahead with perjured testimony. While the Court in *Nix v. Whiteside* decided that there is no Sixth Amendment claim of ineffective assistance of counsel when an attorney threatens to withdraw from the case and expose the perjury if the client lies on the stand, the Court did not decide whether such a withdrawal violates the lawyer's ethical duty not to reveal confidential information or whether a refusal to call the defendant to the stand violates the client's due process right to testify in his or her own behalf. Furthermore, lawyers are usually not allowed to withdraw from a case without giving the judge a good reason for doing so. But the lawyer cannot tell the judge the reasons for withdrawing without revealing confidential information about the client.

In summary, the issue of client perjury presents many difficult issues for the advocate. As one court has stated:

> The problem of representing a defendant who insists on testifying falsely has been called, correctly, one of the hardest questions a criminal defense lawyer faces. The attorney is faced simultaneously with a duty to represent [the] client effectively, a duty to protect [the] client's right to testify, a duty not to disclose the confidential communications of [the] client, a duty to reveal fraud on the court, and a duty not to knowingly use perjured testimony. . . . Experienced and conscientious people can come to different conclusions about the best way to deal with the conflict.[15]

DISCUSSION QUESTIONS

9. Under the Model Rules an attorney has an obligation not to present false evidence, but there is no affirmative obligation to reveal truthful material *facts* unless asked to do so by the other side. However, attorneys are under an obligation to disclose to the court *legal authority* in the controlling jurisdiction that is directly adverse to their clients' position if it has not already been disclosed by the opposing counsel. While there can be arguments as to why the obligation only runs to law from the "controlling jurisdiction" (the state or federal district in which the case is being tried) and what it means for the law to be "directly" adverse, this raises an even more fundamental question: If the goal of a trial is the search for truth, why is there an affirmative obligation to reveal law but not facts?

10. Former Supreme Court Justice Byron White said that if a defense attorney "can confuse a witness, even a truthful one, or make him appear at a disadvantage, unsure or indecisive, that will be his normal course." But is it ethical for an attorney to impeach the credibility of a witness when the attorney knows that the testimony given was in fact truthful? In essence, how is that different from putting on the stand a client the attorney knows is going to lie?

f. Inadvertent Disclosure of Confidential Information

Under our adversarial system, attorneys are expected to serve as zealous advocates for their clients. However, there may be times when zealous advocacy should give way to other interests, such as professionalism, respect for the

---

[15]Maddox v. State, 613 S.W.2d 275, 280 (Tex. Crim. App. 1980).

courts, and respect for innocent bystanders. We have already discussed the requirement that lawyers not use false evidence to help win their cases. An additional limitation on zealous representation involves the decision regarding what to do with confidential information that the other side has inadvertently disclosed.

Consider the following fact scenario. You are an attorney working on a major case. Things are not going so well. Imagine your surprise and delight when in opening the day's mail you find the proverbial smoking gun: the one piece of evidence that seals your opponent's fate and guarantees victory for your side. Unfortunately, the piece of paper that contains this information is a letter from the opposing attorney to her client. Apparently, this letter was accidentally mixed in with a group of other documents that you had legitimately received through a document request. Should you try to forget what the letter said, notify the opposing attorney you have the letter, and then return or destroy it at the opposing attorney's direction? Or should you remind yourself that you are a zealous advocate, that your first duty is to your client, keep the fact that you have it secret, and then use the information to win your case?

The receipt of such misdirected confidential information raises this fundamental question. In an adversarial system, just how adversarial do the adversaries have to be? Is there a place for cooperation and even assistance when one adversary makes a mistake?

When an adversary fails to make a crucial motion or ask the right questions on cross-examination, it is not incumbent on the other attorney to point out or even correct the mistake. However, in the area of inadvertent disclosure of confidential information, ethics committees and courts seem to be moving in the direction of saying an attorney should "help out the opponent" when that opponent makes a mistake, even though that assistance interferes with the attorney's loyalty to the client. As first fax and now e-mail have become major modes of communication, the danger of misdialing a fax number or hitting "reply all" rather than "reply" to an e-mail are obvious. But are these errors fundamentally different from other mistakes that attorneys make? The leading ethics opinion on this issue was issued by the ABA in 1992.

American Bar Association Standing Committee on Ethics and Professional Responsibility Formal Opinion 92-368

The Committee has been asked to opine on the obligations under the Model Rules of Professional Conduct of a lawyer who comes into possession of materials that appear on their face to be subject to the attorney-client privilege or otherwise confidential, under circumstances where it is clear that the materials were not intended for the receiving lawyer. . . . This opinion is intended to answer a question which has become increasingly important as the burgeoning of multi-party cases, the availability of xerography and the proliferation of facsimile machines and electronic mail make it technologically ever more likely that through inadvertence, privileged or confidential materials will be produced to opposing counsel by no more than the pushing of the wrong speed dial number on a facsimile machine.

A satisfactory answer to the question posed cannot be drawn from a narrow, literalistic reading of the black letter of the Model Rules. But it is useful, and necessary, to bear in mind the thoughts in the Preamble to the Model Rules that "many difficult issues of professional discretion . . . must be resolved through the exercise of sensitive professional and moral judgment guided by the basic principles underlying the Rules," and that "the Rules do not exhaust the moral and ethical considerations that should inform a lawyer, for no worthwhile human activity can be completely defined by legal rules." . . .

[I]t is the view of the Committee that the receiving lawyer, as a matter of ethical conduct contemplated by the precepts underlying the Model Rules, (a) should not examine the materials once the inadvertence is discovered, (b) should notify the sending lawyer of their receipt and (c) should abide by the sending lawyer's instructions as to their disposition. . . .

The concept of confidentiality is a fundamental aspect of the right to the effective assistance of counsel. As reflected in each iteration of the rules of professional responsibility, the obligation of the lawyer to maintain and to refuse to divulge client confidences is virtually absolute.

The confidentiality principle rests on the vital importance society places upon the "full, free and frank" exchange between lawyer and client, shielded from the intrusive eyes and ears of adverse parties, the government, the media and the public. The principle's primary basis is that, absent the guarantee of confidentiality, critical discussions will be either proscribed, circumscribed or intruded upon in a way that will impact directly on the ability of the lawyer to serve his or her client. If the lawyer cannot gather all the necessary information and is not free to explore with the client the client's options, free from the threat that these confidential communications will be shared with those whose interests may be adverse to the client, the chilling effect on the lawyer-client relationship becomes plain. . . .

A. Competing Principles

. . . First, it might be argued that keeping the confidential materials and not letting the sending lawyer know they were received will punish carelessness on the part of the sending lawyer and those with whom that lawyer works. However, loss of confidentiality is a very high penalty to pay for a mere slip, particularly when the person or entity paying the "price" is not the individual lawyer responsible for the inadvertent conduct, but rather the client who presumably had nothing to do with the mis-sending of the materials.

Second, it could be asserted that letting the receiving lawyer keep the confidential materials in this situation will encourage more careful conduct on the part of other counsel in the future. Once the catastrophic consequences of a misstep are recognized, lawyers and their clients will conform their future conduct to avoid such an unfortunate result. . . . The argument . . . ignores the persistence of human frailty. The possibility of "punishment," no matter how severe, will never prevent, in this modern age of electronic transmission, unlimited photocopies and cases with hundreds of parties, accidents from occurring. The wrong number on the facsimile machine will still be "mis-speed-dialed;" the contents of two envelopes will get switched; "send copies to all defense counsel" will be misunderstood as "send copies to all counsel." . . .

IV. Good Sense and Reciprocity

. . . The immediate reaction of receiving counsel might be that the use of the missent materials can only serve to advantage his client. Nonetheless, it is clear there are advantages to doing just the opposite. First, instances of inadvertent production of documents tend not to occur only on one side. While a lawyer today may be the beneficiary of the opposing lawyer's misstep, tomorrow the shoe could be on the other foot. Second, when it is discovered that the confidential materials were retained and used the result could be similar to that which occurred recently in Baltimore when the court learned after jury selection that defendants' jury selection strategy was misdirected to plaintiffs' counsel by fax. "I find that the plaintiffs' attorneys have an advantage over the defense attorneys. Specifically, the plaintiffs know pretty well which prospective jurors the defense is going to strike. . . . They knew the inner-most thinking of the defense counsel." The judge struck the jury and ordered the entire process to begin again, at no small cost to plaintiffs, a cost that would have been expanded exponentially if the judge had not learned of this fact until the trial was over or when it was on appeal. . . . "Taking a bet" on what reaction a court may have when an inadvertent disclosure becomes known can be a risky proposition indeed. Third, the credibility and professionalism inherent in doing the right thing can, in some significant ways, enhance the strength of one's case, one's standing with the other party and opposing counsel, and one's stature before the Court.

Conclusion

The preamble to the Model Rules correctly notes that "virtually all difficult ethical problems arise from the conflict between a lawyer's responsibility to clients, to the legal system and to the lawyer's interest in remaining an upright person while earning a satisfactory living." Similarly, the same introduction observes that "a lawyer is also guided by personal conscience and the approbation of professional peers." . . . [R]eceiving counsel's obligations under those circumstances are to avoid reviewing the materials, notify sending counsel if sending counsel remains ignorant of the problem and abide sending counsel's direction as to how to treat the disposition of the confidential materials. This result not only fosters the important principle of confidentiality [and] avoids punishing the innocent client, . . . but also achieves a level of professionalism which can only redound to the lawyer's benefit.

CASE DISCUSSION QUESTIONS

1. The American Bar Association concluded that an attorney should not read inadvertently received confidential documents. Instead, the attorney should notify the other lawyer and comply with any request, such as to return the unread documents. Do you agree?

2. The Committee discussed the need for protecting client confidentiality, but generally that right is seen as running from the client to the client's attorney, not from the client to the opposing attorney. How does that factor into your thinking about the Committee's conclusion?

3. If attorneys are not to follow the "narrow, literalistic reading" of the Model Rules but rather, as the Committee suggests, are to be governed by "basic principles," is there any value in having a set of specific rules?

4. Many attorneys see a move toward "professionalism" as a misguided attempt to subvert the adversarial system. What do you suppose is the basis of their argument?

DISCUSSION QUESTIONS

11. In the ABA Opinion, the Committee raised the following hypotheticals to bolster its position that it would be unethical for an attorney to use mis-sent information. Example 1: During a lunch break in a deposition, Lawyer B left notes in a conference room either in an unlocked briefcase or on the conference room table. Lawyer A, arriving back from lunch early, could not ethically review the materials to which he now has easy access. Example 2: After a closing at Lawyer A's office, Lawyer B accidentally leaves a file or a briefcase behind. Lawyer A could not ethically take advantage of this inadvertence and rifle the file or inspect the briefcase before returning it. Example 3: In positioning an overhead projector on a shared counsel table in a courtroom during a recess, court personnel inadvertently moved the prosecutor's notes into a position in front of the defense counsel's place at the table. Again, ethically the defendant's attorney could not take a quick peek at those notes. If an attorney were to take advantage of any of the above situations and read the confidential information, do you

think it would present a different situation than the one presented in the Ethics Opinion? Why?

12. In this day of fax machines and e-mails, it is all too easy to pick the wrong fax number off a list or the wrong address from a computerized address book. Is it fair to penalize attorneys when they mistakenly dial the wrong number?

Not all state bars have agreed with the ABA approach. For example, the Massachusetts Bar Association's Committee on Professional Ethics advised that a lawyer's primary ethical duty is to zealously advocate for the client's interests, and therefore, the documents do not have to be returned. In Opinion No. 99-4, the Committee stated that the attorney's main ethical obligation is to "represent [the] client zealously within the bounds of the law." A lawyer had received a letter written by the opposing attorney to that attorney's client. An associate thought their firm had simply been copied on the letter and filed it in the firm's file. When preparing for a hearing, the lawyer reviewed the file and read the letter for the first time. The Committee determined that not only did the attorney not have to return the letter but that it would be unethical to do so as that would conflict with the lawyer's ethical obligation to represent his client "zealously within the bounds of the law."[16]

The Maine Board of Bar Overseers was presented with a similar issue when it was asked to decide whether an attorney (Counsel Z) who received from Counsel A a number of documents, one of which was clearly privileged, could use that information and whether Counsel Z had to notify Counsel A of the error. Their response is strikingly different from that of the ABA.

Professional Ethics Commission of the
Maine Board of Overseers of the Bar Opinion No. 146 (1994)

... For the reasons stated herein, the Commission concludes that Counsel Z may use the document and the information contained in it ... but that she should notify Counsel A, the sending lawyer, of the fact that the document has been received and provide a copy of the document to Counsel A on request.

In so holding, we are mindful that the ABA Standing Committee on Ethics and Professional Responsibility reached a contrary result in Formal Opinion 92-368. We do not find that Opinion to be persuasive. The ABA Committee was unable to cite any specific provision of the Model Rules of Professional Conduct in support of its conclusion. Indeed, Committee Opinion 92-368 expressly acknowledged that it was not based on any "black letter of the Model Rules." ...

The fundamental purpose behind the creation of the Bar Rules was to establish a clear codified set of standards for attorneys, the violation of which could result in professional sanctions. With that purpose ... in mind, we strongly believe that this Commission is not free to add ethical limitations not expressed by the Bar Rules....

Rule 3.2(f)(4) states that "A lawyer shall not: ... (4) engage in conduct that is prejudicial to the administration of justice." While that rule is very broad, nothing in its history suggests that the language of the Rule on its face would apply to

---

[16]Mass. R. Prof. C. 1.3 (Opinion No. 99-4).

the question before us. . . . We do not believe that Rule 3.2(f)(4), standing alone, requires Counsel Z to return the document to the sending lawyer, nor does that rule prohibit a lawyer from taking advantage of any other mistake of opposing counsel such as the failure to (1) plead an affirmative defense, (2) assert a counterclaim, (3) argue a theory of law, (4) assert an evidentiary objection at trial, (5) introduce an essential piece of evidence or (6) demand an important provision during contract negotiations. . . .

The ABA Committee opinion . . . [is] based in part on the view that lawyers owe to each other a level of courtesy that obligates them to return an inadvertently disclosed privileged document. . . . However appealing such rationale is in theory, we find no support for that conclusion in the Maine Bar Rules. . . .

We join the   concern for maintaining and improving the level of civility, honor and common courtesy in the profession, however we do not believe that we can enforce those values through the Bar Rules in the absence of specific provisions to that effect. . . .

Dissent

. . . In the debate about how the ethical question discussed in the majority opinion should be resolved, several Commission members indicated that, acting as individuals, they would return the papers as requested. However, absent any specific disciplinary rule which required otherwise, these members felt constrained to follow the client's wishes that they retain the documents even though they would have preferred to do otherwise.

In an article entitled "uncivil Law," . . . former B.C. Law School Dean Dan Coquillette states that the "legal culture" must change before the public's perception of lawyers will improve. He suggests that attorneys cannot separate their private views of justice and morality from the standards which they practice as professionals:

One lawyer I talked to who was very embarrassed about the profession said to me, "You know, one thing I keep telling myself is that being a lawyer is what I do. It's not what I am." I said, "You've got it wrong. Aristotle said you are what you do every day. You are the product of what you do day in, day out, hour in, hour out. You can't say that being a lawyer is what you do and not what you are. . . . There's no way you can split these roles. If you act like a jerk in court, you're not an aggressive advocate pursuing an assertive strategy—you're just a jerk."

. . . Indeed, Dean Coquillette attributes much of the profession's present image problem to its failure to maintain a proper balance between the duty to uphold the system of justice embodied in the lawyers' oath, and the obligation to promote the interests of individual clients.

The foregoing considerations suggest that conduct which attorneys would find repugnant in their private lives, e.g., refusing to return something which clearly belongs to another, should not be tolerated on a professional level.

CASE DISCUSSION QUESTIONS

1. The majority opinion seems to be that an attorney should not be responsible for correcting the mistakes of the opposing attorney. Even the dissent stated, "After all, Attorney Z should not be expected to rectify every mistake made by opposing counsel in the course of litigation." Do you agree? Are there some mistakes that so fundamentally alter the adversarial process that an attorney should be required to rectify opposing counsel's errors?

2. Why should the lawyer be required to notify the sending lawyer of the document's receipt? See *Aerojet General Corp. v. Transport Indemnity Insurance,* 22 Cal. Rptr. 2d 862 (Cal. App. 1993), in which the court stated that the attorney had not violated any ethical rules by not notifying the opposing attorneys immediately after he inadvertently received documents originating from them, including a memorandum that revealed the existence of a witness about whom he had not known and whom he subsequently deposed.

3. Do you think a different result should occur if an attorney left a file folder behind during a break in a deposition and while out of the room, the opposing attorney took the folder and surreptitiously copied it? What if a disgruntled staff member working in the opposing attorney's firm had sent the document to the attorney?

When the ABA's Ethics 2000 Commission reviewed the Rules, they added this provision to Rule 4.4:

> (b) A lawyer who receives a document relating to the representation of the lawyer's client and knows or reasonably should know that the document was inadvertently sent shall promptly notify the sender.

Notice that the new rule only addresses part of the issue—that is, the need to notify the opposing side of the receipt of the document. It gives no guidance as to whether the attorney may use the information contained in the document nor whether the attorney must return it if requested to do so.

This revised rule was adopted by the ABA in February of 2002. It will not be in effect in any state, however, until that state accepts the recommendation as binding on the attorneys in that state. In states that choose to do so, because the rule uses the mandatory verb "shall," attorneys who fail to follow Rule 4.4(b) will be subject to discipline including suspension and possible disbarment.

DISCUSSION QUESTIONS

13. When an attorney receives information that the opposing side has sent accidentally, that attorney has four options:

- to refrain from reading the information, and then to contact the opposing attorney and return the document unread;
- to read the information, contact the opposing attorney, and return the document;
- to read the information, contact the opposing attorney, and refuse to return the document; or
- to read the information and use it.

Given our adversarial system and your own sense of justice, which approach do you think is best?

14. Attorney White represents the plaintiff, who was injured in an automobile accident. She and her client have decided to settle the case if they can obtain at least $200,000. The settlement talks are set to begin tomorrow, and her strategy is to start by asking for $300,000, hoping to end up at $200,000. As attorney White is reviewing the files in preparation for the settlement talks, she discovers a one-page fax that she had not noticed before. It is from the defendant's insurer and was obviously intended to reach the defendant's attorney. It contains just one line: "Offer $100,000, but you have authority to settle for up to $500,000."

    a. What should attorney White do?

    b. Do you think that it should matter whether the fax was intermixed with other documents?

c. What if attorney White was wandering by the fax machine as it came in? As she pulled it out, she saw the cover sheet that contained the following language:

> Privileged and Confidential—All information transmitted hereby is intended only for the use of the addressee(s) named above. If the reader of this message is not the intended recipient or the employee or agent responsible for delivering the message to the intended recipient(s), please note that any distribution or copying of this communication is strictly prohibited. Anyone who receives this communication in error should notify us immediately by telephone and return the original to us at the above address via the U.S. mail.

The cover sheet showed that the fax was to be sent to the opposing attorney, but the fax number was for Ms. White's office. What should she do?

2. Avoiding Conflict of Interest

In an adversarial system, an attorney may not represent both sides. By representing both the plaintiff and the defendant in a negligence action, or acting as both prosecutor and defense attorney in a criminal case, an attorney would have a clear conflict of interest. Any action that would help the plaintiff or the government would at the same time hurt the defendant.

However, many conflicts are not this obvious. Take, for example, a situation in which the chief executive officer (CEO) of a corporation comes to the corporation's attorney for advice. Is the corporation's attorney supposed to be representing the interests of the CEO, the interests of the board of directors, the interests of the employees, or the interests of the shareholders?

Conflicts of interest can generally be divided into two categories. The first involves situations in which lawyers have a personal or business interest that suggests they cannot give their undivided loyalty to a client. The second involves either present or past client representation that presents a conflict with the representation of a new client.

Conflicts of the first type can occur when a lawyer is related to another lawyer who represents the opposite side of a case. Other examples include entering into certain types of business relationships with clients, preparing instruments for a client that give some benefit to the lawyer or a family member of the lawyer (such as a bequest in a will), providing financial assistance to a client in connection with pending litigation, and accepting compensation from third parties. Each of these situations poses either a real or a potential conflict of interest.

As an example of the first type of conflict, assume Mrs. Abbot is an attorney working for a defendants' firm. Her husband is an attorney who works for a plaintiffs' firm. One of Mr. Abbot's clients is suing the local grocery store for allegedly selling tainted meat. Mrs. Abbot represents the grocery store. See Figure 13-3 on page 548. Mr. and Mrs. Abbot had been hoping for some time to get away from the pressures of work for a week or so, but their lack of finances was standing in their way. If Mr. Abbot wins his case against the grocery store (through either a settlement or a court judgment), he will earn 33 percent of the amount awarded to his client. Defendants' attorneys, however, usually receive a fee that does not vary based on whether their clients win. Can you see any potential conflict of interest? Would anyone knowing all the facts think that

Conflict of interest
The ethical rule prohibiting attorneys and paralegals from working for opposite sides in a case.

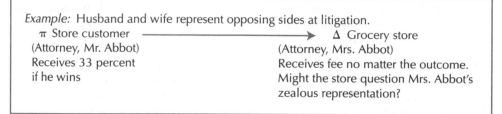

Figure 13-3 Personal Conflict

perhaps Mrs. Abbot might not be quite as diligent in her representation of the grocery store as she would be if another attorney were representing the plaintiff? In addition, do you think anyone might be concerned that in a careless moment either Mr. or Mrs. Abbot might let some confidential information slip?

Because of the ever-increasing number of women entering the legal profession and because of the variety of lifestyle choices other than traditional marriage that are becoming commonplace, one type of personal conflict that we may expect to see more frequently is the one created when the opposing attorneys share a close personal relationship. One such case was *Commonwealth v. Croken*.

Commonwealth v. Croken
432 Mass. 266, 733 N.E.2d 1005 (2000)

SPINA, J.

The defendant, Richard H. Croken, was convicted on two indictments charging forcible rape of a child under sixteen years, G. L. c. 265, § 22A, and one indictment charging indecent assault and battery on a child under fourteen years, G. L. c. 265, § 13B. Represented by new counsel on appeal the defendant filed a motion for a new trial raising claims . . . that trial counsel was impaired by a conflict of interest due to an undisclosed intimate relationship he had at the time of representation with an assistant district attorney (to whom he is now married) employed by the office which prosecuted the defendant. The motion was denied by the trial judge without an evidentiary hearing. . . . The Appeals Court held that the defendant was entitled to an evidentiary hearing on his motion and ordered that the case be remanded to the Superior Court. We granted the Commonwealth's application for further appellate review. We . . . remand the case to the Superior Court for an evidentiary hearing on that motion.

We summarize the evidence. . . . The defendant frequently babysat for the victims, whom we shall call Steve and Chris. Steve and Chris are cousins, and they are related to the defendant by marriage. One night when Chris was eight years old he slept at the defendant's home during a February vacation. The defendant fondled the boy's penis during the night and performed fellatio on him. Chris struck the defendant, then ran into the bathroom. The next morning the defendant told Chris not to tell anyone what happened or he would get hurt and disappear, and his mother would never find him. On several other occasions the defendant put his fingers or his penis into Chris's anus. When Chris was ten or eleven years old the defendant again fondled his penis and performed fellatio on him during the night. He also put his penis into the boy's anus. Chris first disclosed these events after Steve made a similar disclosure in 1993. . . .

2. Motion for a new trial. The defendant argues that the motion judge, who was also the trial judge, erred by denying his motion for a new trial without an evidentiary hearing after concluding that it did not raise a substantial issue. The thrust of the motion was that trial counsel was impaired by an actual conflict of interest created by his intimate relationship with an assistant district attorney, now his wife, who was employed by the same office that prosecuted the defendant, and that he never disclosed the conflict to the defendant. . . .

Affidavits of the defendant and his appellate counsel were filed with his motion. An affidavit by the prosecutor was filed with the Commonwealth's opposition to the motion. The following facts are undisputed or appear from those affidavits. Attorney Robert LaLiberte was appointed to represent the defendant from his arraignment in the District Court on June 3, 1993, through sentencing in the Superior Court on July 18, 1996, and until August 13, 1996, when appellate counsel was appointed. For much if not all of that time, LaLiberte was involved in a close relationship with an assistant district attorney whom we, like the Appeals Court, shall call Jane Doe.

Doe was employed as an assistant district attorney for the Plymouth district from 1989 through December, 1994. Thereafter she practiced law in the private sector until April, 1997; then served as an attorney for the Department of Social Services until February, 1998. In March, 1998, she returned to a position of supervising assistant district attorney in the District Court for the Plymouth district. At the start of LaLiberte's representation, one of Doe's colleagues was James M. Sullivan, the assistant district attorney in Plymouth County who was responsible for prosecuting the defendant throughout the proceedings in the trial court. Area telephone directories for July, 1996, through June, 1998, listed LaLiberte and Doe at the same residential address, a home purchased by LaLiberte in July, 1995. Doe and LaLiberte lived together during a portion of the time that LaLiberte represented the defendant.

Much more than this we do not know. Nor, apparently, does the defendant, whose affidavit states that he knew during the representation that LaLiberte had a girl friend with whom he was living, but that he did not know her name or her occupation. The defendant avers that he would never have consented to LaLiberte's representing him had he known that she worked for the district attorney's office for the Plymouth district. He became aware of this fact only by chance. His appellate counsel was speaking casually one day at a courthouse with an assistant district attorney, who informed her that Doe and LaLiberte were now married. The date of that marriage is not known. Appellate counsel investigated and brought to light some of the few details that are known. . . .

At the time LaLiberte represented the defendant, the Canons of Ethics and Disciplinary Rules were still in effect. . . . Disciplinary Rule 5-101(A), as appearing in *382 Mass. 779 (1981)*, provided: "Except with the consent of his client after full disclosure, a lawyer shall not accept employment if the exercise of his professional judgment on behalf of his client will be or reasonably may be affected by his own financial, business, property, or personal interests." A lawyer's personal interests surely include his interest in maintaining amicable relations with his relatives, his spouse, and anyone with whom he is comparably intimate. This interest is, of course, often significantly pecuniary in character, but it also has irreducible emotional and moral dimensions, and it heavily bears on how any ordinary human being goes about making important decisions. It follows that in a case where a lawyer's representation of a client may be significantly limited by his ties to his relatives and intimate companions, professional ethics are implicated just as they would in a case where the lawyer represents a second client with litigation interests potentially adverse to those of the first client. . . .

Before agreeing to represent the defendant, LaLiberte should have determined whether he reasonably believed his representation would be adversely affected by his relationship with Doe. If he concluded that it would, then he should have withdrawn from the case. If, on the other hand, he determined that he could represent the defendant vigorously, LaLiberte should then have asked the defendant whether he consented to being represented by him in light of his relationship with Doe. Informed consent would of course include disclosure of the fact that Doe was an assistant district attorney who worked in the same office as the prosecutor who was trying to convict the defendant.[4]

We think that the motion and affidavits raise a substantial question as to whether there was an actual conflict. The issue is certainly serious. Although factually underdeveloped, the papers demonstrate sufficient basis for a reasonable belief that the core of the attorney-client relationship might have been impaired, and that some probing of the matter by way of an evidentiary hearing was required. . . .

Marital and similar intimate relationships between lawyers have potential for creating unique problems. "The marriage relationship may be conducive to inadvertent breaches of confidentiality. A spouse may have knowledge of out-of-town investigative trips at or around the time of preparation for a particular case; clients and witnesses may contact the lawyer at home or leave messages on the home answering machine that may reveal a tactic or a confidence. Working papers left at home or work performed at home may reveal confidences of a client. The needs of a lawyer to work early or late or on weekends may give rise to the need for explanation in a marriage relationship that could inadvertently reveal client confidences or secrets." ABA Criminal Justice Section, Ethical Problems Facing the Criminal Defense Lawyer at 248 (1995). In addition, a "potential conflict of interest that may arise can be financial or personal. A district attorney or public defender may have a special interest in the outcome of a case based on a concern for a promotion or political benefit for one's spouse. A lawyer's loyalty to a client may be impaired by a personal interest in the success of a spouse. . . ." Id. at 249. We see no appreciable difference between marriage and other intimate relationships in this regard.

Sullivan's affidavit leaves some key questions unanswered, and it raises serious questions because of what it does not say. Sullivan simply did not have the information to tell what Doe knew and did. . . .

The Commonwealth would have done better in this case to submit an affidavit by Doe, who at present is in its employ. Doe could aver—assuming, of course, that the averments were true—that she never worked on the case, that she never discussed the case with LaLiberte or anyone from the district attorney's office, that no information concerning the case was ever made known to her or conveyed by her to the office or to LaLiberte, and that she had never understood that whether she regained employment with the district attorney's office would depend in any way on how LaLiberte handled his representation of the defendant. The existence of a strictly observed office policy designed to eliminate even inadvertent breaches of confidence in circumstances involving interoffice relationships, whose numbers appear to be increasing significantly, is also something that could have been included in an affidavit. Similarly, LaLiberte could have submitted an affidavit stating—again, assuming it were true—that he never discussed the case with Doe, and that he never expected that his performance in this case would affect Doe's chances of becoming reemployed by the district attorney's office. . . . We do not imply that affidavits addressing these particular issues would have obviated the need for a hearing. That is a question that can only be answered on a case-by-case basis. There are obvious and serious questions in this case that should have been addressed, but were not. The woeful inadequacy of the Commonwealth's response to the defendant's motion and affidavits compel the need for an evidentiary hearing. . . .

The hearing must not intrude unnecessarily on the privacy of LaLiberte and Doe. The details of their relationship need not be explored, as it is not disputed that LaLiberte and Doe were involved in an intimate relationship during most of LaLiberte's representation of the defendant. We think the hearing should focus upon (1) whether an actual conflict of interest existed between LaLiberte and the defendant; and (2) whether the potential conflict, i.e., the relationship between LaLiberte and Doe caused any material prejudice to the defendant, including (a) whether LaLiberte and Doe discussed the defendant's case, and if so,

---

[4]"A possible conflict does not itself preclude the representation. The critical questions are the likelihood that a conflict will eventuate and, if it does, whether it will materially interfere with the lawyer's independent professional judgment in considering alternatives or foreclose courses of action that reasonably should be pursued on behalf of the client. Consideration should be given to whether the client wishes to accommodate the other interest involved." Mass. R. Prof. C. 1.7 comment [4], *426 Mass. 1330 (1998)*.

what was said; (b) whether Doe discussed the case with anyone in the district attorney's office, or in the office of the Department of Social Services if that office had any involvement in this matter, and if so, what information was disclosed which may have harmed the defense; (c) whether, during LaLiberte's representation of the defendant, Doe had any expectation of returning to the district attorney's office, and if so, whether LaLiberte's representation was directly or indirectly affected thereby (e.g., did LaLiberte show any special deference to the prosecutor that harmed the defense). . . .

The . . . matter is remanded to the Superior Court for an evidentiary hearing consistent with this opinion. . . .

So ordered.

After the case was remanded for an evidentiary hearing, the trial court determined that there was no actual conflict, finding Jane Doe and Attorney LaLiberte's testimony credible when they stated that they had no conversations regarding the case and that the prosecuting attorney never discussed the case with Doe. Finally, the court concluded that any potential conflict that may have arisen did not result in any showing of ineffective assistance of counsel. When the case was once again appealed, the court found that there was nothing in the record to show that LaLiberte's "independent professional judgment" was impaired by his own personal interest arising from his relationship with Doe.[17]

CASE DISCUSSION QUESTIONS

1. What is the danger to a client when his or her attorney is having a personal relationship with another attorney who works for the same organization that is prosecuting the client?

2. Do you think this case would have been decided differently if Jane Doe had been the prosecuting attorney instead of simply being an attorney working in the office?

3. The defendant stated that he would never have retained attorney LaLiberte as his attorney had he known of LaLiberte's and Ms. Doe's relationship. Why is this statement and the attorney's total failure to reveal the potential conflict not enough to form the basis for a new trial?

4. How is a client ever truly to know whether confidences and secrets were shared if the majority of the evidentiary hearing is based on the testimony of the two individuals who have the alleged conflict?

The second type of conflict of interest occurs when the attorney has information about the client on the opposite side of the case and therefore may know something that will be detrimental to that person. For example, assume attorney Smith worked for Mr. Brown when he was getting a divorce. During the divorce proceedings, attorney Smith naturally became quite informed on Mr. Brown's financial state, including his partnership interest in a local gymnasium. It is now two years later, and one of Mr. Brown's partners has approached the firm seeking representation in a case he wants to bring against Mr. Brown. If attorney Smith is allowed to take the case, his knowledge of

---

[17]Commonwealth v. Croken, 797 N.E.2d 403 (Mass. App. C. 2003).

Mr. Brown's finances that he gained while he represented him in his divorce might put Mr. Brown at an unfair disadvantage.

As you can see, client confidentiality and conflicts of interest are very closely related. In the situation involving Mr. and Mrs. Abbot and the *Croken* case, there is the fear that confidentiality might be breached because of the close relationship between the attorneys representing the two sides. In the situation involving information gained from a client, the fear is more real, as attorney Smith actually knows confidential information and the only issue is whether he might use it against his former client. Because of this possibility, the ethics codes require that attorney Smith either obtain Mr. Brown's consent to proceed as the attorney representing the partner or resign from the case. In addition, all other attorneys at attorney Smith's firm would be barred from representing Mr. Brown's partner.

To summarize, in cases of actual conflict, an attorney can never represent both sides. In those situations involving potential conflict, a court might allow the representation so long as the client consented after being fully informed of the potential problems. However, the court could still disallow the representation if the court thought that there was in fact an actual conflict or that the client had not been fully informed.

DISCUSSION QUESTIONS

15. Why should Mr. Brown's partner be penalized in his choice of attorney just because attorney Smith happened to represent Mr. Brown years ago in an unrelated matter?

16. Model Rule 1.7 states that "notwithstanding the existence of a concurrent conflict of interest . . . a lawyer may represent a client if the lawyer reasonably believes that the lawyer will be able to provide competent and diligent representation." Is that a bit like asking the fox to guard the hen house?

D. ACCESS TO JUSTICE

In this chapter we have discussed the key role lawyers play in the adversary system. But what if no lawyer wants to take the person's case? Can a lawyer be forced to represent a guilty client or to advocate for a cause that is contrary to the lawyer's personal beliefs? What if a person cannot afford to hire a lawyer? While the Constitution guarantees the right to an attorney in criminal matters, that is not true in civil cases. In this section we will explore these access to justice issues.

1. Providing Services to Unpopular Clients and Causes

Generally, lawyers are free to accept or reject clients. However, lawyers who work for others, whether it is in a law firm, public agency, corporation, or advocacy group, generally lose the ability to pick and choose the individuals they wish to represent. Perhaps the most obvious example of this is the lawyer who works for the public defenders' office representing individuals who have been charged with a crime. That lawyer is not free to represent only those whom the lawyer believes are innocent.

One of the most common questions asked of lawyers is, "How can you defend a guilty client?" There are several possible responses to this question.[18] The first response is to point out that guilt is a legal concept that is determined by a judge or a jury and not by the lawyer. A person is not considered guilty until after the trial has been completed. The second response is that in representing a guilty client, the attorney is just playing a role, similar to the actor who plays the part of the villain in a movie. The third response is based on the belief that the very legitimacy of our adversary system depends upon having lawyers willing to represent the "guilty" as well as the innocent. If criminal defendants cannot find attorneys willing to represent them, "the foundation of the judicial system is eroded and the lawyers become the judges of guilt or innocence by their very decision to accept or reject those criminal clients."[19] The importance of attorneys being willing to accept court appointments is stated in Model Rule 6.2: "A lawyer shall not seek to avoid appointment by a tribunal to represent a person except for good cause." Examples of good cause include where the lawyer is not competent to handle the particular type of case or the representation would result in a conflict of interest.

NETNOTE

An excellent site for up-to-date information on legal ethics is *www.legalethics.com.*

One exception to Rule 6.2 provides that an attorney may decline representation if "the client or the cause is so repugnant to the lawyer as to be likely to impair the client-lawyer relations or the lawyer's ability to represent the client."[20] Because of this provision, no doubt there are limits as to the types of situations in which a court would order an attorney to represent a client. For example, it is not likely that a court would force an African American attorney to represent a member of the Ku Klux Klan accused of placing a burning cross on the front lawn of an integrated church. Similarly, a court would not order a Jewish attorney to defend a Nazi organization that wished to march in a town parade. Nonetheless, some attorneys who have found themselves in such

---

[18]For an interesting discussion of this topic found in the world of fiction, you might enjoy reading A Cinderella Affidavit by Michael Fredrickson. In that novel, when discussing the difficulties that confront attorneys, the main character concludes that attorneys must proceed on "the curious faith that the localized permissible evil we do on behalf of our clients will dissolve in the higher justice served by the adversary system." Id. at 446.

[19]Stephen Jones, A Lawyer's Ethical Duty to Represent the Unpopular Client, 1 Chap. L. Rev. 105, 107 (1998).

[20]Model Rule 6.2(c).

situations have voluntarily chosen to represent such unpopular clients in order to defend constitutional principles, such as freedom of speech and assembly.[21]

DISCUSSION QUESTION

17. Attorney Judith Nathanson is an attorney who earned her law degree with the purpose of helping to advance the status of women in the legal system. In her divorce practice, she only represents wives. As she only has a certain amount of time and energy to devote to her clients, she feels it essential to use her resources to redress social and legal wrongs done to women. Therefore, when Mr. Stropnicky asked her to represent him in his divorce, she refused. Should she be required to represent him? Should it matter that in his marriage he had assumed the role of homemaker and childcare giver? Is this analogous to an attorney with white supremacist views arguing that she should be able to decline to represent nonwhite clients?

2. Making Legal Services Available to Low-Income Clients

Over the past twenty years there has been an increasingly large unmet need for legal services, particularly among the poor and middle class. One American Bar Association study concluded that at least 70 to 80 percent of low-income persons who require legal assistance are unable to obtain it.[22]

Legal services agencies that were created in the 1970s by the federal government to serve the poor have not been able to keep up with this demand for legal assistance. They lack sufficient funding and typically can represent only the very poor. Attorney pro bono work is also not filling this need for legal services. Rule 6.1 of the Model Rules of Professional Conduct states that every lawyer should "aspire to render at least (50) hours of pro bono publico legal services per year," but this provision has not been adopted in all states, and even in the ones where it has, the rule is aspirational only. It does not require attorneys to provide pro bono representation.

Contingency fee
Attorney compensation as a percentage of the amount recovered rather than a flat amount of money or an hourly fee.

The traditional method that attorneys have used in order to provide representation to those who have been injured and who could not otherwise afford an attorney is the **contingency fee**. Clients can hire an attorney and only owe a fee "contingent upon" the attorney's winning the case. If the plaintiff loses, the plaintiff is responsible for the costs of litigation but owes the attorney nothing. If the plaintiff wins, however, then the attorney's fee is a percentage of what the plaintiff has won. Typically that amount is 33 percent of the plaintiff's recovery. Because typically lower-income clients do not have enough money to pay an attorney on an hourly basis, many argue that contingency fees make it possible for those clients to pursue claims that they would otherwise have to abandon.

However, some have questioned if it is ethical for an attorney to take one-third of the money that would otherwise be going to compensate the client for his or her injuries. If the goal in awarding a plaintiff money, either through a

---

[21]See, for example, the case of Anthony Griffin, an attorney for the NAACP who represented the Grand Dragon of the Texas Knights of the Ku Klux Klan, and David Goldberger, an ACLU lawyer who defended the Nazis' right to march in Skokie, Illinois.

[22]Commission on Nonlawyer Practice, American Bar Association, Nonlawyer Activity in Law-Related Situations (1995).

jury award or settlement, is to compensate the plaintiff 100 percent for the plaintiff's loss, that will not happen if the attorney takes one-third of the payment. Consider the following case.

Attorney Goodman represented Donald Gagnon, who was severely injured in a highway accident. At the time of the accident, Gagnon was trying to help another motorist. The driver of a tractor-trailer had pulled completely off the travel lane of the highway and was parked in the breakdown lane. The driver had stopped because she had noticed that the mud flaps on her truck were rubbing against her rear trailer wheels. To help the woman, Gagnon pulled off the highway behind the truck in the breakdown lane. He then went underneath the rear of the trailer to attempt to correct the problem. While he was in that position, Donald Shoblom, driving a loaded garbage truck, veered off the highway into the breakdown lane and crashed into the tractor-trailer. The woman was killed as the result of the collision, and Gagnon sustained massive injuries, leaving him a paraplegic.

Gagnon v. Shoblom
409 Mass. 63, 565 N.E.2d 775 (1991)

On June 9, 1988, at 1 PM, a truck operated by Donald Shoblom crashed into a parked trailer, killing Susan J. Thompson and severely injuring Donald Gagnon. Gagnon retained Attorney Alan R. Goodman in pursuit of his claim against Shoblom and Shoblom's employer, and for his workers' compensation claim. Gagnon and Mr. Goodman signed a contingent fee agreement in which Gagnon agreed that Mr. Goodman's compensation would amount to $33\frac{1}{3}\%$ of the recovery in his personal injury claim. The entire contingent fee agreement is set forth as an appendix to this opinion.

Mr. Goodman commenced an action and, after extensive discovery and investigation, a structured settlement of $2,925,000 (present cash value) was reached.[3] . . .

A Superior Court judge conducted a hearing and indicated his approval of the terms of the settlement agreement except the provision for recovery of $33\frac{1}{3}\%$ of the settlement which amounted to $975,000. The judge called this fee unconscionable. There was an evidentiary hearing on the reasonableness of the settlement agreement. Gagnon testified that he voluntarily signed

the contingent fee agreement and that he was satisfied that Mr. Goodman had earned his agreed fee. Additionally, a leading member of the bar who specializes in prosecuting personal injury claims for plaintiffs testified as to the reasonableness of the fee. The attorney who defended the action in the case testified as to the impressive work performed by Mr. Goodman. There was no evidence tending to prove that the fee was anything but reasonable.

However, the judge filed a carefully crafted memorandum and order in which he ordered payment of legal fees to Mr. Goodman as follows: "Mr. Goodman handled the case expeditiously and well. He obtained what I consider to be a very fine result. As stated above, he is entitled to handsome compensation.

"Taking those factors into account, as well as Mr. Goodman's ability and reputation (both of which are good) the demand for his services by others, the time reasonably spent, the expenses reasonably incurred by him and the charges usually made for similar services by others in Western Massachusetts, I am satisfied that the $33\frac{1}{3}\%$ maximum rate provided for in his contingent fee

---

[3]The settlement called for immediate cash payment of $ 800,000 to Gagnon and . . . for substantial annual payments to Gagnon for life and deferred payments to Gagnon and his daughter.

agreement should only be applied to the first $300,000.00 of the recovery. A rate of 25% of the next $1,200,000.00, plus a rate of 20% of all amounts in excess of $1,500,000 would be reasonable. At those rates Mr. Goodman is entitled to an attorney's fee of $695,000.00, which I consider to be 'handsome' compensation. Anything in excess of that amount would be unreasonable and excessive."

We allowed Mr. Goodman's request for direct appellate review of the correctness of the judge's order regarding the fee. We hold that it was error for the judge to disapprove the agreed fee. . . .

The courts are not powerless to act in disapproving a fee which exceeds the percentage in the agreement, a fee to which the client never agreed, or a fee which is plainly unreasonable. . . . However, we need not discuss the court's inherent power in this case because no one is challenging the fee.

Accordingly, an order shall enter approving the entire settlement, including the amount of compensation due to Mr. Goodman under the contingent fee agreement.

So ordered.

GREANEY, J. (concurring). . . . I agree with the court that the attorney's fee in this case should not have been reduced. The evidence before the judge sufficiently indicated that the contingent fee agreement was reasonable "in light of the circumstances prevailing at the time of [the] making [of the agreement]." This conclusion is reinforced by the fact that the client, Gagnon, has made no objection to the contingent fee agreement and has affirmatively stated his satisfaction both with the work done and the percentage charged by Goodman. It is also a consideration that the one-third percentage has become institutionalized in the practice of the litigation bar as the minimum rate to be charged in the typical tort case. Change, if it is to come, should not come suddenly and to the disappointment of long-standing expectations.

The judge, however, has touched upon a larger issue. His memorandum frames that issue in this manner:

> "Contingent fee agreements . . . serve a very beneficial public purpose. They have been said to be the 'poor man's key to the courthouse' because they do provide a method whereby civil claims can be filed and litigated by persons who would otherwise be unable to afford the assistance of counsel. . . ."

> "I am satisfied (both on the basis of my own experience as a practicing attorney and as a trial judge as well as by the evidence presented at the hearings) that in the case of a civil tort action in which damages are sought for personal injuries a contingent fee of $33\frac{1}{3}\%$ of the amount recovered is reasonable to a point; depending (among other factors of course) upon the size of the recovery ultimately obtained. I am also satisfied, however, that as the size of the recovery (and hence the size of the fee) increases, the spread between the attorney's fee and the fair value of the time, effort and skill that he devoted to earning that fee widens—and at some point the fee becomes unreasonable and even (if the spread becomes wide enough) outrageous or unconscionable.

> "One should not lose sight of the fact that under our law a recovery for a personal injury is limited, at least in theory, to the fair and reasonable value of the pain and suffering, mental anguish, reasonable medical expenses, disfigurement, disability and lost earning capacity, both past and future, *sustained by the client*. However, attorney's fees incurred by the client are not recoverable in such a case, either as part of or in addition to his damages. Any fee that the attorney exacts from the client under a contingent fee agreement must therefore reduce the client's compensation for his injury below what is fair and reasonable. When, as in this case, the injury sustained by the client is catastrophic, the amount of the reduction can become enormous unless some rule of reason is applied to the application of the contingent fee. It is, after all, Mr. Gagnon and not Mr. Goodman who must spend the remainder of his life confined to a wheelchair with no bowel or bladder control and with constant dependence upon others to assist him in the normal tasks of day-to-day living . . ." (Emphasis in original; citation omitted). . . .

At a time when the gap between the service and the fee in tort cases appears to be becoming more and more pronounced, there may be a need to establish a better sense of proportion. This case is illustrative of the problem. The question raised by the judge deserves honest debate.

LOW FIRM OF

ALAN R. GOODMAN

CONTINGENT FEE AGREEMENT

Date .... 6-23-88 ....

The Client .... Donald A. Gagnon   38 Felicia St., Springfield, MA ......
      (Name)   (Street & Number)   (City or Town)

retains the Law Firm of   ALAN R. GOODMAN   1350 Main Street   Springfield, MA 01103
to perform the legal services mentioned in paragraph (1) below. The attorney agrees to perform them faithfully and with due diligence.

(1) The claim, controversy, and other matters with reference to which the services are to be performed are:
an accident which occurred on or about   6 / 9 /88

(2) The contingency upon which compensation is to be paid is:
33.3% if settled before suit
15% if settled after suit before trial or after arbitration/mediation
40% if settled after trial but before verdict or judgement
45% if verdict or judgement
50% if appeal taken
An additional 15% (minimum $100.00) of PIP and Med. Pay collected in auto cases.

(3) The client is not to be liable to pay compensation otherwise than from amounts collected for him by the attorney, except that is responsible for following costs:
Out of pocket expenses, such as costs of medical reports and opinions, filing fees, sheriff's fees, service of subpoena, witness fees, photographs, excessive postage and photocopying, long distance telephone calls, research materials, expert witness opinions and fees, file initialization, travel costs, investigator's reports. Said costs are deducted from gross settlement after calculation of attorney's fees.   to be included in

(4) Reasonable compensation on the foregoing contingency is to be paid by the client to the attorney, but such compensation (including that of any associated counsel) is not to exceed the maximum percentages of the gross amount collected as specified in (2) above.

(5) The client is in any event to be liable to the attorney for his reasonable expenses and disbursements (3) above even if no settlement is made.

(6) If the attorney is discharged by the client prior to the conclusion of this representation, the attorney is entitled to be then compensated for his reasonable expenses and disbursements. Further, the attorney is to be compensated for the fair value of the services rendered to the client up to the time of discharge, but the amount of the fee shall not be due to the attorney until the subject matter litigation is concluded pursuant to Paragraphs 2 and 3 above.

This agreement and its performance are subject to Rule 3:05 of the Supreme Judicial Court of Massachusetts.

WE EACH HAVE READ THE ABOVE AGREEMENT BEFORE SIGNING IT.
CLIENT ACKNOWLEDGES RECEIPT OF CARBON COPY.

Witness to Signatures: Nancy L. Hall
(To Client) ....

                               Donald A. Gagnon
                                   (Signature of Client)

(To Attorney) ....

                                   (Signature of Client)
                 6/25/88   Alan R. Goodman
                                   (Signature of Attorney)

Practice Limited to Personal Injury Law

350 MAIN STREET, BANK OF BOSTON BUILDING 12th FLOOR, SPRINGFIELD, MA 01103 413-736-1616
APP-60
Form No. D-100 Rev. 6-87

Exhibit 13-1   Contingent Fee Agreement

CASE DISCUSSION QUESTIONS

1. Why did the Massachusetts Supreme Judicial Court think the trial court had erred in disapproving the agreed-upon fee?

2. Mr. Gagnon received a structured settlement in this case. How do you think that might have affected his ability to pay his attorney's fees?

3. Do you agree with the trial court judge that the percentage an attorney earns should decrease as the size of the client's award increases? Why or why not?

4. Specifically, how do you answer the trial judge's assertion that "[a]ny fee that the attorney exacts from the client under a contingent fee agreement must therefore reduce the client's compensation for his injury below what is fair and reasonable"?

5. What do you think of the contingency fee agreement in this particular case? Given the facts outlined before the case, it seems apparent that when Goodman had his client sign the contingent fee agreement, he knew that the liability aspect of Gagnon's case would not be difficult to prove, that his client's injuries were catastrophic, and as Shoblom was employed as a driver for a large corporate employer, that it was likely Gagnon would receive a very substantial judgment or settlement from that corporate employer.

6. In addition to representing Donald Gagnon, attorney Goodman had also been retained to represent the administrator of the dead woman's estate in her claim for wrongful death and the dead woman's mother for her claim of negligent infliction of emotional distress. Clearly, Goodman could make use of much of the work he had already done on the *Gagnon* case in preparing those additional cases, for which he was also charging a fee. Do you think those clients should receive some sort of a discount for work that had already been done and paid for?

SUMMARY

In this chapter we have focused on some of the most important ethical and moral issues related to the role of attorneys in our adversarial system of justice. We have seen how the need to protect the interests of their clients may come in direct conflict with the needs and even safety of others. Specifically, we examined these conflicts in the context of client confidentiality, conflict of interest, and access to justice.

In dealing with these issues, attorneys often have to choose between competing values and interests. While the ABA and state bar associations have addressed many of these issues in their ethical guidelines, we saw that the provisions of these codes do not always provide individual attorneys with the answers they need.

Clearly, knowing and following a code of ethics does not ensure moral behavior. In fact, at times it could even be argued that it leads to immoral or at least amoral behavior. However, if attorneys follow general rules, the belief is that over the long run more morally right than wrong choices will be made. The only other alternative is the anarchy that would result if each individual attorney were allowed to decide on a course of action based on his or her individual conscience. A compromise position acknowledges that the rules are meant to govern the "normal," while attorneys must exercise discretion in cases of the extraordinary.

We ended the chapter with a look at the issue of access to justice. In this context we considered an attorney's responsibility for taking on unpopular clients and the contingency fee as a way to increase access to justice for those who otherwise could not afford legal services.

CRITICAL THINKING EXERCISES

1. As you can see, there is substantial disagreement as to when an attorney should be required or even allowed to report a client's future crime. Do you think there are any instances when such reporting should be required instead of merely permitted?[23] Classify each of the following according to whether you think an attorney should be required to report the future crime, allowed to do so at his or her discretion, or prohibited from disclosing it at all. You should also consider whether the test should be a subjective one, based on what the attorney actually thought was likely to happen, or an objective test, based on what a reasonable person would think would happen.
   a. A deliberately wrongful act
   b. Harm to a financial or property interest
   c. Substantial harm to a financial or property interest
   d. Any crime
   e. A serious violent crime
   f. Bodily harm
   g. Substantial bodily harm
   h. Death
   i. Imminent death

2. In *Belge* (page 526), the principal harm had already been done. The client had committed the crime of murder, and the girl was dead. Nothing the attorney could do would change that. In *Spaulding* (page 530), the harm had also been done, but revealing it would serve to save a life and would not lead to the client's trial for murder. Suppose, however, that a case arose in which the attorney had a chance to still "save the girl" but that his actions would lead to the criminal conviction of his client. Consider the following.[24] On December 17, Gary Krist went to the motel room of Barbara Mackle. He told her he was a detective and that there had been an accident involving a young man driving a white Ford. The young man was in the hospital and asking for her. As her boyfriend owned a white Ford, she believed Krist and opened the door. Krist entered brandishing a knife and forced her into the backseat of his car where he then tied her up. After driving her out into the country, he ordered her into a coffin-like box, equipped with a method for getting air, and buried her alive. He

---

[23]*See, e.g.,* the argument presented in Harry L. Subin, The Lawyer as Superego: Disclosure of Client Confidences to Prevent Harm, 70 Iowa L. Rev. 1091 (July 1985), to the effect that in the case of threatened criminal activity the rules should provide for mandatory disclosure because the present rules give attorneys no guidance as to how and when to exercise their discretion. Contrast this with the position of others who view the duty of confidentiality as a sacred trust between attorney and client. Therefore, almost always the balance should be tipped toward silence. This may cause individualized harm, but it will prevent harm to the system as a whole. Allegiance to that system is viewed as necessary. Without the maintenance of client confidences, the attorney-client relationship, the very foundation of the adversary system, would be destroyed.

[24]These facts are based on the case of Krist v. State, 179 S.E.2d 56 (Ga. 1970).

then called her father, told him he had kidnapped his daughter, and demanded $500,000 in ransom. Arrangements were made for Krist to receive the money. On December 19 following Krist's instructions, the father left the money in a suitcase. Krist retrieved the money and left without revealing the whereabouts of Barbara. Two days later on December 21 Krist was arrested when he tried to spend part of the money in order to rent a boat and motor at a local marina.

Assume that Krist meets with his court-appointed attorney and reveals where Barbara is located. He thinks she is still alive but does not know. He said that he left her with a limited amount of food and water but does not know how long it will last. The attorney encourages Krist to tell the police where Barbara is buried. Krist refuses to do so, feeling that so long as they do not find Barbara, the police have no direct proof that he was the kidnapper. What should the attorney do? What are his options under the Model Code, the Model Rules, and the recently proposed changes to the Model Rules?

3. Consider the case of Leo Frank. Although innocent, he had been convicted of the rape and murder of a fourteen-year-old girl. While he was waiting to be executed, an attorney, who was not involved in the *Frank* case, found out from a prospective client the name of the true murderer. The attorney never revealed the information, and Frank was killed when a mob kidnapped him from prison and lynched him. Later in his memoirs, the attorney wrote, "I am one of the few people who know that Leo Frank was innocent of the crime for which he was convicted and lynched. . . . [B]ut the information came to me in such a way that, though I wish I could do so, I can never reveal it so. . . . We lawyers . . . take an oath never to reveal the communications made to us by our clients; and this includes facts revealed in an attempt to employ the lawyer, though he refuses the employment."[25]

4. William Macumber was on trial for first-degree murder. His attorney wanted to call attorney Brown to the stand. Attorney Brown had been the attorney for James Smith in a different murder trial. During his representation of Smith, Smith had confessed to attorney Brown that he was the murderer and had acted alone in the case for which Macumber was on trial. Sometime prior to the Macumber trial, Smith died. After his death, attorney Brown approached Macumber's attorney and volunteered to testify as to what Brown had told him. Should the court allow this testimony?[26]

||| REVIEW QUESTIONS

Pages 517 through 521
1. Describe the adversarial system. How does it vary from a system based on the inquisitorial model?
2. Explain the relationship between the rights contained in the Fourth, Fifth, and Sixth Amendments and our adversarial system.
3. Some have described litigation as a battleground. Why is that?

---

[25]Arthur G. Powell, I Can Go Home Again 291 (1943).
[26]These facts are based on State v. Macumber, 544 P.2d 1084 (Ariz. 1976).

Pages 521 through 547

4. Why does our legal system place such a high value on attorneys' maintaining their clients' confidences?

5. How does the attorney-client privilege differ from the ethical rules regarding confidentiality?

6. Mrs. Smith, who is seeking a divorce, entered attorney Black's office for her first interview. Because she was very disturbed over the prospect of a divorce, Mrs. Smith brought her best friend along with her to the interview. Should attorney Black let Mrs. Smith's best friend sit in on the interview? Why?

7. At a cocktail party attorney Sims sees one of his firm's clients kissing someone not the client's wife. At the client's divorce hearing could attorney Sims be required to testify about what he saw at the party? Could attorney Sims ethically tell his own wife about what he saw at the party? Why?

8. For each of the following discuss whether you think the attorney should reveal the information:
   a. A client tells her attorney that she murdered her husband.
   b. A client tells her attorney that she is planning to murder her husband.
   c. A client tells her attorney that at the end of the week she is planning to steal all of her employer's cash receipts as she has access to his safe.
   d. A client tells her attorney that her husband is so upset with how the litigation is going that he is planning to kill the opposing attorney.
   e. A client tells her attorney that it was she, and not the woman who is on trial for murder, who killed the victim.

9. If a client tells an attorney she is going to commit perjury, what are the attorney's options?

10. If an attorney suspects but does not know that a client is going to commit perjury, what should the attorney do? Does it matter if the client is the defendant in a criminal case?

11. What should attorneys do when they inadvertently receive confidential information from the other side?

12. Give some examples of when an attorney might find her duty of loyalty to her client to be in conflict with other values she holds.

Pages 547 through 552

13. What are the two major causes of conflict of interest?

14. In each of the following situations determine whether you see any potential conflict of interest problems.
   a. Sam was injured in an automobile accident when the car he was riding in was struck in an intersection by a pickup truck. Both Sam and the driver of the car want attorney Black to represent them against the driver of the pickup truck.
   b. Sara and Emily were arrested for the attempted robbery of United Bank. They would like attorney Jones to represent both of them.
   c. Attorney Lacy is the prosecuting attorney for the murder trial of Tom Black. Jim White represents the defendant. Halfway through the murder trial, attorney Lacy and attorney White start dating.

Pages 552 through 558

15. What reasons do attorneys usually give for why they are willing to represent guilty or unpopular clients?

16. What is a contingency fee and how does it arguably increase access to justice?

Appendix A

The Constitution of the United States

We the People of the United States, in Order to form a more perfect Union, establish Justice, insure domestic Tranquility, provide for the common defense, promote the general Welfare, and secure the Blessings of Liberty to ourselves and our Posterity, do ordain and establish this Constitution for the United States of America.

Article I

Section 1. All legislative Powers herein granted shall be vested in a Congress of the United States, which shall consist of a Senate and House of Representatives.

Section 2. The House of Representatives shall be composed of Members chosen every second Year by the People of the several States, and the Electors in each State shall have the Qualifications requisite for Electors of the most numerous Branch of the State Legislature.

No Person shall be a Representative who shall not have attained to the Age of twenty five Years, and been seven Years a Citizen of the United States, and who shall not, when elected, be an Inhabitant of that State in which he shall be chosen.

Representatives and direct Taxes shall be apportioned among the several States which may be included within this Union, according to their respective Numbers, which shall be determined by adding to the whole Number of free Persons, including those bound to Service for a Term of Years, and excluding Indians not taxed, three fifths of all other Persons. The actual Enumeration shall be made within three Years after the first Meeting of the Congress of the United States, and within every subsequent Term of ten Years, in such Manner as they shall by Law direct. The Number of Representatives shall not exceed one for every thirty Thousand, but each State shall have at Least one Representative; and until such enumeration shall be made, the State of New Hampshire shall be entitled to chuse three, Massachusetts eight, Rhode-Island and Providence Plantations one, Connecticut five, New-York six, New Jersey four, Pennsylvania eight, Delaware one, Maryland six, Virginia ten, North Carolina five, South Carolina five, and Georgia three.

When vacancies happen in the Representation from any State, the Executive Authority thereof shall issue Writs of Election to fill such Vacancies.

The House of Representatives shall chuse their Speaker and other Officers; and shall have the sole Power of Impeachment.

Section 3. The Senate of the United States shall be composed of two Senators from each State, chosen by the Legislature thereof, for six Years; and each Senator shall have one Vote.

Immediately after they shall be assembled in Consequence of the first Election, they shall be divided as equally as may be into three Classes. The Seats of the Senators of the first Class shall be vacated at the Expiration of the second Year, of the second Class at the Expiration of the fourth Year, and of the third Class at the Expiration of the sixth Year, so that one third may be chosen every second Year; and if Vacancies happen by Resignation, or otherwise, during the Recess of the Legislature of any State, the Executive thereof may make temporary Appointments until the next Meeting of the Legislature, which shall then fill such Vacancies.

No Person shall be a Senator who shall not have attained to the Age of thirty Years, and been nine Years a Citizen of the United States, and who shall not, when elected, be an Inhabitant of that State for which he shall be chosen.

The Vice President of the United States shall be President of the Senate, but shall have no Vote, unless they be equally divided.

The Senate shall chuse their other Officers, and also a President pro tempore, in the Absence of the Vice President, or when he shall exercise the Office of President of the United States.

The Senate shall have the sole Power to try all Impeachments. When sitting for that Purpose, they shall be on Oath or Affirmation. When the President of the United States is tried, the Chief Justice shall preside: And no Person shall be convicted without the Concurrence of two thirds of the Members present.

Judgment in Cases of Impeachment shall not extend further than to removal from Office, and disqualification to hold and enjoy any Office of honor, Trust or Profit under the United States: but the Party convicted shall nevertheless be liable and subject to Indictment, Trial, Judgment and Punishment, according to Law.

Section 4. The Times, Places and Manner of holding Elections for Senators and Representatives, shall be prescribed in each State by the Legislature thereof; but the Congress may at any time by Law make or alter such Regulations, except as to the Places of chusing Senators.

The Congress shall assemble at least once in every Year, and such Meeting shall be on the first Monday in December, unless they shall by Law appoint a different Day.

Section 5. Each House shall be the Judge of the Elections, Returns and Qualifications of its own Members, and a Majority of each shall constitute a Quorum to do Business; but a smaller Number may adjourn from day to day, and may be authorized to compel the Attendance of absent Members, in such Manner, and under such Penalties as each House may provide.

Each House may determine the Rules of its Proceedings, punish its Members for disorderly Behaviour, and, with the Concurrence of two thirds, expel a Member.

Each House shall keep a Journal of its Proceedings, and from time to time publish the same, excepting such Parts as may in their Judgment require Secrecy; and the Yeas and Nays of the Members of either House on any question shall, at the Desire of one fifth of those Present, be entered on the Journal.

Neither House, during the Session of Congress, shall, without the Consent of the other, adjourn for more than three days, nor to any other Place than that in which the two Houses shall be sitting.

Section 6. The Senators and Representatives shall receive a Compensation for their Services, to be ascertained by Law, and paid out of the Treasury of the United States. They shall in all Cases, except Treason, Felony and Breach of the Peace, be privileged from Arrest during their Attendance at the Session of their respective Houses, and in going to and returning from the same; and for any Speech or Debate in either House, they shall not be questioned in any other Place.

No Senator or Representative shall, during the Time for which he was elected, be appointed to any civil Office under the Authority of the United States, which shall have been created, or the Emoluments whereof shall have been increased during such time; and no Person holding any Office under the United States, shall be a Member of either House during his Continuance in Office.

Section 7. All Bills for raising Revenue shall originate in the House of Representatives; but the Senate may propose or concur with Amendments as on other Bills.

Every Bill which shall have passed the House of Representatives and the Senate, shall, before it become a Law, be presented to the President of the United States: If he approve he shall sign it, but if not he shall return it, with his Objections to that House in which it shall have originated, who shall enter the Objections at large on their Journal, and proceed to reconsider it. If after such Reconsideration two thirds of that House shall agree to pass the Bill, it shall be sent, together with the Objections, to the other House, by which it shall likewise be reconsidered, and if approved by two thirds of that House, it shall become a Law. But in all such Cases the Votes of both Houses shall be determined by Yeas and Nays, and the Names of the Persons voting for and against the Bill shall be entered on the Journal of each House respectively. If any Bill shall not be returned by the President within ten Days (Sundays excepted) after it shall have been presented to him, the Same shall be a Law, in like Manner as if he had signed it, unless the Congress by their Adjournment prevent its Return, in which Case it shall not be a Law.

Every Order, Resolution, or Vote to which the Concurrence of the Senate and House of Representatives may be necessary (except on a question of Adjournment) shall be presented to the President of the United States; and before the Same shall take Effect, shall be approved by him, or being disapproved by him, shall be repassed by two thirds of the Senate and House of Representatives, according to the Rules and Limitations prescribed in the Case of a Bill.

Section 8. The Congress shall have Power To lay and collect Taxes, Duties, Imposts and Excises, to pay the Debts and provide for the common Defence and general Welfare of the United States; but all Duties, Imposts and Excises shall be uniform throughout the United States; To borrow Money on the credit of the United States; To regulate Commerce with foreign Nations, and among the several States, and with the Indian Tribes; To establish an uniform Rule of Naturalization, and uniform Laws on the subject of Bankruptcies throughout the United States; To coin Money, regulate the Value thereof, and of foreign Coin, and fix the Standard of Weights and Measures; To provide for the Punishment of counterfeiting the Securities and current Coin of the United States; To establish Post Offices and post Roads; To promote the Progress of Science and useful Arts, by securing for limited Times to Authors and Inventors the exclusive Right to their respective Writings and Discoveries; To constitute Tribunals inferior to the supreme Court; To define and punish Piracies and Felonies committed on the high Seas, and Offences against the Law of Nations; To declare War, grant Letters of Marque and Reprisal, and make Rules concerning Captures

on Land and Water; To raise and support Armies, but no Appropriation of Money to that Use shall be for a longer Term than two Years; To provide and maintain a Navy; To make Rules for the Government and Regulation of the land and naval Forces; To provide for calling forth the Militia to execute the Laws of the Union, suppress Insurrections and repel Invasions; To provide for organizing, arming, and disciplining, the Militia, and for governing such Part of them as may be employed in the Service of the United States, reserving to the States respectively, the Appointment of the Officers, and the Authority of training the Militia according to the discipline prescribed by Congress; To exercise exclusive Legislation in all Cases whatsoever, over such District (not exceeding ten Miles square) as may, by Cession of particular States, and the Acceptance of Congress, become the Seat of the Government of the United States, and to exercise like Authority over all Places purchased by the Consent of the Legislature of the State in which the Same shall be, for the Erection of Forts, Magazines, Arsenals, dock-Yards, and other needful Buildings;—And To make all Laws which shall be necessary and proper for carrying into Execution the foregoing Powers, and all other Powers vested by this Constitution in the Government of the United States, or in any Department or Officer thereof.

Section 9. The Migration or Importation of such Persons as any of the States now existing shall think proper to admit, shall not be prohibited by the Congress prior to the Year one thousand eight hundred and eight, but a Tax or duty may be imposed on such Importation, not exceeding ten dollars for each Person.

The Privilege of the Writ of Habeas Corpus shall not be suspended, unless when in Cases of Rebellion or Invasion the public Safety may require it.

No Bill of Attainder or ex post facto Law shall be passed.

No Capitation, or other direct, Tax shall be laid, unless in Proportion to the Census or enumeration herein before directed to be taken.

No Tax or Duty shall be laid on Articles exported from any State.

No Preference shall be given by any Regulation of Commerce or Revenue to the Ports of one State over those of another; nor shall Vessels bound to, or from, one State, be obliged to enter, clear, or pay Duties in another.

No Money shall be drawn from the Treasury, but in Consequence of Appropriations made by Law; and a regular Statement and Account of the Receipts and Expenditures of all public Money shall be published from time to time.

No Title of Nobility shall be granted by the United States: And no Person holding any Office of Profit or Trust under them, shall, without the Consent of the Congress, accept of any present, Emolument, Office, or Title, of any kind whatever, from any King, Prince, or foreign State.

Section 10. No State shall enter into any Treaty, Alliance, or Confederation; grant Letters of Marque and Reprisal; coin Money; emit Bills of Credit; make any Thing but gold and silver Coin a Tender in Payment of Debts; pass any Bill of Attainder, ex post facto Law, or Law impairing the Obligation of Contracts, or grant any Title of Nobility.

No State shall, without the Consent of the Congress, lay any Imposts or Duties on Imports or Exports, except what may be absolutely necessary for executing it's inspection Laws: and the net Produce of all Duties and Imposts, laid by any State on Imports or Exports, shall be for the Use of the Treasury of the United States; and all such Laws shall be subject to the Revision and Controul of the Congress.

No State shall, without the Consent of Congress, lay any Duty of Tonnage, keep Troops, or Ships of War in time of Peace, enter into any Agreement or Compact with another State, or with a foreign Power, or engage in War, unless actually invaded, or in such imminent Danger as will not admit of delay.

Article II

Section 1. The executive Power shall be vested in a President of the United States of America. He shall hold his Office during the Term of four Years, and, together with the Vice President, chosen for the same Term, be elected, as follows:

Each State shall appoint, in such Manner as the Legislature thereof may direct, a Number of Electors, equal to the whole Number of Senators and Representatives to which the State may be entitled in the Congress: but no Senator or Representative, or Person holding an Office of Trust or Profit under the United States, shall be appointed an Elector.

The Electors shall meet in their respective States, and vote by Ballot for two Persons, of whom one at least shall not be an Inhabitant of the same State with themselves. And they shall make a List of all the Persons voted for, and of the Number of Votes for each; which List they shall sign and certify, and transmit sealed to the Seat of the Government of the United States, directed to the President of the Senate. The President of the Senate shall, in the Presence of the Senate and House of Representatives, open all the Certificates, and the Votes shall then be counted. The Person having the greatest Number of Votes shall be the President, if such Number be a Majority of the whole Number of Electors appointed; and if there be more than one who have such Majority, and have an equal Number of Votes, then the House of Representatives shall immediately chuse by Ballot one of them for President; and if no Person have a Majority, then from the five highest on the List the said House shall in like Manner chuse the President. But in chusing the President, the Votes shall be taken by States, the Representation from each State having one Vote; A quorum for this purpose shall consist of a Member or Members from two thirds of the States, and a Majority of all the States shall be necessary to a Choice. In every Case, after the Choice of the President, the Person having the greatest Number of Votes of the Electors shall be the Vice President. But if there should remain two or more who have equal Votes, the Senate shall chuse from them by Ballot the Vice President.

The Congress may determine the Time of chusing the Electors, and the Day on which they shall give their Votes; which Day shall be the same throughout the United States.

No Person except a natural born Citizen, or a Citizen of the United States, at the time of the Adoption of this Constitution, shall be eligible to the Office of President; neither shall any Person be eligible to that Office who shall not have attained to the Age of thirty five Years, and been fourteen Years a Resident within the United States.

In Case of the Removal of the President from Office, or of his Death, Resignation, or Inability to discharge the Powers and Duties of the said Office, the Same shall devolve on the Vice President, and the Congress may by Law provide for the Case of Removal, Death, Resignation or Inability, both of the President and Vice President, declaring what Officer shall then act as President, and such Officer shall act accordingly, until the Disability be removed, or a President shall be elected.

The President shall, at stated Times, receive for his Services, a Compensation, which shall neither be increased nor diminished during the Period for which he shall have been elected, and he shall not receive within that Period any other Emolument from the United States, or any of them.

Before he enter on the Execution of his Office, he shall take the following Oath or Affirmation: "I do solemnly swear (or affirm) that I will faithfully execute the Office of President of the United States, and will to the best of my Ability, preserve, protect and defend the Constitution of the United States."

Section 2. The President shall be Commander in Chief of the Army and Navy of the United States, and of the Militia of the several States, when called into the actual Service of the United States; he may require the Opinion, in writing, of the principal Officer in each of the executive Departments, upon any Subject relating to the Duties of their respective Offices, and he shall have Power to grant Reprieves and Pardons for Offences against the United States, except in Cases of Impeachment.

He shall have Power, by and with the Advice and Consent of the Senate, to make Treaties, provided two thirds of the Senators present concur; and he shall nominate, and by and with the Advice and Consent of the Senate, shall appoint Ambassadors, other public Ministers and Consuls, Judges of the supreme Court, and all other Officers of the United States, whose Appointments are not herein otherwise provided for, and which shall be established by Law: but the Congress may by Law vest the Appointment of such inferior Officers, as they think proper, in the President alone, in the Courts of Law, or in the Heads of Departments.

The President shall have Power to fill up all Vacancies that may happen during the Recess of the Senate, by granting Commissions which shall expire at the End of their next Session.

Section 3. He shall from time to time give to the Congress Information of the State of the Union, and recommend to their Consideration such Measures as he shall judge necessary and expedient; he may, on extraordinary Occasions, convene both Houses, or either of them, and in Case of Disagreement between them, with Respect to the Time of Adjournment, he may adjourn them to such Time as he shall think proper; he shall receive Ambassadors and other public Ministers; he shall take Care that the Laws be faithfully executed, and shall Commission all the Officers of the United States.

Section 4. The President, Vice President and all civil Officers of the United States, shall be removed from Office on Impeachment for, and Conviction of, Treason, Bribery, or other high Crimes and Misdemeanors.

Article III

Section 1. The judicial Power of the United States shall be vested in one supreme Court, and in such inferior Courts as the Congress may from time to time ordain and establish. The Judges, both of the supreme and inferior Courts, shall hold their Offices during good Behaviour, and shall, at stated Times, receive for their Services a Compensation, which shall not be diminished during their Continuance in Office.

Section 2. The Judicial Power shall extend to all Cases, in Law and Equity, arising under this Constitution, the Laws of the United States, and Treaties made, or which shall be made, under their Authority;—to all Cases affecting Ambassadors, other public Ministers and Consuls;—to all Cases of admiralty and maritime Jurisdiction;—to Controversies to which the United States shall be a Party;—to Controversies between two or more States;—between a State and Citizens of another State;—between Citizens of different States;—between Citizens of the same State claiming Lands under Grants of different States, and between a State, or the Citizens thereof, and foreign States, Citizens or Subjects.

In all Cases affecting Ambassadors, other public Ministers and Consuls, and those in which a State shall be Party, the supreme Court shall have original Jurisdiction. In all the other Cases before mentioned, the supreme Court shall have appellate

Jurisdiction, both as to Law and Fact, with such Exceptions, and under such Regulations as the Congress shall make.

The Trial of all Crimes, except in Cases of Impeachment, shall be by Jury; and such Trial shall be held in the State where the said Crimes shall have been committed; but when not committed within any State, the Trial shall be at such Place or Places as the Congress may by Law have directed.

Section 3. Treason against the United States, shall consist only in levying War against them, or in adhering to their Enemies, giving them Aid and Comfort. No Person shall be convicted of Treason unless on the Testimony of two Witnesses to the same overt Act, or on Confession in open Court.

The Congress shall have Power to declare the Punishment of Treason, but no Attainder of Treason shall work Corruption of Blood, or Forfeiture except during the Life of the Person attainted.

Article IV

Section 1. Full Faith and Credit shall be given in each State to the public Acts, Records, and judicial Proceedings of every other State. And the Congress may by general Laws prescribe the Manner in which such Acts, Records and Proceedings shall be proved, and the Effect thereof.

Section 2. The Citizens of each State shall be entitled to all Privileges and Immunities of Citizens in the several States.

A Person charged in any State with Treason, Felony, or other Crime, who shall flee from Justice, and be found in another State, shall on Demand of the executive Authority of the State from which he fled, be delivered up, to be removed to the State having Jurisdiction of the Crime.

No Person held to Service or Labour in one State, under the Laws thereof, escaping into another, shall, in Consequence of any Law or Regulation therein, be discharged from such Service or Labour, but shall be delivered up on Claim of the Party to whom such Service or Labour may be due.

Section 3. New States may be admitted by the Congress into this Union; but no new State shall be formed or erected within the Jurisdiction of any other State; nor any State be formed by the Junction of two or more States, or Parts of States, without the Consent of the Legislatures of the States concerned as well as of the Congress.

The Congress shall have Power to dispose of and make all needful Rules and Regulations respecting the Territory or other Property belonging to the United States; and nothing in this Constitution shall be so construed as to Prejudice any Claims of the United States, or of any particular State.

Section 4. The United States shall guarantee to every State in this Union a Republican Form of Government, and shall protect each of them against Invasion; and on Application of the Legislature, or of the Executive (when the Legislature cannot be convened), against domestic Violence.

Article V

The Congress, whenever two thirds of both Houses shall deem it necessary, shall propose Amendments to this Constitution, or, on the Application of the Legislatures of two thirds of the several States, shall call a Convention for proposing Amendments, which, in either Case, shall be valid to all Intents and Purposes, as Part of this Constitution, when ratified by the Legislatures of three fourths of the several States, or by Conventions in three fourths thereof, as the one or the other Mode of Ratification may be proposed by the Congress; Provided that no Amendment which may be made prior to the Year One thousand eight hundred and eight shall in any Manner affect the first and fourth Clauses in the Ninth Section of the first Article; and that no State, without its Consent, shall be deprived of its equal Suffrage in the Senate.

Article VI

All Debts contracted and Engagements entered into, before the Adoption of this Constitution, shall be as valid against the United States under this Constitution, as under the Confederation.

This Constitution, and the Laws of the United States which shall be made in Pursuance thereof; and all Treaties made, or which shall be made, under the Authority of the United States, shall be the supreme Law of the Land; and the Judges in every State shall be bound thereby, any

Thing in the Constitution or Laws of any State to the Contrary notwithstanding.

The Senators and Representatives before mentioned, and the Members of the several State Legislatures, and all executive and judicial Officers, both of the United States and of the several States, shall be bound by Oath or Affirmation, to support this Constitution; but no religious Test shall ever be required as a Qualification to any Office or public Trust under the United States.

Article VII

The Ratification of the Conventions of nine States, shall be sufficient for the Establishment of this Constitution between the States so ratifying the Same. Done in Convention by the Unanimous Consent of the States present the Seventeenth Day of September in the Year of our Lord one thousand seven hundred and Eighty seven and of the Independence of the United States of America the Twelfth.

ARTICLES IN ADDITION TO, AND AMENDMENT OF THE CONSTITUTION OF THE UNITED STATES OF AMERICA, PROPOSED BY CONGRESS, AND RATIFIED BY THE LEGISLATURES OF THE SEVERAL STATES, PURSUANT TO THE FIFTH ARTICLE OF THE ORIGINAL CONSTITUTION

Amendment I [1791]

Congress shall make no law respecting an establishment of religion, or prohibiting the free exercise thereof; or abridging the freedom of speech, or of the press; or the right of the people peaceably to assemble, and to petition the Government for a redress of grievances.

Amendment II [1791]

A well regulated Militia, being necessary to the security of a free State, the right of the people to keep and bear Arms, shall not be infringed.

Amendment III [1791]

No Soldier shall, in time of peace be quartered in any house, without the consent of the Owner, nor in time of war, but in a manner to be prescribed by law.

Amendment IV [1791]

The right of the people to be secure in their persons, houses, papers, and effects, against unreasonable searches and seizures, shall not be violated, and no Warrants shall issue, but upon probable cause, supported by Oath or affirmation, and particularly describing the place to be searched, and the persons or things to be seized.

Amendment V [1791]

No person shall be held to answer for a capital, or otherwise infamous crime, unless on a presentment or indictment of a Grand Jury, except in cases arising in the land or naval forces, or in the Militia, when in actual service in time of War or public danger; nor shall any person be subject for the same offence to be twice put in jeopardy of life or limb; nor shall be compelled in any criminal case to be a witness against himself, nor be deprived of life, liberty, or property, without due process of law; nor shall private property be taken for public use, without just compensation.

Amendment VI [1791]

In all criminal prosecutions, the accused shall enjoy the right to a speedy and public trial, by an impartial jury of the State and district wherein the crime shall have been committed, which district shall have been previously ascertained by law, and to be informed of the nature and cause of the accusation; to be confronted with the witnesses against him; to have compulsory process for obtaining witnesses in his favor, and to have the Assistance of Counsel for his defence.

Amendment VII [1791]

In suits at common law, where the value in controversy shall exceed twenty dollars, the right of trial by jury shall be preserved, and no fact tried by a jury, shall be otherwise reexamined in any Court of the United States, than according to the rules of the common law.

Amendment VIII [1791]

Excessive bail shall not be required, nor excessive fines imposed, nor cruel and unusual punishments inflicted.

Amendment IX [1791]

The enumeration in the Constitution, of certain rights, shall not be construed to deny or disparage others retained by the people.

Amendment X [1791]

The powers not delegated to the United States by the Constitution, nor prohibited by it to the States, are reserved to the States respectively, or to the people.

Amendment XI [1798]

The Judicial power of the United States shall not be construed to extend to any suit in law or equity, commenced or prosecuted against one of the United States by Citizens of another State, or by Citizens or Subjects of any Foreign State.

Amendment XII [1804]

The Electors shall meet in their respective states and vote by ballot for President and Vice-President, one of whom, at least, shall not be an inhabitant of the same state with themselves; they shall name in their ballots the person voted for as President, and in distinct ballots the person voted for as Vice-President, and they shall make distinct lists of all persons voted for as President, and of all persons voted for as Vice-President, and of the number of votes for each, which lists they shall sign and certify, and transmit sealed to the seat of the government of the United States, directed to the President of the Senate;—the President of the Senate shall, in the presence of the Senate and House of Representatives, open all the certificates and the votes shall then be counted;—The person having the greatest number of votes for President, shall be the President, if such number be a majority of the whole number of Electors appointed; and if no person have such majority, then from the persons having the highest numbers not exceeding three on the list of those voted for as President, the House of Representatives shall chuse immediately, by ballot, the President. But in chusing the President, the votes shall be taken by states, the representation from each state having one vote; a quorum for this purpose shall consist of a member or members from two-thirds of the states, and a majority of all the states shall be necessary to a choice. [And if the House of Representatives shall not chuse a President whenever the right of choice shall devolve upon them, before the fourth day of March next following, then the Vice-President shall act as President, as in case of the death or other constitutional disability of the President.— The person having the greatest number of votes as Vice-President, shall be the Vice-President, if such number be a majority of the whole number of Electors appointed, and if no person have a majority, then from the two highest numbers on the list, the Senate shall choose the Vice-President; a quorum for the purpose shall consist of two-thirds of the whole number of Senators, and a majority of the whole number shall be necessary to a choice. But no person constitutionally ineligible to the office of President shall be eligible to that of Vice-President of the United States.

Amendment XIII [1865]

Section 1. Neither slavery nor involuntary servitude, except as a punishment for crime whereof the party shall have been duly convicted, shall exist within the United States, or any place subject to their jurisdiction.

Section 2. Congress shall have power to enforce this article by appropriate legislation.

Amendment XIV [1868]

Section 1. All persons born or naturalized in the United States, and subject to the jurisdiction thereof, are citizens of the United States and of the State wherein they reside. No State shall make or enforce any law which shall abridge the privileges or immunities of citizens of the United States; nor shall any State deprive any person of life, liberty, or property, without due process of law; nor deny to any person within its jurisdiction the equal protection of the laws.

Section 2. Representatives shall be apportioned among the several States according to their respective numbers, counting the whole number of persons in each State, excluding Indians not taxed. But when the right to vote at any election for the choice of electors for President and Vice-President of the United States, Representatives in Congress, the Executive and Judicial officers of a State, or the members of the Legislature thereof, is denied to any of the male inhabitants of such State, being twenty-one years of age, and citizens of the United States, or in any way abridged, except for participation in rebellion, or other crime, the basis of representation therein shall be reduced in the proportion which the number of such male citizens shall bear to the whole number of male citizens twenty-one years of age in such State.

Section 3. No person shall be a Senator or Representative in Congress, or elector of President and Vice-President, or hold any office, civil or military, under the United States, or under any State, who, having previously taken an oath, as a member of Congress, or as an officer of the United States, or as a member of any State legislature, or as an executive or judicial officer of any State, to support the Constitution of the United States, shall have engaged in insurrection or rebellion against the same, or given aid or comfort to the enemies thereof. But Congress may by a vote of two-thirds of each House, remove such disability.

Section 4. The validity of the public debt of the United States, authorized by law, including debts incurred for payment of pensions and bounties for services in suppressing insurrection or rebellion, shall not be questioned. But neither the United States nor any State shall assume or pay any debt or obligation incurred in aid of insurrection or rebellion against the United States, or any claim for the loss or emancipation of any slave; but all such debts, obligations and claims shall be held illegal and void.

Section 5. The Congress shall have the power to enforce, by appropriate legislation, the provisions of this article.

Amendment XV [1870]

Section 1. The right of citizens of the United States to vote shall not be denied or abridged by the United States or by any State on account of race, color, or previous condition of servitude.

Section 2. The Congress shall have the power to enforce this article by appropriate legislation.

Amendment XVI [1913]

The Congress shall have power to lay and collect taxes on incomes, from whatever source derived, without apportionment among the several States, and without regard to any census or enumeration.

Amendment XVII [1913]

The Senate of the United States shall be composed of two Senators from each State, elected by the people thereof, for six years; and each Senator shall have one vote. The electors in each State shall have the qualifications requisite for electors of the most numerous branch of the State legislatures.

When vacancies happen in the representation of any State in the Senate, the executive authority of such State shall issue writs of election to fill such vacancies: *Provided*, That the legislature of any State may empower the executive thereof to make temporary appointments until the people fill the vacancies by election as the legislature may direct.

This amendment shall not be so construed as to affect the election or term of any Senator chosen before it becomes valid as part of the Constitution.

Amendment XVIII [1919]

Section 1. After one year from the ratification of this article the manufacture, sale, or transportation of intoxicating liquors within, the importation thereof into, or the exportation thereof from the United States and all territory subject to the jurisdiction thereof for beverage purposes is hereby prohibited.

Section 2. The Congress and the several States shall have concurrent power to enforce this article by appropriate legislation.

Section 3. This article shall be inoperative unless it shall have been ratified as an amendment to the Constitution by the legislatures of the several States, as provided in the Constitution, within seven years from the date of the submission hereof to the States by the Congress.

Amendment XIX [1920]

The right of citizens of the United States to vote shall not be denied or abridged by the United States or by any State on account of sex.

Congress shall have power to enforce this article by appropriate legislation.

Amendment XX [1933]

Section 1. The terms of the President and the Vice President shall end at noon on the 20th day of January, and the terms of Senators and Representatives at noon on the 3d day of January, of the years in which such terms would have ended if this article had not been ratified; and the terms of their successors shall then begin.

Section 2. The Congress shall assemble at least once in every year, and such meeting shall begin at noon on the 3d day of January, unless they shall by law appoint a different day.

Section 3. If, at the time fixed for the beginning of the term of the President, the President elect shall have died, the Vice President elect shall become President. If a President shall not have been chosen before the time fixed for the beginning of his term, or if the President elect shall have failed to qualify, then the Vice President elect shall act as President until a President shall have qualified; and the Congress may by law provide for the case wherein neither a President elect nor a Vice President shall have qualified, declaring who shall then act as President, or the manner in which one who is to act shall be selected, and such person shall act accordingly until a President or Vice President shall have qualified.

Section 4. The Congress may by law provide for the case of the death of any of the persons from whom the House of Representatives may chuse a President whenever the right of choice shall have devolved upon them, and for the case of the death of any of the persons from whom the Senate may chuse a Vice President whenever the right of choice shall have devolved upon them.

Section 5. Sections 1 and 2 shall take effect on the 15th day of October following the ratification of this article.

Section 6. This article shall be inoperative unless it shall have been ratified as an amendment to the Constitution by the legislatures of three-fourths of the several States within seven years from the date of its submission.

Amendment XXI [1933]

Section 1. The eighteenth article of amendment to the Constitution of the United States is hereby repealed.

Section 2. The transportation or importation into any State, Territory, or Possession of the United States for delivery or use therein of intoxicating liquors, in violation of the laws thereof, is hereby prohibited.

Section 3. This article shall be inoperative unless it shall have been ratified as an amendment to the Constitution by conventions in the several States, as provided in the Constitution, within seven years from the date of the submission hereof to the States by the Congress.

Amendment XXII [1951]

Section 1. No person shall be elected to the office of the President more than twice, and no person who has held the office of President, or acted as President, for more than two years of a term to which some other person was elected President shall be elected to the office of President more than once. But this Article shall not apply to any person holding the office of President when this Article was proposed by Congress, and shall not prevent any person who may be holding the office of President, or acting as President, during the term within which this Article becomes operative from holding the office of President or acting as President during the remainder of such term.

Section 2. This article shall be inoperative unless it shall have been ratified as an amendment to the Constitution by the legislatures of three-fourths of the several States within seven years from the date of its submission to the States by the Congress.

Amendment XXIII [1961]

Section 1. The District constituting the seat of Government of the United States shall appoint in such manner as Congress may direct: A number of electors of President and Vice President equal to the whole number of Senators and Representatives in Congress to which the District would be entitled if it were a State, but in no event more than the least populous State; they shall be in addition to those appointed by the States, but they shall be considered, for the purposes of the election of President and Vice President, to be electors appointed by a State; and they shall meet in the District and perform such duties as provided by the twelfth article of amendment.

Section 2. The Congress shall have power to enforce this article by appropriate legislation.

Amendment XXIV [1964]

Section 1. The right of citizens of the United States to vote in any primary or other election for President or Vice President, for electors for President or Vice President, or for Senator or Representative in Congress, shall not be denied or abridged by the United States or any State by reason of failure to pay poll tax or other tax.

Section 2. The Congress shall have power to enforce this article by appropriate legislation.

Amendment XXV [1967]

Section 1. In case of the removal of the President from office or of his death or resignation, the Vice President shall become President.

Section 2. Whenever there is a vacancy in the office of the Vice President, the President shall nominate a Vice President who shall take office upon confirmation by a majority vote of both Houses of Congress.

Section 3. Whenever the President transmits to the President pro tempore of the Senate and the Speaker of the House of Representatives his written declaration that he is unable to discharge the powers and duties of his office, and until he transmits to them a written declaration to the contrary, such powers and duties shall be discharged by the Vice President as Acting President.

Section 4. Whenever the Vice President and a majority of either the principal officers of the executive departments or of such other body as Congress may by law provide, transmit to the President pro tempore of the Senate and the Speaker of the House of Representatives their written declaration that the President is unable to discharge the powers and duties of his office, the Vice President shall immediately assume the powers and duties of the office as Acting President.

Thereafter, when the President transmits to the President pro tempore of the Senate and the Speaker of the House of Representatives his written declaration that no inability exists, he shall resume the powers and duties of his office unless the Vice President and a majority of either the principal officers of the executive department or of such other body as Congress may by law provide, transmit within four days to the President pro tempore of the Senate and the Speaker of the House of Representatives their written declaration that the President is unable to discharge the powers and duties of his office. Thereupon Congress shall decide the issue, assembling within forty-eight hours for that purpose if not in session. If the Congress, within twenty-one days after receipt of the latter written declaration, or, if Congress is not in session, within twenty-one days after Congress is required to assemble, determines by two-thirds vote of both Houses that the President is unable to discharge the powers and duties of his office, the Vice President shall continue to discharge the same as Acting President; otherwise, the President shall resume the powers and duties of his office.

Amendment XXVI [1971]

Section 1. The right of citizens of the United States, who are eighteen years of age or older, to vote shall not be denied or abridged by the United States or by any State on account of age.

Section 2. The Congress shall have power to enforce this article by appropriate legislation.

Amendment XXVII [1992]

No law, varying the compensation for the services of the Senators and Representatives, shall take effect, until an election of representatives shall have intervened.

NetNotes

ALTERNATIVE DISPUTE RESOLUTION (ADR)

American Arbitration Association at *www.adr.org*.

The Mediation Information and Resource Center at *www.mediate.com*.

The ABA Section on Dispute Resolution at *www.abanet.org/dispute*.

The Victim Offender Mediation Association at *www.voma.org*.

BUSINESS INFORMATION

Business ownership information, such as the names of the resident agent and the corporate officers at *www.westlaw.com* (Westlaw) or *www.lexis.com* (Lexis).

The Electronic Data Gathering, Analysis, and Retrieval (EDGAR) system at *www.sec.gov/edgar.shtml* or *www.freeedgar.com*.

Information on the Americans with Disabilities Act—Go to the U.S. Department of Justice site at *www.usdoj.gov/crt/ada/adahom1.htm* or the Americans with Disabilities Act Document Center at *www.jan.wvu.edu/links/adalinks.htm*.

COMMERCIALON-LINE PROVIDERS

Lexis at *www.lexis.com*.

Westlaw at *www.westlaw.com*.

Findlaw at *www.findlaw.com*.

VersusLaw at *www.versuslaw.com.*

LoisLaw at *www.loislaw.com.*

GOVERNMENT SITES

The EEOC home page is located at *www.eeoc.gov.*

The FBI maintains a web site at *www.fbi.gov.*

The U.S. Department of Justice maintains statistics about crimes and victims at *www.ojp.usdoj.gov/bjs.*

INFORMATION ON THE COURT SYSTEM

Map of the federal circuits with links to their cases—Go to *www.law.emory. edu/FEDCTS.* Note that FEDCTS must be typed in all caps.

Biographies of the U.S. Supreme Court justices—Go to *http://supremecourtus. gov/about/biographiescurrent.pdf.*

Information on specific state courts—Go to the National Center for State Courts, *www.ncsconline.org/D_KIS/info_court_web_sites.html.*

Information on federal courts—Go to either the federal judiciary home page at *www.uscourts.gov* or the Federal Judicial Center home page at *www.fjc.gov.*

The U.S. Supreme Court—Go to *www.supremecourtus.gov.*

Read about and see video clips of current trials at *www.cnn.com/crime.*

LEGAL ETHICS

Developments in legal ethics and links to the states' Rules of Professional Conduct or Code of Professional Responsibility and to their ethics opinions—Go to *www.law.cornell.edu/ethics* and *www.legalethics.com.*

You can locate the ABA Model Rules of Professional Conduct at *www.abanet. org/cpr/mrpc/mrpc_toc.html.*

LEGAL NEWS

Start at Findlaw: *www.findlaw.com.* Click on "News."

LEGAL SEARCH ENGINES

There are various search engines that can assist you with your Internet legal research. Two that have been designed specifically for legal research are *www.lawcrawler.com* and *http://gsulaw.gsu.edu/metaindex*.

ORGANIZATIONS

American Anti-Defamation League (AADL) at *www.adl.org*.

American Arbitration Association (AAA) at *www.adr.org*.

American Bar Association (ABA) at *www.abanet.org*.

American Civil Liberties Union (ACLU) at *www.aclu.org*.

Court Appointed Special Advocates (CASA) at *www.nationalcasa.org*.

Southern Center for Human Rights (SCHR) at *www.schr.org*.

PRIMARY MATERIAL

U.S. Supreme Court opinions dating back to the 1800 at *www.findlaw.com/casecode/supreme.html*.

Federal appellate court opinions at *www.findlaw.com/ casecode/index.html*. Select your circuit.

State court opinions at *www.findlaw.com/casecode/index.html*. Select your state.

Federal statutes and regulations at *www.findlaw.com/casecode/index.html*. Select the US Code or the Code of Federal Regulations.

State statutes and regulations at *www.findlaw.com/casecode/indexhtml*. Select your state.

Current information on federal legislation—A good source is *http://thomas.loc.gov*, provided by the Library of Congress.

The Declaration of Independence at the National Archives web site: *www.archives.gov exhibits/charters/declaration.html*.

The Constitution at *www.archives.gov/exhibits/charters/constitution.html* or *http://caselaw.findlaw.com/data/constitution/articles.html*.

The Bill of Rights at *www.archives.gov/exhibits/charters/bill_of_rights.html* or *http://caselaw.findlaw.com/data/Constitution/amendments.html*.

TORTS

Medical information—You can find current medical news at *www.medscape.com*. The Cancer Web at *cancerweb.ncl.ac.uk/omd* contains an on-line medical dictionary.

Consumer Product Safety Commission at *www.cpsc.gov*.

UNIFORM LAWS

The Uniform Commercial Code as revised through 2001 at *www.law.cornell.edu/ucc/ucc.table.html*.

The Uniform Probate Code at *www.law.cornell.edu/uniform/probate.html*.

Various uniform laws governing the family, such as the Uniform Child Custody Jurisdiction Act, the Uniform Interstate Family Support Act, the Uniform Premarital Agreement Act, and the Uniform Marriage and Divorce Act can be found at *www.law.cornell.edu/uniform/vol9.html*.

Glossary

Abstract A condensed history of the title to real property, which includes the chain of ownership and a record of all liens, taxes, or other encumbrances that may impair the title.

Abuse of process Misusing the criminal or civil court process.

Accessory Also referred to as an **accomplice**; a person who assists the principal in the preparation of the crime.

Accessory after the fact A person who aids the principal after the commission of the crime.

Accomplice Also known as a *principal in the second degree;* a person who assists the principal with the crime or with the preparation of the crime.

Accord and satisfaction An accord is an agreement to do something different than originally promised. The satisfaction is the performance of the accord.

Acquit To determine that a criminal defendant is not guilty of the crime with which he or she is charged.

Actual cause Also known as **cause in fact**; this is measured by the "but for" standard: But for the defendant's actions, the plaintiff would not have been injured.

Actual damages See **Compensatory damages.**

Actus reus Bad act.

Adhesion contract A contract formed where the weaker party has no realistic bargaining power. Typically a form contract is offered on a "take it or leave it" basis.

Adjudicatory hearing A mechanism through which parties to a dispute can present arguments and evidence about their case to an administrative law judge.

Administrative law Rules and regulations created by administrative agencies.

Administrative law judge Another name for a **hearing officer.**

Administrative regulations Rules, regulations, orders, and decisions created by administrative agencies under their authority to interpret specific statutes.

Administrator/administratrix A person appointed by the court to carry out the directions and requests of someone's will.

ADR See **Alternative dispute resolution.**

Advance sheets The first printing of a court decision before it appears in a hardbound reporter.

Adverse possession A transfer of real property rights that occurs after someone other than the owner has had actual, open, adverse, and exclusive use of the property for a statutorily determined number of years.

Affinity Persons related to the decedent by marriage.

Affirm A decision is affirmed when the litigants appeal the trial court decision and the higher court agrees with what the lower court has done.

Affirmative defense A defense whereby the defendant offers new evidence to avoid judgment.

Agency adoption An adoption in which a licensed agency assumes responsibility for screening adoptive parents and matching them with available children.

Agent Someone who has the power to act in the place of another.

Alibi defense A defense requiring proof that the defendant could not have been at the scene of the crime.

Alien corporation A corporation formed in another country.

Alimony Also known as **maintenance** or **support**; financial support and other forms of assistance required to supply the "necessities" of life.

Alternative dispute resolution (ADR) Techniques for resolving conflicts that are alternatives to full-scale litigation. The two most common are **arbitration** and **mediation.**

American Bar Association (ABA) A national voluntary organization of lawyers.

American Jurisprudence Second (Am. Jur. 2d) A general legal encyclopedia that summarizes the entire body of American law.

American Law Reports (ALR) ALR contains the full text of leading court opinions, followed by a discussion of the issue with references to cases from around the country. Only selected topics are covered, but they are covered in more depth than you will find in an encyclopedia.

Amicus curiae Someone who, with the court's permission, intervenes in litigation, usually on appeal, to influence the decision. Also known as a **friend of the court**.

Analogize To find similarities between two situations.

Analogous Similar; analogous cases involve similar facts and rules of law.

Annotated codes Private publications that include not only the statutes arranged by subject matter but also editorial material, such as legislative history and summaries of court decisions that have interpreted the statutes.

Annotated statutes See **Annotated codes**.

Annotations Editorial features, such as court decision summaries and references to other sources of information, added by the editor to assist the researcher.

Annulment A legal (or religious) judgment that a valid marriage never existed.

Answer The defendant's reply to the complaint. It may contain statements of denial, admission, or lack of knowledge and affirmative defenses.

Antecedent When a pronoun (*hers, her, his, him, it, its, them, their, theirs*) substitutes for a noun that has preceded it, the noun is known as an antecedent.

Anti-heart-balm statute A law that prohibits lawsuits for such things as breach of a promise of marriage, alienation of affection, and seduction of a person over the legal age of consent.

Appeal To ask a higher court to review the actions of a lower court.

Appealable issues Questions that can form the basis for an appeal.

Appellant or **petitioner** The party in a lawsuit who has initiated an appeal.

Appellate brief An attorney's written argument presented to an appeals court, setting forth a statement of the law as it should be applied to the client's facts.

Appellate courts Courts that determine whether lower courts have made errors of law.

Appellate jurisdiction The power of a higher court to review and modify the decision of a lower court.

Appellee or **respondent** The party in a lawsuit against whom an appeal has been filed.

Appropriation An intentional unauthorized exploitive use of another person's personality, name, or picture for the defendant's benefit.

Arbitration An ADR mechanism whereby the parties submit their disagreement to a third party whose decision is binding.

Arraignment A criminal proceeding at which the court informs the defendant of the charges being brought against him or her and the defendant enters a plea.

Arrest Occurs when the police restrain a person's freedom and charge the person with a crime.

Arrest warrant A court order directing the arrest of a person.

Arson The malicious burning of the house or property of another.

Articles of incorporation The primary document needed to form a corporation.

Artisan's lien The right to retain an interest in property until a worker has been paid for his or her labor.

Assault An intentional act that creates a reasonable apprehension of an immediate harmful or offensive physical contact.

Assigned counsel A private attorney paid by the state on a contractual basis to represent an indigent client.

Assignee A person to whom contract rights are assigned.

Assignment The transfer by one of the original parties to the contract of part or all of his or her interest to a third party.

Assignor A person who assigns contract rights.

Assumption In logic, a belief that justifies one in arguing a conclusion.

Assumption of the risk Voluntarily and knowingly subjecting oneself to danger.

At-will employment When an employee has not signed a formal contract with the employer governing the employment relationship.

Attachment If a creditor either possesses the collateral or has a signed **security agreement** and gave something of value and if the debtor has rights in the collateral, the creditor's interest in the security is said to have attached.

Attorney Lawyer; a person licensed by a court to practice law.

Attorney-client privilege A rule of evidence that prevents an attorney or a paralegal from being compelled to testify about confidential client information.

Attorney general The chief legal officer of the federal or a state government.

Bail Money or something else of value that is held by the government to ensure the defendant's appearance in court.

Bailee The party taking temporary control of personal property during a bailment.

Bailiff An officer of the court who is responsible for maintaining order in the courtroom.

Bailment   A temporary transfer of personal property to someone other than the owner for a specified purpose.

Bailor   The owner of the personal property that is being temporarily transferred as part of a bailment.

Bankruptcy judges   Appointed for set terms, they handle bankruptcy matters.

Battered woman's or spouse's syndrome   Being the victim of repeated attacks, self-defense sometimes is allowed to the victim, even when the victim is not in immediate danger.

Battery   An intentional act that creates a harmful or offensive physical contact. Can form the basis for either a tort or a criminal action.

Bearer paper   Has written on its front a statement that it is payable to cash or payable to the bearer, or has a signature on the back, causing it to be indorsed in blank.

Bench trial   A trial conducted without a jury.

Beneficiary   The person named in a will, insurance policy, or trust who receives a benefit.

Bequest   Also known as a **legacy**; a gift of personal property in a will.

Beyond a reasonable doubt   The standard of proof used in criminal trials. The evidence presented must be so conclusive and complete that there are no reasonable doubts regarding the guilt of the accused.

Bilateral contract   A contract where a promise is exchanged for a promise.

Bill   A proposed law as presented to a legislature.

Bill of Rights   The first ten amendments to the U.S. Constitution.

Black letter law   Generally accepted legal principles.

Bluebook   A book originally written by a group of law students to provide a uniform method for citations in law reviews; contains detailed rules for all forms of citation.

Board of directors   The group responsible for the management of a corporation.

Boilerplate   Standard language found in a particular type of legal document.

Bona fide occupational qualification (BFOQ)   A defense to an overt discrimination claim, alleging that the qualification is necessary to the essence of the business operation.

Booking   The process after arrest that includes taking the defendant's personal information, giving the defendant an opportunity to read and sign a *Miranda* card, and allowing the defendant the opportunity to use a telephone.

Bribery   Offering something of value to a public official with the purpose of influencing that official's actions.

Brief   Either a short written summary of a court opinion or a written argument presented to a court. See **Appellate brief.**

Brief answer   In a law office memorandum, the brief answer gives the reader a short, specific answer to the question presented.

Broad holding   A statement of the court's decision in which the facts are either omitted or given in very general terms so that it will apply to a wider range of cases.

Burden of production   The necessity to produce some evidence, but it need not be so strong as to convince the trier of fact of its truth.

Burden of proof   The necessity of proving the truth of the matter asserted.

Bureau of National Affairs (BNA)   A private publishing company that publishes legal materials, including United States Law Week.

Burglary   Breaking into and entering a building with the intent of committing a felony.

"But for" standard   See **Actual cause.**

Buyer in the ordinary course of business   Someone who buys a product in good faith and without knowledge that someone else has a security interest in the goods.

Canons of construction   General principles that guide the courts in their interpretation of statutes.

Capital crime   A crime for which the death sentence can be imposed.

Caption   The heading section of a pleading that contains the names of the parties, the name of the court, the title of the action, the docket or file number, and the name of the pleading.

Case briefing   A method for summarizing court opinions.

Case citation   Information that tells the reader the name of the case, where it can be located, the court that decided it, and the year it was decided. The Bluebook gives precise rules as to how case citations are to be written.

Case history   Either prior or subsequent procedural history of the case cited.

Case management   Managing the flow of paperwork involved in handling client cases.

Case of first impression   A type of case that the court has never faced before.

Case reporters   Books that contain appellate court decisions. There are both official and unofficial reporters.

Cause of action   A claim that based on the law and the facts is sufficient to support a lawsuit. If the plaintiff does not state a valid cause of action in the complaint, the court will dismiss it.

Cause in fact   See **Actual cause.**

Caveat emptor   Let the buyer beware.

Censure   A public or private statement that an attorney's conduct violated the code of ethics.

Certiorari   See **Writ of certiorari.**

Challenge for cause   A method for excusing a prospective juror based on the juror's inability to serve in an unbiased manner.

Charging the jury   The judge informs the jurors of the law they need to know to make their decision.

Charitable immunity   The prohibition against suing charitable institutions.

Chattel   Personal property.

Check   A specialized form of a draft in which a bank depositor names a specific payee to whom funds are to be paid from the drawer's account.

Checks and balances   Division among governmental branches so that each branch acts as a check on the power of the other two, thereby maintaining a balance of power among the three branches.

Child abuse   Intentional harm to a child's physical or mental well-being.

Child neglect   The negligent failure to provide a child with the necessaries of life.

Child support   Money that the noncustodial parent contributes to assist the custodial parent in paying for a child's food, shelter, clothing, medical care, and education.

Citation   A stylized form for giving the reader information about a legal authority, generally including the name of the authority, its date, and specifics such as volume and page numbers to help the reader locate it. For court opinions, a citation includes the name of the case, where it can be located, the name of the court that decided it, and the year it was decided. A statutory citation is a formalized method for referring to a statute's chapter (or title) and section numbers. The Bluebook gives precise rules as to how citations are to be written. See **Bluebook**.

Civil action   A lawsuit brought to enforce an individual right or gain payment for an individual wrong.

Civil law   Law that deals with harm to an individual.

Civil liberties   Legal guarantees that the government will not interfere with aspects of people's personal lives.

Civil rights   Legal rights that (1) are associated with being a citizen or an inhabitant of a country and are enforced by the government of that country, and (2) involve having the government do something for its citizens.

Class action suit   A lawsuit brought by a person as a representative for a group of people who have been similarly injured.

Clear and convincing   An evidentiary standard that requires more than a preponderance of the evidence but less than beyond a reasonable doubt.

Clear title   Also known as **marketable title**; an ownership right that is free from encumbrances or other defects.

Clearly erroneous   Standard used by appellate courts when reviewing a trial court's findings of fact.

Client confidentiality   An ethical rule requiring that attorneys and paralegals maintain their clients' secrets.

Client trust account   A bank account used to hold money belonging to a client or to a third party.

Closely held corporation   A relatively small business operation in which one person or the members of a family own all the stock.

Closing statement   An itemized allocation of all the costs and moneys exchanged among the various parties, including financial institutions and real estate brokers, when a property is sold.

Code   A compilation of federal or state statutes in which the statutes are organized by subject matter rather than by year of enactment.

Code of Federal Regulations (C.F.R.)   A compilation of federal administrative regulations arranged by agency.

Codicil   A supplement or addition to a will that modifies, explains, or adds to its provisions.

Codification   The process of organizing statutes by subject matter.

Codification of the common law   The process of legislative enactment of areas of the law previously governed solely by the common law.

Collateral heir   One who has the same ancestors, but does not descend from the decedent.

Comma splice   A type of run-on sentence; two independent clauses joined by a comma.

Commercial impracticability   An argument that a contract has become too costly for one of the parties.

Commercial paper   A written promise or order to pay a certain sum of money.

Committee hearing   Legislative committees often hold public hearings where interested parties can testify about a proposed law. The transcript of the hearing becomes a part of the statute's legislative history.

Committee report   When a legislative committee holds public hearings on proposed legislation, the result of those hearings is sometimes published in a committee report, which becomes part of the statute's legislative history.

Common law   Law created by the courts.

Common-law marriage   A marriage that has not been solemnized but in which the parties have mutually agreed to enter into a relationship in which they accept all the duties and responsibilities that correspond to those of marriage.

Community property states   States that classify all property acquired by either the husband or the wife during the marriage, with the exception of gifts or inheritance, as marital property to be equally distributed between the spouses at the time of the divorce.

Comparative negligence   A method for measuring the relative negligence of the plaintiff and the defendant, with a commensurate sharing of the compensation for the injuries.

Compelling interest test See **Strict scrutiny test.**

Compensatory damages Money awarded to a plaintiff in payment for his or her actual losses. Compare **punitive damages.**

Complaint The pleading that begins a lawsuit.

Complete defense A defense that, if proven, relieves the defendant of all criminal responsibility.

Compulsory joinder When a person must be brought into a lawsuit as either a plaintiff or a defendant.

Concurrent conflict of interest Simultaneously representing adverse clients.

Concurrent jurisdiction When more than one court has jurisdiction to hear a case.

Concurring opinion An opinion that agrees with the majority's result but disagrees with its reasoning.

Conditional fee estate The current owner of the land retains ownership only as long as certain conditions are met.

Cone of silence See **Ethical wall.**

Confidentiality The ethical rule prohibiting attorneys and paralegals from disclosing information regarding a client or a client's case.

Conflict of interest The ethical rule prohibiting attorneys and paralegals from working for opposing sides in a case.

Consanguinity See **Kindred.**

Consequential damages See **Special damages.**

Consideration Something of value exchanged to form the basis of a contract; each side must give consideration for a valid contract to exist.

Consortium See **Loss of consortium.**

Conspiracy An agreement to commit an unlawful act.

Constitution The fundamental law of a nation or state.

Constitutional court A court established by Article III of the U.S. Constitution.

Constitutional law The study of the U.S. Constitution, the legal framework it established, and the rights it protects; a body of principles and rules either explicitly stated in, or inferred from, the U.S. Constitution and those of the individual states.

Constructive Not factually true, but accepted by the courts as being legally true.

Constructive delivery When actual delivery is impossible but the court decides that enough was done to prove intent to relinquish title and control.

Constructive eviction An act by a landlord that makes the premises unfit or unsuitable for occupancy.

Constructive knowledge Not actual knowledge but the knowledge the person should have if reasonable care is taken to be informed.

Contextual analysis An approach to constitutional interpretation whereby judges examine other parts of the same document or similar documents to see how the same words or phrases were used in those related contexts. Also a form of statutory analysis in which meaning is inferred from the statement of legislative purpose and other sections of the statute.

Contingency fee Attorney compensation as a percentage of the amount recovered rather than a flat amount of money or an hourly fee.

Contract An agreement supported by consideration.

Contract reformation An equitable remedy that allows the courts to "rewrite" contract provisions.

Contributory negligence Negligence by the plaintiff that contributed to his or her injury. Normally, any finding of contributory negligence acts as a complete bar to the plaintiff's recovery. See **Comparative negligence.**

Conversion The taking of someone else's property with the intent of permanently depriving the owner; the civil side of theft.

Copyright An author or artist's right to control the use of his or her works.

Corporation A business entity formed by an association of shareholders.

Corpus Juris Secundum (C.J.S.) West's law encyclopedia. Contains cross-references to West digest topics and key numbers.

Count In a complaint, one cause of action.

Counterclaim A claim by the defendant against the plaintiff. A compulsory counterclaim relates to the facts alleged in the complaint. A permissive counterclaim can relate to an entirely different factual setting.

Court A unit of the judicial branch of government that has the authority to decide legal disputes.

Court clerk A court official responsible for keeping the court files in proper condition and ensuring that the various motions filed by lawyers and the actions taken by judges are properly recorded.

Court commissioner A title given in some states to a public official with limited judicial powers.

Court of record A court where a permanent record is kept of the testimony, lawyers' remarks, and judges' rulings.

Court reporter A person trained to take a verbatim transcript of a courtroom proceeding or deposition.

Covenant not to compete A promise not to compete within a given geographical area for a specific time period.

Cover Finding substitute goods.

Crime An activity that has been prohibited by the legislature as violating a duty owed to society and hence prosecutable, with the possibility of resulting incarceration or the payment of a fine.

Criminal complaint A document charging a person with a crime.

Criminal justice system Used to refer to a combination of legislative, administrative, and judicial agencies that are involved in the development and enforcement of criminal law in the United States.

Criminal law   Law that deals with harm to society as a whole.

Criminal procedure   The way in which criminal prosecutions are handled; governed by the federal or state rules of criminal procedure.

Critical Legal Studies (CLS)   An offshoot of legal realism that seeks to identify ways in which the law protects certain groups and ideas at the expense of others.

Cross-claim   A claim by one defendant against another defendant or by one plaintiff against another plaintiff.

Cross-examination   The questioning of an opposing witness.

Custodial interrogation   Questioning that occurs after a defendant has been deprived of his or her freedom in a significant way.

Custody   Occurs when the defendant has been deprived of freedom in a significant way.

Damages   Monetary compensation, including compensatory, punitive, and nominal damages.

Deadly force   A force that would cause serious bodily injury or death.

Decedent   A person who died.

Deductive reasoning   A form of logical reasoning based on a major premise, a minor premise, and a conclusion.

Deed   The legal document that formally conveys title to the property to the new owner.

Defamation   The publication of false statements that harm a person's reputation.

Defamation per se   Remarks considered to be so harmful that they are automatically viewed as defamatory.

Default judgment   A judgment entered against a party who fails to complete a required step, such as answering the complaint.

Defendant   In a lawsuit, the person who is sued; in a criminal case, the person who is charged with a crime.

Defense   A fact or legal argument that would relieve the defendant of liability in a civil case or guilt in a criminal case.

Delegatee   A person who owes an obligation to the obligee in a contractual situation.

Delegation   The transfer by one of the original parties to the contract of his or her obligations to a third party.

Delegator   A person who delegates duties under a contract.

Demand letter   A letter from an attorney demanding that some action be taken, with either an implicit or an explicit threat to take the matter to court if the requested action is not forthcoming.

Dependent clause   A clause that contains a subject and a verb but that cannot stand alone, as it does not contain a complete thought. Dependent clauses always begin with subordinating conjunctions.

Deponent   The person who is being asked questions at a deposition.

Deposition   The pretrial oral questioning of a witness under oath.

Derogation of the common law   Used to describe legislation that changes the common law.

Descendants   Also known as issue; lineal heirs who descend from, or issue from, the decedent, such as children and grandchildren.

Detrimental reliance   See **Promissory estoppel.**

Devise   A gift of real estate that is given to someone through a will.

Dicta   Plural of dictum.

Dictum   A statement in a judicial opinion not necessary for the decision of the case.

Digest   A book that contains court opinion headnotes arranged by subject matter.

Direct appellate review   Occurs when the courts think a case is so significant that the middle step of going through an intermediate appellate court should be skipped; the case proceeds directly from a trial court to the highest appellate court.

Direct examination   The questioning of your own witness.

Directed verdict   A verdict ordered by a trial judge if the plaintiff fails to present a prima facie case or if the defendant fails to present a necessary defense.

Disability   Under the Americans with Disabilities Act, a physical or mental impairment that substantially limits a major life activity. An individual with a disability is one who has such an impairment, has a record of such an impairment, or is regarded as having such an impairment.

Disaffirm   The ability to take back one's contractual obligations.

Disbarment   The revocation of an attorney's license.

Disclosure   The intentional publication of embarrassing private affairs.

Discovery   The modern pretrial procedure by which one party gains information from the adverse party.

Disillusionment   See **divorce.**

Dismissal with prejudice   A court order that ends a lawsuit; the suit cannot be refiled by the same parties.

Dismissal without prejudice   A court order that ends a lawsuit; the suit can be refiled by the same parties.

Disparate impact   The legal theory applied when the use of a neutral standard has a disproportionate impact on one protected group.

Disparate treatment   The legal theory applied when a rejected applicant claims the reason for rejection was based on a discriminatory intent but the employer alleges a nondiscriminatory reason.

Disposition   The result reached in a particular case.

Dissenting opinion   An opinion that disagrees with the majority's decision and reasoning.

Distinguish   To find differences (distinctions) between two situations.

Distinguishable   Different; distinguishable cases involve dissimilar facts and/or rules of law.

District attorney   An attorney appointed to prosecute crimes.

Diversity jurisdiction   The power of the federal courts to hear matters of state law if the opposing parties are from different states and the amount in controversy exceeds $75,000.

Divided custody   A situation in which the court separates the children so that each parent is awarded custody of one or more of the children.

Dividend   A distribution of the corporate profit as ordered by the board of directors.

Divorce   Also called disillusionment; a legal judgment that dissolves a marriage.

Doctrine of equitable distribution   A system for distributing property acquired during a marriage on the basis of such factors as the contributions of the spouses, the length of the marriage, the age and health of the spouses, and their ability to make a living.

Doctrine of implied powers   Powers not stated in the Constitution but that are necessary for Congress to carry out other, expressly granted powers.

Documents clerk   Someone who organizes and files legal documents.

Domestic corporation   A corporation doing business in its own state.

Donor   Also known as a **grantor** or **settlor**; a person who creates a trust.

Double jeopardy   A constitutional protection against being tried twice for the same crime.

Draft   A three-party instrument in which the **drawer** orders the drawee, usually a bank, to pay money to the **payee**.

Dramshop laws   Statutes making bar owners responsible if intoxicated patrons negligently injure third parties.

Drawee   On the face of a check or draft, the party that is ordering payment to be made.

Drawer   On the face of a check or draft, the party that is ordered to pay.

Due process   Fifth and Fourteenth Amendment guarantees that notice and a hearing must be provided before depriving someone of property or liberty.

Durable power of attorney   See **Health care proxy.**

Duress   In criminal law, a defense requiring proof that force or a threat of force was used to cause a person to commit a criminal act. In contract law, pressure that is so great as to overwhelm the contracting party's ability to make a free choice.

Earnest money   The money the buyer turns over to the real estate agent to be applied to the purchase price of property.

Easement   A right to use property owned by another for a limited purpose.

Ejusdem generis   A canon of construction meaning "of the same class."

Element   A separable part of a statute that must be satisfied for the statute to apply.

Emancipated minor   Someone who is still under the legal age of adulthood but who has nevertheless been released from parental authority and given the legal rights of an adult.

Eminent domain   The power of government to take private property for public purposes.

Employee   A person working for another. Compare **Independent contractor.**

En banc   When an appellate court that normally sits in panels sits as a whole.

Enabling act   A statute establishing and setting out the powers of an administrative agency.

Encumbrance   A lien or other type of security interest that signifies that some other party has a legitimate claim to the property.

Entrapment   A defense requiring proof that the defendant would not have committed the crime but for police trickery.

Equity   Fairness; a court's power to do justice. Equity powers allow judges to take action when otherwise the law would limit their decisions to monetary awards. Equity powers include a judge's ability to issue an injunction and to order specific performance.

Escheat   A reversion of property to the state when there are no heirs.

Escrow account   A bank account used to hold money belonging to a client or a third party.

Establishment of religion clause   A clause in the First Amendment that restricts the types of actions government can take to recognize and support religious groups and religious principles.

Estate   An interest in or title to real property. In probate law, the total property of whatever kind, both real and personal, that a person owns at the time of his or her death.

Ethical wall   Also known as a **screen** or **cone of silence**; a system developed to shield an attorney or a paralegal from a case that otherwise would create a conflict of interest.

Evict   To remove a tenant from possession of rental property.

Evidence   The way in which a question of fact is established. Evidence can consist of witness testimony or documents and exhibits. It is the proof presented at a trial.

Evolutionary approach   An approach to constitutional interpretation in which judges seek to determine the underlying purpose that the drafters had in mind at the time they wrote the law and the modern-day option that best advances that purpose.

Exception   An attorney's objection to a trial court's ruling in order to preserve it as grounds for an appeal.

Exclusionary rule   A rule that states that evidence obtained in violation of an individual's constitutional rights cannot be used against that individual in a criminal trial.

Exclusive jurisdiction   When only one court has the power to hear a case.

Exculpatory clause   A provision that purports to waive liability.

Exculpatory evidence   Evidence that suggests the defendant's innocence; opposite of **inculpatory evidence.**

Execute   To perform or to sign; in contract law an executed contract is one that has been completely performed.

Executive privilege   A legal doctrine that exempts some members of the executive branch from having to disclose information in situations where nondisclosure is deemed necessary to the discharge of executive responsibilities.

Executor/executrix   A person appointed by the testator to carry out the directions and requests in his or her will.

Executory contract   A contract that has not been fully performed.

Exemplary damages   See **Punitive damages.**

Exhaustion   The requirement that certain preliminary steps be taken.

Exhaustion of administrative remedies   The requirement that relief be sought from an administrative agency before proceeding to court.

Exigent circumstances   Generally, an emergency situation that allows a search to proceed without a warrant.

Explanatory parenthetical   A parenthetical located at the end of a case citation containing information about the case.

Express contracts   Contracts that are formed through words, either oral or written.

Express warranty   An express warranty or promise can be created by an affirmation of fact or a promise made by the seller, a description of the goods being sold (including technical specifications and blueprints), or a sample or model provided.

Extradition   The transportation of an individual from one state to another so that person can be tried on criminal charges.

Fact bound   When even a minor change in the facts can change the outcome.

False arrest   Occurs when a person is arrested (by either a law officer or a citizen) without probable cause and the arrest is not covered by special privilege.

False imprisonment   Occurs whenever one person, through force or the threat of force, unlawfully detains another person against his or her will.

False light   The intentional false portrayal of someone in a way that would be offensive to a reasonable person.

Family law   The area of the law that covers marriage, divorce, and parent-child relationships.

Federal courts of appeals   The intermediate appellate courts in the federal system.

Federal district courts   The trial courts in the federal system.

Federal question jurisdiction   The power of the federal courts to hear matters of federal law.

Federal Register   A daily newspaper in which proposed federal regulations are first printed.

Federal Reporter   The West reporter that contains decisions from the U.S. courts of appeals.

Federal Rules of Civil Procedure   The rules governing the stages of civil litigation in federal courts.

Federal Supplement   The West reporter that contains decisions from the U.S. district courts.

Federalism   A system of government in which the authority to govern is split between a single, nationwide central government and several regional governments that control specific geographical areas.

Fee simple absolute estate   An ownership of land that is free from any conditions or restrictions.

Felony   A serious crime, usually carrying a prison sentence of one or more years.

Fiduciary   A person who has a legally imposed obligation to act in the best interests of another party.

Fiduciary duty   A legally imposed obligation to act in the best interests of the party to whom the duty is owed.

Financing statement   A public record of a security interest.

Fine   A penalty requiring the payment of money.

Floating lien   A security interest in proceeds or after-acquired property.

Floor debate   Debate that takes place in the legislature before a vote is taken on a proposed statute. It becomes part of the statute's legislative history.

Follow precedent   When a court bases its decision on prior similar cases.

Forcible entry and detainer   In some states, a summary civil action by a landlord to regain possession of the premises from a tenant who disputes the landlord's right to possession. Also, an action by anyone with the right to possession who has been unlawfully evicted.

Foreclosure   The process by which a creditor who holds a mortgage or some other form of a lien on real property can force the sale of that property in order to satisfy the debt to the mortgagee or lien holder.

Foreign corporation   A corporation incorporated in one state doing business in another state.

Forfeiture   The loss of money or property as a result of committing a criminal act.

Forgery   The alteration or falsification of documents with the intent to defraud.

Formal contract A contract requiring certain formalities, such as a seal, to be valid.

Formal will A will that has been prepared on a word processor or typewriter and that has been properly signed by the testator and the required witnesses.

Fourth branch of government Administrative agencies.

Fraud A false representation of facts or intentional perversion of the truth to induce someone to take some action or give up something of value.

Freedom of expression A term used to include a group of First Amendment provisions designed to protect people's ability to inform and influence others.

Freedom of religion See **Free exercise of religion clause** and **Establishment of religion clause**.

Free exercise of religion clause A clause in the First Amendment that prohibits government from taking actions to prevent people from adopting any type of religious beliefs or following religious practices that do nto violate general, religiously neutral laws.

Freehold estate A right of title or ownership to real property that extends for life or some other indeterminate period of time.

Free speech See **Freedom of expression**.

Friend of the court See **Amicus curiae**.

Fruit of the poisonous tree doctrine Evidence that is derived from an illegal search or interrogation is inadmissible.

Full-text search A computer search that identifies every place in which the search term appears in the actual text of the document being searched.

Garnishment A process through which a court can require an employer to withhold money from an employee's wages and turn this money over to the party to whom a debt is owed.

General damages Damages that you would naturally expect to occur given the type of harm suffered.

General intent An intention to act without regard to the results of the act.

General jurisdiction A court's power to hear any type of case arising within its geographical area.

General partnership A type of partnership in which all partners have the right to manage the business.

Grand jury A group of people, usually twenty-three, whose function is to determine if probable cause exists to believe that a crime has been committed and that the defendant committed it.

Grantor The prior owner.

Guardian A person appointed by the court to manage the affairs or property of a person who is incompetent due to age or some other reason.

Guardian ad litem Someone appointed by the court to speak for the interests of a child.

Guilty Convicted of a crime.

Harmless error A trial court error that is not sufficient to warrant reversing the decision.

Headnote A summary of one legal point in a court opinion; written by the editors at West.

Health care proxy Also known as a **durable power of attorney**; a document in which an individual delegates legal authority to make medical or financial decisions for that person if he or she is too incapacitated to make such decisions.

Hearing officer Holds administrative hearings, administers oaths, issues subpoenas, oversees depositions, and holds settlement conferences.

Hearsay Testimony or evidence introduced in court regarding what someone said out of court for the purpose of establishing the truth of what was said.

Heightened scrutiny See **Intermediate scrutiny test.Heir** Someone entitled to inherit property left by the decedent.

History The prior or subsequent history of the case you are Shepardizing. It is always preceded by a one-letter abbreviation.

Holder Someone who receives negotiable paper through proper delivery.

Holder in due course Someone who gives value in good faith (a subjective standard) and without notice that the instrument is overdue or has been dishonored or has any claims against it or defenses to it (an objective standard).

Holding In a case brief, the court's answer to the issue presented to it; the new legal principle established by a court opinion.

Holographic will A will that was handwritten by the testator, without the witness signatures necessary for a formal will; an informal will.

Homicide The killing of one human being by another.

Hostile work environment Occurs when unwelcome sexual conduct has the purpose or effect of unreasonably interfering with an individual's work performance or creating an intimidating, hostile, or offensive working environment.

Human rights Legal rights that all human beings are thought to have regardless of where they live.

Id. A short citation form indicating reference is to the immediately preceding authority.

Immunity For policy reasons, protection from being sued for negligent acts.

Implied warranty of fitness An implied promise that the goods being sold will satisfy a special purpose.

Implied warranty of habitability A requirement that property be fit for the purpose for which it is being rented. Owners are required to repair and maintain the premises at certain minimum levels.

Implied warranty of merchantability An implied promise that the goods being sold will be usable for the purpose for which they were sold.

Implied-in-fact contracts Contracts formed through conduct.

Inchoate crimes Attempted crimes.

Incidental beneficiary Someone who the original contracting parties did not explicitly intend to benefit from the contract.

Inculpatory evidence Evidence that suggests the defendant's guilt; opposite of **exculpatory evidence.**

Independent adoption An adoption that involves a private agreement between the birth parents and the adoptive parents.

Independent contractor A person who works for another but who retains the right to control the manner of producing the end result; not an employee.

Indictment A grand jury's written accusation that a given individual has committed a crime. Compare **Presentment.**

Indorsement in blank When an indorser simply signs his or her name and does not specify to whom the instrument is payable.

Infant In the law, a name sometimes used to mean any minor child.

Inference A conclusion reached based on the facts given.

Inferior courts In the federal system, all courts other than the U.S. Supreme Court.

Informal contract A contract not requiring any particular formalities to be valid.

Information A prosecutor's written accusation that a person has committed a crime.

Infra Below; used to refer to authority cited later in the document. May not be used with citations to cases, statutes, or constitutions.

Initial appearance The first court hearing for a person charged with committing a crime.

Injunction A court order requiring a party to perform a specific act or to cease doing a specific act.

Insanity defense A defense requiring proof that the defendant was not mentally responsible.

Intangible property Personal property that cannot be touched.

Intellectual property Intangible assets, such as trademarks, copyrights, and patents.

Intended beneficiary A person the contractual parties intend to benefit.

Intentional infliction of emotional distress An intentional tort that occurs through an extreme and outrageous act that causes severe emotional distress.

Intentional tort A tort committed by one who intends to do the act that creates the harm.

Inter vivos trust A trust that is created before a person's death.

Interference with a contractual relationship An intentional tort that occurs if someone induces a party to breach a contract or interferes with the performance of a contract.

Intermediate scrutiny test Usually applied to cases of alleged gender discrimination; the government must show the challenged action was substantially related to an important government interest. Also known as **Heightened scrutiny.**

Interrogatories Written questions sent by one side to the opposing side, answered under oath.

Intestate When a person dies without a valid will.

Intoxication defense A defense requiring proof that the defendant was not able to form the requisite mens rea due to intoxication.

Intrusion The intentional unjustified encroachment into another person's private activities.

Intrusive phrase A phrase placed between a sentence's subject and verb.

Invasion of privacy An intentional tort that covers a variety of situations, including disclosure, intrusion, appropriation, and false light.

IRAC A method for organizing legal writing: issue, rule, analysis, and conclusion.

Irresistible impulse test A test that provides that the defendant is not guilty due to insanity if, at the time of the killing, the defendant could not control his or her actions.

Irrevocable trust A form of inter vivos trust that the grantor cannot alter.

Issue Arises when the law is applied to specific facts and the result is not obvious. In a case brief, the statement of the problem facing the court. In an IRAC analysis, the statement of the client's problem. In probate law, a lineal heir; see **Decedent.**

Issue of first impression An issue that the court has never faced before.

Jails City or county places of confinement.

J.N.O.V. Shorthand for **judgment notwithstanding the verdict.**

Joint and several liability Liability shared collectively and individually.

Joint legal custody Both parents have an equal say in making major decisions, such as those regarding the education of the child.

Joint liability Shared liability, so that if one party is sued, others must be sued also.

Joint tenancy Ownership by two or more persons who have equal rights in the use of that property. When a joint tenant dies, that person's share passes to the other joint tenant(s).

Joint tenancy with right of survivorship Another term for **joint tenancy.**

Judge A court official who presides over courtroom proceedings and decides all legal questions. In a bench trial the judge also decides the facts.

Judgment The decision of the court regarding the claims of each side. It may be based on a jury's verdict.

Judgment notwithstanding the verdict (J.N.O.V.) A judgment that reverses the verdict of the jury when the verdict had no reasonable factual support or was contrary to law.

Judgment proof When the defendant does not have sufficient money or other assets to pay the judgment.

Judicial activism A judicial philosophy that supports an active role for the judiciary in changing the law.

Judicial history See **Procedural facts.**

Judicial restraint A judicial philosophy that supports a limited role for the judiciary in changing the law, including deference to the legislative branch.

Judicial review The court's power to review statutes to decide if they conform to the U.S. Constitution

Judicial self-restraint A self-imposed restraint that judges exercise to avoid political confrontations and having to decide controversial issues.

Jurisdiction The power of a court to hear a case.

Jurisprudence The study of law and legal philosophy.

Jury trial When a jury decides the facts and determines liability or guilt.

Just compensation The amount of money the government must pay the owner of property it seizes through eminent domain.

Justice of the peace A title given to the presiding officer (judge) in limited jurisdiction minor courts operated by some states.

Kidnapping An unlawful movement and confinement of the victim.

Kindred Also known as **consanguinity**; persons related to the decedent by blood.

Knowingly Not intending to cause a specific harm but being aware that such harm would be caused.

Land contract An installment contract for the sale of land.

Landmark decision A court opinion that establishes new law in an important area.

Larceny Another term for **theft.**

Last clear chance The doctrine that states that despite the plaintiff's contributory negligence, the defendant should still be liable if the defendant was the last one in a position to avoid the accident.

Law clerk A law student or a recent law school graduate whose duties usually focus on legal research.

Law review A journal generally published by a law school editorial board or by a bar association. The articles usually contain in-depth analyses of current legal topics.

Laws Rules of conduct promulgated and enforced by the government, based on policy decisions that determine legal rights and duties between people or between people and the government.

Lay advocate A nonlawyer who provides legal services directly to the public without being under the supervision of an attorney; also known as a **legal technician.** Absent a statute allowing this activity, it constitutes the unauthorized practice of law.

Leading question A question that suggests the answer; generally, leading questions may not be asked during direct examination of a witness.

Lease An agreement in which the property owner gives someone else the right to use that property for a designated period of time.

Leasehold A parcel of real estate held under a lease.

Leasehold estate A right to use real property for a limited period of time.

Legacy See **Bequest.**

Legal aid services See **Legal Services Corporation.**

Legal analysis The process of applying the law to a client's facts. Also known as **legal reasoning.**

Legal assistant Synonym for **paralegal**; may also refer to other nonlawyers who assist attorneys.

Legal custody The designated parent or guardian who has authority to make legal decisions for the child relating to such matters as health care and education.

Legal fiction An assumption that something that is not real is real—for example, assuming that a corporation is a person for purposes of its being able to sue and be sued.

Legal issue Question about the interpretation and application of the law.

Legal formalism A legal theory that views the law as a complete and autonomous system of logically consistent principles within which judges find the correct result by simply making logical deductions.

Legal malpractice The failure of an attorney to act reasonably.

Legal positivism A legal theory whose proponents believe that the validity of a law is determined by the process through which it was made rather than by the degree to which it reflects natural law principles.

Legal realism A legal philosophy whose proponents think that judges decide cases based on factors other than logic and preexisting rules, such as economic and sociological factors.

Legal reasoning The application of legal rules to a client's specific factual situation; also known as **legal analysis.**

Legal research The process of finding the law.

Legal right A legally enforceable claim to use something or to be treated in a particular way.

Legal scrivener The provider of a typing service.

Legal Services Corporation   A federally funded program to deliver legal assistance to the indigent.

Legal technician   A nonlawyer who provides legal services directly to the public without being under the supervision of an attorney; also known as a **lay advocate.** Absent a statute allowing this activity, it constitutes the unauthorized practice of law.

Legal writing   Examples of legal writing include case briefs, law office memoranda, and documents filed with the court.

Legislative courts   Courts created under Congress's Article I powers.

Legislative history   The background documents created during the process of a bill becoming a statute. These documents can include alternative versions of the legislation, proceedings of committee hearings, committee reports, and transcripts of floor debates.

Legislative intent   The purpose of the legislature at the time it enacted a statute. In interpreting statutes the role of the court is to try to discover the intent of the legislature at the time it enacted the statute.

Lessee or tenant   The person with right of possession during the term of the lease.

Lesser included offense   A crime whose elements are contained within a more serious crime. Theft is a lesser included offense of robbery.

Lessor or landlord   The owner of the property being leased.

Lexis   An on-line legal database containing court decisions and statutes from the entire country, as well as secondary authority; a competitor to **Westlaw.**

Liable   A finding in a civil suit that a defendant is responsible.

Libel   Written defamation.

Liberal construction   An approach whereby the courts give a statute a broad interpretation.

Licensing   Governmental permission to engage in a profession.

Life estate   An ownership right to real property that lasts only as long as that person, or some other named individual, lives.

Life tenant   A person who has ownership under a life estate.

Limited jurisdiction   A court's power to hear only specialized cases.

Limited liability company (LLC)   A new form of business ownership that gives small businesses the advantage of liability limited to the amount of the owner's investment along with single taxation.

Limited liability partnership (LLP)   A form of business ownership similar to a general partnership except the partners do not have unlimited personal liability for the wrongful acts of other partners. Unlike a limited liability company, however, the partners remain personally liable for other business debts, such as rent and utilities.

Limited partnership   A partnership of at least one general partner and one or more limited partners. The limited partners' liability is limited to their investments so long as they do not participate in management decisions.

Lineal heir   Someone who is a grandparent, parent, child, grandchild, or great-grandchild of the decedent.

Liquidated damages clause   A contract provision that specifies what will happen in case of breach.

Listing agreement   A document that spells out the nature of the services a real estate agent will perform with respect to selling real property and how the agent will be compensated for those services.

Literal interpretation   An approach to constitutional interpretation in which judges use common dictionary definitions for terms used in the document they are interpreting.

Litigation   A lawsuit; a controversy to be settled in a court.

Living Constitution   Judicial philosophy that seeks to interpret the Constitution in light of existing societal values.

Living trust   A form of inter vivos trust that allows a person, while still living, to benefit another.

Living will   Also known as a **medical directive;** a document expressing a person's wishes regarding the withholding or withdrawal of life-support equipment and other heroic measures to sustain life if the individual has an incurable or irreversible condition that will cause death.

Loss of consortium   The loss by one spouse of the other spouse's companionship, services, or affection.

Magistrate   A title sometimes given to a public official exercising limited judicial power.

Magistrate judges   In the federal district courts they supervise court calendars, hear procedural motions, issue subpoenas, hear minor criminal offense cases, and conduct civil pretrial hearings.

Maintenance   See **Alimony.**

Major premise   In deductive reasoning, the statement of a broad proposition that forms the starting point; in law, the statement of a legal rule that you can find in a statute or court opinion.

Majority opinion   An opinion in which a majority of the court joins.

Maker   On the face of a note, the person who signs, promising to pay.

Malice   Making a defamatory remark either knowing the material was false or acting with a "reckless disregard" for whether or not it was true.

Malicious prosecution   A lawsuit that can be brought against someone who unsuccessfully and maliciously brought an action without probable cause.

Mandatory authority or decisions Court decisions from a higher court in the same jurisdiction.

Marital property Property that is subject to court distribution upon termination of the marriage.

Market share theory A legal theory that allows plaintiffs to recover proportionately from a group of manufacturers when the identity of the specific manufacturer responsible for the harm is unknown.

Marketable title See **Clear title.**

Master In law, the name that is sometimes given to an employer.

Material breach Such a grave failure to fulfill the contractual terms that the other party is relieved of all contractual obligations.

Mechanic's lien A claim filed by a contractor or repair person who had done work on a building for which he or she has not been fully paid.

Mediation An ADR mechanism whereby a neutral third party assists the parties in reaching a mutually agreeable, voluntary compromise.

Medical directive See **Living will.**

Mens rea Bad intent.

Merchant's firm offer An offer made by a merchant in a signed writing that assures the buyer that the offer will remain open for a specific period of time. It does not require consideration to be binding.

Minimum contacts A constitutional fairness requirement that a defendant have at least a certain minimum contact with a state before the state courts can have jurisdiction over the defendant.

Minor A child who is under the age of legal competence.

Minor premise In deductive reasoning, the second proposition, which along with the major premise leads to the conclusion; in law, the minor premise consists of the client's facts.

Miranda warnings The requirement that defendants be notified of their rights to remain silent and to have an attorney present prior to being questioned by the police.

Mirror image rule The requirement that the acceptance exactly mirror the offer or the acceptance will be viewed as a counteroffer.

Misdemeanor A minor crime not amounting to a felony, usually punishable by a fine or a jail sentence of less than a year.

Misfeasance Acting in an improper or a wrongful way.

Mistrial A trial ended by the judge because of a major problem, such as a prejudicial statement by one of the attorneys.

Mitigation of damages The requirement that the non-breaching party take reasonable steps to limit his or her damages.

M'Naghten test A test that provides that the defendant is not guilty due to insanity if, at the time of the killing, the defendant suffered from a defect or disease of the mind and could not understand whether the act was right or wrong.

Model Code of Professional Responsibility An older set of standards governing attorney ethics developed by the American Bar Association.

Model Penal Code and Commentaries The American Law Institute's proposal for a uniform set of criminal laws; not the law unless adopted by a state's legislature.

Model Rules of Professional Conduct A set of ethical rules developed by the American Bar Association in the 1980s. The Model Rules have been adopted by more than half the states.

Motion A request made to the court.

Motion for acquittal A request that the court end the trial by finding for the defendant.

Motion for a continuance A request that the court postpone the proceeding to a later time.

Motion for a directed verdict A request that the court find for the moving party because either the plaintiff failed to present a prima facie case or the defendant failed to present a necessary defense.

Motion for further appellate review In Massachusetts, the process whereby the Supreme Judicial Court agrees to hear a case.

Motion for judgment notwithstanding the verdict A request that the court reverse the jury's verdict when the verdict had no reasonable factual support or was contrary to law.

Motion for leave to obtain further appellate review In Massachusetts, a request that the Supreme Judicial Court hear a case.

Motion in limine A request that the court order that certain information not be mentioned in the presence of the jury.

Motion for a new trial A request that the court order a rehearing of a lawsuit because irregularities, such as errors of the court or jury misconduct, make it probable that an impartial trial did not occur.

Motion to dismiss See **12(b)(6) motion.**

Motion to require a finding of not guilty The defense's request that the court find the prosecution failed to meet its burden and that it remove the case from the jury by finding the defendant not guilty.

Motion to suppress A request that the court prohibit the use of certain evidence at the trial.

Narrow holding A statement of the court's decision that contains many of the case's specific facts, thereby limiting its future applicability to a narrow range of cases.

National Reporter System West's system for reporting court decisions from every state and the federal courts.

Natural law A legal philosophy whose proponents think there are ideal laws that can be discovered through careful thought and humanity's innate sense of right and wrong.

Necessaries Normally food, clothing, shelter, and medical treatment.

Necessity A defense requiring proof that the defendant was forced to take an action to avoid a greater harm.

Negligence The failure to act reasonably under the circumstances.

Negotiable instrument Commercial paper that can be transferred by indorsement or delivery. It must meet the requirements of UCC §3-104 to be negotiable. If it does not, a transferee cannot become a holder, but only gets the rights along with the liabilities of a contract assignee.

New trial A rehearing of a lawsuit granted when irregularities such as errors of the court or jury misconduct make it probable that an impartial trial did not occur.

Next friend A person who represents the interests of someone in court without being that person's legal guardian.

No-fault divorce A form of divorce that allows a couple to end their marital relationship without having to assess blame for the breakup.

No-knock warrant A warrant that allows the police to enter without announcing their presence in advance.

Nolo contendere A defendant's plea meaning that the defendant neither admits nor denies the charges.

Nominal damages A token sum awarded when liability has been found but monetary damages cannot be shown.

Nonfeasance Failing to act.

Nonrestrictive phrase A phrase that is not essential to the sense of a sentence; it should be set off with commas.

Note A promise to pay money.

Notice Being informed of some act done or about to be done.

Notice pleading A method adopted by the federal rules in which the plaintiff simply informs the defendant of the claim and the general basis for it.

Novation In a contract, when a third party is substituted for one of the original parties.

Nuncupative will An oral will.

Obiter dictum See **Dictum.**

Obligee A person owed a contractual benefit.

Obligor A person under a contractual obligation.

Obscenity Sexually explicit material without redeeming artistic, scientific, or political worth.

Official reporter A governmental publication of court opinions.

On all fours A term used to describe two cases that are almost identical, with similar facts and legal issues.

On point A term used to describe a case that is similar to another case.

Option contract A contract in which the buyer gives the seller consideration to keep the offer open for a stated period of time.

Order paper An instrument that is payable to the order of a specific party.

Ordinance A law enacted by a local government; a subcategory of statutory law.

Originalism An approach to constitutional interpretation that narrowly interprets the text of the Constitution in a manner that is consistent with what most people understood those words to mean at the time that they were written.

Original jurisdiction The authority of a court to hear a case when it is initiated, as opposed to appellate jurisdiction.

Output contract A contract in which one party agrees to deliver its entire output of a particular product to the other party.

Overbreadth A reason for invalidating a statute where it covers both protected and criminal activity.

Overrule A decision is overruled when a court in a later case changes the law so that its prior decision is no longer good law. Compare with **Reverse.**

Overt discrimination When an employer openly refuses to treat all applicants or employees equally.

Paralegal A person who assists an attorney and, working under the attorney's supervision, does tasks that, absent the paralegal, the attorney would do. A paralegal cannot give legal advice or appear in court.

Parallel citation When reference to two or more reporters is required, each citation is known as a parallel citation. For example, 333 Mass. 99 is the parallel citation for 89 N.E.2d 488; the reverse is also true.

Parental immunity The prohibition against allowing children to sue their parents.

Parenthetical The parenthetical that occurs at the end of a court citation always contains the year of decision and also the name of the court if that information is not obvious from the name of the reporter.

Parol evidence rule An evidentiary rule that a written contract cannot be modified or changed by prior verbal agreements.

Parole Conditional early release from custody.

Partial defense A defense that reduces a crime to a lesser included offense.

Partnership A business run by two or more persons as co-owners.

Partnership by estoppel A partnership created by the words or actions of persons acting as though they were a partnership.

Patent A right to exclude others from making, using, or selling one's invention.

Pattern jury instructions A set of standardized jury instructions.

Payee The person who will receive payment.

Penal system Also known as the *correctional system;* the system of jails, prisons, and other places of confinement, as well as the pardon and parole systems.

Per stirpes Also known as the **right of representation;** a method of dividing an intestate estate whereby a person takes in place of the dead ancestor.

Peremptory challenge A method for excusing a prospective juror; no reason need be given.

Perfect tender rule The requirement that the goods delivered exactly meet the contractual specifications.

Perfected security interest A creditor's interest in security is perfected if the creditor possesses the security, files a financing statement, or gives money to purchase consumer goods.

Perfection In secured transactions, a security interest is perfected when notice of an attached security interest has been given, usually by filing a financing statement, thereby protecting the secured party from claims of third parties.

Periodic tenancy A tenancy established at a set interval, such as week to week, month to month, or year to year. At the end of each rental period the lease can be terminated with proper notice.

Perjury Lying to the court while under oath.

Perpetrator A person who commits a crime.

Personal defense In negotiable instrument law, a defense that is good against everyone except a holder in due course. Compare **Real defense.**

Personal jurisdiction The power of a court to force a person to appear before it.

Personal property All property that is not **real property.**

Personal recognizance bond A defendant's personal promise to appear in court.

Persuasive authority or decisions Court decisions from an equal or a lower court from the same jurisdiction or from a higher court in a different jurisdiction. Also includes secondary authority.

Petitioner A person who initiates an appeal.

Physical custody The child lives with and has day-to-day activities supervised by the designated parent or guardian.

Piercing the corporate veil When a court sets aside the unlimited liability protection normally given to corporate shareholders.

Pinpoint cite The reference to a particular page within an opinion.

Plain meaning A method for interpreting statutes in which the ordinary meaning of the statute's language is examined.

Plain view doctrine Without the need for a warrant, the police may seize objects that are openly visible.

Plaintiff A person who initiates a lawsuit.

Plea bargaining A process whereby the prosecutor and the defendant's attorney agree for the defendant to plead guilty in exchange for the prosecutor's promise to charge him or her with a lesser offense, drop some additional charges, or request a lesser sentence.

Pleading in the alternative Including more than one count in a complaint; the counts do not need to be consistent.

Pleadings The papers that begin a lawsuit—generally, the complaint and the answer.

Pocket part A pamphlet inserted into the back of a book containing information new since the volume was published.

Political question doctrine The practice of not deciding cases in situations where their resolution is committed to another branch of government or because those issues are not capable of judicial resolution.

Popular name table Located in most codified statutes, this table lists statutes by their popular names along with their citations.

Potential conflict A situation in which a conflict of interest may arise in the future—for example, representing business partners.

Power of judicial review A court's power to review statutes to decide if they conform to the federal or state constitution.

Power of sale clause A clause authorizing a private foreclosure sale that does not require court action.

Practice of law An activity that requires professional judgment, or the educated ability to relate law to a specific legal problem.

Practitioners' Notes A section of the Bluebook devoted to citation information for the practicing attorney.

Precedent One or more prior court decisions.

Preemption The power of the federal government to prevent the states from passing conflicting laws, and sometimes even to prohibit states from passing any laws on a particular subject.

Prejudicial error A trial court error so serious as to require reversal of the trial court's decision.

Preliminary hearing The first time a judge considers the criminal charge and decides whether there is enough evidence for the government to continue with the case.

Prenuptial agreement Also known as an antenuptial agreement; a document that prospective spouses sign prior to marriage regarding financial and other arrangements should the marriage end.

Preponderance of the evidence The standard of proof most commonly used in civil trials. The evidence presented must prove that it is more likely than not that the defendant committed the wrongful act.

Presentment   Acting on its own initiative, a grand jury's charging a person with a crime. Compare **Indictment**.

Presidential immunity   A legal doctrine that exempts the President of the United States from being criminally prosecuted or from being civilly sued for actions taken as President.

Pretrial conference   A meeting of the attorneys and the judge prior to the beginning of the trial.

Pretrial motion   A motion brought before the beginning of a trial either to eliminate the necessity for a trial or to limit the information that can be heard at the trial.

Prima facie case   What the prosecution or the plaintiff must be able to prove in order for the case to go to the jury—that is, the elements of the prosecution's case or the plaintiff's cause of action.

Primary authority   The law itself, such as statutes and court opinions.

Principal   In agency law, a person who permits or directs another person to act on the principal's behalf; in criminal law, the person who commits the crime.

Prior case history   Information about what happened procedurally to the cited case before it was heard by the cited court. Do not include this information in a citation.

Prisons   Places of confinement for those convicted of the more serious crimes.

Privity of contract   The relationship that exists between the contracting parties.

Pro bono work   Legal representation done without charge.

Pro se   One who represents himself or herself in a legal action.

Probable cause   Not susceptible to a precise definition; a belief based on specific facts that a crime has been or is about to be committed; more than a reasonable suspicion.

Probate   The process of court supervision over the distribution of a deceased person's property.

Probation   An alternative sentence to incarceration that releases the defendant upon agreeing to certain conditions.

Probation officers   Government employees who administer the probation system.

Procedural due process   The requirement that governments follow certain procedures when seeking to deprive people of life, liberty, or property.

Procedural facts   In a case brief, the facts that relate to what happened procedurally in the lower courts or administrative agencies before the case reached the court issuing the opinion and how the appellate court disposed of the case. Examples include aff'd and rev'd.

Procedural law   Law that regulates how the legal system operates.

Product misuse   When the product was not being used for its intended purpose or was being used in a dangerous manner; it is a defense to a products liability claim so long as the misuse was not foreseeable.

Products liability   The theory holding manufacturers and sellers liable for defective products when the defects make the products unreasonably dangerous.

Professional judgment   The educated ability to apply law to specific facts.

Promissory estoppel   Occurs when the courts allow detrimental reliance to substitute for consideration.

Property   A tangible object or a right or ownership interest.

Property law   Law dealing with ownership.

Prosecuting attorney   The attorney responsible for presenting the state's evidence against the defendant; called *United States attorneys* on the federal level and **district attorneys** or **state's attorneys** on the state level.

Prostitution   Participating in sexual activity for a fee.

Protected categories   Under Title VII, race, color, religion, sex, and national origin.

Protection order   A court order issued in domestic violence and abuse cases to keep one spouse away from the other, the children, or the home.

Proving a case within a case   The requirement in a legal malpractice case that the plaintiff-client prove that but for the attorney's negligence, the client would have won.

Proximate cause   Once actual cause is found, as a policy matter, the court must also find that the act and the resulting harm were so foreseeably related as to justify a finding of liability.

Public defender   An attorney employed by the state to represent indigent defendants.

Punitive damages   Money awarded to a plaintiff in cases of intentional torts in order to punish the defendant and serve as a warning to others.

Purchase money security interest   Arises when a seller gives credit to a debtor so that the debtor can purchase an item.

Purposeful   Intending to cause a specific harm.

Qualified individual   Under the Americans with Disabilities Act, someone who can perform the essential job functions.

Quasi-contract   Although no contract was formed, the courts will fashion an equitable remedy to avoid unjust enrichment.

Question of fact   Relates to what happened: who, what, when, where, and how. Disputed factual issues are normally for the jury or trial court to decide and cannot be appealed.

Question of law   Relates to the application or interpretation of the law. Disputed legal issues are initially for the trial court to decide but can be appealed.

Quid pro quo sexual harassment   A situation involving an exchange of sexual favors for employment benefits.

Quiet enjoyment   The tenant's right to be free from interference from the landlord with respect to how the property is used.

Quitclaim deed   A deed in which the grantor gives up any claims to the property without making any assertions about there being a clear title.

Ratio decidendi   The court's reasoning for its decision.

Rational basis test   Applied to cases of alleged discrimination when there is no suspect classification nor fundamental right involved; the plaintiff must prove the challenged action is not reasonably related to achieving a legitimate government purpose. Also known as **Standard scrutiny.**

Real defense   In negotiable instrument law, a defense inherent in the instrument itself, such as forgery. Compare **Personal defense.**

Real estate closing   A meeting at which the buyer and the seller or their representatives sign and deliver a variety of legal documents associated with the sale and transfer of the property.

Real property   Land and items growing on or permanently attached to that land; also known as real estate.

Reasonable accommodation   Under the Americans with Disabilities Act, an accommodation that would not create an undue hardship for the employer.

Reasonable suspicion   A suspicion based on specific facts; less than probable cause.

Receiving stolen property   Knowingly possessing stolen property.

Recidivist   A repeat offender; one who continues to commit more crimes.

Recklessness   Disregarding a substantial and unjustifiable risk that harm will result.

Reformation   An equitable remedy whereby the court rewrites a contract.

Registered agent   The person designated to receive service of legal documents.

Registration   The process by which individuals or organizations have their names placed on an official list kept by some private organization or governmental agency.

Regulation   A law promulgated by an administrative agency.

Remand   When an appellate court sends a case back to the trial court for a new trial or other action.

Remedial statute   A statute enacted to correct a defect in prior law or to provide a remedy where none existed.

Removal   The transfer of a case from one state court to another or from state court to federal court.

Reporters   Books that contain court decisions. There are both official and unofficial reporters.

Reprimand or censure   A public or private statement that an attorney's conduct violated the code of ethics.

Request for admissions   A document that lists statements regarding specific items for the other party to admit or deny.

Request for documents   A discovery tool whereby one party asks for documents in the other party's possession or control.

Requirements contract   A contract in which one party agrees to buy all its requirements for a particular product from the other party.

Res ipsa loquitur   "The thing speaks for itself"; the doctrine that suggests negligence can be presumed if an event happens that would not ordinarily happen unless someone was negligent.

Rescission   The act of canceling the contract and returning the parties to the positions they were in prior to the contract having been formed.

Respondeat superior   The tort theory that an employer can be sued for the negligent acts of its employees.

Respondent   The party in a lawsuit against whom an appeal has been filed.

Restatement of the Law of Torts, Second   An authoritative secondary source, written by a group of legal scholars, summarizing the existing common law, as well as suggesting what the law should be.

Restatements   A series of books—the Restatements of the Law—summarizing the basic principles of the common law, written by the American Law Institute (ALI).

Restitution   Repaying the victim for harm caused.

Restrictive covenant   A provision in a deed that prohibits specified uses of the property.

Retreat exception   The rule that in order to claim self-defense there must have been no possibility of retreat.

Reversal   When an appellate court reverses a lower court decision.

Reverse   A decision is reversed when an appellate court disagrees with the decision of a lower court. Compare with **Overrule.**

Reversible error   An error made by the trial judge sufficiently serious to warrant reversing the trial court's decision.

Revocable trust   A form of inter vivos trust that the grantor can alter.

RICO   The federal Racketeer Influenced and Corrupt Organizations Act.

Right of representation   See **Per stirpes.**

Robbery   Theft through the use of force.

Rule   In a case brief, the general legal principle in existence before the case began.

Rule 8   The rule of civil procedure that sets forth the general pleading requirements.

Rule 11 A requirement that attorneys sign a pleading only after conducting a reasonable inquiry into the circumstances supporting it.

Rule 12(b)(6) motion A request that the court find the plaintiff has failed to state a valid claim and dismiss the complaint. Also known as a **motion to dismiss.**

Rule 56 motion A request that the court grant judgment in favor of the moving party because there is no genuine issue as to any material fact and the moving party is entitled to judgment as a matter of law. It is similar to a **12(b)(6) motion** except that the court also considers matters outside the pleadings. Also known as a **summary judgment motion.**

Rulemaking hearing An administrative agency hearing that resembles a legislative hearing in which interested parties present evidence and arguments to an administrative agency about what the general law should be.

Rules of criminal procedure Federal and state rules that regulate how criminal proceedings are conducted.

Rules of evidence Federal and state rules that govern the admissibility of evidence in court.

Said Legalese for "the."

Screen See **Ethical wall.**

Search engine A computer program that allows the user to retrieve web documents that match the key words entered by the searcher.

Secondary authority Information about the law, such as that contained in encyclopedias and law review articles.

Secured transaction An arrangement whereby a creditor asks for and receives a guarantee of repayment from the debtor in the form of collateral.

Security agreement An agreement granting a creditor a security interest in specific property.

Security deposit An amount of money, usually equal to one month's rent, that is collected at the time the lease is signed and then held by the landlord to cover the cost of repairs that may be needed when the tenant moves out.

Security interest A security interest is created when a debtor agrees to put up something as collateral that the creditor can then claim if the debtor fails to pay the debt.

Self-defense The justified use of force to protect oneself or others.

Self-proving clause A notarized affidavit, signed by the attesting witnesses, that may eliminate the need to call witnesses during the probate process to attest to the validity of the will.

Sentencing hearing A hearing held after a finding of guilt to determine the appropriate sentence.

Separation of powers The division of governmental power among the legislative, executive, and judicial branches.

Servant In law, an archaic term sometimes used to mean employee.

Service The delivery of a pleading or other paper in a lawsuit to the opposing party.

Service mark A mark used to identify a service-oriented business.

Service of process See **Service.**

Session laws Statutes that are enacted and published for a particular session of the legislature

Settlement An agreement between the parties to end the lawsuit on mutually satisfactory terms.

Settlement agreement A document that contains the arrangements agreed on by the parties to a dispute.

Settlor See **Donor.**

Shareholders The owners of a corporation.

Shepardizing The process of using **Shepard's Citations** to check a court citation to see whether there has been any subsequent history or treatment by other court decisions.

Shepard's Citations A book that contains nothing but citations. It serves three purposes: (1) as a source for parallel citations; (2) as a source for subsequent history for a case or statute; and (3) as a source for treatment by later courts of the case or statute you are Shepardizing.

Short citation form A partial citation that may be used after you have given a complete citation.

Signal A word or a phrase that precedes a citation to indicate the purpose for which the citation is being given.

Signing Statement A written pronouncement issued by the President at the time a bill is signed into law.

Simultaneous death clause A clause that states that if a person named as a beneficiary in the will dies within a short period of time after the decedent dies, it will be assumed for purposes of the will that the person in question failed to survive the decedent.

Slander Spoken defamation.

Slip laws A form in which statutes are published; they are printed individually at the time they are first enacted.

Sole custody An individual has both physical and legal custody of the child.

Sole proprietorship A business owned by a single owner.

Solemnized marriage A marriage in which the couple has obtained the proper marriage license from a local government official and has then taken marriage vows before either a recognized member of the clergy or a judge and a designated number of witnesses.

Solicitation Encouraging someone to commit a crime.

Sovereign immunity The prohibition against suing the government without the government's consent.

Special damages Indirect damages that must be foreseeable to be recovered.

Specific intent An intention to act and to cause a specific result.

Specific performance When money damages are inadequate, a court may use this equitable remedy and order the breaching party to perform his or her contractual obligations.

Split custody One parent has both physical and legal custody during one part of the year, and the other parent gets both physical and legal custody during the rest of the year.

Spousal immunity The prohibition against one spouse suing the other.

Stalking The intentional or knowing course of conduct that places a person in fear of imminent physical injury or death to that person or that person's family.

Standard scrutiny See **Rational basis test.**

Standing The principle that courts cannot decide abstract issues or render advisory opinions; rather they are limited to deciding cases that involve litigants who are personally affected by the court's decision.

Standing to sue The requirement that a potential litigant have a sufficient stake in the outcome of the case before being accepted as a party in the case.

Stare decisis The doctrine stating that normally once a court has decided one way on a particular issue, it and other courts in the same jurisdiction will decide the same way on that issue in future cases given a similar set of facts, unless they can be convinced of the need for change.

State action requirement A court-imposed requirement that most constitutional protections apply only if a governmental entity is involved.

State's attorney A law officer who represents the state in criminal cases. Also known as a **district attorney.**

Statute A law enacted by a state legislature or by Congress.

Statute in derogation of the common law A statute that changes the common law.

Statute of frauds A statutory requirement that in order to be enforceable certain contracts must be in writing.

Statute of limitations The law that sets the length of time from when something happens to when a lawsuit must be filed before the right to bring it is lost.

Statutes at large or session laws The chronological publication of statutes at the end of a legislative session.

Statutory element A separable part of a statute that must be satisfied for the statute to apply.

Stay the judgment A suspension of the judgment. It is often requested when the trial court judgment is being appealed.

Stipulate To agree.

Stop and frisk The right of the police to detain an individual for a brief period of time and to search the outside of the person's clothing if the police have a reasonable suspicion that the individual has committed or is about to commit a crime.

Strict construction An approach whereby the courts give a statute a narrow interpretation.

Strict liability Liability without having to prove fault.

Strict scrutiny test Applied to cases of alleged discrimination when there is a suspect classification or a fundamental right involved; the government must prove the challenged action was necessary to achieve a compelling government interest and was the least restrictive means available. Also known as **Compelling interest test.**

String citation A series of citations in a row.

Subject matter jurisdiction The power of a court to hear a particular type of case.

Subpoena A court order requiring a person to appear to testify at a trial or deposition. (Administrative agencies also usually have subpoena powers.)

Subpoena duces tecum A court order that a person who is not a party to litigation appear at a trial or deposition and bring requested documents.

Subsequent case history Information about what happened procedurally to the litigation after the case cited. Include this information in a citation.

Substantial capacity test Part of the Model Penal Code; a test that provides that the defendant is not guilty due to insanity if, at the time of the killing, the defendant lacked either the ability to understand that the act was wrong or the ability to control the behavior.

Substantial performance Although a breach of contract, performance of all the essential terms of the contract will entitle the breaching party to the contractual price minus any damages caused by the breach.

Substantive due process The requirement that governments not deprive anyone of life, liberty, or property where the law being violated is found to be arbitrary or unreasonable.

Substantive facts In a case brief, facts that deal with what happened to the parties before the litigation began.

Substantive law Law that creates rights and duties.

Successive conflict of interest Representing someone who is in a position adverse to a prior client.

Summary judgment A judgment based on a finding that there is no genuine issue as to any material fact and that the moving party is entitled to judgment as a matter of law.

Summary judgment motion A request for a summary judgment. Also known as a **Rule 56 motion.**

Summary jury trial A nonbinding process in which attorneys for both sides present synopses of their cases to a jury, which renders an advisory opinion on the basis of these presentations.

Summons A notice informing the defendant of the lawsuit and requiring the defendant to respond or risk losing the suit.

Superseding cause In negligence, an intervening cause that relieves the defendant of liability.

Support See **Alimony.**

Supra Above; used to refer to authority already cited in the document. May not be used with citations to cases, statutes, or constitutions.

Supreme Court Reporter A West publication containing U.S. Supreme Court decisions.

Surrogacy contract A document in which a woman agrees to conceive and give birth to a child, deliver the child to its natural father, and terminate her parental rights so the father's wife can become its adoptive mother.

Suspension A determination that an attorney may not practice law for a set period of time.

Symbolic speech The use of physical actions, rather than words, to express a point of view.

Syllabus A summary of a court opinion that appears at the beginning of the case.

Synthesis The process of integrating a series of cases in such a way that their interrelationship is explained to the reader.

Tangible personal property Also known as **chattel**; personal property that can be touched and moved.

Temporary restraining order (TRO) A court order of limited duration designed to maintain the status quo pending further court action at a later date.

Tenancy in common Ownership by two or more people. Ownership shares do not have to be equal, but each has an undivided interest in the property. When a tenant in common dies, that person's share passes either by will or by intestate statute.

Tenancy by the entirety A special type of joint tenancy applicable only to married couples.

Tenancy at sufferance A situation in which the person in possession of the land has no legal right to be there.

Tenancy for a term or estate for years A right to control real property for a set period of time.

Tenancy at will An arrangement in which no time period is specified and the lessee can leave or the lessor can reclaim the land at any time.

Testamentary capacity The mental capacity, also known as *sound mind*, whereby the testator understands the nature of his or her property and the identity of those most closely related to him or her.

Testamentary trust A trust that is created by a will and does not become effective until after the testator's death.

Testator/testatrix The person making a will to direct how his or her assets will be distributed at death.

Theft Also known as **larceny**; the taking of another's property with the intent to permanently deprive the owner.

Third-party claim A claim by a defendant against someone in addition to the persons the plaintiff has already sued.

Time and place restrictions Governmental restrictions that limit when and where free expression activities can take place.

Title insurance Insurance against any loss due to a defective title.

Title search An examination of documents recording title to a property to ensure the owner has a clear title.

Tort Harm to a person or a person's property.

Tort law Law that deals with harm to a person or a person's property.

Tortfeasor A person who commits a tort.

Trademark A name, combination of letters or numbers, or logo that identifies a particular product.

Transferred intent A legal fiction that if a person directs a tortious action toward A but instead harms B, the intent to act against A is transferred to B.

Treason Attempting to overthrow the government or betraying the government to a foreign power.

Treatise A book that summarizes, interprets, and evaluates the law.

Treatment How subsequent cases have affected the case you are Shepardizing. It is sometimes indicated by a one-letter abbreviation before the Shepard's citation.

Trespass The unauthorized intrusion onto the land of another.

Trespass to personal property Occurs when someone harms or interferes with the owner's exclusive possession of the property but has no intention of keeping the property.

Trial The process of deciding a dispute by presenting evidence and witness testimony either to a jury or to a judge.

Trial courts Courts that determine the facts and apply the law to the facts.

Trust A legal relationship in which one party holds property for the benefit of another.

Trustee The person appointed to administer a trust.

12(b)(6) motion A request that the court find the plaintiff has failed to state a valid claim and dismiss the complaint.

Ultrahazardous activities Those activities that have an inherent risk of injury and therefore may result in strict liability.

Unauthorized practice of law When nonlawyers do things that only lawyers are allowed to do. In most states this is a crime.

Unconscionable contract A contract formed between parties of very unequal bargaining power where the terms are so unfair as to "shock the conscience."

Undue influence When one party is in a position of trust and misuses that trust to influence the actions of another.

Unenforceable contract A valid contract that cannot be enforced, for example, because the statute of limitations has passed.

Uniform Commercial Code (UCC)   Originally drafted by the National Conference of Commissioners on Uniform State Law, it governs commercial transactions and has been adopted by all states entirely or in part.

Uniform Partnership Act (UPA)   Known as a gap filler, the UPA comes into play only if terms are left out of a partnership agreement.

Unilateral contract   A contract where a promise is exchanged for an act.

United States Code (U.S.C.)   Federal statutes arranged by subject matter.

United States Code Annotated (U.S.C.A.)   Federal statutes arranged by subject matter, published by West.

United States Code Service (U.S.C.S.)   Federal statutes arranged by subject matter, published by Lexis Law Publishing.

United States Constitution   Drafted in 1787, it established the structure of the federal government and the relationship between the federal and state governments.

United States courts of appeals   The intermediate appellate courts in the federal system.

United States district courts   The general jurisdiction trial courts in the federal system.

United States Law Week   BNA's publication of U.S. Supreme Court decisions.

United States Reports   The official federal government publication of U.S. Supreme Court decisions.

United States Sentencing Guidelines   Government guidelines that specify an appropriate range of sentences for each class of convicted persons based on factors related to the offense and the offender.

United States Supreme Court   The highest appellate court in the federal system; consists of nine appointed members; established by Article III of the U.S. Constitution.

United States Supreme Court Reports, Lawyers' Edition   U.S. Supreme Court decisions published by Lexis Law Publishing.

Unlawful detainer   A civil action brought to recover use of property.

Unofficial reporter   A private publication of court opinions—for example, the regional reporters, such as N.E.2d, published by West.

Valid   In logic, an argument is considered to be valid or sound if the assumptions underlying the argument are true.

Valid contract   A contract having all the essential elements needed for a binding agreement.

Verdict   The opinion of a jury on a question of fact.

Verification   An affidavit signed by the client indicating that he or she has read the complaint and that its contents are correct.

Vicarious representation   The rule whereby all members of a law firm are treated as though they had represented the former client.

Void   In law, if an action is void, it has no legal effect.

Void contract   A contract that is invalid even if it is not repudiated by either party; for example, a contract formed for an illegal purpose.

Void for vagueness   A reason for invalidating a statute where a reasonable person could not determine a statute's meaning.

Void marriage   A marriage that is invalid from its inception and that does not require court action for the parties to be free of any marital obligations.

Voidable   A valid contract that can be set aside at the option of one of the parties.

Voidable contract   A contract that can be disaffirmed by one of the parties.

Voidable marriage   A marriage that was valid when it was entered into and that remains valid until either party obtains a court order dissolving it.

Voir dire   An examination of a prospective juror to see if he or she is fit to serve as a juror.

Warrant   A court's prior permission for the police to search and seize.

Warranty   A guarantee, made by the seller or implied by law, regarding the character, quality, or title of the goods being sold.

Warranty deed   A deed in which the seller promises clear title to the property.

West Group   A major private publisher of legal materials. Its logo is the key symbol.

Westlaw   An on-line legal database containing court decisions and statutes from the entire country, as well as secondary authority; a competitor to **Lexis.**

Will   The document used to express a person's wishes as to how his or her property should be distributed upon death.

Writ   A judge's order requiring that something be done.

Writ of certiorari   A means of gaining appellate review; in the U.S. Supreme Court the writ is discretionary and will be issued to another court to review a federal question if four of the nine justices vote to hear the case.

Writ of execution   A court order authorizing a sheriff to take property in order to enforce a judgment.

Writ of habeas corpus   A request that the court release the defendant because of the illegality of the incarceration.

Wrongful birth   Also known as *wrongful life;* liability for negligently causing a child's birth.

Table of Cases

Index